THE SECRET DOCTRINE

THE ARYAN THEOSOPHICAL PRESS
Point Loma, California

THE SECRET DOCTRINE

THE SYNTHESIS OF
SCIENCE, RELIGION, AND PHILOSOPHY

BY

H. P. BLAVATSKY

Author of *Isis Unveiled*

सत्यात् नास्ति परो धर्मः ।

" There is no Religion Higher than Truth "

VOLUME II
ANTHROPOGENESIS

SECOND POINT LOMA EDITION

THE ARYAN THEOSOPHICAL PRESS
POINT LOMA, CALIFORNIA
1917

"Entered according to Act of Congress in the year 1888, by H. P. Blavatsky, in the Office of the Librarian of Congress at Washington, D. C."

This Work

I Dedicate to all True Theosophists,

In Every Country,

And of Every Race,

For they called it forth, and for them it was recorded.

TABLE OF CONTENTS

VOLUME SECOND

BOOK II — PART I
ANTHROPOGENESIS

BOOK II — PART II
THE ARCHAIC SYMBOLISM OF THE WORLD-RELIGIONS

BOOK II — PART III

ADDENDA

SCIENCE AND THE SECRET DOCTRINE CONTRASTED

§§

INDEX

'Η ἐμὴ διδαχὴ οὐκ ἔστιν ἐμή, ἀλλὰ τοῦ πέμψαντός με.

"My doctrine is not mine, but his that sent me."
—*John* vii. 16.

MODERN science insists upon the doctrine of evolution; so do human reason and the " Secret Doctrine," and the idea is corroborated by the ancient legends and myths, and even by the Bible itself when it is read between the lines. We see a flower slowly developing from a bud, and the bud from its seed. But whence the latter, with all its predetermined program of physical transformation, and its invisible, therefore *spiritual* forces which gradually develop its form, color, and odor? The word *evolution* speaks for itself. The germ of the present human race must have pre-existed in the parent of this race, as the seed, in which lies hidden the flower of next summer, was developed in the capsule of its parent flower; the parent may be but *slightly* different, but it still differs from its future progeny. The antediluvian ancestors of the present elephant and lizard were, perhaps, the mammoth and the plesiosaurus; why should not the progenitors of our human race have been the "*giants*" of the *Vedas*, the *Völuspa*, and the Book of *Genesis?* While it is positively absurd to believe the " transformation of species " to have taken place according to some of the more materialistic views of the evolutionists, it is but natural to think that each genus, beginning with the molluscs and ending with man, had modified its own primordial and distinctive forms.—" *Isis Unveiled*," Vol. I, pp. 152–3.

PRELIMINARY NOTES

―――――――

ON THE ARCHAIC STANZAS, AND THE FOUR PRE-HISTORIC CONTINENTS

Facies totius Universi, quamvis infinitis modis variet,
Manet tamen semper eadem.

— Spinoza

THE Stanzas, with the Commentaries thereon, in this Book, the second, are drawn from the same Archaic Records as the Stanzas on Cosmogony in Book I. As far as possible a verbatim translation is given; but some of the Stanzas were too obscure to be understood without explanation. Hence, as was done in Book I, while they are first given in full as they stand, when taken verse by verse with their Commentaries an attempt is made to make them clearer, by words added in brackets, in anticipation of the fuller explanation of the Commentary.

As regards the evolution of mankind, the Secret Doctrine postulates three new propositions, which stand in direct antagonism to modern science as well as to current religious dogmas: it teaches (a) the simultaneous evolution of seven human groups on seven different portions of our globe; (b) the birth of the *astral*, before the *physical* body: the former being a model for the latter; and (c) that man, in this Round, preceded every mammalian — the anthropoids included — in the animal kingdom.[1]

The Secret Doctrine is not alone in speaking of primeval MEN born

―――――――

1. See *Genesis* ch. ii, v. 19. Adam is formed in verse 7, and in verse 19 it is said: "Out of the *ground* the Lord God formed *every beast of the field, and every fowl of the air; and brought them unto Adam* to see what he would call them." Thus man was created *before* the animals; for the animals mentioned in chapter i. are the signs of the Zodiac, while the man, "male and female," is not *man*, but the Host of the Sephiroth; FORCES, or Angels, "made in his (God's) image and after his likeness." The Adam, man, is not made in that likeness, nor is it so asserted

simultaneously on the seven divisions of our Globe. In the *Divine* "*Pymander*" of Hermes we find the same Seven primeval men[2] evolving from Nature and "Heavenly Man," in the collective sense of the word, namely, from the Creative Spirits; and in the fragments (collected by George Smith) of Chaldaean tablets on which is inscribed the Babylonian Legend of Creation, in the first column of the *Cutha* tablet, seven human beings with the faces of ravens (black, swarthy complexions), whom "the [Seven] great gods created," are mentioned. Or, as explained in lines 16 and 18 — "In the midst of the Earth they grew up and became great ... Seven kings, brothers of the same family."[3] These are the Seven Kings of Edom to whom reference is made in the Kabala; the first race, which was *imperfect, i. e.,* was born before the "balance" (sexes) existed, and which was therefore destroyed.[4] "*Seven Kings,* brethren, appeared and begat children. 6000 in number were their peoples."[5] The god Nergas (death) destroyed them. "How did he destroy them?" "By bringing into equilibrium (or balance) those who did not yet exist." (*Siphrah Dzeniouta.*) They were "destroyed," as a race, by being merged in their own progeny (by exudation); that is to say, the sexless race reincarnated in the bisexual (potentially); the latter in the Androgynes; these again in the sexual,

in the Bible. Moreover, the Second Adam is esoterically a septenary which represents seven men, or rather groups of men. For the first Adam — the Kadmon — is the synthesis of the *ten* Sephiroth. Of these, the upper triad remains in the Archetypal World as the future "Trinity," while the seven lower Sephiroth create the manifested material world; and *this septennate is the second Adam. Genesis,* and the mysteries upon which it was fabricated, came from Egypt. The "God" of the 1st chapter of *Genesis* is the *Logos,* and the "Lord God" of the 2nd chapter the Creative *Elohim* — the *lower* powers.

2. Thus saith Pymander —"This is the mystery that to this day was hidden. Nature being mingled with the Heavenly man [Elohim, or Dhyânis], brought forth a wonder. ... *Seven men,* all males and females [Hermaphrodite] . . . according to the nature of the seven Governors "— (Book II, 29) — or the seven Hosts of the *Pitris*

or Elohim, who projected or created him. This is very clear, but yet, see the interpretations of even our modern theologians, men supposed to be intellectual and learned! In the *Theological and philosophical works of Hermes Trismegistus, Christian* [?] *Neoplatonist,* a work compiled by John David Chambers, of Oriel College, Oxford, the translator wonders "for whom these *seven men* are intended?" He solves the difficulty by concluding that, as "the original pattern man [*Adam Kadmon of ch. i. Genesis*] was masculine-feminine, . . . the seven may signify the succeeding patriarchs named in *Genesis*" (p. 9). . . . A truly theological way of cutting the Gordian knot.

3. *Chaldean Account of Genesis,* p. 103.

4. *Zohar, Siphrah Dzeniouta, Idrah Sutah,* 292b, *La Kabale,* p. 205.

5. *Hibbert Lectures,* Prof. Sayce, pp. 372, 373.

the later third Race; (for further explanation, *vide infra*). Were the tablets less mutilated, they would be found to contain word for word the same account as given in the archaic records and in Hermes, at least as regards the fundamental facts, if not as regards minute details; for Hermes is a good deal disfigured by mistranslations.

It is quite certain that the seeming supernaturalism of these teachings, although allegorical, is so diametrically opposed to the dead-letter statements of the Bible[6] as well as to the latest hypotheses of science, that it will evoke passionate denial. The Occultists, however, know that the traditions of Esoteric Philosophy must be the right ones, simply because they are the most logical, and reconcile every difficulty. Besides, we have the Egyptian "*Books of Thoth*," and "*Book of the Dead*," and the Hindû Purânas with the seven Manus, as well as the Chaldaeo-Assyrian accounts, whose tiles mention seven primitive men, or Adams, the real meaning of which name may be ascertained through the Kabala. Those who know anything of the Samothracian mysteries will also remember that the generic name of the Kabiri was the "Holy Fires," which created on seven localities of the island of *Electria* (or Samothrace) the "Kabir born of the Holy Lemnos" (the island sacred to *Vulcan*).

According to Pindar,[7] this Kabir, whose name was Adamas, was, in the traditions of Lemnos, the type of the primitive man born from the bosom of the Earth. He was the Archetype of the first males in the order of generation, and was one of the seven autochthonous ancestors or progenitors of mankind.[8] If, while coupling with this the fact that Samothrace was colonized by the Phoenicians, and before them by the mysterious Pelasgians who came from the East, one remembers also the identity of the *mystery* gods of the Phoenicians, Chaldaeans, and Israelites, it will be easy to discover whence came also the confused account of the Noachian deluge. It has become undeniable of late that the Jews, who obtained their primitive ideas about creation from Moses, who had them from the Egyptians, compiled

6. As it is now asserted that the Chaldaean tablets, which give the allegorical description of Creation, the Fall, and the Flood, even to the legend of the Tower of Babel, were written "before the time of Moses" (See G. Smith's *Chaldean Account* of *Genesis*, p. 86), how can the Pentateuch be called a *revelation?* It is simply another version of the same story.

7. See *Philosophumena*, Miller's edition, p. 98.

8. *Ibid.*, p. 108.

their *Genesis* and first Cosmogonic traditions — when these were re-written by Ezra and others — from the Chaldaeo-Akkadian account. It is, therefore, sufficient to examine the Babylonian and Assyrian cuneiform and other inscriptions to find also therein, scattered here and there, not only the original meaning of the name Adam, Admi, or Adami,[9] but also the creation of seven Adams or roots of men, born of Mother Earth, physically, and of the *divine fire* of the progenitors, spiritually or astrally. The Assyriologists, ignorant of the esoteric teachings, could hardly be expected to pay any greater attention to the mysterious and ever-recurring number seven on the Babylonian cylinders, than they paid to it on finding the same in *Genesis* and the Bible. Yet the number of the ancestral spirits and their seven groups of human progeny are there, notwithstanding the dilapidated condition of the fragments, as plainly as they are to be found in *Pymander* and in the *Book of the Concealed Mystery* of the Kabala. In the latter Adam Kadmon is the Sephirothal TREE, as also the "Tree of the Knowledge of Good and Evil." And that "*Tree*," says verse 32, "hath around it seven columns," or palaces, of the seven creative Angels operating in the spheres of the seven planets on our Globe. As Adam Kadmon is a *collective* name, so also is the name of the man Adam. Says George Smith in his *Chaldean Account of Genesis:*

The word Adam used in these legends for the first human being is evidently *not a proper name, but is only used as a term for mankind.* Adam appears as a proper name in *Genesis,* but certainly in some passages is only used in the same sense as the Assyrian word.[10]

Moreover, neither the Chaldaean nor the Biblical deluge (the stories of Xisuthrus and Noah) is based on the universal or even on the Atlantean deluges, recorded in the Indian allegory of Vaivasvata Manu. They are the *exoteric allegories based on the esoteric mysteries* of Samothrace. If the older Chaldees knew the esoteric truth concealed in the Purânic legends, the other nations were aware only of the Samothracian mystery, and allegorized it. They adapted it to their astronomical and anthropological, or rather phallic, notions. Samothrace is known *historically* to have been famous in antiquity for a deluge, which submerged the country and reached the top of the highest mountains; an event which happened before the age of the Argonauts. It was over-

9. *Vide* " Adam-Adami," in Part II, § XVI of this volume.   10. Page 86.

flowed very suddenly by the waters of the Euxine, regarded up to that time as a lake.[11] But the Israelites had, moreover, another legend upon which to base their allegory: the "deluge," that transformed the present Gobi Desert into a sea *for the last time,* some 10 or 12,000 years ago, and which drove many Noahs and their families on to the surrounding mountains. As the Babylonian accounts are now only restored from hundreds of thousands of broken fragments (the mound of *Kuyunjik* alone having yielded to Layard's excavations over twenty thousand fragments of inscriptions), the proofs here cited are comparatively scanty; yet such as they are, they corroborate almost every one of our teachings, certainly three, at least. These are:—

(1) That the race which was the first to fall into generation was a *dark Race* (*Zalmat-qaqadi*), which they call the *Adami* or dark Race, and that *Sarku,* or the light Race, remained pure for a long while subsequently.

(2) That the Babylonians recognized *two principal Races* at the time of the Fall, the Race of the Gods (the Ethereal *doubles of the Pitris*), having preceded these two. This is Sir H. Rawlinson's opinion. These "Races" are our second and third Root-races.

(3) That these seven Gods, each of whom created a *man,* or group of men, were "the gods *imprisoned* or incarnated." These gods were: the god *Zi;* the god *Ziku* (noble life, Director of purity); the god *Mirku* (noble crown) "Savior from death of the gods [later on] imprisoned," and the creator of "the dark Race which his hand has made"; the god *Libzu* "wise among the gods"; the god *Nissi* . . . and the god *Suhhab;* and *Hea* or *Sa,* their synthesis, the god of wisdom and of the Deep, identified with Oannes-Dagon, at the time of the fall, and called (collectively) the Demiurge, or Creator.[12]

There are two "Creations" so called, in the Babylonian fragments, and *Genesis* having adhered to this, one finds its first two chapters distinguished as the Elohite and the Jehovite creations. Their proper order, however, is not preserved in these or in any other exoteric accounts. Now these "Creations," according to the occult teachings, refer respectively to the formation of the primordial seven *men* by the

11. See Pliny, IV, c. 12; Strabo X; Herodotus, VII, c. 108; Pausanias, VII, c. 4, etc.
12. See *Chaldean Account of Genesis,* p. 82.

progenitors (the Pitris, or Elohim) : and to that of the human groups after the fall.

All this will be examined in the light of science and comparisons drawn from the scriptures of all the ancient nations, the Bible included, as we proceed. Meanwhile, before we turn to the *Anthropogenesis* of the prehistoric Races, it may be useful to agree upon the names to be given to the Continents on which the four great Races, which preceded our *Adamic* Race, were born, lived, and died. Their archaic and esoteric names were many, and varied with the language of the nationality which mentioned them in its annals and scriptures. That which in the *Vendîdâd*, for instance, is referred to as Airyanem Vaejo[13] wherein was born the original Zoroaster,[14] is called in the Purânic literature " Śveta-Dvipa," " Mount Meru," the abode of Vishnu, etc., etc.; and in the Secret Doctrine is simply named the land of the " Gods " under their chiefs the " Spirits of this Planet."

Therefore, in view of the possible, and even very probable confusion, that may arise, it is considered more convenient to adopt, for each of the four Continents constantly referred to, a name more familiar to the cultured reader. It is proposed, then, to call the first continent, or rather the first *terra firma* on which the first Race was evolved by the divine progenitors :—

I. " The Imperishable Sacred Land."

The reasons for this name are explained as follows : This " Sacred Land "— of which more later on — is stated never to have shared the fate of the other continents; because it is the only one whose destiny it is to last from the beginning to the end of the Manvantara throughout each Round. It is the cradle of the first man and the dwelling of the last *divine* mortal, chosen as a *Sishta* for the future seed of humanity. Of this mysterious and sacred land very little can be said, except, perhaps, according to a poetical expression in one of the Commentaries, that the " pole-star has its watchful eye upon it, from the dawn to the close of the twilight of ' a day ' of the GREAT BREATH." [15]

13. See *Bundahiś*, 79, 12.

14. By "original" we mean the "Amshâspend," called "Zarathustra, the lord and ruler of the Vara made by Yima in that land." There were several Zarathustra or Zertusts, the *Dabistân* alone enumerating thirteen; but these were all the reincarnations of the first one. The last Zoroaster was the founder of the Fire temple of Azareksh and the writer of the works on the primeval sacred Magian religion destroyed by Alexander.

15. In India called "The Day of Brahmâ,"

II. The "HYPERBOREAN" will be the name chosen for the Second Continent, the land which stretched out its promontories southward and westward from the North Pole to receive the Second Race, and comprised the whole of what is now known as Northern Asia. Such was the name given by the oldest Greeks to the far-off and mysterious region, whither their tradition made Apollo the "Hyperborean" travel every year. *Astronomically*, Apollo is of course the Sun, who, abandoning his Hellenic sanctuaries, loved to visit annually his far-away country, where the Sun was said never to set for one half of the year. Ἐγγὺς γὰρ νυκτός τε καὶ ἤματός εἰσι κέλευθοι, says a verse in the *Odyssey*.[16]

But *historically*, or better, perhaps, ethnologically and geologically, the meaning is different. The land of the Hyperboreans, the country that extended beyond Boreas, the frozen-hearted god of snows and hurricanes, who loved to slumber heavily on the chain of Mount Rhipaios was neither an ideal country, as surmised by the mythologists, nor yet a land in the neighborhood of Scythia and the Danube.[17] It was a real Continent, a *bona fide* land which knew no winter in those early days, nor have its sorry remains more than one night and day during the year, even now. The nocturnal shadows never fall upon it, said the Greeks; for it is the *land of the Gods*, the favorite abode of Apollo, the god of light, and its inhabitants are his beloved priests and servants. This may be regarded as poetized *fiction* now; but it was poetized *truth* then.

III. The third Continent, we propose to call "Lemuria." The name is an invention, or an idea, of Mr. P. L. Sclater, who asserted, between 1850 and 1860, on zoological grounds the actual existence, in prehistoric times, of a Continent which he showed to have extended from Madagascar to Ceylon and Sumatra. It included some portions of what is now Africa; but otherwise this gigantic Continent, which stretched from the Indian Ocean to Australia, has now wholly disappeared beneath the waters of the Pacific, leaving here and there only some of its highland tops which are now islands. Mr. A. R. Wallace, the naturalist, "extends the Australia of tertiary periods to New Guinea and the Solomon Islands, and perhaps to Fiji"; and from its Marsupial types he infers "a connexion with the Northern Continent

16. X, 86.   17. See Völcker, *Mythological Geography*, pp. 145 to 170.

during the Secondary period," writes Mr. C. Gould.[18] The subject is treated at length elsewhere.[19]

IV. "Atlantis" is the Fourth Continent. It would be the first historical land, were the traditions of the ancients to receive more attention than they have hitherto. The famous island of Plato of that name was but a fragment of this great Continent.[20]

V. The Fifth Continent was America; but, as it is situated at the Antipodes, it is Europe and Asia Minor, almost coeval with it, which are generally referred to by the Indo-Aryan Occultists as the fifth. If their teaching followed the appearance of the Continents in their geological and geographical order, then this classification would have to be altered. But as the sequence of the Continents is made to follow the order of evolution of the Races, from the first to the fifth, our Aryan Root-race, Europe must be called the fifth great Continent. The Secret Doctrine takes no account of islands and peninsulas, nor does it follow the modern geographical distribution of land and sea. Since the day of its earliest teachings and the destruction of the great Atlantis, the face of the earth has changed more than once. There was a time when the delta of Egypt and Northern Africa belonged to Europe, before the formation of the Straits of Gibraltar, and a further upheaval of the continent, changed entirely the face of the map of Europe. The last serious change occurred some 12,000 years ago,[21] and was followed

---

18. In *Mythical Monsters*, page 47.

19. It is to be remarked, however, that Mr. Wallace does not accept Mr. Sclater's idea, and even opposes it. Mr. Sclater supposes a land or continent formerly uniting Africa, Madagascar, and India (but not Australia and India); and Mr. A. R. Wallace shows, in his *Geographical Distribution of Animals* and *Island Life*, that the hypothesis of such a land is quite uncalled for on the alleged zoological grounds. But he admits that a much closer proximity of India and Australia did certainly exist, and at a time so very remote that it was "certainly pre-tertiary," and he adds in a private letter that "no name has been given to this supposed land." Yet the land did exist, and was of course *pre-tertiary*, for "Lemuria" (accepting this name for the

third Continent) had perished before Atlantis had fully developed; and the latter sank and its chief portions had disappeared before the end of the Miocene period.

20. See "*Esoteric Buddhism.*"

21. One more "coincidence"—

"Now it is proved that in geologically recent times, *this region of North Africa was in fact a peninsula of Spain,* and that its union with Africa (proper) was effected on the North by the rupture of Gibraltar, and on the South by an *upheaval to which the Sahara owes its existence.* The shores of this former sea of Sahara are still marked by the shells of the same Gastropoda that live on the shores of the Mediterranean." (Prof. Oscar Schmidt, *Doctrine of Descent and Darwinism,* page 244.)

by the submersion of Plato's little Atlantic island, which he calls Atlantis after its parent continent. Geography was part of the mysteries, in days of old. Says the *Zohar*:[22] "These secrets [of land and sea] were divulged *to the men of the secret science*, but not to the geographers."

The claim that physical man was originally a colossal pre-tertiary giant, and that he existed 18,000,000 years ago, must of course appear preposterous to admirers of, and believers in, modern learning. The whole *posse comitatus* of biologists will turn away from the conception of this third race Titan of the Secondary age, a being fit to fight as successfully with the then gigantic monsters of the air, sea, and land, as his forefathers — the ethereal prototype of the Atlantean — had little need to fear that which could not hurt him. The modern anthropologist is quite welcome to laugh at our Titans, as he laughs at the Biblical Adam, and as the theologian laughs at his pithecoid ancestor. The Occultists and their severe critics may feel that they have pretty well mutually squared their accounts by this time. Occult sciences claim less and give more, at all events, than either Darwinian Anthropology or Biblical Theology.

Nor ought the Esoteric Chronology to frighten any one; for, with regard to figures, the greatest authorities of the day are as fickle and as uncertain as the Mediterranean wave. As regards the duration of the geological periods alone, the learned men of the Royal Society are all hopelessly at sea, and jump from one million to five hundred millions of years with the utmost ease, as will be seen more than once during this comparison.

Take one instance for our present purpose — the calculations of Mr. Croll. Whether, according to this authority, 2,500,000 years represent the time since the beginning of the tertiary age, or the Eocene period, as an American geologist makes him say;[23] or whether again Mr. Croll "allows fifteen millions since the beginning of the Eocene period," as quoted by an English geologist,[24] both sets of figures cover the claims made by the Secret Doctrine.[25] For assigning as the latter

22. iii, fol. 10a.

23. A. Winchell, Professor of Geology, *World-Life*, page 369.

24. Mr. Charles Gould, late Geological surveyor of Tasmania, in *Mythical Monsters*, page 84.

25. Sir Charles Lyell, who is credited with having "*happily* invented the terms Eocene, Miocene, and Pliocene," to mark

does from four to five million years between the incipient and the
final evolution of the Fourth Root-Race, on the Lemuro-Atlantean
Continents; one million years for the Fifth, or Aryan Race, to the present date; and about 850,000 since the submersion of the last large
peninsula of the great Atlantis — all this may have easily taken place
within the 15,000,000 years conceded by Mr. Croll to the Tertiary
Age. But, *chronologically* speaking, the duration of the period is of
secondary importance, as we have, after all, certain American scientists
to fall back upon. These gentlemen, unmoved by the fact that their
assertions are called not only dubious but absurd, yet maintain that
man existed so far back as in the Secondary Age. They have found
human footprints on rocks of that formation; and furthermore, M. de
Quatrefages finds no valid *scientific* reason why man should not have
existed during the Secondary Age.

The " Ages " and periods in geology are, in sober truth, purely con-
ventional terms, as they are still hardly delineated, and, moreover,
no two geologists or naturalists agree as to the figures. Thus, there is
a wide margin for choice offered to the Occultist by the learned fraternity. Shall we take for one of our supports Mr. T. Mellard Reade?
This gentleman, in a paper on " Limestone as an Index of Geological
Time," read by him in 1878 before the Royal Society, claims that the

---

the three divisions of the Tertiary age,
ought really to have settled upon some approximate age for his " Mind-offspring."
Having left the duration of these periods,
however, to the speculations of specialists,
the greatest confusion and perplexity are
the result of that happy thought. It seems
like a hopeless task to quote one set of
figures from one work, without the risk of
finding it contradicted by the same Author
in an earlier or a subsequent volume. Sir
W. Thomson, one of the most eminent
among the modern authorities, has changed,
about half-a-dozen times, his opinion upon
the age of the Sun and the date of the consolidation of the Earth's crust. In Thomson and Tait's *Natural Philosophy*, one finds
only ten million years allowed, since the
time when the temperature of the Earth permitted vegetable life to appear on it (*App.
D, et seq.; also Trans. Roy. Soc. Edin.* xxiii,
Pt. 1, 157, 1862, where 847 is cancelled).
Mr. Darwin gives Sir W. Thomson's estimate as " a minimum of 98 and a maximum
of 200 millions of years since the consolidation of the crust " (See Ch. Gould). In the
same work (*Nat. Phil.*) 80 millions are given
from the time of incipient incrustation to the
present state of the world. And in his last
lecture, as shown elsewhere, Sir W. Thomson declares (1887) that the Sun is not
older than 15 *millions* of years! Meanwhile,
basing his arguments as to the limits to the
age of the Sun's heat, on figures previously
established by Sir W. Thomson, Mr. Croll
allows 60 *millions* of years since the beginning of the Cambrian period. This is
hopeful for the lovers of *exact* knowledge.
Thus, whatever figures are given by Occult
Science, they are sure to be corroborated by
those of some one among the modern men of
Science who are considered as authorities.

minimum time required for the formation of the sedimentary *strata* and the elimination of the calcareous matter is in round numbers 600 million years;[26] or shall we ask support for our chronology from Mr. Darwin's works, wherein he demands for the organic transformations according to his theory from 300 to 500 million years? Sir C. Lyell and Professor Houghton were satisfied with placing the beginning of the Cambrian Age at 200 and 240 millions of years back respectively. Geologists and zoologists claim the maximum time, though Mr. Huxley, at one time, placed the beginning, of the incrustation of the earth 1,000 million years ago, and would not surrender a millennium of it.

But the main point for us lies not in the agreement or disagreement of the Naturalists as to the duration of geological periods, but rather in their perfect accord on one point, for a wonder, and this a very important one. They all agree that during " The Miocene Age " — whether one or ten million years ago — Greenland and even Spitzbergen, the remnants of our Second or Hyperborean Continent, " had *almost a tropical climate.*" Now the pre-Homeric Greeks had preserved a vivid tradition of this " Land of the Eternal Sun," whither their Apollo journeyed yearly. " During the Miocene Age, Greenland (in N. Lat. 70°) developed an abundance of trees, such as the Yew, the Redwood, a Sequoia, allied to the Californian species, Beeches, Planes, Willows, Oaks, Poplars and Walnuts, as well as a Magnolia and a Zamia," says Science;[26a] in short Greenland had Southern plants unknown to Northern regions.

And now this natural question rises. If the Greeks knew, in the days of Homer, of a Hyperborean land, *i. e.,* a blessed land beyond the reach of Boreas, the god of winter and of the hurricane, an ideal region which the later Greeks and their classics have vainly tried to locate by searching for it beyond Scythia, a country where nights were short and days long, and beyond that land a country where the sun never set and the palm grew freely — if they knew of all this, who then told them of it? In their day, and for ages previously, Greenland must certainly have been already covered with perpetual snows, with never-thawing ice, just as it is now. Everything tends to

26. See *Proceedings of Royal Society*, London, Vol. XXVIII, p. 281.
26a. *Mythical Monsters*, page 91.

show that the land of the short nights and the long days was Norway or Scandinavia, *beyond* which was the blessed land of eternal light and summer; and to know of this, their tradition must have descended to the Greeks from some people more ancient than themselves, who were acquainted with those climatic details of which the Greeks themselves could know nothing. Even in our day, science suspects beyond the Polar seas, at the very circle of the Arctic Pole, the existence of a sea which never freezes and a continent which is ever green. The archaic teachings, and likewise the Purânas — for one who understands the allegories of the latter — contain the same statements. Suffice, then, to us the strong probability that a people, now unknown to history, lived during the Miocene period of modern science, at a time when Greenland was an almost tropical land.

NOTE. The reader is requested to bear in mind that the first and the following sections are not strictly consecutive in order of time. In the first Section the Stanzas which form the skeleton of the exposition are given, and certain important points commented upon and explained. In the subsequent sections various additional details are gathered, and a fuller explanation of the subject is attempted.

BOOK II — PART I

ANTHROPOGENESIS

STANZAS TRANSLATED WITH COMMENTARIES

FROM THE

SECRET BOOK OF DZYAN

In primeval times, a maiden,
Beauteous Daughter of the Ether,
Passed for ages her existence
In the great expanse of Heaven.
   .   .   .   .   .   .

Seven hundred years she wandered,
Seven hundred years she labored,
Ere her first-born was delivered.
   .   .   .   .   .   .

Ere a beauteous duck descending,
Hastens toward the water-mother.
   .   .   .   .   .

Lightly on the knee she settles,
Finds a nesting-place befitting,
Where to lay her eggs in safety.
Lays her eggs within, at pleasure,
Six, the golden eggs she lays them,
Then a *Seventh*, an egg of iron. . . . .
             (*Kalevala*, Rune I.)

ANTHROPOGENESIS IN THE SECRET VOLUME
(VERBATIM EXTRACTS [27])

I

1. THE LHA WHICH TURNS THE FOURTH IS SUBSERVIENT TO THE LHA OF THE SEVEN, THEY WHO REVOLVE DRIVING THEIR CHARIOTS AROUND THEIR LORD, THE ONE EYE. HIS BREATH GAVE LIFE TO THE SEVEN; IT GAVE LIFE TO THE FIRST.

2. SAID THE EARTH:—"LORD OF THE SHINING FACE; MY HOUSE IS EMPTY . . . . SEND THY SONS TO PEOPLE THIS WHEEL. THOU HAST SENT THY SEVEN SONS TO THE LORD OF WISDOM. SEVEN TIMES DOTH HE SEE THEE NEARER TO HIMSELF, SEVEN TIMES MORE DOTH HE FEEL THEE. THOU HAST FORBIDDEN THY SERVANTS, THE SMALL RINGS, TO CATCH THY LIGHT AND HEAT, THY GREAT BOUNTY TO INTERCEPT ON ITS PASSAGE. SEND NOW TO THY SERVANT THE SAME."

3. SAID THE "LORD OF THE SHINING FACE":—"I SHALL SEND THEE A FIRE WHEN THY WORK IS COMMENCED. RAISE THY VOICE TO OTHER LOKAS; APPLY TO THY FATHER, THE LORD OF THE LOTUS, FOR HIS SONS . . . . THY PEOPLE SHALL BE UNDER THE RULE OF THE FATHERS. THY MEN SHALL BE MORTALS. THE MEN OF THE LORD OF WISDOM, NOT THE LUNAR SONS, ARE IMMORTAL. CEASE THY COMPLAINTS. THY SEVEN SKINS ARE YET ON THEE . . . . THOU ART NOT READY. THY MEN ARE NOT READY."

4. AFTER GREAT THROES SHE CAST OFF HER OLD THREE AND PUT ON HER NEW SEVEN SKINS, AND STOOD IN HER FIRST ONE.

II.

5. THE WHEEL WHIRLED FOR THIRTY CRORES MORE. IT CONSTRUCTED RÛPAS: SOFT STONES THAT HARDENED; HARD PLANTS THAT SOFTENED. VISIBLE FROM INVISIBLE, INSECTS AND SMALL LIVES. SHE SHOOK THEM OFF HER BACK WHENEVER THEY OVERRAN THE MOTHER.

27. Only forty-nine Ślokas out of several hundred are here given. Not every verse is translated verbatim. A periphrasis is sometimes used for the sake of clearness and intelligibility, where a literal translation would be quite unintelligible.

. . . . AFTER THIRTY CRORES SHE TURNED ROUND. SHE LAY ON HER BACK; ON HER SIDE . . . SHE WOULD CALL NO SONS OF HEAVEN, SHE WOULD ASK NO SONS OF WISDOM. SHE CREATED FROM HER OWN BOSOM. SHE EVOLVED WATER-MEN, TERRIBLE AND BAD.

6. THE WATER-MEN TERRIBLE AND BAD SHE HERSELF CREATED FROM THE REMAINS OF OTHERS, FROM THE DROSS AND SLIME OF HER FIRST, SECOND, AND THIRD, SHE FORMED THEM. THE DHYÂNI CAME AND LOOKED — THE DHYÂNI FROM THE BRIGHT FATHER-MOTHER, FROM THE WHITE REGIONS THEY CAME, FROM THE ABODES OF THE IMMORTAL MORTALS.

7. DISPLEASED THEY WERE. OUR FLESH IS NOT THERE. NO FIT RÛPAS FOR OUR BROTHERS OF THE FIFTH. NO DWELLINGS FOR THE LIVES. PURE WATERS, NOT TURBID, THEY MUST DRINK. LET US DRY THEM.

8. THE FLAMES CAME. THE FIRES WITH THE SPARKS; THE NIGHT FIRES AND THE DAY FIRES. THEY DRIED OUT THE TURBID DARK WATERS. WITH THEIR HEAT THEY QUENCHED THEM. THE LHAS OF THE HIGH, THE LHAMAYIN OF BELOW, CAME. THEY SLEW THE FORMS WHICH WERE TWO- AND FOUR-FACED. THEY FOUGHT THE GOAT-MEN, AND THE DOG-HEADED MEN, AND THE MEN WITH FISHES' BODIES.

9. MOTHER-WATER, THE GREAT SEA, WEPT. SHE AROSE, SHE DISAPPEARED IN THE MOON WHICH HAD LIFTED HER, WHICH HAD GIVEN HER BIRTH.

10. WHEN THEY WERE DESTROYED, MOTHER-EARTH REMAINED BARE. SHE ASKED TO BE DRIED.

III

11. THE LORD OF THE LORDS CAME. FROM HER BODY HE SEPARATED THE WATERS, AND THAT WAS HEAVEN ABOVE, THE FIRST HEAVEN.

12. THE GREAT CHOHANS CALLED THE LORDS OF THE MOON, OF THE AIRY BODIES. "BRING FORTH MEN, MEN OF YOUR NATURE. GIVE THEM THEIR FORMS WITHIN. SHE WILL BUILD COVERINGS WITHOUT. MALES-FEMALES WILL THEY BE. LORDS OF THE FLAME ALSO . . . ."

13. THEY WENT EACH ON HIS ALLOTTED LAND: SEVEN OF THEM EACH ON HIS LOT. THE LORDS OF THE FLAME REMAIN BEHIND. THEY WOULD NOT GO, THEY WOULD NOT CREATE.

IV

14. THE SEVEN HOSTS, THE "WILL-BORN LORDS," PROPELLED BY THE SPIRIT OF LIFE-GIVING, SEPARATE MEN FROM THEMSELVES, EACH ON HIS OWN ZONE.

15. SEVEN TIMES SEVEN SHADOWS OF FUTURE MEN WERE BORN, EACH OF HIS OWN COLOR AND KIND. EACH INFERIOR TO HIS FATHER. THE FATHERS, THE BONELESS, COULD GIVE NO LIFE TO BEINGS WITH BONES. THEIR PROGENY WERE BHÛTA, WITH NEITHER FORM NOR MIND. THEREFORE THEY ARE CALLED THE CHHÂYÂ.

16. HOW ARE THE MANUSHYA BORN? THE MANUS WITH MINDS, HOW ARE THEY MADE? THE FATHERS CALLED TO THEIR HELP THEIR OWN FIRE; WHICH IS THE FIRE THAT BURNS IN EARTH. THE SPIRIT OF THE EARTH CALLED TO HIS HELP THE SOLAR FIRE. THESE THREE PRODUCED IN THEIR JOINT EFFORTS A GOOD RÛPA. IT COULD STAND, WALK, RUN, RECLINE, OR FLY. YET IT WAS STILL BUT A CHHÂYÂ, A SHADOW WITH NO SENSE . . . .

17. THE BREATH NEEDED A FORM; THE FATHERS GAVE IT. THE BREATH NEEDED A GROSS BODY; THE EARTH MOLDED IT. THE BREATH NEEDED THE SPIRIT OF LIFE; THE SOLAR LHAS BREATHED IT INTO ITS FORM. THE BREATH NEEDED A MIRROR OF ITS BODY; "WE GAVE IT OUR OWN," SAID THE DHYÂNIS. THE BREATH NEEDED A VEHICLE OF DESIRES; "IT HAS IT," SAID THE DRAINER OF WATERS. BUT BREATH NEEDS A MIND TO EMBRACE THE UNIVERSE; "WE CANNOT GIVE THAT," SAID THE FATHERS. "I NEVER HAD IT," SAID THE SPIRIT OF THE EARTH. "THE FORM WOULD BE CONSUMED WERE I TO GIVE IT MINE," SAID THE GREAT FIRE . . . . MAN REMAINED AN EMPTY SENSELESS BHÛTA . . . . THUS HAVE THE BONELESS GIVEN LIFE TO THOSE WHO BECAME MEN WITH BONES IN THE THIRD.

V

18. THE FIRST WERE THE SONS OF YOGA. THEIR SONS THE CHIL-DREN OF THE YELLOW FATHER AND THE WHITE MOTHER.

19. THE SECOND RACE WAS THE PRODUCT BY BUDDING AND EXPAN-

SION, THE A-SEXUAL FROM THE SEXLESS.[28] THUS WAS, O LANOO,
THE SECOND RACE PRODUCED.

20. THEIR FATHERS WERE THE SELF-BORN. THE SELF-BORN, THE
CHHÂYÂ FROM THE BRILLIANT BODIES OF THE LORDS, THE FATHERS,
THE SONS OF TWILIGHT.

21. WHEN THE RACE BECAME OLD, THE OLD WATERS MIXED WITH
THE FRESHER WATERS. WHEN ITS DROPS BECAME TURBID, THEY VAN-
ISHED AND DISAPPEARED IN THE NEW STREAM, IN THE HOT STREAM OF
LIFE. THE OUTER OF THE FIRST BECAME THE INNER OF THE SECOND.
THE OLD WING BECAME THE NEW SHADOW, AND THE SHADOW OF
THE WING.

VI

22. THEN THE SECOND EVOLVED THE EGG-BORN, THE THIRD. THE
SWEAT GREW, ITS DROPS GREW, AND THE DROPS BECAME HARD AND
ROUND. THE SUN WARMED IT; THE MOON COOLED AND SHAPED IT;
THE WIND FED IT UNTIL ITS RIPENESS. THE WHITE SWAN FROM THE
STARRY VAULT OVERSHADOWED THE BIG DROP. THE EGG OF THE FUTURE
RACE, THE MAN-SWAN OF THE LATER THIRD. FIRST MALE-FEMALE,
THEN MAN AND WOMAN.

23. THE SELF-BORN WERE THE CHHÂYÂS: THE SHADOWS FROM
THE BODIES OF THE SONS OF TWILIGHT.

VII

24. THE SONS OF WISDOM, THE SONS OF NIGHT, READY FOR RE-
BIRTH, CAME DOWN, THEY SAW THE VILE FORMS OF THE FIRST THIRD,
"WE CAN CHOOSE," SAID THE LORDS, "WE HAVE WISDOM." SOME
ENTERED THE CHHÂYÂ. SOME PROJECTED THE SPARK. SOME DEFERRED
TILL THE FOURTH. FROM THEIR OWN RÛPA THEY FILLED THE KÂMA.
THOSE WHO ENTERED BECAME ARHATS. THOSE WHO RECEIVED BUT
A SPARK, REMAINED DESTITUTE OF KNOWLEDGE; THE SPARK BURNED
LOW. THE THIRD REMAINED MIND-LESS. THEIR JÎVAS WERE NOT

---

28. The idea and the spirit of the sentence is here given, as a verbal translation
would convey very little to the reader.

READY. THESE WERE SET APART AMONG THE SEVEN. THEY BECAME NARROW-HEADED. THE THIRD WERE READY. "IN THESE SHALL WE DWELL," SAID THE LORDS OF THE FLAME.

25. HOW DID THE MÂNASA, THE SONS OF WISDOM, ACT? THEY REJECTED THE SELF-BORN. THEY ARE NOT READY. THEY SPURNED THE SWEAT-BORN. THEY ARE NOT QUITE READY. THEY WOULD NOT ENTER THE FIRST EGG-BORN.

26. WHEN THE SWEAT-BORN PRODUCED THE EGG-BORN, THE TWO-FOLD AND THE MIGHTY, THE POWERFUL WITH BONES, THE LORDS OF WISDOM SAID: "NOW SHALL WE CREATE."

27. THE THIRD RACE BECAME THE VÂHANA OF THE LORDS OF WISDOM. IT CREATED "SONS OF WILL AND YOGA," BY KRIYÂSAKTI IT CREATED THEM, THE HOLY FATHERS, ANCESTORS OF THE ARHATS. .

VIII

28. FROM THE DROPS OF SWEAT; FROM THE RESIDUE OF THE SUB-STANCE; MATTER FROM DEAD BODIES OF MEN AND ANIMALS OF THE WHEEL BEFORE; AND FROM CAST-OFF DUST, THE FIRST ANIMALS WERE PRODUCED.

29. ANIMALS WITH BONES, DRAGONS OF THE DEEP, AND FLYING SARPAS WERE ADDED TO THE CREEPING THINGS. THEY THAT CREEP ON THE GROUND GOT WINGS. THEY OF THE LONG NECKS IN THE WATER BECAME THE PROGENITORS OF THE FOWLS OF THE AIR.

30. DURING THE THIRD RACE THE BONELESS ANIMALS GREW AND CHANGED: THEY BECAME ANIMALS WITH BONES, THEIR CHHÂYÂS BECAME SOLID.

31. THE ANIMALS SEPARATED THE FIRST. THEY BEGAN TO BREED. THE TWO-FOLD MAN SEPARATED ALSO. HE SAID: "LET US AS THEY; LET US UNITE AND MAKE CREATURES." THEY DID.

32. AND THOSE WHICH HAD NO SPARK TOOK HUGE SHE-ANIMALS UNTO THEM. THEY BEGAT UPON THEM DUMB RACES. DUMB THEY WERE THEMSELVES. BUT THEIR TONGUES UNTIED. THE TONGUES OF THEIR PROGENY REMAINED STILL. MONSTERS THEY BRED. A RACE OF CROOKED RED-HAIR-COVERED MONSTERS GOING ON ALL FOURS. A DUMB RACE TO KEEP THE SHAME UNTOLD.

IX

33. SEEING WHICH, THE LHAS WHO HAD NOT BUILT MEN, WEPT, SAYING: —

34. "THE AMÂNASA HAVE DEFILED OUR FUTURE ABODES. THIS IS KARMA. LET US DWELL IN THE OTHERS. LET US TEACH THEM BETTER, LEST WORSE SHOULD HAPPEN." THEY DID . . . .

35. THEN ALL MEN BECAME ENDOWED WITH MANAS. THEY SAW THE SIN OF THE MINDLESS.

36. THE FOURTH RACE DEVELOPED SPEECH.

37. THE ONE BECAME TWO; ALSO ALL THE LIVING AND CREEPING THINGS THAT WERE STILL ONE, GIANT FISH-BIRDS AND SERPENTS WITH SHELL-HEADS.

———

X

38. THUS TWO BY TWO ON THE SEVEN ZONES, THE THIRD RACE GAVE BIRTH TO THE FOURTH-RACE MEN; THE GODS BECAME NO-GODS; THE SURA BECAME A-SURA.

39. THE FIRST, ON EVERY ZONE, WAS MOON-COLORED; THE SECOND YELLOW LIKE GOLD; THE THIRD RED; THE FOURTH BROWN, WHICH BECAME BLACK WITH SIN. THE FIRST SEVEN HUMAN SHOOTS WERE ALL OF ONE COMPLEXION. THE NEXT SEVEN BEGAN MIXING.

40. THEN THE FOURTH BECAME TALL WITH PRIDE. WE ARE THE KINGS, IT WAS SAID; WE ARE THE GODS.

41. THEY TOOK WIVES FAIR TO LOOK UPON. WIVES FROM THE MINDLESS, THE NARROW-HEADED. THEY BRED MONSTERS. WICKED DEMONS, MALE AND FEMALE, ALSO KHADO (DÂKINÎ), WITH LITTLE MINDS.

42. THEY BUILT TEMPLES FOR THE HUMAN BODY. MALE AND FEMALE THEY WORSHIPED. THEN THE THIRD EYE ACTED NO LONGER.

———

XI

43. THEY BUILT HUGE CITIES. OF RARE EARTHS AND METALS THEY BUILT, AND OUT OF THE FIRES VOMITED, OUT OF THE WHITE STONE OF

THE MOUNTAINS AND OF THE BLACK STONE, THEY CUT THEIR OWN
IMAGES IN THEIR SIZE AND LIKENESS, AND WORSHIPED THEM.

44. THEY BUILT GREAT IMAGES NINE YATIS HIGH, THE SIZE OF
THEIR BODIES. INNER FIRES HAD DESTROYED THE LAND OF THEIR
FATHERS. THE WATER THREATENED THE FOURTH.

45. THE FIRST GREAT WATERS CAME. THEY SWALLOWED THE
SEVEN GREAT ISLANDS.

46. ALL HOLY SAVED, THE UNHOLY DESTROYED. WITH THEM
MOST OF THE HUGE ANIMALS, PRODUCED FROM THE SWEAT OF THE
EARTH.

XII

47. FEW MEN REMAINED: SOME YELLOW, SOME BROWN AND BLACK,
AND SOME RED REMAINED. THE MOON-COLORED WERE GONE FOREVER.

48. THE FIFTH PRODUCED FROM THE HOLY STOCK REMAINED; IT
WAS RULED OVER BY THE FIRST DIVINE KINGS.

49. . . . . WHO RE-DESCENDED, WHO MADE PEACE WITH THE FIFTH,
WHO TAUGHT AND INSTRUCTED IT. . . . . .

STANZA I [29]

BEGINNINGS OF SENTIENT LIFE

§§ (1) THE LHA, or Spirit of the Earth.   (2) Invocation of the Earth to the Sun.   (3) What the Sun answers.   (4) Transformation of the Earth.

1. THE LHA (*a*) WHICH TURNS THE FOURTH (*Globe, or our Earth*) IS SERVANT TO THE LHA(S) OF THE SEVEN (*the planetary Spirits*) (*b*), THEY WHO REVOLVE, DRIVING THEIR CHARIOTS AROUND THEIR LORD, THE ONE EYE (*Loka-Chakshus*) OF OUR WORLD. HIS BREATH GIVES LIFE TO THE SEVEN (*gives light to the planets*). IT GAVE LIFE TO THE FIRST (*c*). "THEY ARE ALL DRAGONS OF WISDOM," adds the Commentary (*d*).

(*a*) Lha is the ancient word in trans-Himâlayan regions for "Spirit," any celestial or *superhuman* Being, and it covers the whole series of heavenly hierarchies, from Archangel, or Dhyâni, down to an angel of darkness, or terrestrial Spirit.

(*b*) This expression shows in plain language that the Spirit-Guardian of our globe, which is the fourth in the chain, is subordinate to the chief Spirit (or God) of the Seven Planetary Genii or Spirits. As already explained, the ancients had, in their Kyriel of gods, seven chief Mystery-gods, whose chief was, *exoterically*, the visible Sun, or the eighth, and, *esoterically*, the *second Logos*, the Demiurge. The seven (who have now become the "Seven Eyes of the Lord" in the Christian religion) were the regents of the seven *chief* planets; but these were

29. All the words and sentences placed in brackets in the Stanzas and Commentaries are the writer's. In some places they may be incomplete and even inadequate from the Hindû standpoint; but in the meaning attached to them in Trans-Himâlayan Esotericism they are correct. In every case the writer takes any blame upon herself. Having never claimed personal infallibility, that which is given on her own authority may leave much to be desired, in the very abstruse cases where too deep metaphysic is involved. The teaching is offered as it is understood; and as there are seven keys of interpretation to every symbol and allegory, that which may not fit a meaning, say from the psychological or astronomical aspect, will be found quite correct from the physical or metaphysical.

not reckoned according to an enumeration devised later by people who had forgotten, or who had an inadequate notion of, the real *Mysteries,* and included neither the sun, the moon, nor the earth. The sun was the chief, exoterically, of the twelve great gods or zodiacal constellations; and, esoterically, the Messiah, the Christos (the subject *anointed* by the Great BREATH, or the ONE) surrounded by his twelve subordinate powers, also subordinate, in turn, to each of the seven " Mystery-gods " of the planets.

" The seven higher make the Seven Lhas create the world," states a Commentary; which means that our Earth, leaving aside the rest, was *created* or fashioned by terrestrial spirits, the " Regents " being simply the supervisors. This is the first germ, the seed of that which grew later into the Tree of Astrology and Astrolatry. The Higher ones were the *Kosmokratores,* the fabricators of our solar system. This is borne out by all the ancient Cosmogonies: that of Hermes, of the Chaldees, of the Aryans, of the Egyptians, and even of the Jews. Heaven's belt, the signs of the Zodiac (the *Sacred animals*), are as much the Bne' Alhim (Sons of the Gods or the Elohim) as the Spirits of the Earth; but they are prior to them. Soma and Sin, Isis and Diana, are all lunar gods or goddesses, called the fathers and mothers of our Earth, which is subordinate to them. But these, in their turn, are subordinate to their " Fathers " and " Mothers " — the latter interchangeable and varying with each nation — the gods and their planets, such as Jupiter, Saturn, Bel, Brihaspati, etc.

(*c*) " His breath gave life to the seven," refers as much to the sun, who gives life to the Planets, as to the " High One," the *Spiritual Sun,* who gives life to the whole Kosmos. The astronomical and astrological keys opening the gate leading to the mysteries of Theogony can be found only in the later glossaries, which accompany the Stanzas.

In the apocalyptic Ślokas of the Archaic Records, the language is as symbolical, if less mystical, than in the Purânas. Without the help of the later *commentaries,* compiled by generations of adepts, it would be impossible to understand the meaning correctly. In the ancient Cosmogonies, the visible and the invisible worlds are the double links of one and the same chain. As the invisible *Logos,* with its seven hierarchies (represented or personified each by its chief angel or rector), form one POWER, the inner and the invisible; so, in the world of Forms, the Sun and the seven chief Planets constitute the visible and active potency; the latter " Hierarchy " being, so to speak, the visible and objective *Logos* of the invisible and (except in the lowest grades) ever-subjective angels.

Thus — to anticipate a little by way of illustration — every Race in its evolution is said to be born under the direct influence of one of the Planets: Race the first receiving its breath of life from the Sun, as will be seen later on; while the third humanity — those who fell into generation, or from androgynes became separate entities, one male and the other female — are said to be under the direct influence of Venus, "*the little sun* in which the solar orb stores his light."

The summation of the Stanzas in Book I showed the genesis[30] of Gods and men taking rise in, and from, one and the same Point, which is the One Universal, Immutable, Eternal, and absolute UNITY. In its primary manifested aspect we have seen it become: (1) in the sphere of objectivity and Physics, Primordial Substance and Force (centripetal and centrifugal, positive and negative, male and female, etc., etc.); (2) in the world of Metaphysics, the SPIRIT OF THE UNIVERSE, or Cosmic Ideation, called by some the LOGOS.

This LOGOS is the apex of the Pythagorean triangle. When the triangle is complete it becomes the Tetraktys, or the Triangle in the Square, and is the dual symbol of the four-lettered *Tetragrammaton* in the manifested Kosmos, and of its radical triple RAY in the unmanifested, or its *noumenon*.

Put more metaphysically, the classification given here of Cosmic Ultimates, is more one of convenience than of absolute philosophical accuracy. At the commencement of a great Manvantara, Parabrahm manifests as Mûlaprakriti and then as the Logos. This Logos is equivalent to the "Unconscious Universal Mind," etc., of Western Pantheists. It constitutes the Basis of the SUBJECT-side of manifested Being, and is the source of all manifestations of individual consciousness. Mûlaprakriti or Primordial Cosmic Substance, is the foundation of the OBJECT-side of things — the basis of all objective evolution and Cosmogenesis. Force, then, does not emerge with Primordial Substance from Parabrahmic Latency. It is *the transformation into energy of the supra-conscious thought of the Logos*, infused, so to speak, into the objectivation of the latter out of potential latency in the One Reality. Hence spring the wondrous laws of matter: hence the "primal impress" so vainly discussed by Bishop Temple. Force thus is *not synchronous with the first objectivation of Mûlaprakriti*. But as, apart from it, the latter is absolutely and necessarily inert — *a mere abstraction* — it is unnecessary to weave too fine a cobweb of subtleties as to the order of succession of the Cosmic Ultimates. Force *succeeds*

30. According to Dr. A. Wilder's learned definition, Genesis, γένεσις, is not generation, but "*a coming out of the eternal* into the Kosmos and Time": "a coming from *esse* into *existere*," or "from BE-NESS into 'being'" — as a Theosophist would say.

Mûlaprakriti; but, *minus* Force, Mûlaprakriti is for all practical intents and purposes non-existent.[31]

The "Heavenly Man" (Tetragrammaton) who is the Protogonos, Tikkun, the firstborn from the passive deity and the first manifestation of that deity's shadow, is the universal form and idea, which engenders the manifested Logos, Adam Kadmon, or the four-lettered symbol, in the Kabala, of the *Universe itself*, also called the *second Logos*. The second springs from the first and develops the third triangle (see the Sephirothal Tree); from the last of which (the lower host of Angels) MEN are generated. It is with this third aspect that we shall deal at present.

The reader must bear in mind that there is a great difference between the LOGOS and the *Demiourgos*, for one is *Spirit* and the other is *Soul;* or as Dr. Wilder has it: "*Dianoia* and *Logos* are synonymous, *Nous* being superior and closely in affinity with Tὸ ἀγαθόν, one being the superior apprehending, the other the comprehending — one noetic and the other phrenic."

Moreover, Man was regarded in several systems as the *third Logos*. The esoteric meaning of the word *Logos* (speech or word, *Verbum*) is the rendering in objective expression, as in a photograph, of the concealed thought. The *Logos* is the mirror reflecting DIVINE MIND, and the Universe is the mirror of the Logos, though the latter is the *esse* of that Universe. As the *Logos* reflects *all* in the Universe of Pleroma, so man reflects in himself all that he sees and finds in *his* Universe, the Earth. It is the three Heads of the Kabala: "*Unum intra alterum, et alterum super alterum.*"[32] "Every Universe (world or planet) has its own Logos," says the doctrine. The Sun was always called by the Egyptians "the eye of Osiris," and was himself the *Logos,* the first-begotten, or light made manifest to the world, "which is the Mind and divine intellect of the Concealed." It is only by the sevenfold Ray of this light that we can become cognizant of the Logos through the Demiurge, regarding the latter as the *creator* of our planet and everything pertaining to it, and the former as the guiding Force of that "Creator" — good and bad at the same time, the origin of good and the origin of evil. This "Creator" is neither good nor bad *per se,* but its differentiated aspects in nature make it assume one or the other character. With the invisible and the unknown Universes disseminated through space, none of the sun-gods had anything to do. The idea is expressed very clearly in the "Books of Hermes," and in every ancient folk lore. It is symbolized generally by the Dragon and the Serpent —

---

31. For a clearer explanation of the origins, as contained in the esotericism of the *Bhagavad Gîtâ,* see the Notes thereon published in the *Theosophist* for February, March and June, 1887, Madras.

32. *Zohar, Idrah Sutah,* sec. VII.

the Dragon of Good and the Serpent of Evil, represented on Earth by
the right and the left-hand Magic. In the epic poem of Finland, the
Kalevala,[33] the origin of the Serpent of Evil is given: it is born from
the "spittle of Suoyatar . . . and endowed with a living Soul by the
Principle of Evil," Hisi. A strife is described between the two, the
"thing of Evil" (the Serpent or Sorcerer), and Ahti, the Dragon,
"Magic Lemminkainen." The latter is one of the seven sons of Ilmatar,
the virgin "daughter of the air," she "who fell from heaven into the
sea," before Creation, i. e., Spirit transformed into the matter of sen-
suous life. There is a world of meaning and Occult thought in these
few lines, admirably rendered by Dr. J. M. Crawford, of Cincinnati.
The hero Lemminkainen, the good magician,

> Hews the wall with might of magic,
> Breaks the palisade in pieces,
> Hews to atoms *seven* pickets,
> Chops the *Serpent wall* to fragments.
>
> . . . .
>
> When the monster little heeding,
>
> . . . .
>
> Pounces with his mouth of venom
> At the head of Lemminkainen.
> But the hero, quick recalling,
> Speaks the *Master words of Knowledge*,
> Words that came from distant ages,
> Words his ancestors had taught him. . . .

(*d*) In China the men of Fohi (or the "Heavenly Man") are called
the twelve *T'ien-Hoang*, the twelve hierarchies of Dhyânis or Angels,
with human Faces, and Dragon bodies; the dragon standing for *divine
Wisdom* or Spirit;[34] and they create men by incarnating themselves in

33. J. W. Alden, New York.

34. It has been repeatedly stated that
the Serpent is the symbol of wisdom and of
Occult knowledge. "The Serpent has been
connected with the god of wisdom from the
earliest times of which we have any historical notice," writes Staniland Wake. "This
animal was the especial symbol of Thoth or
Taut . . . and of all those *gods*, such as
Hermes [?] and Seth who can be connected
with him. This is also the primitive Chal-
dæan triad Ilea or Hoa." According to
Sir Henry Rawlinson, the most important
titles of this deity refer to "his functions
as the source of all knowledge and science."
Not only is he "the intelligent fish," but
his name may be read as signifying both
"life" and a serpent (an initiated adept),
and he may be considered as "figured by
the great serpent which occupies so conspicu-
ous a place among the symbols of the gods
on the black stones recording Babylonian
benefactions." Aesculapius, Serapis, Pluto,
Khnûm and Kneph, are all deities with the
attributes of the serpent. Says Dupuis,
"They are all *healers*, givers of health, spiritual and physical, and of *enlightenment*."
The crown formed of an asp, the *Thermuthis*,
belongs to Isis, goddess of Life and Healing.
The Upanishads have a treatise on the
Science of Serpents — in other words, the
Science of Occult knowledge; and the *Nâgas*
of the exoteric Buddhist are not "the fabulous *creatures* of the nature of serpents . . .

seven figures of clay — earth and water — made in the shape of those *T'ien-hoang*, a third allegory.[35] The twelve ÆSERS of the Scandinavian Eddas do the same. In the Secret Catechism of the Druses of Syria — a legend which is repeated word for word by the oldest tribes about and around the Euphrates — men were created by the " Sons of God " descending on Earth, where, after culling seven *Mandragoras*, they animated these roots, which became forthwith men.[36]

All these allegories point to one and the same origin — to the dual and the triple nature of man; dual, as male and female; triple — as being of spiritual and psychic essence *within*, and of a material fabric without.

---

2. SAID THE EARTH, "LORD OF THE SHINING FACE (*the Sun*) MY HOUSE IS EMPTY. . . . SEND THY SONS TO PEOPLE THIS WHEEL (*Earth*). THOU HAST SENT THY SEVEN SONS TO THE LORD OF WISDOM (*a*). SEVEN TIMES DOTH HE SEE THEE NEARER TO HIMSELF; SEVEN TIMES MORE DOTH HE FEEL THEE. THOU HAST FORBIDDEN THY SERVANTS, THE SMALL RINGS, TO CATCH THY LIGHT AND HEAT, THY GREAT BOUNTY TO INTERCEPT ON ITS PASSAGE (*b*). SEND NOW TO THY SERVANT THE SAME!" (*c*).

(*a*) The " Lord of Wisdom " is Mercury, or *Budha*.

(*b*) The modern Commentary explains the words as a reference to a well-known astronomical fact, " that Mercury receives seven times more

---

beings superior to men and the protectors of the law of Buddha," as Schlagintweit believes, but real living men, some superior to men by virtue of their Occult knowledge, and the *protectors of Buddha's law*, inasmuch as *they interpret his metaphysical tenets correctly*, others inferior morally as being *black* magicians. Therefore it is truly declared that Gautama Buddha " is said to have taught them a more philosophical religious system than to men, who were not sufficiently advanced to understand it at the time of his appearance." (Schlagintweit's *Buddhism in Tibet*, p. 31.)

35. Compare the *Symbols of the Bonzes*.

36. The Mandragora is the *mandrake* of the Bible, of Rachel and Leah. They are the roots of a plant, fleshy, hairy, and forked below, representing roughly the limbs of a man, the body and even a head. Its magical and mysterious properties have been proclaimed in fable and play from the most archaic ages. From Rachel and Leah, who indulged in witchcraft with them, down to Shakespeare, who speaks of *shrieking* —

" Like mandrakes torn out of the earth
That living mortals, hearing them, run mad "

— the mandragora was *the* magic plant *par excellence*.

These roots, without any stalk, and with large leaves growing out of the head of the root, like a gigantic crop of hair, present little similitude to man when found in Spain, Italy, Asia Minor, or Syria. But on the Isle of Candia, and in Karamania near the city of Adan, they have a wonderfully human form; being very highly prized as amulets. They are also worn by women as a charm against sterility, and for other purposes. They are especially effective in *Black Magic*.

light and heat from the Sun than Earth, or even the beautiful Venus, which receives but twice that amount more than our insignificant Globe." Whether the fact was known in antiquity may be inferred from the prayer of the " Earth Spirit " to the Sun as given in the text.[37] The Sun, however, refuses to people the globe, as it is not ready to receive life as yet.

Mercury is, as an astrological planet, still more occult and mysterious than Venus. It is identical with the Mazdean Mithra, the genius, or god, "established between the Sun and the Moon, the perpetual companion of ' Sun' of Wisdom." Pausanias shows him as having an altar in common with Jupiter.[38] He had wings to express his attendance upon the Sun in its course; and he was called the *Nuntius*, or Sun-wolf, " *solaris luminis particeps.*" He was the leader of and the evocator of Souls, the " great Magician " and the Hierophant. Virgil depicts him as taking " his wand to evoke from Orcus the souls plunged therein " — *tum virgam capit, hac animas ille evocat Orco.* (See also the 21st Fargard of the *Vendîdâd* on the celestial militia.) He is the golden-colored Mercury, the χρυσοφαὴς Ἑρμῆς whom the Hierophants forbade to name. He is symbolized in Grecian mythology by one of the *dogs* (vigilance), which watch over the celestial flock (occult wisdom), or Hermes Anubis, or again Agathodaimon. He is the Argus watching over the Earth, and which the latter mistakes for the Sun itself. It is through the intercession of Mercury that the Emperor Julian prayed to the Occult Sun every night; for, as says Vossius: "All the theologians agree to say that *Mercury and the Sun are one.* . . . He was the most eloquent and the most wise of all the gods, which is not to be wondered at, since *Mercury is in such close proximity to the Wisdom and the Word of God* [the Sun] that he was confused with both." [39] Vossius utters here a greater occult truth than he suspected. The *Hermes-Sarameyas* of the Greeks is closely related to the Hindû *Saramâ and Sârameya*, the divine watchman, " who watches over the golden flock of stars and solar rays."

In the clearer words of the Commentary :—

" *The Globe, propelled onward by the Spirit of the Earth and his six*

---

37. Copernicus wrote his theories on the " Revolution of the Heavenly Bodies " in the xvith century, and the *Zohar*, even if compiled by Moses de Leon in the xiiith century, states that: " In the book of Hammannunah, the Old, we learn . . . that the earth turns upon itself in the form of a circle; that some are on top, the others below, . . . that there are some countries which are lightened, whilst others are in darkness; these have the day, when for the former it is night; and there are countries in which it is constantly day, or in which at least the night continues only some instants." (*Zohar*, iii, fol. 10a; Myer's *Qabbalah*, page 139.)

38. Book v.

39. *Idolatry*, Vol. ii, page 373.

assistants, gets all its vital forces, life, and powers through the medium of the seven planetary Dhyânis from the Spirit of the Sun. They are his messengers of Light and Life."

" Like each of the seven regions of the Earth, each of the seven [40] *First-born* (the primordial human groups) *receives its light and life from its own especial Dhyâni — spiritually, and from the palace* (house, the planet) *of that Dhyâni physically; so with the seven great Races to be born on it. The first is born under the Sun; the second under Brihaspati* (Jupiter) *; the third under Lohitânga* (the " fiery-bodied," Venus, or Śukra) *; the fourth, under Soma* (the Moon, our Globe also, the Fourth Sphere being born under and from the Moon) *and Sani, Saturn,* [41] *the Krûra-lochana* (evil-eyed) *and the Asita* (the dark) *; the fifth, under Budha* (Mercury)."

" So also with man and every 'man' in man (every principle). *Each gets its specific quality from its primary* (the planetary spirit), *therefore every man is a septenate* (or a combination of principles, each having its origin in a quality of that special Dhyâni). *Every active power or force of the earth comes to her from one of the seven Lords. Light comes through Śukra* (Venus), *who receives a triple supply, and gives one-third of it to the Earth. Therefore the two are called ' Twin-sisters;' but the Spirit of the Earth is subservient to the ' Lord' of Śukra. Our wise men represent the two Globes, one over, the other under the double Sign* (the primeval Svastika bereft of its four arms, or the cross $+$)." [42]

The " double sign " is, as every student of Occultism knows, the symbol of the male and the female principles in Nature, of the positive and the negative, for the Svastika or ⌐┐ is all that and much more. All antiquity, ever since the birth of Astronomy — imparted to the Fourth Race by one of its divine kings of the Divine Dynasty — and also of Astrology, represented Venus in its astronomical tables as a

40. Science teaches that Venus receives from the sun twice as much light and heat as the earth. Thus the planet, precursor of the dawn and the twilight, the most radiant of all the planets, said to give the earth one-third of the supply she receives, has two parts left for herself. This has an occult as well as an astronomical meaning.

41. "As it is above so it is below" is the fundamental axiom of occult philosophy. As the logos is seven-fold, i. e., throughout Kosmos it appears as seven logoi under seven different forms, or, as taught by learned Brâhmans, "each of these is the central figure of one of the seven main branches of the ancient wisdom religion "; and, as the seven principles which correspond to the seven distinct states of *Prajñâ,* or consciousness, are allied to seven states of matter and the seven forms of force, the division must be the same in all that concerns the earth.

42. Venus is thus ♀, the Earth ♁.

Globe poised over a Cross, and the Earth, as a *Globe under a Cross.*
The esoteric meaning of this is: " Earth fallen into generation, or into
the production of its species through sexual union." But the later
Western nations did not fail to give quite a different interpretation.
They explained this sign through their mystics — guided by the light
of the Latin Church — as meaning that our Earth and all on it were
redeemed *by the Cross,* while Venus (otherwise *Lucifer* or Satan) was
trampling upon it. Venus is the most occult, powerful, and mysterious
of all the planets; the one whose influence upon, and relation to the
Earth is most prominent. In exoteric Brâhmanism, Venus or *Sukra*
— a male deity [43] — is the son of Bhrigu, one of the Prajâpati and a
Vedic sage, and is Daitya-Guru, or the priest-instructor of the primeval
giants. The whole history of " Śukra " in the Purânas, refers to the
Third and to the Fourth Races.

*" It is through Sukra that the ' double ones' (the Hermaphrodites)
of the Third* (Root-Race) *descended from the first ' Sweat-born,' "*
says the Commentary. Therefore it is represented under the symbol of
$\ominus$ (the circle and diameter) *during the Third (Race) and of* $\oplus$
during the Fourth.

This needs explanation. The *diameter,* when found isolated in a
circle, stands for female nature, for the first *ideal* World, *self-generated
and self-impregnated* by the universally diffused Spirit of Life — referring thus to the primitive Root-Race also. It becomes androgynous as
the Races and all on Earth develop into their physical forms, and the
symbol is transformed into a circle with a diameter from which runs a
vertical line: expressive of male and female, not separated as yet — the
first and earliest Egyptian *Tau* T ; after which it becomes $+$'
or male-female separated[44] and fallen into generation. Venus (the
planet) is symbolized by the sign of a globe over the cross, which shows
it as presiding over the natural generation of man. The Egyptians
symbolized *Ankh,* "life," by the ansated cross, or $\,\stackrel{\circ}{\mathsf{T}}\,$ which is only another form of Venus (Isis) $\,\female\,$, and meant, esoterically, that mankind
and all animal life had stepped out of the divine spiritual circle and
fallen into physical male and female generation. This sign, from the
end of the Third Race, has the same phallic significance as the *"tree*

---

43. In the esoteric philosophy it is male
and female, or hermaphrodite; hence the
bearded Venus in mythology.
44. Therefore, putting aside its religio-

metaphysical aspect, the Cross of the Christians is symbolically far more *phallic* than
the pagan Svastika.
See first pp. of Book I.

of life" in Eden. *Anuki*, a form of Isis, is the goddess of life; and *Ankh* was taken by the Hebrews from the Egyptians and introduced by Moses, one learned in the Wisdom of the priests of Egypt, with many other mystical words. The word *Ankh* in Hebrew, with the personal suffix, means "my life," my being, which "is the personal pronoun Anochi," from the name of the Egyptian goddess *Anuki*.[45]

In one of the most ancient Catechisms of Southern India, Madras Presidency, the hermaphrodite goddess Ardhanâri[46] has the ansated cross, the Svastika, the "male and female sign," right in the central part, to denote the pre-sexual state of the Third Race. Vishnu, who is now represented with a lotus growing out of his navel — or the Universe of Brahmâ evolving out of the central point *Nara* — is shown in one of the oldest carvings as double-sexed (Vishnu and Lakshmi) standing on a lotus-leaf floating on the water; which water rises in a semicircle and pours through the Svastika, "the source of generation" or of the descent of man.

Pythagoras calls Śukra-Venus the *Sol alter*, "the other Sun." Of the "seven palaces of the Sun," that of Lucifer Venus is the *third* one in Christian and Jewish Kabala, the *Zohar* making of it the abode of *Samael*. According to the Occult Doctrine, this planet is our Earth's *primary*, and its spiritual prototype. Hence, Śukra's car (Venus-Lucifer's) is said to be drawn by an *ogdoad of "earth-born horses,"* while the steeds of the chariots of the other planets are different.

"*Every sin committed on Earth is felt by Uśanas-Śukra. The Guru of the Daityas is the Guardian Spirit of the Earth and Men. Every change on Śukra is felt on, and reflected by, the Earth.*"

Śukra, or Venus, is thus represented as the preceptor of the Daityas, the giants of the Fourth Race, who, in the Hindû allegory, obtained at one time the sovereignty of all the Earth, and defeated the minor gods. The *Titans* of the Western allegory are as closely connected with Venus-Lucifer, identified by later Christians with Satan. Therefore, as Venus, equally with Isis, was represented with Cow's horns on her head, the symbol of mystic Nature, and one that is convertible with, and significant of, the moon, since all these were lunar goddesses, the configuration of this planet is now placed by theologians between the horns of the mystic Lucifer.[47] It is owing to the fanciful interpretation of the

45. The ansated Cross is the astronomical planetary sign of Venus, "signifying the existence of *parturient energy* in the sexual sense, and this was one of the attributes of Isis, the *Mother*, of Eve, Hauvah, or Mother-Earth, and was so recognized among all the ancient peoples in one or another mode of expression." (From a modern Kabalistic MS.)

46. See also *Indian Pantheon*.
47. Athenaeus shows that the first letter of Satan's name was represented in days of old by an arc and crescent; and some Roman Catholics, good and kind men, would persuade the public that it is in honor of Lucifer's crescent-like horns that Mussulmans have chosen the Crescent for their national arms. Venus has always been iden-

archaic tradition, which states that Venus changes simultaneously (geologically) with the Earth; that whatever takes place on the one takes place on the other; and that many and great were their common changes — it is for these reasons that St. Augustine repeats it, applying the several changes of configuration, color, and even of the orbital paths, to that theologically-woven character of Venus-Lucifer. He even goes so far in his pious fancy as to connect the last changes of the planet with the Noachian and mythical Deluge alleged to have taken place 1796 years B. C.[48]

As Venus has no satellites, it is stated allegorically, that " Åsphujit " (this " planet ") adopted the Earth, the progeny of the Moon, " who overgrew its parent and gave much trouble," a reference to the occult connexion between the two. The Regent (of the planet) Śukra [49] loved his adopted child so well that he incarnated as Uśanas and gave it perfect laws, which were disregarded and rejected in later ages. Another allegory, in *Harivanśa,* is that Śukra went to Śiva asking him to protect his pupils, the Daityas and Asuras, from the fighting gods; and that to further his object he performed a Yoga rite " imbibing the *smoke* of chaff with his *head downwards* for 1000 years." This refers to the great inclination of the axis of Venus (amounting to 50 degrees), and to its being enveloped in eternal clouds. But it relates only to the physical constitution of the planet. It is with its Regent, the informing Dhyân Chohan, that Occult mysticism has to deal. The allegory which

tified, since the establishment of Roman Catholic dogmatism, with Satan and Lucifer, or the great Dragon, contrary to all reason and logic. As shown by the symbologists and astronomers, the association between the serpent and the idea of darkness had an astronomical foundation. The position which the constellation of Draco at one time occupied showed that the great serpent was the ruler of the night. This constellation was formerly at the very center of the heavens, and is so extensive that it was called the Great Dragon. Its body spreads over seven signs of the Zodiac; and Dupuis, " who," says Staniland Wake, " sees in the Dragon of the Apocalypse a reference to the celestial serpent," remarks that " it is not astonishing that a constellation so extended should be represented by the author of that book as a Great Dragon with seven heads, who drew the third part of the stars from heaven and cast them to Earth "; (Dupuis, tome III, p. 255). Only Dupuis never knew *why* Draco, once the *pole-star*

— the symbol of " Guide," Guru and director — had been thus degraded by posterity. " The gods of our fathers are our devils," says an Asiatic proverb. When Draco ceased to be the *lode-star,* the guiding sidereal divinity, it shared the fate of all the fallen gods. Seth and Typhon was at one time, Bunsen tells us, " a great god universally adored throughout Egypt, who conferred on the sovereigns of the 18th and 19th Dynasties the symbols of life and power. But subsequently, in the course of the 20th Dynasty, he is suddenly treated as an evil Demon, insomuch that his effigies and name are obliterated on all the monuments and inscriptions that could be reached." The real occult reason will be given in these pages.

48. See *City of God,* lxxi, ch. viii.

49. Śukra is the son of Bhrigu the great Rishi, and one of the Seven *Prajâpati,* the founder of the Race of Bhârgavas, in which Paraśu Râma is born.

states that for killing Śukra's mother, Vishnu was cursed by him to be *reborn seven times* on the Earth, is full of occult philosophical meaning. It does not refer to Vishnu's Avatârs, since these number nine, the tenth being still to come, but to the Races on Earth. Venus, or Lucifer (also Śukra and Uśanas) the planet, is the light-bearer of our Earth, in both its physical and mystic sense. The Christians knew it well in early times, since one of the earliest popes of Rome is known by his Pontiff name as Lucifer.

"*Every world has its parent star and sister planet. Thus Earth is the adopted child and younger brother of Venus, but its inhabitants are of their own kind. . . . All sentient complete beings* (full septenary men or higher beings) *are furnished, in their beginnings, with forms and organisms in full harmony with the nature and state of the sphere they inhabit.*" [50]

"*The Spheres of Being, or centers of life, which are isolated nuclei breeding their men and their animals, are numberless; not one has any resemblance to its sister-companion or to any other in its own special progeny.*" [51]

"*All have a double physical and spiritual nature.*"

"*The nucleoles are eternal and everlasting; the nuclei periodical and finite. The nucleoles form part of the absolute. They are the embrasures of that black impenetrable fortress, which is for ever concealed from human or even Dhyânic sight. The nuclei are the light of eternity escaping therefrom.*"

"*It is that* LIGHT *which condenses into the forms of the 'Lords of Being'* — *the first and the highest of which are, collectively,* JÎVÂTMÂ, *or Pratyagâtmâ* (said figuratively to issue from Paramâtmâ. It is the Logos of the Greek philosophers — appearing at the beginning of every new Manvantara). *From these downwards — formed from the ever-consolidating waves of that light, which becomes on the objective*

---

50. This is a flat contradiction of Sweden-borg, who *saw*, in "the *first harth of the astral world*," inhabitants *dressed as are the peasants in Europe*; and on the *Fourth Earth* women clad as are the shepherdesses in a *bal masqué*. Even the famous astronomer Huyghens labored under the mistaken idea that other worlds and planets have the same identical beings as those who live on our Earth, possessing the same figures, senses, brain-power, arts, sciences, dwellings and even to the same fabric for their wearing apparel! (*Théorie du Monde.*) For the clearer comprehension of the statement that the Earth "is the progeny of the Moon," see Book I, Stanza VI.

51. This is a modern gloss. It is added to the old Commentaries for the clearer comprehension of those disciples who study esoteric Cosmogony after having passed through Western learning. The earlier Glosses are too redundant with adjectives and figures of speech to be easily assimilated.

plane gross matter — proceed the numerous hierarchies of the Creative Forces, some formless, others having their own distinctive form, others, again, the lowest (Elementals), having no form of their own, but assuming every form according to the surrounding conditions."

"Thus there is but one Absolute Upâdhi (basis) in the spiritual sense, from, on, and in which, are built for Manvantaric purposes the countless basic centers on which proceed the Universal, cyclic, and individual Evolutions during the active period."

"The informing Intelligences, which animate these various centers of Being, are referred to indiscriminately by men beyond the Great Range[52] as the Manus, the Rishis, the Pitris,[53] the Prajâpati, and so on; and as Dhyâni Buddhas, the Chohans, Melhas (fire-gods), Bodhisattvas,[54] and others, on this side. The truly ignorant call them gods; the learned profane, the one God; and the wise, the Initiates, honor in them only the Manvantaric manifestations of THAT *which neither our Creators (the Dhyân Chohans) nor their creatures can ever discuss or know anything about. The* ABSOLUTE *is not to be defined, and no mortal or immortal has ever seen or comprehended it during the periods of Existence. The mutable cannot know the Immutable, nor can that which lives perceive Absolute Life."*

Therefore, man cannot know higher beings than his own "progenitors." *"Nor shall he worship them,"* but he ought to learn *how* he came into the world.

(*c*) Number Seven, the fundamental figure among all other figures in every national religious system, from Cosmogony down to man, must have its *raison d'être*. It is found among the ancient Americans, as prominently as among the archaic Aryans and Egyptians. The question will be fully dealt with in the second part of this Book; meanwhile a few facts may be given here. Says the author of the *Sacred Mysteries among the Mayas and Quichés, 11,500 Years Ago:*[55]

52. "Beyond" the Great Range, means, in our case, India, as being the Trans-Himâlayan region for the Cis-Himâlayan region.

53. The term Pitris is used by us in these Slokas to facilitate their comprehension, but it is not so used in the original Stanzas, where they have distinct appellations of their own, besides being called "Fathers" and "Progenitors."

54. It is erroneous to take literally the *worship* of the human Bodhisattvas, or Manjuśri. It is true that, exoterically, the Mahâyâna school teaches adoration of these

without distinction, and that Hiuen-Tsang speaks of some disciples of Buddha as being worshiped. But esoterically it is not the disciple or the learned Manjuśri *personally* that received honors, but the divine Bodhisattvas and Dhyâni Buddhas that animated (*Amilakha*, as the Mongolians say) the human forms.

55. The author of this work is Augustus Le Plongeon. He and his wife are well known in the United States for their untiring labors in Central America. It is they who discovered the sepulcher of the royal Kan Coh, at Chichen-Itza. The author seems

Seven seems to have been the sacred number *par excellence* among all civilized nations of antiquity. Why? Each separate people has given a different explanation, according to the peculiar tenets of their [*exoteric*] religion. That it was the *number of numbers for those initiated into the sacred mysteries, there can be no doubt.* Pythagoras . . . calls it the "Vehicle of Life" containing body and soul, since it is formed of a Quaternary, that is Wisdom and intellect, and of a *Trinity* or *action and matter.* The Emperor Julian, "*In Matrem, etc.*," expresses himself thus: "Were I to touch upon the initiation into our Sacred Mysteries, which the Chaldees Bacchized, respecting the *seven-rayed* god, lighting up the soul through him, I should say things unknown to the rabble, very unknown, but well known to the blessed Theurgists." [56]

And who, acquainted with the Purânas, the *Book of the Dead,* the *Zendavesta,* the Assyrian tiles, and finally the Bible, and who has observed the constant occurrence of the number seven, in these records of people living from the remotest times unconnected and so far apart, can regard as a coincidence the following fact, given by the same explorer of ancient Mysteries? Speaking of the prevalence of seven as a mystic number, among the inhabitants of the " Western continent " (of America), he adds that it is not less remarkable. For:—

It frequently occurs in the *Popol Vuh* . . . we find it besides in the *seven families* said by Sahagún and Clavigero to have accompanied the mystical personage named *Votan,* the reputed founder of the great city of Nachan, identified by some with Palenque. In the *seven caves* [57] from which the ancestors of the Nahuatl are reported to have emerged. In the *seven cities* of Cibola, described by Coronado and Niza. . . . In the *seven Antilles;* in the *seven heroes* who, we are told, escaped the Deluge. . . .

" Heroes," moreover, whose number is found the same in every " Deluge " story — from the seven Rishis who were saved with Vaivasvata Manu, down to Noah's ark, into which beasts, fowls, and living creatures were taken by " Sevens." Thus we see the figures 1, 3, 5, 7, as perfect, because thoroughly mystic, numbers playing a prominent part in every Cosmogony and evolution of living Beings. In China, 1, 3, 5, 7, are called "celestial numbers" in the canonical *Book of Changes.* [58]

The explanation of it becomes evident when one examines the ancient

to believe and to seek to prove that the esoteric learning of the Aryans and the Egyptians was derived from the Mayas. But, though certainly coeval with Plato's Atlantis, the Mayas belonged to the Fifth Continent, which was preceded by Atlantis and Lemuria.

56. Page 141.
57. These *seven caves, seven cities,* etc., etc., stand in every case for the seven centers, or zones, upon which the seven primitive groups of the first Root-race were born.
58. *Yi King,* or *transformation,* as in " Evolution."

Symbols: all these are based upon and start from the figures given
from the Archaic Manuscript in the proem of Book I. ⊕, the symbol
of evolution and fall into generation or matter, is reflected in the old
Mexican sculptures or paintings, as it is in the Kabalistic Sephiroth,
and the Egyptian *Tau*. Examine the Mexican MS.;[59] you will find
in it a tree whose trunk is covered with *ten* fruits ready to be plucked
by a male and female, one on each side of it, while from the top of the
trunk two branches shoot horizontally to the right and left, thus forming a perfect T (tau), the ends of the two branches, moreover, each
bearing a triple bunch, with a bird — the bird of immortality, Atman
or the divine Spirit — sitting between the two, and thus making the
seventh. This represents the same idea as the Sephirothal Tree, *ten in
all*, yet, when separated from its upper triad, leaving *Seven*. These are
the celestial fruits, the ten or ⓪ 10, born out of the two invisible male
and female seeds, making up the 12, or the Dodecahedron of the
Universe. The mystic system contains the •, the central point; the
3 or △ ; the five, ☆, and the seven or △ , or again ✡ ; the
triangle in the square and the synthesizing point in the interlaced
double triangles. This for the world of the archetypes. The phenomenal world receives its culmination and the reflex of all in MAN.
Therefore he is the mystic square — in his metaphysical aspect — the
Tetraktys; and becomes the *Cube* on the creative plane. His symbol
is the cube unfolded [60] and 6 becoming 7, or the ⊞, *three* crossways
(the female) and *four* vertically; and this is man, the culmination of
the deity on Earth, whose body is the cross of flesh, *on, through*, and *in*
which he is ever crucifying and putting to death the divine Logos or
his HIGHER SELF.

"The universe," says every Philosophy and Cosmogony, "hath a
Ruler (Rulers collectively) set over it, which is called the WORD
(Logos); the fabricating Spirit is its Queen: which two are the
First Power after the ONE."

These are the Spirit and Nature, which two form our illusory universe. The two inseparables remain in the *Universe of Ideas* so long as
it lasts, and then merge back into Parabrahm, the One ever changeless.
"The Spirit, whose essence is eternal, one and self-existent," emanates

59. *Add. MSS.* Brit. Mus. 9789. The   60. See *Source of Measures*, p. 50 to 53
engraving is reproduced in the *Sacred Mys-*   and also Book II, Part II.
teries of the Mayas and Quichés, on p. 134.

a pure ethereal LIGHT — a dual light not perceptible to the elementary senses — in the Purânas, in the Bible, in the Sepher Jetzirah, the Greek and Latin hymns, in the Book of Hermes, in the Chaldaean Book of Numbers, in the esotericism of Lao-tze, everywhere. In the Kabala, which explains the secret meaning of *Genesis,* this light is the DUAL-MAN, or the Androgyne (rather the sexless) angels, whose generic name is ADAM KADMON. It is they who complete man, whose ethereal form is emanated by other divine, but far lower beings, who solidify the body with clay, or the " dust of the ground " — an allegory indeed, but as scientific as any Darwinian evolution and more *true.*

The author of the *Source of Measures* says that the foundation of the Kabala and all its mystic books is made to rest upon the *ten Sephiroth;* which is a fundamental truth.[61] He shows these ten Sephiroth or the ten numbers in the following diagram :—

wherein the circle is the *naught,* its vertical diameter line is the first or primal ONE (the *Word* or *Logos*), from which springs the series of the other numbers up to 9, the limit of the digits. The 10 is the first Divine Manifestation[62] containing "every possible power of exact expression of proportion." By this Kabalistic speculation we are taught that the Sephiroth " were the numbers or emanations of the Heavenly Light (figures 20612 to 6561), they were the 10 ' Words,' DBRIM, 41224, the light, of which they were the flux, was the Heavenly Man, the Adam KDM (the 144-144) ; and the Light, by the New Testament or Covenant (or 41224) created God ; just as, by the Old Testament God (Alhim, 31415) creates light (20612 to 6561)."

Now there are three kinds of light in Occultism, as in the Kabala. (1) The Abstract and Absolute Light, which is Darkness ; (2) The Light of the Manifested-Unmanifested, called by some the Logos : and (3) The latter light reflected in the Dhyân Chohans, the minor *logoi* (the Elohim, collectively), who, in their turn, shed it on the objective Universe. But in the Kabala — re-edited and carefully adjusted to fit the Christian tenets by the Kabalists of the XIIIth century — the three lights are described as :— (1) The clear and penetrating, that of Jehovah ; (2) reflected light ; and (3) light in the *abstract.* " This

61. See *Masonic Review,* Cincinnati, June, 1886, Art, " The Cabbalah," No. 6.

62. See " *Isis Unveiled,*" Vol. II, pp. 300 *et seq.,* for a proof of the antiquity of the decimal system of figures.

light abstractly taken (in a metaphysical or symbolical sense) is Alhim (Elohim God), while the clear penetrating light is Jehovah. The light of Alhim belongs to the world in general, in its allness and general fulness, but the light of Jehovah is that pertaining to the chiefest production, man, whom this light penetrated and made." The author of the *Source of Measures* pertinently refers the reader to Inman's *Ancient Faiths embodied in Ancient Names.*[63] There, an engraving of " the *vesica piscis,* Mary and the female emblem, copied from a rosary of the blessed Virgin . . . printed at Venice, 1542," and therefore, as Inman remarks, " with a license from the Inquisition, consequently orthodox," will show the reader what the Latin Church understood by this *" penetrating power of light and its effects."* How sadly disfigured — applied as they were to the grossest anthropomorphic conceptions — have become, under Christian interpretation, the noblest and grandest, as the most exalted, ideas of deity of the Eastern philosophy!

The Occultists call this light *Daiviprakriti* in the East, and light of *Christos* in the West. It is the light of the LOGOS, the direct reflection of the ever Unknowable on the plane of Universal manifestation. But here is the interpretation thereof given by the modern Christians from the Kabala. As declared by the author just cited :—

To the fulness of the world in general with its chiefest content, man, the term Elohim-Jehovah applies. In extracts from the *Zohar,* the Rev. Dr. Cassell [a Kabalist], to prove that the Cabbalah sets forth the doctrine of the Trinity, among other things says: "Jehovah is Elohim (Alhim) . . . by three steps God (Alhim), and Jehovah become the same, and though separated each and together, they are of the same one."

Similarly, Vishnu becomes the Sun, the visible symbol of the impersonal deity. Vishnu is described as "striding through the seven regions of the Universe in *three steps."* But with the Hindûs this is an *exoteric* account, a surface tenet and an allegory, while the Kabalists give it out as the esoteric and final meaning. But to proceed :—

Now light, [explains the author] as shown, is 20612 to 6561, as the proper enunciation of the integral and numerical relation of diameter to circumference of a circle. God (Alhim, *i. e..* 3.1415 to one, a modified form of the above) is the reduction of this, so as to obtain a standard unit *one,* as the basis, in general, cf all calculation and all mensuration. But, for the production of animal life, and for especial *time measure* or the lunar year, that influence which causes conception and embryotic development, the numbers of the Jehovah measure (" *man even Jehovah*" measure), viz., 113 to 355, have to be specialized.[64] But this last ratio is but a modified form of light or 20612 to 6561, as a " π " *value,* being only a variation of the same (that is 20612 to 6561, is 31415 to one, or

63. Vol. II. p. 648.   64. See *Source of Measures,* pp. 276, *et seq.* App. VII.

Alhim or God) — and in such a manner that one can be made to flow into and be derived from the other, and these are the three steps by which the *Unity* and sameness can be shown of the divine names. That is, the two are but variations of the same ratio, viz, that of "π." The object of this comment is to show the same measuring use for the Cabbalah as was employed in the three Covenants of the Bible, and in the symbols of Masonry, as just noticed.

First then, the Sephiroth are described as *Light,* that is, they themselves are a function of, indeed, the same as, the manifestation of Ain-Soph; and they are so from the fact that *Light* represents the ratio of 20612 to 6561, as part of the " Words," DBRIM, 41224, or as to the Word, Debar, 206 (= 10 cubits). *Light* is so much the burden of the Kabbalah, in explaining the Sephiroth, that the most famous book on the Kabbalah is called *Zohar* or *Light.* In this we find expressions of this kind: — " The Infinite was entirely unknown and diffused no light before the luminous point violently broke through into vision. . . ." " When he first assumed the form (of the Crown, or the first Sephira), he caused 9 splendid lights to emanate from it, which, shining through it, diffused a bright light in all directions": that is, these 9 with his one (which was the origin, as above, of the nine), together made the 10, that is $\bigodot$ or $\bigotimes$, or *the sacred Ten (numbers or Sephiroth),* or *Jod* — and these numbers were *" the Light."* Just as in the Gospel of St. John, God (Alhim, 31415 to one) was that light (20612 to 6561) by which (Light) all things were made.

In *Sepher Jetzirah,* or Numbers of Creation, the whole process of evolution is given out in Numbers. In its " 32 paths of Wisdom " the number 3 is repeated four times, and the number 4 five times. Therefore, the Wisdom of God is contained in numbers (Sephrim or Sephiroth), for Sepher (or S-ph-ra when unvoweled) means " to cipher." And therefore, also, we find Plato stating that the deity *geometrizes* in fabricating the Universe.

The Kabalistic book, the *Sepher Jetzirah,* opens with a statement of the hidden wisdom of *Alhim* in *Sephrim, i. e.,* the Elohim in the Sephiroth.

" In thirty and two paths, hidden wisdom, established Jah, JHVH, Tzabaoth, Elohi of Israel, Alhim of Life, El of Grace and Mercy — exalted, uplifted Dweller on high, and King of Everlasting, and his name — Holy! in three Sephrim: viz: — B-S'ph-r, V-S'ph-r, V-Siph-o-r."

This Comment sets forth "the *Hidden Wisdom*" of the original text by hidden Wisdom, that is, by the use of words carrying a special set of Numbers and a special phraseology, which will set forth the very explanatory system which we find to fit so accurately in the Hebrew Bible. . . . . In setting forth his scheme, to enforce it, and to finish out his detailed exposition in a general postulate, viz., the one word *Sephrim (Sephiroth)* of the Number Jezirah, the author explains the separation of this word in the three subordinate ones, a play upon a common word *s-ph-r,* or number.

The prince Al-Chazari says to the Rabbi [65] : — " I wish now that thou
wouldest impart to me some of the chiefest or leading principles of
Natural Philosophy, which as thou sayest were in former times worked
out by them (the Ancient Wise Ones) "; to which the Rabbi makes
answer: — " To such principles appertains the Number of Creation of
our Race-father Abraham " (that is Abram and Abraham, or numbers
41224 and 41252).   He then says that this book of Number treats of
teaching the *Alhim-ness* and *One-ness* through " DBRIM," viz., the
numbers of the Word *" Words."*   That is, it teaches the use of the
ratio 31415 to one, through 41224, which last, in the description of the
Ark of the Covenant, was divided into two parts by two tables of stone,
on which these DBRIM, or 41224, were written or engraved — or 20612
by 2. He then comments on these three subordinately used words, and
takes care as to one of them to make the comment: — "And *Alhim*
(31415 to 1) said: Let there be Light (20612 to 6561)."

The three words as given in the text are : ספר ספר סיפור   And the
Rabbi in commenting upon them says:

It teaches the *Alhim-ness* (31415) and One-ness (the diameter to Alhim)
through Words (DBRIM, 41224), by which on the one side there is infinite
expression in heterogeneous creations, and on the other a final harmonic
tendency to *One-ness*

(which as everyone knows is the mathematical function of "π" of the
schools, which measures, and weighs and numbers the stars of heaven,
and yet resolves them back into the final Oneness of the Universe
through Words).

Their final accord perfects itself in that Oneness that ordains them and which
consists in   ספר ספר ספור   (Book of *Al-Chazari*), that is, the Rabbi, in his
first comment, leaves the jod, or *i*, out of one of the words, whereas afterwards
he restores it again. If we take the values of those subordinate words, we find
them to be 340, 340, 346; together these are 1026, and the division of the general
word into these has been to produce these numbers, which by Temurah may be
changed in various ways for various purposes.[66]

The reader is asked to turn to Stanza IV of Book I and its fourth
commentary to find that the 3, 4 — (7), and the thrice seven, or 1065,
the number of Jehovah, is the number of the 21 Prajâpati mentioned in
the *Mahâbhârata*, or the three *Sephrim* (words in cipher or figures).
And this comparison between the Creative Powers of Archaic philosophy and the anthropomorphic Creator of *exoteric* Judaism (since their
esotericism shows its identity with the Secret Doctrine) will lead the
student to perceive and discover that, in truth, Jehovah is but a *lunar*

65. In the Book *Al-Chazari*, by Jehuda-ba-Levi, translated by Dr. D. Cassell.
66. *Masonic Review*, Art. " The Cabbalah."

and " generation " god.[67] It is a fact well known to every conscientious
student of the Kabala, that the deeper he dives into it, the more he feels
convinced that unless the Kabala — or what is left of it — is read by
the light of the Eastern esoteric philosophy, its study leads only to the
discovery that on the lines traced by exoteric Judaism and Christianity,
the monotheism of both is nothing more exalted than ancient Astrolatry,
now vindicated by modern Astronomy. The Kabalists never cease to
repeat that *primal intelligence* can never be understood. It cannot be
comprehended, nor can it be located, therefore it has to remain nameless
and negative. Hence the Ain-Soph — the " UNKNOWABLE " and the
" UNNAMABLE " — which, as *it* could not be made manifest, was conceived to emanate manifesting Powers. It is then with its *emanations
alone that human intellect has to, and can deal.* Christian theology
having rejected the doctrine of emanations and replaced them with
direct, conscious creations of angels and the rest out of *nothing*, now
finds itself hopelessly stranded between Supernaturalism, or miracle,
and materialism. An *extra*-cosmic god is fatal to philosophy, an *intra*-
cosmic Deity — *i.e.* Spirit and matter inseparable from each other —
is a philosophical necessity. Separate them and that which is left is
a gross superstition under a mask of emotionalism. But why " geo-
metrize," as Plato has it, why represent these emanations under the
form of an immense arithmetical table? The question is well answered
by the author just cited. His remarks are quoted in Vol. I, Part II,
§ XII, " The Theogony of the Creative Gods." He says:

> Mental perception to become physical perception, must have the Cosmic prin-
> ciple of *light:* and by this, our mental circle must become visible through light;
> or, for its complete manifestation, the Circle must be that of physical visibility,
> or Light itself. Such conceptions, thus formulated, became the groundwork of
> the philosophy of the divine manifesting in the Universe.

This is philosophy. It is otherwise when we find the Rabbi in
Al-Chazari saying that —

> under s'ph-r is to be understood *calculation* and *weighing* of created bodies.
> For the *calculation*, by means of which a body must be constructed in harmony
> or symmetry, by which it must be in construction rightly arranged and made
> to correspond to the object in design, consists at last in *number, extension, mass,
> weight;* co-ordinate relation of movements, then harmony of music, must con-
> sist altogether by number, that is (S'ph-r). . . . By Sippor (s'phor) is to
> be understood the words of Alhim whereunto joins or adapts itself the design
> of the frame or form of construction; for example, it was said " Let Light be."
> The *work became as the* WORDS *were spoken,* that is, as the numbers of the
> work came forth. . . .

This is *materializing the Spiritual* without scruple. But the Kabala

67. See Book I, Part II, § IX, " Deus Lunus."

was not always so well adapted to anthropo-monotheistic conceptions. Compare this with any of the six schools of India. For instance, in Kapila's "Sânkhya" Philosophy, unless, allegorically speaking, Purusha mounts on the shoulders of Prakriti, the latter remains irrational, while the former remains inactive without her. Therefore Nature (in man) must become a compound of Spirit and Matter before he becomes what he is; and the Spirit latent in Matter must be awakened to life and consciousness gradually. The Monad has to pass through its mineral, vegetable and animal forms, before the Light of the Logos is awakened in the animal man. Therefore, till then, the latter cannot be referred to as "MAN," but has to be regarded as a Monad imprisoned in ever changing forms. *Evolution*, not *creation*, by means of WORDS is recognized in the philosophies of the East, even in their exoteric records. *Ex oriente lux.* Even the name of the first man in the Mosaic Bible had its origin in India, Professor Max Müller's negation notwithstanding. The Jews got their Adam from Chaldaea; and Adam-Adami is a compound word and therefore a manifold symbol, and proves the occult dogmas.

This is no place for philological disquisitions. But the reader may be reminded that the words *Ad* and *Adi* mean in Sanskrit "the first"; in Aramaean, "One" (*Ad-ad*, "the only one") ; in Assyrian, "father" whence *Ak-Ad* or "father-creator." [68] And once the statement is found correct it becomes rather difficult to confine Adam to the Mosaic Bible alone, and to see therein simply a Jewish name. [69]

There is frequent confusion in the attributes and genealogies of the gods in their theogonies, as given to the world by the half-initiated writers, Brâhmanical and Biblical, the Alpha and the Omega of the records of that symbolical science. Yet there could be no such confusion made by the earliest nations, the descendants and pupils of the divine instructors: for both the attributes and the genealogies were inseparably linked with cosmogonical symbols, the "gods" being the life and animating "soul-principle" of the various regions of the Universe. Nowhere and by no people was speculation allowed to range *beyond* those *manifested* gods. The boundless and infinite UNITY remained with every nation a virgin forbidden soil, untrodden by man's

---

68. The appellation *Ak-ad* (or Akkadiars) is of the same class as *Ad-m, Ha-va* (Eve) * Acd-en* (Eden); Ak-Ad meaning " Son of *Ad*" (like the sons of Ad in Ancient Arabia). *Ad-ad*, the "Only One" and the First, was the *Ad-on* or " Lord " of Syria and consort of *A-tar-gat* or Aster't, the Syrian goddess. And Gan-Aeden (Eden) or Gandunia was Babylonia and Mesopotamia.

In Assyrian *Ak* meant Creator, the letter K pronounced Kh (Ah) gutturally. According to Swedenborg's mysticism Adam was not a man but a church (?) of primitive light. In the Vedas *Ad-iti* is the primitive light, the Akâsa of the phenomenal world.

69. *Vide* Part II, § xvi of this Volume, " Adam-Adami."

thought, untouched by fruitless speculation. The only reference made to it was the brief conception of its diastolic and systolic property, of its periodical expansion or dilatation, and contraction. In the Universe with all its incalculable myriads of systems and worlds disappearing and re-appearing in eternity, the anthropomorphized powers, or gods, their Souls, had to disappear from view with their bodies: —" The breath returning to the eternal bosom which exhales and inhales them," says our Catechism.

" *Ideal nature,*" the abstract Space in which everything in the Universe is mysteriously and invisibly generated, is the same female side of procreative power in Nature in the Vedic as in every other Cosmogony. Aditi is Sephira, and the Sophia-Achamoth of the Gnostics, and Isis, the virgin Mother of Horus. In every Cosmogony, behind and higher than the *creative* deity, there is a superior deity, a planner, an Architect, *of whom* the Creator is but the executive agent. And still higher, *over* and *around, within* and *without,* there is the UNKNOWABLE and the *unknown,* the Source and Cause of all these Emanations. . . . .

It thus becomes easy to account for the reason why *"Adam-Adami"* is found in the Chaldaean scripture, certainly earlier than the Mosaic Books. In Assyrian *Ad* is the father, and in Aramaean *Ad* is " One," and *Ad-ad* the " only one," while *Ak* is in Assyrian " creator." Thus *Ad-am-ak-ad-mon* became Adam Kadmon in the Kabala (*Zohar*), meaning as it did, the " One (Son) of the divine Father, or the creator," for the words *"am"* and *"om"* meant at one time in nearly every language the *divine,* or the *deity.* Thus Adam Kadmon and Adam-Adami came to mean : — " The first emanation of the Father-Mother or divine nature," and literally " the first divine one." And it is easy to see that *Ad*-Argat (or *Aster't,* the Syrian goddess, the consort of *Ad-on,* the lord god of Syria or the Jewish Adonai), and Venus, Isis, Ister, Mylitta, Eve, etc., etc., are identical with the *Aditi* and Vâch of the Hindûs. They are all the " Mothers of all living " and " of the gods." On the other hand — cosmically and astronomically — all the male gods became at first " Sun-gods," then, theologically, the " Suns of Righteousness " and the Logoi, all symbolized by the Sun.[70] They are all *Protogonoi* (the first-born) and *Mikroprosopoi.* With the Jews Adam Kadmon

70. Adam-Jehovah, Brahmâ and Mars are, in one sense, identical; they are all symbols for primitive or initial *generative powers* for the purposes of human procreation. Adam is red, and so also are Brahmâ-Virâj and Mars — god and planet. Water is the blood of the Earth; therefore, all these names are connected with Earth and Water. " It takes *earth and water* to create a *human* soul," says Moses. Mars is identical with *Kârttikeya* God of War (in one sense) — which god is born of the Sweat of Śiva, *Śiva-Gharmaja,* and the Earth. In the *Mahâbhârata* he is shown as born without the intervention of a woman. And he is also called " Lohita," the *red,* like Adam, and the other " first men." Hence, the author of *The Source of Measures* is quite right in thinking that Mars (and all the other gods of like attributes), " being the

was the same as Athamaz, Tamaz, or the Adonis of the Greeks — "the One *with,* and *of* his father" — the "Father" becoming during the later Races *Helios,* the Sun, as Apollo *Karneios,*[71] for instance, who was the "Sun born"; Osiris, Ormazd, and so on, were all followed by, and found themselves transformed later on into still more earthly types: such as Prometheus, the crucified of Mount Kazbek, Hercules, and so many others, sun-gods and heroes, until all of them came to have no better significance than phallic symbols.

In the *Zohar* it is said "Man was created by the Sephiroth (Elohim-Javeh, also) and they engendered by common power the *earthly* Adam." Therefore in *Genesis* the Elohim say: — "Behold Man is become *as one of us.*" But in Hindû Cosmogony or "Creation," Brahmâ-Prajâ-pati *creates* Virâj and the Rishis, spiritually; therefore the latter are distinctly called "the Mind-born Sons of Brahmâ"; and this specified mode of *engendering* precluded every idea of *Phallicism,* at any rate in the earlier human nations. This instance well illustrates the respective *spirituality* of the two nations.

———

3. SAID THE "LORD OF THE SHINING FACE." "I SHALL SEND THEE A FIRE WHEN THY WORK IS COMMENCED. RAISE THY VOICE TO OTHER LOKAS, APPLY TO THY FATHER THE LORD OF THE LOTUS (*Kumuda-Pati*) (*a*) FOR HIS SONS . . . . THY PEOPLE SHALL BE UNDER THE RULE OF THE FATHERS (*Pitri-pati*). THY MEN SHALL BE MORTALS. THE MEN OF THE LORD OF WISDOM (*Budha, Mercury*) NOT THE SONS OF SOMA (*the Moon*) ARE IMMORTAL. CEASE THY COMPLAINTS (*b*). THY SEVEN SKINS ARE YET ON THEE. . . . THOU ART NOT READY. THY MEN ARE NOT READY (*c*).

(*a*) *Kumuda-Pati* is the Moon, the Earth's parent, in his region of Soma-loka. Though the Pitris (Pitaras or "Fathers") are sons of the Gods, elsewhere sons of Brahmâ and even Rishis, they are generally known as the "lunar" ancestors.

(*b*) Pitri-pati is the lord or king of the *Pitris,* Yama, the god of Death and the Judge of mortals. The men of Budha (Mercury) are

god *of war* and of *bloodshed,* was but a secondary idea flowing out of the primary one of shedding of blood in *conception* for the first time." Hence Jehovah became later a *fighting* god, "Lord of Hosts," and one who commands war. He is the aggressive Zodh — or Cain by permutation who *slew* his (female) "*brother*," whose "blood crieth from the ground," the *Earth* having opened *her mouth* to receive *the blood.* (*Genesis* iv.)

71. Apollo *Karneios* is certainly a Greek transformation from the Hindû Krishna *Karna.* "Karna" means *radiant,* from "karn," "*a ray,*" and *Karneios,* which was a title of Apollo with the Celts as with the Greeks, meant "Sun-born."

metaphorically *immortal* through their Wisdom. Such is the common belief of those who credit every star or planet with being inhabited. (And there are men of science — M. Flammarion among others — who believe in this fervently, on logical as well as on astronomical data). The Moon being an inferior body to the Earth even, to say nothing of other planets, the terrestrial men produced by her sons — the lunar men or "ancestors" — from her shell or body, cannot be immortal. They cannot hope to become real, self-conscious and intelligent men, unless they are *finished*, so to say, by other creators. Thus in the Purânic legend, the son of the Moon (*Soma*) is *Budha* (Mercury), "the intelligent" and the Wise, because he is the offspring of Soma, the "regent" of the visible Moon, not of Indu, the physical Moon. Thus Mercury is the elder brother of the Earth, metaphorically — his step-brother, so to say, the offspring of *Spirit* — while she (the Earth) is the progeny of the *body*. These allegories have a deeper and more scientific meaning (astronomically and geologically) than our modern physicists are willing to admit. The whole cycle of the "first War in Heaven," the Târakâ-maya, is as full of philosophical as of Cosmogonical and astronomical truths. One can trace therein the biographies of all the planets by the history of their gods and rulers. Uśanas (Śukra, or Venus), the bosom-friend of Soma and the foe of Brihaspati (Jupiter) the instructor of the gods, whose wife Târâ (or Târakâ) had been carried away by the Moon, *Soma* — "of whom he begat Budha " — took also an active part in this war against "the gods" and forthwith was degraded into a *demon* (Asura) deity, and so he remains to this day.[72]

Here the word "men" refers to the celestial men, or what are called in India the PITARAS or *pitris*, the Fathers, the progenitors of men. This does not remove the seeming difficulty, in view of modern hypotheses, of the teaching, which shows these progenitors or ancestors

72. Uśanas-Śukra or Venus is our "Lucifer," the morning star, of course. The ingenuity of this allegory in its manifold meanings is great indeed. Thus *Brihaspati* (the planet Jupiter) or Brahmanaspati is, in the *Rig Veda*, a deity who is the symbol and the prototype of the *exoteric* or ritualistic worship. He is priest sacrificer, suppliant, and the medium through which the prayers of mortals reach the gods. He is the *Purohita* (family priest, or Court Chaplain) of the Hindû Olympus and the spiritual *Guru* of the Gods. Soma is the mystery god and presides over the mystic and occult nature in man and the Universe. Târâ, the priest's wife, who symbolizes the worshiper, prefers esoteric truths to their mere shell, exotericism; hence she is shown as carried off by Soma. Now Soma is the sacred juice of that name, giving mystic visions and trance revelations, the *result of which union is Budha* (Wisdom), Mercury, Hermes, etc., etc.; that science in short which to this day is proclaimed by the Brihaspatis of Theology as devilish and *Satanic*. What wonder that by expanding the cycle of this allegory we find Christian theology espousing the quarrel of the Hindû gods, and regarding *Uśanas* (Lucifer), who helped Soma against that ancient personification of ritualistic worship (Brahmanaspati, the lord of the Brâhmans, now become "Jupiter-Jehovah") as SATAN, the "enemy of God"!

creating the first Adams out of their sides: as astral shadows. And though it is an improvement on Adam's rib, still geological and climatic difficulties will be brought forward. Such, however, is the teaching of Occultism.

(*c*) Man's organism was adapted in every race to its surroundings. The first Root-Race was as ethereal as ours is material. The progeny of the seven Creators, who evolved the seven primordial Adams,[73] surely required no purified gases to breathe and live upon.[74] Therefore, however strongly the impossibility of this teaching may be urged by the devotees of modern science, the Occultist maintains that the case was as stated *aeons of years* before even the evolution of the Lemurian, the first physical man, which itself took place 18,000,000 years ago.[75]

Preliminary evolution is described in one of the BOOKS OF DZYAN and the Commentaries thereon in this wise: —

Archaic Scripture teaches that at the commencement of every local Kalpa, or Round, the earth is reborn; "as the human *Jiva* (monad), when passing into a new womb, gets re-covered with a new body, so does the Jiva of the Earth; it gets a more perfect and solid covering with each Round after re-emerging once more from the matrix of space into objectivity" (Commentary). This process is attended, of course, by the throes of the new birth or geological convulsions.

Thus the only reference to it is contained in one verse of the volume of the *Book of Dzyan* before us, where it says:

———

4. AND AFTER GREAT THROES SHE (*the Earth*) CAST OFF HER OLD THREE AND PUT ON HER NEW SEVEN SKINS, AND STOOD IN HER FIRST ONE (*a*).

(*a*) This refers to the growth of the Earth, whereas in the Stanza treating of the First Round it is said (given in the Commentary): —

"*After the changeless* (avikâra) *immutable nature* (Essence, sadai-karûpa) *had awakened and changed* (differentiated) *into* (a state of) *causality* (avyakta), *and from cause* (Kârana) *had become its own discrete effect* (vyakta), *from invisible it became visible. The smallest of the small* (the most atomic of atoms, or aniyâmsam aniyasâm) *be-*

73. As shown elsewhere, it is only the "Heavenly Man," Adam Kadmon, of the first chapter of *Genesis*, who is made "in the image and likeness of God." Adam, of chapter ii, is not said to be made in that *image* nor in the divine likeness, before he ate of the forbidden fruit. The former Adam is the Sephirothal Host; the second Adam is the Mindless first human Root-race; the third Adam is the race that separated, whose eyes are opened.

74. See Part III of this Volume.

75. For a discussion of the scientific objections to the views and figures here enunciated, the reader is referred to the Addenda, which form Part III of this book.

came one and the many (ekânekarûpa); *and producing the Universe produced also the Fourth Loka* (our Earth) *in the garland of the seven lotuses. The Achyuta then became the Chyuta.*[16]

The Earth is said to cast off her old *three* skins, because this refers to the three preceding Rounds she has already passed through; the present being the *fourth* Round out of the seven. At the beginning of every new ROUND, after a period of " obscuration," the earth (as do also the other six " earths ") casts off, or is supposed to cast off, her old skins as the Serpent does: therefore she is called in the *Aitareya-Brâhmana* the *Sarpa Râjñî*, " the Queen of the Serpents," and " the mother of all that moves." The " Seven Skins," in the first of which she now stands, refer to the seven geological changes which accompany and correspond to the evolution of the Seven Root-Races of Humanity.

Stanza II, which speaks of this Round, begins with a few words of information concerning the age of our Earth. The chronology will be given in its place. In the Commentary appended to the Stanza, two personages are mentioned: Nârada and Asura Maya, especially the latter. All the calculations are attributed to this archaic celebrity; and what follows will make the reader superficially acquainted with some of these figures.

TWO ANTEDILUVIAN ASTRONOMERS

To the mind of the Eastern student of Occultism, two figures are indissolubly connected with mystic astronomy, chronology, and their cycles. Two grand and mysterious figures, towering like two giants in the Archaic Past, emerge before him, whenever he has to refer to Yugas and Kalpas. When, at what period of pre-history they lived, none save a few men in the world know, or ever can know with that certainty which is required by exact chronology. It may have been 100,000 years ago, it may have been 1,000,000, for all that the outside world will ever know. The mystic West and Freemasonry talk loudly of Enoch and Hermes. The mystic East speaks of NÂRADA, the old Vedic Rishi, and of ASURAMAYA, the Atlantean.

It has already been hinted that of all the incomprehensible characters in the *Mahâbhârata* and the Purânas, Nârada, the son of Brahmâ in *Matsya Purâna*, the progeny of Kaśyapa and the daughter of Daksha

---

76. Achyuta is an almost untranslatable term. It means that which is not subject to fall or change for the worse: the *Unfalling;* and it is the reverse of *chyuta,* "the Fallen."

The Dhyânis who incarnate in the human forms of the *Third* Root-Race and endow them with intellect (Manas) are called the *chyuta,* for they fall into generation.

in the *Vishnu Purâna,* is the most mysterious. He is referred to by the honorable title of Deva Rishi (divine Rishi, more than a demi-god) by Parâśara, and yet he is cursed by Daksha and even by Brahmâ. He informs Kanśa that Bhagavat (or Vishnu in exotericism) would incarnate in the eighth child of Devaki, and thus brings the wrath of the Indian *Herod* upon Krishna's mother; and then, from the cloud on which he is seated — invisible as a true *Mânasaputra* — he lauds Krishna, in delight at the Avatâr's feat of killing the monster Keśin. Nârada is here, there, and everywhere; and yet, none of the Purânas gives the true characteristics of this great enemy of physical procreation. Whatever those characteristics may be in Hindû Esotericism, Nârada — who is called in Cis-Himâlayan Occultism *Pesh-Hun,* the "Messenger," or the Greek *Angelos* — is the sole confidant and the executor of the universal decrees of Karma and *Âdi-Budh:* a kind of active and ever incarnating logos, who leads and guides human affairs from the beginning to the end of the Kalpa.

"Pesh-Hun" is a general not a special Hindû possession. He is the mysterious guiding intelligent power, which gives the impulse to, and regulates the impetus of cycles, Kalpas and universal events.[77] He is Karma's visible adjuster on a general scale; the *inspirer* and the leader of the greatest heroes of this Manvantara. In the exoteric works he is referred to by some very uncomplimentary names; such as "Kali-Kâraka," *strife-maker,* "Kapi-vaktra," *monkey-faced,* and even "Piśuna," the spy, though elsewhere he is called Deva-Brahmâ. Even Sir W. Jones was strongly impressed with this mysterious character from what he gathered in his Sanskrit Studies. He compares him to Hermes and Mercury, and calls him "the eloquent messenger of the gods."[78] All this led the late Dr. Kenealy,[79] on the ground that the Hindûs believe him to be a great Rishi, "who is for ever wandering about the earth, giving good counsel," to see in him one of his twelve *Messiahs.* He was, perhaps, not so far off the real track as some imagine.

What Nârada *really is,* cannot be explained in print; nor would the modern generations of the profane gather much from the information. But it may be remarked, that if there is in the Hindû Pantheon a deity which resembles Jehovah, in tempting by "suggestion" of thoughts and "hardening" of the hearts of those whom he would make his tools and victims, it is Nârada. Only with the latter it is no desire to obtain a pretext for "plaguing," and thus showing that *"I am the Lord God."*

77. This is perhaps the reason why, in the *Bhagavad Gîtâ,* we are told that Brahmâ had communicated to Nârada in the beginning that all men whatsover, even Mlechchhas, outcasts and barbarians, might know the true nature of Vâsudeva and learn to have faith in that deity.

78. See *Asiat. Res.,* I. p. 264.

79. *Book of God:* The Apocalypse of Adam-Oannes, p. 60.

Nor is it through any ambitious or selfish motive; but, verily, to serve and guide universal progress and evolution.

Nârada is one of the few prominent characters, save some gods, in the Purânas, who visits the so-called nether or infernal regions, Pâtâla. Whether or not it was from his intercourse with the thousand-headed Sesha, the serpent who bears the seven Pâtâlas and the entire world like a diadem upon his heads, and who is the great teacher of astronomy,[80] that Nârada learned all that he knew, certain it is that he surpasses Garga's Guru in his knowledge of cyclic intricacies. It is he who has charge of our progress and national weal or woe. It is he who brings on wars and puts an end to them. In the old Stanzas Pesh-Hun is credited with having calculated and recorded all the astronomical and cosmic cycles to come, and with having taught the Science to the first gazers at the starry vault. And it is Asuramaya, who is said to have based all his astronomical works upon those records, to have determined the duration of all the past geological and cosmical periods, and the length of all the cycles to come, till the end of this life-cycle, or the end of the seventh Race.

There is a work among the Secret Books, called the " Mirror of Futurity," wherein all the Kalpas within Kalpas and cycles within the bosom of Sesha, or infinite Time, are recorded. This work is ascribed to *Pesh-Hun* Nârada. There is another old work which is attributed to various Atlanteans. It is these two Records which furnish us with the figures of our cycles, and the possibility of calculating the date of cycles to come. The chronological calculations which will presently be given are, however, those of the Brâhmans as explained further on; but most of them are also those of the Secret Doctrine.

The chronology and computations of the Brâhman Initiates are based upon the Zodiacal records of India, and the works of the above-mentioned astronomer and magician — Asuramaya. The Atlantean zodiacal records cannot err, as they were compiled under the guidance of those who first taught astronomy, among other things, to mankind.

But here again we are deliberately and recklessly facing a new difficulty. We shall be told that our statement is contradicted by *science,* in the person of a man regarded as a great authority (in the West) upon all subjects of Sanskrit literature — Professor Albrecht Weber, of Berlin. This, to our great regret, cannot be helped; and we are ready to maintain what is now stated. Asuramaya, to whom the epic tradition points as the earliest astronomer in Âryâvarta, one to whom " the Sun-

---

80. Sesha, who is also Ananta, the infinite, and the " Cycle of Eternity " in esotericism, is credited with having given his astronomical knowledge to Garga, the oldest astronomer of India, who propitiated him, and forthwith knew all about the planets and how to read omens.

god imparted the knowledge of the stars," *in propria persona*, as Dr. Weber himself states, is identified by him, in some very mysterious way, with the " Ptolemaios " of the Greeks.   No more valid reason is given for this identification than that "this latter name (Ptolemaios), as we see from the inscription of Piyadasi, became the Indian ' Turamaya,' out of which the name 'Asuramaya' *might* very easily grow." No doubt it *" might,"* but the vital question is — Are there any good proofs that it *has* thus *grown?*   The only evidence that is given for it is, that it *must* be so: "since this Maya is distinctly assigned to Romaka-pura in the West."[81]   The Maya is evident, since no Sanskritist among Europeans can tell where that locality of " Romaka-pura " was, except, indeed, that it was somewhere "in the West."   Anyhow, as no member of the Asiatic Society, or Western Orientalist, will ever listen to a Brâhmanical teaching, it is useless to take the objections of European Orientalists into consideration.   " Romakapura " was in " the West," certainly, since it was part and parcel of the last continent of ATLANTIS.   And it is equally certain that it is Atlantis which is assigned in the Hindû Purânas as the birth-place of Asuramaya, " as great a magician as he was an Astrologer and an Astronomer."   Moreover, Professor Weber refuses to assign any great antiquity to the Indian Zodiac, and feels inclined to think that the Hindûs never knew of a Zodiac at all till "they had borrowed one from the Greeks."[82] This statement clashes with the most ancient traditions of India, and must therefore be ignored.[83]   We are the more justified in ignoring it, as the learned German Professor himself tells us in the introduction to his work[84] that "in addition to the natural obstacles which impede investigation [in India], there still prevails a dense mist of prejudices and preconceived opinions hovering over the land, and enfolding it as with a veil."   Caught in that veil, it is no wonder that Dr. Weber should himself have been led into involuntary errors.   Let us hope that he knows better now.

Now whether Asuramaya is to be considered a modern myth, a personage who flourished in the day of the Macedonian Greeks, or as that which he is claimed to be by the Occultists, in any case his calculations agree entirely with those of the Secret Records.

From fragments of immensely old works attributed to the Atlantean astronomer, and found in Southern India, the calendar elsewhere men-

81. See *Lectures on the History of Indian Literature*, p. 253, by Prof. A. Weber; in Trübner's Oriental Series.

82. Even the Maya Indians of Guatemala had their Zodiac from untold antiquity. And "primitive man acted in the same manner independently of time or locality in every age," observes a French writer.

83. *Vide* Vol. I, Part III, § xvii, "The Zodiac and its Antiquity."

84. *History of Indian Literature.*

tioned was compiled by two very learned Brâhmans [85] in 1884 and 1885. The work is proclaimed by the best Pandits as faultless — from the Brâhmanical standpoint — and thus far relates to the chronology of the orthodox teachings. If we compare its statements with those made several years earlier in " *Isis Unveiled,*" with the fragmentary teachings published by some Theosophists, and with the present data derived from the Secret Books of Occultism, the whole will be found to agree perfectly, save in some details which may not be explained; for secrets of higher Initiation — as unknown to the writer as they are to the reader — would have to be revealed, and that *cannot be done.*[86]

85. The *Tirukkanda Pañchanga* for the Kali Yuga 4986, by Chintamany Raghanaracharya, son of the famous Government astronomer of Madras, and Tartakamala Venkata Krishna Rao.
86. But see " Chronology of the Brâhmans," page 66, at the close of Stanza II.

STANZA II

NATURE UNAIDED FAILS

§§ (5) After enormous periods the Earth creates monsters. (6) The "Creators" are displeased. (7) They dry the Earth. (8) The forms are destroyed by them. (9) The first great tides. (10) The beginning of incrustation.

5. THE WHEEL WHIRLED FOR THIRTY CRORES (*of years, or* 300,000,000 [87]). IT CONSTRUCTED RÛPAS (*forms*). SOFT STONES, THAT HARDENED (*minerals*); HARD PLANTS, THAT SOFTENED (*vegetation*). VISIBLE FROM INVISIBLE, INSECTS AND SMALL LIVES (*sarîsripa, svapada*). SHE (*the Earth*) SHOOK THEM OFF HER BACK, WHENEVER THEY OVERRAN THE MOTHER (*a*). AFTER THIRTY CRORES OF YEARS, SHE TURNED ROUND. SHE LAY ON HER BACK; ON HER SIDE. . . . . SHE WOULD CALL NO SONS OF HEAVEN, SHE WOULD ASK NO SONS OF WISDOM. SHE CREATED FROM HER OWN BOSOM. SHE EVOLVED WATERMEN TERRIBLE AND BAD (*b*).

(*a*) This relates to an inclination of the axis — of which there were several — to a consequent deluge and chaos on Earth (having, however, no reference to primeval chaos), in which monsters, half-human, halfanimal, were generated. We find it mentioned in the *"Book of the Dead,"* and also in the Chaldaean account of creation, on the Cutha Tablets, however mutilated.

87. 300 million years, or Three Occult Ages. The *Rig Veda* has the same division. In the *"Physician's Hymn,"* (X, 97, 1) it is said that "the plants came into being *three ages* (Triyugam) before the gods" on our Earth (See "Chronology of the Brâhmans" at the end of this Stanza).

It is not even allegory. Here we have *facts,* that are found repeated in the account of *Pymander,* as well as in the Chaldaean tablets of creation. The verses may almost be checked by the Cosmogony, as given by Berosus, which has been disfigured out of recognition by Eusebius, but some of the features of which may yet be found in fragments left by ancient ·Greek authors — Apollodorus, Alexander Polyhistor, etc., etc. "The water-men terrible and bad," who were the production of physical nature alone, a result of the "evolutionary impulse" and the first attempt to create *man* the "crown," and the aim and goal of all animal life on Earth — are shown to be failures in our Stanzas. Do we not find the same in the Berosian Cosmogony, denounced with such vehemence as the culmination of heathen absurdity? And yet who of the Evolutionists can say that things in the beginning have not come to pass as they are described? That, as maintained in the Purânas, the Egyptian and Chaldaean fragments, and even in *Genesis,* there have not been two, and even more, "creations" before the last formation of the Globe; which, changing its geological and atmospheric conditions, changed also its flora, its fauna, and its men? This claim agrees not only with every ancient Cosmogony, but also with modern science, and even, to a certain degree, with the theory of evolution, as may be demonstrated in a few words.

There is no "dark creation," no "Evil Dragon" conquered by a Sun-God, in the earliest World-Cosmogonies. Even with the Akkads, the great Deep (the Watery Abyss, or SPACE) was the birthplace and abode of Ea, Wisdom, the incognizable infinite Deity. But with the Semites and the later Chaldaeans, the fathomless Deep of Wisdom becomes gross matter, sinful Substance, and Ea is changed into Tiamat, the dragon slain by Merodach, or Satan, in the astral waves.

In the Hindû Purânas, Brahmâ, the creator, is seen recommencing *de novo* several creations after as many failures; and two great creations are mentioned,[88] the Padma and the Varâha, the present, when the Earth was lifted out of the water by Brahmâ, in the shape of a boar, or "Varâha-Avatâra." Creation is shown as a sport, an amusement (Lîlâ) of the creative god. The *Zohar* speaks of primordial worlds, which perished as soon as they came into existence. And the same is said in Midrash, Rabbi Abahu explaining distinctly[89] that "the Holy One" had successively created and destroyed sundry worlds, before he succeeded in the present one. This does not relate only to other

88. These two must not be confused with the seven creations or divisions in each Kalpa (See Book I, Part II, § xiii, "The Seven Creations"). The *primary* and *secondary* creations are here meant.
89. In *Bereshith Rabbah,* Parsha IX.

worlds in space, but to a mystery of our own globe contained in the allegory about the " kings of Edom." For the words, " This one pleases me," are repeated in *Genesis* i. 31, though in disfigured terms, as usual. The Chaldaean fragments of Cosmogony on the Cuneiform inscriptions, and elsewhere, show two distinct creations of animals and men, the first being destroyed, as it was a failure. The Cosmogonical tablets prove that this our actual creation was preceded by others;[90] and as shown by the author of " *The Qabbalah,*" in the *Zohar, Siphrah Dzeniouta,* in *Idrah Rabbah,* 128*a*, etc., etc., the Kabala states the same.[91]

(*b*) Oannes (or Dagon, the Chaldaean " Man-fish ") divides his Cosmogony and Genesis into two portions. First the abyss of waters and darkness, wherein resided most hideous beings — men with wings, four and two-faced men, human beings with two heads, with the legs and horns of a goat (our "goat-men"),[92] hippocentaurs, bulls with the heads of men, and dogs with tails of fishes. In short, combinations of various animals and men, of fishes, reptiles and other monstrous animals assuming each other's shapes and countenances. The feminine element they resided in, is personified by Thalatth — the Sea, or " Water " — which was finally conquered by Belus, the male principle. And Polyhistor says : " Belus came and cut the woman asunder, and of one half of her he formed the Earth, and of the other half the heavens, and at the same time he destroyed the animals within her." [92a] As pertinently remarked by I. Myer, " with the Akkadians each object and power of Nature had its *Zi*, Spirit. The Akkadians formed their deities into triads, usually males [sexless, rather?] ; the Semites also had triadic deities, but introduced sex" [91] — or phallicism. With the Aryans and the earliest Akkadians all things are emanations *through*, not *by*, a creator or logos. With the Semites everything is *begotten.*

---

90. See *Hibbert Lectures*, 1887, Professor Sayce, p. 390.

91. Myer's *The Qabbalah.* p. 246.

92. Whence the identity of the ideas? The Chinese have the same traditions. According to the commentator Kwoh P'oh, in the work called *Shan-Hai-King,* " Wonders by Sea and Land," a work which was written by the historiographer Chung Ku from engravings on nine urns made by the Emperor Yü (a. c., 2255), an interview is mentioned with men *having two distinct faces on their heads,* before and behind, monsters with bodies of goats and human faces, etc. Gould, in his *Mythical Monsters,* p. 27, giving the names of some authors on Natural History, mentions *Shan-Hai-King.* According to Kwoh P'oh (a. d. 276–324) this work was compiled three thousand years before his time, or at seven dynasties distance. Yang Sun of the Ming Dynasty (commencing a. d. 1368) states that it was compiled by Kung Chia and Chung Ku (as stated above). Chung Ku at the time of the last emperor of the Hia dynasty, a. c. 1818, fearing that the emperor might destroy the books treating of the ancient time, carried them in his flight to Yin. (See *Mythical Monsters,* by C. Gould, p. 27.)

92a. Cf. Cory's *Ancient Fragments,* ed. of 1828, p. 27.

6. The Water-men terrible and bad she herself created. From the remains of others (*from the mineral, vegetable and animal remains*) from the first, second, and third (*Rounds*) she formed them. The Dhyâni came and looked. . . . . The Dhyâni from the bright Father-Mother, from the white (*Solar-lunar*) regions they came,[93] from the abodes of the Immortal-Mortals (*a*).

(*a*) The explanations given in our Stanzas are far more clear than that which the legend of creation from the *Cutha* tablet would give, even were it complete. What is preserved on it, however, corroborates them. For, in the tablet, " the Lord of Angels " destroys the men in the abyss, when "there were not left the carcasses and waste" after they were slaughtered. After which they, the Great Gods, create men with the bodies of birds of the desert, human beings, " seven kings, brothers of the same family," etc., which is a reference to the locomotive qualities of the primary ethereal bodies of men, which could fly as well as they could walk,[94] but who " were destroyed " because they were not "*perfect*," *i. e.*, they " were sexless, like the Kings of Edom."

Weeded of metaphors and allegories, what will science say to this idea of a primordial creation of species? It will object to the "Angels" and " Spirits " having anything to do therewith: but if it is nature and the physical law of evolution that are the creators of all there is now on Earth, why could there be " no such abyss " when the globe was covered with waters, in which numbers of monstrous beings were generated? Is it the " human beings " and animals with human heads and double faces, which are a point of the objection? But if man is only a higher animal and has evolved from the brute species by an infinite series of transformations, why could not the "missing links" have had human heads attached to the bodies of animals, or, being two-headed, have heads of beasts and *vice versa*, in Nature's early efforts? Are we not shown during the geological periods, in the ages of the reptiles and the mammalia, lizards with birds' wings, and serpents' heads on animal bodies.[95] And, arguing from the standpoint of science, does not even our modern human race occasionally furnish us with monster-specimens: two-headed children, animal bodies with human heads, dog-headed babies, etc., etc.? And this proves that, if nature

93. Gods and planetary Spirits, especially the Ribhus. " The three Ribhus " who yet become " thrice seven in number " of their gifts.

94. Remember the " winged Races " of Plato; and the *Popol Vuh* accounts of the first human race, which could walk, fly and see objects, however distant.

95. See *Mythical Monsters*, by Charles Gould.

will still play such freaks now that she has settled for ages into the order of her evolutionary work, monsters, like those described by Berosus, were a possibility in her opening program; which possibility may even have existed once upon a time as a law, before she sorted out her species and began regular work upon them; which indeed now admits of definite proof by the bare fact of " REVERSION," as science puts it.

This is what the doctrine teaches and demonstrates by numerous proofs. But we shall not wait for the approval of either dogmatic theology or materialistic science, but proceed with the Stanzas. Let these speak for themselves, with the help of the light thrown by the Commentaries and their explanations; the scientific aspect of these questions will be considered later on.

Thus physical nature, when left to herself in the creation of animal and man, is shown to have failed. She can produce the first two and the lower animal kingdoms, but when it comes to the turn of man, spiritual, independent and intelligent powers are required for his creation, besides the " coats of skin " and the " Breath of animal Life." The human Monads of preceding Rounds need something higher than purely physical materials to build their personalities with, under the penalty of remaining even below any " Frankenstein " animal.[96]

96. In the first volume of the lately published *Introduction à l'Etude des Races Humaines*, by M. de Quatrefages, there is proof that since the post-tertiary period and even before that time — since many Races were already scattered during that age on the face of the Earth — man has not altered one iota in his physical structure. And if, surrounded for ages by a fauna that altered from one period or cycle to another, which died out, which was reborn in other forms — so that now there does not exist one single animal on Earth, large or small, contemporary with the man of that period — if, then, every animal has been transformed save man himself, this fact goes to prove not only his antiquity, but that he is a *distinct Kingdom.* Why should he alone have escaped transformation? Because, says de Quatrefages, the weapon used by him, in his struggle with nature and the ever-changing geological conditions and elements, was " his *psychic force, not his physical strength or body,*" as in the case of animals. Give man only that dose of intelligence and reason with which other mammalia are endowed, and with his present bodily organization he will show himself the most helpless of creatures of Earth. And as everything goes to prove that the *human organism with all its characteristics, peculiarities and idiosyncrasies existed already on our Globe in those far distant geological periods when there was not yet one single specimen of the now-existing forms of mammalia,* what is the unavoidable conclusion? Why this: Since all the human races are of one and the same species, it follows that this species is the *most ancient of all* the now-living mammalia. Therefore it is the most stable and persevering of all, and was already as fully developed as it is now when all the other mammalia now known had not made even their first approach to appearance on this Earth. Such is the opinion of the great French Naturalist, who gives thereby a terrible blow to Darwinism.

7. DISPLEASED THEY WERE. OUR FLESH IS NOT THERE (*they said*). THIS IS NO FIT RÛPA FOR OUR BROTHERS OF THE FIFTH. NO DWELLINGS FOR THE LIVES.[97] PURE WATERS, NOT TURBID, THEY MUST DRINK (*a*). LET US DRY THEM (*the waters*).

(*a*) Says the Catechism (Commentaries) :—

"*It is from the material Worlds that descend they, who fashion physical man at the new Manvantaras. They are inferior Lha (Spirits), possessed of a dual body* (an astral within an ethereal form). *They are the fashioners and creators of our body of illusion.*" . . . .

"*Into the forms projected by the Lha* (Pitris) *the two letters*[98] (the Monad, called also 'the Double Dragon') *descend from the spheres of expectation.*[99] *But they are like a roof with no walls, nor pillars to rest upon.*" . . . .

"*Man needs four flames and three fires to become one on Earth, and he requires the essence of the forty-nine fires*[100] *to be perfect. It is those who have deserted the Superior Spheres, the Gods of Will,*[101] *who complete the Manu of illusion. For the 'Double Dragon' has no hold upon the mere form. It is like the breeze where there is no tree or branch to receive and harbor it. It cannot affect the form where there is no agent of transmission* (Manas, 'Mind') *and the form knows it not.*"

"*In the highest worlds, the three are one,*[102] *on Earth* (at first) *the one becomes two. They are like the two* (side) *lines of a triangle that has lost its bottom line — which is the third fire.*" (Catechism, Book III, sec. 9.)

Now this requires some explanation before proceeding any further.

97. The Monads of the *presentments* of men of the *Third* Round, the huge Ape-like forms.

98. In the esoteric system the seven principles in man are represented by seven letters. The first two are *more* sacred than the four letters of the Tetragrammaton.

99. The intermediate spheres, wherein the Monads, which have not reached Nirvâna, are said to slumber in unconscious inactivity between the Manvantaras.

100. Explained elsewhere. The "Three Fires," Pâvaka, Pavamâna, and Śuchi, who had forty-five sons, who, with their three fathers and their Father Agni, constitute the 49 fires. Pavamâna (fire produced by friction) is the parent of the *fire of the Asuras*; Śuchi (Solar fire) is the parent of the fire of the gods; and Pâvaka (electric fire) is the father of the fire of the *Pitris* (See *Vâyu Purâna*). But this is an explanation on the material and the terrestrial plane. The flames are evanescent and only periodical; the fires — eternal in their triple unity. They correspond to the *four* lower, and the *three* higher human principles.

101. The *Suras*, who become later the A-Suras.

102. Atmâ, Buddhi and Manas. In Devachan the higher element of the Manas is needed to make it a state of perception and consciousness for the disembodied *Monad*.

To do so especially for the benefit of our Aryan Hindū brethren —
whose esoteric interpretations may differ from our own — we shall
have to explain to them the foregoing by certain passages in their own
exoteric books, namely, the Purânas. In the allegories of the latter,
Brahmâ, who is collectively the creative Force of the Universe, is said
to be "at the beginning of the Yugas (cycles). . . . *Possessed of the
desire and of the power to create, and, impelled by the potencies of
what is to be created,* again and again does he, at the outset of a Kalpa,
put forth a similar creation."[103] It is now proposed to examine the
exoteric account in the *Vishnu Purâna,* and see how much it may agree
or disagree with our occult version.

CREATION OF DIVINE BEINGS IN THE EXOTERIC ACCOUNTS

In the *Vishnu Purâna* — which is certainly the earliest of all the
scriptures of that name — we find, as in all the others, Brahmâ assuming
as the male God, for purposes of creation, "*four bodies invested by
three qualities.*"[104] It is said: "In this manner, Maitreya, *Jyotsnâ*
(dawn), *Râtri* (night), *Ahan* (day), and *Sandhyâ* (evening twilight)
are the four bodies of Brahmâ." . . .[105] As Parâsara explains it,
when Brahmâ wants to create the world anew and construct progeny
through his will, in the fourfold condition (or the four orders of
beings) termed gods (Dhyân Chohans), Demons[106] (*i. e.,* more material Devas), Progenitors (Pitris) and men, "he collects Yoga-like
(Yuyuje) his mind."
Strange to say, he begins by creating DEMONS, who thus take prece-
dence over the angels or gods. This is no incongruity, nor is it due to
inconsistency, but has, like all the rest, a profound esoteric meaning,
quite clear to one free from Christian theological prejudice. He who
bears in mind that the principle MAHAT, or Intellect, the "Universal
Mind" (literally "the great"), which esoteric philosophy explains as
the "manifested Omniscience" — the "first product" of Pradhâna
(primordial matter) as *Vishnu Purâna* says, but the first Cosmic
aspect of Parabrahm or the esoteric SAT, the Universal Soul,[107] as

---

103. See *Vishnu Purâna,* Book I, ch. v,
closing Sloka: Also *Mânava-Dharma-Sâstra,*
I, 30.

104. This has in *esotericism* a direct
bearing upon the seven principles of the
manifested Brahmâ, or universe, in the same
order as in man. Exoterically, it is only
four principles.

105. Page 81, vol. I, Wilson's translation.

106. *Demons* is a very loose word to

use, as it applies to a great number of inferior — *i. e.,* more material — Spirits, or
minor Gods, who are so termed because they
"war" with the higher ones; but they are
no devils.

107. The same order of principles in
man:— *Atmâ* (Spirit), *Buddhi* (Soul), its
vehicle, as Matter is the *Vâhana* of Spirit,
and *Manas* (mind), the third, or the fifth
microcosmically. On the *plane of personality, Manas* is the first.

Occultism teaches — is at the root of SELF-Consciousness, will understand the reason why. The so-called "Demons" — who are (esoterically) the Self-asserting and (intellectually) active Principle — are the *positive poles of creation*, so to say; hence, the first produced. This is in brief the process as narrated allegorically in the Purânas.

Having concentrated his mind into itself and the quality of darkness pervading Brahmâ's assumed body, the Asuras, issuing from his thigh, were first produced; after which, abandoning this body, it was transformed into NIGHT.[**]

Two important points are involved herein:— (a) Primarily in the *Rig-Veda*, the "Asuras" are shown as *spiritual divine beings;* their etymology is derived from *asu* (breath), the "Breath of God," and they mean the same as the Supreme Spirit or the Zoroastrian *Ahura*. It is later on, for purposes of theology and dogma, that they are shown issuing from Brahmâ's thigh, and that their name began to be derived from *a* privative, and *sura*, god (solar deities), or *not-a-god*, and that they became the enemies of the gods. Every ancient theogony without exception — from the Âryan and the Egyptian down to that of Hesiod — places, in the order of Cosmogonical evolution, Night before the Day; even *Genesis*, where "darkness is upon the face of the deep" before "the *first day*." The reason for this is that every Cosmogony — except in the Secret Doctrine—begins by the "Secondary Creation" so-called: to wit, the *manifested* Universe, the Genesis of which has to open by a marked differentiation between the eternal Light of *Primary* Creation, whose mystery must remain for ever "Darkness" to the prying finite conception and intellect of the profane, and the Secondary Evolution of manifested visible nature. The Veda contains the whole philosophy of that division without having ever been correctly explained by our Orientalists, because it has *never been understood* by them.

Continuing to create, Brahmâ assumes another form, that of the Day, and creates from his breath the gods, who are endowed with the quality of goodness (passivity).[109] In his next body the quality of great passivity prevailed, which is also (negative) goodness, and from the side of that personage issued the Pitris, the progenitors of men, because, as the text explains, "Brahmâ thought of himself (during the process) as the father of the world." [110] This is *Kriyâ-śakti* — the mysterious *Yoga*

108. See Part II, § xviii, "The Fallen Angels."

109. Thus, says the Commentary, the saying "by day the gods are most powerful, and by night the demons," is purely allegorical.

110. This *thinking of oneself* as this, that, or the other, is the chief factor in the production of every kind of psychic or even physical phenomena. The words " whosoever shall say to this mountain be thou removed and cast into the sea, and *shall not doubt* . . . that thing will come to pass," are no vain words. Only the word " faith " ought to be translated by WILL. Faith without Will is like a wind-mill without *wind* — barren of results.

power explained elsewhere. This body of Brahmâ when cast off became the *Sandhyâ* (evening twilight), the interval between day and night.

Finally Brahmâ assumed his last form pervaded by the *quality of foulness,* " and from this MEN, in whom foulness and passion predominate, were produced." This body when cast off became the dawn, or morning twilight — the twilight of Humanity. Here Brahmâ stands esoterically for the *Pitris.* He is collectively the Pitar, " father."

The true esoteric meaning of this allegory must now be explained. Brahmâ here symbolizes personally the collective creators of the World and Men — the universe with all its numberless productions of things movable and (seemingly) immovable.[111] He is collectively the Prajâpatis, the Lords of Being; and the four bodies typify the four classes of creative powers or Dhyân Chohans, described in the Commentary directly following Stanza VII in Book I. The whole philosophy of the so-called " Creation " of the good and evil in this world and of the whole cycle of Manvantaric results therefrom, hangs on the correct comprehension of these Four bodies of Brahmâ.

The reader will now be prepared to understand the real, the esoteric significance of what follows. Moreover there is an important point to be cleared up. Christian theology having arbitrarily settled and agreed that Satan with his Fallen Angels belonged to the earliest creation, Satan being the first-created, the wisest and most beautiful of God's Archangels, the word was given, the key-note struck. Henceforth all the *pagan* scriptures were made to yield the same meaning, and all were shown to be demoniacal, and it *was* and *is* claimed that *truth and fact* belong to, and commence only with, Christianity. Even the Orientalists and Mythologists, some of them no Christians at all but " infidels," or men of science, entered unconsciously to themselves, and by the mere force of association of ideas and habit, into the theological groove. Purely Brâhmanical considerations, based on greed of power and ambition, allowed the masses to remain in ignorance of great truths; and the same causes led the Initiates among the early Christians to remain silent, while those who had never known the truth disfigured the order of things, judging of the hierarchy of " Angels " by their exoteric form. Thus as the *Asuras* had become the rebellious inferior gods fighting the higher ones in popular creeds, so the highest archangel, in truth the Agathodaimon, the eldest benevolent Logos, became with theology the " Adversary " or *Satan.* But is this warranted by the correct interpretation of any old Scripture? The answer is, *most certainly not.* As the Mazdean Scriptures of the *Zend-Avesta,* the *Vendîdâd* and others correct and expose the later cunning shuffling

111. The same idea is found in the first four chapters of *Genesis,* with their " Lord " and " God," which are the *Elohim* and the Androgynous *Eloha.*

of the gods in the Hindû Pantheon, and restore through AHURA the *Asuras* to their legitimate place in theogony, so the recent discoveries of the Chaldaean tablets vindicate the good name of the first divine Emanations. This is easily proved. Christian Angelology is directly and solely derived from that of the Pharisees, who brought their tenets from Babylonia. The Sadducees, the real guardians of the Laws of Moses, knew not of, and rejected, any angels, opposing even the immortality of the human *Soul* (not impersonal Spirit). In the Bible the only "Angels" spoken of are the "Sons of God" mentioned in *Genesis* vi (who are now regarded as the *Nephilim*, the Fallen Angels), and several angels in human form, the "Messengers" of the Jewish God, whose own rank needs a closer analysis than heretofore given. (*Vide supra*[112] where it is shown that the early Akkadians called *Ea*, Wisdom, that which was disfigured by the later Chaldees and Semites into *Tiamat*, Tisalat and the Thalatth of Berosus, the female Sea Dragon, now Satan.) Truly — "How art thou fallen (by the hand of man), O bright star and son of the morning"!

Now what do the Babylonian accounts of "Creation," as found on the Assyrian fragments of tiles, tell us; those very accounts upon which the Pharisees built their angelology? But compare Mr. G. Smith's *Assyrian Discoveries*,[113] and his *Chaldean Account of Genesis*.[114] The "*Tablet with the story of the Seven Wicked Gods or Spirits*," has the following account — we print the important passages in italics:—

1. In the *first days* the evil Gods,
2. the *angels, who were in rebellion*, who *in the lower part of heaven*
3. *had been created*,
4. they caused their evil work
5. devising with wicked heads . . . etc.

Thus we are shown, as plainly as can be, on a fragment which remained unbroken, so that there can be no dubious reading, that the " rebellious angels " had been created in the *lower part of heaven, i. e.,* that they belonged and do belong to a *material plane of evolution,* although as it is not the plane of which we are made cognizant through our senses, it remains generally invisible to us, and is thus regarded as subjective. Were the Gnostics so wrong, after this, in affirming that this our visible world, and especially the Earth, had been created by *lower* angels, the inferior Elohim, of which, as they taught, the God of Israel was one. These Gnostics were nearer in time to the records of the Archaic Secret Doctrine, and therefore ought to be allowed to have known better than non-initiated Christians, who took upon themselves,

112. Stanza I, sub-sections 2, 3, *et seq.*   113. Page 398.   114. Page 107.

hundreds of years later, to remodel and *correct* what was said. But let us see what the same Tablet says further on :—

7. There were seven of them (the wicked gods) . . . (then follows the description of these, the fourth being a "serpent," the phallic symbol of the *fourth* Race in human Evolution).

15. The seven of them, messengers of the God Anu, their king.

Now Anu belongs to the Chaldaean trinity, and is identical with Sin, the "Moon," in one aspect. And the Moon in the Hebrew Kabala is the Argha of the seed of all material life, and is still more closely connected, kabalistically, with Jehovah, who is double-sexed as Anu is. They are both represented in Esotericism and viewed from a dual aspect : male or spiritual, female or material, or Spirit and Matter, the two antagonistic principles. Hence the "Messengers of Anu," (who is Sin, the "Moon,") are shown, in verses 28 to 41, as being finally overpowered by the same Sin with the help of Bel (the Sun) and Ishtar (Venus). This is regarded as a contradiction by the Assyriologists, but is simply *metaphysics* in the esoteric teaching.

There is more than one interpretation, for there are seven keys to the mystery of the Fall. Moreover there are two "Falls" in Theology : the rebellion of the Archangels and their "Fall," and the "Fall" of Adam and Eve. Thus the lower as well as the higher Hierarchies are charged with a supposed crime. The word "supposed" is the true and correct term, for in both cases it is founded on misconception. Both are considered in Occultism as Karmic effects, and both belong to the law of Evolution : intellectual and spiritual on the one hand, physical and psychic on the other. The "Fall" is a universal allegory. It sets forth at one end of the ladder of Evolution the "rebellion," *i. e.*, the action of differentiating intellection or consciousness on its various planes, seeking union with matter ; and at the other, the lower end, the rebellion of matter against Spirit, or of action against spiritual inertia. And here lies the germ of an error which has had such disastrous effects on the intelligence of civilized societies for over 1800 years. In the original allegory it is matter — hence the more material angels — which was regarded as the conqueror of Spirit, or the Archangels who "fell" on this plane. "They of the *flaming sword* (or animal passions) had put to flight the Spirits of Darkness." Yet it is the latter who fought for the supremacy of the conscious and divine spirituality on Earth and failed, succumbing to the power of matter. But in theological dogma we see the reverse. It is Michael, "who is like unto God," the representative of Jehovah, who is the leader of the celestial hosts — as Lucifer, in Milton's fancy, is of the infernal hosts — who has the best of Satan. It is true that the nature of Michael depends upon that of his Creator and Master. Who the latter is, one may find out by carefully studying the allegory of the " War in Heaven " with the astronomical key. As shown by Bentley, the " War of the Titans against the gods " in Hesiod, and also the war of the Asuras (or the Târakâmaya) against the devas in Purânic legend, are identical in all save the names. The aspects of the stars show (Bentley taking the year 945 B. C. as the nearest date for such conjunction) that " all the planets, except Saturn, were on the same side of the heavens as the Sun and Moon," and hence were his opponents. And yet it is Saturn, or the Jewish "Moon-god," who is shown as prevailing, both by Hesiod and Moses, neither of whom was understood. Thus it was that the real meaning became distorted.

STANZA II—*Continued.*

8. THE FLAMES CAME. THE FIRES WITH THE SPARKS; THE NIGHT FIRES AND THE DAY FIRES (*a*). THEY DRIED OUT THE TURBID DARK WATERS. WITH THEIR HEAT THEY QUENCHED THEM. THE LHAS (*Spirits*) OF THE HIGH; THE LHAMAYIN (*those*) OF BELOW, CAME (*b*). THEY SLEW THE FORMS, WHICH WERE TWO- AND FOUR-FACED. THEY FOUGHT THE GOAT-MEN, AND THE DOG-HEADED MEN, AND THE MEN WITH FISHES' BODIES.

(*a*) The " Flames " are a Hierarchy of Spirits parallel to, if not identical with, the " burning " fiery *Saraph* (Seraphim) mentioned by Isaiah,[118] those who attend, according to Hebrew Theogony, " the Throne of the Almighty." Melha is the Lord of the " Flames." When he appears on Earth, he assumes the personality of a Buddha, says a popular legend. He is one of the most ancient and revered *Lhas*, a Buddhist St. Michael.

(*b*) The word " Below " must not be taken to mean infernal regions, but simply a spiritual, or rather ethereal, Being of a lower grade, because nearer to the Earth, or one step higher than our terrestrial sphere; while the Lhas are Spirits of the highest Spheres — whence the name of the capital of Tibet, *Lha-ssa*.

Besides a statement of a purely physical nature and belonging to the evolution of life on Earth, there may be another allegorical meaning attached to this Śloka, or indeed, as is taught, several. The FLAMES, or " Fires," represent Spirit, or the male element, and " Water," matter, or the opposite element. And here again we find, in the action of the Spirit slaying the purely material form, a reference to the eternal struggle, on the physical and psychic planes, between Spirit and Matter, besides a scientific cosmic fact. For, as said in the next verse:—

----

9. MOTHER-WATER, THE GREAT SEA WEPT. SHE AROSE, SHE DIS-APPEARED IN THE MOON, WHICH HAD LIFTED HER, WHICH HAD GIVEN HER BIRTH (a).

(a) Now what can this mean? Is it not an evident reference to tidal action in the early stage of the history of our planet in its fourth Round? Modern research has been busy of late in its speculations on the Palaeozoic high-tides. Mr. Darwin's theory was that not less than 52,000,000 years ago—and probably much more—the Moon originated from the Earth's plastic mass. Starting from the point where research was left by Helmholtz, Ferrel, Sir William Thomson and others, he retraced the course of tidal retardation of the earth's rotary motions far back into the very night of time, and placed the Moon during the infancy of our planet at only " a fraction of its present distance." In short, his theory was that it is the Moon which separated from the Earth. The tidal elevation concurring with the swing of the globular mass — centrifugal tendency being then nearly equal to gravity — the latter was overcome, and the tidally elevated mass could thus separate completely from the Earth.[116]

The Occult teaching is the reverse of this. The Moon is far older than the Earth; and, as explained in Book I, it is the latter which owes its being to the former, however astronomy and geology may explain the fact. Hence, the tides and the attraction to the Moon, as shown by the liquid portion of the Globe ever striving to raise itself towards its parent. This is the meaning of the sentence that "the Mother-Water arose and disappeared in the Moon, which had lifted her, which had given her birth."

----

116. But see the difficulties suggested later, in the works of various geologists, against this theory. Compare Sir R. S. Ball's article in *Nature* (Dec. 1, 1881), and also what the American geologists say.

10. WHEN THEY (the Rûpas) WERE DESTROYED, MOTHER-EARTH REMAINED BARE,[117] SHE ASKED TO BE DRIED (a).[118]

(a) The time for its incrustation had arrived. The waters had separated and the process was started. It was the beginning of a new life. This is what one key divulges to us. Another key teaches the origin of Water, its admixture with Fire (liquid fire it calls it),[119] and enters upon an alchemical description of the progeny of the two — solid matter such as minerals and earths. From the " Waters of Space," the progeny of the male Spirit-Fire and the female (gaseous) Water has become the Oceanic expanse on Earth. Varuna is dragged down from the infinite Space, to reign as Neptune over the finite Seas. As always, the popular fancy is found to be based on a strictly scientific foundation.

Water is the symbol of the female element everywhere; mater, from which the letter M, is derived pictorially from ⟨∿∿⟩, a water hieroglyph. It is the universal matrix or the " Great Deep." Venus, the great Mother-Virgin, issues forth from the Sea-wave, and Cupid or Eros is her son. But Venus is the later mythological variant of Gaia (or Gaea), the Earth, which, in its higher aspect is Nature (Prakriti), and metaphysically Aditi, and even Mûlaprakriti, the root of Prakriti or its noumenon.

Hence Cupid or Love in his primitive sense is Eros, the Divine Will, or Desire of manifesting itself through visible creation. Thence Fohat, the prototype of Eros, becomes on Earth the great power " Life-electricity," or the Spirit of " Life-giving." Let us remember the Greek Theogony and enter into the spirit of its philosophy. We are taught by the Greeks[120] that all things, gods included, owe their being to the Ocean and his wife Tethys, the latter being Gaia, the Earth or Nature. But who is Ocean? Ocean is the immeasurable SPACE (Spirit in Chaos), which is the Deity;[121] and Tethys is not the Earth, but primordial matter in the process of formation. In our case it is no longer Aditi-Gaia who begets Ouranos or Varuna, the chief Âditya among the seven planetary gods, but Prakriti, materialized and localized. The Moon, masculine in its theogonic character, is, in its cosmic aspect only,

117. The goddess who gave birth to these primordial monsters, in the account of Berosus, was Thalatth, in Greek Thalassa, " the Sea."

118. See, for comparison, the account of creation by Berosus (Alexander Polyhistor) and the hideous beings born from the twofold principle (Earth and Water) in the Abyss of primordial creation: Naras (Centaurs, men with the limbs of horses and human bodies), and Kinnaras (men with the heads of horses) created by Brahmâ in the commencement of the Kalpa.

119. See Commentary following Sloka 18.

120. See Iliad, XIV, 201, 246.

121. See Book I.

the female generative principle, as the Sun is the male emblem thereof. Water is the progeny of the Moon, an androgyne deity with every nation.

Evolution proceeds on the laws of analogy in Kosmos as in the formation of the smallest globe. Thus the above, applying to the *modus operandi* at the time when the Universe was appearing, applies also in the case of our Earth's formation.

This Stanza opens by speaking of thirty crores, 300,000,000, of years. We may be asked — What could the ancients know of the duration of geological periods, when no modern scientist or mathematician is able to calculate their duration with anything like approximate accuracy? Whether they had or had not better means (and it is maintained that they had them in their Zodiacs), still the chronology of the ancient Brâhmans shall now be given as faithfully as possible.

The Chronology of the Brâhmans

No greater riddle exists in science, no problem is more hopelessly insoluble, than the question: How old — even approximately — are the Sun and Moon, the Earth and Man? What does modern science know of the duration of the ages of the World, or even of the length of geological periods?

Nothing; *absolutely nothing.*

If one turns to science for chronological information, one is told by those who are straightforward and truthful, as for instance Mr. Pengelly, the eminent geologist, " We do not know." [122] One will learn that, so far, no trustworthy numerical estimate of the ages of the world and man could be made, and that both geology and anthropology are at sea. Yet when a student of esoteric philosophy presumes to bring forward the teachings of Occult Science, he is at once sat upon. Why should this be so, since, when reduced to their own physical methods, the greatest scientists have failed to arrive even at an approximate agreement?

It is true that science can hardly be blamed for it. Indeed, in the Cimmerian darkness of the prehistoric ages, the explorers are lost in a labyrinth, whose great corridors are as doorless, allowing no visible exit into the Archaic past. Lost in the maze of their own conflicting speculations, rejecting, as they have always done, the evidence of Eastern tradition, without any clue, or one single certain milestone to guide them, what can geologists or anthropologists do but pick up the slender

122. For a similar admission see Professor Lefèvre's *Philosophy*, p. 481.

thread of Ariadne where they first perceive it, and then proceed at perfect random? Therefore we are first told that the farthest date to which documentary record extends is now generally regarded by Anthropology as but " the earliest distinctly visible point of the pre-historic period." [123]

At the same time it is confessed that " beyond that period stretches back a vast indefinite series of prehistoric ages." [124]

It is with those specified "Ages" that we shall begin. They are "prehistoric" to the naked eye of matter only. To the spiritual eagle eye of the seer and the prophet of every race, Ariadne's thread stretches beyond that "historic period " without break or flaw, surely and stead-ily, into the very night of time; and the hand which holds it is too mighty to drop it, or even let it break. Records exist, although they may be rejected as fanciful by the profane; though many of them are tacitly accepted by philosophers and men of great learning, and meet with an unvarying refusal only from the official and collective body of orthodox science. And since the latter refuses to give us even an approximate idea of the duration of the geological ages — save in a few conflicting and contradictory hypotheses — let us see what Āryan philosophy can teach us.

Such computations as are given in Manu and the Purânas — save trifling and most evidently intentional exaggerations — are, as already stated, almost identical with those taught in esoteric philosophy. This may be seen by comparing the two in any Hindû calendar of recognized orthodoxy.

The best and most complete of all such calendars, at present, as vouched for by the learned Brâhmans of Southern India, is the already mentioned Tamil calendar called the " Tirukkanda Pañchanga," com-piled, as we are told, from, and in full accordance with, secret frag-ments of Asuramaya's data. As Asuramaya is said to have been the greatest astronomer, so he is whispered to have also been the most powerful " Sorcerer " of the " WHITE ISLAND, which had become BLACK with sin," i. e., of the islands of Atlantis.

The " White Island " is a symbolical name. Asuramaya is said to have lived (see the tradition of Jñâna-bhâskara) in Romaka-pura in the West: because the name is an allusion to the land and cradle of the " Sweat-born " of the Third Race. That land or continent had dis-appeared ages before Asuramaya lived, since he was an Atlantean; but he was a direct descendant of the Wise Race, the Race that never dies. Many are the legends concerning this hero, the pupil of Sûrya (the Sun-God) himself, as the Indian accounts allege. It matters little whether he lived on one or another island, but the question is to prove

123. Encyclopaedia Britannica.   124. Ibid.

that he was no myth, as Dr. Weber and others would make him. The fact of " *Romaka-pura* in the West " being named as the birthplace of this hero of the archaic ages, is the more interesting because it is so very suggestive of the esoteric teaching about the " Sweat-born " Races, the men born from the *pores of their parents*. " ROMAKÛPAS " means " hair-pores " in Sanskrit. In *Mahâbhârata*,[125] a people named Raumyas are said to have been created from the pores of Virabhadra, the terrible giant, who destroyed Daksha's sacrifice. Other tribes and people are also represented as born in this way. All these are references to the later Second and the earlier Third Root Races.

The following figures are from the calendar just referred to; a footnote marks the points of disagreement with the figures of the Ârya Samâj school:—

I. From the beginning of cosmic evolution,[126] up to the Hindû year *Tarana* (or 1887) . 1,955,884,687 years.

II. The (astral) mineral, vegetable and animal kingdoms up to Man, have taken to evolve[127]   300,000,000 years.

III. Time, from the first appearance of " Humanity " (on planetary chain) . . . . . 1,664,500,987 years.[128]

125. XII, 10,308.

126. The esoteric doctrine says that this " cosmic evolution " refers only to our solar system; while exoteric Hindûism makes the figures refer, if we do not mistake, to the whole Universal System.

127. Another point of disagreement. Occultism says: " The astral prototypes of the mineral, vegetable and animal kingdoms up to man have taken that time (300 million years) to evolve, re-forming out of the cast-off materials of the preceding Round, which, though very dense and physical in their own cycle, are relatively ethereal as compared with the materiality of our present middle Round. At the expiration of these 300 million years, Nature, on the way to the physical and material, down the arc of descent, begins with mankind and works downwards, hardening or materializing forms as it proceeds. Thus the fossils found in strata, to which an antiquity, not of eighteen, but of many hundreds of millions of years, must be ascribed, belong in reality to forms of the preceding Round, which, while living, were far more ethereal than physical, as *we know the physical*. That we perceive and disinter them as tangible forms, is due to

the process of materialization or crystallization referred to, which took place subsequently, at the beginning of the Fourth Round, and reached its maximum after the appearance of man, proceeding parallel with his physical evolution. This alone illustrates the fact that the degree of materiality of the Earth changes *pari passu* with that of its inhabitants. And thus man now finds, as tangible fossils, what were once the (to his present senses) ethereal forms of the lower kingdoms. The above Brâhmanical figures refer to evolution beginning on Globe A, and in the First Round. In this Volume we speak only of this, the Fourth Round."

128. This difference and the change of ciphers in the last three triplets of figures, the writer cannot undertake to account for. According to every calculation, once the three hundred millions are subtracted, the figures ought to stand, 1,655,884,687. But they are given as stated in the Tamil calendar above-named and as they were translated. The school of the late Pandit Dayânand Sarasvatî, founder of the Arya Samâj, gives a date of 1,960,852,987. See the *Arya Magazine* of Lahore, the cover of which bears the words: "Aryan era 1,960,852,987."

IV. The number that elapsed since the "*Vai-vasvata Manvantara*" [129] — or the *human* period — up to the year 1887, is just.... 18,618,728 years.

V. The full period of one *Manvantara* is.... 308,448,000 years.

VI. 14 "Manvantaras" *plus* the period of one *Satya Yuga* make ONE DAY OF BRAHMÂ, or a complete Manvantara, and make...... 4,320,000,000 years. Therefore a *Mahâ-Yuga* consists of..... 4,320,000 years. [130] The year 1887 is from the commencement of Kali-Yuga........................ 4,989 years.

To make this still clearer in its details, the following computations by Rao Bahadur P. Srinivas Rao, are given from the *Theosophist* of November, 1885.

	Mortal years.
360 days of mortals make a year..........	1
Krita Yuga contains.........................	1,728,000
Tretâ Yuga contains.........................	1,296,000
Dvâpara Yuga contains......................	864,000
Kali Yuga contains.........................	432,000
The total of the said four Yugas constitute a Mahâ-Yuga................................	4,320,000
Seventy-one of such Mahâ-Yugas form the period of the reign of one Manu..........	306,720,000
The reign of 14 Manus embraces the duration of 994 Mahâ-Yugas, which is equal to.......	4,294,080,000

129. VAIVASVATA Manu is the one human being — some versions add to him the seven Rishis — who in the *Matsya*-Avatâra allegory is saved from the Deluge in a boat, like Noah in the Ark. Therefore, this *Vaivasvata Manvantara* would be the "post-Diluvian" period. This, however, does not refer to the later "Atlantean" or Noah's Deluge, nor to the Cosmic *Deluge* or *Pralaya* of obscuration, which preceded our Round, but to the appearance of mankind in the latter Round. There is a great difference made, however, between the "*Naimittika*," occasional or incidental, "*Prâkritika*," elemental, "*Atyantika*," the absolute, and "*Nitya*," the perpetual Pralaya; the latter being described as "Brahmâ's contingent recoalescence of the Universe at the end of Brahmâ's DAY." The question was raised by a learned Brâhman Theosophist: "Whether there is such a thing as Cosmic Pralaya; because, otherwise, the *Logos* (Krishna) would have to be reborn, and he is *Aja* (unborn)." We cannot see why. The *Logos* is said to be born only metaphorically, as the Sun is born daily, or rather a beam of that Sun is born in the morning and is said to die when it disappears, whereas it is simply reabsorbed into the parent essence. Cosmic *Pralaya* is for things visible, not for the *Arûpa*, formless, world. The Cosmic or Universal *Pralaya* comes only at the end of one hundred years of Brahmâ; when the Universal dissolution is said to take place. Then the *Avyaya*, say the exoteric scriptures, the eternal life symbolized by Vishnu, assuming the character of Rudra, the *Destroyer*, enters into the *Seven* Rays of the Sun and drinks up all the waters of the Universe. "Thus fed, the seven solar Rays dilate to *seven suns* and set fire to the whole Cosmos. . . ."

130. Since a Mahâ-Yuga is the 1000th part of a day of Brahmâ.

Add *Sandhis, i. e.,* intervals between the reign of each Manu, which amount to six Mahâ-Yugas, equal to............................	25,920,000
The total of these reigns and interregnums of 14 Manus, is 1000 Mahâ-Yugas, which constitute a Kalpa, *i. e.,* one day of Brahmâ....	4,320,000,000
As Brahmâ's Night is of equal duration, one Day and Night of Brahmâ would contain....	8,640,000,000
360 of such days and nights make one year of Brahmâ, equal to............................	3,110,400,000,000
100 such years constitute the whole period of Brahmâ's age, *i. e.,* Mahâ-Kalpa.............	311,040,000,000,000

These are the exoteric figures accepted throughout India, and they dovetail pretty nearly with those of the Secret works. The latter, moreover, amplify them by a division into a number of esoteric cycles, never mentioned in Brâhmanical popular writings — one of which, the division of the Yugas into racial cycles, is given elsewhere as an instance. The rest, in their details, have of course never been made public. They are, nevertheless, known to every *"Twice-born"* (Dvija, or Initiated) Brâhman, and the Purânas contain references to some of them in veiled terms, which no matter-of-fact Orientalist has yet endeavored to make out, nor could if he would.

These sacred astronomical cycles are of immense antiquity, and most of them pertain, as stated, to the calculations of Nârada and Asuramaya. The latter has the reputation of a giant and a sorcerer. But the antediluvian giants (the Gibborim of the Bible) were not all bad or Sorcerers, as Christian Theology, which sees in every Occultist a servant of the Evil one, would have it; nor were they worse than many of " the faithful sons of the Church." A Torquemada and a Catherine de Médicis certainly did more harm in their day and in the name of their Master than any Atlantean giant or demigod of antiquity ever did; whether his name was Cyclops, or Medusa, or yet the Orphic Titan, the *anguipedal* monster known as Ephialtes. There were *good* "giants" in days of old just as there are *bad* "pigmies" now; and the Râkshasas and Yakshas of Lankâ are no worse than our modern dynamiters, and certain Christian and civilized generals during modern wars. Nor are they myths. " He who would laugh at Briareus and Orion ought to abstain from going to, or even talking of, Karnac or Stonehenge," remarks somewhere a modern writer.

As the Brâhmanical figures given above are approximately the basic calculations of our esoteric system, the reader is requested to carefully keep them in mind.

In the *Encyclopaedia Britannica* one finds, as the last word of science, that the antiquity of man is allowed to stretch *only over* " tens of thous-

ands of years." [131]   It becomes evident that as these figures may be
made to fluctuate between 10,000 and 100,000, therefore they mean very
little if anything, and only render still denser the darkness surrounding
the question.   Moreover, what matters it that science places the birth
of man in the " pre- or post-glacial drift," if we are told at the same
time that the so-called " ice age " is simply a long succession of ages
which " shaded without abrupt change of any kind into what is termed
the human or Recent period . . . the overlapping of geological periods
having been the rule from the beginning of time."   The latter " rule "
only results in the still more puzzling, even if strictly *scientific* and
correct, information, that " even today man is contemporary with the
ice-age in the Alpine valleys and in the Finmark." [132]

Thus, had it not been for the lessons taught by the *Secret Doctrine*,
and even by exoteric Hindûism and its traditions, we should be left to
this day to float in perplexed uncertainty between the indefinite ages of
one school of science, the " tens of thousands " of years of the other,
and the 6000 years of the Bible interpreters.   This is one of the several
reasons why, with all the respect due to the conclusions of the men of
learning of our modern day, we are forced to ignore them in all such
questions of pre-historic antiquity.

Modern Geology and Anthropology must, of course, disagree with
our views.   But Occultism will find as many weapons against these two
sciences as it has against astronomical and physical theories, in spite
of Mr. Laing's assurances that " in [chronological] calculations of this
sort, concerning older and later formations, there is no *theory*, and they
are based upon positive *facts*, limited only by a certain possible [?]
amount of error either way," [133] occultism will prove, scientific confessions in hand, that geology is very much in error, and very often
even more so than Astronomy.   In this very passage by Mr. Laing,
which gives to Geology pre-eminence for correctness over Astronomy,
we find a passage in flagrant contradiction to the admissions of the
best Geologists themselves.   Says the author —

In short, the conclusions of Geology, at any rate up to the Silurian period, [134]
when the present order of things was fairly inaugurated, are approximate
[truly so] *facts* and not *theories*, while the astronomical conclusions are *theories*
based on *data so uncertain*, that while in some cases they give results incredibly
short . . . in others they give results almost incredibly long.

131. See article " Geology," in *Encyclopaedia Britannica.*
132. This allows a chance even to the
Biblical " Adam Chronology " of 6000 years.
(*Ibid.*)

133. See his *Modern Science and Modern
Thought,* p. 48.
134. To the Silurian period as regards
Molluscs and Animal life — granted; but
what do they know of man?

After which, the reader is advised that the safest course
seems to be to *assume* that Geology really proves the *duration of the present
order of things* to have been somewhere over 100 millions of years, [as] Astronomy gives an enormous though unknown time in the past, and to come in the
future, for the birth, growth, maturity, decline, and death of the Solar System,
of which our Earth is a small planet now passing through the habitable phase.[135]

Judging from past experience, we do not entertain the slightest doubt
that, once called upon to answer " the absurd unscientific and preposterous claims of exoteric (and esoteric) Âryan chronology," the scientist
of " the results incredibly short," *i. e.*, only 15,000,000 years, and the
scientist, who " would require 600,000,000 years," together with those
who accept Mr. Huxley's figures of 1,000,000,000 " since sedimentation
began in Europe," [136] would all be as dogmatic one as the other. Nor
would they fail to remind the Occultist and the Brâhman, that it is
the modern men of science alone who represent exact science, whose
duty it is to fight *inaccuracy* and *superstition*.

The earth is passing through the " habitable phase " only for the
present order of things, and as far as our present mankind is concerned
with its actual " coats of skin " and phosphorus for bones and brain.

We are ready to concede the 100 millions of years offered by Geology,
since we are taught that our present physical mankind — or the *Vaivasvata* humanity — began only 18 millions of years ago. But Geology has
no facts to give us for the duration of geological periods, as we have
shown, no more indeed than has Astronomy. The authentic letter
from Mr. W. Pengelly, F. R. S., quoted elsewhere, says that: " It is
at present, and perhaps always will be, IMPOSSIBLE to reduce, even
approximately, geological time into years or even into millenniums."
And having never, hitherto, excavated a fossil man of any other than
the *present form* — what does Geology know of him? It has traced
zones or strata and, with these, primordial zoological life, down to
the Silurian. When it has, in the same way, traced man down to his
primordial protoplasmic form, then we will admit that it may know
something of primordial man. If it is not very material " to the
bearings of modern scientific discovery on modern thought," whether
" man has existed in a state of constant though slow progression for
the last 50,000 years of a period of 15 millions, or for the last 500,000
years of a period of 150 millions," [137] as Mr. S. Laing tells his readers,
it is very much so for the claims of the Occultists. Unless the latter
show that it is *a possibility,* if not a perfect certainty, that man lived
18 millions of years ago, the Secret Doctrine might as well have
remained unwritten. An attempt must, therefore, be made in this

135. Page 49.   136. *World-Life,* p. 180.   137. *Mod. Sc. and Mod. Th.,* p. 49.

direction, and it is our modern geologists and men of science generally who will be brought to testify to this fact in the third part of this volume. Meanwhile, and notwithstanding the fact that Hindû Chronology is constantly represented by the Orientalists as a fiction based on no *"actual* computation,"[138] but simply a "childish boasting," it is nevertheless often twisted out of recognition to make it yield to, and fit in with, Western theories. No figures have ever been more meddled with and tortured than the famous 4, 3, 2, followed by cyphers of the Yugas and Mahâ-Yugas.

As the whole cycle of prehistoric events, such as the evolution and transformation of Races and the extreme antiquity of man, hangs upon the said Chronology, it becomes extremely important to check it by other existing calculations. If the Eastern Chronology is rejected, we shall at least have the consolation of proving that no other — whether the figures of Science or of the Churches — is one whit more reliable. As Professor Max Müller expresses it, it is often as useful to prove what a thing is not as to show what it may be. And once we succeed in pointing out the fallacies of both Christian and scientific computations — by allowing them a fair chance of comparison with our Chronology — neither of the two will have a reasonable ground to stand upon, in pronouncing the esoteric figures less reliable than its own.

We may here refer the reader to our earlier work " *Isis Unveiled*," [139] for some remarks concerning the figures which were cited a few pages back.

Today a few more facts may be added to the information there given, which is already known to every Orientalist. The sacredness of the cycle of 4320, with additional cyphers, lies in the fact that the figures which compose it, taken separately or joined in various combinations, are each and all symbolical of the greatest mysteries in Nature. Indeed, whether one takes the 4 separately, or the 3 by itself, or the two together making 7, or again the three added together and yielding 9, all these numbers have their application in the most sacred and occult things, and record the workings of Nature in her eternally periodical phenomena. They are never erring, perpetually recurring numbers, unveiling, to him who studies the secrets of Nature, a truly divine System, an *intelligent* plan in Cosmogony, which results in natural cosmic divisions of times, seasons, invisible influences, astronomical phenomena, with their action and reaction on terrestrial and even moral nature; on birth, death, and growth, on health and disease. All these natural events are based and depend upon cyclical processes in the Kosmos itself, producing periodic agencies which, acting from without,

138. Wilson's Translation of *Vishnu Purâna*, Vol. I, pp. 50, 51.   139. Vol. I, p. 32.

affect the Earth and all that lives and breathes on it, from one end to
the other of any Manvantara. Causes and effects are esoteric, exoteric,
and *endexoteric,* so to say.

In *Isis Unveiled* we wrote that which we now repeat:—" *We are at
the bottom of a cycle and evidently in a transitory state.* Plato divides
the intellectual progress of the universe during every cycle into fertile
and barren periods. In the sublunary regions, the spheres of the various elements remain eternally in perfect harmony with the divine nature, he says; 'but their parts,' owing to a too close proximity to
earth, and their commingling with the *earthly* (which is matter, and
therefore the realm of evil), 'are sometimes according, and sometimes
contrary to (divine) nature.' When those circulations — which Éliphas Lévi calls 'currents of the astral light' — in the universal ether
which contains in itself every element, take place in harmony with the
divine spirit, our earth and everything pertaining to it enjoys a fertile
period. The occult powers of plants, animals, and minerals magically
sympathize with the 'superior natures,' and the divine soul of man is
in perfect intelligence with these 'inferior' ones. But during the barren periods, the latter lose their magic sympathy, and the spiritual sight
of the majority of mankind is so blinded as to lose every notion of the
superior powers of its own divine spirit. We are in a barren period:
the eighteenth century, during which the malignant fever of scepticism
broke out so irrepressibly, has entailed unbelief as a hereditary disease
upon the nineteenth. The divine intellect is veiled in man; his animal
brain alone *philosophizes.*" And philosophizing alone, how can it understand the " SOUL DOCTRINE "?

In order not to break the thread of the narrative we shall give some
striking proofs of these cyclic laws in Part II, proceeding meanwhile
with our explanations of geological and racial cycles.

STANZA III

ATTEMPTS TO CREATE MAN

§§ (11) The Descent of the Demiurge. (12) The lunar gods ordered to create. (13) The higher gods refuse.

11. THE LORD OF THE LORDS CAME. FROM HER BODY HE SEPARATED THE WATERS, AND THAT WAS HEAVEN ABOVE, THE FIRST HEAVEN (*the atmosphere, or the air, the firmament*) (*a*).

(*a*) Here tradition falls again into the Universal. As in the earliest version, repeated in the Purânas, so in the latest, the Mosaic account. In the first it is said: "He the Lord" (the god who has the form of Brahmâ) "when the world had become one ocean [140] concluding that within the waters lay the earth, and desirous to raise it up," to separate it, "created himself in another form. As in the preceding Kalpa (Manvantara) he had assumed the shape of a tortoise, so in this one he took the shape of a boar, etc., etc." In the Elohistic "creation" [141] "God" creates a firmament in the midst of the waters . . . and says "let *dry land* appear." And now comes the traditional peg whereunto is hung the esoteric portion of the Kabalistic interpretation.

12. THE GREAT CHOHANS (*Lords*), CALLED THE LORDS OF THE MOON, OF THE AIRY BODIES (*a*). "BRING FORTH MEN, (*they were told*), MEN OF YOUR NATURE. GIVE THEM (*i. e., the Jîvas or Monads*) THEIR FORMS WITHIN. SHE (*Mother Earth or Nature*) WILL BUILD COVERINGS WITHOUT (*external bodies*). (*For*) MALES-FEMALES WILL THEY BE. LORDS OF THE FLAME, ALSO."

(*a*) Who are the Lords of the Moon? In India they are called *Pitris* or "lunar ancestors," but in the Hebrew scrolls it is Jehovah himself who is the "Lord of the Moon," collectively as the Host, and also as one of the Elohim. The astronomy of the Hebrews and their observance of *times* was regulated by the moon. A Kabalist, having shown that "Daniel . . . told off God's providence by *set times*," and that the "Revelation" of John "speaks of a carefully measured *cubical* city descending out of the heavens," etc., adds—

140. *Harivamśa*, I, 36.   141. *Genesis*, i, verses 6, 7, 8, and 9.

But the vitalizing power of heaven lay chiefly *with the moon*. . . . It was the Hebrew יהוה (Jehovah), and St. Paul enjoins: "Let no man judge you for your observance of the seventh day, and the *day of the new moon, which are a shadow of things to come;* but the body [or substance] is of Christ" or Jehovah, that function of this power that "made the barren woman . . . a mother . . . for they are the gift of Jehovah" . . . which is a key to the objection which her husband made to the Shunamite, as to her going to the man of God — "for it is neither the seventh day nor the *day of the new moon.* . . ."[142]

The living spiritual powers of the constellations had mighty wars, marked by the movements and positions of the stars and planets, and especially as the result of the conjunction of the moon, earth, and sun. Bentley comments on the Hindû "War between the gods and the giants," as marked by the eclipse of the Sun at the ascending node of the Moon, 945 B. C. (!!), at which time was born[143] or produced from the sea, Śrî (Sarai, S-r-i, the wife of the Hebrew A-bram[144]). Śrî is also Venus-Aphrodite the Western emblem "of the luni-solar year or the moon (as Śrî is the wife of the moon; *vide* foot-note), the goddess of increase[145] . . ." Therefore . . .

the grand monument and landmark of the exact period of the lunar year and month, by which this cycle [of 19 tropical years and 235 revolutions of the moon] could be calculated, was Mount Sinai — the Lord Jehovah coming down thereon. . . . Paul speaks [then] as a mystagogue, when he says concerning the freed woman and bond woman of Abraham: "For this Hagar [the bond-woman] is Mount Sinai in Arabia." How could a woman be a mountain? and such a mountain! Yet ... she was. ... Her name was Hagar, Hebrew הגר, whose numbers re-read 235, or in exact measure, the very number of lunar months to equal nineteen tropical years to complete this cycle. . . . Mount Sinai being, in the esoteric language of the wisdom, the monument of the exact time of the lunar years and months, by which this spiritual vitalizing cycle

---

142. II *Kings*, iv. 23.

143. According to the wonderful chronology of Bentley, who wrote in days when Biblical chronology was still undisputed; and also according to that of those modern Orientalists who dwarf the Hindû dates as far as they can.

144. Now *Śrî* is the daughter of Bhrigu, one of the Prajâpatis and Rishis, the chief of the Bhrigus, "the Consumers," the aerial class of gods. She is Lakshmi, the wife of Vishnu, and she is "the bride of Śiva," (Gaurî), and she is Sarasvatî, "the watery," the wife of Brahmâ, because the three gods and goddesses are one, under three aspects.

Read the explanation by Parâśara, in *Vishnu Purâna* in Bk. I, ch. viii. (Vol. I, Wilson's trans., p. 119), and you will understand. "The Lord of Śrî" is the moon, he says, and "Śrî" is the wife of Nârâyana, the God of Gods"; Śrî or Lakshmi (Venus) is Indrânî, as she is Sarasvatî, for in the words of Parâśara: "Hari (or Îśvara, "the Lord") is all that is called male in the Universe; Lakshmî is all that is termed female. There is nothing else than they." Hence she is "female," and "God" is male Nature.

145. Śrî is goddess of, and herself "Fortune and Prosperity."

could be computed — and which mountain, indeed, was called (see Fuerst), "the Mountain of the Moon" (Sin). So also Sarai (SRI), the wife of Abram, could have no child until her name was changed to Sarah, שָׂרָה, giving to her the property of this lunar influence.[146]

This may be regarded as a digression from the main subject; but it is a very necessary one with a view to Christian readers. For who, after studying dispassionately the respective legends of Abram or Abraham, Sarai, or Sarah, who was "fair to look upon," and those of Brahmâ and Sarasvati, or Śrî, Lakshmî-Venus, with the relations of all all these to the Moon and Water;— and especially one who understands the real Kabalistic meaning of the name Jehovah and its relation to, and connexion with, the moon — who can doubt that the story of Abram is based upon that of Brahmâ, or that *Genesis* was written upon the old lines used by every ancient nation? All in the ancient Scriptures is allegorical — all based upon and inseparably connected with Astronomy and Cosmolatry.

---

13. THEY (*the Moon-gods*) WENT, EACH ON HIS ALLOTTED LAND: SEVEN OF THEM, EACH ON HIS LOT. THE LORDS OF THE FLAME RE-MAINED BEHIND. THEY WOULD NOT GO, THEY WOULD NOT CREATE (*a*).

(*a*) The Secret teachings show the divine Progenitors creating men on seven portions of the globe "each on his lot" — *i. e.*, each a different race of men externally and internally, and on different zones. This polygenistic claim is considered elsewhere.[147] But who are "They" who create, and the "Lords of the Flame," "who do not"? Occultism divides the "Creators" into twelve classes; of which four have reached *liberation* to the end of the "Great Age," the fifth is ready to reach it, but still remains active on the intellectual planes, while seven are still under direct Karmic law. These last act on the man-bearing globes of our chain.

Exoteric Hindû books mention seven classes of Pitris, and among them two distinct kinds of Progenitors or Ancestors: the *Barhishad* and the *Agnishvâtta;* or those possessed of the "sacred fire" and those devoid of it. Hindû ritualism seems to connect them with sacrificial fires, and with *Grihastha* Brâhmans in earlier incarnations: those who have, and those who have *not* attended as they should to their household sacred fires in their previous births. The distinction, as said, is derived from the *Vedas.* The first and highest class (esoterically) the *Agnishvâtta*, are represented in the exoteric allegory as *Grihastha*

---

146. *Masonic Review*, Cincinnati, June, 1886; art. "The Cabbalah."
147. *Vide* Stanza VII.

(Brâhman-householders) who, in their past births in other Manvantaras having failed to maintain their domestic fires and to offer burnt sacrifices, have lost every right to have oblations with fire presented to them. Whereas the Barhishad, being Brâhmans who have kept up their household sacred fires, are thus honored to this day. Thence the *Agnishvâtta* are represented as devoid of, and the *Barhishad* as possessed of, fires.

But esoteric philosophy explains the original qualifications as being due to the difference between the natures of the two classes: the *Agnishvâtta* Pitris are devoid of fire (*i.e.*, of creative passion), because too divine and pure;[148] whereas the Barhishad, being the lunar spirits more closely connected with Earth, became the creative Elohim of form, or the Adam of dust.

The allegory says that Sanandana and other *Vedhas*, the Sons of Brahmâ, *his first progeny*, "were without desire or passion, inspired with the holy wisdom, estranged from the Universe and *undesirous of progeny.*"[149] This also is what is meant in Śloka 13 by the words: "They would not create," and is explained as follows:— " The primordial Emanations from the creative Power are too near the absolute Cause. They are transitional and latent forces, which will develop only in the next and subsequent removes." This makes it plain. Hence Brahmâ is said to have felt wrathful when he saw that those " embodied spirits, produced from his limbs (*gâtra*), would not multiply themselves." After which, in the allegory, he creates other seven *mind-born* Sons,[150] namely, *Marîchi, Atri, Angiras, Pulastya, Pulaha, Kratu* and *Vasishtha*, the latter being often replaced by *Daksha*, the most prolific of the creators. In most of the texts these Seven Sons of *Vasishtha-Daksha* are called the seven Rishis of the *Third* Manvantara; the latter referring both to the Third Round and also to the third Root-Race and its branch-Races in the Fourth Round. These are all the creators of the various beings on this Earth, the Prajâpatis, and at the same time they appear as divers reincarnations in the early Manvantaras or races.

It thus becomes clear why the *Agnishvâtta*, devoid of the grosser *creative fire*, hence unable to create physical man, having no *double*, or astral body, to project, since they were without any *form*, are shown in exoteric allegories as Yogis, Kumâras (chaste youths), who became " rebels," *Asuras*, fighting and opposing gods,[151] etc., etc. Yet it is they

148. *Vide supra*, Śloka 13.
149. *Vishnu Purâna*, Book I, vii.
150. See *Moksha-Dharma, Mahâbhârata.*
151. Because, as the allegory shows, the Gods who had no personal merit of their own, dreading the sanctity of those self-striving incarnated Beings who had become ascetics and Yogis, and thus threatened to upset the power of the former by their *self-acquired* powers — denounced them. All this has a deep philosophical meaning and refers

alone who could complete man, *i. e.*, make of him a self-conscious, almost a divine being — a god on Earth. The *Barhishad*, though possessed of creative fire, were devoid of the higher MAHAT-mic element. Being on a level with the lower principles — those which precede gross objective matter — they could only give birth to the outer man, or rather to the model of the physical, the astral man. Thus, though we see them intrusted with the task by Brahmâ (the collective *Mahat* or Universal Divine Mind), the " Mystery of Creation " is repeated on Earth, only in an inverted sense, as in a *mirror*. It is those who are unable to create the spiritual immortal man, who project the senseless model (the *Astral*) of the physical Being; and, as will be seen, it was those who would not multiply, who sacrificed themselves to the good and salvation of *Spiritual Humanity*. For, to complete the *septenary man*, to add to his three lower principles and cement them with the spiritual Monad — which could never dwell in such a form otherwise than in an *absolutely latent state* — two connecting principles are needed: *Manas* and *Kâma*. This requires a living *Spiritual Fire* of the middle principle from the *fifth* and *third states* of Pleroma. But this fire is the possession of the *Triangles*, not of the (perfect) *Cubes*, which symbolize the Angelic Beings:[152] the former having from the first creation got hold of it and being said to have appropriated it for themselves, as in the allegory of Prometheus. These are the active, and therefore — in Heaven — no longer " pure " Beings. They have become the independent and free Intelligences, shown in every Theogony as fighting for that independence and freedom, and hence — in the ordinary sense — " rebellious to the divine passive law." These are then those " Flames " (the *Agnishvâtta*) who, as shown in Śloka 13, " remain behind " instead of going along with the others to create men on Earth. But the true esoteric meaning is that most of them were destined to incarnate as the *Egos* of the forthcoming crop of Mankind. The human *Ego* is neither Âtman nor Buddhi, but the higher *Manas:* the intellectual fruition and the efflorescence of the intellectual self-conscious *Egotism* — in the higher spiritual sense. The ancient works refer to it as *Kârana Śarîra* on the plane of *Sûtrâtmâ*, which is the golden thread on which, like beads, the various personalities of this higher *Ego* are strung. If the reader were told, as in the *semi-esoteric* allegories, that these Beings were returning *Nirvânîs*, from preceding *Mahâ-Manvantaras* — ages of incalculable duration which have rolled away in the Eternity, a still more incalculable

to the evolution and acquirement of divine powers through *self-exertion*. Some Rishi-Yogis are shown in the Purânas to be far more powerful than the gods. Secondary gods or temporary powers in Nature (the Forces) are doomed to disappear; it is only

the spiritual potentiality in man which can lead him to become one with the INFINITE and the ABSOLUTE.

152. See Book I, Stanzas III to V. The triangle becomes a Pentagon (five-fold) on Earth.

time ago — he would hardly understand the text correctly; while some Vedântins might say: " This is not so; the Nirvâni can never return "; which is true during the Manvantara he belongs to, and erroneous where Eternity is concerned. For it is said in the Sacred Slokas:

" The thread of radiance which is imperishable and dissolves only in Nirvâna, re-emerges from it in its integrity on the day when the Great Law calls all things back into action. . . ."

Hence, as the higher " Pitris or Dhyânis " had no hand in his physical creation, we find primeval man, issued from the bodies of his *spiritually fireless* progenitors, described as aeriform, devoid of compactness, and MINDLESS. He had no middle principle to serve him as a medium between the *highest* and the *lowest*, the spiritual man and the physical brain, for he lacked *Manas.* The Monads which incarnated in those *empty* SHELLS, remained as unconscious as when separated from their previous incomplete forms and vehicles. There is no potentiality for creation, or self-Consciousness, in a *pure* Spirit on this our plane, unless its too homogeneous, perfect, because divine, nature is, so to say, mixed with, and strengthened by, an essence already differentiated. It is only the lower line of the Triangle — representing the first triad that emanates from the Universal MONAD — that can furnish this needed consciousness on the plane of differentiated Nature. But how could these pure Emanations, which, on this principle, must have originally been themselves *unconscious* (in our sense), be of any use in supplying the required principle, as they could hardly have possessed it themselves? The answer is difficult to comprehend, unless one is well acquainted with the philosophical metaphysics of a beginningless and endless series of Cosmic Re-births; and becomes well impressed and familiarized with that immutable law of Nature which is ETERNAL MOTION, cyclic and spiral, therefore progressive even in its seeming retrogression. The one divine Principle, the nameless THAT of the Vedas, is the universal Total, which, neither in its spiritual aspects and emanations, nor in its physical atoms, can ever be at *" absolute rest "* except during the " Nights " of Brahmâ. Hence, also, the " first-born " are those who are first set in motion at the beginning of a Manvantara, and thus the first to fall into the lower spheres of materiality. They who are called in Theology " the Thrones," and are the " Seat of God," must be the first incarnated men on Earth; and it becomes comprehensible, if we think of the endless series of past Manvantaras, to find that the last had to come first, and the first last. We find, in short, that the higher Angels had broken, countless aeons before, through the " Seven Circles," and thus *robbed* them of the Sacred fire; which means in plain words, that they had assimilated during their past incarnations, in lower as well as in higher worlds, all the wisdom there-from — the reflection of MAHAT in its various degrees of intensity. No Entity, whether angelic or human, can reach the state of Nirvâna, or of absolute purity, except through aeons of suffering and the *knowledge* of EVIL as well as of good, as otherwise the latter remains incomprehensible.

Between man and the animal — whose Monads (or Jivas) are funda-mentally identical — there is the impassable abyss of Mentality and Self-consciousness. What is human mind in its higher aspect, whence comes it, if it is not a portion of the essence — and, in some rare cases of incarnation, the *very essence*—of a higher Being: one from a higher and divine plane? Can man — a god in the animal form — be the pro-duct of Material Nature by evolution alone, even as is the animal, which differs from man in external shape, but by no means in the materials of its physical fabric, and is informed by the same, though undeveloped, Monad — seeing that the intellectual potentialities of the two differ as the Sun does from the Glow-worm? And what is it that creates such difference, unless man is an animal *plus* a *living god* within his physical shell? Let us pause and ask ourselves seriously the question, regardless of the vagaries and sophisms of both the materialistic and the psychological modern sciences.

To some extent, it is admitted that even the esoteric teaching is alle-gorical. To make the latter comprehensible to the average intelligence, requires the use of symbols cast in an intelligible form. Hence the allegorical and semi-mythical narratives in the exoteric, and the (only) *semi*-metaphysical and objective representations in the esoteric teach-ings. For the purely and transcendentally spiritual conceptions are adapted only to the perceptions of those who "see without eyes, hear without ears, and sense without organs," according to the graphic expression of the Commentary. The too puritan idealist is at liberty to spiritualize the tenet, whereas the modern psychologist would simply try to spirit away our " fallen," yet still divine, human Soul in its connexion with *Buddhi*.

The mystery attached to the highly spiritual ancestors of the *divine* man within the earthly man is very great. His dual creation is hinted at in the Purânas, though its esoteric meaning can be approached only by collating together the many varying accounts, and reading them in their symbolical and allegorical character. So it is in the Bible, both in *Genesis* and even in the *Epistles* of Paul. For that *creator*, who is called in the second chapter of *Genesis* the " Lord God," is in the ori-ginal the *Elohim*, or *Gods* (the Lords), in the plural; and while one of them makes the earthly Adam of dust, the other breathes into him the breath of life, and the third makes of him a *living soul* (ii. 7), all of

which readings are implied in the plural number of the Elohim.[153]
" The first man is of the Earth, the second [the last, or rather highest]
is from heaven," says Paul.[154]

In the Aryan allegory the rebellious Sons of Brahmâ are all represented as holy ascetics and Yogis. Re-born in every Kalpa, they
generally try to impede the work of human procreation. When
Daksha, the chief of the *Prajâpatis* (creators), brings forth 10,000 sons
for the purpose of peopling the world, Nârada — a son of Brahmâ,
the great Rishi, and *virtually* a " Kumâra," if not so in name — inter-
feres with, and twice frustrates Daksha's aim, by persuading those Sons
to remain holy ascetics and eschew marriage. For this, Daksha curses
Nârada to be *re-born as a man*, as Brahmâ had cursed him before for
refusing to marry, and obtain progeny, saying :— " Perish in thy present [*Deva* or angelic] form and take up thy abode in the womb,"
i.e., become a man.[155] Notwithstanding several conflicting versions of
the same story, it is easy to see that Nârada belongs to that class of
Brahmâ's " first-born," who have all ·proven rebellious to the law of
animal procreation, for which they had to incarnate as *men*. Of all
the Vedic Rishis, Nârada, as already shown, is the most incomprehensible, because the most closely connected with the occult doctrines
— especially with the secret cycles and Kalpas.[156]

Certain contradictory statements about this Sage have much dis-
tracted the Orientalists. Thus he is shown as refusing positively to
create (have progeny), and even as calling his father Brahmâ "a false
teacher " for advising him to get married (*Nârada-Pañcha-Râtra*) ;
nevertheless, he is referred to as one of the Prajâpatis, "progenitors"!
In *Nâradîya Purâna*, he describes the laws and the duties of the celibate adepts ; and as these occult duties do not happen to be found in
the fragment of about 3000 Stanzas in the possession of European
museums, the Brâhmans are proclaimed liars ; the Orientalists forgetting that the *Nâradîya* is credited with containing 25,000 Stanzas,
and it is not very likely that any such MSS. should be found in the
hands of the Hindû profane, those who are ready to sell any precious
olla for a red pottage. Suffice it to say, that Nârada is *the* Deva-

153. Seth, as Bunsen and others have
shown, is not only the *primitive god* of the
Semites — early Jews included — but also
their " semi-divine ancestor." For, says Bunsen (*God in History*, vol. i, pp. 233, 234),
the Seth of *Genesis*, the father of Enoch
(*the* man) must be considered as originally
running parallel with that derived from the
Elohim, Adam's father." "According to Bunsen, the Deity (the god Seth) was the *prim-*

itive god of Northern Egypt and Palestine "
(Staniland Wake, *The Great Pyramid*). And
Seth became considered in the later Theology of the Egyptians as " AN EVIL DAEMON,"
says the same Bunsen, for he is one with
Typhon and one with the Hindû demons as
a logical sequel.
154. In I *Corinthians* xv. 47.
155. *Vâyu Purâna; Harivamśa*, 170.
156. *Vide supra*.

Rishi of Occultism *par excellence;* and that the Occultist who does not ponder, analyse, and study Nârada from his seven esoteric facets, will never be able to fathom certain anthropological, chronological, and even Cosmic Mysteries. He is one of the *Fires* above-mentioned, and plays a part in the evolution of this Kalpa from its incipient, down to its final stage. He is an actor who appears in each of the successive acts (Root-Races) of the present Manvantaric drama, in the world allegories which strike the key-note of esotericism, and are now becoming more familiar to the reader. But shall we turn to other ancient Scriptures and documents for the corroboration of the " Fires," " Sparks," and " Flames "? They are plentiful, if one only seeks for them in the right places. In the *Book of the Concealed Mystery,* they are clearly enunciated, as also in the *Ha Idra Zuta Qadisha,* or the Lesser Holy Assembly. The language is very mystical and veiled, yet still comprehensible. Therein, among the sparks of Prior Worlds, " vibrating Flames and Sparks," from the divine flint, the *workmen* proceed to create man, "male and female" (427); which " Flames and Sparks " (Angels and their Worlds, Stars and Planets) are said, figuratively, to " become extinct and die," that is to say, remain *unmanifested* until a certain process of nature is accomplished. To show how thickly veiled from public view are the most important facts of anthropogenesis, two passages are now quoted from two Kabalistic books. The first is from the *Ha Idra Zuta Qadisha:*—

(429) From a Light-Bearer [one of the seven sacred planets] of insupportable brightness proceeded a radiating Flame, dashing off, like a vast and mighty hammer, those sparks which were the prior worlds.

(430) And with most subtle ether were these intermingled and bound mutually together, but *only when they were conjoined together,* even the great Father and great Mother.

(431) From *Hoa,* himself, is AB, the Father; and from *Hoa,* himself, is RUACH, the Spirit; who are hidden in the Ancient of Days, and therein is that Ether concealed.

(432) And it was connected with a Light-Bearer [a planet and its angel or regent], which went forth from that Light-Bearer of insupportable brightness, which is hidden in the bosom of *Aima,* the Great Mother.[157]

Now the following extract from the *Zohar*[158] also deals with the same mystery:—

The Pre-Adamite Kings. " We have learned in the *Siphrah D'Tznioothah:* That the *At-tee'kah D'At-tee'keen,* Ancient of Ancients, before He prepared his Form, built Kings, and engraved Kings, and sketched out Kings [men, the Kings of the animals], and they could not exist: till he overthrew them *and hid them until after a time*, therefore it is written: 'And these are the Kings which reigned in the land of Edom' . . . And they could not exist till *Resha' Hiv'rah*, the White Head, the *At'-tee'kah D'At-tee'keen*, Ancient of Ancients, arranged Himself . . . and formed all forms above and below. . . . Before He arranged himself in his Form had not been formed all those whom he desired to form, and all worlds have been destroyed." . . . "they did not remain in their places, because the form of the Kings had not been formed as it ought to be, and *the Holy City had not been prepared*." [159]

Now the plain meaning of these two allegorical and metaphysical disquisitions is simply this: Worlds and men were in turn formed and destroyed, *under the law of evolution* and *from pre-existing material*, until both the planets and their men, in our case our Earth and its animal and human races, became what they are now in the present cycle: opposite polar forces, an equilibrized compound of Spirit and Matter, of the positive and the negative, of the male and the female. Before man could become male and female *physically*, his prototype, the creating Elohim, had to arrange his Form on this sexual plane *astrally*. That is to say, the atoms and the organic forces, descending into the plane of the given differentiation, had to be marshaled in the order intended by Nature, so as to be ever carrying out, in an immaculate way, that law which the Kabala calls the *Balance*, through which everything that exists does so as male and female in its final perfection, in this present stage of materiality. *Chochmah*, Wisdom, the Male Sephiroth, had to diffuse itself *in*, and *through*, *Binah*, intelligent Nature, or Understanding. Therefore the First Root-race of men, sexless and mindless, had to be overthrown and "hidden until after a time"; *i.e.*, the first race, instead of dying, disappeared *in the second race*, as certain lower lives and plants do in their progeny. It was a wholesale transformation. The First became the Second Root-race, without either begetting it, procreating it, or dying. "*They passed by together*," as it is written: "And he died and another reigned in his stead." [160] Why? Because "the *Holy City* had not been prepared." And what is the "Holy City"? The *Maqom* (the Secret *Place* or the Shrine) on Earth: in other words, the human womb, the microcosmic copy and reflection of the *Heavenly Matrix*, the female space or primeval Chaos, in which the male Spirit fecundates the germ of the Son, or the visible Universe. [161] So much so, that in the paragraph on "the Emanation of the Male and Female Principles" in the *Zohar*, [162] it is

159. *Zohar* iii, 135a; 292a *Idra Zutah*, Brody ed., etc.
160. *Genesis* xxxvi, 31, *et seq. Zohar* iii, 292a.
161. *Vide* "The Holy of Holies: its Esoteric Meaning," in Part II of this Vol., § xvii.
162. *Ibid*.

said that, on this earth, the WISDOM from the " Holy Ancient " " does not shine except in male and female."

Hokhmah, Wisdom, is the Father, and BINAH, understanding, is the Mother . . . and when they connect one with the other they bring forth and diffuse and emanate truth. In the sayings of Rabbi Ye-yeva Sabah, *i. e.,* the Old, we learned this: What is Binah Understanding? But when they connect in one another, the ‏ (Yod) in the ‏ (Heh), they become impregnated and produce a Son. And, therefore, it is called *Binah,* Understanding. It means BeN YaH, *i e.,* Son of YaH. This is the completeness of the whole.[163]

This is also the [164] " completeness " of phallicism by the Rabbis, its perfect apotheosis, the divine being dragged into the animal, the sublime into the grossness of the terrestrial. Nothing so graphically gross exists in Eastern Occultism, nor in the primitive Kabala — the " Chaldaean Book of Numbers." We have said so in " *Isis Unveiled* ":

We find it rather unwise on the part of Catholic writers to pour out their vials of wrath in such sentences as these: "In a multitude of pagodas, the phallic stone, ever and always assuming, like the Grecian *baitylos,* the brutally indecent form of the *lingam* . . . the Mahâ Deva." Before casting slurs on a symbol whose profound metaphysical meaning is too much for the modern champions of that religion of sensualism *par excellence,* Roman Catholicism, to grasp, they are in duty bound to destroy their oldest churches, and change the form of the cupolas of their own temples. The Mahody of Elephanta, the Round Tower of Bhagalpur, the minarets of Islâm — either rounded or pointed — are the originals of the *Campanile* column of San Marco, at Venice, of the Rochester Cathedral, and of the modern Duomo of Milan. All of these steeples, turrets, domes, and Christian temples, are the reproductions of the primitive idea of the *lithos,* the upright phallus.[164]

Nevertheless, and however it may be, the fact that all these Hebrew Elohim, Sparks, and Cherubs are identical with the Devas, Rishis and the Fires and Flames, the Rudras and the forty-nine Agnis of the ancient Âryas, is sufficiently proven by and in the Kabala.

163. *Zohar* iii, 290a, quoted in Isaac Myer's *Qabbalah,* p. 387.   164. Vol. II, p. 5.

STANZA IV

CREATION OF THE FIRST RACES

---

§§ (14) Creation of men. (15) They are empty shadows. (16) The Creators are perplexed how to create a THINKING man. ♪(17) What is needed for the formation of a perfect Man.

---

14. THE SEVEN HOSTS, THE "WILL (or Mind)-BORN" LORDS, PROPELLED BY THE SPIRIT OF LIFE-GIVING (Fohat), SEPARATE MEN FROM THEMSELVES, EACH ON HIS OWN ZONE (a).

(a) They threw off their "shadows" or *astral bodies* — if such an ethereal being as a "lunar Spirit" may be supposed to rejoice in an astral, besides a hardly tangible body. In another Commentary it is said that the "Ancestors" *breathed* out the first man, as Brahmâ is explained to have breathed out the *Suras* (Gods), when they became "*Asuras*" (from *Asu*, breath). In a third it is said that they, the newly-created men, "were the shadows of the Shadows."

With regard to this sentence — "They were the shadows of the Shadows" — a few more words may be said and a fuller explanation attempted. This first process of the evolution of mankind is far easier to accept than the one which follows it, though one and all will be rejected and doubted even by some Kabalists, especially the Western, who study the present effects, but have neglected to study their primary causes. Nor does the writer feel competent to explain a mode of procreation so difficult of appreciation save for an Eastern Occultist. Therefore it is useless to enter here into details concerning the process, though it is minutely described in the Secret Books, as it would only lead to speaking of facts hitherto unknown to the profane world, and hence to their being misunderstood. An "Adam" made of the dust of the ground will always be found preferable, by a certain class of students, to one projected out of the ethereal body of his creator; though the former process has never been heard of, while the latter is familiar, as all know, to many Spiritualists in Europe and America, who, of all men, ought to understand it. For who of those who have witnessed the phenomenon of a materializing form oozing out of the pores of a medium or, at other times, out of his *left side*, can fail to credit the possibility, at least, of such a *birth?* If there are in the Universe such beings as Angels or Spirits, whose *incorporeal* essence may constitute an intelligent entity notwithstanding the absence of any (to us) solid organism; and if there are those who believe that a god made the first man out of dust, and breathed into him a living Soul — and there are millions upon millions who believe both — what does this doctrine of ours contain that is so impossible? Very soon the day will dawn, when the world will have to choose whether it will accept the miraculous creation of man (and Kosmos too) out of *nothing*, according to the dead letter of *Genesis*, or a first man born from a fantastic link — absolutely *" missing "* so far — the common ancestor of man, and of the " true ape." [165] Between these two falla-cies,[166] Occult philosophy steps in. It teaches that the first human stock was projected by higher and semi-divine Beings out of their own essences. If the latter process is to be considered as abnormal or even inconceivable — because obsolete in Nature at this point of evolution — it is yet proven possible on the authority of certain " Spiritualistic " FACTS. Which, then, we ask of the three hypotheses or theories is the most reasonable and the least absurd? Certainly no one — provided he is not a soul-blind materialist — can ever object to the occult teaching.

Now, as shown, we gather from the latter that man was not " cre-ated " the complete being he is now, however imperfect he still remains. There was a spiritual, a psychic, an intellectual, and an animal evolu-tion, from the highest to the lowest, as well as a physical development — from the simple and homogeneous, up to the more complex and heter-ogeneous; though not quite on the lines traced for us by the modern evolutionists. This double evolution in two contrary directions, re-quired various ages, of divers natures and degrees of spirituality and intellectuality, to fabricate the being now known as man. Furthermore, the one absolute, ever acting and never erring law, which proceeds on

165. " . . . Huxley, supported by the most evident discoveries in Comparative Anatomy, could utter the momentous sen-tence that the anatomical differences between man and the highest apes are less than those between the latter and the lowest apes. In relation to our genealogical tree of man, the necessary conclusion follows that the human race has *evolved gradually from the true apes.*" (*The Pedigree of Man*, by Ernst Haeckel, translated by Ed. B. Aveling, p. 49.)

What may be the scientific and *logical* objections to the opposite conclusion — we would ask? The anatomical resemblances between Man and the Anthropoids — grossly exaggerated as they are by Darwinists, as M. de Quatrefages shows — are simply enough " accounted for " when the origin of the latter is taken into consideration.

" Nowhere in the older deposits, is an ape to be found that approximates more closely to man, or a man that approximates more closely to an ape. . . ."

166. " . . . The same gulf which is found today between Man and Ape, goes back with undiminished breadth and depth to the Tertiary period. This fact alone is enough to make its untenability clear." (Dr. F. Pfaff, Prof. of Natural Science in the University of Erlangen.)

the same lines from one eternity (or Manvantara) to the other — ever
furnishing an ascending scale for the manifested, or that which we
call the great Illusion (*Mahâ-Mâyâ*), but plunging Spirit deeper and
deeper into materiality on the one hand, and then *redeeming it through
flesh* and liberating it — this law, we say, uses for these purposes the
Beings from other and higher planes, men, or *Minds* (Manus), in
accordance with their Karmic exigencies.

At this juncture, the reader is again asked to turn to the Indian
philosophy and religion. The Esotericism of both is at one with our
Secret Doctrine, however much the form may differ and vary.

On the Identity and Differences of the Incarnating Powers

THE Progenitors of Man, called in India "Fathers," Pitaras or
Pitris, are the creators of our bodies and lower principles. They are
ourselves, as the *first personalities,* and *we are they*. Primeval man
would be "the bone of their bone and the flesh of their flesh," if
they had body and flesh. As stated, they were "*lunar* Beings."

The Endowers of man with his conscious, immortal EGO, are the
"Solar Angels" — whether so regarded metaphorically or literally.
The mysteries of the Conscious EGO or human Soul are great. The
esoteric name of these "Solar Angels" is, literally, the "Lords"
(*Nâthas*) of "persevering ceaseless devotion" (*pranidhâna*). Therefore they of the *fifth* principle (*Manas*) seem to be connected with,
or to have originated the system of the Yogis who make of *pranidhâna*
their *fifth* observance.[167] It has already been explained why the trans-
Himâlayan Occultists regard them as evidently identical with those
who in India are termed *Kumâras, Agnishvâttas,* and the *Barhishads*.

How precise and true is Plato's expression, how profound and philosophical his remark on the (human) soul or EGO, when he defined it as
"a compound of the *same* and the *other*." And yet how little this hint
has been understood, since the world took it to mean that the soul was
the breath of God, of Jehovah. It is "the *same* and the *other*," as the
great Initiate-Philosopher said; for the EGO (the "Higher Self" when
merged with and in the Divine Monad) is Man, and yet the *same* as the
"OTHER," the Angel in him incarnated, as the same with the universal
MAHAT. The great classics and philosophers felt this truth, when
saying that "there must be something within us which produces our

167. See *Yoga Sâstra*, II, 32.

PITRIS OF THE GODS AND DEMONS   89

thoughts. Something very subtle; it is a breath; it is fire; it is ether;
it is quintessence; it is a slender likeness; it is an intellection; it is
a number; it is harmony. . . ."[168]

All these are the *Mânasam* and *Rajasas:* the *Kumâras, Asuras,* and
other rulers and *Pitris,* who incarnated in the Third Race, and in this
and various other ways endowed mankind with Mind.

There are seven classes of Pitris, as shown below, three incorporeal
and four corporeal; and two kinds, the Agnishvâtta and the Barhishad.
And we may add that, as there are two kinds of Pitris, so there is a
double and a triple set of Barhishad and Agnishvâtta. The former,
having given birth to their astral doubles, are reborn as *Sons of
Atri,* and are the " Pitris of the Demons," or corporeal beings, on
the authority of *Manu;*[169] while the Agnishvâtta are reborn as Sons of
Marichi (a son of Brahmâ), and are the Pitris of the Gods (*Manu*
again, *Matsya* and *Padma Purânas* and Kullûka in the *Laws of the
Mânavas*[170]).[171] Moreover, the *Vâyu Purâna* declares all the seven
orders to have originally been the *first gods,* the *Vairâjas,* whom Brahmâ " with the eye of Yoga, beheld in the eternal spheres, and who are
the *gods of gods* "; and the *Matsya* adds that the Gods worshiped them;
while the *Harivansa*[172] distinguishes the Virâjas as one class of the
Pitris only — a statement corroborated in the Secret Teachings, which,
however, identify the Virâjas with the *elder Agnishvâttas*[173] and the
Rajasas, or *Abhûtarajasas,* who are incorporeal without even an astral
phantom. Vishnu is said, in most of the MSS., to have incarnated in
and through them. " In the *Raivata Manvantara,* again, Hari, best of
gods, was born of Sambhûti, as the divine Mânasas — originating with
the deities called Rajasas." Sambhûti was a daughter of Daksha, and
wife of Marichi, the father of the *Agnishvâtta,* who, along with the
Rajasas, are ever associated with *Mânasas.* As remarked by a far
more able Sanskritist than Wilson, Mr. Fitzedward Hall, " Mânasa is
no inappropriate name for a deity associated with the Rajasas. We
appear to have in it Manasam — the same as *Manas* — with the change
of termination required to express male personification."[174] All the
sons of *Virâja* are *Mânasa,* says *Nîlakantha.* And Virâja is Brahmâ,

168. Voltaire.

169. III, 196.
170. III, 195.
171. We are quite aware that the *Vâyu*
and *Matsya Purânas* identify (agreeably to
Western interpretation) the Agnishvâtta with
the seasons, and the Barhishad Pitris with
the months; adding a fourth class — the
Kâvyas — cyclic years. But do not Christian
Roman Catholics identify their Angels with

planets, and are not the seven Rishis become
the *Saptarshi* — a constellation? They are
deities presiding over all the cyclic divisions.
172. S. 1, 935.
173. The *Vâyu Purâna* shows the region
called Virâja-loka inhabited by the Agnishvâttas.
174. *Vishnu Purâna,* Bk. III, ch. 1, p. 17,
footnote.

and, therefore, the *incorporeal* Pitris are called Vairâjas from being the sons of Virâja, says *Vâyu Purâna.*

We could multiply our proofs *ad infinitum,* but it is useless. The wise will understand our meaning, the *unwise* are not required to. There are thirty-three crores, or 330 millions, of gods in India. But, as remarked by the learned lecturer on the *Bhagavad Gîtâ,* "they may be all devas, but are by no means all 'gods', in the high spiritual sense one attributes to the term." "This is an unfortunate blunder," he remarks, "generally committed by Europeans. Deva is a kind of spiritual being, and because the same word is used in ordinary parlance to mean god, it by no means follows that we have to worship thirty-three crores of gods." And he adds suggestively: "These beings, as may be naturally inferred, have a *certain affinity* with one of the three component *Upâdhis* [basic principles] into which we have divided man." [175]

The names of the deities of a certain mystic class change with every Manvantara. Thus the twelve great gods, *Jayas,* created by Brahmâ to assist him in the work of creation in the very beginning of the Kalpa, and who, lost in Samâdhi, neglected to create — whereupon they were cursed to be repeatedly born in each Manvantara till the seventh — are respectively called *Ajitas, Tushitas, Satyas, Haris, Vaikunthas, Sâdhyas,* and *Adityas:* they are *Tushitas* (in the second Kalpa), and *Adityas* in this *Vaivasvata* period (see *Vâyu Purâna*), besides other names for each age. But they are identical with the *Mânasa* or *Rajasas,* and these with our incarnating Dhyân Chohans. They are all classes of the *Jñâna-devas.*

Yes; besides those beings, who, like the Yakshas, Gandharvas, Kinnaras, etc., etc., taken in their *individualities,* inhabit the astral plane, there are real *Devajñânams,* and to these classes of *Devas* belong the *Adityas,* the *Vairâjas,* the *Kumâras,* the *Asuras,* and all those high celestial beings whom Occult teaching calls *Manasvin,* the Wise, foremost of all, and who would have made all men the *self-conscious* spiritually intellectual beings they will be, had they not been "cursed" to fall into generation, and to be reborn themselves as mortals for their neglect of duty.

STANZA IV — (*Continued*)

15. SEVEN TIMES SEVEN SHADOWS (*chhâyâs*) OF FUTURE MEN (*or Amânasas*) (*a*) WERE (*thus*) BORN, EACH OF HIS OWN COLOR (*complexion*) AND KIND (*b*). EACH (*also*) INFERIOR TO HIS FATHER (*creator*). THE FATHERS, THE BONELESS, COULD GIVE NO LIFE TO BEINGS

175. See *Theosophist,* February and March (p. 360), 1887.

WITH BONES. THEIR PROGENY WERE BHÛTA (*phantoms*) WITH NEI-
THER FORM NOR MIND. THEREFORE THEY WERE CALLED THE CHHÂYÂ
(*image or shadow*) RACE (*c*).

(*a*) *Manu*, as already remarked, comes from the root *"man"* to
think, hence "a thinker." It is from this Sanskrit word very likely
that sprang the Latin *"mens,"* mind, the Egyptian *"Menes,"* the
"Master-Mind," the Pythagorean *Monas*, or conscious *"thinking unit,"*
mind also, and even our "Manas" or mind, the fifth principle in man.
Hence these shadows are called *amânasa*, "mindless."

With the Brâhmans the Pitris are very sacred, because they are the
Progenitors,[176] or ancestors of men — the first *Manushya* on this Earth
— and offerings are made to them by the Brâhman when a son is born
unto him. They are more honored and their ritual is more important
than the worship of the gods.[177]

May we not now search for a philosophical meaning in this dual
group of progenitors?

The Pitris being divided into *seven classes*, we have here the mystic
number again. Nearly all the Purânas agree that three of these are
arûpa, formless, while four are corporeal; the former being intellectual
and spiritual, the latter material and devoid of intellect. Esoterically,
it is the *Asuras* who form the first three classes of Pitris — "born in
the body of night" — whereas the other four were produced from the
body of twilight. Their fathers, the gods, were doomed to be born
fools on Earth, according to *Vâyu Purâna*. The legends are purposely
mixed up and made very hazy: the Pitris being in one the sons of the
gods, and, in another those of Brahmâ; while a third makes them instructors of their own fathers. It is the Hosts of the four material
classes who create men simultaneously on the seven zones.

Now, with regard to the seven classes of Pitris, each of which is
again divided into seven, a word to students and a query to the profane.
That class of the "Fire Dhyânis," which we identify on undeniable
grounds with the Agnishvâttas, is called in our school the "Heart" of
the Dhyân-Chohanic Body; and it is said to have incarnated in the
third race of men and made them perfect. The esoteric Mystagogy
speaks of the mysterious relation existing between the hebdomadic
essence or substance of this angelic Heart and that of man, whose

---

176. This was hinted at in *Isis Unveiled*, Vol. I, p. xxxviii, though the full
explanation could not then be given: "The
Pitris are not the ancestors of the present
living men, but those of the first human kind
or Adamic race; the spirits of *human* races,
which, on the great scale of descending

evolution, preceded our races of men, and
were physically as well as spiritually, far
superior to our modern pigmies. In *Mânava-
Dharma-Sâstra* they are called the *Lunar*
ancestors."

177. See the *Laws of Manu*, Book III,
p. 203.

every physical organ, and psychic, and spiritual function, is a reflection, so to say, a copy on the terrestrial plane of the model or prototype *above*. Why, it is asked, should there be such a strange repetition of the number seven in the anatomical structure of man? Why should the heart have *four lower* "cavities and *three higher* divisions," answering so strangely to the septenary division of the human principles, separated into two groups, the higher and the lower; and why should the same division be found in the various classes of Pitris, and especially our Fire Dhyânis? For, as already stated, these Beings fall into four corporeal (or grosser) and three incorporeal (or subtler) "principles," or call them by any other name you please. Why do the seven nervous plexuses of the body radiate *seven* rays? Why are there these seven plexuses, and why seven distinct layers in the human skin?

"*Having projected their shadows and made men of one element* (ether), *the progenitors re-ascend to Mahâ-loka, whence they descend periodically, when the world is renewed, to give birth to new men.*

"*The subtle bodies remain without understanding* (Manas) *until the advent of the Suras* (Gods) *now called Asuras* (not Gods)," says the Commentary.

"*Not-gods*," for the Brâhmans, perhaps, but the highest *Breaths*, for the Occultist; since those Progenitors (*Pitaras*), the formless and the intellectual, refuse to build man, but endow him with mind; the four corporeal classes creating only his body.

This is very plainly shown in various texts of the *Rig Veda* — the highest authority for a Hindû of any sect whatever. Therein *Asura* means "spiritual divine," and the word is used as a synonym for Supreme Spirit, while in the sense of a "God," the term "Asura" is applied to Varuna and Indra and pre-eminently to Agni — the three having been in days of old the *three highest gods*, before Brâhmanical Theo-Mythology distorted the true meaning of almost everything in the Archaic Scriptures. But, as the key is now lost, the Asuras are hardly mentioned.

In the *Zendavesta* the same is found. In the Mazdean, or Magian, religion, "Asura" is the lord *Asura Viśvavedas*, the "all-knowing" or "omniscient Lord"; and *Asura-Mazdhâ*, become later *Ahura-Mazdhâ*, is, as Benfey shows, "the Lord who *bestows Intelligence*" — Asura-Medhâ, and Ahura-Mazdâo. Elsewhere in this work it is shown, on equally good authority, that the Indo-Iranian Asura was always regarded as *sevenfold*. This fact, combined with the name Mazdhâ, as above, which makes of the sevenfold Asura the "Lord," or "Lords" collectively "who *bestow Intelligence*," connects the *Amshâspends* with the Asuras and with our incarnating Dhyân Chohans, as well as with the Elohim, and the seven informing gods of Egypt, Chaldaea, and every other country.

Why these " gods " refused to create men is not, as stated in exoteric accounts, because their pride was too great to share the celestial power of their essence with the children of Earth, but for reasons already suggested. However, allegory has indulged in endless fancies and theology taken advantage thereof in every country to make out its case against these first-born, or the *logoi*, and to impress it as a truth on the minds of the ignorant and credulous. (Compare also what is said about Makara and the Kumâras in connexion with the Zodiac.)

The Christian system is not the only one which has degraded them into demons. Zoroastrianism and even Brâhmanism have profited thereby to obtain hold over the people's mind. Even in Chaldaean exotericism, Beings who *refuse to create, i. e.,* who are said to oppose thereby the *Demiourgos,* are also denounced as the Spirits of Darkness. The Suras, who win their intellectual independence, fight the Suras who are devoid thereof, who are shown as passing their lives in profitless ceremonial worship based on blind faith — a hint now ignored by the *orthodox* Brâhmans — and forthwith the former become *A-Suras.* The first and *mind-born* Sons of the Deity refuse to create progeny, and are *cursed* by Brahmâ to be *born as men.* They are hurled *down to Earth,* which, later on, is transformed, in theological dogma, into the *infernal* regions. Ahriman destroys the Bull created by Ormazd — which is the emblem of terrestrial *illusive* life, the "germ of sorrow" — and, forgetting that the perishing finite seed must die, in order that the plant of immortality, the plant of spiritual, eternal life, should sprout and live, Ahriman is proclaimed the enemy, the opposing power, the devil. Typhon cuts Osiris into fourteen pieces, in order to prevent his peopling the world and thus creating misery; and Typhon becomes, in the exoteric, theological teaching, the Power of Darkness. But all this is the exoteric shell. It is the worshipers of the latter who attribute to disobedience and rebellion the effort and self-sacrifice of those who would help men to their original status of divinity through *self-conscious* efforts; and it is these worshipers of Form who have made demons of the Angels of Light.

Esoteric philosophy, however, teaches that *one third* [178] of the Dhyânis — *i. e.,* the three classes of the *Arûpa* Pitris, endowed with intelligence, " which is a formless breath, composed of *intellectual* not elementary substances " [179] — was simply *doomed by the law of Karma and evolu-*

178. Whence the subsequent assertions of St. John's vision, referred to in his *Apocalypse,* about "the great red Dragon having seven heads and *ten* horns, and seven crowns upon his heads," whose "tail drew the *third part* of the stars of heaven and did cast them to the earth." (ch. xii.)

179. See *Harivansa,* 932.

tion to be reborn (or incarnated) on Earth.[180] Some of these were *Nirmânakâyas* from other Manvantaras. Hence we see them, in all the Purânas, reappearing on this globe, in the *third Manvantara,* as Kings, Rishis and heroes (read Third Root-Race). This tenet, being too philosophical and metaphysical to be grasped by the multitudes, was, as already stated, disfigured by the priesthood for the purpose of preserving a hold over them through superstitious fear.

The supposed "rebels," then, were simply those who, compelled by Karmic law to drink the cup of gall to its last bitter drop, *had to incarnate* anew, and thus make responsible thinking entities of the astral statues projected by their inferior brethren. Some are said to have refused, because they had not in them the requisite materials — *i. e.,* an astral body — since they were *arûpa.* The refusal of others had reference to their having been Adepts and Yogis of long past preceding Manvantaras; another mystery. But, later on, as *Nirmânakâyas,* they sacrificed themselves for the good and salvation of the *Monads* which were waiting for their turn, and which otherwise would have had to linger for countless ages in irresponsible, animal-like, though in appearance human, forms. It may be a parable and an allegory *within an allegory.* Its solution is left to the intuition of the student, if he only reads that which follows with his *spiritual eye.*

As to their fashioners or "Ancestors" — those Angels who, in the exoteric legends, obeyed the law — they must be identical with the Barhishad Pitris, or the Pitar-Devatâs, *i. e.,* those *possessed of the physical creative fire.* They could only create, or rather clothe, the human Monads with their own astral Selves, but they could not make man in their image and likeness. "Man must not be like one of us," say the *creative* gods, entrusted with the fabrication of the lower animal, but higher; (see *Genesis* and Plato's *Timaios*). Their creating the semblance of men out of their own divine Essence means, esoterically, that

---

180. The verse "did cast them to the Earth," plainly shows its origin in the grandest and oldest allegory of the Aryan mystics, who, after the destruction of the Atlantean *giants* and *sorcerers,* concealed the truth — *astronomical, physical,* and *divine,* as it is a page out of *pre-cosmic* theogony — under various allegories. Its esoteric, true interpretation is a veritable Theodice of the "Fallen Angels," so called; the *willing* and the *unwilling,* the *creators* and those who *refused to create,* being now mixed up most perplexingly by Christian Catholics, who forget that their highest Archangel, St. Michael, who is shown to conquer (to master and to assimilate) the DRAGON OF WISDOM and of divine Self-sacrifice (now miscalled and calumniated as Satan), WAS THE FIRST TO REFUSE TO CREATE! This led to endless confusion. So little does Christian theology understand the paradoxical language of the East and its symbolism, that it even explains, in its *dead letter sense,* the Chinese Buddhist and Hindû exoteric rite of raising a noise during certain eclipses to scare away the "great red Dragon," which laid a plot to carry away the light! But here "Light" means esoteric Wisdom, and we have sufficiently explained the secret meaning of the terms *Dragon, Serpent,* etc., etc., all of which refer to Adepts and Initiates.

it is they who became the first Race, and thus shared its destiny and further evolution. They *would* not, simply because they *could* not, give to man that sacred spark which burns and expands into the flower of human reason and self-consciousness, for they had it not to give. This was left to that class of Devas who became symbolized in Greece under the name of Prometheus, to those who had nought to do with the physical body, yet everything with the purely spiritual man.[181]

Each class of Creators endows man with what it has to give: the one builds his external form; the other gives him its essence, which later on becomes the Human *Higher Self* owing to the *personal exertion of the individual;* but they could not make men as they were themselves — perfect, because sinless; sinless, because having only the first, pale shadowy outlines of attributes, and these all perfect — from the human standpoint — white, pure and cold as the virgin snow. Where there is no struggle, there is no merit. Humanity, " of the Earth earthy," was not destined to be created by the angels of the first divine Breath: therefore they are said to *have refused* to do so, and man had to be formed by more material creators,[182] who, in their turn, could give only what they had in their own natures, and no more. Subservient to eternal law, the pure gods could only project out of themselves *shadowy* men, a little less ethereal and spiritual, less *divine and perfect* than themselves — shadows still. The first humanity, therefore, was a pale copy of its progenitors; too material, even in its ethereality, to be a hierarchy of gods; too spiritual and pure to be MEN, endowed as it is with every *negative* (*Nirguna*) perfection. Perfection, to be fully such, must be born out of imperfection, the *incorruptible* must grow out of the corruptible, having the latter as its vehicle and basis and contrast. Absolute light is absolute darkness, and *vice versa*. In fact, there is neither light nor darkness in the realms of truth. Good and Evil are twins, the progeny of Space and Time, under the sway of

181. See Part II, of this volume, § xviii, "The Fallen Angels "; also " The Gods of Light proceed from the Gods of Darkness."

182. In spite of all efforts to the contrary, Christian theology — having burdened itself with the Hebrew esoteric account of the creation of man, which is understood *literally* — cannot find any reasonable excuse for its " *God*, the Creator," who produces a man devoid of mind and sense; nor can it justify the punishment following an act, for which Adam and Eve might plead *non compos*. For if the couple is admitted to be ignorant of good and evil before the eating of the forbidden fruit, how could it be expected to know that *disobedience was evil?* If primeval man was meant to remain a half-witted, or rather witless, being, then his creation was aimless and even *cruel*, if produced by an omnipotent and perfect God. But Adam and Eve are shown, even in *Genesis*, to be created by a class of lower divine Beings, the *Elohim*, who are so jealous of their personal prerogatives as reasonable and intelligent creatures, that they will not allow man to become " as one of us." This is plain, even from the dead-letter meaning of the Bible. The Gnostics, then, were right in regarding the Jewish God as belonging to a class of lower, material, and not very holy denizens of the invisible World.

Mâyâ. Separate them, by cutting off one from the other, and they will both die. Neither exists *per se*, since each has to be generated and created out of the other, in order to come into being; both must be known and appreciated before becoming objects of perception, hence, in mortal mind, they must be divided.

Nevertheless, as the illusionary distinction exists, it requires a *lower order of creative angels* to "create" inhabited globes — especially ours — or to deal with matter on this earthly plane. The philosophical Gnostics were the first to think so, in the historical period, and to invent various systems upon this theory. Therefore in their schemes of creation, one always finds their *Creators* occupying a place at the very foot of the ladder of spiritual Being. With them, those who created our earth and its mortals were placed on the very limit of *mâyâvic* matter, and their followers were taught to think — to the great disgust of the Church Fathers — that for the creation of those wretched races, in a spiritual and moral sense, which grace our globe, no high divinity could be made responsible, but only angels of a *low hierarchy,*[183] to which class they relegated the Jewish God, Jehovah.

Mankinds different from the present are mentioned in all the ancient Cosmogonies. Plato speaks, in the *Phaidros,* of a *winged race of men.* Aristophanes (in Plato's *Banquet*), speaks of a race androgynous and with round bodies. In *Pymander,* all the animal kingdom even is double-sexed. Thus in § 18, it is said: " The circuit having been accomplished, *the knot was loosened* . . . and all the animals, which were equally androgynous, were *untied* [separated] together with man . . ." for ". . . the causes had to produce effects on earth."[184] Again, in the ancient Quiché Manuscript, the *Popol Vuh* — published by the late Abbé Brasseur de Bourbourg — the first men are described as a race " whose sight was unlimited, and who knew all things at once ": thus showing the *divine knowledge of Gods,* not mortals. The Secret Doctrine, correcting the unavoidable exaggerations of popular fancy, gives the facts as they are recorded in the Archaic symbols.

(*b*) These "shadows" were born "each of his own color and kind," each also " inferior to his creator," because the latter was a complete

---

183. In *Isis Unveiled* several of these Gnostic systems are given. One is taken from the *Codex Nazaraeus,* the Scriptures of the Nazarenes, who, although they existed long before the days of Christ, and even before the laws of Moses, were Gnostics, and many of them Initiates. They held their " Mysteries of Life " in Nazara (ancient and modern Nazareth), and their doctrines are a faithful echo of the teachings of the Secret Doctrine — some of which we are now endeavoring to explain.

184. See the translation from the Greek by François, Monsieur de Foix, Evesque d'Ayre: the work dedicated to Marguerite de France, Reine de Navarre. Edition of 1579, Bordeaux.

being of his kind. The Commentaries refer the first sentence to the color or complexion of each human race thus evolved. In *Pymander*, the Seven primitive men, created by Nature from the "heavenly Man," all partake of the qualities of the "Seven *Governors*," or Rulers, who loved Man — their own reflection and synthesis.

In the Norse Legends, one recognizes in Asgard, the habitat of the gods, as also in the *Ases* themselves, the same mystical *loci* and personifications woven into the popular "myths," as in our Secret Doctrine; and we find them in the Vedas, the Purânas, the Mazdean Scriptures and the Kabala. The *Ases* of Scandinavia, the rulers of the world which preceded ours, whose name means literally the "pillars of the world," its "supports," are thus identical with the Greek *Kosmokratores*, the "Seven Workmen or Rectors" of *Pymander*, the seven Rishis and Pitris of India, the seven Chaldaean gods and seven evil spirits, the seven Kabalistic Sephiroth synthesized by the upper triad, and even the seven Planetary Spirits of the Christian mystics. The Ases create the earth, the seas, the sky and the clouds, the whole visible world, from the remains of the slain giant Ymir; but they do not create MAN, but only his form from the *Ask* or ash-tree. It is Odin who endows him with life and soul, after Lodur had given him blood and bones, and finally it is Hönir who furnishes him with his intellect (*manas*) and with his conscious senses. The Norse Ask, the Hesiodic Ash-tree, whence issued the men of the generation of bronze, the Third Root-Race, and the *Tzïté* tree of the *Popol Vuh*, out of which the Mexican *third* race of men was created, are all one.[185] This may be plainly seen by any reader. But the Occult reason why the Norse Yggdrasil, the Hindû Aśvattha, the Gogard, the Hellenic tree of life, and the Tibetan Zampun, are one with the Kabalistic Sephirothal Tree, and even with the Holy Tree made by Ahura Mazda, and the Tree of Eden — who among the western scholars can tell?[186] Nevertheless, the fruits of all those "Trees," whether Pippala or Haoma or yet the more prosaic apple, are the "plants of life," in fact and verity. The prototypes of our races were all enclosed in the microcosmic tree, which grew and developed *within and under* the great mundane macrocosmic tree;[187] and the mystery is half revealed in the *Dîrghatamas*, where it is said: "Pippala, the sweet fruit of that tree upon which come *spirits who love the science*, and where the gods produce all marvels." As in the Gogard, among the luxuriant branches of all those mundane trees, the "Serpent" dwells. But while the Macrocosmic tree is the

185. See Max Müller's review of the *Popol Vuh* (*Chips*, vol. I, p. 336 *et seq.*).
186. Mr. James Darmesteter, the translator of the *Vendîdâd*, speaking of it says: "*The tree, whatever it is . . .*" (Sacred Books of the East, vol. IV, p. 209).
187. Plato's *Timaios*.

Serpent of Eternity and of absolute Wisdom itself, those who dwell in the Microcosmic tree are the Serpents of the manifested Wisdom. One is the One and All; the others are its *reflected* parts. The "tree" is man himself, of course, and the Serpents dwelling in each, the conscious *Manas*, the connecting link between Spirit and Matter, heaven and earth.

Everywhere, it is the same. The *creating* powers produce Man, but fail in their final object. All these logoi strive to endow man with *conscious* immortal spirit, reflected in the Mind (*manas*) alone; they fail, and they are all represented as being punished for the failure, if not for the attempt. What is the nature of the punishment? A sentence of imprisonment in the lower or nether region, which is *our earth; the lowest in its chain;* an "eternity" — meaning the duration of the life-cycle—in the *darkness* of matter, or *within animal Man.* It has pleased the half ignorant and half designing Church Fathers to disfigure the graphic symbol. They took advantage of the metaphor and allegory found in every old religion to turn them to the benefit of the new one. Thus man was transformed into the darkness of a material hell; his divine consciousness, obtained from his indwelling Principle (the Mânasa), or the incarnated Deva, became the glaring flames of the infernal region; and our globe that Hell itself. *Pippala, Haoma,* the fruit of the Tree of Knowledge, were denounced as the *forbidden* fruit, and the "Serpent of Wisdom," the Voice of reason and consciousness, remained identified for ages with the Fallen Angel, which is the old Dragon, the Devil! [188]

The same for the other high symbols. The *Svastika,* the most sacred and mystic symbol in India, the "Jaina-Cross" as it is now called by the Masons, notwithstanding its direct connexion, and even identity with the Christian Cross, has become dishonored in the same manner. It is the "devil's sign," we are told by the Indian missionaries. "Does it not shine on the head of the great *Serpent* of Vishnu, on the thousand headed Śesha-Ananta, in the depths of Pâtâla, the Hindû *Naraka* or Hell?" It does; but what is Ananta? As Śesha, it is the almost endless Manvantaric cycle of time, and becomes *infinite* Time itself, when called Ananta, the great seven-headed Serpent, on which rests Vishnu, the *eternal Deity,* during *Pralayic* inactivity. What has Satan to do with this highly metaphysical symbol? The *Svastika* is the most philosophically scientific of all symbols, as also the most comprehensible. It is the summary in a few lines of the whole work of *creation,* or evolution, as one should rather say, from Cosmo-theogony down to Anthropogony, from the indivisible unknown Parabrahm to the humble

188. *Vide* Part II, § xviii, "The Evil Spirit, Who, or What?"

moneron of materialistic science, whose *genesis is as unknown* to that science as is that of the All-Deity itself. The *Svastika* is found heading the religious symbols of every old nation. It is the "Worker's Hammer" in the Chaldaean *Book of Numbers*, the "Hammer" just referred to in the *Ha Idra Zuta Qadisha*,[189] "which striketh sparks from the flint" (Space), those sparks becoming worlds. It is "Thor's Hammer," the magic weapon forged by the dwarfs against the Giants, or the *pre-cosmic* Titanic forces of Nature, which rebel and, while alive in the region of matter, will not be subdued by the Gods, the Agents of Universal Harmony, but have first to be destroyed. This is why the world is formed out of the relics of the murdered Ymir. The Svastika is the Miölnir, the "storm-hammer"; and therefore it is said that when the Ases, the holy gods, after having been purified by fire (the fire of passions and suffering in their life-incarnations), become fit to dwell in Ida in eternal peace, then Miölnir will become useless. This will be when the bonds of Hel (the goddess-queen of the region of the Dead) will bind them no longer, for the kingdom of evil will have passed away. " Surtur's flames had not destroyed them, nor yet had the raging waters " of the several deluges. . . . " Then came the sons of Thor. They brought *Miölnir* with them, no longer as a weapon of war, but as the hammer with which to consecrate the new heaven and the new Earth. . . ."[190]

Verily many are its meanings! In the *Macrocosmic* work, the "HAMMER OF CREATION," with its four arms bent at right angles, refers to the continual *motion* and revolution of the invisible Kosmos of Forces. In that of the manifested Kosmos and our Earth, it points to the rotation in the cycles of Time of the world's axes and their equatorial belts; the two lines forming the *Svastika* ⊥⌐ meaning Spirit and Matter, the four hooks suggesting the motion in the revolving cycles. Applied to the *Microcosm*, Man, it shows him to be a link between heaven and Earth: the right hand being raised at the end of a horizontal arm, the left pointing to the Earth. In the *Smaragdine Tablet of Hermes*, the uplifted right hand is inscribed with the word "*Solve*," the left with the word "*Coagula*." It is at one and the same time an Alchemical, Cosmogonical, Anthropological, and Magical sign, with seven keys to its inner meaning. It is not too much to say that the compound symbolism of this universal and most suggestive of signs contains the key to the seven great mysteries of Kosmos. Born in the mystical conceptions of the early Aryans, and by them placed at the very threshold of eternity, on the head of the serpent Ananta, it found

189. *Cf. Book of the Concealed Mystery*, ch. I, §§ 1, 2, 3, 4, etc.
190. See *Asgard and the Gods:* "The Renewal of the World" (page 305).

its spiritual death in the scholastic interpretations of medieval Anthropomorphists. It is the *Alpha* and the *Omega* of universal creative Force, evolving from pure Spirit and ending in gross Matter. It is also the key to the cycle of Science, divine and human; and he who comprehends its full meaning is for ever liberated from the toils of *Mahâmâyâ*, the great Illusion and Deceiver. The light that shines from under the divine hammer, now degraded into the mallet or gavel of the Grand Masters of Masonic Lodges, is sufficient to dissipate the darkness of any human schemes or fictions.

How prophetic are the songs of the three Norse Goddesses, to whom the ravens of Odin whisper of the past and the future, as they flutter around in their abode of crystal beneath the flowing river. The songs are all written down in the "*Scrolls* of Wisdom," of which many are lost but some still remain: and they repeat in poetical allegory the teachings of the archaic ages. To summarize from Dr. Wagner's *Asgard and the Gods*, the " renewal of the world," which is a prophecy about the seventh Race of our Round told in the past tense.

The Miölnir had done its duty in this Round, and:—

> . . . on the field of Ida, the field of resurrection [for the Fifth Round], the sons of the highest gods assembled, and *in them their fathers rose again* [the *Egos* of all their past incarnations]. They talked of the Past and the Present, and remembered the wisdom and prophecies of their ancestor which had all been fulfilled. Near them, but *unseen of them*, was the strong, the mighty One, who rules all things . . . and ordains the eternal laws that govern the world. They *all knew he was there, they felt his presence and his power, but were ignorant of his name. At his command the new Earth rose out of the Waters of Space.* To the South above the Field of Ida, he made another heaven called Audlang, and further off, a third, Widblain. Over Gimil's cave, a wondrous palace was erected, covered with gold and shining brighter than the sun.

These are the three gradually ascending planets of our " Chain." There the Gods were enthroned, as *they used to be.* . . . From Gimil's heights (the *seventh* planet or globe, the highest and the purest), they looked down upon the happy descendants of LIF and LIFTHRASIR (the coming Adam and Eve of purified *humanity*), and signed to them to CLIMB *up higher, to rise in knowledge and wisdom,* step by step, from one " heaven to another," until they were at last fit to be united to the Gods in the house of All-Father.[191]

He who knows the doctrines of Esoteric *Budhism* (or Wisdom), though so imperfectly sketched hitherto, will see clearly the allegory contained in the above.

Its more philosophical meaning will be better understood if the reader thinks carefully over the myth of Prometheus. It is examined

191. Page 305.

further on in the light of the Hindû *Pramantha*. Degraded into a purely *physiological* symbol by some Orientalists, and taken in connexion with terrestrial fire only, their interpretation is an insult to every religion, including Christianity, whose greatest mystery is thus dragged down to matter. The "friction" of divine Pramantha and Arani could suggest itself under this image only to the brutal conceptions of the German materialists — than whom there are none worse. It is true that the Divine babe, *Agni* with the Sanskrit-speaking Race, who became *Ignis* with the Latins, is born from the conjunction of Pramantha and Arani (Svastika) during the sacrificial ceremony. But what of that? *Tvashtri* (Viśvakarman) is the "divine artist and *carpenter*" [192] and is also the Father of the gods and of *creative fire* in the Vedas. So ancient is the symbol and so sacred, that there is hardly an excavation made on the sites of old cities without its being found. A number of such *terra cotta* discs, called *fusaïoles*, were found by Dr. Schliemann *under* the ruins of ancient Troy. Both these forms ⊞ and ⊞ were excavated in great abundance, their presence being one more proof that the ancient Trojans and their ancestors were pure Âryans.

(*c*) Chhâyâ, as already explained, is the astral image. It bears this meaning in Sanskrit works. Thus Sanjñâ (Spiritual Consciousness), the wife of Sûrya, the Sun, is shown retiring into the jungle to lead an ascetic life, and leaving behind to her husband her Chhâyâ, shadow or image.

192. The "Father of the Sacred Fire," writes Professor Joly, "is Twashtri . . . his mother was Mâyâ. He himself was styled Akta (anointed, χριστός) after the priest had poured upon his head the *spirituous* [?] Soma, and on his body butter purified by sacrifice"; (*Man Before Metals*, p. 190). The source of his information is not given by the French Darwinist. But the lines are quoted to show that light begins to dawn even upon the materialists. Adalbert Kühn, in his *Die Herabkunft des Feuers*, identifies the two signs ⊞ and ⊞ with *Arani*, and designates them under this name. He adds: "This process of kindling fire naturally led men to the idea of sexual reproduction," etc. Why could not a more dignified idea, and one more occult, have led man to invent that symbol, in so far as it is connected, in one of its aspects, with human reproduction? But its chief symbolism refers to Cosmogony.

"*Agni*, in the condition of *Akta*, or anointed, is suggestive of Christ," remarks Professor Joly. "*Mâyâ*, Mary, his mother; *Twashtri*, St. Joseph, the carpenter of the Bible." In the *Rig Veda*, Viśvakarman is the highest and oldest of the Gods and their "Father." He is the "carpenter or builder," because God is called even by the monotheists, "the Architect of the Universe." Still, the original idea is purely metaphysical, and had no connexion with the later Phallicism,

16. HOW ARE THE (*real*) MANUSHYAS BORN? THE MANUS WITH MINDS, HOW ARE THEY MADE? (*a*) THE FATHERS (*Barhishad* (?)) CALL TO THEIR HELP THEIR OWN FIRE (*the Kavyavâhana, electric fire*), WHICH IS THE FIRE WHICH BURNS IN EARTH. THE SPIRIT OF THE EARTH CALLED TO HIS HELP THE SOLAR FIRE (*Suchi, the spirit in the Sun*). THESE THREE (*the Pitris and the two fires*) PRODUCED IN THEIR JOINT EFFORTS A GOOD RÛPA. IT (*the form*) COULD STAND, WALK, RUN, RECLINE AND FLY. YET IT WAS STILL BUT A CHHÂYÂ, A SHADOW WITH NO SENSE (*b*) . . . . . .

(*a*) Here an explanation again becomes necessary in the light, and with the help of the exoteric added to the esoteric scriptures. The "*Manushyas*" (men) and the *Manus* are here equivalent to the Chaldaean "Adam" — this term not meaning at all the first man, as with the Jews, or one solitary individual, but *mankind* collectively, as with the Chaldaeans and Assyrians. It is the four orders or classes of Dhyân Chohans out of the seven, says the Commentary, " who were the progenitors of the *concealed* man," *i. e.*, the subtle inner man. The " Lha " of the Moon, the lunar spirits, were, as already stated, only the *ancestors of his form, i. e.*, of the model according to which Nature began her external work upon him. Thus primitive man was, when he appeared, only a senseless Bhûta[193] or a "phantom." This " creation " was a failure, the reason of which will be explained in the Commentary on Sloka 20.

(*b*) This attempt was again a failure. It allegorizes the vanity of *physical* nature's unaided attempts to construct even a perfect *animal* — let alone man. For the " Fathers," the lower Angels, are all Nature-Spirits and the higher Elementals also possess an intelligence of their own ; but this is not enough to construct a THINKING man. "*Living* Fire" was needed, that fire which gives the human mind its self-perception and self-consciousness, or *Manas;* and the progeny of *Pâvaka* and *Suchi* are the *animal electric* and solar fires, which create animals, and could thus furnish but a physical living constitution to that first astral model of man. The first creators, then, were the Pygmalions of primeval man: they failed to animate the statue — *intellectually.*

This Stanza we shall see is very suggestive. It explains the mystery of, and fills the gap between, the informing principle in man — the HIGHER SELF or human Monad — and the animal Monad, both one and

193. It is not clear why " *Bhûtas* " should be rendered by the Orientalists as meaning "evil Spirits" in the Purânas. In the *Vishnu Purâna*, Book I, ch. 5, the Sloka simply says: " Bhûtas—fiends, frightful from being monkey-colored and carnivorous "; and the word in India now means *ghosts,* ethereal or *astral* phantoms, while in esoteric teaching it means *elementary substances,* something made of attenuated, non-compound essence, and, specifically, the astral *double* of any man or animal. In this case these primitive men are the *doubles* of the first ethereal Dhyânis or Pitris.

the same, although the former is endowed with *divine* intelligence, the latter with *instinctual* faculty alone. How is the difference to be explained, and the presence of that HIGHER SELF in man accounted for?

"*The Sons of* MAHAT *are the quickeners of the human Plant. They are the Waters falling upon the arid soil of latent life, and the Spark that vivifies the human animal. They are the Lords of Spiritual Life eternal.*" . . . ."*In the beginning* (in the Second Race) *some* (of the Lords) *only breathed of their essence into Mānushya* (men); *and some took in man their abode.*"

This shows that not all men became incarnations of the "divine *Rebels,*" but only a few among them. The remainder had their fifth principle simply quickened by the spark thrown into it, which accounts for the great difference between the intellectual capacities of men and races. Had not the "sons of Mahat," speaking allegorically, skipped the intermediate worlds, in their impulse toward intellectual freedom, the animal man would never have been able to reach upward from this earth, and attain through self-exertion his ultimate goal. The cyclic pilgrimage would have to be performed through all the planes of existence half unconsciously, if not entirely so, as in the case of the animals. It is owing to this rebellion of intellectual life against the morbid inactivity of pure spirit, that we are what we are — self-conscious, thinking men, with the capabilities and attributes of Gods in us, for good as much as for evil. Hence the REBELS are our saviors. Let the philosopher ponder well over this, and more than one mystery will become clear to him. It is only by the attractive force of the contrasts that the two opposites — Spirit and Matter — can be cemented on Earth, and, smelted in the fire of self-conscious experience and suffering, find themselves wedded in Eternity. This will reveal the meaning of many hitherto incomprehensible allegories, foolishly called "fables."[194]

It explains, to begin with, the statement made in *Pymander:* that the "heavenly MAN," the "Son of the Father," who partook of the nature and essence of the Seven Governors, or *creators* and *Rulers* of the material world, "peeped through the *Harmony* and, breaking through the *Seven Circles of Fire,* made manifest the downward-born nature."[195] It explains every verse in that Hermetic narrative, as also the Greek allegory of Prometheus. Most important of all, it explains the many allegorical accounts about the "Wars in Heaven," including that of *Revelation* with respect to the Christian dogma of the *fallen angels.* It explains the "rebellion" of the oldest and highest Angels, and the meaning of their being cast down from Heaven into the depths of Hell, *i. e.,* MATTER. It even solves the recent perplexity of the Assyriologists, who express their wonder through the late George Smith.

194. *Vide infra,* "The Secret of Satan."   195. See *Pymander,* Bk. II, v. 17 to 29.

"My first idea of this part" (of the rebellion), he says, "was that the wars with the powers of Evil *preceded the Creation;* I now think it followed the account of the fall." [196]   In this work Mr. George Smith gives an engraving, from an early Babylonian cylinder, of the Sacred Tree, the Serpent, man and woman.   The tree has seven branches: *three* on the man's side, *four* on that of the female.   These branches are typical of the seven Root-Races, in the *third* of which, at its very close, occurred the separation of the sexes and the so-called FALL into generation.   The three earliest Races were sexless, then hermaphrodite; the other four, male and female, as distinct from each other.   "The Dragon," says Mr. G. Smith, "which in the Chaldaean account of the creation leads man to sin, is the creation of Tiamat, the living principle of the Sea, or Chaos . . . which was opposed to the deities at the creation of the world."   This is an error. The Dragon is the male principle, or Phallus, personified, or rather *animalized;* and Tiamat, "the embodiment of the Spirit of Chaos," of the deep, or Abyss, is the female principle, the Womb.   The "Spirit of *Chaos* and *Disorder*" refers to the mental perturbation which it led to.   It is the sensual, attractive, magnetic principle which fascinates and seduces, the ever living active element which throws the whole world into disorder, chaos, and sin.   The Serpent seduces the woman, but it is the latter who seduces man, and both are included in the Karmic curse, though only as a natural result of a cause produced.   Says George Smith:

It is clear that the Dragon is included in the curse for the Fall, and that the Gods [the Elohim, jealous at seeing the man of clay becoming a Creator in his turn, like all the animals] invoke on the head of the human Race all the evils which afflict humanity.   Wisdom and knowledge shall injure him, he shall have family quarrels, he will anger the gods, he shall submit to tyranny . . . he shall be disappointed in his desires, he shall pour out *useless prayers,* he shall commit future sin.   No doubt subsequent lines continue this topic, but again our narrative is broken, and it reopens only where the gods are preparing for war with the powers of evil, which are led by Tiamat [the woman]. . . . [197]

This account is omitted in *Genesis,* for monotheistic purposes.   But it is a mistaken policy — born no doubt of fear, and regard for dogmatic religion and its superstitions — to have sought to restore the Chaldaean fragments by *Genesis,* whereas it is the latter, far younger than any of the fragments, which ought to be explained by the former.

17.   THE BREATH (*human Monad*) NEEDED A FORM; THE FATHERS GAVE IT.   THE BREATH NEEDED A GROSS BODY; THE EARTH MOLDED

196.   *Chaldean Account of Genesis,* p. 92.
197.   *Op. cit.,* Babylonian Legend of Creation, p. 92.

IT. THE BREATH NEEDED THE SPIRIT OF LIFE; THE SOLAR LHAS BREATHED IT INTO ITS FORM. THE BREATH NEEDED A MIRROR OF ITS BODY (*astral shadow*); "WE GAVE IT OUR OWN," SAID THE DHYÂNIS. THE BREATH NEEDED A VEHICLE OF DESIRES (*Kâma Rûpa*); "IT HAS IT," SAID THE DRAINER OF WATERS (*Suchi, the fire of passion and animal instinct*). THE BREATH NEEDS A MIND TO EMBRACE THE UNIVERSE; "WE CANNOT GIVE THAT," SAID THE FATHERS. "I NEVER HAD IT," SAID THE SPIRIT OF THE EARTH. "THE FORM WOULD BE CONSUMED WERE I TO GIVE IT MINE," SAID THE GREAT (*solar*) FIRE . . . . (*nascent*) MAN REMAINED AN EMPTY, SENSELESS BHÛTA . . . . THUS HAVE THE BONELESS GIVEN LIFE TO THOSE WHO BECAME (*later*) MEN WITH BONES IN THE THIRD (*race*) (*a*).

(*a*) As a full explanation is found in Stanza V,[198] a few remarks will now suffice. The " Father " of primitive physical man, or of his body, is the vital electric principle residing in the Sun. The Moon is its Mother, because of that mysterious power in the Moon which has as decided an influence upon human gestation and generation, which it regulates, as it has on the growth of plants and animals. The " Wind " or Ether, standing in this case for the agent of transmission by which those influences are carried down from the two luminaries and diffused upon Earth, is referred to as the " nurse "; while " Spiritual Fire " alone makes of man a divine and perfect entity.

Now what is that " Spiritual Fire "? In alchemy it is HYDROGEN, in general; while in esoteric actuality it is the emanation or the Ray which proceeds from its *noumenon*, the " Dhyân of the first Element." Hydrogen is *gas* only on our terrestrial plane. But even in chemistry hydrogen " would be the only existing form of matter, in 'our sense of the term," [199] and is very nearly allied to *protyle*, which is our *layam*. It is the father and generator, so to say, or rather the *Upâdhi* (basis), of both AIR and WATER, and is " fire, air and water," in fact: *one* under three aspects; hence the chemical and alchemical trinity. In the world of manifestation or matter it is the objective symbol and the material emanation from the subjective and purely spiritual entitative Being in the region of *noumena*. Well might Godfrey Higgins have compared Hydrogen to, and even identified it with, the To on, the " One " of the Greeks. For, as he remarks, Hydrogen is *not* Water, though it generates it; Hydrogen is not fire, though it manifests or creates it; nor is it Air, though air may be regarded as a product of the union of Water and Fire — since Hydrogen is found in the aqueous element of the atmosphere. It is three in one.

If one studies comparative Theogony, it is easy to find that the

198. *Vide* paragraph (*a*) Sloka 18.
199. See *Genesis of the Elements*, by Prof. W. Crookes, p. 21.

secret of these "Fires" was taught in the *Mysteries* of every ancient people, pre-eminently in Samothrace. There is not the smallest doubt that the Kabeiroi, the most arcane of all the ancient deities, gods and men, great deities and Titans, are identical with the Kumâras and Rudras headed by Kârttikeya—a Kumâra also. This is quite evident even exoterically; and these Hindû deities were, like the Kabeiroi, the *personified sacred fires of the most occult powers of Nature.* The several branches of the Aryan Race, the Asiatic and the European, the Hindû and the Greek, did their best to conceal their true nature, if not their importance. As in the case of the Kumâras, the number of the Kabeiroi is uncertain. Some say that there were three or four only; others say seven. Axieros, Axiokersa, Axiokersos, and Kadmilos, may very well stand for the *alter egos* of the four Kumâras—Sanat-Kumâra, Sananda, Sanaka, and Sanâtana. The former deities, whose reputed father was Vulcan, were often confounded with the Dioscuri, Corybantes, Anakes, etc., etc.; just as the Kumâras, whose reputed father is Brahmâ (or rather, the "Flame of his Wrath," which prompted him to perform the ninth or Kumâra creation, resulting in Rudra or Nilalohita (Śiva) and the Kumâras), were confounded with the Asuras, the Rudras, and the Pitris, for the simple reason that they are all one — *i. e.*, correlative Forces and Fires. There is no space to describe these "fires" and their real meaning here, though we may attempt to do so if the third and fourth volumes of this work are ever published. Meanwhile a few more explanations may be added.

The foregoing are all mysteries which must be left to the personal intuition of the student for solution, rather than described. If he would learn something of the secret of the FIRES, let him turn to certain works of the Alchemists, who very correctly connect fire with every element, as do the Occultists. The reader must remember that the ancients considered religion, and the natural sciences along with philosophy, to be closely and inseparably linked together. Aesculapius was the Son of Apollo — the Sun or FIRE of Life; at once *Helios, Pythios,* and the god of oracular Wisdom. In exoteric religions, as much as in esoteric philosophy, the Elements — especially fire, water, and air — are made the progenitors of our *five physical senses,* and hence are directly connected (in an occult way) with them. These physical senses pertain even to a lower creation than the one called in the Purânas *Pratisarga,* or secondary Creation. "Liquid fire proceeds from indiscrete fire," says an Occult axiom.

"The Circle is the THOUGHT; the diameter (or the line) is the WORD; and their union is LIFE." In the Kabala, Bath-Kol is the daughter of the *Divine Voice,* or primordial light, Shekinah. In the Purânas and

Hindû exotericism, Vâch (the Voice) is the female *Logos* of Brahmâ
— a permutation of Aditi, *primordial light*. And if Bath-Kol, in Jewish
mysticism is an articulate praeter-natural voice from heaven, revealing
to the "chosen people" the sacred traditions and laws, it is only
because Vâch was called, before Judaism, the "Mother of the Vedas,"
who entered into the Rishis and inspired them by her revelations; just
as Bath-Kol is said to have inspired the prophets of Israel and the
Jewish High-Priests. And both exist to this day, in their respective
sacred symbologies, because the ancients associated sound or Speech
with the Ether of Space, of which Sound is the characteristic. Hence
Fire, Water and Air are the primordial Cosmic Trinity. "I am thy
Thought, thy God, more ancient than the moist principle, the *light
that radiates within Darkness* [Chaos], and the shining *Word* of God
[Sound] is the Son of the Deity." [200]

Thus we have to study well the "Primary creation," before we can
understand the Secondary. The first Race had three *rudimentary*
elements in it; and *no fire* as yet; because, with the Ancients, the
evolution of man, and the growth and development of his spiritual
and physical senses, were subordinate to the evolution of the elements
on the Cosmic plane of this Earth. All proceeds from *Prabhavâpyaya*,
the evolution of the creative and sentient principles in the gods, and
even of the so-called creative deity himself. This is found in the
names and appellations given to Vishnu in exoteric scriptures. As
the *Protologos* (the Orphic), he is called *Pûrvaja*, "pregenetic," and
then the other names connect him in their descending order more and
more with matter.

The following order on parallel lines may be found in the evolution
of the Elements and the Senses; or in Cosmic terrestrial " MAN " or
" Spirit," and mortal physical man:—

1. Ether	...	Hearing...	Sound.
2. Air	...	Touch ...	Sound and Touch.
3. Fire, or Light		Sight ...	Sound, Touch and Color.
4. Water	...	Taste ...	Sound, Touch, Color and Taste.
5. Earth	...	Smell ...	Sound, Touch, Color, Taste and Smell.

As seen, each Element adds to its own characteristics, those of its
predecessor; as each Root-Race adds the characterizing sense of the

200. *Pymander*, i, § 6.
The opponents of Hindûism may call the
above Pantheism, Polytheism, or anything
they may please. If Science is not entirely blinded by prejudice, it will see in
this account a profound knowledge of *natural
Sciences and Physics*, as well as of Metaphysics and Psychology. But to find this
out, one has to study the personifications,
and then convert them into chemical atoms.
It will then be found to satisfy both physical and even purely materialistic *Science*, as
well as those who see in evolution the work
of the "Great Unknown Cause" in its phenomenal and illusive aspects.

preceding Race. The same is true in the *septenary* creation of man, who evolves gradually in seven stages, and on the same principles, as will be shown further on.

Thus, while Gods or Dhyân Chohans (Devas) proceed from the First Cause — which is not Parabrahm, for the latter is the ALL CAUSE, and cannot be referred to as the "*First* Cause," — which First Cause is called in the Brâhmanical Books Jagad-Yoni, "the womb of the world," mankind emanates from these active agents in Kosmos. But men, during the first and the second races, were not physical beings, but merely *rudiments* of the future men: *Bhûtas*, which proceeded from Bhûtâdi, "origin," or the "original place whence sprung the Elements." Hence they proceeded with all the rest from *Prabhavâpyaya*, "the place whence is the origination, and into which is the resolution of all things," as explained by the Commentator. Whence also our physical senses. Whence even the highest "created" deity itself, in our philosophy. As one with the Universe, whether we call him Brahmâ, Îśvara, or Purusha, he is a manifested deity, — hence created, or limited and conditioned. This is easily proven, even from the exoteric teachings.

After being called the *incognizable*, eternal Brahma (neuter or abstract), the Pundarîkâksha, "supreme and imperishable glory," once that instead of *Sadaika-Rûpa*, "changeless" or "immutable" Nature, he is addressed as *Ekâneka-Rûpa*, "both single and manifold," he, the cause, becomes merged with his own effects; and his names, if placed in esoteric order, show the following descending scale:—

1. Mahâpurusha or Paramâtman... Supreme Spirit.
2. Âtman or Pûrvaja (Protologos).. The living Spirit of Nature.
3. Indriyâtman, or Hrishikeśa...... Spiritual or intellectual soul (One with the senses).
5. Bhûtâtman .... The living, or Life Soul.
6. Kshetrajña .... Embodied soul, or the Universe of Spirit and Matter.
7. Bhrântidarśanatah .... False perception — Material Universe.

The last name means something perceived or conceived of, owing to false and erroneous apprehension, as a material form; but, in fact, only *Mâyâ*, illusion, as all is in our physical universe.

It is in strict analogy with ITS attributes in both the spiritual and material worlds, that the evolution of the Dhyân Chohanic Essences takes place; the characteristics of the latter being reflected, in their turn, in *Man,* collectively, and in each of his principles; *every one of which contains in itself, in the same progressive order, a portion of their various "fires" and elements.*

STANZA V

THE EVOLUTION OF THE SECOND RACE

§§ (18) The Sons of Yoga. (19) The Sexless Second Race. (20) The Sons of the Sons of Twilight. (21) The "Shadow," or the Astral Man, retires within, and man develops a physical body.

18. THE FIRST (*Race*) WERE THE SONS OF YOGA. THEIR SONS, THE CHILDREN OF THE YELLOW FATHER AND THE WHITE MOTHER.

In the later Commentary, the sentence is translated:—
"*The Sons of the Sun and of the Moon, the nursling of ether* (or the wind) (a) . . . .
"*They were the shadows of the shadows of the Lords* (b). *They* (the shadows) *expanded. The Spirits of the Earth clothed them; the solar Lhas warmed them* (*i. e.*, preserved the vital fire in the nascent physical forms). *The Breaths had life, but had no understanding. They had no fire nor water of their own* (c).

(a) Remember in this connexion the *Tabula Smaragdina* of Hermes, the esoteric meaning of which has seven keys to it. The Astro-Chemical is well known to students, the anthropological may be given now. The "One thing" mentioned in it is MAN. It is said: "The Father of THAT ONE ONLY THING is the Sun; its Mother the Moon; the Wind carries it in his bosom, and its nurse is the Spirituous Earth." In the occult rendering of the same it is added: "and *Spiritual* Fire is its instructor (Guru)."

This fire is the higher Self, the Spiritual Ego, or that which is eternally reincarnating under the influence of its lower personal Selves, changing with every re-birth, full of *Tanhâ* or desire to live. It is a strange law of Nature that, on this plane, the higher (Spiritual) Nature should be, so to say, in bondage to the lower. Unless the Ego takes refuge in the Âtman, the ALL-SPIRIT, and merges entirely into the essence thereof, the personal Ego may goad it to the bitter end. This cannot be thoroughly understood unless the student makes himself familiar with the mystery of evolution, which proceeds on triple lines — spiritual, psychic and physical.

That which propels towards, and forces evolution, *i. e.*, compels the growth and development of Man towards perfection, is (a) the MONAD, or that which acts in it unconsciously through a force inherent in itself; and (b) the lower astral body or the *personal* SELF. The former, whether imprisoned in a vegetable or an animal body, is endowed with, is indeed itself, that force. Owing to its identity with the ALL-FORCE, which, as said, is inherent in the Monad, it is all-potent on the *Arûpa*, or formless plane. On our plane, its essence being too pure, it remains all-potential, but individually becomes inactive: *e. g.*, the rays of the Sun, which contribute to the growth of vegetation, do not select this or that plant to shine upon. Uproot the plant and transfer it to a piece of soil where the sunbeam cannot reach it, and the latter will not follow it. So with the Âtman: unless the higher Self or EGO gravitates towards its Sun — the Monad — the lower *Ego,* or *personal* Self, will have the upper hand in every case. For it is this Ego, with its fierce Selfishness and animal desire to live a Senseless life (*Tanhâ*), which is " the maker of the tabernacle," as Buddha calls it in *Dhammapada* (153 and 154). Hence the expression, " the Spirits of the Earth clothed the shadows and expanded them." To these " Spirits " belong temporarily the human astral selves; and it is they who give, or build, the physical tabernacle of man, for the Monad and its conscious principle, Manas, to dwell in. But the " Solar " *Lhas,* Spirits, warm them, the shadows. This is physically and literally true; metaphysically, or on the psychic and spiritual plane, it is equally true that the Âtman alone *warms* the inner man; *i. e.,* it enlightens it with the ray of divine life and alone is able to impart to the inner man, or the reincarnating Ego, its immortality. Thus, as we shall find, for the first three and a half Root-Races, up to the middle or turning point, it is the astral shadows of the " progenitors," the lunar Pitris, which are the formative powers in the Races, and which build and gradually force the evolution of the physical form towards perfection — this, at the cost of a proportionate loss of spirituality. Then, from the turning point, it is the Higher Ego, or incarnating principle, the *nous* or *Mind*, which reigns over the animal Ego, and rules it whenever it is not carried down by the latter. In short, Spirituality is on its ascending arc, and the animal or physical impedes it from steadily progressing on the path of its evolution only when the selfishness of the *personality* has so strongly infected the real *inner* man with its lethal *virus*, that the upward attraction has lost all its power on the thinking reasonable man. In sober truth, vice and wickedness are an *abnormal, unnatural* manifestation, at this period of our human evolution — at least they ought to be so. The fact that mankind was never more selfish and vicious than it is now, civilized nations having succeeded in making of the first an ethical characteristic, of the second an art, is an additional proof of the exceptional nature of the phenomenon.

The entire scheme is in the *Chaldaean Book of Numbers*, and even in the *Zohar*, if one only understood the meaning of the apocalyptic hints. First comes En-Soph, the "Concealed of the Concealed," then the *Point*, Sephira and the later Sephiroth; then the *Atzilatic* World, a *World of Emanations* that gives birth to three other worlds — called the Throne, the abode of pure Spirits; the second, the *World of Formation*, or Jetzirah, the habitat of the Angels who sent forth the Third, or World of Action, the Asiatic *World*, which is the Earth or *our* World; and yet it is said of it that this world, also called *Kliphoth*, containing the (six other) Spheres, גלגלים, and matter, is the residence of the "Prince of Darkness." This is as clearly stated as can be; for *Metatron*, the Angel of the second or *Briatic* World, means Messenger, ἄγγελος, Angel, called the great Teacher; and under him are the Angels of the third World, *Jetzirah*, whose ten and seven classes are the *Sephiroth*,[201] of whom it is said that "they inhabit and vivify this world as Essential *Entities* and *Intelligences*, whose *correlatives* and *contraries* inhabit the third or *Asiatic World*." These "Contraries" are called "the *Shells*," קליפות, or *demons*,[202] who inhabit the seven habitations called *Sheba Haichaloth*, which are simply the seven zones of our globe. Their prince is called in the Kabala Samael, the Angel of Death, who is also the seducing serpent Satan; but that Satan is also Lucifer, the bright angel of Light, the *Light* and *Life-bringer*, the "Soul" alienated from the Holy *Ones*, the other angels, and for a period, *anticipating the time* when they would have descended on Earth to incarnate in their turn.

"The *Souls* [Monads] are pre-existent in the world of Emanations";[203] and the *Zohar* teaches that in the "Soul" "is the *real man, i. e.,* the Ego and the conscious I AM: '*Manas.*'"

"They descend from the pure air to be *chained to bodies*," says Josephus repeating the belief of the Essenes.[204] "The air is full of Souls," states Philo, "*they descend to be tied to mortal bodies, being desirous to live in them*";[205] because through, and in, the human form they will become *progressive* beings, whereas the nature of the angel is purely *intransitive*, therefore man has in him the potency of transcending the faculties of the Angels. Hence the Initiates in India say

---

201. See Vol. I, Part III, § xv, "Gods, Monads, and Atoms." It is symbolized in the Pythagorean Triangle, the 10 dots within, and the seven points of the Triangle and the Cube.

202. Whence the Kabalistic name of *Shells* given to the astral form, the body called *Kâma Rûpa*, left behind by the higher angels in the shape of the higher *Manas*, when the

latter leaves for Devachan, forsaking its residue.

203. *Book of Wisdom*, viii, 20.
204. *De Bello Judaico*, II, viii, 11.
205. *De Gigant.*, 222c; *De Somniis*, p. 455. 455.

Which shows that the Essenes believed in re-birth and many re-incarnations on Earth, as Jesus himself did, a fact we can prove from the New Testament itself.

that it is the Brâhman, the twice-born, who rules the gods or devas; and Paul repeated it in: "Know ye not that we [the Initiates] shall judge angels?" [206]

Finally, it is shown in every ancient scripture and Cosmogony that man evolved primarily as a *luminous incorporeal form,* over which, like the molten brass round the clay model of the sculptor, the physical frame of his body was built by, through, and from, the lower forms and types of animal terrestrial life. "The Soul and the *Form* when descending on Earth put on an earthly garment," says the *Zohar.* His protoplastic body was not formed of that matter of which our mortal frames are fashioned. "When Adam dwelt in the garden of Eden, he was clothed in the celestial garment, which is the garment of heavenly light ... *light of that light which was used in the garden of Eden.*" [207] "Man (the heavenly Adam) *was created* by the ten Sephiroth of the Jetziric world, and by the *common power* they [the seven angels of a still lower world] *engendered the earthly Adam.* . . . First Samael fell, and then *deceiving* [?] man, caused his fall also."

(b) The sentence: "They were the shadows of the shadows of the Lords," *i. e.,* the progenitors created man out of their own astral bodies, explains a universal belief. The *Devas* are credited in the East with having no shadows of their own. "The devas cast no shadows," and this is the sure sign of a *good holy Spirit.*

Why had they "no fire or water of their own"? [208] Because:—

(c) That which Hydrogen is to the elements and gases on the objective plane, its noumenon is in the world of mental or subjective phenomena; since its trinitarian latent nature is mirrored in its three active emanations from the three higher principles in man, namely, "Spirit, Soul, and Mind," or *Atmâ, Buddhi,* and *Manas.* It is the spiritual and

---

206. I *Corinthians,* vi, 3.
207. *Zohar* II, 229 ꜩ.
208. It is corroborated, however, as we have shown, by the esotericism of *Genesis.* Not only are the animals created therein after the "Adam of Dust," but vegetation is shown *in* the Earth before "the heavens and the Earth were created." "Every plant of the field before it (the day that the heavens and the Earth were made, ii, 4,) was in the Earth" (5). Now, unless the Occult interpretation is accepted, which shows that in this 4th Round the Globe was covered with vegetation, and the first (*astral*) humanity was produced before almost anything could grow and develop thereon, what can the dead letter mean? Simply that the grass was in the earth of the Globe before that Globe was created? And yet the meaning of verse 6, which says that "there went up a mist from the Earth" and watered the whole face of the Earth before it rained, and caused the trees, etc., to grow, is plain enough. It shows also in what geological period it occurred, and further what is meant by "Heaven and Earth." It meant the firmament and dry *incrustated* land, separated and ridden of its vapors and exhalations. Moreover, the student must bear in mind that, as Adam Kadmon, "the male and female being" of *Genesis,* ch. 1, is no physical human being but the host of the Elohim, among which was Jehovah himself — so the animals mentioned in that chapter as "created" before man in the dead letter text, were no animals, but the Zodiacal signs and other sidereal bodies.

also the material human basis. Rudimentary man, having been nursed by the "air" or the "wind," becomes the perfect man later on; when, with the development of " Spiritual fire," the *noumenon* of the " Three in One " within his Self, he acquires from his inner Self, or Instructor, the Wisdom of Self-Consciousness, which he does not possess in the beginning. Thus here again divine Spirit is symbolized by the Sun or Fire; divine Soul by Water and the Moon, both standing for the Father and Mother of *Pneuma*, human Soul, or Mind, symbolized by the Wind or air, for *Pneuma* means " breath."

Hence in the *Smaragdine Tablet*, disfigured by Christian hands:—

" The Superior agrees with the Inferior; and the Inferior with the Superior; to effect that one truly wonderful Work " — which is MAN. For the secret work of Chiram, or King Hiram in the Kabala, " one in Essence, but three in Aspect," is the Universal Agent or *Lapis Philosophorum*. The culmination of the Secret Work is Spiritual Perfect Man, at one end of the line; the union of the three elements is the Occult Solvent in the " Soul of the World," the *Cosmic* Soul or Astral Light, at the other; and, on the material plane, it is *Hydrogen* in its relation to the other gases. The To ON, truly; the ONE " whom no person has seen except the Son "; this sentence applying both to the metaphysical and physical Kosmos, and to the spiritual and material Man. For how could the latter understand the To ON the " One Father," if his *Manas*, the " Son," does not become (*as*) " One with the Father," and through this absorption receive enlightenment from the " divine instructor," Guru — *Atmâ-Buddhi?*

" *If thou wouldst understand the SECONDARY* (" Creation," so-called), *oh Lanoo, thou shouldst first study its relation to the PRIMARY.*" [209]

The first Race had three elements, but no *living* Fire. Why? Because:—

" We say *four* elements, my Son, but ought to say three," says Hermes Trismegistos. " In the Primary Circle " (creation) that which is marked 卌 reads " Root," as in the Secondary likewise.

Thus in Alchemy or Western Hermetism (a variant on Eastern Esotericism) we find:—

X.	卌	X.
Sulphur	Flamma	Spiritus
Hydrargyrum	Natura	Aqua
Sal	Mater	Sanguis

And these three are all quaternaries completed by their Root, Fire.

209. Commentary, *Book of Dzyan*, III, 19.

The Spirit, beyond manifested Nature, is the fiery BREATH in its absolute Unity. In the manifested Universe, it is the Central Spiritual Sun, the electric Fire of all Life. In our System it is the visible Sun, the Spirit of Nature, the terrestrial god. And in, on, and around the Earth, the fiery Spirit thereof — air, fluidic fire; *water*, liquid fire; *Earth*, solid fire. All is fire — *ignis*, in its ultimate constitution, or I, the root of which is O (*nought*) in our conceptions, the All in nature, and its mind. *Pro-Mater* is divine fire. It is the Creator, the Destroyer, the Preserver. The primitive names of the gods are all connected with fire, from AGNI, the Āryan, to the Jewish god who "is a consuming fire." In India, God is called in various dialects, *Eashoor, Esur, Iswur* and *IśVara*, in Sanskrit the Lord, from Îśa, but this is primarily the name of Śiva, the Destroyer; and the three Vedic chief gods are Agni (*ignis*), Vâyu, and Sûrya — Fire, Air, and the Sun, three occult degrees of fire. In the Hebrew אזא (*aza*), means to illuminate, and אשא (*asha*) is fire. In Occultism, "to kindle a fire" is synonymous with evoking one of the three great fire-powers, or "to call on God." In Sanskrit *Ush* or *Ash* is fire or heat; and the Egyptian word Osiris is compounded (as shown by Schelling) of the two primitives *aish* and *asr*, or a "fire-enchanter." *Aesar* in the old Etruscan meant a God (being perhaps derived from *Asura* of the Vedas). *Aesar* and *Îsvara* are analogous terms, as Dr. Kenealy thought. In the *Bhagavad Gîtâ* we read, Îśvara "resides in every mortal being and puts in motion, by his supernatural power, all things which mount on the Wheel of Time." It is the creator and the destroyer, truly.

The primitive fire was supposed to have an insatiable appetite for devouring. Maximus of Tyre relates that the ancient Persians threw into the fire combustible matter, crying: "Devour, O Lord!" In the Irish language *Easam*, or *Asam*, means "to create," and *Aesar* was the name of an ancient Irish god, meaning "to light a fire."[210]

The Christian Kabalists and symbologists who disfigured *Pymander* — prominent among them the Bishop of Ayre, François de Tours, in the 16th century — divide the elements in this way:—

The four elements formed from divine substances and the Spirits of the Salts of Nature represented by —

חֹם	St. Matthew	Angel-Man	Water (Jesus-Christ, Angel-Man, Mikael)
A - ω	St. Mark	The Lion	Fire
E - Y	St. Luke	The Bull	Earth
I - O	St. John	The Eagle	Air [211]

210. Kenealy, *The Book of God*: The Apocalypse of Adam-Oannes, pp. 114, 115.

211. To those who would inquire "What has Hydrogen to do with air or oxygena-

H, THE QUINTESSENCE, 'H ΦΑΟΣ, FLAMMA-VIRGO (virgin-oil), FLAMMA DURISSIMA, VIRGO, LUCIS ÆTERNA MATER.

The first race of men were, then, simply the images, the astral doubles, of their Fathers, who were the pioneers, or the most progressed Entities from a preceding though *lower* sphere, the shell of which is now our Moon. But even this shell is all-potential, for, having generated the Earth, it is the *phantom* of the Moon which, attracted by magnetic affinity, sought to form its first inhabitants, the pre-human monsters.[212] To assure himself of this, the student has again to turn to the Chaldaean Fragments, and read what Berosus says. Berosus obtained his information, he tells us, from *Ea*, the male-female deity of Wisdom. While the gods were generated in its androgynous bosom (Svabhâvat, Mother-space) its (the Wisdom's) reflections became on Earth the woman Omoroka, who is the Chaldaean Thavatth, or the the Greek Thalassa, the Deep or the Sea, which esoterically and even exoterically is *the Moon*. It was the Moon (Omoroka) who presided over the monstrous creation of nondescript beings which were slain by the Dhyânis.[213]

Evolutionary law compelled the lunar "Fathers" to pass, in their monadic condition, through all the forms of life and being on this globe; but at the end of the Third Round, they were already human in their divine nature, and were thus called upon to become the creators of the forms destined to fashion the tabernacles of the less progressed Monads, whose turn it was to incarnate. These "Forms" are called "Sons of Yoga," because Yoga (union with Brahmâ exoterically) is the supreme condition of the passive infinite deity, since it contains all the divine energies and is the essence of Brahmâ, who is said (as Brahmâ) to create everything through Yoga power. Brahmâ, Vishnu and Śiva are the most powerful energies of God, Brahma, the Neuter, says a Purânic text. Yoga here is the same as Dhyâna, which word is again

---

tion?" it is answered: "Study first the ABC of Occult Alchemy." In their anxiety, however, to identify Pymander, "the mouth of Mystery," with St. John the Baptist prophetically, they thus identified also the 7 *Kabeiroi* and the Assyrian Bulls with the Cherubs of the Jews and the Apostles. Having, moreover, to draw a line of demarcation between the *four* and the *three* — the latter being the *Fallen Angels;* and furthermore to avoid connecting these with the "Seven Spirits of the Face," the Archangels, they unceremoniously threw out all they did not choose to recognize. Hence the perversion in the order of the Elements, in order to make them dovetail with the order of the

Gospels, and to identify the Angel-Man with Christ. With the Chaldees, the Egyptians, from whom Moses adopted the *Chroub* (Cherubs in their animal form), and the Ophites; with all these, the Angels, the Planets, and the Elements, were symbolized mystically and alchemically by the *Lion* (Mikael); the *Bull* (Suriel); the *Dragon* (Raphael); the *Eagle* (Gabriel); the *Bear* (Thantabaoth); the *Dog* (Erataoth); the *Mule* (Onioth or Zartaoth). All these have a qualificative meaning.

212. *Vide supra*, Stanza II.

213. See *Hibbert Lectures* (1887), p. 370 *et seq.;* also in Part II, "Adam-Adami."

synonymous with Yoga in the Tíbetan text, where the " Sons of Yoga " are called " Sons of Dhyâna," or of that abstract meditation through which the Dhyâni-Buddhas create their celestial sons, the Dhyâni-Bodhisattvas. All the creatures in the world have each a superior above. " This superior, whose inner pleasure it is *to emanate into them,* cannot impart efflux until they have adored " — *i. e.,* meditated as during Yoga.[214]

---

19. The second race (*was*) the product by budding and expansion; the a-sexual (*form*) from the sexless (*shadow*). Thus was, O Lanoo, the second race produced (*a*).

(*a*). What will be most contested by scientific authorities is this a-sexual Race, the Second, the fathers of the " Sweat-born " so-called, and perhaps still more the Third Race, the " Egg-born " androgynes. These two modes of procreation are the most difficult to comprehend, especially for the Western mind. It is evident that no explanation can be attempted for those who are not students of Occult metaphysics. European language has no words to express things which Nature repeats no more at this stage of evolution, things which therefore can have no meaning for the materialist. But there are analogies. It is not denied that in the beginning of physical evolution there must have been processes in Nature, spontaneous generation, for instance, now extinct, which are repeated in other forms. Thus we are told that microscopic research shows no permanence of any particular mode of reproducing life. For it shows that —

the same organism may run through various metamorphoses in the course of its life-cycle, during some of which it may be *sexual,* and in others *a-sexual;* *i. e.,* it may reproduce itself alternately by the co-operation of two beings of opposite sex, and also by fissure or *budding* from one being only, which is of no sex.[215]

" Budding " is the very word used in the Stanza. How could these Chhâyâs reproduce themselves otherwise; viz., procreate the Second Race, since they were ethereal, a-sexual, and even devoid, as yet, of the vehicle of desire, or Kâma Rûpa, which evolved only in the Third Race? They evolved the Second Race unconsciously, as do some plants. Or, perhaps, as the *Amoeba,* only on a more ethereal, impressive, and larger scale. If, indeed, the cell-theory applies equally to Botany and Zoology, and extends to Morphology, as well as to the Physiology of

214. Sepher *M'bo She-arim,* translated by   215. See Laing's *Modern Science and*
Isaac Myer, *Qabbalah,* pp. 109-111.   *Modern Thought,* p. 90.

organisms, and if the microscopic cells are looked upon by physical science as independent living beings — just as Occultism regards the " fiery lives " [216] — there is no difficulty in the conception of the primitive process of procreation.

Consider the first stages of the development of a germ-cell. Its *nucleus* grows, changes, and forms a double cone or spindle, thus, ✕ *within* the cell. This spindle approaches the surface of the cell, and one half of it is *extruded* in the form of what are called the "*polar cells.*" These polar cells *now* die, and the embryo develops from the growth and segmentation of the remaining part of the nucleus which is *nourished* by the substance of the cell. Then why could not beings have lived thus, and been created in *this* way — at the very beginning of *human and mammalian evolution?*

This may, perhaps, serve as an analogy to give some idea of the process by which the Second Race was formed from the First.

The astral form clothing the Monad was surrounded, as it still is, by its egg-shaped sphere of *aura*, which here corresponds to the substance of the germ-cell or *ovum*. The astral form itself is the nucleus, now, as then, instinct with the principle of life.

When the season of reproduction arrives, the *sub*-astral " *extrudes* " a miniature of itself from the egg of surrounding aura. This germ grows and feeds on the aura till it becomes fully developed, when it gradually separates from its parent, carrying with it its own sphere of aura; just as we see living cells reproducing their like by growth and subsequent division into two.

The analogy with the "*polar cells*" would seem to hold good, since their death would *now* correspond to the change introduced by the separation of the sexes, when gestation *in utero, i. e., within the cell,* became the rule.

"*The early Second* (Root) *Race were the Fathers of the 'Sweat-born'; the later Second* (Root) *Race were 'Sweat-born' themselves.*"

This passage from the Commentary refers to the work of evolution from the beginning of a Race to its close. The "Sons of Yoga," or the primitive astral race, had seven stages of evolution *racially*, or collectively; as every individual Being in it had, and has now. It is not Shakespeare only who divided the ages of man into a series of seven, but Nature herself. Thus the first sub-races of the Second Race were born at first by the process described on the law of analogy; while the last began gradually, *pari passu* with the evolution of the human body, to be formed otherwise. The process of reproduction had seven stages

216. See Book I, Part I, Stanza VII, Commentary.

also in each Race, each covering aeons of time. What physiologist or biologist could tell whether the present mode of generation, with all its phases of gestation, is older than half a million, or at most one million of years, since their cycle of observation began hardly half a century ago?

Primeval human hermaphrodites are a fact in Nature well known to the ancients, and form one of Darwin's greatest perplexities. Yet there is certainly no impossibility, but, on the contrary, a great probability that hermaphroditism existed in the evolution of the early races; while on the grounds of analogy, and on that of the existence of one universal law in physical evolution, acting indifferently in the construction of plant, animal, and man, it must be so. The mistaken theories of monogenesis, and the descent of man from the mammals instead of the reverse, are fatal to the completeness of evolution as taught in modern schools on Darwinian lines, and they will have to be abandoned in view of the insuperable difficulties which they encounter. Occult tradition — if the terms Science and Knowledge are denied in this particular to antiquity — can alone reconcile the inconsistencies and fill the gap. " If thou wilt know the invisible, open thine eye wide on the visible," says a Talmudic axiom.

In the *Descent of Man* [217] occurs the following passage; which shows how near Darwin came to the acceptance of this ancient teaching:

> It has long been known that in the vertebrate kingdom one sex bears rudiments of various accessory parts appertaining to the reproductive system, which properly belong to the opposite sex. . . . Some remote progenitor of the whole vertebrate kingdom appears to have been hermaphrodite or androgynous.[218] . . . But here we encounter a *singular difficulty*. In *the mammalian class the males possess rudiments of a uterus with the adjacent passages in the vesiculae prostaticae; they bear also rudiments of mammae, and some male marsupials have traces of a marsupial sac*. Other analogous facts could be added. Are we then to suppose that some extremely ancient mammal continued androgynous after it had acquired the chief distinctions of its class, and therefore after it had diverged from the lower classes of the vertebrate kingdom? This seems very improbable,[219] for *we have to look to fishes, the lowest of all the classes, to find any still existent androgynous forms*.

Mr. Darwin is evidently strongly disinclined to adopt the hypothesis which the facts so forcibly suggest, viz., that of a primeval androgynous stem from which the mammalia sprang. His explanation runs:—

217. Second Edition, p. 161.
218. And why not all the progenitive first Races, human as well as animal; and why one " remote progenitor "?
219. Obviously so, on the lines of Evolutionism, which traces the mammalia to some amphibian ancestor.

The fact that various accessory organs proper to each sex, are found in a rudimentary condition in the opposite sex may be explained by such organs having been gradually acquired by the one sex and then transmitted in a more or less imperfect condition to the other.

He instances the case of "spurs, plumes, and brilliant colors, acquired for battle or for ornament by male birds " and only *partially* inherited by their female descendants. In the problem to be dealt with, however, the need of a more satisfactory explanation is evident, the facts being of so much more prominent and important a character than the mere superficial details with which they are compared by Darwin. Why not candidly admit the argument in favor of the hermaphroditism which characterizes the old fauna? Occultism proposes a solution which embraces the facts in a most comprehensive and simple manner. These relics of a prior androgyne stock must be placed in the same category as the pineal gland, and other organs as mysterious, which afford us silent testimony as to the reality of functions which have long since become atrophied in the course of animal and human progress, but which once played a signal part in the general economy of primeval life.

The occult doctrine, anyhow, can be advantageously compared with that of the most liberal men of science, who have theorized upon the origin of the first man.

Long before Darwin, Naudin, who gave the name of *Blastema* to that which the Darwinists call protoplasm, put forward a theory half occult and half scientifico-materialistic. He made Adam, the *a-sexual*, spring suddenly from the *clay*, as it is called in the Bible, the *Blastema* of Science.

It is from this larval form of mankind that the evolutive force effected the completion of species. For the accomplishment of this great phenomenon, Adam had to pass through a phase of immobility and unconsciousness, very analogous to the nymphal state of animals undergoing metamorphosis,[219a]

explains Naudin. For the eminent botanist, Adam was not one man, however, but *mankind*, " which remained concealed within a temporary organism . . . distinct from all others and never contracting alliance with any of these." He shows the differentiation of sexes accomplished by " a process of germination similar to that of Medusae and Ascidians." Mankind, thus constituted physiologically, "would retain a sufficient evolutive force for the rapid production of the various great human races."

De Quatrefages criticises this position in the *Human Species*. It is *unscientific*, he says, or, properly speaking, Naudin's ideas " do not form a scientific theory," inasmuch as primordial *Blastema* is connected in his theory with the *First Cause*, which is credited with having made

219a. *The Human Species*, p. 124, de Quatrefages.

potentially in the Blastema all past, present, and future beings, and
thus of having in reality *created* these beings *en masse;* moreover,
Naudin does not even consider the *secondary* Causes, or their action
in this evolution of the organic world. Science, which is only occupied
with Secondary Causes, has thus "nothing to say to the theory of
Naudin." [220]

Nor will it have any more to say to the occult teachings, which
are to some extent approached by Naudin. For if we but see in his
"primordial Blastema" the Dhyân-Chohanic essence, the *Chhâyâ* or
double of the *Pitris,* which contains within itself the potentiality of
all forms, we are quite in accord. But there are two real and vital
differences between our teachings. M. Naudin declares that evolution
has progressed by sudden leaps and bounds, instead of extending slowly
over millions of years; and his primordial Blastema is endowed only
with blind instincts — a kind of *unconscious* First Cause in the *manifested Kosmos* — which is an absurdity. Whereas it is our Dhyân
Chohanic essence — the *causality* of the *primal cause* which creates
physical man — which is the living, active and potential matter, pregnant *per se* with that animal consciousness of a superior kind, such
as is found in the ant and the beaver, which produces the long series
of physiological differentiations. Apart from this his "ancient and
general process of *creation*" from *proto-organisms* is as occult as
any theory of Paracelsus or Kunrath could be.

Moreover, the Kabalistic works are full of the proof of this. The
Zohar, for instance, says that every type in the visible has its prototype
in the invisible Universe.

All that which is in the lower [our] world is found in the upper. The Lower
and the Upper act and react upon each other. [221]

----

20. THEIR FATHERS WERE THE SELF-BORN. THE SELF-BORN, THE
CHHÂYÂ FROM THE BRILLIANT BODIES OF THE LORDS, THE FATHERS,
THE SONS OF TWILIGHT (*a*).

(*a*) The "shadows," or *Chhâyâs,* are called the sons of the "self-
born," as the latter name is applied to all the gods and Beings born
through the WILL, whether of Deity or Adept. The *Homunculi* of
Paracelsus would, perhaps, be also given this name, though the latter
process is on a far more material plane. The name "Sons of Twilight"
shows that the "Self-born" progenitors of our doctrine are identical

220. *Op. cit.,* page 125.   "Esoteric Tenets corroborated in every
221. *Zohar,* fol. 186. *Vide infra,* Part II,   Scripture."

with the Pitris of the Brâhmanical system, as the title is a reference to their mode of birth, these Pitris being stated to have issued from Brahmâ's " body of twilight." (*See the Purânas.*)

———

21. WHEN THE RACE BECAME OLD, THE OLD WATERS MIXED WITH THE FRESHER WATERS (*a*) ; WHEN THE DROPS BECAME TURBID, THEY VANISHED AND DISAPPEARED, IN THE NEW STREAM, IN THE HOT STREAM OF LIFE. THE OUTER OF THE FIRST BECAME THE INNER OF THE SECOND (*b*). THE OLD WING BECAME THE SHADOW, AND THE SHADOW OF THE WING (*c*).

(*a*) The old (primitive) Race merged in the second race, and became one with it.

(*b*) This is the mysterious process of transformation and evolution of mankind. The material of the first forms — shadowy, ethereal, and negative — was drawn or absorbed into, and thus became the complement of the forms of the Second Race. The *Commentary* explains this by saying that, as the First Race was simply composed of the astral shadows of the creative progenitors, having of course neither astral nor physical bodies of their own — this Race *never died*. Its " men " melted gradually away, becoming absorbed in the bodies of their own "sweat-born" progeny, more solid than their own. The old form vanished and was absorbed by, disappeared in, the new form, more human and physical. There was no death in those days of a period more blissful than the Golden Age; but the first, or parent material was used for the formation of the new being, to form the body and even the inner or *lower* principles or bodies of the progeny.

(*c*) When the shadow retires, *i. e.,* when the astral body becomes covered with more solid flesh, man develops a physical body. The " wing," or the ethereal form that produced its shadow and image, became the shadow of the astral body and its own progeny. The expression is queer but original.

As there may be no occasion to refer to this mystery later, it is as well to point out at once the dual meaning contained in the Greek myth bearing upon this particular phase of evolution. It is found in the several variants of the allegory of Leda and her two sons Castor and Pollux, which variants have each a special meaning. Thus in Book XI of the *Odyssey*, Leda is spoken of as the spouse of Tyndareus, who gave birth by her husband " to two sons of valiant heart " — Castor and Pollux. Jupiter endows them with a marvelous gift and privilege. They are semi-immortal; they live and die, each in turn, and every alternate day; (ἐτερήμεροι[222]). As the Tyndaridae, the twin brothers are an astronomical symbol, and stand for *Day* and *Night;* their two wives, Phoebe and Hilaeira, the daughters of Apollo or the Sun, personifying the Dawn and the Twilight.[223] Again, in the allegory where Zeus is shown as the father of the two heroes — born from the egg to which Leda gives birth — the myth is entirely theogonical. It relates to that group of cosmic allegories in which the world is described as born from an egg. For Leda assumes in it the shape of a white swan when uniting herself to the Divine Swan.[224] Leda is the mythical bird, then, to which, in the traditions of various peoples of the Aryan race, are attributed various ornithological forms of birds which all lay golden eggs.[225] In the *Kalevala* (the Epic Poem of Finland), the beauteous daughter of the Ether, "the Water Mother," creates the world in conjunction with a "Duck" (another form of the Swan or Goose, Kâla-hansa), who lays six golden eggs, and the seventh, "an egg of iron," in her lap. But the variant of the Leda allegory which has a direct reference to mystic man is found in Pindar[226] only, with a slighter reference to it in the Homeric hymns.[227] Castor and Pollux are in it no longer the *Dioskouroi*[228]; but become the highly significant symbol of the dual man, the Mortal and the Immortal. Not only this, but as will now be seen, they are also the symbol of the Third Race, and its transformation from the animal man into a god-man with only an animal body.

Pindar shows Leda uniting herself in the same night to her husband and also to the father of the gods — Zeus. Thus Castor is the son of the Mortal, Pollux the progeny of the Immortal. In the allegory made up for the occasion, it is said that in a riot of vengeance against the *Apharides*[229] Pollux kills Lynkeus—"of all mortals he whose sight is the most penetrating"— but Castor is wounded by *Idas,* "he who sees and knows." Zeus puts an end to the fight by hurling his thunderbolt and killing the last two combatants. Pollux finds his brother dying.[230] In his despair he calls upon Zeus to slay him also. "Thou canst not die

222. *Odyssey*, xi, 298 to 305; *Iliad*, iii, 236.

223. *Chants Cypriaques*, Hyg. *Fab.*, 80. Ovid, *Fasti*, v, 700 *et seqq.*, etc. See Decharme's *Mythologie de la Grèce Antique*.

224. See Brahmâ Kâlahamsa in Book I, Stanza III, p. 78.

225. See Decharme's *Mythologie*, etc., p. 652.

226. *Nem.*, x, 80 *et seq.* Theocritus, xxiv, 131.

227. xxxi, v. 5; Theocritus, xxii, 1.

228. Apollodorus. III, 10, 7.

229. Apollodorus, III, ii, 1.

230. Castor's tomb was shown in Sparta, in days of old, says Pausanias (III, 13, 1); and Plutarch says that he was called at Argos the demi-mortal or demi-hero μιξαρχαγέτας. (See Plutarch, *Quæstiones Græcae*, 23.)

altogether," answers the master of the Gods; " thou art of a divine race." But he gives him the choice: Pollux will either remain immortal, living eternally in Olympos; or, if he would share his brother's fate in all things, he must pass half his existence underground, and the other half in the golden heavenly abodes. This semi-immortality, which is also to be shared by Castor, is accepted by Pollux.[231] *And thus the twin brothers live alternately, one during the day, and the other during the night.*[232]

Is this a poetical fiction only? An allegory, one of those "solar myth" interpretations, higher than which no modern Orientalist seems able to soar? Indeed, it is much more. Here we have an allusion to the " Egg-born," *Third* Race; the first half of which is mortal, *i.e.*, unconscious in its personality, and having nothing within itself to survive;[233] and the latter half of which becomes immortal in its individuality, by reason of its fifth principle being called to life by the *informing gods,* and thus connecting the Monad with this Earth. This is Pollux; while Castor represents the *personal,* mortal man, an animal of not even a superior kind, when unlinked from the divine individuality. " Twins " truly; yet divorced by death forever, unless Pollux, moved by the voice of twinship, bestows on his less favored mortal brother a share of his own divine nature, thus associating him with his own immortality.

Such is the occult meaning of the metaphysical aspect of the allegory. The widely spread modern interpretation of it — so celebrated in antiquity, Plutarch tells us,[234] as symbolical of brotherly devotion—namely, that it was an image borrowed from the spectacle of Nature — is weak and inadequate to explain the secret meaning. Besides the fact that the Moon, with the Greeks, was feminine in exoteric mythology, and could therefore hardly be regarded as Castor — and at the same time be identified with Diana — ancient symbologists who held the Sun, the King of all sidereal orbs, as the visible image of the highest deity, would not have personified it by Pollux, a demi-god only.[235]

231. Pindar, *Nem.* x, 60, Dissen.

232. Scholia on Euripides: *Orestes,* 463, Dindorf. See Decharme's *Mythol.* etc, page 654.

233. The *Monad* is impersonal and a god *per se,* albeit unconscious on this plane. For, divorced from its third (often called fifth) principle, Manas, which is the horizontal line of the first manifested triangle or trinity, it can have no consciousness or perception of things on this earthly plane. " The highest sees through the eye of the lowest " in the manifested world; *Purusha* (Spirit) remains blind without the help of Prakriti (matter) in the material spheres; and so does Atmâ-Buddhi without Manas.

234. *Morals,* p. 484f,

235. This strange idea and interpretation are accepted by Decharme in his *Mythologie de la Grèce Antique.* " Castor and Pollux," he says, "are nothing but the Sun and Moon,

If from Greek mythology we pass to the Mosaic allegories and symbolism, we shall find a still more striking corroboration of the same tenet under another form. Unable to trace in *Genesis* the "Egg-born," we shall still find there unmistakably the androgynes, and the first three races of the Secret Doctrine hidden under most ingenious symbology in the first four chapters of *Genesis*.

THE DIVINE HERMAPHRODITE

An impenetrable veil of secrecy was thrown over the occult and religious mysteries taught, after the submersion of the last remnant of the Atlantean race, some 12,000 years ago, lest they should be shared by the unworthy, and so desecrated. Of these sciences several have now become exoteric — such as Astronomy, for instance, in its purely mathematical and physical aspect. Hence their dogmas and tenets, being all symbolized and left to the sole guardianship of parable and allegory, have been forgotten, and their meaning has become perverted. Nevertheless, one finds the hermaphrodite in the scriptures and traditions of almost every nation; and why such unanimous agreement if the statement is only a fiction?

It is this secrecy which lead the Fifth Race to the establishment, or rather the re-establishment of the religious mysteries, in which ancient truths might be taught to the coming generations under the veil of allegory and symbolism. Behold the imperishable witness to the evolution of the human race from the divine, and especially from the androgynous Race — the Egyptian Sphinx, that riddle of the Ages! Divine wisdom incarnating on earth, and forced to taste of the bitter fruit of personal experience of pain and suffering, generated under the shade of the tree of the knowledge of Good and Evil — a secret first known only to the Elohim, the SELF-INITIATED, "*higher gods*" — on earth only.[236]

In the *Book of Enoch* we have Adam,[237] the first divine androgyne,

conceived as twins. . . . The Sun, the immortal and powerful being that disappears every evening from the horizon and descends under the Earth, as though he would make room for the fraternal orb which comes to life with night, is Pollux, who sacrifices himself for Castor; Castor, who, inferior to his brother, owes to him his immortality: for the Moon, says Theophrastus, is only another, but feebler Sun." (*De Ventis*, 17. See Decharme, p. 655.)

236. See *Book of Enoch*.

237. Adam (Kadmon) is, like Brahmâ and Mars, the symbol of the *generative* and *creative power* typifying Water and Earth — an alchemical secret. "It takes Earth and Water to create a human soul," said Moses. Mars is the Hindû *Mangala*, the planet Mars, identical with *Kârttikeya*, the "War-God," born of Śiva's *sweat* (*Gharma-ja*) and of the Earth. He is *Lohita*, the red, like Brahmâ also and Adam. The Hindû Mars is, like Adam, born from no woman and mother. With the Egyptians, Mars was the

or *Race,* and Cain and Abel [238] (male and female) in its other form or *Race* — the double-sexed Jehovah [239] — an echo of its Aryan prototype, Brahmâ-Vâch.   After which come the Third and Fourth Root-Races of mankind [240] — that is to say, Races of men and women, or individuals of opposite sexes, no longer sexless semi-spirits and androgynes, as were the two Races which precede them.   This fact is hinted at in every Anthropogony.   It is found in fable and allegory, in myth and *revealed* Scriptures, in legend and tradition.   Because, of all the great Mysteries, inherited by Initiates from hoary antiquity, this is *one of the greatest.*   It accounts for the bi-sexual element found in every creative deity, in Brahmâ-Virâj-Vâch, as in Adam-Jehovah-Eve, also in "Cain-Jehovah-Abel."   For " The Book of the Generations of Adam " does not even mention Cain and Abel, but says only: " Male and female created he them . . . and called their name Adam." [241]   Then it proceeds to say: "And Adam begat a son in *his own likeness,* after his image, and called his name Seth";[242] after which he begets other sons and daughters, thus proving that Cain and Abel are his own allegorical permutations.   Adam stands for the primitive *human* race, especially in its cosmo-sidereal sense.   Not so, however, in its theo-anthropological meaning.   The compound name of Jehovah, or *Jah-Hovah,* meaning *male life* and female life — first androgynous, then separated into sexes — is used in this sense in *Genesis* from ch. v. on-wards.   As the author of *The Sources of Measures* says:[243] " The two words of which Jehovah is composed make up the original idea of male-female, as the birth originator (for the Hebrew letter *Jod* was the *membrum virile* and *Hovah* was Eve)," the mother of all living, or the procreatrix, Earth and Nature.   The author believes, therefore, that " It is seen that the *perfect one* " (the perfect female circle or *Yoni,* 20612, *numerically*), " as *originator of measures,* takes also the form of *birth*-origin, as *Hermaphrodite one*; hence the phallic form and use."

Precisely; only " the phallic form and use " came long ages later; and the first and original meaning of Enos, the son of Seth, was the First *Race* born in the present usual way from man and woman — for Seth is no man, but a *race.*   Before him humanity was hermaphrodite. While Seth is the first result (physiologically) after the FALL, he is also separating into man and woman, and becoming JAH-HEVA in one form,

---

primeval generative Principle, and so are Brahmâ, in exoteric teaching, and Adam, in the Kabala.

238. Abel is Chebel, meaning " Pains of Birth," conception.

239. See *"Isis Unveiled,"* Vol. II, p. 398, where Jehovah is shown to be Adam and Eve

blended, and *Hevah,* and Abel, the *feminine serpent.*

240. See *" Isis Unveiled,"* Vol. I, 305: " The union of the two creates a *third* Race," etc.

241. *Genesis,* v. 2.

242. *Genesis,* v. 3.

243. Page 159.

the *first man;* hence his son Enos is referred to as the " Son of man." (*Vide infra*)   Seth represents the *later* Third Race.

To screen the real mystery name of AIN-SOPH — the Boundless and Endless *No-Thing* — the Kabalists have brought forward the compound *attribute*-appellation of one of the personal creative Elohim, whose name was *Yah* and *Jah*, the letters *i* or *j* or *y* being interchangeable, or *Jah-Hovah, i. e., male* and *female;*[244] *Jah-Eve* a *hermaphrodite*, or the *first form of humanity*, the original Adam of Earth, not even *Adam Kadmon*, whose " mind-born son " is the earthly Jah-Hovah, mystically.   And knowing this, the crafty Rabbin-Kabalist has made of it a name so secret, that he could not divulge it later on without exposing the whole scheme; and thus he was obliged to make it *sacred*.

How close is the identity between Brahmâ-Prajâpati and Jehovah-Sephiroth, between Brahmâ-Virâj and Jehovah-Adam, the Bible and the Purânas compared can alone show.   Analysed and read in the same light, they afford cogent evidence that they are two copies of the same original — made at two periods far distant from each other.   Compare once more in relation to this subject *Genesis* ch. iv, verses 1 and 26 and *Manu* I, and they will both yield their meaning.   In *Manu*[246] Brahmâ, who is also both man and god, and divides his body into male and female, stands in his esoteric meaning, as does Jehovah or Adam in the Bible, for the symbolical personification of creative and *generative* power, both divine and human.   The *Zohar* affords still more convincing proof of identity, while some Rabbins repeat word for word certain original Purânic expressions; *e. g.*, the "creation" of the world is generally considered in the Brâhmanical books to be the Lîlâ, delight or sport, the amusement of the Supreme Creator.

Vishnu being thus discrete and indiscrete substance, spirit, and time, sports like a playful boy in frolics.[246]

Now compare this with what is said in the Book, *Nobeleth 'Hokhmah:*

The Qabbalists say that the entering into existence of the worlds happens through *delight*, in that Ain-Soph [?!] *rejoiced* in Itself, and flashed and beamed from Itself to Itself . . . which are all called delight. [etc.] [247]

Thus it is not a " curious idea of the Qabbalists," as the author just quoted remarks, but a purely Purânic, Aryan idea.   Only, why make of Ain-Soph a Creator?

The " Divine Hermaphrodite " is then Brahmâ-Vâch-Virâj ; and that of the Semites, or rather of the Jews, is Jehovah-Cain-Abel.   Only the

244. *Jod* in the Kabala has for symbol the hand, the forefinger and the *lingam*, while numerically it is the perfect one; but it is also the number 10, male and female, when divided.

245. Book I, 32.

246. *Vishnu Purâna*, Book I, ch. ii.

247. Quoted in Myer's *Qabbalah*, page 110.

"Heathen" were, and are, more sincere and frank than were the later Israelites and Rabbis, who undeniably knew the real meaning of their exoteric deity. The Jews regard the name given to them — the Yah-oudi — as an insult. Yet they have, or would have if they only wished it, as undeniable a right to call themselves the ancient Yah-oudi, "Jah-hovians," as the Brâhmans have to call themselves Brâhmans, *after their national deity.* For Jah-hovah is the generic name of that group or hierarchy of creative planetary angels, under whose star their nation has evolved. He is one of the planetary *Elohim* of the regent group of Saturn. Verse 26 of *Genesis,* ch. iv, when read correctly, would alone give them such a right, for it calls the new race of men sprung from Seth and Enos, *Jehovah,* something quite different from the translation adopted in the Bible: — " To him also, was born a son, Enos; then began men to call themselves *Jah* or Yah-hovah," to wit, *men and women,* the "lords of creation." One has but to read the above-mentioned verse in the original Hebrew text and by the light of the Kabala, to find that, instead of the words as they now stand translated, it is: — " Then began men to *call themselves Jehovah,"* which is the correct translation, and not " Then began men to call upon the name of the Lord "; the latter being a mistranslation, whether deliberate or not. Again the well-known passage: "I have gotten a man from the Lord," should read: " I have gotten a man, even Jehovah."[248] Luther translated the passage one way, the Roman Catholics quite differently. Bishop Wordsworth renders it: "Cain — *I have gotten.* Kain, from *Kânithi,* I have gotten." Luther: "I have gotten a man — even the Lord " (Jehovah); and the author of *The Source of Measures:* " I have *measured a man,* even *Jehovah."* The last is the correct rendering, because (*a*) a famous Rabbin, a Kabalist, explained the passage to the writer in precisely this way, and (*b*) because this rendering is identical with that in the Secret Doctrine of the East with regard to Brahmâ. In *" Isis Unveiled,"* [249] it was explained by the writer that "Cain . . . is the son of the 'Lord' not of Adam."[250] The "Lord" is Adam Kadmon, the "father" of *Yodcheva,* "Adam-Eve," or Jehovah, the son of sinful thought, not the progeny of flesh and blood. Seth on the other hand, is the *leader and the progenitor of the Races of the Earth;* for he is the son of Adam, exoterically, but esoterically he is the progeny of Cain and Abel, since Abel or Hebel is a female, the counterpart and female half of the male Cain, and Adam is the collective name for man and woman: "male and female (*Zachar va Nakobeh*) created he them . . . and called *their* name Adam." The verses in *Genesis* from chs. i. to v., are purposely mixed up for Kabalistic reasons. After MAN of

248. See *Source of Measures,* p. 277.   249. Vol. II, p. 464, *et seq.*   250. *Genesis,* iv. 1.

Genesis ch. i. 26 and *Enos*, Son of Man of ch. iv. 26, after Adam, the first androgyne, after Adam Kadmon, the sexless (the first) *Logos*, Adam and Eve once separated, come finally Jehovah-Eve and Cain-Jehovah. These represent distinct Root-Races, for millions of years elapsed between them.

Hence the Aryan and the Semitic Theo-anthropographies are two leaves on the same stem; their respective personifications and symbolic personages standing in relation to each other in this way.

1. The *Unknowable*, referred to in various ways in *Rig Vedic* verse, such as "*Nought* Was," called later on " Parabrahm "; the אין (*Ain*, nothing, or the "Ain-Soph" of the Kabalists), and again, the " Spirit " (of God) that moves upon the face of the waters, in *Genesis*. All these are *identical*. Moreover, in *Genesis*, ch. i. 2 is placed as verse 1 in the *secret* Kabalistic texts, where it is followed by the *Elohim* "creating the Heaven and the Earth." This deliberate shifting of the order of the verses was necessary for *monotheistic* and Kabalistic purposes. Jeremiah's curse against those Elohim (gods) who *have not created* the Heavens and the Earth (ch. x. 11), shows that there were other Elohim who had.

II. The " Heavenly " *Manu-Svâyambhuva*, who sprang from Svayambhû-Nârâyana, the " Self-existent," and Adam Kadmon of the Kabalists, and the androgyne MAN of *Genesis* ch. i., are also identical.

III. Manu-svâyambhuva is Brahmâ, or the Logos; and he is Adam Kadmon, who in *Genesis* iv. separates himself into two halves, male and female, thus becoming Jah-Hovah or Jehovah-Eve; as Manu Svâyambhuva or Brahmâ separates himself to become " Brahmâ-Virâj and Vâch-Virâj," male and female; all the rest of the texts and versions being *blinds*.

IV. Vâch is the daughter of Brahmâ and is named *Sata-Rûpâ*, " the hundred-formed," and *Sâvitrî*, " *generatrix*," the mother of the gods and of all living. She is identical with Eve, " the mother (of all the lords or gods or) of all living." Besides this there are many other occult meanings.

What is written in " *Isis*," although scattered about and very cautiously expressed at the time, is correct:

Explaining esoterically Ezekiel's wheel,[251] it is said of *Jodheva* or Jehovah:—

When the ternary is taken in the beginning of the Tetragram, it expresses the divine creation *spiritually*, without any carnal sin; taken at its opposite end it expresses the latter: it is feminine. The name of Eve is composed of three letters, that of the primitive or heavenly Adam is written with one letter,

251. *Isis Unveiled*, Vol. II, p. 462.

Jod or Yodh; therefore it must not be read Jehovah but Ieva, or Eve. The Adam of the first chapter is the spiritual, therefore pure, androgyne Adam Kadmon. When woman issues from the rib of the second Adam (of dust), the pure *Virgo* is separated, and falling "into generation," or the downward cycle, becomes *Scorpio,* emblem of sin and matter. While the ascending cycle points to the purely spiritual races, or the ten prediluvian patriarchs, the Prajâpatis and Sephiroth are led on by the creative Deity itself, who is Adam Kadmon or Yod-cheva. Spiritually, the lower one (Jehovah) is that of the terrestrial races, led on by Enoch or *Libra,* the seventh; who, because he is half-divine, half-terrestrial, is said to have been taken by God alive. Enoch, Hermes, and Libra, are one.

This is only one of the several meanings. No need to remind the scholar that *Scorpio* is the astrological sign of the organs of reproduction. Like the Indian Rishis, the Patriarchs are all convertible in their numbers, as well as interchangeable. According to the subject to which they relate they become ten, twelve, seven or five, and even *fourteen,* and they have the same esoteric meaning as the *Manus* or Rishis.

Moreover, Jehovah, as may be shown, has a variety of etymologies, but only those are *true* which are found in the Kabala. יהוה (*Ieve*) is the Old Testament term, and was pronounced *Ya-va.* Inman suggests that it is contracted from the two words יהו יה *Yaho-Iah, Jaho-Jah,* or *Jaho is Jah.* Punctuated it is יְהוָֹה which is, however, a Rabbinical caprice to associate it with the name *Adoni* or אֲדֹנָי, which has the same points. It is curious, and indeed hardly conceivable, that the Jews anciently read the name יהוה (*Adoni*), when they had so many names of which *Jeho* and *Jah* and *Iah* constituted a part. But so it was; and Philo Byblius, who gives us the so-called fragment of Sanchoniathon, spelled it in Greek letters ΊΕΥΩ, *Javo* or *Jevo.* Theodoret says that the Samaritans pronounced *Yahva,* and the Jews *Yaho.* Professor Gibbs, however, suggests its punctuation thus: יְהֹוֶה (*Ye-hou-vih*); and he cut the Gordian knot of its true occult meaning. For in this last form, as a Hebrew verb, it means "he will — be."[252] It was also derived from the Chaldaic verb הוא or הוה *eue* (*eva*) or *eua* (*Eva*) "to be." And so it was, since from *Enosh,* the "Son of Man," only, were the truly human races to begin and "to be," as males and females. This statement receives further corroboration, inasmuch as Parkhurst makes the verb הוה to mean: (1) "To fall down" (*i. e.,* into generation or matter); and (2) "*To be, to continue*" — as

___

252. See for comparison *Hosea,* xii. 6, where it is so punctuated.

a *race*. The aspirate of the word *eua* (*Eva*) "to be" being הוה *Heve* (*Eve*), which is the feminine of יהוה and the same as Hebe, the Grecian goddess of youth and the Olympian bride of Herakles, makes the name Jehovah appear still more clearly in its primitive double-sexed form.

Finding in Sanskrit such syllables as *Jah* and *Yah*, *e. g., Jôh-*(*navî*) "Ganges," and *Jagan-nâtha*, "Lord of the World," it becomes clear why Mr. Rawlinson is so very confident in his works of an *Aryan* or *Vedic* influence on the early mythology of Babylon. Nor is it to be much wondered at that the alleged ten tribes of Israel disappeared during the captivity period, without leaving a trace behind them, when we are informed that the Jews had *de facto* but two tribes — those of *Judah* and of *Levi*. The *Levites,* moreover, were not a tribe at all, but a priestly caste. The descendants have only followed their progenitors, the various patriarchs, into thin, sidereal air. There were *Brahms* and *A-brahms,* in days of old, truly, and before the first Jew had been born. Every nation held its first god and gods to be androgynous; nor could it be otherwise, since they regarded their distant primeval progenitors, their dual-sexed ancestors, as divine Beings and Gods, just as do the Chinese to this day. And they were divine in one sense, as also were their first human progeny, the "mind-born" primitive humanity, which were most assuredly bi-sexual, as all the more ancient symbols and traditions show. "Under the emblematical devices and peculiar phraseology of the priesthood of old, lie latent hints of sciences as yet undiscovered during the present cycle. Well acquainted as may be a scholar with the hieratic writing and hieroglyphical system of the Egyptians, he must first of all learn to sift their records. He has to assure himself, compasses and rule in hand, that the picture-writing he is examining fits, to a line, *certain fixed geometrical figures* which are the hidden keys to such records, before he ventures on an interpretation.

"But there are myths which speak for themselves. In this class we may include the double-sexed first creators of every Cosmogony. The Greek Zeus-Zen (Aether), and Chthonia (the chaotic earth) and Metis (water), his wives; Osiris and Isis-Latona — the former god also representing Aether, the first emanation of the Supreme Deity, Amun, the primeval source of Light; the goddess Earth and Water again; Mithras, the rock-born god, the symbol of the male mundane fire, or the personified primordial light, and Mithra, the fire goddess, at once his mother and his wife; the pure element of fire (the active, or male principle) regarded as light and heat, in conjunction with Earth and Water, or Matter, the female or passive element of cosmical generation "[252a]— all these are records of the primeval divine Hermaphrodite.

[252a]. *Isis Unveiled,* I, 156.

STANZA VI

THE EVOLUTION OF THE "SWEAT-BORN"

§§ (22) The evolution of the three races continued. (23) The second race creates the Third and perishes.

22. THEN THE SECOND EVOLVED THE SWEAT-BORN, THE THIRD (*Race*). THE SWEAT GREW, ITS DROPS GREW, AND THE DROPS BECAME HARD AND ROUND. THE SUN WARMED IT; THE MOON COOLED AND SHAPED IT; THE WIND FED IT UNTIL ITS RIPENESS. THE WHITE SWAN FROM THE STARRY VAULT (*the Moon*), OVERSHADOWED THE BIG DROP. THE EGG OF THE FUTURE RACE, THE MAN-SWAN (*Hamsa*) OF THE LATER THIRD (*a*). FIRST MALE-FEMALE, THEN MAN AND WOMAN (*b*).

(*a*) The text of the Stanza clearly implies that the human embryo was nourished *ab extra* by Cosmic forces, and that the "Father-Mother" furnished apparently the germ that ripened: in all probability a "sweat-born egg," to be hatched out, in some mysterious way, disconnected from the "double" parent. It is comparatively easy to conceive of an oviparous humanity, since even now man is, in one sense, "egg-born." Magendie, moreover,[253] citing "a case where the umbilical cord was ruptured and perfectly cicatrized," yet the infant was born alive, pertinently asks, "How was the circulation carried on in this organ?" On the next page he says: "Nothing is at present known respecting the use of digestion in the fetus"; and respecting its nutrition, propounds this query: "What, then, can we say of the nutrition of the fetus? Physiological works contain only *vague conjectures* on this point." "Ah, but," the sceptic may urge, "Magendie's book belongs to the last generation, and Science has since made such strides that his stigma of ignorance can no longer be fixed upon the profession." Indeed; then let us turn to a very great authority upon Physiology, viz., Sir M. Foster;[254] and to the disadvantage of modern Science we shall find him saying:

Concerning the rise and development of the functional activities of the embryo, our knowledge is almost a blank. We know scarcely anything about the various steps by which the primary fundamental qualities of the protoplasm of the ovum are differentiated into the complex phenomena which we have attempted in this book to explain.

253. In his *Précis Élémentaire de Physiologie*.

254. *Text-Book of Physiology*, third edition, 1879, p. 623.

The students of Trin. Coll. Cantab. will now kindly draw a veil before the statue of Hygieia and bandage the eyes of the busts of Galen
and Hippokrates, lest they should look reproachfully at their degenerate descendants. One further fact we must note. Sir M. Foster is
discreetly silent about the case of the ruptured umbilical cord cited
by his great French *confrère*.

This is a very curious statement as explained in the Commentaries.
To make it clear: The First Race having created the Second by " budding," as just explained, the Second Race gives birth to the Third —
which itself is separated into three distinct divisions, consisting of men
differently procreated. The first two of these are produced by an
oviparous method, presumably unknown to modern Natural History.
While the early sub-races of the Third Humanity procreated their
species by a kind of exudation of moisture or vital fluid, the drops of
which coalescing formed an oviform ball—or shall we say egg?—which
served as an extraneous vehicle for the generation therein of a *fetus*
and child, the mode of procreation by the later races changed, in its
results at all events. The little ones of the earlier races were entirely
sexless — shapeless even for all one knows;[255] but those of the later
races were born androgynous. It is in the Third Race that the separation of sexes occurred. From being previously a-sexual, Humanity
became distinctly hermaphrodite or bi-sexual; and finally the man-
bearing eggs began to give birth, gradually and almost imperceptibly in
their evolutionary development, first, to Beings in which one sex pre-
dominated over the other, and, finally, to distinct men and women. And
now let us search for corroboration of these statements in the religious
legends of East and West. Let us take the " Egg-born Race " first.
Think of Kaśyapa, the Vedic sage, and the most prolific of creators.
He was the son of Marîchi, Brahmâ's mind-born son; and he is made
to become the father of the *Nâgas*, or Serpents, among other beings.
Exoterically, the *Nâgas* are semi-divine beings which have a human
face and the tail of a serpent. Yet there was a race of *Nâgas*, said to
be a thousand in number only, born or rather sprung from Kadrû,
Kaśyapa's wife, for *the purpose of peopling Pâtâla,* which is undeniably
America, as will be shown; and there was a NâGA-Dvîpa, one of the
seven divisions of Bhârata-Varsha, India, inhabited by a people bearing the same name, who are allowed, even by some Orientalists, to be
historical, and to have left many a trace behind them to this day.

Now the point most insisted upon at present is that, whatever origin
be claimed for man, his evolution took place in this order: (1) Sexless,
as all the earlier forms are; (2) then, by a natural transition, he

255. See the *Timaios.*

became, "a solitary hermaphrodite," a bi-sexual being; and (3) finally separated and became what he is now. Science teaches us that all the primitive forms, though sexless, "still retained the power of undergoing the processes of A-Sexual multiplication"; why, then, should man be excluded from that law of Nature? Bi-sexual reproduction is an evolution, a specialized and perfected form on the scale of matter of the fissiparous act of reproduction. Occult teachings are preeminently panspermic, and the early history of humanity is hidden only "from ordinary mortals"; nor is the history of the primitive Races buried from the Initiates in the tomb of time, as it is for profane science. Therefore, supported on the one hand by that science which shows to us progressive development and an internal cause for every external modification, as a law in Nature; and, on the other hand, by an implicit faith in the wisdom — we may say pansophia even — of the universal traditions gathered and preserved by the Initiates, who have perfected them into an almost faultless system — thus supported, we venture to state the doctrine clearly.

In an able article, written some fifteen years ago, our learned and respected friend, Prof. Alex. Wilder, of New York, shows the absolute logic and necessity of believing "The Primeval Race Double-Sexed," and gives a number of scientific reasons for it.[256] He argues firstly,

that a large part of the vegetable creation exhibits the phenomenon of bisexuality . . . the Linnaean classification enumerating thus almost all plants. This is the case in the superior families of the vegetable kingdoms as much as in the lower forms, from the Hemp to the Lombardy Poplar and Ailantus. In the animal kingdom, in insect life, the moth generates a worm, as in the *Mysteries* the great secret was expressed: "*Taurus Draconem genuit, et Taurum Draco.*" The coral-producing family, which, according to Agassiz, "has spent many hundreds of thousands of years, during the present geological period, in building out the peninsula of Florida . . . produce their offspring from themselves like the buds and ramifications in a tree." Bees are somewhat in the same line. . . . The Aphides or plant lice, keep house like Amazons, and *virgin parents* perpetuate the Race for ten successive generations.

What say the old sages, the philosopher-teachers of antiquity? Aristophanes speaks thus on the subject in Plato's *Banquet:*

Our nature of old was not the same as it is now. It was *androgynous*, the form and name partaking of, and being common to both the male and female. . . . Their bodies were round, and the manner of their running circular.[257]

They were terrible in force and strength and had prodigious ambition. Hence Zeus *divided each of them into two*, making them weaker; Apollo, under his direction, closed up the skin.

Meshia and Meshiane were but a single individual with the old Persians.

They also taught that man was the product of the tree of life, growing in androgynous pairs, till they were separated at a subsequent modification of the human form.[258]

In the *Toleduth* (generations) of Adam, the verse "God created (*bara*, brought forth) man in his image, in the image of God created he him, male and female created he them," if read esoterically will yield the true sense, viz.: "The *Elohim* [Gods] brought forth from themselves [by modification] man in their image . . . created they *him* [collective humanity, or *Adam*], male and female created *he* [collective deity] them."[259] This will show the esoteric point. The *sexless* Race was their first production, a modification *of* and *from* themselves, the pure spiritual existences; and this was Adam *solus*. Thence came the *second* Race: Adam-Eve or *Jod-Heva*, inactive androgynes; and finally the *Third*, or the "*Separating* Hermaphrodite," Cain and Abel, who produce the Fourth, Seth-Enos, etc. It is that Third, the last semi-spiritual *race*, which was also the last vehicle of the divine and innate Wisdom, ingenerate in the Enochs, the Seers of that Mankind. The *Fourth*, which had tasted from the fruit of the Tree of Good and Evil — Wisdom united already to earthy, and therefore *impure* intelligence[260] — had consequently to acquire that Wisdom by initiation and great struggle. And the union of Wisdom and Intelligence, the former *ruling* the latter, is called in the Hermetic books "the God possessing the double fecundity of the two sexes." Mystically Jesus was held to be man-woman. See also in the *Orphic Hymns*, sung during the

---

258. See Professor Wilder's Essay, *The Primeval Race Double-Sexed.*

259. Eugibinus, a Christian, and the Rabbis Samuel, Manasseh ben Israel, and Maimonides taught that "Adam had *two faces* and *one* person, and from the beginning he was both male and female — male on one side and female on the other [like Manu's Brahmâ], but afterwards the parts were separated." The one hundred and thirty-ninth Psalm of David recited by Rabbi Jeremiah ben Eliazar is evidence of this, "Thou hast *fashioned* me behind and before," not *beset* as in the Bible, which is absurd and meaningless, and this shows, as Professor Wilder thinks, "that the primeval form of mankind was androgynous."

260. See the union of *Chochmah*, Wisdom, with *Binah*, Intelligence, or Jehovah, the *Demiurge*, called *Understanding* in the *Proverbs of Solomon*, ch. vii. Unto men Wisdom (divine occult Wisdom) crieth: "Oh, ye simple, understand Wisdom; and ye fools, be *of an understanding heart.*" It is *spirit* and *matter*, the *nous* and the *psyche*; of the latter of which St. James says that it is "earthly, sensual, and devilish."

Mysteries, we find: "Zeus is a male, Zeus is an immortal maid." The Egyptian Amen was the goddess Neïth, in his other half. Jupiter has female breasts, Venus is bearded in some of her statues, and Ilâ, the goddess, is also Su-Dyumna, the god, as Vaivasvata's progeny. Says Professor A. Wilder:—

The name *Adam,* or man, itself implies this double form of existence. It is identical with *Athamas,* or *Thomas* (Tamil *Tam*), which is rendered by the Greek *Didumos,* a twin; if, therefore, the first woman was formed subsequently to the first man, she must, as a logical necessity, be "taken out of man" . . . and the *side* which the *Elohim* had taken from man, "made he a woman." [260a] The Hebrew word here used is *Tzala,* which bears the translation we have given. It is easy to trace the legend in Berosus, who says that *Thalatth* (the *Omoroka,* or Lady of Urka) was the beginning of creation. She was also Melita, the queen of the Moon. . . . The two twin births of *Genesis,* that of Cain and Abel, and of Esau and Jacob, shadow the same idea. *The name "Hebel" is the same as Eve,* and its characteristic seems to be feminine,

continues the author. "Unto thee shall be his desire," said the Lord God to Cain, "and thou shalt rule over him." The same language had been uttered to Eve: "Thy desire shall be to thy husband, and he shall rule over thee." . . .

Thus the pristine bi-sexual unity of the human *Third* Root-Race is an axiom in the Secret Doctrine. Its virgin individuals were raised to "Gods," because that Race represented their "divine Dynasty." The moderns are satisfied with worshiping the male heroes of the Fourth Race, who created gods after their own sexual image, whereas the gods of primeval mankind were "male and female."

As stated in Book I, the humanities developed co-ordinately, and on parallel lines with the four Elements, every new Race being physiologically adapted to meet the additional element. Our Fifth Race is rapidly approaching the Fifth Element — call it interstellar ether, if you will — which has more to do, however, with psychology than with physics. We men have learned to live in every climate, whether frigid or tropical, but the first two Races had nought to do with climate, nor were they subservient to any temperature or change therein. And thus, we are taught, men lived down to the close of the Third Root-Race, when eternal spring reigned over the whole globe, such as is now enjoyed by the inhabitants of Jupiter; a "world," says M. Flammarion, "which is not subject like our own to the vicissitudes of seasons nor to abrupt alternations of temperature, but which is enriched with all the treasures of eternal spring." [261] Those astronomers who maintain that Jupiter is in a molten condition, in our sense of the term, are invited

260a. *Genesis,* ii.   261. *Pluralité des Mondes,* p. 69.

to settle their dispute with this learned French Astronomer.[262]   It must, however, be always borne in mind that the "eternal spring" referred to is only a condition *cognized as such by the Jovians*. It is not "spring" *as we know it*. In this reservation is to be found the reconciliation between the two theories here cited. Both embrace *partial* truths.

It is thus a universal tradition that mankind has evolved gradually into its present shape from an almost transparent condition of texture, and neither by miracle nor by sexual intercourse. Moreover, this is in full accord with the ancient philosophies; from those of Egypt and India with their Divine Dynasties down to that of Plato. And all these universal beliefs must be classed with the "presentiments" and "obstinate conceptions," some of them ineradicable, in popular faiths. Such beliefs, as remarked by Louis Figuier, are "frequently the outcome of the wisdom and observation of an infinite number of generations of men." For, "*a tradition which has a uniform and universal existence,*

---

262. A hypothesis evolved in 1881 by Mr. Mattieu Williams seems to have impressed Astronomers but little. Says the author of "The Fuel of the Sun," in *Knowledge*, Dec. 23, 1881: "Applying now the researches of Dr. Andrews to the conditions of Solar existence . . . I conclude that the Sun has *no nucleus*, either solid, liquid, or gaseous, but is composed of dissociated matter in the critical state, surrounded, first, by a flaming envelope, due to the recombination of the dissociated matter, and outside of this, by another envelope of vapors due to this combination."

This is a novel theory to be added to other hypotheses, *all scientific and orthodox*. The meaning of the "*critical* state" is explained by Mr. M. Williams in the same journal (Dec. 9, 1881), in an article on "Solids, Liquids, and Gases." Speaking of an experiment by Dr. Andrews on carbonic acid, the scientist says that "when 88° is reached, the boundary between liquid and gas vanished; *liquid and gas have blended into one mysterious intermediate fluid; an indefinite fluctuating something is there filling the whole of the tube — an etherealised liquid or a visible gas.* Hold a red-hot poker between your eye and the light; you will see an upflowing wave of movement of what appears like liquid air. The appearance of

the *hybrid* fluid in the tube resembles this, but is sensibly denser, and evidently stands between the liquid and gaseous states of matter, as pitch or treacle stands between solid and liquid."

The *temperature at which this occurs has been named by Dr. Andrews the "critical temperature"*; here the gaseous and the liquid states are "*continuous*," and it is probable that *all other substances capable of existing* in both states have their own particular critical temperatures.

Speculating further upon this "critical" state, Mr. Mattieu Williams emits some quite *occult* theories about Jupiter and other planets. He says : "*Our notions of solids, liquids, and gases are derived from our experiences of the state of matter here upon this Earth. Could we be removed to another planet, they would be curiously changed.* On Mercury water would rank as one of the condensible gases; on Mars, as a fusible solid; but what on Jupiter?"

"Recent observations justify us in regarding this as a miniature sun, with an external envelope of cloudy matter, apparently of partially-condensed water, but red-hot, or probably still hotter within. His vaporous atmosphere is evidently of enormous depth, and the force of gravitation being on his visible outer surface two-and-a-half times

has all the weight of scientific testimony." [263]   And there is more than one such tradition in the Purânic allegories, as has been shown. Moreover, the doctrine that the first Race of mankind was formed out of the *chhâyâs* (astral images) of the Pitris, is fully corroborated in the *Zohar.* " In the *Tzalam,* shadow image, of Elohim [the Pitris], was made Adam (man)." [264]

It has been repeatedly urged as an objection that, however high the degree of metaphysical thought in ancient India, yet the old Egyptians had nothing but crass idolatry and zoolatry to boast of; Hermes, as alleged, being the work of mystic Greeks who lived in Egypt.   To this, one answer can be given — a direct proof that the Egyptians believed in the Secret Doctrine is, that it was taught to them at Initiation. Let the objectors open the *Eclogae Physicae et Ethicae* of Stobaeus, the Greek compiler of ancient fragments, who lived in the fifth century, A. D.   The following is a transcription by him of an old Hermetic fragment, showing the Egyptian theory of the Soul.   Translated word for word, it says:—

From one Soul, that of ALL, spring all the Souls, which spread themselves as if purposely distributed through the world. These souls undergo many transformations; those which are already creeping creatures turn into aquatic animals; from these aquatic animals are derived land animals; and from the latter the birds. From the beings who live aloft in the air (heaven) men

greater than that on our Earth's surface, the atmospheric pressure, in descending below this visible surface, must soon reach that at which the vapor of water would be brought to its critical condition.   Therefore we may infer that *the oceans of Jupiter are neither of frozen, liquid, nor gaseous water, but are oceans or atmospheres of critical water.   If any fish or birds swim or fly therein, they must be very critically organised."*

As the whole mass of Jupiter is 300 times greater than that of the Earth, and its compressing energy towards the center proportional to this, its materials, if similar to those of the Earth, and no hotter, would be considerably more dense, and the whole planet would have a higher specific gravity; but we know by the movement of its satellites that, instead of this, its specific gravity is less than a fourth of that of the Earth. This justifies the conclusion that it is intensely hot; for even hydrogen, if cold,

would become denser than Jupiter under such pressure.

" As all elementary substances may exist as solids, liquids, or gases, or critically, according to the conditions of temperature and pressure, I am justified in hypothetically concluding that *Jupiter is neither a solid, a liquid, nor a gaseous planet, but a critical planet, or an orb composed internally of associated elements in the critical state, and surrounded by a dense atmosphere of their vapors* and those of some of their compounds such as water. The same reasoning applies to Saturn and other large and rarefied planets."

It is gratifying to see how *scientific imagination* approaches every year more closely to the borderland of our occult teachings.

263. *The Day After Death,* p. 23.

264. Cremona Ed., iii, 76a; Brody Ed., iii, 159a; *Qabbalah,* Isaac Myer, p. 420.

are born. On reaching that status of men, the Souls receive the principle of (conscious) immortality, become Spirits, then pass into the choir of gods.

---

23. THE SELF-BORN WERE THE CHHÂYÂS, THE SHADOWS FROM THE BODIES OF THE SONS OF TWILIGHT. NEITHER WATER NOR FIRE COULD DESTROY THEM. THEIR SONS WERE (*so destroyed*) (*a*).

(*a*) This verse cannot be understood without the help of the Commentaries. It means that the First Root-Race, the " Shadows " of the Progenitors, could not be injured, or destroyed by death. Being so ethereal and so little human in constitution, they could not be affected by any element — flood or fire. But their " Sons," the Second Root-Race, could be and were so destroyed. As the "progenitors" merged wholly in their own astral bodies, which were their progeny; so that progeny was absorbed in its descendants, the " Sweat-born." These were the second Humanity—composed of the most heterogeneous gigantic semi-human monsters—the first attempts of material nature at building human bodies. The ever-blooming lands of the Second Continent (Greenland, among others) were transformed, in order, from Edens with their eternal spring, into hyperborean Hades. This transformation was due to the displacement of the great waters of the globe, to oceans changing their beds; and the bulk of the Second Race perished in this first great throe of the evolution and consolidation of the globe during the human period. Of such great cataclysms there have already been four.[265] And we may expect a fifth for ourselves in due course of time.

A FEW WORDS ABOUT " DELUGES " AND " NOAHS "

The accounts in the various Purânas about our Progenitors are as contradictory *in their details* as everything else. Thus while, *in the Rig Veda*, Idâ (or Ilâ) is called the Instructress of Vaivasvata Manu, Sâyana makes of her a goddess presiding over the Earth, and the *Satapatha Brâhmana* shows her to be the Manu's daughter, an *offspring of his sacrifice*, and, later on, his (Vaivasvata's) *wife, by whom he begat the race of Manus.* In the Purânas, again, she is Vaivasvata's daughter, yet the wife of Budha (Wisdom), the illegitimate son of the Moon (Soma) and the planet Jupiter's (*Brihaspati's*) wife, Târâ.

---

265. The first occurred when what is now the North Pole was separated from the later Continents.

All this, which seems a jumble to the profane, is full of philosophical meaning to the Occultist. On the very face of the narrative a secret and sacred meaning is perceivable, all the details, however, being so purposely mixed up that the experienced eye of an Initiate alone can follow them and place the events in their proper order.

The story as told in the *Mahâbhârata*[265a] strikes the key-note, and yet it needs to be explained by the secret sense contained in the *Bhagavad Gîtâ*. It is the *prolog to the drama* of our (Fifth) Humanity. While Vaivasvata was engaged in devotion on the river bank, a fish craves his protection from a bigger fish. He saves and places it in a jar, where, growing larger and larger, it communicates to him the news of the forthcoming deluge. It is the well-known " Matsya-Avatâra," the first Avatâr of Vishnu, the *Dagon*[266] of the Chaldaean Xisuthrus, and many other things besides. The story is too well known to need repetition. Vishnu orders a ship to be built, in which Manu is said to be saved along with the seven Rishis, the latter, however, being absent from other texts. Here the seven Rishis stand for the *seven Races,* the seven principles, and various other things; for there is again a double mystery involved in this manifold allegory.

We have said elsewhere that the great Flood had several meanings, and that it referred, as also does the FALL, to both spiritual and physical, cosmic and terrestrial, events: as above, so it is below. The ship or ark — *navis* — in short, being the symbol of the female generative principle, is typified in the heavens by the Moon, and on Earth by the Womb: both being the vessels and bearers of the seeds of life and being, which the sun, or Vishnu, the male principle, vivifies and fructifies.[267] The First Cosmic Flood refers to primordial creation, or the formation of Heaven and the Earths; in which case Chaos and the great Deep stand for the " Flood," and the Moon for the " Mother," from whom proceed all the life-germs.[268] But the terrestrial Deluge

265a. Vana-parva, clxxxvi.

266. We must remember that at the head of all the Babylonian gods were Ea, Anu, and the primeval Bel; and that Ea, the first, was the God of Wisdom, the great "God of Light" and of the DEEP, and that he was identified with Oannes, or the Biblical Dagon — the man-fish who rose out of the Persian Gulf.

267. See Part II, § xvii, "The Holy of Holies."

268. It is far later on that the Moon became a male god; with the Hindûs it was Soma, with the Chaldeans Nannak or Nannar, and Sin, the son of Mulil, the older Bel. The "Akkadians" called him the "Lord of Ghosts"; and he was the god of Nippur

(Niffer) in northern Babylonia. It is Mulil who caused the waters of the Flood to fall from heaven on Earth, for which Xisuthrus would not allow him to approach his altar. As the modern Assyriologists have now ascertained, it is the northern Nippur which is the center whence Chaldean (black) magic spread; and Eridu (the Southern) which was the primitive seat of the worship of the culture god, the god of divine wisdom — the Sun-God being the supreme deity everywhere. With the Jews, the Moon is connected with Israel's Jehovah and his seed, because Ur was the chief seat of the worship of the Moon-god, and because Abraham is said to have come from Ur, when from A-bra(h)m, he becomes Abraham.

and its story has also its dual application. In one case it has reference to that mystery when mankind was saved from utter destruction, by the mortal woman being made the receptacle of the human seed at the end of the Third Race,[269] and in the other to the real and historical Atlantean submersion. In both cases the "Host"—or the Manu which saved the *seed*—is called Vaivasvata Manu. Hence the diversity between the Purânic and other versions; while in the *Satapatha Brâhmana*, Vaivasvata produces a daughter and begets from her the race of Manu; which is a reference to the first human *Manushyas*, who had to create women by will (*Kriyâśakti*), before they were naturally born from the hermaphrodites as an independent sex, and who were, therefore, regarded as their creator's *daughters*. The Purânic accounts make of her (*Idâ* or *Ilâ*) the wife of Budha (Wisdom), the latter version referring to the events of the Atlantean flood, when Vaivasvata, the great Sage on Earth, saved the Fifth Root-race from being destroyed along with the remnants of the Fourth.

This is shown very clearly in the *Bhagavad Gîtâ*, where Krishna is made to say:—

The Seven great Rishis, the *four preceding Manus,* partaking of my essence, were born from my mind: from them sprang (were born) the human races and the world.[270]

Here the four preceding "Manus," out of the seven, are the four Races [271] which have already lived, since Krishna belongs to the Fifth Race, his death having inaugurated the Kali Yuga. Thus Vaivasvata Manu, the son of Sûrya (the Sun), and the savior of our Race, is

269. When Nârada, the virgin-ascetic, threatened to put an end to the human race by preventing Daksha's sons from pro-creating it.

270. Chapter x, verse 6.

271. This is corroborated by a learned Brâhman. In his most excellent lectures on the *Bhagavad Gîtâ* (see *Theosophist,* April, 1887, page 444) the lecturer says: "There is a peculiarity to which I must call your attention. He (Krishna) speaks here of four Manus. Why does he speak of four? We are now in the seventh Man-vantara, that of Vaivasvata. If he is speak-ing of the past Manus, he ought to speak of six, but he only mentions four. In some commentaries an attempt has been made to interpret this in a peculiar manner. The word 'Chatvârah' is separated from the word 'Manavah,' and is made to refer to Sanaka, Sanandana, Sanatkumâra, and Sa-natsujâta, who are also included among the mind-born sons of Prajâpati. But this in-terpretation will lead to a most absurd con-clusion, and make the sentence contradict itself. The persons alluded to in the text have a qualifying clause in the sentence. It is well known that Sanaka and the other three refused to create, though the other sons had consented to do so; therefore, in speaking of those persons from whom hu-manity has sprung into existence, it would be absurd to include these four also in the list. The passage must be interpreted with-out splitting the compound into two nouns. The number of Manus will then be four, and the statement would then contradict the Purânic account, though it would be in har-mony with the occult theory. You will recollect that it is stated [in Occultism] that we are now in the Fifth Root-Race. Each Root-Race is considered as the *San-tati* of a particular Manu. Now, the Fourth Race has passed, or, in other words, there have been four past Manus. . . ."

connected with the *Seed of Life,* both physically and spiritually. But, at present, while speaking of all, we have to concern ourselves only with the first two.

The " Deluge " is undeniably a *universal tradition.* " Glacial periods " were numerous, and so were the " Deluges," for various reasons. Stockwell and Croll enumerate some half dozen Glacial Periods and subsequent Deluges — the earliest of all being dated by them 850,000, and the last about 100,000 years ago.[272] But which was *our* Deluge? Assuredly the former, the one which to this date remains recorded in the traditions of all the peoples, from the remotest antiquity; the one that finally swept away the last peninsulas of Atlantis, beginning with Ruta and Daitya and ending with the (comparatively) small island mentioned by Plato. This is shown by the agreement of certain details in all the legends. It was the last of its gigantic character. The little deluge, the traces of which Baron Bunsen found in Central Asia, and which he places at about 10,000 years B. C., had nothing to do with either the *semi*-universal Deluge, or Noah's flood — the latter being a purely mythical rendering of old traditions — nor even with the submersion of the last Atlantean island; at least, only a moral connexion.

Our Fifth Race (the non-initiated portions), hearing of many deluges, confused them, and now know of but one. This one altered the whole aspect of the globe in its interchange and shifting of land and sea.

We may compare the traditions of the Peruvians: — " The Incas, *seven* in number, have repeopled the Earth after the deluge," they say;[273] Humboldt mentions the Mexican version of the same legend, but confuses somewhat the details of the still-preserved legend concerning the American Noah. Nevertheless, the eminent Naturalist mentions *twice seven* companions and the *divine bird* which preceded the boat of the Aztecs, and thus makes fifteen elect instead of the seven and the fourteen. This was written probably under some involuntary reminiscence of Moses, who is said to have mentioned fifteen grandsons of Noah, who escaped with their grandsire. Then again Xisuthrus, the Chaldaean Noah, is saved and translated *alive* to heaven — like Enoch — with the seven gods, the *Kabirim,* or the seven divine Titans; again the Chinese *Yao* has *seven* figures which sail with him and which he will *animate* when he lands, and use for " human seed." Osiris, when he enters the ark, or solar boat, takes *seven* Rays with him, etc., etc.

Sanchoniathon makes the *Aletae* or Titans (the Kabirim) contempo-

---

272. *Smithsonian Contributions to Knowledge,* xviii; *American Journal of Science,* III, xi, 456; and Croll's *Climate and Time.*

273. Acosta, bk. VI, chap. 19.

Lemuria was not submerged by a flood, but was destroyed by volcanic action, and afterwards sank.

rary with Agruerus, the great Phoenician god (whom Faber sought to identify with Noah [274]); further, it is suspected that the name of " Titan " is derived from *Tit-Ain* — " the fountains of the chaotic abyss " [275] (Tit-theus, or Tityus is " the *divine deluge* "); and thus the Titans, who are *seven,* are shown to be connected with the Flood and the seven Rishis saved by Vaivasvata Manu.[276]

They are the sons of Kronos (Time) and Rhea (the Earth); and as Agruerus, Saturn and Sydyk are one and the same personage, and as the seven Kabiri are said to be the sons of Sydyk or Kronos-Saturn, the Kabiri and Titans are identical. For once the pious Faber was right in his conclusions when he wrote: " I have no doubt of the seven Titans and Cabiri being the same as the seven Rishis of the Hindû *mythology* [?], who are said to have escaped in a boat along with Manu, the head [?] of the family."

But he is less fortunate in his speculations when he adds " The Hindûs, in their *wild* legends have *variously perverted the history of the Noachidae* [?!], yet it is remarkable that they seem to have religiously adhered to the number seven." [277] Hence Captain (Col.) Wilford very judiciously observes that:

Perhaps the seven Manus, the seven Brahmâdicas and the seven Rishis are the same, and make only seven individual persons.[278] The seven Brahmâdicas were Prajâpatis, or lords "of the prajas or creatures." From them mankind was born, and they are probably the same with the seven Manus. . . . These seven grand ancestors of the human race were created for the purpose of replenishing the Earth with inhabitants.[279]

and Faber adds that:— " the mutual resemblance of the Cabiri, the Titans, the Rishis, and the Noetic family, is too striking to be the effect of mere accident." [280]

Faber was led into this mistake, and subsequently built his entire theory concerning the Kabiri, on the fact that the name of the scriptural Japhet is on the list of the Titans contained in a verse of the Orphic hymns. According to Orpheus the names of the seven

274. Agruerus is *Kronos,* or Saturn, and the prototype of the Israelitish Jehovah. As connected with *Argha,* the Moon or Ark of salvation, Noah is mythologically one with Saturn. But then this cannot relate to the terrestrial flood. (*But see Faber's* " *Cabiri,*" *Vol. I, pp.* 35, 43, *and* 45.)
275. See *ibid.,* Vol. II, p. 240.
276. Sanchoniathon says that the Titans were the sons of Kronos, and seven in number; and he calls them fire-worshipers, Aletae (sons of Agni?), and diluvians. Al-ait is the god of fire.

277. Of which *seven,* let us remark, the Aryans, and not the Semites, were the originators, while the Jews got that number from the Chaldaeans.
278. Seven individual sons of God, or Pitars and Pitris; also in this case the sons of Kronos or Saturn (*Kâla* " time ") and *Arkites,* like the Kabiri and Titans, as their name — "*lunar* ancestors " — shows, the Moon being the Ark, or *Argha,* on the watery abyss of space.
279. *Asiatic Researches,* Vol. V, p. 246.
280. See *Cabiri,* Vol. I, p. 131.

"Arkite" Titans (whom Faber refuses to identify with the *impious* Titans, their descendants) were Koios, Krios, Phorkys, Kronos, Okeanos, Hyperion, and *Iapetos:* —

Κοίόν τε, Κρίόν τε μέγαν, Φόρκυν τε κραταιόν,
Καὶ Κρόνον, Ὠκεανόν θ', Ὑπερίονά τ', Ἰαπετόν τε.[281]

But why could not the Babylonian Ezra have adopted the name of *Iapetos* for one of Noah's sons? The Kabiri, who are the Titans, are also called Manes and their mother Mania, according to Arnobius.[282] The Hindûs can therefore claim with far more reason that the Manes mean their Manus, and that Mania is the *female* Manu. (See *Râmâyana*.) Mania is Ilâ or Idâ, the wife and daughter of Vaivasvata Manu, from whom "he begat the race of Manus." Like *Rhea*, the mother of the Titans, she is the Earth (Sâyana making her the goddess of the Earth), and she is but the second edition and repetition of Vâch. Both *Idâ* and *Vâch* are turned into males and females; Idâ becoming Sudyumna, and Vâch, "the female Virâj," turning into a woman in order to punish the Gandharvas; one version referring to cosmic and divine theogony, the other to the later period. The *Manes* and Mania of Arnobius are names of Indian origin, appropriated by the Greeks and Latins and disfigured by them.

Thus it is no accident, but the result of one archaic doctrine common to all, of which the Israelites, through Ezra, the author of the modernized Mosaic books, were the latest adapters. So unceremonious were they with other people's property, that Berosus [283] shows that *Titea* — of whom Diodorus makes the mother of the Titans or *Diluvians* [284] — was the *wife of Noah*. For this Faber calls him the "*pseudo-Berosus*," yet accepts the information in order to register one proof more that the pagans have borrowed all their gods from the Jews, by transforming patriarchal material. According to our humble opinion, this is one of the best proofs possible of exactly the reverse. It shows as clearly as facts can show, that it is the Biblical *pseudo*-personages which are all borrowed from pagan myths, if myths they must be. It shows, at any rate, that Berosus was well aware of the source of *Genesis*, and that it bore the same cosmic astronomical character as the allegories of Isis-Osiris, and the Ark, and other older "Arkite" symbols. For, Berosus says that "Titea Magna" was afterwards called *Aretia*,[285] and worshiped with the Earth; and this identifies

281. *Orph. apud Proclum.* In *Tim.*, lib. v, p. 295.
282. *Adversum Gentes*, lib. III, p. 124.
283. *Antiquitates Libyae* 1, fol. 8.
284. See *Bibl.*, lib. III, p. 170.
285. Aretia is the female form of Artes (Egyptian Mars). Thence the Chaldaean (and now Hebrew) word ארץ (*Aretz*) "Earth." The author of *Beiträge zur Kenntniss* (Art. under "*Artes*" Mars) quotes: "*Addit Cedrenus (Salem I, 3): Stella Martis ab Egyptiis vocatur Ertosi*

" Titea," Noah's consort, with *Rhea*, the mother of the Titans, and with *Idâ* — both being goddesses who preside over the Earth, and the mothers of the Manus and Manes (or Tit-an-Kabiri). And " Titea-Aretia " was worshiped as *Horchia*, says the same Berosus, and this is a title of Vesta, goddess of the Earth. " *Sicanus deificavit Aretiam, et nominavit eam lingua Janigena Horchiam.*" [286]

Scarce an ancient poet of historic or prehistoric days who failed to mention the sinking of the two continents — often called isles — in one form or another. Hence the destruction, besides Atlantis, of the Phlegyae. (See Pausanias and Nonnus, who both tell how:

> From its deep-rooted base the Phlegyan isle
> Stern Neptune shook, and plunged beneath the waves
> Its impious inhabitants. . . .) [287]

Faber felt convinced that the " insulae Phlegyae " were Atlantis. But all such allegories are more or less distorted echoes of the Hindû tradition about that great Cataclysm, which befell the Fourth, really human, though gigantic, Race, the one which preceded the Aryan. Yet, as just said, like all other legends, that of " the Deluge has more than one meaning. It refers in Theogony, to *pre-cosmic transformations*, to *spiritual correlations* — however absurd the term may sound to a scientific ear — and also to subsequent Cosmogony; to the great FLOOD of WATERS (matter) in CHAOS, awakened and fructified by those Spirit-Rays which were swamped by, and *perished* in, the mysterious differentiation — a pre-cosmic mystery, the Prolog to the drama of Being. Anu, Bel, and Noah preceded Adam Kadmon, Adam the Red, and Noah; just as Brahmâ, Vishnu, and Śiva preceded Vaivasvata and the rest." [288]

All this goes to show that the *semi*-universal deluge known to geology (first glacial period) must have occurred just at the time allotted to it by the Secret Doctrine: namely, 200,000 years (in round numbers) after the commencement of our FIFTH RACE, or about the time assigned by Messrs. Croll and Stockwell for the first glacial period: *i. e.*, about 850,000 years ago. Thus, as the latter disturbance is attributed by geologists and astronomers to " an extreme eccentricity of the Earth's

---

(plantare, generare). Significat autem hoc omnis generis procreationem et vivificationem, omnisque substantiae et materiae naturam et vim ordinantem atque procreantem." It is Earth as " source of being "; or, as explained by the author of *The Source of Measures*, Arts is the same in *Hebrew* and *Egyptian*, and both combine the primeval idea of *Earth as source*; precisely as in the Hebrew itself, under another form, *Adam* and *Madim* (Mars) are the same, and combine the idea of Earth with Adam under the form of *H-Adam-H*.

286. *Ibid*, lib. V, fol. 64.
287. *Dionysiaka*, xviii, 319.
288. See " *Isis Unveiled*," Vol. II, pp. 420 *et seq.*, where one or two of the seven meanings are hinted at.

orbit," and as the Secret Doctrine attributes it to the same source, but with the addition of another factor, the shifting of the Earth's axis — a proof of which may be found in the *Book of Enoch*,[289] if the veiled language of the Purânas is not understood — all this should tend to show that the ancients knew something of the "modern discoveries" of Science. Enoch, when speaking of "the great inclination of the Earth," which "is in travail," is quite significant and clear.

Is not this evident? Nuah is Noah, *floating* on the waters in his ark; the latter being the emblem of the Argha, or Moon, the feminine principle; Noah is the "spirit" falling into matter. We find him, as soon as he descends upon the Earth, planting a vineyard, drinking of the wine, and getting drunk on it, *i. e.*, the pure spirit becomes intoxicated as soon as it is finally imprisoned in matter. The seventh chapter of *Genesis* is only another version of the First. Thus, while the latter reads: "and darkness was upon the face of the deep. And the spirit of God moved upon the face of the waters," in ch. 7 it is said ". . . and the waters prevailed . . . and the ark went [with Noah, the spirit] upon the face of the waters." Thus Noah, if identical with the Chaldaean Nuah, is the spirit vivifying *matter*, which latter is Chaos, represented by the DEEP, or the Waters of the Flood. In the Babylonian legend (the pre-cosmical blended with the terrestrial event) it is Istar (Astaroth or Venus, the lunar goddess) who is shut up in the ark and sends out "a *dove* in search of dry land."[290]

George Smith notes in the "*Tablets*," first the creation of the moon, and then that of the sun: "Its beauty and perfection are extolled, and the regularity of its orbit, which led to its being considered the type of a judge and the regulator of the world." If this story related simply to a cosmogonical cataclysm — even were this latter universal — why should the goddess Ishtar or Astoreth, the Moon, speak of the *creation of the sun* after the deluge? The waters might have reached as high as the mountain of *Nizir* (Chaldaean version), or Jebel Judi (the deluge mountains of the Arabian legend), or yet Ararat (of the Biblical narrative), and even the Himâlaya (of the Hindû tradition), and yet not reach the sun: the Bible itself stopped short of such a miracle! It is evident that the deluge of the people who first recorded it had another meaning, less problematical and far more philosophical than that of a *universal* deluge, of which there are no geological traces whatever.

As all such Cataclysms are periodical and cyclical, and as Manu Vaivasvata figures as a *generic* character, under various circumstances and events,[291] there seems to be no serious objection to the supposition

289. Chapter lxiv, Section xi.
290. "*Isis Unveiled*," vol. II, pp. 423 and 424.
291. *Vide infra*: "The Seven Manus of Humanity."

that the first "great flood" had an allegorical, as well as a cosmic meaning, and that it happened at the end of the Satya Yuga, the "age of Truth," when the *Second* Root Race, "The Manu with bones," made its primeval appearance as "the Sweat-Born." [292]

The Second Flood—the so-called "universal"—which affected the Fourth Root Race (now conveniently regarded by theology as "the accursed race of giants," the CAINITES, and "the sons of Ham") is that flood which was first perceived by geology. If one carefully compares the accounts in the various legends of the Chaldees and other exoteric works of the nations, it will be found that all of them agree with the orthodox narratives given in the Brâhmanical books. And it may be perceived that while, in the first account, "there is no God or mortal yet on Earth," when Manu Vaivasvata lands on the Himâvan; in the second, the Seven Rishis are allowed to keep him company: thus showing that whereas some accounts refer to the sidereal and cosmic FLOOD before the so-called creation, the others treat, one of the Great Flood of Matter on Earth, and the other of a real watery deluge. In the *Satapatha Brâhmana*, Manu finds that "the Flood had swept away all living creatures, and he alone was left"—*i.e., the seed of life* alone remained from the previous dissolution of the *Universe*, or *Mahâpralaya*, after a "Day of Brahmâ"; and the *Mahâbhârata* refers simply to the geological cataclysm which swept away nearly all the Fourth Race to make room for the Fifth. Therefore is Vaivasvata Manu shown under three distinct attributes in our esoteric Cosmogony: [293] (*a*) as the "Root-Manu" on Globe A in the First Round; (*b*) as the "*seed of life*" on Globe D in the Fourth Round; and (*c*) as the "Seed of Man" at the beginning of every Root-Race—in our Fifth Race

292. All such expressions are explained in the "Anthropogenesis" of this Book, and elsewhere.

293. One has to remember that, in the Hindû philosophy, every differentiated unit is such only through the cycles of Mâyâ, being one in its essence with the Supreme or One Spirit. Hence arises the seeming confusion and contradiction in the various Purânas, and at times in the same Purâna, about the same individual. Vishnu — as the many-formed Brahmâ, and as Brahma (neuter) — is one, and yet he is said to be all the 28 Vyâsas (*Vishnu Purâna*). "In every Dvâpara (third) age, *Vishnu, in the person of Vyâsa*, divides the Veda, which is one, into four and many portions. Twenty-eight times have the Vedas been arranged by the great Rishis in the Vaivasvata Manvantara, in the Dvâpara Yuga ... and, consequently, twenty-eight Vyâsas have passed away ... they who were all *in the form of Veda-Vyâsas,* who were the Vyâsas of their respective eras...." (*Op. cit.,* Bk. III, ch. iii.) "This world is Brahmâ in Brahmâ, from Brahmâ ... nothing further to be known." Then, again "... There were in the First Manvantara seven celebrated sons of Vasishtha, who, in the *Third* Manvantara, were sons of Brahmâ (*i. e.,* Rishis), the illustrious progeny of Ûrjâ." This is plain: the Humanity of the First Manvantara is that of the seventh and of all the intermediate ones. The mankind of the First Root-Race is the mankind of the *second, third, fourth, fifth,* etc. To the last it forms a cyclic and constant reincarnation of the Monads belonging to the Dhyân Chohans of our Planetary chain.

especially. The very commencement of the latter witnesses, during the Dvâpara Yuga,[294] the destruction of the accursed sorcerers; " of that island [Plato speaking only of its last island] beyond the Pillars of Hercules, in the Atlantic Ocean, from which there was an easy transition to other islands in the neighborhood of another *large Continent* " (America).[294a] It is this "Atlantic" land which was connected with the " *White Island*," and this White Island was Ruta; but it was not the Atala and the " *White Devil* " of Colonel Wilford,[295] as already shown. It may well be remarked here that the Dvâpara Yuga lasts 864,000 years, according to the Sanskrit texts; and that, if the *Kali Yuga* began only about 5000 years ago, that it is just 869,000 since that destruction took place. Again, these figures are not very widely different from those given by the geologists, who place their " glacial period " 850,000 years ago.

Then " a woman was produced who came to Manu and declared *herself his daughter, with whom he lived and begat the offspring of Manu.*" This refers to the physiological transformation of sexes during the Third Root-Race. And the allegory is too transparently clear to need much explanation. Of course, as already remarked, in the separation of sexes an androgyne being was supposed to divide his body into two halves (as in the case of Brahmâ and Vâch, and even of Adam and Eve), and thus the female is, in a certain sense, his daughter, just as he will be her son, " the flesh of his (and her) flesh and the bone of his (and her) bone." Let it be also well remembered that not one of our Orientalists have yet learned to discern in those " contradictions and amazing nonsense," as some call the Purânas, that a reference to a Yuga may mean a Round, a Root-Race, and often a *Sub-Race*, as well as form a page torn out of pre-cosmic theogony. This double and triple meaning is proved by various references to one and the same individual apparently, under an identical name, while it refers, in fact, to events divided by entire Kalpas. A good instance is that of Ilâ. She is first represented as one thing and then as another. In the exoteric legends it is said that Manu Vaivasvata, desiring to create sons, instituted a sacrifice to Mitra and Varuna; but, through a mistake of the officiating

294. The Dvâpara Yuga differs for each Race. All races have their own cycles, which fact causes a great difference. For instance, the Fourth Sub-Race of the Atlanteans was in its Kali-Yuga, when destroyed, whereas the Fifth was in its Satya or *Krita* Yuga. The Aryan Race is now in its Kali Yuga, and will continue to be in it for 427,000 years longer, while various " family Races," called the Semitic, Hamitic, etc., are in their own special cycles. The forthcoming 6th Sub Race — which may begin very soon — will be in its Satya (golden) age while we reap the fruit of our iniquity in our Kali Yuga.

294a. *Timaios*, 25.

295. See *Asiatic Researches*, Vol. viii, page 280.

Brâhman, a daughter only was obtained — Ilâ. Then, " through the favor of the gods," her *sex is changed* and she becomes a man, *Su-dyumna*. Then she is again turned into a woman, and so on; the fable adding that Śiva and his consort were pleased that "she would be male one month and female another." This has a direct reference to the Third Root-Race, whose men were androgynes. But some very learned Orientalists think [296] and have declared that " Ilâ was primarily food, nourishment, or a libation of milk; thence a stream of praise, personi-fied as the goddess of speech." The "profane" are not told, however, the reason why " a libation of milk," or " a stream of praise," should be *male* and *female* by turn: unless, indeed there is some " internal evidence " which the occultists fail to perceive.

In their most mystical meanings, the union of Svâyambhuva Manu with Vâch-Śata-Rûpâ, his own daughter (this being the first " euhem-erization " of the dual principle of which Vaivasvata Manu and Ilâ are a secondary and a third form), stands in Cosmic symbolism as the Root-life, the germ from which spring all the Solar Systems, the worlds, angels and the gods. For, as says Vishnu:—

From Manu all creation, gods, Asuras, man must be produced,
By him the world must be created, that which moves and moveth not. . . .

But we may find worse opponents than even the Western Scientists and Orientalists. If, on the question of figures, Brâhmans may agree with our teaching, we are not so sure that some of them, orthodox conservatives, may not raise objections to the modes of procreation attributed to their *Pitar-Devatâs*. We shall be called upon to produce the works from which we quote, while they will be invited by us to read their own Purânas a little more carefully and with an eye to the esoteric meaning. And then, we repeat again, they will find, under the veil of more or less transparent allegories, every statement made herein cor-roborated by their own works. One or two instances have already been given as regards the appearance of the Second Race, which is called the " Sweat-Born." This allegory is regarded as a fairy-tale, and yet it conceals a psycho-physiological phenomenon, and one of the greatest mysteries of Nature.

But in view of the chronological statements made herein, it is natural to ask:—

COULD MEN EXIST 18,000,000 YEARS AGO?

To this Occultism answers in the affirmative, notwithstanding all scientific objectors. Moreover, this duration covers only the Vaivas-vata-Manu *Man*, *i. e.*, the male and female entity already separated into

296. See *Hindû Classical Dictionary.*

distinct sexes. The two and a half Races that preceded that event may have lived 300,000,000 years ago for all that science can tell. For the geological and physical difficulties in the way of the theory could not exist for the *primeval, ethereal* man of the Occult teachings. *The whole issue of the quarrel between the profane and the esoteric sciences depends upon the belief in, and demonstration of, the existence of an astral body within the physical,* the former independent of the latter. Paul d'Assier, the Positivist, seems to have proven the fact pretty plainly,[297] not to speak of the accumulated testimony of the ages, and that of the modern spiritualists and mystics. It will be found difficult to reject this fact in our age of proofs, tests, and ocular demonstrations.

The Secret Doctrine maintains that, notwithstanding the general cataclysms and disturbances of our globe, which — owing to its being the period of its greatest physical development, for the Fourth Round is the middle-point of the life allotted to it — were far more terrible and intense than during any of the three preceding Rounds (the cycles of its earlier psychic and spiritual life and of its semi-ethereal conditions) physical Humanity has existed upon it for the last 18,000,000 years.[298] This period was preceded by 300,000,000 years of the mineral and vegetable development. To this, all those who refuse to accept the theory of a " boneless," purely ethereal, man, will object. Science, which knows only of physical organisms, will feel indignant; and materialistic theology still more so. The first will object on logical and reasonable grounds, based upon the preconception that all animate organisms have always existed on the same plane of materiality in all the ages; the last on a tissue of most absurd fictions. The ridiculous claim usually brought forward by theologians, is based on the virtual assumption that mankind (read Christians) on this planet have the honor of being the only human beings in the whole Kosmos, who dwell on a globe, and that they are consequently, the best of their kind.[299]

The Occultists, who believe firmly in the teachings of the mother-

297. *Posthumous Humanity* — translated by H. S. Olcott, London, 1887.

298. Professor Newcomb says: " The heat evolved by contraction would last only 18,000,000 years" (*Popular Astronomy*, page 500); but " a temperature permitting the existence of water could not be reached earlier than 10,000,000 years ago." (Winchell's *World-Life*, p. 356.) But Sir W. Thomson says that the whole age of the incrustation of the Earth is 18,000,000 years, though, this year, he has again altered his opinion and allows only 15,000,000 years as the age of the Sun. As will be shown in the

Addenda, the divergence of scientific opinions is so great that no reliance can ever be placed upon *scientific* speculation.

299. The essay on *The Plurality of Worlds* (1853) — an anonymous work, yet well known to have been the production of Dr. Whewell — is a good proof of this. No Christian ought to believe in either the plurality of worlds or the geological age of the globe, argues the Author; because, if it is asserted that this world is only one among the many of its kind, which are all the work of God, as it is itself; that all are the

philosophy, repel the objections of both theologians and scientists. They maintain, on their side, that, during those periods when there must have been insufferable heat, even at the two poles, successive floods, upheaval of the valleys and constant shifting of the great waters and seas, none of these circumstances could form an impediment to human life and organization, such *as is assigned by them to the early mankind*. Neither the heterogeneity of ambient regions, full of deleterious gases, nor the perils of a crust hardly consolidated, could prevent the First and Second Races from making their appearance even during the Carboniferous, or the Silurian age itself.

Thus the *Monads* destined to animate future Races were ready for the new transformation. They had passed their phases of immetalization, of plant and animal life, from the lowest to the highest, and were waiting for their human, more intelligent form. Yet, what could the plastic modelers do but follow the laws of evolutionary Nature? Could they, as claimed by the Biblical dead-letter, form " Lord-God "-like, or as Pygmalion in the Greek allegory, Adam-Galatea out of volcanic dust, and breathe a *living soul* into Man? No: because the soul was already there, latent in its *Monad*, and needed but a *coating*. Pygmalion, who fails to *animate his statue*, and Bahak-Zivo of the Nazaraean Gnostics, who fails to construct " a human soul in the creature," are as conceptions, far more philosophical and scientific than Adam, taken in the dead-letter sense, or the Biblical Elohim-Creators. Esoteric philosophy, which teaches spontaneous generation — after the Sishta and Prajâpati have thrown the seed of life on the Earth — shows the lower angels able to *construct physical* man only, even with the help of Nature, after having evolved the ethereal form out of themselves, and leaving the physical form to evolve gradually from its ethereal, or what would now be called, *protoplasmic* model.

This will again be objected to: " Spontaneous Generation " is an exploded theory, we shall be told. Pasteur's experiments disposed of it twenty years ago, and Professor Tyndall is against it. Well, suppose he is? He ought to know that, should spontaneous generation be

---

seat of life, all the realm and dwelling of intelligent creatures endowed with will, subject to law and capable of free-will; then, it would become extravagant to think that *our* world should have been the subject of God's favors and His special interference, of His communications and His *personal visit*. . . . Can the Earth presume to be considered the center of the moral and religious Universe, he asks, if it has not the slightest distinction to rely upon in the physical Universe? Is it not as absurd to uphold such an assertion (of the plurality of inhabited worlds), as it would be today to uphold the old hypothesis of Ptolemy, who placed Earth in the center of our system? . . . The above is quoted from memory, yet *almost textually*. The author fails to see that he is bursting his own soap-bubble with such a defense.

indeed proven impossible in our present world-period and actual conditions — which the Occultists deny — still it would be no demonstration that it could not have taken place under different cosmic conditions,
not only in the seas of the Laurentian period, but even on the then
convulsed Earth. It would be interesting to know how Science could
ever account for the appearance of species and life on Earth, especially
of *Man*, once that she rejects both the Biblical teachings and spontaneous generation. Pasteur's observations, however, are far from being
perfect or proven. Blanchard and Dr. Lutaud reject their importance
and show that they have none. The question is so far left *sub judice*,
as well as that other one "when, at what period, life appeared on the
Earth?" As to the idea that Haeckel's Moneron — a pinch of salt!
— has solved the problem of the origin of life, it is simply absurd.
Those materialists, who feel inclined to pooh-pooh the theory of the
"Self-existent," the "Self-born heavenly man," represented as an
ethereal, astral man, must excuse even a tyro in Occultism laughing,
in his turn, at some speculations of modern thought. After proving
most learnedly that the primitive speck of *protoplasm* (moneron) is
neither animal nor plant, but both, and that it *has no ancestors* among
either of these, since it is that moneron which serves as a point of
departure for all organized existence, we are finally told that *the
Monera are their own ancestors*. This may be very scientific, but
it is very metaphysical also; too much so, even for the Occultist.

If spontaneous generation has changed its methods now, owing
perhaps to accumulated material on hand, so as to almost escape detection, it was in full swing in the genesis of terrestrial life. Even the
simple physical form and the evolution of species show how Nature
proceeds. The scale-bound, gigantic sauria, the winged pterodactyl,
the Megalosaurus, and the hundred-feet long Iguanodon of the later
period, are the transformations of the earliest representatives of the
animal kingdom found in the sediments of the primary epoch. There
was a time when all those above enumerated "antediluvian" monsters
appeared as filamentoid infusoria without shell or crust, with neither
nerves, muscles, organs nor sex, and reproduced their kind by gemmation: as do microscopical animals also, the architects and builders of
our mountain ranges, agreeably to the teachings of science. Why not
man in this case? Why should he not have followed the same law in
his growth, *i. e.*, gradual condensation? Every unprejudiced person
would prefer to believe that primeval humanity had at first an ethereal
— or, if so preferred, a huge filamentoid, jelly-like form, evolved by
gods or natural "forces," which grew, condensed throughout millions
of ages, and became gigantic, in its physical impulse and tendency,
until it settled into the huge, physical form of the Fourth Race Man,

— rather than believe him created of the dust of the Earth (*literally*), or from some unknown anthropoid ancestor.

Nor does our esoteric theory clash with scientific data, except on first appearance, as Dr. A. Wilson, F. R. S., says, in a letter to *Knowledge*.[300] "Evolution — rather Nature, in the light of evolution — has only been studied for some *twenty-five years or so.* That is, of course, a mere fractional space in the history of human thought." And just because of that we do not lose all hope that materialistic science will amend its ways, and will gradually accept the esoteric teachings — if even at first divorced from their (to science) too metaphysical elements.

Has the last word on the subject of Human evolution yet been said? Professor Huxley writes:

Each . . . answer to the great Question [Man's Real Place in Nature], invariably asserted by the followers of its propounder, if not by himself, to be *complete and final*, remains in high authority and esteem, *it may be for one century*, it may be for twenty, but, as invariably, time proves each reply to have been a *mere approximation to the truth — tolerable chiefly on account of the ignorance of those by whom it was accepted, and wholly intolerable when tested by the larger knowledge of their successors.* [!!]

Will this eminent Darwinian admit the possibility of his *pithecoid ancestry* being assignable to the list of "wholly intolerable beliefs," in the "larger knowledge" of Occultists? *But whence the savage?* Mere "rising to the civilized state" does not account for the evolution of form.

In the same letter, "The Evolution of Man," Dr. Wilson makes other strange confessions. Thus, he observes, in answer to the queries put to *Knowledge* by "G. M.":—

"Has evolution effected any change in man? If so, what change? If not, why not?" . . . If we refuse to admit (as science does) that man was created a perfect being, and then became degraded, there exists only another supposition — that of evolution. If man has arisen from a savage to a civilized state, that surely is evolution. *We do not yet know, because such knowledge is difficult to acquire, if the human frame is subject to the same influences as those of lower animals.* But there is little doubt that elevation from savagery to civilized life means and implies "evolution," and that of considerable extent. Mentally, man's evolution cannot be doubted; the ever-widening sphere of thought has sprung from small and rude beginnings, like language itself. But man's ways of life, his power of adaptation to his surroundings, and countless other circumstances, have made the facts and course of his "evolution" very difficult to trace.

This very difficulty ought to make the Evolutionists more cautious in their affirmations. But why is evolution *impossible*, if "man was

300, Dec. 23, 1881,

created a perfect being, and then became degraded"? At best it can only apply to the *outward, physical man*. As remarked in "*Isis Unveiled*," Darwin's evolution begins at the middle point, instead of commencing for man, as for everything else, from the universals. The Aristotle-Baconian method may have its advantages, but it has undeniably already demonstrated its defects. Pythagoras and Plato, who proceeded from the Universals downwards, are now shown more learned, in the light of modern science, than was Aristotle. For he opposed and denounced the idea of the revolution of the earth, and even of its rotundity. "Almost all those," he wrote, "who affirm that they have studied heaven in its uniformity, claim that the earth is in the center, but the philosophers of the Italian School, otherwise called the Pythagoreans, teach entirely the contrary. . . ." Because (*a*) the Pythagoreans were Initiates, and (*b*) they followed the deductive method. Whereas, Aristotle, the father of the inductive system, complained of those who taught that "the center of our system was occupied by the Sun, and the earth was only a star, which by a rotatory motion around the same center, produces night and day."[301] The same with regard to man. The theory taught in the Secret Doctrine, and now expounded, is the only one, which can — without falling into the absurdity of a "miraculous" man created out of the dust of the Earth, or the still greater fallacy of man evolving from a pinch of lime-salt, (the ex-protoplasmic moneron) — account for his appearance on Earth.

Analogy is the guiding law in Nature, the only true Ariadne's thread that can lead us, through the inextricable paths of her domain, toward her primal and final mysteries. Nature, as a creative potency, is infinite, and no generation of physical scientists can ever boast of having exhausted the list of her ways and methods, however uniform the laws upon which she proceeds. If we can conceive of a ball of Fire-mist becoming gradually — as it rolls through aeons of time in the interstellar spaces — a planet, a self-luminous globe, to settle into a *man-bearing* world or Earth, thus having passed from a soft plastic body into a rock-bound globe; and if we see on it everything evolving from the non-nucleated jelly-speck that becomes the sarcode[302] of the *moneron*, then passes from its *protistic* state[303] into the form of an animal, to grow into a gigantic reptilian monster of the Mesozoic times; then

---

301. Vide *De Coelo*, Book II, chapter 13.

302. Or what is more generally known as *Protoplasm*. This substance received its name of "*Sarcode*" from Prof. Dujardin Beaumetz far earlier.

303. The Monera are indeed *Protista*.

They are neither animals "nor plants," writes Haeckel; ". . . the whole body of the Moneron represents nothing more than a single thoroughly homogeneous particle of albumen in a firmly adhesive condition." (*Journal of Microscopical Science*, Jan. 1869, page 28.)

dwindles again into the (comparatively) dwarfish crocodile, now confined solely to tropical regions, and the universally common lizard [304] — how can man alone escape the general law? "There were giants on earth in those days," says *Genesis,* repeating the statement of all the other Eastern Scriptures; and the *Titans* are founded on anthropological and physiological fact.

And, as the hard-shelled crustacean was once upon a time a jelly-speck, "a thoroughly homogeneous particle of albumen in a firmly adhesive condition," so was the outward covering of primitive man, his early "coat of skin," *plus* an immortal spiritual monad, and a psychic temporary form and body within that shell. The modern, hard, muscular man, almost impervious to any climate, was, perhaps, some 25,000,000 years ago, just what the Haeckelian Moneron is, strictly "an organism without organs," an entirely homogeneous substance with a structureless albumen body within, and a human form only outwardly.

No man of science has the right, in this century, to find the figures of the Brâhmans preposterous in the question of Chronology; for their own calculations often exceed by far the claims made by esoteric science. This may easily be shown.

Helmholtz calculated that the cooling of our Earth from a temperature of 2000° to 200° Cent. must have occupied a period of no less than 350,000,000 years. Western science (including geology) seems generally to allow our globe an age of about 500,000,000 years altogether. Sir W. Thomson, however, limits the appearance of the earliest vegetable life to 100,000,000 years ago — a statement respectfully contradicted by the archaic records. Speculations, furthermore, vary daily in the domains of science. Meanwhile, some geologists are very much opposed to such limitation. "Volger . . . calculates, that the time requisite for the deposit of the strata known to us must at least have amounted to 648 millions of years . . ." Both time and space are infinite and eternal. "The Earth, as a material existence, is indeed infinite; the changes only which it has undergone can be determined by finite periods of time" (*Burmeister*). "We must therefore assume that the starry heaven is not merely in space, what no astronomer doubts, but also in time, without beginning or end; that it never was created, and is imperishable." (See *Czolbe.*) [305]

Czolbe repeats exactly what the Occultists say. But the Âryan Occultists, we may be told, knew nothing of these later speculations.

304. Behold the *Iguanodon* of the Mesozoic ages — the monster 100 feet long — now transformed into the small Iguana lizard of South America. Popular traditions about *giants* in days of old, and their mention in every mythology, including the Bible, may some day be shown to be founded on fact. In nature, the logic of analogy alone ought to make us accept these *traditions* as scientific verities.

305. *Force and Matter,* by L. Büchner, edited by J. F. Collingwood, P. R. S. L., p. 61.

"They were even ignorant of the globular form of our earth" (Coleman). To this the *Vishnu Purâna* contains a reply, which has forced certain Orientalists to open their eyes very widely.

. . . The Sun is stationed, for all time, in the middle of the day, and over against midnight, in all the *Dvipas* (continents), Maitreya! But the rising and the setting of the *Sun* being perpetually *opposite to each other* — and in the same way, all the cardinal points, and so the cross-points, Maitreya; people speak of the rising of the Sun where they see it; and where the Sun disappears, there, to them, is his setting. Of the Sun, which is always in *one and the same place*, there is neither setting nor rising, for what is called rising and *setting* are only the seeing and the *not* seeing the Sun.[306]

To this Fitzedward Hall remarks, "The Heliocentricism taught in this passage is remarkable. It is contradicted, however, a little further on." Contradicted *purposely*, because it was a secret temple-teaching. Martin Haug remarked the same teaching in another passage. It is useless to calumniate the Âryans any longer.

To return to the Chronology of the geologists and anthropologists. We are afraid Science has no reasonable grounds on which she could oppose the views of the Occultists in this direction. Except that "of man, the highest organic being of creation, not a trace was found in the primary strata; only in the uppermost, the so-called alluvial layer," is all that can be urged, so far. That man was *not the last member in the mammalian family*, but the first in *this Round*, is something that science will be forced to acknowledge one day. A similar view also has already been mooted in France on very high authority.

That man can be shown to have lived in the mid-Tertiary period, and in a geological age *when there did not yet exist one single specimen of the now known species of mammals*, is a statement that science *cannot* deny and which has now been proven by de Quatrefages.[307] But even supposing his existence in the Eocene period is not yet demonstrated, what period of time has elapsed since the Cretaceous period? We are aware of the fact that only the boldest geologists dare to place man further back than the Miocene age. But how long, we ask, is the duration of those ages and periods since the Mesozoic time? On this, after a good deal of speculation and wrangling, science is silent, the greatest authorities upon the subject being compelled to answer to the question: "We do not know." This ought to show that the men of science are no greater authorities in this matter than are the profane. If, according to Professor Huxley, "the time represented by the coal formation would be six millions of years," [308] how many more millions

306. *Vishnu Purâna*, Book II, ch. viii.
307. *Introduction à l'Étude des Races Humaines.*
308. *Modern Science and Modern Thought*, by S. Laing, page 32.

would be required to cover the time from the Jurassic period, or the middle of the so-called "Reptilian" age (when the Third Race appeared), up to the Miocene, when the bulk of the Fourth Race was submerged?[309]

The writer is well aware that those specialists, whose computations of the ages of the globe and man are the most liberal, always had the shyer majority against them. But this proves very little, since the majority rarely, if ever, turns out to be right in the long run. Harvey stood alone for many years. The advocates for crossing the Atlantic with steamers were in danger of ending their days in a lunatic asylum. Mesmer is classed to this day (in the Encyclopaedias) along with Cagliostro and St. Germain, as a charlatan and impostor. And now that Messrs. Charcot and Richet have vindicated Mesmer's claims, and that "Mesmerism" under its new name of Hypnotism — a false nose on a very old face — is accepted by science, it does not strengthen one's respect for that majority, when one sees the ease and unconcern with which its members treat of "Hypnotism," "Telepathic Impacts," and its other phenomena. They speak of it, in short, as if they had believed in it since the days of Solomon, and had never called its votaries, only a few years ago, "lunatics and impostors!"[310]

The same revulsion of thought is in store for the long period of years, claimed by esoteric philosophy as the age of sexual and physiological mankind. Therefore even the Stanza which says:—

"The mind-born, the boneless, gave being to the will-born with bones"; adding that this took place in the middle of the *Third* Race 18,000,000 years ago — has yet a chance of being accepted by future scientists.

As far as XIXth century thought is concerned, we shall be told, even by some personal friends who are imbued with an abnormal respect for the shifting conclusions of science, that such a statement is absurd. How much more improbable will appear our further assertion, to the effect that the antiquity of the *First* Race dates back millions of years beyond this again. For, although the exact figures are withheld, and it is out of the question to refer the incipient evolution of the primeval

---

309. "*Esoteric Buddhism,*" page 70.

310. The same fate is in store for spiritualistic phenomena and all the other psychological manifestations of the *inner* Man. Since the days of Hume, whose researches culminated in a nihilistic idealism, Psychology has gradually shifted its position to one of crass *materialism*. Hume is regarded as a psychologist, and yet he denied *a priori* the possibility of phenomena in which millions now believe, including many men of science. The Hylo-idealists of today are rank *Annihilationists*. The schools of Spencer and Bain are respectively positivist and materialist, and not metaphysical at all. It is *psychism* and not *psychology;* it reminds one as little of the Vedântic teaching as the pessimism of Schopenhauer and von Hartmann recalls the esoteric philosophy, the heart and soul of true Buddhism.

Divine Races with *certainty* to either the early Secondary, or the Primary ages of geology, one thing is clear: that the figures 18,000,000 of years, which embrace the duration of *sexual, physical,* man, have to be enormously increased if the whole process of spiritual, astral and physical development is taken into account. Many geologists, indeed, consider that the duration of the Quaternary and Tertiary Ages demands the concession of such an estimate; and it is quite certain that no terrestrial conditions whatever negative the hypothesis of an Eocene Man, if evidence for his reality is forthcoming. Occultists, who maintain that the above date carries us far back into the secondary or "Reptilian" age, may refer to M. de Quatrefages in support of the possible existence of man in that remote antiquity. But with regard to the earliest Root-Races the case is very different. If the thick agglomeration of vapors, charged with carbonic acid, that escaped from the soil or was held in suspension in the atmosphere since the commencement of sedimentation, offered a fatal obstacle to the life of human organisms as now known, how, it will be asked, could the primeval men have existed? This consideration is, in reality, out of court. Such terrestrial conditions as were then operative had no touch with the plane on which the evolution of the *ethereal astral* races proceeded. Only in relatively recent geological periods, has the spiral course of cyclic law swept mankind into the lowest grade of physical evolution — the plane of gross material causation. In those early ages, *astral* evolution was alone in progress, and the two planes, the astral and the physical,[311] though developing on parallel lines, had no direct point of contact with one another. It is obvious that a shadow-like *ethereal* man is related by virtue of his organization — if such it can be called — only to that plane from which the substance of his *Upâdhi* is derived.

There are things, perhaps, that may have escaped the *far-seeing* — but not *all-seeing* — eyes of our modern naturalists; yet it is Nature herself who undertakes to furnish the missing links. Agnostic speculative thinkers have to choose between the version given by the Secret Doctrine of the East, and the hopelessly materialistic Darwinian and Biblical accounts of the origin of man; between no soul and no spiritual evolution, and the Occult doctrine which repudiates "Special creation" and the "Evolutionist" Anthropogenesis equally.

Again, to take up the question of "Spontaneous generation"; life — as science shows — has not always reigned on this terrestrial plane.

311. It must be noted that, though the astral and physical planes of matter ran parallel with one another even in the earliest geological ages, yet they were not in the same phases of manifestation in which they are *now.* The Earth did not reach its present *grade of density* till 18,000,000 years ago. Since then *both* the physical and astral planes have become grosser.

There was a time when even the Haeckelian Moneron — that simple globule of Protoplasm—had not yet appeared at the bottom of the seas. Whence came the *Impulse* which caused the molecules of Carbon, Nitrogen, Oxygen, etc., to group themselves into the *Urschleim* of Oken, that organic " slime," now christened protoplasm. What were the prototypes of the Monera? They, at least, could not have fallen in meteorites from other globes already formed, Sir W. Thomson's wild theory to this effect, notwithstanding. And if *they have* so fallen; if our Earth got its supply of life-germs from other planets; who, or *what*, had carried them into those planets? Here, again, unless the Occult teaching is accepted, we are compelled once more to face a *miracle;* to accept the theory of a *personal, anthropomorphic Creator*, the attributes and definitions of whom, as formulated by the Monotheists, clash as much with philosophy and logic, as they degrade the ideal of an infinite Universal deity, before whose incomprehensible awful grandeur the highest human intellect feels dwarfed. Let not the modern philosopher, while arbitrarily placing himself on the highest pinnacle of human intellectuality hitherto evolved, show himself spiritually and intuitionally so far below the conceptions of even the ancient Greeks, themselves on a far lower level, in these respects, than the philosophers of Eastern Åryan antiquity. Hylozoism, when philosophically understood, is the highest aspect of Pantheism. It is the only possible escape from idiotic atheism based on lethal materiality, and the still more idiotic anthropomorphic conceptions of the monotheists; between which two it stands on its own entirely neutral ground. Hylozoism *demands* absolute Divine Thought, which would *pervade* the numberless active, creating Forces, or " Creators "; which *entities* are moved by, and have their being in, from, and through that Divine Thought; the latter, nevertheless, having no more personal concern in them or *their* creations, than the Sun has in the sun-flower and its seeds, or in vegetation in general. Such active " Creators " are known to exist and are believed in, because perceived and sensed by the *inner* man in the Occultist. Thus the latter says that an ABSOLUTE Deity, having to be unconditioned and unrelated, cannot be thought of at the same time as an active, creating, one living god, without immediate degradation of the ideal.[312] A Deity that manifests in *Space* and *Time* — these two being simply the forms of THAT which is the Absolute ALL — can be but a fractional part of the whole. And since that " all "

312. The conception and definition of the *Absolute* by Cardinal Cusa may satisfy only the Western mind, prisoned, so unconsciously to itself, and entirely degenerated by long centuries of scholastic and theological sophistry. But this " Recent philosophy of the Absolute," traced by Sir W. Hamilton to Cusa, would never satisfy the more acutely metaphysical mind of the Hindû Vedântin.

cannot be divided in its absoluteness, therefore that *sensed* creator (we say *Creators*) can be at best but the mere *aspect* thereof. To use the same metaphor — inadequate to express the full idea, yet well adapted to the case in hand — these creators are like the numerous rays of the solar orb, which remains unconscious of, and unconcerned in, the work; while its mediating agents, the rays, become the instrumental media every spring — the Manvantaric dawn of the Earth — in fructifying and awakening the dormant vitality inherent in Nature and its differentiated matter. This was so well understood in antiquity, that even the moderately religious Aristotle remarked that such work of direct creation would be quite *unbecoming* to God — ἀπρεπὲς τῷ Θεῷ. Plato and other philosophers taught the same: deity cannot set its own hand to creation,— αὐτουργεῖν ἄπαντα. This Cudworth calls " Hylozoism." As old Zeno is credited by Laertius with having said,

> Nature is a habit moved from itself, according to seminal principles; perfecting and containing those several things which in determinate times are produced from it, and acting agreeably to that from which it was secreted.[313]

Let us return to our subject, pausing to think over it. Indeed, if there was vegetable life during those periods that could feed on the then deleterious elements; and if there was even animal life whose aquatic organization could be developed, notwithstanding the supposed scarcity of Oxygen, why could there not be human life also, in its incipient physical form, *i.e.*, in a race of beings adapted for that geological period and its surroundings? Besides, science confesses that it knows nothing of the real length of " geological periods."

But the chief question before us is, whether it is quite certain that, from the time of that which is called the "Azoic" age, there ever was such an atmosphere as that hypothesized by the Naturalists. Not all the physicists agree with this idea. Were the writer anxious to corroborate the teachings of the Secret Doctrine by exact science, it would be easy to show, on the admission of more than one physicist, that the atmosphere has changed little, if at all, since the first condensation of the oceans—*i.e.*, since the Laurentian period, the *Pyrolithic* age. Such, at any rate, is the opinion of Blanchard, S. Meunier, and even of Bischof — as the experiments of the latter scientist with basalts have shown. For were we to take the word of the majority of scientists as to the quantity of deadly gases, and of elements entirely saturated with carbon and nitrogen, in which the vegetable and animal kingdoms are shown to have lived, thriven, and developed, then one would have to come to the curious conclusion that there were, in those days, oceans of *liquid carbonic acid*, instead of water. With such an element, it be-

313. Cudworth's *Intellectual System*, I, p. 328; Diog. Laert. *s. v.*, lxxiii.

comes doubtful whether the Ganoids, or even the Primitive Trilobites themselves could live in the oceans of the primary age — let alone in those of the Silurian, as shown by Blanchard.

The conditions that were necessary for the earliest race of mankind, however, require no elements, whether simple or compound. That which was stated at the beginning is maintained. The spiritual ethereal Entity which lived in Spaces unknown to Earth, before the first sidereal "jelly-speck" evolved in the ocean of crude Cosmic Matter,— billions and trillions of years before our globular speck in infinity, called Earth, came into being and generated the *Moneron* in its drops, called Oceans — needed no " elements." The " Manu with soft bones " could well dispense with calcic phosphate, as he had no bones, save in a figurative sense. And while even the Monera, however homogeneous their organism, still required physical conditions of life that would help them toward further evolution, the being which became primitive Man and the " Father of man," after evolving on planes of existence undreamt of by science, could well remain impervious to any state of atmospheric conditions around him. The primitive ancestor, in Brasseur de Bourbourg's " *Popul Vuh*," who — in the Mexican legends — could act and live with equal ease under ground and water as upon the Earth, answers only to the Second and early Third Races in our texts. And if the three kingdoms of Nature were so different in *pre*-diluvian ages, why should not man have been composed of materials and combinations of atoms now entirely unknown to physical science? The plants and animals now known, in almost numberless varieties and species, have all developed, according to scientific hypotheses, from primitive and far fewer organic forms. Why should not the same have occurred in the case of man, the elements, and the rest? " Universal Genesis starts from the one, breaks into three, then five, and finally culminates into seven, to return into four, three, and one." (Commentary.)

For additional proofs consult Part II. of this Volume, " The Septenary in Nature."

STANZA VII

FROM THE SEMI-DIVINE DOWN TO THE FIRST

HUMAN RACES

---

§ § (24) The higher creators reject in their pride the forms evolved by the "Sons of Yoga." (25) They will not incarnate in the early "Egg-born." .. (26) They select the later androgynes. (27) The first man endowed with mind.

---

24. THE SONS OF WISDOM, THE SONS OF NIGHT (*issued from the body of Brahmâ when it became Night*), READY FOR RE-BIRTH, CAME DOWN. THEY SAW THE (*intellectually*) VILE FORMS OF THE FIRST THIRD (*still senseless Race*) (*a*). "WE CAN CHOOSE," SAID THE LORDS, "WE HAVE WISDOM." SOME ENTERED THE CHHÂYÂS. SOME PROJECTED A SPARK. SOME DEFERRED TILL THE FOURTH (*Race*). FROM THEIR OWN ESSENCE THEY FILLED (*intensified*) THE KÂMA (*the vehicle of desire*). THOSE WHO RECEIVED BUT A SPARK REMAINED DESTITUTE OF (*higher*) KNOWLEDGE. THE SPARK BURNT LOW (*b*). THE THIRD REMAINED MINDLESS. THEIR JÎVAS (*Monads*) WERE NOT READY. THESE WERE SET APART AMONG THE SEVEN (*primitive human species*). THEY (*became the*) NARROW-HEADED. THE THIRD WERE READY. IN THESE SHALL WE DWELL, SAID THE LORDS OF THE FLAME AND OF THE DARK WISDOM (*c*).

This Stanza contains, in itself, the whole key to the mysteries of evil, the so-called Fall of the angels, and the many problems that have puzzled the brains of the philosophers from the time that the memory of man began. It solves the secret of the subsequent inequalities of intellectual capacity, of birth or social position, and gives a logical explanation to the incomprehensible Karmic course throughout the aeons which followed. The best explanation which can be given, in view of the difficulties of the subject, shall now be attempted.

(*a*) Up to the Fourth Round, and even to the later part of the Third Race in this Round, Man — if the ever-changing forms that clothed the Monads during the first three Rounds and the first two and a half races of the present one can be given that misleading name — is, so far, only an animal intellectually. It is only in the actual *midway* Round that he developes in himself entirely the fourth principle as a fit vehicle for the fifth. But Manas will be relatively *fully* developed only in the following Round, when it will have an opportunity of becoming entirely divine until the end of the Rounds. As Christian Schoettgen says in *Horae Hebraicae,* etc., the first terrestrial Adam " had only the breath of life," *Nephesh, but not the living Soul.*

(*b*) Here the *inferior* Races, of which there are still some analogs left — as the Australians (now fast dying out) and some African and Oceanic tribes — are meant. " *They were not ready* " signifies that the *Karmic* development of these Monads had not yet fitted them to occupy the forms of men destined for incarnation in higher intellectual Races. But this is explained later on.

(*c*) The *Zohar* speaks of " Black Fire," which is *Absolute* Light-Wisdom. To those who, prompted by old theological prejudice, may say : " But the *Asuras* are the rebel Devas, the *opponents of the Gods—* hence devils, and the spirits of Evil," it is answered : Esoteric philosophy admits neither good nor evil *per se,* as existing independently in nature. The cause for both is found, as regards the Kosmos, in the necessity of contraries or contrasts, and with respect to man, in his human nature, his ignorance and passions. There is no *devil* or the utterly depraved, as there are no Angels absolutely perfect, though there may be spirits of Light and of Darkness ; thus LUCIFER — the spirit of Intellectual Enlightenment and Freedom of Thought—is metaphorically the guiding beacon, which helps man to find his way through the rocks and sand-banks of Life, for Lucifer is the LOGOS in his highest, and the " Adversary " in his lowest aspect — both of which are reflected in our *Ego.* Lactantius, speaking of the Nature of Christ, makes the LOGOS, the *Word, the first-born brother of Satan,* the " *first of all creatures." * [314]

The *Vishnu Purâna* describes these primeval creatures (the *Tiryak-srotas*) with *crooked* digestive canals : They were "endowed with inward manifestations, but mutually in ignorance about *their kind and nature.*" The twenty-eight kinds of *Bâdhas,* or imperfections, do not apply, as Wilson thought, to the animals now known and specified by him,[315] for these did not exist in those geological periods. This is quite plain in the said work, in which the first created (on this globe) are the " five-fold immovable creation," minerals and vegetables ; then come those fabulous animals, *Tiryaksrotas,* (the monsters of the abyss slain by the " Lords" [316]) ; then the *Ûrdhvasrotas,* the happy celestial beings, which

314. *Inst. Div.,* Book II, chap. viii ; I. Myer's *Qabbalah,* 116.
315. See Book I, chap. v, 71, *Vishnu Purâna,* Wilson's translation.
316. See Stanzas II and III.

feed on ambrosia; then lastly, the *Arvâksrotas,* human beings —
Brahmâ's seventh creation so-called. But these " creations," including
the latter, did not occur on this globe, wherever else they may have taken
place. It is not Brahmâ who creates things and men on this Earth, but
the chief and Lord of the Prajâpati, the Lords of Being and terrestrial
Creation.[317] Obeying the command of Brahmâ, Daksha (the synthesis,
or the aggregate, of the terrestrial creators and progenitors, Pitris
included) made superior and inferior (*vara* and *avara*) things "referring to *putra*" progeny, and "*bipeds* and *quadrupeds,* and subsequently
by his will (the Sons of Will and Yoga) made females," *i. e.,* separated the androgynes. Here again, we have " bipeds " or men, created
before the " quadrupeds " as in the esoteric teachings.[318]

Since, in the exoteric accounts, the *Asuras* are the first beings created
from the " body of night," while the *Pitris* issue from that of *Twilight;*
the " gods " being placed by Parâśara [319] between the two, and shown
to evolve from the " body of the day," it is easy to discover a determined purpose to veil the order of creation. Man is the *Arvâksrotas*
coming from the " Body of the Dawn "; and elsewhere, man is again
referred to, when the creator of the world, Brahmâ, is shown " creating
fierce beings, denominated Bhûtas and eaters of flesh," or as the text
has it, " fiends frightful from being monkey-colored and carnivorous." [320] Whereas the Râkshasas are generally translated by " Evil
Spirits " and " the enemies of the gods," which identifies them with the
Asuras. In the *Râmâyana,* when Hanumân is reconnoitering the enemy
in Lankâ, he finds there Râkshasas, some hideous, " while some were
beautiful to look upon," and, in *Vishnu Purâna,* there is a direct reference to their becoming the Saviors of " Humanity," or of Brahmâ.

The allegory is very ingenious. Great intellect and too much knowledge are a two-edged weapon in life, and instruments for evil as well
as for good. When combined with Selfishness, they will make of the
whole of Humanity a footstool for the elevation of him who possesses
them, and a means for the attainment of his objects; while, applied to
altruistic humanitarian purposes, they may become the means of the
salvation of many. At all events, the absence of self-consciousness and
intellect will make of man a idiot, a brute in human form. Brahmâ is
Mahat — the universal Mind — hence the too-selfish among the Râkshasas showing the desire to become possessed of it all — to "devour"
Mahat. The allegory is transparent.

At any rate, esoteric philosophy identifies the pre-Brahmânical Asu-

317. *Vishnu Purâna,* Book I, chap. xv of vol. 2.
318. *Vide supra* and Stanza XII as explained.
319. *Vishnu Purâna.*   320. *Ibid.,* Book I, chap. v.

ras, Rudras,[321] Râkshasas and all the "Adversaries" of the Gods in the allegories, with the Egos, which, by incarnating in the still witless man of the Third Race, made him *consciously* immortal. They are, then, during the cycle of Incarnations, the true *dual Logos* — the conflicting and two-faced divine Principle in Man. The Commentary that follows, and the next Stanzas may, no doubt, throw more light on this very difficult tenet, but the writer does not feel competent to give it out fully. Of the succession of Races, however, they say:—

"*First come the SELF-EXISTENT on this Earth. They are the 'Spiritual Lives' projected by the absolute WILL and LAW, at the dawn of every rebirth of the worlds. These LIVES are the divine 'Sishta,'* (the seed-Manus, or the Prajâpati and the Pitris)."

From these proceed —

1. *The First Race, the "Self-born," which are the* (astral) *shadows of their progenitors.*[322] *The body was devoid of all understanding* (mind, intelligence, and will). *The inner being* (the higher self or Monad), *though within the earthly frame, was unconnected with it. The link, the Manas, was not there as yet.*

2. *From the First* (race) *emanated the second, called the "Sweat-born"*[323] *and the "Boneless." This is the Second Root-Race, endowed*

321. Whom Manu calls "our paternal grandfathers" (III, 284). The Rudras are the seven manifestations of Rudra-Siva, "the destroying god," and *also* the grand Yogi and ascetic.

322. See § II, ¶¶ 1, Commentary.

323. To speak of *life* as having arisen, and of the human race as having originated, in this *absurdly unscientific* way, in the face of the modern Pedigrees of Man, is to court instantaneous annihilation. The esoteric doctrine risks the danger, nevertheless, and even goes so far as to ask the impartial reader to compare the above hypothesis (if it is one) with Haeckel's theory — now fast becoming an axiom with science — which is quoted verbatim:—

". . . How did life, the living world of organisms, arise? And, secondly, the special question: How did the human race originate? The first of these two inquiries, that as to the first appearance of living beings, can only be decided empirically [!!] by proof of the so-called Archebiosis, or equivo-

cal generation, or the spontaneous production of organisms of the simplest conceivable kind. Such are the Monera (Protogenes, Protamoeba, etc.), exceedingly simple microscopic masses of protoplasm without structure or organization, which take in nutriment and *reproduce themselves by division.* Such a Moneron as that primordial organism *discovered* by the renowned English zoologist Huxley, and named Bathybius Haeckelii, appears as a continuous thick protoplasmic covering at the greatest depths of the ocean, between 3000 and 30,000 feet. *It is true that the first appearance of such Monera has not up to the present moment been actually observed;* but there is nothing intrinsically improbable in such an evolution." (*The Pedigree of Man,* Aveling's transl. p. 33.)

The Bathybius protoplasm having recently turned out to be no organic substance at all, there remains little to be said. Nor, after reading this, does one need to consume further time in refuting the further assertion that . . . "in that case man also has *beyond by the preservers* (Râkshasas) [324] *and the incarnating gods* (Asuras and the Kumâras) *with the first primitive and weak spark* (the germ of intelligence) . . *And from these in turn proceeds:—*

3. *The Third Root-Race, the* " *Two-fold* " (Androgynes). *The first Races hereof are shells, till the last is* " *inhabited* " (*i. e.,* informed) *by the Dhyânis.*

The Second Race, as stated above, being also sexless, evolved out of itself, at its beginning, the Third Androgyne Race by an analogous, but already more complicated process. As described in the *Commentary,* the very earliest of that race were:—

" *The ' Sons of Passive Yoga.'* [325] *They issued from the second*

a doubt [to the minds of Haeckel and his like] arisen from the lower mammalia, apes and the earlier simian creatures, the still earlier Marsupialia, Amphibia, Pisces, by progressive transformations," all produced by " a series of *natural forces working blindly,* . . . *without aim, without design* " (p. 36).

The above-quoted passage bears its criticism on its own face. Science is made to teach that which, up to the present time, " *has never been actually observed.*" She is made to deny the phenomenon of an *intelligent* nature and a vital force independent of form and matter, and to find it more scientific to teach the miraculous performance of " natural forces *working blindly without aim or design.*" If so, then we are led to think that the *physico-mechanical* forces of the brains of certain eminent Scientists are leading them on as blindly to sacrifice logic and common sense on the altar of mutual admiration. Why should the protoplasmic *Moneron* producing the first living creature through *self-division* be held as a very scientific hypothesis, and an ethereal *pre-human* race generating the primeval men in the same fashion be tabooed as *unscientific* superstition? Or has materialism obtained a sole monopoly in Science?

324. The *Râkshasas,* regarded in Indian popular theology as demons, are called the " Preservers " beyond the Himâlayas. This double and contradictory meaning has its origin in a philosophical allegory, which is variously rendered in the Purânas. It is stated that when Brahmâ created the demons, Yakshas (from *Yaksh,* to eat) and the Râk-

shasas, both of which kinds of demons, as soon as born, wished to devour their creator, those among them that called out " Not so! oh, let him be saved (preserved)" were named Râkshasas (*Vishnu Purâna,* Book I, ch. v). The *Bhâgavata Purâna* (III, 20, 19–21) renders the allegory differently. Brahmâ transformed himself into night (or ignorance) invested with a body, upon which the Yakshas and Râkshasas seized, exclaiming " Do not spare it; devour it." Brahmâ then cried out, " Do not devour me, spare me." This has an inner meaning of course. The " body of Night " is the darkness of ignorance, and it is the darkness of silence and secrecy. Now the Râkshasas are shown in almost every case to be Yogis, pious Sâdhus and Initiates, a rather unusual occupation for *demons.* The meaning then is that while we have power to dispel the darkness of ignorance, "*devour it,*" we have to preserve the sacred truth from profanation. " Brahmâ is for the Brâhmans alone," says that proud caste. The moral of the *fable* is evident.

325. The gradual evolution of man in the Secret Doctrine shows that all the later (to the profane the earliest) Races have their *physical* origin in the early Fourth Race. But it is the sub-race, which preceded the one that separated sexually, that is to be regarded as the *spiritual* ancestors of our present generations, and especially of the Eastern Aryan Races. Weber's idea that the Indo-Germanic Race preceded the Aryan *Vedic* Race is, to the Occultist, grotesque to the last degree.

Manushyas (human race), *and became oviparous. The emanations that came out of their bodies during the seasons of procreation were ovulary; the small spheroidal nuclei developing into a large soft, egg-like vehicle, gradually hardened, when, after a period of gestation, it broke and the young human animal issued from it unaided, as the fowls do in our race."*

This must seem to the reader ludicrously absurd. Nevertheless, it is strictly on the lines of evolutionary analogy, which science perceives in the development of the living animal species. First the *moneron*-like procreation by self-division (*vide Haeckel*); then, after a few stages, the oviparous, as in the case of the reptiles, which are followed by the birds; then, finally, the mammals with their *ovoviviparous* modes of producing their young ones.

If the term *ovoviviparous* is applied to some fish and reptiles, which hatch their eggs within their bodies, why should it not be applied to female mammalians, including woman? The ovule, in which, after impregnation, the development of the fetus takes place, is an egg.

At all events, this conception is more philosophical than that of Eve with a suddenly created placenta giving birth to Cain, because of the Apple, when even the marsupial, the earliest of mammals, *is not placental* yet.

Moreover, the *progressive* order of the methods of reproduction as unveiled by science, is a brilliant confirmation of esoteric Ethnology. It is only necessary to tabulate the data in order to prove our assertion.[326]

I. *Fission:*—

(*a*) As seen in the division of the homogeneous speck of protoplasm, known as Moneron or Amoeba, into two.

(*b*) As seen in the division of the nucleated cell, in which the cell-nucleus splits into two sub-nuclei, which either develop within the original cell-wall or burst it, and multiply outside as independent entities. (*Cf., the First Root-Race.*)

II. *Budding:*—

A small portion of the parent structure swells out at the surface and finally parts company, growing to the size of the original organism; *e. g.*, many vegetables, the sea-anemone, etc. (*Cf., the Second Root-Race.*) [327]

---

326. *Cf.* especially Schmidt's *Doctrine of Descent and Darwinism,* p. 39, et seq., and Laing's *A Modern Zoroastrian,* pages 102-111.

327. Every process of healing and cica-trization in the higher animal groups — even in the case of reproduction of mutilated limbs with the Amphibians — is effected by *fission* and *gemmation* of the elementary morphological elements.

III. *Spores:—*

A single cell thrown off by the parent organism, which develops into a multicellular organism reproducing the features of the latter, *e. g.,* bacteria and mosses.

IV. *Intermediate Hermaphroditism:—*

Male and female organs inhering in the same individual; *e. g.,* the majority of plants, worms, and snails, etc.; allied to budding. (*Cf., Second and early Third Root-Races.*)

V. *True sexual union:—*

(*Cf., later Third Root-Race.*)

We now come to an important point with regard to the double evolution of the human race. The Sons of Wisdom, or the *spiritual* Dhyânis, had become "intellectual" through their contact with matter, because they had already reached, during previous cycles of incarnation, that degree of intellect which enabled them to become independent and self-conscious entities, *on this plane* of matter. They were reborn only by reason of Karmic effects. They *entered* those who were "ready," and became the Arhats, or *sages,* alluded to above. This needs explanation.

It does not mean that *Monads* entered forms in which other Monads already were. They were "Essences," "Intelligences," and *conscious spirits;* entities seeking to become still more conscious by uniting with more developed matter. Their essence was too pure to be distinct from the universal essence; but their "Egos," or *Manas* (since they are called *Mânasaputra,* born of "Mahat," or Brahmâ) had to pass through earthly human experiences to become *all-wise,* and be able to start on the returning ascending cycle. The *Monads* are not *discrete* principles, limited or conditioned, but rays from that one universal *absolute* Principle. The entrance into a dark room through the same aperture of one ray of sunlight following another will not constitute *two* rays, but one ray intensified. It is not in the course of natural law that man should become a *perfect* septenary being, before the seventh race in the seventh Round. Yet he has all these principles latent in him from his birth. Nor is it part of the evolutionary law that the Fifth principle (*Manas*), should receive its complete development before the *Fifth* Round. All such prematurely developed intellects (on the *spiritual* plane) in our Race are *abnormal;* they are those whom we call the "Fifth-Rounders." Even in the coming seventh Race, at the close of this Fourth Round, while our four lower principles will be fully developed, that of *Manas* will be only proportionately so. This limitation, however, refers solely to the spiritual development. The intellectual, on the physical plane, was reached during the Fourth Root-Race. Thus, those who were "half ready," who received "but a spark,"

constitute the average humanity which has to acquire its intellectuality
during the present Manvantaric evolution, after which they will be
ready in the next for the full reception of the "Sons of Wisdom."
While those which "were not ready" at all, the latest Monads, which
had hardly evolved from their last transitional and lower animal forms
at the close of the Third Round, remained the "narrow-brained" of
the Stanza. This explains the otherwise unaccountable degrees of
intellectuality among the various races of men — the savage Bushman
and the European — even now. Those tribes of savages, whose reasoning powers are very little above the level of the animals, are not the
unjustly disinherited, or the *unfavored,* as some may think — nothing
of the kind. They are simply those *latest arrivals* among the human
Monads, which *were not ready:* which have to evolve during the
present Round, as on the three remaining globes (hence on four
different planes of being) so as to arrive at the level of the average
class when they reach the Fifth Round. One remark may prove useful, as food for thought to the student in this connexion. The MONADS
of the lowest specimens of humanity (the "narrow-brained" [328] savage
South-Sea Islander, the African, the Australian) *had no Karma to
work out when first born as men, as their more favored brethren
in intelligence had.* The former are spinning out Karma only now;
the latter are burdened with past, present, and future Karma. In
this respect the poor savage is more fortunate than the greatest genius
of *civilized countries.*

Let us pause before giving any more such strange teachings. Let
us try and find out how far any ancient Scriptures, and even Science,
permit the possibility of, or even distinctly corroborate, such wild
notions as are found in our Anthropogenesis.

Recapitulating that which has been said we find:— That the Secret
Doctrine claims for man, (1) a polygenetic origin. (2) A variety of
modes of procreation before humanity fell into the ordinary method of
generation. (3) That the evolution of animals — of the mammalians
at any rate — follows that of man instead of preceding it. And this
is diametrically opposed to the now generally accepted theories of
evolution and the descent of man from an animal ancestor.

---

328. The term here means neither the
dolicho-cephalic nor the brachy-cephalic,
nor yet skulls of a smaller volume, but
simply brains devoid of intellect generally.
The theory which would judge of the intellectual capacity of a man according to
his cranial capacity, seems absurdly illogical to one who has studied the subject. The
skulls of the stone period, as well as those
of African Races (Bushmen included) show
that the first are above rather than below
the average of the brain capacity of the
modern man, and the skulls of the last are
on the whole (as in the case of Papuans
and Polynesians generally) larger by one
cubic inch than that of the average French-
man. Again, the cranial capacity of the
Parisian of today represents an average of
1437 cubic centimeters compared to 1523 of
the Auvergnat.

Let us, by giving to Caesar what is Caesar's, examine, first of all, the chances for the polygenetic theory among the men of science.

Now the majority of the Darwinian evolutionists incline to a polygenetic explanation of the origin of Races. On this particular question, however, scientists are, as in many other cases, at sixes and sevens; they agree to disagree.

Does man descend from one *single couple* or from *several groups* — monogenism or polygenism? As far as one can venture to pronounce on what in the absence of witnesses [?] will never be known [?], the second hypothesis is far the most probable.[329]

Abel Hovelacque, in his *Science of Language,* comes to a similar conclusion, arguing from the evidence available to a linguistic inquirer.

In an address delivered before the British Association, Professor W. H. Flower remarked on this question :—

The view which appears best to accord with what is now known of the characters and distribution of the races of man . . . is a modification of the monogenistic hypothesis [!]. Without entering into the difficult question of the method of man's first appearance upon the world, we must assume for it a vast antiquity, at all events as measured by any historical standard. *If we had any approach to a complete palaeontological record, the history of Man could be re-constructed, but nothing of the kind is forthcoming.*

Such an admission must be regarded as fatal to the dogmatism of the physical Evolutionists, and as opening a wide margin to occult speculations. The opponents of the Darwinian theory were, and still remain, polygenists. Such "intellectual giants " as John Crawford and James Hunt discussed the problem and favored polygenesis, and in their day there was a far stronger feeling in favor of than against this theory. It is only in 1864 that Darwinians began to be wedded to the theory of unity, of which Messrs. Huxley and Lubbock became the first *coryphaei.*

As regards that other question, of the priority of man to the animals in the order of evolution, the answer is as promptly given. If man is really the Microcosm of the Macrocosm, then the teaching has nothing so very impossible in it, and is but logical. For, man becomes that Macrocosm for the three lower kingdoms under him. Arguing from a physical standpoint, all the lower kingdoms, save the mineral — which is light itself, crystallized and immetallized — from plants to the creatures which preceded the first mammalians, all have been consolidated in their physical structures by means of the " cast-off dust " of those minerals, and *the refuse of the human matter, whether from*

329. A. Lefèvre, *Philosophy,* p. 498.

living or dead bodies, on which they fed and which gave them their outer bodies. In his turn, man grew more physical, by re-absorbing into his system that which he had given out, and which became transformed in the living animal crucibles through which it had passed, owing to Nature's alchemical transmutations. There were animals in those days of which our modern naturalists have never dreamed; and the stronger became physical material man, the giants of those times, the more powerful were his emanations. Once that Androgyne " humanity " separated into sexes, transformed by Nature into childbearing engines, it ceased to procreate its like through drops of vital energy oozing out of the body. But while man was still ignorant of his procreative powers on the human plane, (before his Fall, as a believer in Adam would say,) all this vital energy, scattered far and wide from him, was used by Nature for the production of the first mammal-animal forms. Evolution is *an eternal cycle of becoming,* we are taught; and nature never leaves an atom unused. Moreover, from the beginning of the Round, all in Nature tends to become Man. All the impulses of the dual, centripetal and centrifugal Force are directed towards one point — MAN. The progress in the succession of beings, says Agassiz,

consists in an increasing similarity of the living fauna, and, among the vertebrates, especially, in the increasing resemblance to man. Man is the end towards which all *animal* creation has tended from the first appearance of the first palaeozoic fishes.[330]

Just so; but " the palaeozoic fishes " being at the lower curve of the arc of the evolution of *forms,* this Round began with astral man, the *reflection of the Dhyân Chohans, called the " Builders."* Man *is the alpha and the omega of objective creation.* As said in *" Isis Unveiled,"* " all things had their origin in spirit — evolution having originally begun from above and proceeding downwards, instead of the reverse, as taught in the Darwinian theory." [331] Therefore, the tendency spoken of by the eminent naturalist above quoted, is one inherent in every atom. Only, were one to apply it to both sides of the evolution, the observations made would greatly interfere with the modern theory, which has now almost become (Darwinian) law.

But in citing the passage from Agassiz' work with approval, it must not be understood that the occultists are making *any concession* to the theory, which derives man from the animal kinigdom. The fact that in this Round he preceded the mammalia is obviously not impugned by the consideration that the latter (mammalia) follow in the wake of man.

330. *Principles of Zoology,* p. 206.   331. Vol. L p. 154.

25. How did the Mânasa, the Sons of Wisdom act? They rejected the Self-born, (*the boneless*). They are not ready. They spurned the (*First*) Sweat-Born.[332] They are not quite ready. They would not enter the (*First*) egg-born.[333]

To a Theist or a Christian this verse would suggest a rather theological idea: that of the Fall of the Angels through Pride. In the Secret Doctrine, however, the reasons for the refusal to incarnate in *half-ready* physical bodies seem to be more connected with physiological than metaphysical reasons. Not all the organisms were sufficiently ready. The incarnating powers chose the ripest fruits and spurned the rest.[334]

By a curious coincidence, when selecting a familiar name for the continent on which the first androgynes, the Third Root-Race, separated, the writer chose, on geographical considerations, that of "Lemuria," invented by Mr. P. L. Sclater. It is only later, that reading Haeckel's *Pedigree of Man*, it was found that the German "Animalist" had chosen the name for his late continent. He traces, properly enough, the center of human evolution to "Lemuria," but with a slight scientific variation. Speaking of it as that "cradle of mankind," he pictures the gradual transformation of the anthropoid mammal into the primeval savage!! Vogt, again, holds that in America Man sprang from a branch of the platyrrhine apes, *independently* of the origination of the African and Asian root-stocks from the old world catarrhinians. Anthropologists are, as usual, at loggerheads on this question, as on many others. We shall examine this claim in the light of esoteric philosophy in Stanza VIII. Meanwhile, let us give a few moments of attention to the various consecutive modes of procreation according to the laws of Evolution.

Let us begin by the mode of reproduction of the later sub-races of the Third human race, by those who found themselves endowed with the *sacred fire* from the spark of higher and then independent Beings, who were the psychic and spiritual parents of Man, as the lower *Pitar-Devatâs* (the *Pitris*) were the progenitors of his physical body. That Third and holy Race consisted of men who, at their zenith, were de-

---

332. This is explained in the section which follows this series of Stanzas in the allegory from the Purânas concerning Kandu, the holy sage, and Pramlochâ, the nymph alleged to have hypnotized him. (*Vide* § II, Commentary after St. I), a suggestive allegory, scientifically, as the drops of perspiration, which she exuded, are the symbols of the spores of science (*Vide infra*).

333. This will be explained as we proceed. This unwillingness to fashion men, or create, is symbolized in the Purânas by Daksha having to deal with his opponent Nârada, the "strife-making ascetic."

334. *Vide* Verse 24.

scribed as, "towering giants of godly strength and beauty, and the depositaries of all the mysteries of Heaven and Earth." Have they likewise *fallen,* if, then, incarnation was the *Fall?*

Of this presently. The only thing now to be noted of these is, that the chief gods and heroes of the Fourth and Fifth Races, as of later antiquity, are the *deified images of these men of the Third.* The days of their physiological purity, and those of their so-called Fall, have equally survived in the hearts and memories of their descendants. Hence, the dual nature shown in those gods, both virtue and sin being exalted to their highest degree, in the biographies composed by posterity. They were the *pre-Adamite* and the divine Races, with which even theology, in whose sight they are all "the accursed Cainite Races," now begins to busy itself.

But the action of "spiritual progenitors" of that Race has first to be disposed of. A very difficult and abstruse point has to be explained with regard to Ślokas 26 and 27. These say:—

---

26. WHEN THE SWEAT-BORN PRODUCED THE EGG-BORN, THE TWO-FOLD (*androgyne Third Race*[335]), THE MIGHTY, THE POWERFUL WITH BONES, THE LORDS OF WISDOM SAID: "NOW SHALL WE CREATE" (*a*).

Why "now" — and not earlier? This the following śloka explains.

---

27. (*Then*) THE THIRD (*race*) BECAME THE VÂHANA (*vehicle*) OR THE LORDS OF WISDOM. IT CREATED SONS OF "WILL AND YOGA," BY KRIYÂSAKTI (*b*), IT CREATED THEM, THE HOLY FATHERS, ANCESTORS OF THE ARHATS. . . .

(*a*) How did they *create,* since the "Lords of Wisdom" are identical with the Hindû Devas, who refuse "to create"? Clearly they are the *Kumâras* of the Hindû Pantheon and Purânas, those elder sons of

---

335. The evolutionist Professor Schmidt alludes to "the fact of the separation of sexes, as to the derivation of which from species *once hermaphrodite* all (the believers in creation naturally excepted) are assuredly of one accord." Such indeed is the incontestable evidence drawn from the presence of rudimentary organs. (*Cf.* his *Doctrine of Descent and Darwinism,* page 159.) Apart from such palpable traces of a primeval hermaphroditism, the fact may be noted that, as Laing writes, "a study of embryology . . . shows that in the *human and higher animal* species the distinction of sex is not developed until a *considerable progress* has been made in the growth of the embryo." (*A Modern Zoroastrian,* p. 106.) The Law of Retardation — operative alike in the case of human races, animal species, etc., when a higher type has once been evolved — still preserves hermaphroditism as the reproductive method of the majority of plants and many lower animals.

Brahmâ, " Sanandana and the other sons of *Vedhas,*" who, previously created by him " without desire or passion, remained chaste, full of holy wisdom and undesirous of progeny? " [336]

The power, by which they first created, is just that which has since caused them to be degraded from their high status to the position of evil spirits, of Satan and his Host, created in their turn by the unclean fancy of exoteric creeds. It was by *Kriyâśakti,* that mysterious and divine power latent in the will of every man, and which, if not called to life, quickened and developed by Yogi-training, remains dormant in 999,999 men out of a million, and gets atrophied. This power is explained in the " Twelve Signs of the Zodiac," [337] as follows:—

(*b*) "*Kriyâśakti* — the mysterious *power of thought* which enables it to produce external, perceptible, phenomenal results by its own inherent energy. The ancients held that any idea will manifest itself *externally,* if one's attention (and Will) is deeply concentrated upon it; similarly, an intense volition will be followed by the desired result. A Yogi generally performs his wonders by means of Ichchhâśakti (Will-power) and Kriyâśakti."

The Third Race had thus created the so-called SONS OF WILL AND YOGA, or the "ancestors" (the *spiritual* forefathers) of all the subsequent and present Arhats, or Mahâtmâs, in a truly *immaculate* way. They were indeed *created,* not *begotten,* as were their brethren of the Fourth Race, who were generated sexually after the separation of sexes, the *Fall of Man.* For creation is but the result of will acting on phenomenal matter, the calling forth out of it the primordial divine *Light* and eternal *Life.* They were the " holy seed-grain " of the future Saviors of Humanity.

Here we have to make again a break, in order to explain certain difficult points, of which there are so many. It is almost impossible to avoid such interruptions. For explanations and a philosophical account of the nature of those beings, which are now viewed as the " Evil " and rebellious Spirits, the creators by Kriyâśakti, the reader is referred to the chapters on " The Fallen Angels " and " The Mystic Dragons," in Part II of this Volume.

The order of the evolution of the human Races stands thus in the Fifth Book of the Commentaries, and was already given:—

The First men were Chhâyâs (1); the second, the " Sweat-born " (2); the Third, "Egg-born," and the holy Fathers born by the power of Kriyâśakti (3); the Fourth were the children of the Padmapâni (Chenresi) (4).

336. See *Vishnu Purâna,* Book I, ch. 7, para. 1.   337. See *Five Years of Theosophy,* page 111.

Of course such primeval modes of procreation — by the evolution of one's own image, through drops of perspiration, after that by Yoga, and then by what people will regard as magic (Kriyâśakti) — are doomed beforehand to be regarded as fairy-tales. Nevertheless, beginning with the first and ending with the last, there is really nothing miraculous in them, nor anything which could not be shown natural. This must be proven.

1. *Chhâyâ-birth,* or that primeval mode of *sexless* procreation, the first Race having *oozed out,* so to say, from the bodies of the Pitris, is hinted at in a Cosmic allegory in the Puranas.[338] It is the beautiful allegory and story of Sanjñâ, the daughter of Viśvakarman — married to the Sun, who, "unable to endure the fervors of her lord," gave him her *chhâyâ* (shadow, image, or *astral* body), while she herself repaired to the jungle to perform religious devotions, or *Tapas.* The Sun, supposing the "chhâyâ" to be his wife begat by her children, like Adam with Lilith — an *ethereal shadow* also, as in the legend, though an actual living female monster millions of years ago.

But, perhaps, this instance proves little except the exuberant fancy of the Purânic authors. We have another proof ready. If the materialized forms, which are sometimes seen oozing out of the bodies of certain mediums could, instead of vanishing, be fixed and made solid — the *creation* of the first Race would become quite comprehensible. This kind of procreation cannot fail to be suggestive to the student. Neither the mystery nor the *impossibility* of such a mode is certainly any greater — while it is far more comprehensible to the mind of the true metaphysical thinker — than the mystery of the conception of the fetus, its gestation and birth as a child, as we now know it.

Now to the curious and little understood corroboration in the Purânas about the " Sweat-born."

2. Kandu is a sage and a Yogî, eminent in holy wisdom and pious austerities, which, finally, awaken the jealousy of the gods, who are represented in the Hindû Scriptures as being in never-ending strife with the ascetics. Indra, the " King of the Gods," [339] finally sends one of his female Apsarasas to tempt the sage. This is no worse than Jehovah sending Sarah, Abraham's wife, to tempt Pharaoh; but in truth it is those gods (and god), who are ever trying to disturb ascetics and thus make them lose the fruit of their austerities, who ought to be regarded as " tempting demons," instead of applying the term to the Rudras, Kumâras, and Asuras, whose great sanctity and chastity seem

---

338. See *Vishnu Purâna*, Book III, c. 2.   India, the god is not Indra, but Kâma,
339. In the oldest MS. of *Vishnu-Purâna*   the god of love and desire. See text fur-
in the possession of an Initiate in Southern   ther on.

a standing reproach to the Don Juanic gods of the Pantheon. But it is
the reverse that we find in all the Purânic allegories, and not without
good esoteric reason.

The king of the gods (or Indra) sends a beautiful Apsaras
(nymph) named Pramlochâ to seduce Kandu and disturb his penance.
She succeeds in her unholy purpose and "907 years six months and
three days"[340] spent in her company seem to the sage as one day.
When this psychological or hypnotic state ends, the Muni curses bit-
terly the creature who seduced him, thus disturbing his devotions.
"Depart, begone!" he cries, "vile bundle of illusions!"... And
Pramlochâ, terrified, flies away, *wiping the perspiration from her body*
with the leaves of the trees as she passes through the air. She went
from tree to tree, and as, with the dusky shoots that crowned their
summits, she dried her limbs, the child she had conceived by the Rishi
came forth from the pores of her skin in drops of perspiration. The
trees received the living dews; and the winds collected them into one
mass. "This," said Soma (the Moon), "I matured by my rays; and
gradually it increased in size, till the exhalation that had rested on the
tree tops became the lovely girl named Mârishâ."[341]

Now Kandu stands here for the *First Race*. He is a son of the
Pitris, hence one *devoid of mind*, which is hinted at by his being unable to discern a period of nearly one thousand years from one day;
therefore he is shown to be so easily deluded and blinded. Here is a
variant of the allegory in *Genesis*, of Adam, born an image of clay,
into which the "Lord-god" breathes the *breath of life* but not of intellect and discrimination, which are developed only after he had tasted
of the fruit of the Tree of Knowledge; in other words when he has
acquired the first development of Mind, and had implanted in him
Manas, whose terrestrial aspect is of the Earth earthy, though its
highest faculties connect it with Spirit and the *divine Soul*. Pramlochâ
is the Hindû Lilith of the Âryan Adam; and Mârishâ, the daughter
born of the perspiration from her pores, is the "sweat-born," and
stands as a symbol for the Second Race of Mankind.

As remarked in the foot note (*vide supra*) it is not Indra, who now
figures in the Purânas, but Kâmadeva, the god of love and desire, who
sends Pramlochâ on Earth. Logic, besides the esoteric doctrine, shows
that it must be so. For Kâma is the king and lord of the Apsarasas,
of whom Pramlochâ is one; and, therefore, when Kandu, in cursing

---

340. These are the exoteric figures given
in a purposely reversed and distorted way,
being the figure of the duration of the cycle
between the first and second human race.
All Orientalists to the contrary, there is

not a word in any of the Purânas that has
not a special esoteric meaning.
341. *Vishnu Purâna*, Book I, ch. 15. *Cf.*
also Vivien's temptation of Merlin (Tenny-
son), the same legend in Irish tradition.

her, exclaims " Thou hast performed the office assigned by the monarch of the gods, go!" he must mean by that monarch Kâma and not Indra, to whom the Apsarasas are not subservient. For Kâma, again, is in the *Rig Veda*[342] the personification of that feeling which leads and propels to creation. He was the *first movement* that stirred the ONE, after its manifestation from the purely abstract principle, to create, " Desire first arose in It, which was the *primal germ of mind;* and which sages, searching with their intellect, have discovered to be the bond which connects Entity with Non-Entity." A hymn in the *Atharva Veda* exalts Kâma into a supreme God and Creator, and says: " Kâma was born the first. Him, neither gods nor fathers [Pitaras] nor men have equalled. . . ." The *Atharva Veda* identifies him with *Agni*, but makes him superior to that god. The *Taittirîya Brâhmana* makes him allegorically the son of Dharma (moral religious duty, piety and justice) and of Sraddhâ (faith). Elsewhere Kâma is born from the heart of Brahmâ; therefore he is *Âtma-Bhû* "Self-Existent," and *Aja*, the "unborn." His sending Pramlochâ has a deep philosophical meaning; sent by Indra — the narrative has none. As Eros was connected in early Greek mythology with the world's creation, and only afterwards became the sexual Cupid, so was Kâma in his original Vedic character, (*Harivansa* making him a son of Lakshmî, who is Venus). The allegory, as said, shows the psychic element developing the physiological, before the birth of *Daksha, the progenitor of real physical men,* made to be born from Mârishâ and before whose time living beings and men were procreated "by the will, by sight, by touch and by Yoga," as will be shown.

This, then, is the allegory built on the mode of procreation of the *Second* or the " Sweat-born." The same for the *Third Race* in its final development.

Mârishâ, through the exertions of Soma, the Moon, is taken to wife by the *Prachetasas*, the production of the " Mind-born " sons of Brahmâ also,[343] from whom they beget the Patriarch Daksha, a son of Brahmâ also, in a former *Kalpa* or life, explain and add the Purânas, in order to mislead, yet speaking the truth.

---

342. x. 129.
343. The text has:—" From Brahmâ were born mind-engendered progeny, with forms and faculties derived from his corporeal nature, *embodied spirits* produced from the limbs (*gâtra*) of *Dhîmat* " (all-wise deity). These beings were the abode of the three qualities of *deva-sarga* (divine creation, which, as the five-fold creation, is *devoid of clearness of perception, without reflection,* dull of nature). But as they *did not multiply themselves,* Brahmâ created " other mind-born sons like himself," namely, the

Brahmâ-rishis, or the Prajâpatis (ten and seven). Sanandana and the other sons of Vedhas (Brahmâ) were previously created, but, as shown elsewhere, they were " *without desire or passion,* inspired with holy wisdom, estranged from the universe and undesirous of progeny" (*Vishnu Purâna*, Book I, ch. 7). These Sanandana and other Kumâras are then the Gods, who after refusing to " create progeny " are forced to incarnate in senseless men. The reader must pardon unavoidable repetitions in view of the great number of the facts given.

3. The early Third Race, then, is formed from drops of "sweat," which, after many a transformation, grow into human bodies. This is not more difficult to imagine or realize than the growth of the fetus from an imperceptible germ, which fetus develops into a child, and then into a strong, heavy man. But this race again changes its mode of procreation according to the Commentaries. It is said to have emanated a *vis formativa*, which changed the drops of perspiration into greater drops, which grew, expanded, and became ovoid bodies — huge eggs. In these the human fetus gestated for several years. In the Purânas, Mârishâ, the daughter of Kandu, the sage, becomes the wife of the *Prachetasas* and the mother of Daksha. Now Daksha is the father of the first *human-like* progenitors, having been born in this way. He is mentioned later on. The evolution of man, the microcosm, is analogous to that of the Universe, the macrocosm. His evolution stands between that of the latter and that of the animal, for which man, in his turn, is a macrocosm.

Then the race becomes:—

4. The androgyne, or hermaphrodite. This process of men-bearing explains, perhaps, why Aristophanes[344] describes the nature of the old race as *androgynous*, the form of every individual being rounded, " having the back and sides as *in a circle*," whose " manner of running was circular . . . terrible in force and strength and with prodigious ambition." Therefore, to make them weaker, " Zeus divided them [in the Third Root-Race] into two, and Apollo [the Sun], under his direction, closed up the skin." The Madagascans (the island belonged to Lemuria) have a tradition about the first man, who lived at first without eating, and, having indulged in food, a swelling appeared in his leg; this bursting, there emerged from it a female, who became the mother of their race. Truly . . . " We have our sciences of *Heterogenesis* and *Parthenogenesis*, showing that the field is yet open. . . . The polyps . . . produce their offspring from themselves, like the buds and ramifications of a tree. . . ." Why not the primitive *human* polyp? The very interesting polyp *Stauridium* passes alternately from gemmation into the sex method of reproduction. Curiously enough, though it grows merely as a polyp on a stalk, it produces gemmules, which ultimately develop into a sea-nettle or *Medusa*. The Medusa is utterly dissimilar to its parent-organism, the Stauridium. It also reproduces itself differently, by sexual method, and from the resulting eggs *Stauridia* once more put in an appearance. This striking fact may assist many to understand that a form may be evolved — as in the *sexual* Lemurians from *Hermaphrodite* parentage — quite unlike its

344. See Plato's *Banquet*, 190.

immediate progenitors. It is, moreover, unquestionable that in the case of *human* incarnations the law of Karma, racial or individual, overrides the subordinate tendencies of " Heredity," its servant.

The meaning of the last sentence in the above-quoted Commentary on Śloka 27, namely, that the Fourth Race were the children of Padmapâni, may find its explanation in a certain letter from the Inspirer of " *Esoteric Buddhism* " quoted on p. 68. " The majority of mankind belongs to the seventh sub-race of the Fourth Root-Race — the above-mentioned Chinamen and their off-shoots and branchlets. (Malayans, Mongolians, Tîbetans, Hungarians, Finns, and even the Esquimaux are all remnants of this last offshoot.) "

Padmapâni, or Avalokiteśvara in Sanskrit, is, in Tîbetan, Chenresi. Now, Avalokiteśvara is the great *Logos* in its higher aspect and in the divine regions. But in the manifested planes, he is, like Daksha, the progenitor (in a spiritual sense) of men. Padmapâni-Avalokiteśvara is called *esoterically* Bodhisattva (or Dhyân Chohan) *Chenresi Vanchug,* " the powerful and all-seeing." He is considered now as the greatest protector of Asia in general, and of Tîbet in particular. In order to guide the Tîbetans and Lamas in holiness, and preserve the great Arhats in the world, this heavenly Being is credited with manifesting himself from age to age in human form. A popular legend has it that whenever faith begins to die out in the world, Padmapâni Chenresi, the " lotus-bearer," emits a brilliant ray of light, and forthwith incarnates himself in one of the two great Lamas — the Dalai and Teshu Lamas; finally, it is believed that he will incarnate as " the most perfect Buddha " in Tîbet, instead of in India, where his predecessors, the great Rishis and Manus had appeared in the beginning of our Race, but now appear no longer. Even the exoteric appearance of Dhyâni Chenresi is suggestive of the esoteric teaching. He is evidently, like Daksha, the synthesis of all the preceding Races and the progenitor of all the *human* Races after the Third, the first complete one, and thus is represented as the *culmination of the four primeval* races in his *eleven-faced* form. It is a column built in four rows, each series having three faces or heads of different complexions: the three faces for each race being typical of its three fundamental physiological transformations. The first is white (moon-colored) ; the second is yellow; the third, red-brown; the fourth, in which are only two faces — the third face being left a blank — (a reference to the untimely end of the Atlanteans) is brown-black. Padmapâni (Daksha) is seated on the column, and forms the apex. In this reference compare Śloka 39. The Dhyân Chohan is represented with four arms, another allusion to the four races. For while two are folded, the third hand holds a lotus (*Padmapâni,* " the lotus-bearer "), this flower symbolizing generation, and the fourth holds a serpent, emblem of the Wisdom in his power. On his neck is a rosary, and on his head the sign of water 〰〰〰 — matter, deluge — while on his brow rests the third eye (Śiva's eye, that of spiritual insight). His name is " Protector " (of Tíbet), " Savior of Humanity." On other occasions when he has only two arms, he is Chenresi, the Dhyâni and Bodhisattva, *Chakna-padma-karpo*, " he who holds a lotus." His other name is Chantong, " he of the 1000 eyes," when he is endowed with a thousand arms and hands, on the palm of each of which is represented an eye of Wisdom, these arms radiating from his body like a forest of rays. Another of his names is Lokapati and Lokanâtha (Sanskrit) " Lord of the World "; and Jigten-gonpo (Tíbetan), " Protector and Savior against evil " of any kind.

Padmapâni, however, is the " lotus-bearer " symbolically only for the profane; esoterically, it means the supporter of the Kalpas, the last of which, the present Mahâ-Kalpa (the Varâha), is called Padma, and represents one half of the life of Brahmâ. Though a minor Kalpa, it is called Mahâ, " great," because it comprises the age in which Brahmâ sprang from a lotus. Theoretically, the Kalpas are infinite, but practically they are divided and sub-divided in Space and Time, each division — down to the smallest — having its own Dhyâni as patron or regent. Padmapâni (Avalokiteśvara) becomes, in China, in his female aspect, Kwan-yin, " who assumes any form, at pleasure, in order to save mankind." The knowledge of the astrological aspect of the constellations on the respective " birth-days " of these Dhyânis — Amitabha (the O-mi-t'o Fo, of China) included: *e. g.,* on the 19th day of the second month, on the 17th day of the eleventh month, and on the 7th day of the third month, etc., etc. — gives the Occultist the greatest facilities for performing what are called "magic" feats. The future of an individual is seen, with all its coming events marshalled in order, in a *magic* mirror placed under the ray of certain constellations. But — beware of the reverse of the medal, SORCERY.

STANZA VIII

EVOLUTION OF THE ANIMAL MAMMALIANS — THE FIRST FALL

---

§ § (28) How the first mammals were produced.   (29) A quasi-Darwinian Evolution.   (30) The animals get solid bodies.   (31) Their separation into sexes.   (32) The first sin of the mindless men.

---

28. FROM THE DROPS OF SWEAT (a); FROM THE RESIDUE OF THE SUBSTANCE; MATTER FROM DEAD BODIES AND ANIMALS OF THE WHEEL BEFORE (*previous, Third Round*); AND FROM CAST-OFF DUST; THE FIRST ANIMALS (*of this Round*) WERE PRODUCED.

(a) The Occult doctrine maintains that, in this Round, the mammalians were a later work of evolution than man. Evolution proceeds in cycles. The great Manvantaric cycle of Seven Rounds, beginning in the First Round with mineral, vegetable, and animal, brings its evolutionary work on the descending arc to a dead stop in the middle of the Fourth *Race,* at the close of the first half of the Fourth *Round.* It is on our Earth, then, (the Fourth sphere and the lowest) and in the present *Round,* that this middle point has been reached. And since the Monad has passed, after its " first inmetalization " on Globe A, through the mineral, vegetable, and animal worlds in every degree of the three states of matter, except the last degree of the third or solid state, which it reached only at the "*mid-point of evolution,*" it is but logical and natural that at the beginning of the Fourth Round on Globe D, Man should be the first to appear; and also that his frame should be of the most tenuous matter that is compatible with objectivity. To make it still clearer: if the Monad begins its cycle of incarnations through the three objective kingdoms on the descending curved line, it has necessarily to enter on the re-ascending curved line of the sphere as a man also. On the descending arc it is the spiritual which is gradually transformed into the material. On the middle line of the base, Spirit and Matter are equilibrized in Man. On the ascending arc, Spirit is slowly re-asserting itself at the expense of the physical, or matter, so that, at the close of the seventh Race of the Seventh Round, the Monad will find itself as free from matter and all its qualities as it was in the beginning; having gained in addition the experience and wisdom, the fruition of all its personal lives, without their evil and temptations.

This order of evolution is found also in *Genesis*[345] if one reads it in its true esoteric sense, for chapter i. contains the history of the first Three Rounds, as well as that of the first Three Races of the Fourth, up to that moment when Man is called to conscious life by the Elohim of Wisdom. In the first chapter, animals, whales and fowls of the air, are created before the androgyne Adam.[346] In the second, Adam (the sexless) comes first, and the animals only appear after him. Even the state of mental torpor and unconsciousness of the first two races, and of the first half of the Third Race, is symbolized, in the second chapter of *Genesis*, by the *deep sleep of Adam*. It was the dreamless sleep of mental inaction, the slumber of the Soul and Mind, which was meant by that " sleep," and not at all the physiological process of differentiation of sexes, as a learned French theorist (M. Naudin) imagined.

The Purânas, the Chaldaean and Egyptian fragments, and also the Chinese traditions, all show an agreement with the Secret Doctrine as to the process and order of evolution. We find in them the corroboration of almost all our teaching. For instance: the statement concerning the oviparous mode of procreation of the Third Race, and even a hint at a less innocent mode of the procreation of the first mammal forms, " gigantic, transparent, dumb and monstrous they were," says the Commentary. Study the stories of the several Rishis and their multifarious progeny; *e.g.*, Pulastya is the father of *all the Serpents and Nâgas* — the oviparous brood; Kaśyapa was grandsire, through his wife Tâmrâ, of the birds and of Garuda, king of the feathered tribe; while by his wife Surabhi, he was the parent of cows and buffaloes, etc., etc.

In the Secret Doctrine, the first *Nâgas* — beings wiser than Serpents — are the " Sons of Will and Yoga," born before the complete separation of the sexes, " matured in the man-bearing eggs [347] produced by the power (Kriyâśakti) of the holy sages " of the early Third Race.[348]

---

345. Chapters i and ii.

346. An allegorical reference to the " Sacred Animals " of the Zodiac and other heavenly bodies. Some Kabalists see in them the prototypes of the animals.

347. In Hesiod (*Works and Days*, 144 *et seqq.*), Zeus creates his *third* race of men out of ash-trees. In the *Popol Vuh* the Third Race of Men is created out of the tree *Tzité* and the marrow of the reed called *Sibac*. But Sibac means "egg" in the mystery language of the

Artufas (or Initiation caves). In a report sent in 1812 to the Cortes by Don Baptista Pino it is said: " All the Pueblos have their *Artufas* — so the natives call subterranean rooms with only a single door where they (secretly) assemble. . . . These are impenetrable temples . . . and the doors are always closed to the Spaniards. . . . They adore the Sun and Moon . . . fire and the great SNAKE (the creative power), whose eggs are called *Sibac*."

348. There is a notable difference *esoterically* between the words Sarpa and Nâga,

"... In these were incarnated the Lords of the three [upper] worlds, the various classes of Rudras, who had been *Tushitas,* who had been *Jayas,* who are *Adityas*"; for, as explained by Parâśara, "There are a hundred appellations of the immeasurably mighty Rudras."

Some of the descendants of the primitive Nâgas, the Serpents of Wisdom, peopled America, when its continent arose during the palmy days of the great Atlantis, (America being the *Pâtâla* or Antipodes of Jambu-Dvîpa, not of Bhârata-Varsha). Otherwise, whence the traditions and legends — the latter *always more true than history,* as says Augustin Thierry — and even the identity in the names of certain "medicine men" and priests, who exist to this day in Mexico? We shall have to say something of the *Nargals* and the *Naguals* and also of *Nagualism,* called "devil-worship" by the Missionaries.

In almost all the Purânas, the story of the "Sacrifice of Daksha" is given, the oldest account of which is to be found in *Vâyu Purâna.* Allegorical as it is, there is more meaning and biological revelation in it to a Naturalist, than in all the *pseudo-scientific* vagaries, which are regarded as learned theories and hypotheses.

Daksha, who is regarded as the Chief Progenitor, is, moreover, pointed out as the creator of *physical man* in the "fable," which makes him lose his head from his body in the general strife between the gods and the *Raumas.* This head, being burnt in the fire, is replaced by the *head of a ram* (Kâśi-Khanda[348a]). Now the ram's head and horns are ever the symbol of generating power and of reproductive force, and are *phallic.* As we have shown, it is Daksha who establishes the era of men engendered by sexual intercourse. But this mode of procreation did not occur suddenly, as one may think, and required long ages before it became the one "natural" way. Therefore, his sacrifice to the gods is shown as interfered with by Śiva, the *destroying* deity, *evolution and* PROGRESS *personified,* who is the *regenerator* at the same time; who destroys things under one form but to recall them to life under another more perfect type. Śiva-Rudra creates the terrible Virabhadra (born of his breath) the "thousand-headed, thousand-armed" (etc.) monster, and commissions him to destroy the sacrifice prepared by Daksha. Then Virabhadra, "abiding in the region of the ghosts (ethereal men) .... *created from the pores of the skin*

though they are both used indiscriminately. Sarpa (serpent) is from the root *Srip, serpo,* to creep; and they are called "Ahi," from *Ha,* to abandon. "The sarpa was produced from Brahmâ's hair, which, owing to his fright at beholding the Yakshas, whom he had created horrible to behold, fell off from the head, each hair becoming a serpent. They are called Sarpa from their creeping and *Ahi* because they had deserted the head" (Wilson). But the Nâgas, their serpent's tail notwithstanding, do not creep, but manage to walk, run and fight in the allegories.

348a. *Skanda Purâna.*

(*Romakûpas*), powerful Raumas,[349] (or Raumyas)." Now, however mythical the allegory, the *Mahâbhârata*, which is history as much as is the *Iliad*, shows [350] the Raumyas and other races, as springing in the same manner from the *Romakûpas*, hair or skin pores. This allegorical description of the " sacrifice " is full of significance to the students of the Secret Doctrine who know of the " Sweat-born."

In the *Vâyu Purâna's* account of Daksha's sacrifice, moreover, it is said to have taken place in the presence of creatures *born from the egg*, from the vapor, vegetation, pores of the skin, and, finally only, from the womb.

Daksha typifies the early Third Race, holy and pure, still devoid of an individual *Ego*, and having merely the passive capacities. Brahmâ therefore, commands him to create (in the exoteric texts); when, obeying the command, he made " inferior and superior " (*avara* and *vara*) progeny (*putra*), *bipeds* and *quadrupeds;* and by his *will*, gave birth to females . . . to the gods, the *Daityas* (giants of the Fourth Race), the snake-gods, animals, cattle and the *Dânavas* (Titans and demon Magicians) and other beings.

" . . . From that period forward, *living creatures were engendered by sexual intercourse. Before the time of Daksha, they were variously propagated* — by the *will*, by sight, by touch, and by *Yoga-power*." [351] And now comes the simply zoological teaching.

---

29. ANIMALS WITH BONES, DRAGONS OF THE DEEP AND FLYING SARPAS (*serpents*) WERE ADDED TO THE CREEPING THINGS. THEY THAT CREEP ON THE GROUND GOT WINGS. THEY OF THE LONG NECKS IN THE WATER, BECAME THE PROGENITORS OF THE FOWLS OF THE AIR (*a*).

(*a*) This is a point on which the teachings and modern biological speculation are in perfect accord. The missing links representing this transition process between reptile and bird are apparent to the veriest bigot, especially in the *ornithoscelida*, *hesperornis*, and the archaeopteryx of Vogt.

---

30. DURING THE THIRD (*Race*), THE BONELESS ANIMALS GREW AND CHANGED: THEY BECAME ANIMALS WITH BONES (*a*), THEIR CHHÂYÂS BECAME SOLID (*also*).

349. Wilson translates the word as "demigods" (See his *Vishnu Purâna*, i, page 130); but Raumas or Raumyas are simply a race, a tribe.
350. xii. 10,308.   351. *Vishnu Purâna*.

31. THE ANIMALS SEPARATED THE FIRST (*into male and female*)
(*b*) . . . .

(*a*) Vertebrates, and after that mammalians. Before that the
animals were also ethereal proto-organisms, just as man was.

(*b*) The fact of former hermaphrodite mammals and the subsequent
separation of sexes is now indisputable, even from the stand-point of
Biology. As Professor Oscar Schmidt, an avowed Darwinist, shows:

Use and disuse combined with selection elucidate [?] *the separation of the
sexes*, and the existence, totally incomprehensible, of rudimentary sexual organs.
In the Vertebrata especially, *each sex possesses such distinct traces of the
reproductive apparatus characteristic of the other*, that even antiquity assumed
hermaphroditism as a natural primeval form of mankind. . . . The tenacity
with which the rudiments of sexual organs are inherited is remarkable. In
the class of mammals, actual hermaphroditism is unheard of, although through
the whole period of their development they drag along with them these residues
borne by *their unknown ancestry,* no one can say how long ago.[352]

---

31. . . . . THEY (*the animals*) BEGAN TO BREED. THE TWO-FOLD
MAN (*then*) SEPARATED ALSO. HE (*man*), SAID "LET US AS THEY;
LET US UNITE AND MAKE CREATURES." THEY DID. . . .

---

32. AND THOSE WHICH HAD NO SPARK (*the " narrow-brained " [353]*)
TOOK HUGE SHE-ANIMALS UNTO THEM (*a*). THEY BEGAT UPON THEM
DUMB RACES. DUMB THEY WERE (*the " narrow-brained "*) THEMSELVES.
BUT THEIR TONGUES UNTIED (*b*). THE TONGUES OF THEIR PROGENY
REMAINED STILL. MONSTERS THEY BRED. A RACE OF CROOKED, RED-
HAIR-COVERED MONSTERS, GOING ON ALL FOURS.[354] A DUMB RACE, TO
KEEP THE SHAME UNTOLD.[355]

(*a*) The animals "separated the first," says Śloka 31. Bear in
mind that at that period men were different, even physiologically, from

---

352. *Doctrine of Descent and Darwinism,* pp. 186-7. The "Unknown Ancestry"
referred to are the *primeval* astral prototypes. *Cf.* § II, p. 260 (a).

353. See verse 24.

354. These "animals," or monsters, are

not the anthropoid or any other apes, but
verily what the Anthropologists might call
the "missing link," the primitive lower
man; see *infra.*

355. The shame of their animal origin
which our modern scientists would empha-
size if they could.

what they are now, having passed the middle point of the Fifth Race. We are not told what the " huge she-animals " were; but they certainly were as different from any we know now, as were the men.

This was the first physical " fall into matter " of some of the then existing and lower races. Bear in mind Śloka 24. The " Sons of Wisdom " had spurned the early *Third* Race, *i. e.,* the non-developed, and are shown incarnating in, and thereby endowing with intellect, the *later* Third Race. Thus the sin of the brainless or " mindless " Races, who had no " spark " and were irresponsible, fell upon those who failed to do by them their Karmic duty.

(*b*) See later on concerning the beginning of human speech.

WHAT MAY BE THE OBJECTIONS TO THE FOREGOING

Thus Occultism rejects the idea that Nature developed man from the ape, or even from an ancestor common to both, but traces, on the contrary, some of the most anthropoid species to the Third Race man of the early Atlantean period. As this proposition will be maintained and defended elsewhere, a few words more are all that are needed at present. For greater clearness, however, we shall repeat in brief what was said previously in Book I, Stanza VI.

Our teachings show that, while it is quite correct to say that nature had built, at one time, around the human astral form an *ape-like external* shape, yet it is as correct that this shape was no more that of the " missing link," than were the coverings of that astral form, during the course of its natural evolution through all the kingdoms of nature. Nor was it, as shown in the proper place, on this Fourth Round planet that such evolution took place, but only during the First, Second, and Third Rounds, when MAN was, in turn, " a stone, a plant, and an animal " until he became what he was in the First Root-Race of present humanity. The real line of evolution differs from the Darwinian, and the two systems are irreconcilable, except when the latter is divorced from the dogma of " Natural Selection " and the like. Indeed, between the *Monera* of Haeckel and the *Sarīsripa* of Manu, there lies an impassable chasm in the shape of the *Jîva;* for the " human " Monad, whether *immetalized* in the stone-atom, or *invegetalized* in the plant, or *inanimalized* in the animal, is still and ever a divine, hence also a HUMAN Monad. It ceases to be human only when it becomes *absolutely divine.* The terms " mineral," " vegetable " and " animal " *monad* are meant to create a superficial distinction: there is no such thing as a Monad (jîva) other than divine, and consequently having been, or having to become, human. And the latter term has to remain meaningless unless the difference is well understood. The Monad is a drop out of the shoreless Ocean beyond, or, to be correct, *within* the plane of primeval differentiation. It is divine in its higher and *human* in its lower condition — the adjectives "higher" and "lower" being used for lack of better words — and a monad it remains at all times, save in the Nirvânic state, under whatever conditions, or whatever external forms. As the Logos reflects the Universe in the Divine Mind, and the manifested Universe reflects itself in each of its Monads, as Leibnitz put it, repeating an Eastern teaching, so the MONAD has, during the cycle of its incarnations, to reflect in itself every *root-form* of each kingdom. Therefore, the Kabalists say correctly that "MAN becomes a stone, a plant, an animal, a man, a Spirit, and finally God. Thus accomplishing his cycle or circuit and returning to the point from which he had started as the *heavenly* MAN." But by "Man" the divine Monad is meant, and not the thinking Entity, much less his physical body. While rejecting the immortal Soul, the men of Science now try to trace the latter through a series of animal forms from the lowest to the highest; whereas, in truth, all the present fauna are the descendants of those primordial monsters of which the Stanzas speak. The animals — the creeping beasts and those in the waters that preceded man in this Fourth Round, as well as those contemporary with the Third Race, and again the mammalia that are posterior to the Third and Fourth Races — all are either directly or indirectly the mutual and correlative product (physically) of man. It is correct to say that the man of this Manvantara, *i. e.*, during the three preceding Rounds, has passed through all the kingdoms of nature. That he was "a stone, a plant, an animal." But (*a*) these stones, plants, and animals were the prototypes, the filmy presentments of those of the Fourth Round; and (*b*) even those at the beginning of the Fourth Round were the astral shadows of the present, as the Occultists express it. And finally the forms and *genera* of neither man, animal, nor plant were what they became later. Thus the astral prototypes of the lower beings of the animal kingdom of the Fourth Round, which *preceded* (the chhâyâs of) *Men*, were the consolidated, though still very ethereal *sheaths* of the still more ethereal forms or models produced at the close of the Third Round on Globe D.[356] "Produced from the residue of the substance matter; from dead bodies of men and (other *extinct*) animals of the wheel before," or the previous *Third* Round — as Śloka 28 tells us. Hence, while the nondescript "animals" that

356. *Vide* "*Esoteric Buddhism.*"

preceded the astral man at the beginning of this life-cycle on our Earth were still, so to speak, the progeny of the man of the Third Round, the mammalians of this Round owe their existence, in a great measure, to man again. Moreover, the "ancestor" of the present anthropoid animal, the ape, is the direct production of the yet mindless *Man*, who desecrated his human dignity by putting himself physically on the level of an animal.

The above accounts for some of the alleged physiological proofs, brought forward by the anthropologists as a demonstration of the descent of man from the animals.

The point most insisted upon by the Evolutionists is that, "The history of the embryo is an epitome of that of the race." That

> every organism, in its development from the egg, runs through a series of forms, through which, in like succession, its ancestors have passed in the long course of Earth's history.[357] The history of the embryo . . . is a picture in little, and outline of that of the race. *This conception forms the gist of our fundamental biogenetic law, which we are obliged to place at the head of the study of the fundamental law of organic development.*[358]

This modern theory was known as a fact to, and far more philosophically expressed by, the Sages and Occultists from the remotest ages. A passage from "*Isis Unveiled*" may here be cited to furnish a few points of comparison. In Vol. I,[359] it was asked why, with all their great learning, physiologists were unable to explain teratological phenomena? Any anatomist who has made the development and growth of the embryo "a subject of special study," can tell, without much brain-work, what daily experience and the evidence of his own eyes show him, viz., that up to a certain period, the human embryo is a facsimile of a young batrachian in its first remove from the spawn — a tadpole. But no physiologist or anatomist seems to have had the idea of applying to the development of the human being — from the

---

357. "A very strong argument in favor of variability is supplied by the science of Embryology. Is not a man in the uterus . . . a simple cell, a vegetable with three or four leaflets, a tadpole with branchiae, a mammal with a tail, lastly a primate [?] and a biped? It is scarcely possible not to recognize in the embryonic evolution a rapid sketch, a faithful summary, of the entire organic series." (Lefèvre, *Philosophy*, page 484.)

The summary alluded to is, however, only that of the *store of types* hoarded up in man, the microcosm. This simple explanation meets all such objections, as the presence of the rudimentary tail in the fetus — a fact triumphantly paraded by Haeckel and Darwin as conclusively in favor of the Ape-Ancestor theory. *It may also be pointed out that the presence of a vegetable with leaflets in the embryonic stages is not explained* on ordinary evolutionist principles. Darwinists have not traced man through the vegetable, but Occultists have. *Why then this feature in the embryo,* and how do the former explain it?

358. "*The Proofs of Evolution,*" a lecture by Haeckel.

359. Pages 388-9.

first instant of its physical appearance as a germ to its ultimate formation and birth — the Pythagorean esoteric doctrine of metempsychosis,
so erroneously interpreted by critics. The meaning of the axiom: "A
stone becomes a plant; a plant, a beast; a beast, a man, etc." was
mentioned in another place in relation to the spiritual and physical
evolution of men on this Earth. We will now add a few more words
to make the matter clearer.

What is the primitive shape of the future man? A grain, a corpuscle,
say some physiologists; a molecule, an ovum of the ovum, say others.
If it could be analysed — by the microscope or otherwise — of what
ought we to expect to find it composed? Analogically, we should say,
of a nucleus of inorganic matter, deposited from the circulation at the
germinating point, and united with a deposit of organic matter. In
other words, this infinitesimal nucleus of the future man is composed of
the same elements as a stone—of the same elements as the Earth, which
the man is destined to inhabit. Moses is cited by the Kabalists as
authority for the remark that it required earth and water to make a
living being, and thus it may be said that man first appears as a stone.

At the end of three or four weeks the ovum has assumed a plant-like
appearance, one extremity having become spheroidal and the other
tapering like a carrot. Upon dissection it is found to be composed,
like an onion, of very delicate laminae or coats, enclosing a liquid. The
laminae approach each other at the lower end, and the embryo hangs
from the root of the umbilicus almost like the fruit from the bough.
The stone has now become changed, by " metempsychosis," into a
plant. Then the embryonic creature begins to shoot out, from the
inside outward, its limbs, and develops its features. The eyes are
visible as two black dots; the ears, nose, and mouth form depressions,
like the points of a pineapple, before they begin to project. The
embryo develops into an animal-like fetus — the shape of a tadpole —
and, like an amphibious reptile, lives in water and develops from it.
Its Monad has not yet become either human or immortal, for the
Kabalists tell us that this only occurs at the "fourth hour." One by
one the fetus assumes the characteristics of the human being, the first
flutter of the immortal breath passes through its being; it moves; and
the divine essence settles in the infant frame, which it will inhabit
until the moment of physical death, when man becomes a spirit.

This mysterious process of a nine-months' formation, the Kabalists
call the completion of the "individual cycle of evolution." As the
fetus develops amidst the *liquor amnii* in the womb, so the Earths
germinate in the universal ether, or astral fluid, in the womb of the
Universe. These cosmic children, like their pigmy inhabitants, are at
first nuclei; then ovules; then gradually mature; and becoming

mothers, in their turn, develop mineral, vegetable, animal, and human forms. From center to circumference, from the imperceptible vesicle to the uttermost conceivable bounds of the Kosmos, those glorious thinkers, the Occultists, trace cycle merging into cycle, containing and contained in an endless series. The embryo evolving in its pre-natal sphere, the individual in his family, the family in the state, the state in mankind, the Earth in our system, that system in its central universe, the universe in the Kosmos, and the Kosmos in the ONE CAUSE . . . thus runs *their* philosophy of evolution, differing as we see, from that of Haeckel:—

> "All are but parts of one stupendous whole,
> Whose body Nature is, and (Parabrahm) the soul . . ."

These are the proofs of Occultism, and they are rejected by Science. But how is the chasm between the mind of man and animal to be bridged in this case? How, if the anthropoid and *Homo primigenius* had, *argumenti gratia,* a common ancestor (in the way modern speculation puts it), did the two groups diverge so widely from one another as regards mental capacity? True, the Occultist may be told that in every case Occultism does what Science repeats; it gives a *common* ancestor to ape and man, since it makes the former issue from primeval man. Ay, but that " primeval man " was *man* only in external form. He was *mindless* and *soulless* at the time he begot, with a female animal monster, the forefather of a series of apes. This speculation—if speculation it be — is at least logical, and fills the chasm between the mind of man and animal. Thus it accounts for and explains the hitherto unaccountable and inexplicable. The fact that, in the present stage of evolution, Science is almost certain that no issue can follow from the union of man and animal, is considered and explained elsewhere.

Now what is the fundamental difference between the accepted (or nearly so) conclusions, as enunciated in *The Pedigree of Man,* viz., that man and ape have a common ancestor; and the teachings of Occultism, which deny this conclusion and accept the fact that all things and all living beings have originated from one common source? Materialistic science makes man evolve gradually to what *he is now,* and, starting from the first protoplasmic speck called *Moneron* (which we are told has, like the rest, " originated in the course of immeasurable ages from a few, or from one simple, *spontaneously arising* original form, that has obeyed one law of evolution "), pass through " unknown and unknowable " types up to the ape, and thence to the human being. Where the transitional shapes are discoverable we are not told; for the simple reason that no "missing links" between man and the apes have ever yet been found, though this fact in no way prevents men like Haeckel from inventing them *ad libitum.*

Nor will they ever be met with; simply, again, because that link which unites man with his real ancestry is searched for on the objective plane and in the material world of forms, whereas it is safely hidden from the microscope and dissecting knife *within* the animal tabernacle of man himself. We repeat what we have said in *Isis Unveiled:—*

... All things had their origin in spirit — evolution having originally begun from above and proceeded downward, instead of the reverse, as taught in the Darwinian theory. In other words, there has been a gradual materialization of forms until a fixed ultimate of debasement is reached. This point is that at which the doctrine of modern evolution enters into the arena of speculative hypothesis. Arrived at this period we will find it easier to understand Haeckel's *Anthropogeny,* which traces the pedigree of man "from its protoplasmic root, sodden in the mud of seas which existed before the oldest of the fossiliferous rocks were deposited," according to Professor Huxley's exposition. We may believe the man (of the Third Round) evolved "by gradual modification of an (astral) mammal of ape-like organization" still easier when we remember that (though in a more condensed and less elegant, but still as comprehensible, phraseology) the same theory was said by Berosus to have been taught many thousands of years before his time by the man-fish Oannes or Dagon, the semi-demon of Babylonia [360] (though on somewhat modified lines).

But what lies back of the Darwinian line of descent? So far as he is concerned nothing but "unverifiable hypotheses." For, as he puts it, he views all beings "as the lineal descendants of some few beings which lived long before the first bed of the Silurian system was deposited." [361] He does not attempt to show us who these "few beings" were. But it answers our purpose quite as well, for, in the admission of their existence at all, resort to the ancients for corroboration and elaboration of the idea receives the stamp of scientific approbation.... [361a]

Truly, as also said in our first work: "If we accept Darwin's theory of the development of species, we find that his starting-point is placed in front of an open door. We are at liberty with him, to either remain within, or cross the threshold, beyond which lies the limitless and the incomprehensible, or rather the *Unutterable.* If our mortal language is inadequate to express what our spirit dimly foresees in the great 'Beyond' — while on this earth — it *must* realize it at some point in the timeless Eternity." But what lies "beyond" Haeckel's theory? Why *Bathybius Haeckelii,* and no more!

A further answer is given in Part III, *Addenda.*

360. Cory: *Ancient Fragments.*
361. *Origin of Species,* pp. 448, 489, first edition.
361a. Vol. I, p. 154.

STANZA IX

THE FINAL EVOLUTION OF MAN

§§ (33) The creators repent. (34) They atone for their neglect. (35) Men become endowed with minds. (36) The fourth race develops perfect speech. (37) Every androgynous unit is separated and becomes bisexual.

33. SEEING WHICH (*the sin committed with the animals*), THE LHAS (*the spirits, the "Sons of Wisdom"*) WHO HAD NOT BUILT MEN (*who had refused to create*), WEPT, SAYING:—

34. "THE AMÂNASA (*the 'mindless'*) HAVE DEFILED OUR FUTURE ABODES (*a*). THIS IS KARMA. LET US DWELL IN THE OTHERS. LET US TEACH THEM BETTER, LEST WORSE SHOULD HAPPEN." THEY DID. . . .

35. THEN ALL BECAME ENDOWED WITH MANAS (*minds*). THEY SAW THE SIN OF THE MINDLESS.

But they had already *separated* before the ray of divine reason had enlightened the dark region of their hitherto slumbering minds, and had *sinned*. That is to say, they had committed evil unconsciously, by producing an effect which was unnatural. Yet, like the other six primitive brother or fellow races, even so this seventh, henceforth degenerated race, which will have to bide its time for its final development on account of the *sin* committed,— even this race will *find itself on the last day* on one of the seven paths. For "the wise [362] guard the home of nature's order, they assume excellent forms in secret." [363] But we must see whether the "animals" tampered with, were of the same kind as those known to zoology.

362. This verse in the *Veda* (X, 5–6), "The seven wise ones [rays of wisdom, Dhyânis] fashion seven paths [or lines as also *Races* in another sense]. To one of these may the distressed mortal come "— which is interpreted solely from the astronomical and cosmic aspect — is one of the most pregnant in occult meaning. The "paths" may mean lines (*maryâdâh*), but they are primarily beams of light falling on the paths leading to wisdom. (See *Rig Veda*, IV, 5–13.) It means "ways" or paths. They are, in short, the seven Rays which fall free from the macrocosmic center, the seven principles in the metaphysical, the seven Races in the physical sense. All depends upon the key used.

363. *Rig Veda*, X, 10, 5, 2.

(*a*) The " Fall " occurred, according to the testimony of ancient
Wisdom and the old records, as soon as Daksha (the reincarnated
Creator of men and things in the early Third Race) disappeared to make
room for that portion of mankind which had " separated." This is how
the Commentary explains the details that preceded the " Fall ":—

" *In the initial period of man's Fourth evolution, the human kingdom
branched off in several and various directions. The outward shape of its
first specimens was not uniform, for the vehicles* (the egg-like, external
shells, in which the future fully physical man gestated) *were often tampered with, before they hardened, by huge animals, of species now unknown, and which belonged to the tentative efforts of Nature. The result
was that intermediate races of monsters, half animals, half men, were
produced. But as they were failures, they were not allowed to breathe
long and live, though the intrinsically paramount power of psychic over
physical nature being yet very weak, and hardly established, the ' Egg-
Born' Sons had taken several of their females unto themselves as mates,
and bred other human monsters. Later, animal species and human races
becoming gradually equilibrized, they separated and mated no longer.
Man created no more — he begot. But he also begot animals, as well as
men in days of old. Therefore the Sages (or wise men), who speak of
males who had no more will-begotten offspring, but begat various animals along with Dânavas* (giants) *on females of other species—animals
being as (or in a manner of) Sons putative to them; and they* (the
human males) *refusing in time to be regarded as* (putative) *fathers of
dumb creatures — spoke truthfully and wisely. Upon seeing this* (state
of things), *the kings and Lords of the Last Races* (of the Third and the
Fourth) *placed the seal of prohibition upon the sinful intercourse. It
interfered with Karma, it developed new (Karma).*[364] *They* (the divine
Kings) *struck the culprits with sterility. They destroyed the Red and
Blue Races.*[365]

In another we find:—

" *There were blue and red-faced animal-men even in later times;
not from actual intercourse* (between the human and animal species),
but by descent."

And still another passage mentions:—

" *Red-haired, swarthy men going on all-fours, who bend and unbend*
(stand erect and fall on their hands again) *who speak as their forefathers, and run on their hands as their giant fore-mothers."*

364. It is next to impossible to translate verbally some of these old Commentaries.
We are often obliged to give the meaning only, and thus retranslate the verbatim translations.
365. Rudra, as a Kumâra, is *Nîlalohita* — red and blue.

Perchance in these specimens, Haeckelians might recognize, not the *Homo primigenius*, but some of the lower tribes, such as some tribes of the Australian savages. Nevertheless, even these are not descended from the anthropoid apes, but from human fathers and semi-human mothers, or, to speak more correctly, from human monsters — those " failures " mentioned in the first Commentary. The real anthropoids, Haeckel's *Catarrhini* and *Platyrrhini*, came far later, in the closing times of Atlantis. The orang-outang, the gorilla, the chimpanzee and cynocephalus are the latest and purely physical evolutions from lower anthropoid mammalians. They have a spark of the purely human essence in them; man on the other hand, has not one drop of pithecoid [366] blood in his veins. Thus saith old Wisdom and universal tradition.

How was the separation of sexes effected? it is asked. Are we to believe in the old Jewish fable of the rib of Adam yielding Eve? Even such belief is more logical and reasonable than the descent of man from the Quadrumana without any reservation; as the former hides an esoteric truth under a fabulous version, while the latter conceals no deeper fact than a desire to force upon mankind a materialistic fiction. The rib is bone, and when we read in *Genesis* that Eve was made out of the rib, it only means that the *Race with bones* was produced out of a previous Race and Races, which were "boneless." This is an esoteric tenet spread far and wide, as it is almost universal under its various forms. A Tahitian tradition states that man was created out of *Araea*, " red

366. This, regardless of modern materialistic evolution, which speculates in this wise: " The primitive human form, whence we think all human species sprang, has perished this long time." (This we deny; it has only decreased in size and changed in texture.) " But many facts point to the conclusion that it was hairy and dolichocephalic." (African races are even *now* dolichocephalic in a great measure, but the palaeolithic Neanderthal skull, the oldest we know of, is of a large size, and no nearer to the capacity of the gorilla's cranium than that of any other now-living man.) " Let us, for the time being, call this hypothetical species *Homo primigenius*. . . . This first species, or the Ape-man, the ancestor of all the others, PROBABLY arose in the *tropical regions* of the old world from ANTHROPOID APES." Asked for proofs, the evolutionist, not the least daunted, replies: " Of these NO FOSSIL REMAINS ARE AS YET KNOWN TO US, BUT THEY WERE *probably* AKIN

TO THE GORILLA AND ORANG OF THE PRESENT DAY." And then the Papuan negro is mentioned as the probable descendant in the first line (*Pedigree of Man*, p. 80).

Haeckel holds fast to Lemuria, which with East Africa and South Asia also, he mentions as the possible cradle of the primitive Ape-men; and so do many geologists. Mr. A. R. Wallace admits its reality, though in a rather modified sense, in his *Geographical Distribution of Animals*. But let not Evolutionists speak so lightly of the comparative size of the brains of man and the ape, for this is very *unscientific*, especially when they pretend to see no difference between the two, or very little at any rate. For Vogt himself showed that, while the highest of the Apes, the gorilla, has a brain of only 30 to 51 cubic inches, the brain of the lowest of the Australian aborigines amounts to 99.35 cubic inches. The former is thus "not half of the size of the brain of a new-born babe," says Pfaff.

Earth." Taaroa, the creative power, the chief god, "put man to sleep for long years, for several lives," which means racial periods, and is a reference to his *mental sleep*, as shown elsewhere. During that time the deity pulled an *Ivi* (bone) out of man and she became a woman.[367]

Nevertheless, whatever the allegory may mean, even its exoteric meaning necessitates a *divine* Builder of man—" a Progenitor." Do we then believe in such "supernatural" beings? We say, No. Occultism has never believed in anything, whether animate or inanimate, *outside* nature. Nor are we Cosmolators or Polytheists for believing in "Heavenly Man" and divine men, for we have the accumulated testimony of the ages, with its unvarying evidence on every essential point, to support us in this; the Wisdom of the Ancients and UNIVERSAL tradition. We reject, however, every groundless and baseless tradition, which, having outgrown strict allegory and symbolism, has found acceptance in exoteric creeds. But that which is preserved in *unanimous* traditions, only the wilfully blind could reject. Hence we believe in races of beings other than our own in far remote geological periods; in races of ethereal, following *incorporeal*, "*Arûpa*," men, with form but no solid substance, giants who preceded us pigmies; in dynasties of divine beings, those Kings and Instructors of the Third Race in arts and sciences, compared with which our little modern science stands less chance than elementary arithmetic with geometry.

No, certainly not. We do not believe in the *supernatural* but only in the *superhuman*, or rather *interhuman*, intelligences. One may easily appreciate the feeling of reluctance that an educated person would have to being classed with the superstitious and ignorant; and even realize the great truth uttered by Renan when he says that:

The supernatural has become like the original sin, a blemish that every one seems ashamed of — even those most religious persons who refuse in our day to accept even a *minimum* of Bible miracles in all their crudeness, and who, seeking to reduce them to the *minimum*, hide and conceal it in the furthermost corners of the past.[368]

But the "supernatural" of Renan belongs to dogma and its dead letter. It has naught to do with its Spirit nor with the reality of facts in Nature. If theology asks us to believe that four or five thousand years ago men lived 900 years and more, that a portion of mankind, the enemies of the people of Israel exclusively, was composed of giants

---

367. *Polynesian Researches*, Ellis, Vol. II, p. 38.
Missionaries seem to have pounced upon this name *Ivi* and made of it *Eve*. But, as shown by Professor Max Müller, *Eve* is not the Hebrew name but a European trans- formation of חַוָּה *chavah*, "life," or mother of all living; "while the Tahitian *Ivi* and the Maori *Wheva* meant bone and bone only." (*False Analogies*.)

368. *Chaire d'Hébreu au Collège de France*, p. 20.

and monsters, we decline to believe such a thing existed in Nature 5,000 *years back*. For Nature never proceeds by jumps and starts, and logic and common sense, besides geology, anthropology and ethnology, have justly rebelled against such assertions. But if that same theology, giving up her fantastic chronology, had claimed that men lived 969 years — the age of Methuselah — five million years ago, we would have nothing to say against the claim. For in those days the physical frame of men was, compared to the present human body, as that of a megalosaurus to a common lizard.

A naturalist suggests another difficulty. The human is the only species which, however unequal in its races, can breed together. " There is no question of selection between *human races*," say the antiDarwinists, and no evolutionist can deny the argument— one which very triumphantly proves *specific unity*. How then can Occultism insist that a portion of the Fourth Race humanity begot young ones from females of another, only *semi-human*, if not quite an animal, race, the hybrids resulting from which union not only bred freely but produced the ancestors of the modern anthropoid apes? Esoteric science replies to this that it was in the very beginnings of physical man. Since then, Nature has changed her ways, and sterility is the only result of the crime of man's bestiality. But we have to this day proofs of this. The Secret Doctrine teaches that the *specific unity of mankind* is not without exceptions even now. For there are, or rather still were a few years ago, descendents of these half-animal tribes or races, both of remote Lemurian and Lemuro-Atlantean origin. The world knows them as Tasmanians (now extinct), Australians, Andaman Islanders, etc. The descent of the Tasmanians can be almost proved by a fact, which struck Darwin a good deal, without his being able to make anything of it. This fact deserves notice.

Now de Quatrefages and other naturalists, who seek to prove Monogenesis by the very fact of every race of mankind being capable of crossing with every other, have left out of their calculations *exceptions*, which do not in this case confirm the rule. Human crossing may have been a general rule from the time of the separation of sexes, and yet that other law may assert itself, viz., sterility between two human races, just as between two animal species of various kinds, in those rare cases when a European, condescending to see in a female of a savage tribe a mate, happens to choose a member of such mixed tribes.[369] Darwin

---

369. Of such semi-animal creatures, the sole remnants known to Ethnology were the Tasmanians, a *portion* of the Australians and a mountain tribe in China, the men and women of which are entirely covered with hair. They were the last descendants in a *direct* line of the semi-animal latter-day Lemurians referred to. There are, however, considerable numbers of the mixed LemuroAtlantean peoples produced by various crossings with such semi-human stocks — *e. g.*, the wild men of Borneo, the Veddahs of

notes such a case in a Tasmanian tribe, whose women were suddenly
struck with sterility, *en masse,* some time after the arrival among them
of the European colonists. The great naturalist tried to explain this fact
by change of diet, food, conditions, etc., but finally gave up the solution
of the mystery. For the Occultist it is a very evident one. " Crossing,"
as it is called, of Europeans with Tasmanian women — *i.e.,* the representatives of a race, whose progenitors were a " soulless "[370] and mindless monster and a real human, though still as mindless a man — brought
on sterility. This, not alone as a consequence of a physiological law, but
also as a decree of *Karmic* evolution in the question of further survival
of the abnormal race. In no one point of the above is Science prepared
to believe *as yet* — but it will have to in the long run. Esoteric philosophy, let us remember, only fills the gaps made by science and corrects
her false premisses.

Yet, in this particular, geology and even botany and zoology support
the esoteric teachings. It has been suggested by many geologists that
the Australian native — co-existing as he does with an *archaic fauna
and flora* — must date back to an enormous antiquity. The whole
environment of this mysterious race, about whose origin ethnology is
silent, is a testimony to the truth of the esoteric position.

" It is a very curious fact," says Jukes,[371]

that not only these marsupial animals [the mammals found in the Oxfordshire
Stone-field slates], but several of the shells — as for instance, the *Trigonias*
and even some of the plants found fossil in the Oölitic rocks — much more
nearly resemble those now living in Australia than the living forms of any
other part of the globe. This might be explained on the supposition that,
since the Oölitic [Jurassic] period, *less change has taken place in Australia
than elsewhere,* and that the Australian flora and fauna consequently retain
something of the Oölitic type, *while it had been altogether supplanted and replaced on the rest of the Globe.* [!!]

Ceylon, classed by Prof. Flower among
Aryans (!), most of the remaining Australians, Bushmen, Negritos, Andaman Islanders, etc.
  The Australians of the Gulf of St. Vin-
cent and the neighborhood of Adelaide are
very hairy, and the brown down on the
skin of boys of five or six years of age assumes a *furry appearance.* They are, however, degraded *men* — not the closest approximation to the *"pithecoid* man," as
Haeckel so sweepingly affirms. Only a portion of these men are a Lemurian relic.
(Cf. " *Esoteric Buddhism,*" p. 55)

370. In calling the animal " Soulless,"
it is not depriving the beast, from the humblest to the highest species, of a " soul,"
but only of a conscious surviving *Ego-soul,*
i. e., that principle which survives after a
man, and reincarnates in a like man. The
animal has an astral body, that survives the
physical form for a short period; but its
(animal) Monad does not re-incarnate in the
same, but in a higher species, and has no
" Devachan " of course. It has the *seeds*
of all the human principles in itself, but
they are *latent.*
371. *Manual of Geology,* p. 302.

Now why has less change taken place in Australia than elsewhere? Where is the *raison d'être* for such a "curse of retardation"? It is simply because the nature of the environment develops *pari passu* with the race concerned. Correspondences rule in every quarter. The survivors of those later Lemurians, who escaped the destruction of their fellows when the main continent was submerged, became the ancestors of a portion of the present native tribes. Being a very low sub-race, begotten originally of animals, of monsters, whose very fossils are now resting miles under the sea floors, their stock has since existed in an environment strongly subjected to the *law of retardation*. Australia is one of the oldest lands now above the waters, and in the senile decrepitude of old age, its "*virgin* soil" notwithstanding. It can produce no new forms, unless helped by new and fresh races, and artificial cultivation and breeding.

To return, however, once more to the history of the Third Race, the " Sweat-Born," the " Egg-bearing," and the "Androgyne." Almost sexless, in its early beginnings, it became bisexual or androgynous; very gradually of course. The passage from the former to the latter transformation required numberless generations, during which the simple cell that issued from the earliest parent (the two in one), first developed into a bisexual being; and then the cell, becoming a regular egg, gave forth a unisexual creature. The Third-Race-mankind is the most mysterious of all the hitherto developed five Races. The mystery of the " How " of the generation of the distinct sexes must, of course, be very obscure here, as it is the business of an embryologist and a specialist, the present work giving only faint outlines of the process. But it is evident that the units of the Third Race humanity began to separate in their pre-natal shells, or eggs,[372] and to issue out of them as distinct male and female babes, ages after the appearance of its early progenitors. And, as time rolled on its geological periods, the newly born sub-races began to lose their natal capacities. Toward the end of the fourth *sub-race,* the babe lost its faculty of walking as soon as liberated from its shell, and by the end of the fifth, mankind was born under the same conditions and by the same identical process as our historical generations. This required, of course, millions of years. The reader has been made acquainted with the approximate figures, at least of the exoteric calculations, in Stanza II.

---

372. The "fables" and "myths" about Leda and Jupiter, and such like, could never have sprung up in people's fancy, had not the allegory rested on a fact in nature. Evolution, gradually transforming man into a mammal, did in his case only what it did in that of other animals. But this does not prevent man from having always stood at the head of the animal world and other organic species, and from having preceded the former.

We are approaching the turning-point of the evolution of the Races. Let us see what occult philosophy says on the origin of language.

---

36. THE FOURTH RACE DEVELOPED SPEECH.

The Commentaries explain that the first Race — the ethereal or astral Sons of Yoga, also called " Self-born " — was, in our sense, speechless, as it was devoid of mind on our plane. The Second Race had a " Sound-language," to wit, chant-like sounds composed of vowels alone. The Third Race developed in the beginning a kind of language which was only a slight improvement on the various sounds in Nature, on the cry of gigantic insects and of the first animals, which, however, were hardly nascent in the day of the "Sweat-born" (the *early* Third Race). In its second half, when the " Sweat-born " gave birth to the " Egg-born," (the *middle* Third Race) ; and when these, instead of " hatching out " (may the reader pardon the rather ridiculous expression when applied to human beings in our age) as androgynous beings, began to evolve into separate males and females ; and when the same law of evolution led them to reproduce their kind sexually, an act which forced the creative gods, compelled by Karmic law, to incarnate in *mindless* men ; then only was speech developed. But even then it was still no better than a tentative effort. The whole human race was at that time of " one language and of one lip." This did not prevent the last two Sub-Races of the Third Race [373] from building cities, and sowing far and wide the first seeds of civilization under the guidance of their divine instructors,[374] and their own already awakened minds. Let the reader also bear in mind that, as each of the seven races is divided into four ages — the Golden, Silver, Bronze, and Iron Age — so is every smallest division of such races.[375] Speech then developed, according to occult teaching, in the following order :—

I. Monosyllabic speech ; that of the first approximately fully developed human beings at the close of the Third Root-race, the " golden-colored," yellow-complexioned men, after their separation into sexes, and the full awakening of their minds. Before that, they communicated

---

373. To avoid confusion, let the reader remember that the term Root-Race applies to one of the seven great Races, sub-Race to one of its great Branches, and Family-Race to one of the sub-divisions, which include nations and large tribes.

374. In the Section on the Divine Dynasties, the nature of these " Instructors " is explained.

375. *Vide* Section attached to the " Divisions into Yugas."

through what would now be called "thought-transference," though, with the exception of the Race called the "Sons of Will and Yoga" — the first in whom the "Sons of Wisdom" had incarnated — thought was but very little developed in nascent physical man, and never soared above a low terrestrial level. Their physical bodies belonging to the Earth, their Monads remained on a higher plane altogether. Language could not be well developed before the full acquisition and development of their reasoning faculties. This monosyllabic speech was the vowel parent, so to speak, of the monosyllabic languages mixed with hard consonants, still in use amongst the yellow races which are known to the anthropologist.[376]

II. These linguistic characteristics developed into the agglutinative languages. The latter were spoken by some Atlantean races, while other parent stocks of the Fourth Race preserved the mother-language. And as languages have their cyclic evolution, their childhood, purity, growth, *fall into matter*, admixture with other languages, maturity, decay and finally death,[377] so the primitive speech of the most civilized Atlantean races — that language, which is referred to as "Râkshasî Bhâshâ," in old Sanskrit works — decayed and almost died out. While the "cream" of the Fourth Race gravitated more and more toward the apex of physical and intellectual evolution, thus leaving as an heirloom to the nascent Fifth (the Aryan) Race the inflectional, highly developed languages, the agglutinative decayed and remained as a fragmentary fossil idiom, scattered now, and nearly limited to the aboriginal tribes of America.

376. The present yellow races are the descendants, however, of the early branches of the Fourth Race. Of the third, the only *pure and direct* descendants are, as said above, a portion of the fallen and degenerated Australians, whose far distant ancestors belonged to a division of the seventh Sub-race of the Third. The rest are of mixed Lemuro-Atlantean descent. They have since then entirely changed in stature and intellectual capacities.

377. *Language* is certainly coeval with reason, and could never have been developed before men became one with the informing principles in them — those who fructified and awoke to life the mânasic element dormant in primitive man. For, as Professor Max Müller tells us in his *Science of Thought*, "Thought and language are identical." Yet to add to this the reflection that *thoughts which are too deep for words, do not really exist at all*, is rather risky, as thought impressed upon the astral tablets exists in eternity whether expressed or not. Logos is both reason and speech. But language, proceeding in cycles, is not always adequate to express *spiritual* thoughts. Moreover, in one sense, the Greek Logos is the equivalent of the Sanskrit Vâch, "the immortal (intellectual) ray of spirit." And the fact that Vâch (as Devasenâ, an *aspect* of Sarasvatî, the goddess of hidden Wisdom) is the spouse of the eternal celibate Kumâra, unveils a suggestive, though veiled, reference to the Kumâras, those "who refused to create," but who were compelled later on to complete *divine* Man by incarnating in him. All this will be fully explained in the sections that follow.

III. The inflectional speech — the root of the Sanskrit, very erroneously called " the elder sister " of the Greek, instead of its mother —
was the first language (now the mystery tongue of the Initiates, of the
Fifth Race). At any rate, the " Semitic " languages are the bastard
descendants of the first phonetic corruptions of the eldest children of
the early Sanskrit. The occult doctrine admits of no such divisions as
the Aryan and the Semite, accepting even the Turanian with ample
reservations. The Semites, especially the Arabs, are later Aryans
— degenerate in spirituality and perfected in materiality. To these
belong all the Jews and the Arabs. The former are a tribe descended
from the Chandâlas of India, the outcasts, many of them ex-Brâhmans,
who sought refuge in Chaldaea, in Scinde, and Aria (Iran), and were
truly born from their father A-bram (No Brâhman) some 8000 years
B. C. The latter, the Arabs, are the descendants of those Aryans who
would not go into India at the time of the dispersion of nations, some
of whom remained on the borderlands thereof, in Afghanistan and
Kabul,[378] and along the Oxus, while others penetrated into and in-
vaded Arabia.

But this was when Africa had already been raised as a continent.
We have meanwhile to follow, as closely as limited space will permit,
the gradual evolution of the now truly human species. It is in the
suddenly arrested evolution of certain sub-races, and their forced and
violent diversion into the purely animal line by artificial cross-breeding,
truly analogous to the hybridization, which we have now learned to
utilize in the vegetable and animal kingdoms, that we have to look for
the origin of the anthropoids.

---

378. Ptolemy, speaking in his ninth table
of the *Kabolitae* (Kabul tribes), calls them
'Αριστόφυλοι, *Aristophyli*, the aristocratic
or *noble tribes*. The Afghans call themselves *Ben-Issrael* (children of Is(sa)rael),
from *Issa*, "woman and also earth," Sons
of Mother Earth. But if you call an Af-
ghan *Yahoudi* (*Jew*), he will kill you. The
subject is fully treated elsewhere. The
names of the supposed twelve tribes and the
names of the real tribes, the same in number, of the Afghans, are the same. The
Afghans being far older (at any rate, their
Arabic stock) than the Israelites, no one
need be surprised to find such tribal names
among them as *Youssoufsic*, " Sons of Joseph " in Punjaure and Boonere; the
Zablistanee (Zebulon); Ben-manasseh (sons
of Manasseh) among the Khojar Tartars;
Isaguri, or Issachar (now Ashnagor in Afghanistan), etc., etc. The whole twelve
names of the so-called twelve tribes are
names of the signs of the Zodiac, as is
now well proven. At any rate, the names
of the oldest Arabic tribes, re-transliter-
ated, yield the names of the zodiacal signs,
and of the mythical sons of Jacob likewise.
Where are the traces of the Jewish twelve
tribes? Nowhere. But there is a trace,
and a good one, that the Jews have tried
to deceive people with the help of those
names. For, see what happens *ages after
the ten tribes* had wholly disappeared from
Babylon. Ptolemy Philadelphus, desiring to
have the Hebrew Law translated for him
into Greek (the famous *Septuagint*), wrote
to the high priest of the Jews, Eleazar, to
*send him six men from each of the twelve
tribes;* and the *seventy-two representatives*
(of whom sixty were ghosts apparently)
came to the king in Egypt and translated
the law amid miracles and wonders. See
Butler's *Horae Biblicae*, Josephus, and Philo
Judaeus.

In these red-haired and hair-covered monsters, the fruit of the un-natural connexion between men and animals, the " Lords of Wisdom " did not incarnate, as we see. Thus by a long series of transforma-tions due to unnatural cross-breeding (unnatural " sexual selection "), originated in due course of time the lowest specimens of humanity; while further bestiality and the fruit of their first animal efforts of reproduction begat a species which developed into mammalian apes ages later.[379]

As to the separation of sexes, it did not occur suddenly, as one may think. Nature proceeds slowly in whatever she does.

---

37. THE ONE (*androgyne*) BECAME TWO; ALSO ALL THE LIVING AND CREEPING THINGS, THAT WERE STILL ONE, GIANT-FISH, BIRDS, AND SERPENTS WITH SHELL-HEADS (*a*).

(*a*) This relates evidently to the so-called age of the amphibious reptiles, during which ages science maintains that *no man existed!* But what could the ancients know of antediluvian prehistoric animals and monsters ! Nevertheless, in Book VI of the Commentaries is found a passage which says, freely translated :—

" *When the Third separated and fell into sin by breeding men-animals, these* (the animals) *became ferocious, and men and they mutually destructive. Till then, there was no sin, no life taken. After* (the separation) *the Satya* (Yuga) *was at an end. The eternal spring became constant change and seasons succeeded. Cold forced men to build shelters and devise clothing. Then man appealed to the superior Fathers* (the higher gods or angels). *The Nirmânakâya of the Nâgas, the wise Serpents and Dragons of Light came, and the precursors of the Enlightened* (Buddhas). *Divine Kings descended and taught men sciences and arts, for man could live no longer in the first land* (Âdi-Varsha, the Eden of the first Races), *which had turned into a white frozen corpse.*"

The above is suggestive. We will see what can be inferred from this brief statement. Some may incline to think that there is more in it than is apparent at first sight.

---

379. The Commentary explains that the apes are the only species, among the ani-mals, which has gradually and with every generation and variety tended more and more to return to the original type of its male forefather — the dark gigantic Lemur-ian and Atlantean.

EDENS, SERPENTS, AND DRAGONS

Whence the idea, and the true meaning of the term "Eden"?
Christians will maintain that the Garden of Eden is the holy Paradise,
the place *desecrated by the sin* of Adam and Eve; the Occultist will
deny this dead-letter interpretation, and show the reverse. One need
not believe and see in the Bible divine revelation in order to say that
this ancient book, if read esoterically, is based upon the same universal
traditions. What Eden was is partially shown in *Isis Unveiled*.[380]

It was said that: "The Garden of Eden as a locality is no myth at
all; it belongs to those landmarks of history which occasionally disclose
to the student that the *Bible* is not all mere allegory. Eden, or the
Hebrew נן־עדן Gan-Eden, meaning the park or the garden of Eden,
is an archaic name of the country watered by the Euphrates and its
many branches, from Asia and Armenia to the Erythraean sea."
(Alex. Wilder says that Gan-duniyas is a name of Babylonia.)   In the
Chaldaean *"Book of Numbers,"* the location is designated in numerals,
and in the cypher Rosicrucian manuscript, left by Count St. Germain,
it is fully described.   In the Assyrian *Tablets* it is rendered *Gan-
duniyas*.   "Behold," says the אלהים (*Elohim*) of *Genesis*, "the man
is become as one of us."   The *Elohim* may be accepted in one sense
for *gods* or powers, and in another for *Aleim*, or priests — the hierophants initiated into the good and evil of this world; for there was a
college of priests called the *Aleim*, while the head of their caste, or the
chief of the hierophants was known as *Java-Aleim*.   Instead of becoming a neophyte, and gradually obtaining his esoteric knowledge
through a regular initiation, an *Adam*, or Man, uses his intuitional
faculties and, prompted by the serpent (*Woman* and matter), tastes of
of the Tree of Knowledge — the esoteric or Secret Doctrine — unlawfully. The priests of Hercules, or Mel-karth, the "Lord of the Eden,"
all wore "coats of skin." The text says: "And *Java-Aleim* made for
Adam and his wife כתנותעור 'Chitonuth-our.'" The first Hebrew
word, *"chiton,"* is the Greek χιτών, Chiton. It became a Slavonic word
by adoption from the *Bible* and means a *coat*, an upper garment.

"Though containing the same substratum of esoteric truth as does
every early Cosmogony, the Hebrew Scripture wears on its face the
marks of a double origin. Its *Genesis* is purely a reminiscence of the
Babylonian captivity. The names of places, men and even objects, can
be traced from the original text to the Chaldaeans and the Akkadians,
the progenitors and Aryan instructors of the former. It is strongly
contested that the Akkad tribes of Chaldaea, Babylonia and Assyria

380. Vol. I, pp. 575, *et seq.*

were in any way cognate with the Brâhmans of Hindûstân; but there are more proofs in favor of this opinion than otherwise. The Shemite or Assyrian ought, perchance, to have been called the Turanian, and the Mongolians have been denominated Scyths. But if the Akkadians ever existed, otherwise than in the imagination of some ethnologists and philologists, they certainly would never have been a Turanian tribe, as some Assyriologists have striven to make us believe. They were simply emigrants on their way to Asia Minor from India, the cradle of humanity, and their sacerdotal adepts tarried to civilize and initiate a barbarian people. Halévy proved the fallacy of the Turanian mania in regard to Akkadian people, and other scientists have proved that the Babylonian civilization was neither born nor developed in that country. It was imported from India, and the importers were Brâhmanical Hindûs."

And now, ten years after this was written, we find ourselves corroborated by Professor Sayce, who says in his first Hibbert lecture that the culture of the Babylonian city Eridu was of *foreign importation.* It came from India.

Much of the theology was borrowed by the Semites from the non-Semitic Akkadians or proto-Chaldaeans, whom they supplanted, and whose local cults they had neither the will nor the power to uproot. Indeed, throughout a long course of ages the two races, Semites and Akkadians, lived side by side, their notions and worship of the gods blending insensibly together.

Here, the Akkadians are called "non-Semitic," as we had insisted they were in "*Isis*," which is another corroboration. And we are no less right in always maintaining that the Jewish Biblical history was a compilation of *historical* facts, arranged from other people's history in Jewish garb — *Genesis* excluded, which is esotericism pure and simple. But it is really from the Euxine to Kashmir and beyond, that science has to search for the cradle — or rather one of the chief cradles — of mankind and the sons of Ad-ah; and especially in after times, when the Garden of Ed-en on the Euphrates became the college of the astrologers and magi, the Aleim.

But this "college" and this Eden belong to the Fifth Race, and are simply a faint reminiscence of the Âdi-varsha, of the primeval Third Race. What is the etymological meaning of the word *Eden?* In Greek it is ἡδονή, signifying *voluptuousness.* In this aspect it is no better than the Olympus of the Greeks, Indra's heaven (Svarga) on Mount Meru, and even the paradise full of *Houris,* promised by Mahomet to the faithful. The Garden of Eden was never the property of the Jews; for China, which can hardly be suspected of having known anything of the Jews 2000 B.C., has such a primitive garden in Central Asia inhabited by the "Dragons of Wisdom," the Initiates. And according to Klaproth, the hieroglyphical chart copied from a Japanese Cyclopaedia in the book of *Fo-koue-ky*, places its "Garden of Wisdom" on the plateau of Pamir between the highest peaks of the Himâlayan ranges; and describing it as the culminating point of Central Asia, shows the four rivers — Oxus, Indus, Ganges, and Silo — flowing from a common source, the "*Lake of the Dragons.*"

But this is not the Genetic Eden; nor is it the Kabalistical Garden of Eden. For the former — *Eden Illa-ah* — means in one sense Wisdom, a state like that of Nirvâna, a paradise of Bliss; while in another sense it refers to Intellectual man himself, the container of the Eden in which grows the tree of Knowledege of good and evil: man being the *Knower* thereof.

Renan and Barthélemy St. Hilaire, basing themselves "on the most solid inductions," think it impossible to doubt any longer, and both place the cradle of humanity "in the region of the Timaus." Finally, the Asiatic Journal [381] concludes that:

All the traditions of the human race gathering its primitive families at the region of their birth-place, show them to us grouped around the countries where Jewish tradition places the Garden of Eden; where the Aryans [Zoroastrians] established their Airyana Vaejo or the Meru [?]. They are hemmed in to the North by the countries which join the lake Aral, and to the South by Baltistân, or Little Tibet. Everything concurs in proving that there was the abode of that primitive humanity to which we have to be traced.

That "primitive humanity" was in its Fifth Race, when the "four-mouthed Dragon," the lake, of which very few traces are now left, was the abode of the "Sons of Wisdom," the first mind-born sons of the Third Race. Yet it was neither the only one nor the primitive cradle of humanity, though it was the copy of the cradle, verily, of the first thinking *divine* man. It was the *Paradeśa*, the highland of the first Sanskrit-speaking people, the *Hedone*, the country of delight of the Greeks, but it was not the "*bower* of voluptuousness" of the Chaldaeans, for the latter was only the reminiscence of it; and also because it was not there that the *Fall of Man* occurred after the "separation." The Eden of the Jews was *copied* from the Chaldaean *copy*.

That the Fall of man into generation occurred during the earliest portion of what science calls the Mesozoic times, or the age of the reptiles, is evidenced by the Bible phraseology concerning the serpent, the nature of which is explained in the *Zohar*. The question is not whether Eve's incident with the tempting reptile is allegorical or textual, for no one can doubt that it is the former, but to show the antiquity of the symbolism on the very face of it, and that it was not only a Jewish but a universal idea.

381. *Journal Asiatique*, seventh year, 1855.

Now we find in the *Zohar* a very strange assertion, one that is calculated to provoke the reader to merry laughter by its ludicrous absurdity. It tells us that the serpent, which was used by *Shamael* (the supposed Satan), to seduce Eve, was a kind of *flying camel* (καμηλόμορφον).

A "flying camel" is indeed too much for the most liberal-minded F. R. S. Nevertheless, the *Zohar*, which can hardly be expected to use the language of a Cuvier, was right in its description:[382] for we find it called in the old Zoroastrian MSS. *Ashmogh*, which in the *Avesta* is represented as having lost after the Fall "its *nature and its name*," and is described as a huge serpent with a camel's neck.

"There are no winged serpents, nor veritable dragons," asserts Salverte,[383] ". . . grasshoppers are called by the Greeks *winged serpents,* and this metaphor may have created several narratives on the existence of winged serpents."

There are none *now;* but there is no reason why they should not have existed during the Mesozoic age; and Cuvier, who has reconstructed their skeletons, is a witness to "flying camels." Already, after finding simple fossils of certain saurians, the great naturalist has written, that, "if anything can justify the Hydra and other monsters, whose figures were so often repeated by medieval historians, it is incontestably the *Plesiosaurus.*" [384]

We are unaware if Cuvier had added anything in the way of a further *mea culpa.* But we may well imagine his confusion, for all his slanders against archaic veracity, when he found himself in the presence of a *flying* saurian, "the Pterodactyl" (found in Germany), "78 feet long, and carrying vigorous wings attached to its reptilian body." That fossil is described as a reptile, the *little fingers of whose hands* are so elongated as to bear a long membranous wing. Here, then, the "flying camel" of the *Zohar* is vindicated. For surely, between the long neck of the Plesiosaurus and the membranous wing of the Pterodactyl, or still better the Mosasaurus, there is enough scientific probability to build a "flying camel," or a long-necked dragon. Professor Cope, of Philadelphia, has shown that the Mosasaurus fossil in the chalk was a *winged serpent* of this kind. There are characters in its vertebrae, which indicate union with the Ophidia rather than with the Lacertilia.

And now to the main question. It is well known that Antiquity has never claimed palaeontography and palaeontology among its arts and sciences; and it never had its Cuviers. Yet on Babylonian tiles, and especially in old Chinese and Japanese drawings, in the oldest Pagodas

382. See Moses Maimonides, *More Nevochim.*   383. *Science Occulte,* p. 646.
384. *Révolution du Globe,* vol. v, p. 464.

and monuments, and in the Imperial library at Pekin, many a traveler has seen and recognized perfect representations of Plesiosauri and Pterodactyls in the multiform Chinese dragons.[385]   Moreover, the prophets speak in the Bible of the flying fiery serpents,[386] and Job mentions the Leviathan.[387]   Now the following questions are put very directly:—

I. How could the ancient nations know anything of the extinct monsters of the carboniferous and Mesozoic times, and even represent and describe them orally and pictorially, unless they had either *seen those monsters themselves or possessed descriptions of them in their traditions*, which descriptions necessitate *living and intelligent eye-witnesses?*

II. And if such eye-witnesses are once admitted (unless retrospective clairvoyance is granted), how can humanity and the first palaeolithic men be no earlier than about the middle of the tertiary period? We must bear in mind that most of the men of science will not allow man to have appeared before the Quaternary period, and thus shut him out completely from the Cenozoic times. Here we have extinct species of animals, which disappeared from the face of the Earth millions of years ago, described by, and known to, nations whose civilization, it is said, could hardly have begun a few thousand years ago. How is this? Evidently either the Mesozoic time has to be made to overlap the Quaternary period, or man must be made the contemporary of the Pterodactyl and the Plesiosaurus.

It does not stand to reason, because the Occultists believe in and defend ancient wisdom and science, even though winged saurians are called " flying camels " in the translations of the *Zohar*, that we believe as readily in all the stories which the middle ages give us of such dragons. Pterodactyls and Plesiosauri ceased to exist with the bulk

385. We read in the *Mémoire à l'Académie* of the "naïve astonishment of Geoffroy St. Hilaire, when M. de Paravey showed to him in some old Chinese works and Babylonian tiles dragons . . . saurians and ornithorhyncuses (aquatic animals *found only in Australia*), etc., extinct animals that he had thought unknown on earth . . . till his own day."

386. See *Isaiah*, xxx. 6: " The viper and the flying serpent unto the land of trouble and anguish," and the fiery serpents conquered by the brazen serpent of Moses.

387. The fossils reconstructed by science, which we know ought to be sufficient warrant for the possibility of even a *Leviathan*, let alone Isaiah's flying serpents, or *saraph mehophep*, which words are translated in all the Hebrew Dictionaries as "saraph," enflamed or fiery venom, and "mehophep," *flying*. But, although Christian theology has always connected both (*Leviathan and saraph mehophep*) with the devil, the expressions are metaphorical and have nought to do with the "evil one." But the word *Drakon* has become a synonym for the latter. In Bretagne the word *Drouk* now signifies "devil," whence, as we are told by Cambry (*Monuments Celtiques*, p. 299), the devil's tomb in England. *Droghedanum sepulcrum*. In Languedoc the meteoric fires and *will-o'-the-wisps* are called *Dragg*, and in Bretagne Dreag, *Wraig* (or wraith); the castle of Drogheda in Ireland meaning the devil's castle.

of the Third Race. When, therefore, we are gravely asked by Roman Catholic writers to credit Christopher Scherer's and Father Kircher's cock-and-bull stories of their having seen with their own eyes living fiery and flying dragons, respectively in 1619 and 1669, we may be allowed to regard their assertions as either dreams or fibs.[388] Nor shall we regard otherwise than as a *poetical license* that other story told of Petrarch, who, while following one day his Laura in the woods and passing near a cave, is credited with having found a dragon, whom he forthwith stabbed with his dagger and killed, thus preventing the monster from devouring the lady of his heart.[389] We would willingly believe the story had Petrarch lived in the days of Atlantis, when such antediluvian monsters may still have existed. We deny their existence in our present era. The sea-serpent is one thing, the dragon quite another. The former is denied by the majority because it exists and lives in the very depths of the ocean, is very scarce, and rises to the surface only when compelled, perhaps, by hunger. Thus keeping invisible, it may exist and still be denied. But if there was such a thing as a dragon of the above description, how could it have ever escaped detection? It is a creature contemporary with the earliest Fifth Race, and exists no more.

388. The ultramontane writers accept the whole series of Draconian stories given by Father Kircher (*Oedipus Aegyptiacus*, "*De Genere Draconum*") quite seriously. According to that Jesuit, he himself saw a dragon which was killed in 1669 by a Roman peasant, as the director of the Museo Barberini sent it to him, to take the beast's likeness, which Father Kircher did and had it published in one of his *in-folios*. After this he received a letter from Christopher Scherer, Prefect of the Canton of Soleure, Switzerland, in which that official certifies to his having seen himself *with his own eyes*, one fine summer night in 1619, a living dragon. Having remained on his balcony "to contemplate the perfect purity of the firmament," he writes, "I saw a fiery, shining dragon rise from one of the caves of Mount Pilatus and direct itself rapidly towards Flüelen to the other end of the lake. Enormous in size, his tail was still longer and his neck very extended. His head and jaws were those of a serpent. In flying he emitted on his way numerous sparks [?!] ... I thought at first I was seeing a meteor, but soon looking more attentively, I was convinced by his flight and the conformation of his body that I saw a *veritable dragon*. I am happy to be thus able to enlighten your Reverence on the *very real* existence of those animals"; in *dreams*, the writer ought to have added, of long past ages.

389. As a convincing proof of the reality of the fact, a Roman Catholic refers the reader to the picture of that incident painted by Simon de Sienne, a friend of the poet, on the portal of the Church *Notre Dame du Don* at Avignon; notwithstanding the prohibition of the Sovereign Pontiff, who "would not allow this triumph of love to be enthroned in the holy place"; and adds: "Time has injured and rubbed out the work of art, but has not weakened its tradition." De Mirville's "Dragon-Devils" of our era seem to have no luck, as they disappear most mysteriously from the museums where they are said to have been. Thus the dragon embalmed by Ulisse Aldrovandi and presented to the Musée du Sénat, either in Naples or Bologna, "was there still in 1700, but is there no more." (Vol. II, p. 247, *Pneumatologie*.)

The reader may inquire why we speak of dragons at all? We answer: *firstly*, because the knowledge of such animals is a proof of the enormous antiquity of the human race; and *secondly*, to show the difference between the zoological real meaning of the words " dragon," " *Nâga*," and " Serpent," and the metaphorical one, when used symbolically. The profane reader, who knows nothing of the mystery language, is likely, whenever he finds one of these words mentioned, to accept it literally. Hence, the *quidproquos* and unjust accusations. A couple of instances will suffice.

Sed et serpens? aye: but what was the nature of the serpent? Mystics intuitionally see in the serpent of *Genesis* an animal emblem and a high spiritual essence: a cosmic force superintelligent, a " great fallen light," a spirit sidereal, aerial and tellurian at the same time, " whose influence circumambulates the globe (*qui circumambulat terram*), as a Christian fanatic of the dead-letter (de Mirville) has it, and which only manifested itself under the physical emblem, which was the most convenient " with respect to its moral and intellectual *coils*": *i. e.* under the ophidian form.

But what will Christians make of the Brazen Serpent, the " DIVINE HEALER," if the serpent is to be regarded as the emblem of cunning and evil? The " Evil One " itself? How can the line of demarcation ever be settled, when it is traced arbitrarily in a sectarian theological spirit. For, if the followers of the Roman Church are taught that Mercury and Aesculapius, or Asklepios, who are, in truth, one, are " devils and sons of devils," and the wand and serpent of the latter were " the devil's wand "; how about the " brazen serpent " of Moses? Every scholar knows that both the *heathen* wand and the Jewish " serpent " are one and the same, namely, the *Caduceus of Mercury*, son of APOLLO-PYTHON. It is easy to comprehend why the Jews adopted the ophidian shape for their " seducer." With them it was purely *physiological and phallic;* and no amount of casuistical reasoning on the part of the Roman Catholic Church can give it another meaning, once that the mystery language is well studied, and that the Hebrew scrolls are read numerically. The Occultists know that the serpent, the *Nâga*, and the dragon have each a septenary meaning; that the Sun, for instance, was the *astronomical* and cosmic emblem of the two contrasted lights, and the two serpents of the Gnostics, the good and the evil one; they also know that, when *generalized*, the conclusions of both science and theology present two most ridiculous extremes. For, when the former tells us that it is sufficient to trace the legends of the serpents to their primal source, the astrological legend, and to meditate seriously on the *Sun*, conqueror of Python, and the celestial virgin in the Zodiac forcing back the devouring dragon, if we would have the key of all the subsequent religious dogmas; it is easy to perceive that, instead of generalizing, the author simply has his eye on Christian religion and *Revelation*. We call this one extreme. The other we see in this: when, repeating the famous decision of the Council of Trent, theology seeks to convince the masses that " from the fall of man until the hour of his baptism the devil has full power over him, and *possesses him by right (diabolum dominationem et potestatem super homines habere et jure eos possidere)*." To this Occult philosophy answers: Prove first the existence of the devil *as an entity*, and then we may believe in such congenital possession. A very small amount of observation and know-ledge of human nature may be sufficient to prove the fallacy of this theological dogma. Had SATAN any reality, in the objective or even subjective world (in the ecclesiastical sense), it is the poor devil who would find himself chronically obsessed and even possessed by the wicked — hence by the bulk of mankind. It is humanity itself, and especially the clergy, headed by the haughty, unscrupulous and intol-erant Roman Church, which have begotten, given birth to, and reared in love the evil one; but this is a digression.

The whole world of thought is reproached by the Church with having adored the serpent. The whole of humanity "incensed and at the same time stoned it." The Zend Avesta speaks of it as the Kings and Vedas do, as the Edda and the Bible. . . . Everywhere the sacred serpent, the nâga, and its shrine and its priest; in Rome it is the Vestal who prepares its meal with the same care as she bestows on the sacred fire. In Greece, Aesculapius cannot cure without its assistance, and delegates to it his powers. Every one has heard of the famous Roman embassy sent by the Senate to the god of medicine and its return with the not less famous serpent, which proceeded of its own will and by itself toward its Master's temple on one of the islands of the Tiber. Not a Bacchante that did not wind it [the serpent] in her hair, not an Augur but questioned it oracularly, not a necromancer whose tomb is free from its presence! The Cainites and the Ophites call it Creator, while recognizing, as Schelling did, that the serpent is "evil in substance and its personification." [390]

Yes, the author is right, and if one would have a complete idea of the prestige which the serpent enjoys to our own day, one ought to study the matter in India and learn all that is believed about, and still attri-buted to the *Nâgas* (Cobras) in that country; one should also visit the Africans of Whydah, the Voodoos of Port-au-Prince and Jamaica, the Naguals of Mexico, and the Pa, or men-serpents of China, etc. But why wonder that the serpent is " adored " and at the same time cursed,

390. "Sacred Serpents" on p. 432 of de Mirville's *Mémoire*.

since we know that from the beginning it was a symbol?[391]   In every ancient language the word *dragon* signified what it now does in Chinese — (*lang*) *i. e.,* "*the being who excels in intelligence*" and in Greek δράκων, or "he who sees and watches." And is it to the animal of that name that any of these epithets can apply? Is it not evident, wherever superstition and oblivion of the primitive meaning may have led savages now, that the said qualifications were intended to apply to the human originals, who were symbolized by serpents and dragons? These "originals" — called to this day in China "the Dragons of Wisdom" — were the first disciples of the Dhyânis, who were their instructors; in short, the primitive adepts of the Third Race, and later, of the Fourth and Fifth Races. The name became universal, and no sane man before the Christian era would ever have confounded the man and the symbol.

The symbol of Chnouphis, or the soul of the world, writes Champollion,

is among others that of an enormous serpent standing on human legs; this reptile, the emblem of the good genius, is a *veritable Agathodaimon*. It is often represented bearded. . . .   That sacred animal, identical with the serpent of the Ophites, is found engraved on numerous Gnostic or Basilidean stones . . . The serpent has various heads, but is constantly inscribed with the letters XNOTBIZ.[392]

Agathodaimon was endowed "with the knowledge of good and evil," *i.e.,* with divine Wisdom, as without the former the latter is impossible.[393] Repeating Iamblichos, Champollion shows him to be "the deity called Εἰχτών (or the fire of the celestial gods — the great Thoth-Hermes[394]), to whom Hermes Trismegistos attributes the invention of magic."[395]

391. This is about as just as though — a few millenniums hence — a fanatic of some future new creed, who was bent on glorifying *his* religion at the expense of *ancient* Christianity, were to say: "Everywhere the quadruped lamb was adored. The nun placed it, calling it the Agnus, on her bosom; the priest laid it on the altar. It figured in every paschal meal, and was glorified loudly in every temple. And yet the Christians dreaded it and hated it, for they slew and devoured it. . . ." Heathens, at any rate, do not eat their sacred symbols. We know of no serpent, or reptile-eaters except in Christian civilized countries, where they begin with frogs and eels, and must end with real snakes, as they have begun with lamb and ended with horse-flesh.

392. *Panthéon,* 3.

393. The solar Chnouphis, or *Agathodaimon,* is the Christos of the Gnostics, as

every scholar knows. He is intimately connected with the seven sons of Sophia (Wisdom), the seven sons of Aditi (universal Wisdom), her eighth being Mârttânda, the Sun, which seven are the seven planetary regents or genii. Therefore Chnouphis was the *spiritual Sun of Enlightenment,* of Wisdom, hence the patron of all the Egyptian Initiates, as Bel-Merodach (or Bel-Belitanus) became later with the Chaldaeans.

394. Hermes, or rather Thoth, was a generic name. Abul Feda shows in *Historia Ante-Islamitica* five Hermes, and the names of Hermes, Nebo, Thoth were given respectively in various countries to great Initiates. Thus *Nebo,* the son of Merodach and Zarpanitu (whom Herodotus calls Zeus-Belos), gave his name to all the great prophets, seers and Initiates. They were all "serpents of Wisdom," as connected with the Sun astronomically, and with Wisdom spiritually.

395. *Panthéon,* text 15.

The "*invention of magic*"! A strange term to use, as though the unveiling of the eternal and actual mysteries of nature could be *invented!* As well attribute, millenniums hence, the *invention* instead of the discovery of radiant matter to Professor Crookes. Hermes was not the inventor, or even the discoverer, for, as said in the foot-note, Thoth-Hermes is a generic name, as is Enoch (Enoïchion, the "inner spiritual eye"), *Nebo,* the prophet and seer, etc. It is not the proper name of any one living man, but a generic title of many adepts. Their connexion in symbolic allegories with the serpent is due to their enlightenment by the solar and planetary gods during thé earliest intellectual Race, the Third. They are all the representative patrons of the Secret Wisdom. Asklepios is the son of the Sun-god Apollo — and he is Mercury; Nebo is the son of Bel-Merodach; Vaivasvata Manu, the great Rishi, is the son of Vivasvat — the Sun or Sûrya, etc., etc. And while, astronomically, the Nâgas along with the Rishis, the Gandharvas, Apsarasas, Grâmanis (or Yakshas, minor gods) Yâtudhânas and Devas, are the Sun's attendants throughout the twelve solar months; in theogony, and also in anthropological evolution, they are gods and men — when incarnated in the *nether* world. Let the reader be reminded, in this connexion, of the fact that Apollonius met in Kashmir Buddhist *Nâgas* — which are neither serpents zoologically, nor yet the *Nâgas* ethnologically, but "wise men."

The Bible, from *Genesis* to *Revelation,* is but a series of historical records of the great struggle between white and black Magic, between the Adepts of the right path, the Prophets, and those of the left, the Levites, the clergy of the brutal masses. Even the students of Occultism, though some of them have more archaic MSS. and direct teaching to rely upon, find it difficult to draw a line of demarcation between the *Sodales* of the Right Path and those of the Left. The great schism that arose between the sons of the Fourth Race, as soon as the first Temples and Halls of Initiation had been erected under the guidance of "the Sons of God," is allegorized in the Sons of Jacob. That there were two schools of Magic, and that the orthodox Levites did not belong to the *holy* one, is shown in the words pronounced by the dying Jacob. And here it may be well to quote a few sentences from "*Isis Unveiled.*"

The dying Jacob thus describes his sons: "Dan," he says, "shall be a *serpent* by the way, an *adder* in the path, that biteth the horse-heels, so that his rider shall fall backwards [*i. e.,* he will teach candidates *black* magic]. . . . I have waited for thy salvation, O Lord!" Of Simeon and Levi the patriarch remarks that they ". . . *are* brethren; instruments of *cruelty* are in their habitations. O my soul, come not thou into their *secret;* unto *their assembly.*" [396]   Now in the original, the words " their secret " really are " their SOD." [397]   And Sod was the name for the great mysteries of Baal, Adonis and Bacchus, who were all sun-gods and had serpents for symbols. The Kabalists explain the allegory of the fiery serpents by saying that this was the name given to the tribe of Levi, to all the *Levites,* in short, and that Moses was the chief of the *Sodales.* [398]   It is to the mysteries that the original meaning of the " Dragon-Slayers " has to be traced, and the question is fully treated of hereafter.

Meanwhile it follows that, if Moses was the chief of the Mysteries, he was the Hierophant thereof, and further, if, at the same time, we find the prophets thundering against the " abominations " of the people of Israel, that there were two schools. " Fiery serpents " was, then, simply the epithet given to the Levites of the priestly caste, after they had departed from the *good law,* the traditional teachings of Moses: and to all those who followed *Black Magic.* Isaiah, when referring to the " rebellious children " who will have to carry their riches into the land whence come " the viper and *fiery* flying *serpent,*" [399] or Chaldaea and Egypt, whose Initiates had already greatly degenerated in his day (700 B. C.), meant the sorcerers of those lands. [400]   But these must be carefully distinguished from the " Fiery Dragons of Wisdom " and the " Sons of the Fire Mist."

In the "*Great Book of the Mysteries*" we are told that: " Seven Lords created Seven men; three Lords (Dhyân Chohans or Pitris) were holy and good, four less heavenly and full of passion. . . . The *chhâyâs* (phantoms) of the Fathers were as they."

This accounts for the differences in human nature, which is divided into seven gradations of good and evil. There were seven tabernacles ready to be inhabited by Monads under seven different Karmic conditions. The Commentaries explain on this basis the easy spread of evil,

<hr>

396. *Genesis,* chap. xlix.

397. Dunlap, in his introduction to *Sod, the Mysteries of Adoni,* explains the word " Sod " as *arcanum,* religious mystery, on the authority of Schindler's *Penteglott.* " The secret of the Lord is with them that fear him," says *Psalm* xxv. 14. This is a mistranslation of the Christians, for it ought to read " *Sod Ihoh* (the mysteries of Ihoh) are for *those who fear him* " (Dunlap, *Mysteries of Adoni,* xi). " Al (El) is terrible in the great Sod of the *Kadeshim* (the priests, the holy, the *Initiated*), *Psalm* lxxxix. 7 " (*ibid.*). The Kadeshim were very far from holy. (*Vide* Part II, " The Holy of Holies.")

398. " The members of the *priest-Colleges* were called *Sodales,*" says Freund's *Latin Lexicon* (iv. 448). " Sodalities were constituted in the Idaean Mysteries of the MIGHTY MOTHER," writes *Cicero* in *de Senectute.* (*Mysteries of Adoni.*)

399. Chap. xxx. 6.

400. The priests of Baal who jumped over the fires. But this was a Hebrew term and a local one. " Saraph " — " fiery or flaming venom."

as soon as the human Forms had become real men.   Some ancient philosophers ignored the seven in their genetical accounts and gave only four.   Thus the Mexican local *Genesis* has " four *good* men " described as the four real ancestors of the human race, " who were neither begotten by the gods nor born of woman "; but whose creation was a wonder wrought by the creative Powers, and who were made only after " *three attempts at manufacturing men had failed.*"   The Egyptians had in their theology only " four sons of God," whereas in *Pymander seven* are given — thus avoiding any mention of the evil nature of man;   though when Seth from a god sank into Set-Typhon, he began to be called " the seventh son."   Whence probably arose the belief that " the seventh son of the seventh son " is always a natural-born magician, though, at first, only a *sorcerer* was meant.   APAP, the serpent symbolizing evil, is slain by Aker, Set's serpent;[401] therefore Set-Typhon could not be that evil.   In the "*Book of the Dead*" it is commanded[402] that chapter clxiii should be read " in the presence of a serpent on two legs," which means a high Initiate, a Hierophant, for the discus and ram's horns[403] that adorn his " serpent's " head in the hieroglyphics of the title of the said chapter denote this.   Over the " serpent " are represented the two mystic eyes of Amen,[404] the hidden " mystery god."   This passage corroborates our assertion, and shows what the word " serpent " meant in antiquity.

But as to the Nâgals and Nargals, whence came the similarity of names between the Indian Nâgas and the American Naguals?

The Nargal was the Chaldaean and Assyrian chief of the Magi (Rab-Mag), and the Nagual was the chief sorcerer of the Mexican Indians. Both derive their names from Nergal-Serezer, the Assyrian god, and the Hindû Nâgas. Both have the same faculties and the power to have an attendant *daemon*, with whom they identify themselves completely. The Chaldean and Assyrian Nargal kept his *daemon*, in the shape of some animal considered sacred, inside the temple; the Indian Nagual keeps his wherever he can — in the neighboring lake, or wood, or in the house in the shape of some household animal.[405]

Such similarity cannot be attributed to *coincidence*.   A new world is discovered, and we find that, for our forefathers of the Fourth Race,

---

401. "*Book of the Dead*" xxxix.

402. Verse 13.

403. The same ram's horns are found on the heads of Moses which were on some old medals seen by the writer in Palestine, one of which is in her possession. The horns, made to form part of the shining aureole on the statue of Moses in Rome (Michael Angelo), are vertical instead of being bent down to the ears, but the emblem is the same; hence the Brazen Serpent.

404. But see Harris's "*Magic Papyrus*" No. v; and the ram-headed Amen manu-facturing men on a potter's wheel.

405. Brasseur de Bourbourg: *Mexique*, pp. 135 and 574.

it was already an old one. That Arjuna, Krishna's companion and *chela*, is said to have descended into *Pâtâla*, the "antipodes," and therein married *Ulûpî*,[406] a Nâga (or Nâgî rather), the daughter of the king of the Nâgas, Kauravya.[407]

And now it may be hoped that the full meaning of the serpent emblem is proven. It is neither that of evil, nor, least of all, that of the devil; but is, indeed, the ΣΕΜΕΣ ΕΙΛΑΜ ΑΒΡΑΣΑΞ ("the eternal Sun-Abra-sax"), the central spiritual sun of all the Kabalists, represented in some diagrams by the circle of Tiphereth.

And here, again, we may quote from our earlier volumes and enter into further explanations.

From this region of unfathomable depth (Bythos, Aditi, Shekinah, the veil of the unknown) issues forth a circle formed of spirals. This is Tiphereth; which, in the language of symbolism, means a grand cycle, composed of smaller ones. Coiled within, so as to follow the spirals, lies the serpent — emblem of Wisdom and Eternity — the dual Androgyne; the cycle representing *Ennoia*, or the divine mind (a power which does not create but which must assimilate), and the serpent, the Agathodaimon, the Ophis, *the Shadow of the Light* (non-eternal, yet the greatest divine light on our plane). Both were the *Logoi* of the Ophites: or the Unity as *Logos* manifesting itself as a double principle of Good and Evil.[407a]

Were it light alone, inactive and absolute, the human mind could not appreciate nor even realize it. Shadow is that which enables light to manifest itself, and gives it objective reality. Therefore, shadow is not evil, but is the necessary and indispensable corollary which completes Light or Good: *it is its creator on Earth.*

According to the views of the Gnostics, these two principles are immutable Light and Shadow, Good and Evil being virtually one and having existed through all eternity, as they will ever continue to exist so long as there are manifested worlds.

This symbol accounts for the adoration by this sect of the Serpent, as the Savior, coiled either around the sacramental loaf, or a Tau, the phallic emblem. As a Unity, Ennoia and Ophis are the *Logos*. When separated, one is the Tree of Life (spiritual), the other, the Tree of Knowledge of Good and Evil. Therefore, we find Ophis urging the

---

406. Ulûpî has an entirely Atlantean ring about it. Like Atlantis, it is neither a Greek nor a Sanskrit name, but reminds one of Mexican names.

407. *Mahâbhârata*, Adiparva, Slokas 7788, 7789. The *Bhâgavata Purâna*, ix, xx, 31, as explained by Sridhara, the commentator, makes Ulûpî the daughter of the king of Manipûra; but the late Pandit Dayânand Sarasvati, certainly the greatest Sanskrit and Purânic authority in India on such questions, personally corroborated that Ulûpî was daughter of the king of the Nâgas at Pâtâla, or America, 5000 years ago, and that the Nâgas were Initiates.

407a. *Isis Unveiled*, Vol. II, p. 293.

first human couple — the material production of Ilda-Baoth, but which owed its spiritual principle to Sophia-Achamoth — to eat of the forbidden fruit, although Ophis represents divine Wisdom.

The serpent, the Tree of Knowledge of Good and Evil, and the Tree of Life, are all symbols transplanted from the soil of India. The Arasa-Maram, the banyan tree, so sacred with the Hindûs (since Vishnu during one of his incarnations, reposed under its mighty shade and there taught human philosophy and sciences), is called the Tree of Knowledge and the Tree of Life. Under the protecting foliage of this king of the forests, the Gurus teach their pupils their first lessons on immortality and initiate them into the mysteries of life and death. The *Java*-Aleim of the Sacerdotal College are said, in the Chaldaean tradition, to have taught the sons of men to become like one of them. To the present day Foh-tchou,[408] who lives in his Foh-Maeyu, or temple of Buddha, on the top of the " Kuen-lun-shan,"[409] the great mountain, produces his greatest religious miracles under a tree called in Chinese Sung-Ming-Shú, or the Tree of Knowledge and the Tree of Life, for ignorance is death, and knowledge alone gives immortality. This marvelous display takes place every three years, when an immense concourse of Chinese Buddhists assembles in pilgrimage at the holy place.

Now it may become comprehensible why the earliest Initiates and Adepts, or the " Wise Men," for whom it is claimed that they were initiated into the mysteries of nature by the UNIVERSAL MIND, represented by the highest angels, were named the " Serpents of Wisdom " and " Dragons "; as also how the first physiologically complete couples — after being initiated into the mystery of human creation through Ophis, the *manifested Logos* and the androgyne, by eating of the fruit of knowledge — gradually began to be accused by the material spirit of posterity of having *committed Sin*, of having disobeyed the " Lord God," and of having been tempted by the Serpent.

So little have the first Christians (who despoiled the Jews of their Bible) understood the first four chapters of *Genesis* in their esoteric meaning, that they never perceived that not only was no sin intended in this disobedience, but that actually the " Serpent " was " the Lord God " himself, who, as the Ophis, the Logos, or the bearer of divine creative wisdom, taught mankind to become creators in their turn.[410] They never realized that the *Cross was* an evolution from the " tree

408. Foh-tchou, literally, in Chinese meaning Buddha's lord, or the teacher of the doctrines of Buddha-Foh.

409. This mountain is situated southwest of China, almost between China and Tibet.

410. Let the reader be reminded that in

the *Zohar*, and also in all the Kabalistic works, it is maintained that "Metatron united to *Shekinah*" (or Shekinah as the veil (grace) of Ain-Soph), representing the Logos, is that very *Tree of Knowledge;* while Shamael — the dark aspect of the

and the serpent," and thus *became the salvation of mankind*. By this it would become the very first fundamental symbol of Creative cause, applying to geometry, to numbers, to astronomy, to measure and to animal reproduction. According to the Kabala the *curse on man came with the formation of woman*.[411] The circle was separated from its diameter line.

From the possession of the double principle in one, that is the Androgyne condition, the separation of the dual principle was made, presenting two opposites, whose destiny it was, for ever after, to seek reunion into the original *one* condition. The curse was this, viz.: that nature, impelling the search, evaded the desired result by the production of a new being, distinct from that reunion or oneness desired, by which the natural longing to recover a lost state was and is for ever being cheated. It is by this tantalizing process of a continued curse that Nature lives.[412] (*Vide* " Cross and Circle," Part II, § xxii.)

The allegory of Adam being driven away from the " Tree of Life " means, esoterically, that the newly separated Race abused and dragged the mystery of Life down into the region of animalism and bestiality. For, as the *Zohar* shows, that Matronethath (Shekinah, the wife of Metatron symbolically) " is the way to the great Tree of Life, the Mighty Tree," and Shekinah is divine grace. As explained: This Tree reaches the heavenly vale and is hidden between three mountains (the upper triad of principles, in man). From these three mountains, the Tree ascends above (the adept's knowledge aspires heavenward) and then re-descends below (into the adept's *Ego* on Earth). This Tree is revealed in the day time and is hidden during the night, *i. e.*, revealed to an enlightened mind and hidden to Ignorance, which is night.[413] " The Tree of the Knowledge of the Good and the Evil grows from the roots of the Tree of Life." [414] But then also:

In the Kabala it is plainly to be found that " the *' Tree of Life '* was the

---

Logos — occupies only the rind of that tree, and has the knowledge of ƏVIL alone. As Lacour, who saw in the scene of the Fall (chap. iii, *Genesis*) an incident pertaining to Egyptian Initiation, says: — " The Tree of the *Divination*, or of the *Knowledge* of Good and Evil . . . is the science of *Tryphon*, the genius of doubt, *Try* to teach, and *phon*, doubt. Tryphon is one of the Aleim; we shall see him presently under the name of *Nach*, the tempter" (*Les Eloim*, Vol. II, p. 218). He is now known to the symbologists under the name JƏHOVAH.

411. This is the view taken and adopted by all the Church Fathers, but it is not the real esoteric teaching. The *curse* did not begin with the formation of either man or woman, for their separation was a natural sequence of evolution, but for *breaking the law* (See *supra*).

412. " By which (human) nature lives," not even the animal — but the misguided, sensual and vicious nature, which *men, not nature, created*.

413. See *Zohar* I, 172, *a* and *b*.

414. Commentary.

ansated cross in its sexual aspect, and that the 'Tree of Knowledge' was the separation and the coming together again to fulfil the fatal condition. To display this in numbers the values of the letters composing the word Otz (yy), tree, are 7 and 9, the seven being the holy feminine number and the nine the number of the phallic or male energy. This ansated cross is the symbol of the Egyptian *female-male*, Isis-Osiris, the germinal principle in all forms, based on the primal manifestation applicable in all directions and in all senses."[415]

This is the Kabalistic view of the Western Occultists, and it differs from the more philosophical Eastern or Âryan views upon this subject.[416] The separation of the sexes was in the program of nature and of natural evolution; and the creative faculty in male and female was a gift of Divine wisdom. In the truth of such traditions the whole of antiquity, from the patrician philosopher to the humblest spiritually inclined plebeian, has believed. And as we proceed, we may successfully show that the *relative* truth of such legends, if not their absolute exactness — vouched for by such giants of intellect as were Solon, Pythagoras, Plato, and others — begins to dawn upon more than one modern scientist. He is perplexed; he stands startled and confused before proofs that are being daily accumulated before him; he feels that there is no way of solving the many historical problems that stare him in the face, unless he begins by accepting ancient traditions. Therefore, in saying that we believe absolutely in ancient records and *universal* legends, we need hardly plead guilty before the impartial observer, for other and far more learned writers, among those who belong to the modern scientific school, evidently believe in much that the Occultists do: *e. g.*, in " Dragons," not only symbolically, but also in their actual existence at one time.

It would have indeed been a bold step for anyone, some thirty years ago, to have thought of treating the public to a collection of stories ordinarily reputed fabulous, and of claiming for them the consideration due to genuine realities, or to have advocated tales, believed to be time-honored fictions, as actual facts; and those of the nursery as being, in many instances, legends, more or less distorted, descriptive of real beings or events. Nowadays it is a less hazardous proceeding. . . .

Thus opens the introduction to a recent (1886) and most interesting work by Mr. Charles Gould, called *Mythical Monsters.* He boldly states his belief in most of these monsters. He submits that:—

Many of the so-called mythical animals, which, throughout long ages and in all nations, have been the fertile subjects of fiction and fable, come legitimately

415. *The Source of Measures.*   416. *Vide infra*, " The Septenary," in Part II.

within the scope of plain matter-of-fact natural history; and that they may be considered, not as the outcome of exuberant fancy, but as creatures which really once existed, and of which, unfortunately, only imperfect and inaccurate descriptions have filtered down to us, probably very much refracted, through the mists of time. . . . Traditions of creatures *once co-existing with man, some of which are so weird and terrible as to appear at first sight to be impossible.* . . . For me the major part of those creatures are not chimeras but objects of rational study. The dragon, in place of being a creature evolved out of the imagination of an Aryan man by the contemplation of lightning flashing through the caverns which he tenanted, as is held by some mythologists, is an animal which once lived and dragged its ponderous coils and perhaps flew. . . . To me the specific instance of the Unicorn seems not incredible, and in fact, more probable than that theory which assigns its origin to a lunar myth.[417] . . . For my part I doubt the general derivation of myths from "the contemplation of the visible workings of external nature." It seems to me easier to suppose that the palsy of time has enfeebled the utterance of these oft-told tales until their original appearance is almost unrecognizable, than that *uncultured savages should possess powers of imagination and poetical invention far beyond those enjoyed by the most instructed nations of the present day;* less hard to believe that these wonderful stories of gods and demigods, of giants and dwarfs, of dragons and monsters of all descriptions are *transformations than to believe* them to be inventions.[418]

It is shown by the same geologist that man, " successively traced to periods *variously estimated from thirty thousand to one million years* . . ., co-existed with animals which have long since become extinct."[419] These animals, " weird and terrible," were, to give a few instances — (1) " Of the *genus Cidastes,* whose huge bones and vertebrae show them to have attained a length of nearly two hundred feet . . ." The remains of such monsters, no less than ten in number, were seen by Professor Marsh in the Mauvaises Terres of Colorado, strewn upon the plains. (2) The *Titanosaurus montanus,* reaching fifty or sixty feet in length; (3) the *Dinosaurians* (in the Jurassic beds of the Rocky Mountains), of still more gigantic proportions; (4) the *Atlantosaurus immanis,* a *femur* of which alone is over six feet in length, and which would be thus over one hundred feet in length! But even yet the line has not been reached, and we hear of the discovery of remains of such titanic proportions as to possess a thigh-bone over twelve feet in length.[420] Then we read of the monstrous *Sivatherium* in the Himâlayas, the four-horned stag, as large as an elephant, and exceeding the latter in height; of the gigantic *Megatherium;* of colossal flying lizards, *Pterodactyli,* with crocodile jaws on a duck's head, etc., etc. *All these*

417. *The Unicorn: a Mythological Investigation,* Robert Brown, Jun., F. S. A.
    418. Pages 2 to 4, Introduction to *Mythical Monsters.*
419. Page 20.   420. Page 37.

were co-existent with man, most probably attacked man, as man at-
tacked them; and we are asked to believe that the said man was no
larger then than he is now! Is it possible to conceive that, surrounded
in Nature with such monstrous creatures, man, unless himself a
colossal giant, could have survived, while all his foes have perished?
Is it with his stone hatchet that he had the best of a *Sivatherium* or a
gigantic flying saurian? Let us always bear in mind that at least one
great man of science, de Quatrefages, sees no good scientific reasons
why man should not have been "contemporaneous with the earliest
mammalia and go back as *far as the Secondary Period.*" [421]

"It appears," writes the very conservative Professor Jukes, "that
the flying dragons of romance had something like a real existence in
former ages of the world." [422]   The author goes on to ask:

Does the written history of man, comprising a few thousand years, embrace
the whole course of his intelligent existence? Or have we in the long mythical
eras, extending over hundreds of thousands of years, and recorded in the
chronologies of Chaldaea and China, shadowy mementos of prehistoric man,
handed down by tradition, and perhaps transported by a few survivors to existing lands, from others which, like the fabled (?) Atlantis of Plato, may have
been submerged, or the scene of some great catastrophe which destroyed them
with all their civilization. [423]

The few remaining giant animals, such as elephants, themselves
smaller than their ancestors the Mastodons, and Hippopotami, are the
only surviving relics, and tend to disappear more entirely with every
day. Even they have already had a few pioneers of their future
genus, and have decreased in size in the same proportion as men did.
For the remains of a pigmy elephant were found (*E. Falconeri*) in the
cave deposits of Malta; and the same author asserts that they were
associated with the remains of pigmy Hippopotami, the former being
"only two feet six inches high; or the still-existing *Hippopotamus
(Choeropsis) Liberiensis,* which M. Milne-Edwards figures as little
more than two feet in height." [424]

Sceptics may smile and denounce our work as full of nonsense or
fairy-tales. But by so doing they only justify the wisdom of the
Chinese philosopher Chuang, who said that "the things that men do
know can in no way be compared, numerically speaking, to the things
that are unknown"; [425] and thus they laugh only at their own ignorance.

421. *The Human Species,* p. 52.

422. *Manual of Geology,* p. 301.

423. *Mythical Monsters,* page 19.

424. *Recherches sur les Mammifères,*
plate I.

425. Preface to *Wonders by Land and
Sea* (Shan Hai King).

The " Sons of God " and the " Sacred Island "

The *legend* given in *Isis*[425a] in relation to a portion of the globe
which science now concedes to have been the cradle of humanity —
though it is but one of the *seven* cradles, in truth — ran, condensed,
and now explained, as follows :—

Tradition says, and the records of the *Great Book* [the Book of Dzyan]
explain, that long before the days of Ad-am, and his inquisitive wife, He-va,
where now are found but salt lakes and desolate barren deserts, there was a
vast inland sea, which extended over Middle Asia, north of the proud Himâlayan
range, and its western prolongation. An island, which for its unparalleled
beauty had no rival in the world, was inhabited by the last remnant of the
race which preceded ours.

" The last *remnant* " meant the " Sons of Will and Yoga," who, with
a few tribes, survived the great cataclysm. For it is the *Third* Race
which inhabited the great Lemurian continent, that preceded the veritable and complete human races — the fourth and the fifth. Therefore it was said in *Isis* that —

This race could live with equal ease in water, air, or fire, for it had an
unlimited control over the elements. These were the " Sons of God "; not
those who saw the daughters of men, but the real *Elohim*, though in the oriental
Kabala they have another name. It was they who imparted Nature's most
weird secrets to men, and revealed to them the ineffable, and now *lost* " word."

The " Island," according to belief, exists to the present hour ; now,
as an *oasis* surrounded by the dreadful wildernesses of the great Desert,
the Gobi — whose sands " no foot hath crossed in the memory of man."

This word, which is no word, has traveled once around the globe, and still
lingers as a far-off dying echo in the hearts of some privileged men. The
hierophants of all the Sacerdotal Colleges were aware of the existence of this
island; but the " word " was known only to the *Java Aleim* (Mahâ Chohan in
another tongue), or chief lord of every college, and was passed to his successor
only at the moment of death. There were many such colleges, and the old
classic authors speak of them. . . .

There was no communication with the fair island by sea, but subterranean
passages, known only to the chiefs, communicated with it in all directions.[426]

Tradition asserts, and archaeology accepts the truth of the legend

---

425a. *Isis Unveiled,* vol. I, pp. 589–590.
426. There are archaeologists, who, like
Mr. James Fergusson, deny the great antiquity of even one single monument in India.
In his work, *Illustrations of the Rock-Cut
Temples of India,* the author ventures to express the very extraordinary opinion that
" Egypt had ceased to be a nation before
the earliest of the cave-temples of India
was excavated." In short, he does not admit the existence of any cave anterior to
the reign of Aśoka, and seems anxious to
prove that most of these rock-cut temples
were executed during a period extending
from the time of that pious Buddhist king
until the destruction of the Andhra dynasty
of Magadha, in the beginning of the fifth
century. We believe such a claim perfectly
arbitrary. Further discoveries will show
that it is erroneous and unwarranted.

that there is more than one city now flourishing in India, which is built
on several other cities, making thus a subterranean city of six or seven
stories high. Delhi is one of them; Allahâbâd another — examples of
this being found even in Europe; *e. g.,* in Florence, which is built on
several defunct Etruscan and other cities. Why, then, could not
Ellora, Elephanta, Karli, and Ajunta have been built on subterranean
labyrinths and passages, as claimed? Of course we do not allude to
the caves which are known to every European, whether *de visu* or
through hearsay, notwithstanding their enormous antiquity, though that
is so disputed by modern archaeology. But it is a fact, known to the
Initiated Brâhmans of India and especially to Yogîs, that there is not
a cave-temple in the country but has its subterranean passages running
in every direction, and that those underground caves and endless corridors have in their turn *their* caves and corridors.

Who can tell that the lost Atlantis — which is also mentioned in the *Secret
Book,* but, again, under another name, pronounced in the sacred language — did
not exist yet in those days? —

we went on to ask. It *did* exist most assuredly, as it was fast approaching its greatest days of glory and civilization when the last of
the Lemurian continents went down.

The great lost continent might have, perhaps, been situated south of Asia,
extending from India to Tasmania?[427] If the hypothesis (now so much doubted, and positively denied by some learned authors, who regard it as a joke
of Plato's) is ever verified, then, perhaps, will the scientists believe that the
description of the god-inhabited continent was not altogether a fable.[428] And
they may then perceive that Plato's guarded hints and his attributing the
narrative to Solon and the Egyptian priests, were but a prudent way of imparting the fact to the world, and, by cleverly combining truth and fiction, so
disconnecting himself from a story which the obligations imposed at initiation
forbade him to divulge. . . .

To continue the tradition, we have to add that the class of hierophants was
divided into two distinct categories:[429] those who were instructed by the "Sons
of God," of the island, and who were initiated in the divine doctrine of pure
revelation; and others who inhabited the lost Atlantis — if such must be its
name — and who, being of another race, (born *sexually* but of *divine* parents),
were born with a sight, which embraced all living things, and was independent
of both distance and material obstacle. In short, they were the *Fourth* Race
of men mentioned in the *Popol Vuh,* whose sight was unlimited, and who knew
all things at once.

427. America when discovered, was called
Atlanta by some native tribes.
428. Since then Donnelly's *Atlantis* has
appeared, and soon its actual existence will
have become a scientific fact.

429. It is so divided to this day, and
theosophists and Occultists, who have learned
something of the Occult but undeniable
power of Dugpaship at their own expense,
know this but too well.

In other words, they were the Lemuro-Atlanteans, the first who had a dynasty of *Spirit*-Kings, not of *Manes*, or "ghosts," as some believe (See "*Pneumatologie*"), but of actual living *Devas* (or demi-gods or *Angels*, again) who had assumed bodies to rule over them, and who, in their turn, instructed them in arts and sciences. Only, as they were *rûpa* or material Spirits, these Dhyânis were not always good. Their King *Thevetata* was one of the latter, and it is under the evil influence of this King-Demon that . . . the Atlantis-race became a nation of wicked *magicians*.

In consequence of this, war was declared, the story of which would be too long to narrate; its substance may be found in the disfigured allegories of the race of Cain, the giants, and that of Noah and his righteous family. The conflict came to an end by the submersion of the Atlantis, which finds its imitation in the stories of the Babylonian and Mosaic flood. The giants and magicians " . . . and all flesh died . . . and every man." All except Xisuthrus and Noah, who are substantially identical with the great Father of the Thlinkithians in the *Popol Vuh*, or the sacred book of the Guatemalans, which also tells of his escaping in a large boat like the Hindû Noah — Vaivasvata.

If we believe the tradition at all, we have to credit the further story that, from the intermarrying of the progeny of the hierophants of the island and the descendants of the Atlantean Noah, sprang up a mixed race of righteous and wicked. On the one side the world had its Enochs, Moseses, various Buddhas, its numerous "Saviors," and great hierophants; on the other hand, its "*natural* magicians" who, through lack of the restraining power of proper spiritual enlightenment, . . . perverted their gifts to evil purposes. . . . ◾

We may supplement this by the testimony of some records and traditions. In the *Histoire des Vierges: Les Peuples et les Continents Disparus*, the author says:—

One of the most ancient legends of India, preserved in the temples by oral and written tradition, relates that several hundred thousand years ago there existed in the Pacific ocean an immense continent which was destroyed by geological upheaval, and the fragments of which must be sought in Madagascar, Ceylon, Sumatra, Java, Borneo, and the principal isles of Polynesia.

The high plateaux of Hindûstân and Asia, according to this hypothesis, would only have been represented in those distant epochs by great islands contiguous to the central continent. . . . According to the Brâhmans, this country had attained a high civilization, and the peninsula of Hindûstân, enlarged by the displacement of the waters, at the time of the grand cataclysm, has but continued the chain of the primitive traditions born in this place. These traditions give the name of *Rutas* to the peoples which inhabited this immense equinoctial continent, and from their speech *was derived the Sanskrit*. . . . And the Indo-Hellenic tradition, preserved by the most intelligent population which emigrated from the plains of India, equally relates the existence of a continent and a people to which it gives the name of Atlantis and Atlantides, and which it locates in the Atlantic in the northern portion of the Tropics.

Apart from this fact, the supposition of an ancient continent in those latitudes, the vestiges of which may be found in the volcanic islands and mountainous surface of the Azores, the Canaries and Cape Verdes, is not devoid of geographical probability. The Greeks, who, moreover, never dared to pass beyond the pillars of Hercules, on account of their dread of the mysterious ocean, appeared too late in antiquity for the stories preserved by Plato to be anything else than an echo of the Indian legend. Moreover, when we cast a look on a planisphere, at the sight of the islands and islets strewn from the Malayan Archipelago to Polynesia, from the straits of Sunda to Easter Island, it is impossible, upon the hypothesis of continents preceding those which we inhabit, not to place there the most important of all.

A religious belief, common to Malacca and Polynesia, that is to say, to the two opposite extremes of the Oceanic world, affirms "that all these islands once formed two immense countries, inhabited by yellow men and black men, always at war; and that the gods, wearied with their quarrels, having charged Ocean to pacify them, the latter swallowed up the two continents, and, since, it has been impossible to make him give up his captives. Alone, the mountain-peaks and high plateaux escaped the flood, by the power of the gods, who perceived too late the mistake they had committed."

Whatever there may be in these traditions, and whatever may have been the place where a civilization more ancient than that of Rome, of Greece, of Egypt, and of India was developed, it is certain that this civilization did exist, and it is highly important to science to recover its traces, however feeble and fugitive they may be.[400]

This last tradition corroborates the one given from the " Records of the Secret Doctrine." The war mentioned between the yellow and the black men, relates to a struggle between the " sons of God " and the " sons of giants," or the inhabitants and magicians of Atlantis.

The final conclusion of the author, who personally visited all the islands of Polynesia, and devoted years to the study of the religion, language, and traditions of nearly all the peoples, is as follows:

As to the Polynesian continent which disappeared at the time of the final geological cataclysms, its existence rests on such proofs that to be logical we can doubt no longer.

The three summits of this continent, the Sandwich Islands, New Zealand, Easter Island, are distant from each other from fifteen to eighteen hundred leagues, and the groups of intermediate islands, Viti, Samoa, Tonga, Foutouna, Ouvea, the Marquesas, Tahiti, Paumotu, the Gambiers, are themselves distant from these extreme points from seven or eight hundred to one thousand leagues.

All navigators agree in saying that the extreme and the central groups could never have communicated in view of their actual geographical position, and with the insufficient means they had at hand. It is physically impossible

430. *Histoire des Vierges,* pages 13-15.

to cross such distances in a pirogue . . . without a compass, and travel months without provisions.

On the other hand, the aborigines of the Sandwich Islands, of Viti, of New Zealand, of the central groups, of Samoa, Tahiti, etc., *had never known each other, had never heard of each other,* before the arrival of the Europeans. *And yet each of these people maintained that their island had at one time formed part of an immense stretch of land which extended towards the West on the side of Asia.* And all, brought together, were found to speak the same language, to have the same usages, the same customs, the same religious belief. And all to the question, "Where is the cradle of your race?" for sole response, *extended their hand toward the setting sun.*[431]

Geographically, this description clashes slightly with the facts in the Secret Records; but it shows the existence of such traditions, and this is all one cares for. For, as there is no smoke without fire, so a tradition must be based on some approximate truth.

In its proper place we will show modern Science fully corroborating the above and the traditions of the *Secret Doctrine* with regard to the two lost continents. The Easter Island relics are, for instance, the most astounding and eloquent memorials of the primeval giants. They are as grand as they are mysterious; and one has but to examine the heads of the colossal statues, that have remained unbroken on that island, to recognize in them at a glance the features of the type and character attributed to the Fourth Race giants. They seem of one cast though different in features — that of a *distinctly sensual type,* such as the Atlanteans (the Daityas and "Atalantians") are represented to have in the esoteric Hindû books. Compare these with the faces of some other colossal statues in Central Asia — those near Bamian for instance — the *portrait-statues,* tradition tells us, of Buddhas belonging to *previous Manvantaras;* of those Buddhas and heroes who are mentioned in the Buddhist and Hindû works, as men of fabulous size,[432] the good and holy brothers of their wicked co-uterine brothers generally, as Râvana, the giant King of Lankâ was the brother of Kumbhakarna; all descendants of the gods through the Rishis, and thus, like "Titan and his enormous brood," all "heaven's first born." These "Buddhas," though often spoilt by the symbolical representation of the great pendent ears, show a suggestive difference, perceived at a glance, between the expression of their faces and that of the Easter Isle statues. They may be of one race — but the former are "Sons of Gods"; the latter the brood of mighty sorcerers. All these are re-incarnations, however, and apart from unavoidable ex-

---

431. *Histoire des Vierges,* pp. 307–308.
432. An approach to the statues at Ba-mian — also a Buddha 200 feet high — is found near a Jain settlement in Southern India, and appears to be the only one that remains at present.

aggerations in popular fancy and tradition, they are *historical characters.*[433] When did they live? How long ago lived the two races, the Third and Fourth, and how long after did the various tribes of the Fifth begin their strife, the wars between Good and Evil? We are assured by the Orientalists that chronology is both hopelessly mixed and absurdly exaggerated in the Purânas and other Hindû Scriptures. We feel quite prepared to agree with the accusation. Yet, if Âryan writers did allow their chronological pendulum to swing too far one way occasionally, beyond the legitimate limit of fact; nevertheless, when the distance of that deviation is compared with the distance of the Orientalists' deviation in the opposite direction, moderation will be found on the Brâhmanical side. It is the Pandit who will in the long run be found more truthful and nearer to fact than the Sanskritist. Surely, it is not because the curtailing of the latter — even when proven to have been resorted to in order to fit a personal hobby — is regarded by Western public opinion as " a *cautious* acceptance of facts," whereas the Pandit is brutally treated in print *as a liar,* that everyone has to see this in the same light. An impartial observer may judge it otherwise. He may either proclaim both unscrupulous historians, or justify both, each on his respective ground, and say: Hindû Âryans wrote for their Initiates, who read truth between the lines, not for the masses. If they did mix up events and confuse Ages *intentionally,* it was not in view of deceiving any one, but to preserve their knowledge from the prying eye of the foreigner. Otherwise, to him who *can count the generations from the Manus, and the series of incarnations specified in the cases of some heroes,*[434] the meaning and chronological order are very clear in the Purânas. As for the Western Orientalist, he must be excused, on account of his undeniable ignorance of the methods used by archaic Esotericism.

But such existing prejudices will have to give way and disappear very soon before the light of new discoveries. Already Dr. Weber's and Mr. Max Müller's favorite theories — namely, that writing was not known in India, even in the days of Pânini (!); that the Hindûs

433. Even Wilson admits that Râma and Râvana were personages founded on historical facts:— " The traditions of Southern India uniformly ascribing its civilization and the settlement of civilized Hindûs [the Fifth Race] to the conquest of Lankâ by Râma " (*Vishnu Purâna,* iii, p. 318) — the victory of the " Sons of God " over the Atlantean sorcerers, says the *true* tradition.

434. Thus we are shown one hero, to give an instance, first born as the " unrighteous but valiant monarch " (Purusha) of the Daityas, Hiranyakaśipu, slain by the Avatâr *Nara-Sinha* (Man-lion). Then he was born as Râvana, the giant king of Lankâ, and killed by Râma; after which he is reborn as Śiśupâla, the son of Râja-rishi (King Rishi) Damaghosha, when he is again killed by Krishna, the last incarnation of Vishnu. This parallel evolution of Vishnu (spirit) with a Daitya, as men, may seem meaningless, yet it gives us the key not only to the respective dates of Râma and Krishna but even to a certain psychological mystery.

had all their arts and sciences — even to the Zodiac and their architecture [435] — from the Macedonian Greeks; these and other such
cock-and-bull hypotheses, are threatened with ruin. It is the ghost
of old Chaldaea that comes to the rescue of truth. In his third
Hibbert Lecture (1887) Professor Sayce of Oxford, speaking of newly-
discovered Assyrian and Babylonian cylinders, referred at length to Ea,
the God of Wisdom, now identified with the Oannes of Berosus, the
half-man, half-fish, who taught the Babylonians culture *and the art of
writing*. This Oannes, to whom, thanks only to the Biblical Deluge, an
antiquity of hardly 1500 B. c. had been hitherto allowed, is now spoken
of in these terms:—

His city was Eridu, which stood 6000 years ago on the shores of the
Persian Gulf. The name means "the good city," a particularly holy spot,
since it was the center from which the earliest Chaldaean civilization made its
way to the north. As the culture-god was represented as coming from the sea,
it was possible that the culture of which Eridu was the seat was of foreign
importation. *We now know that there was intercourse at a very early period
between Chaldaea and the Sinaitic peninsula, as well as with India.* The
statues discovered by the French at Tel-loh (dating from at latest B. c. 4000)
were made of the extremely hard stone known as diorite, and the inscriptions
on them stated the diorite to have been brought from Magan — *i. e.*, the Sinaitic
peninsula, which was then ruled by the Pharaohs. The statues are known to
resemble in general style the diorite statue, Kephren, the builder of the second
Pyramid, while, according to Mr. Petrie, the unit of measurement marked on
the plan of the city, which one of the Tel-loh figures holds on his lap, is the
same as that employed by the Pyramid builders. *Teak wood has been found
at Mugheir, or Ur of the Chaldees, although that wood is an Indian special
product; add to this that an ancient Babylonian list of clothing mentions
sindhu, or "muslins," explained as "vegetable cloth."*

Muslin, best known as *Dacca* muslin, known in Chaldaea as Hindu
(Sindhu), and *teak* wood used 4000 years B. c.; and yet the Hindûs,
to whom Chaldaea owes its civilization (as well proven by Colonel
Vans Kennedy), were *ignorant of the art of writing* before the Greeks
taught them their alphabet — if we have to believe Orientalists!

435. Fergusson.

STANZA X

THE HISTORY OF THE FOURTH RACE

§ § (38) The Birth of the Fourth, Atlantean Race. (39) The sub-races of the Fourth Humanity begin to divide and interblend; they form the first mixed races of various colors. (40) The superiority of the Atlantean over other races. (41) They fall into sin and beget children and monsters. (42) The first germs of Anthropomorphism and sexual religion. They lose their "third Eye."

38. THUS TWO BY TWO, ON THE SEVEN ZONES, THE THIRD (*Race*) GAVE BIRTH TO THE FOURTH (*Race men*). THE GODS BECAME NO-GODS (*Sura became a-Sura*) (*a*).

39. THE FIRST (*Race*) ON EVERY ZONE WAS MOON-COLORED (*yellow-white*); THE SECOND, YELLOW, LIKE GOLD; THE THIRD, RED; THE FOURTH, BROWN, WHICH BECAME BLACK WITH SIN.[436] THE FIRST SEVEN (*human*) SHOOTS WERE ALL OF ONE COMPLEXION IN THE BEGINNING. THE NEXT (*seven, the sub-races*) BEGAN MIXING THEIR COLORS (*b*).

(*a*) To understand this verse 38, it must be read together with the three verses of Stanza IX. Up to this point of evolution man belongs more to metaphysical than physical nature. It is only after the so-called FALL, that the races begin to develop rapidly into a purely human shape. And, in order that he may correctly comprehend the full meaning of the Fall, so mystic and transcendental is it in its real significance, the student must be told at once the details which pre-

---

436. Strictly speaking, it is only from the time of the Atlantean, brown and yellow giant Races, that one ought to speak of MAN, since it was the Fourth race only which was the first *completely human species*, however much larger in size than we are now. In *Man* (by two chelas), all that is said of the Atlanteans is quite correct. It is chiefly that race which became "black with sin" that brought the divine names of the Asuras, the Rākshasas and the Daityas into disrepute, and passed them on to posterity as the names of fiends. For, as said, the Suras (gods) or Devas having incarnated in the wise men of Atlantis, the names of *Asuras* and *Rākshasas* were given to the Atlanteans; which names, owing to their incessant conflicts with the last remnants of the Third Race and the "Sons of Will and Yoga," have led to the later allegories about them in the Purānas. "Asura was the generic appellation of all the Atlanteans who were the enemies of the spiritual heroes of the Aryans (gods)."— *Man,* p. 77.

ceded this event; of which event modern theology has formed a pivot
on which its most pernicious and absurd dogmas and beliefs are made
to turn.

The archaic commentaries explain, as the reader must remember,
that, of the Host of Dhyânis, whose turn it was to incarnate as the *Egos*
of the immortal, but, *on this plane, senseless* monads — that some
" obeyed " (the law of evolution) immediately when the men of the
Third Race became physiologically and physically ready, *i.e.,* when
they had separated into sexes. These were those early conscious Beings
who, now adding conscious knowledge and will to their inherent Divine
purity, *created* by *Kriyâśakti* the semi-Divine man, who became the
seed on earth for future adepts.   Those, on the other hand, who,
jealous of their intellectual freedom (unfettered as it then was by the
bonds of matter), said:—" We can choose . . . we have wisdom," [437] and
incarnated far later—these had their first Karmic punishment prepared
for them. They got bodies (physiologically) inferior to their astral
models, because their *chhâyâs* had belonged to progenitors of an inferior degree in the seven classes.   As to those " Sons of Wisdom "
who had " deferred " their incarnation till the Fourth Race, which was
already tainted (physiologically) with sin and impurity, they produced
a terrible cause, the Karmic result of which weighs on them to this day.
It was produced in themselves, and they became the carriers of that
seed of iniquity for aeons to come, because the bodies they had to
inform had become defiled through their own procrastination.[438]

This was the " Fall of the angels," because of their rebellion against
Karmic Law.   The " fall of *man* " was no fall, *for he was irresponsible.*   But " Creation " having been invented on the dualistic
system as the " prerogative of God alone," the legitimate *attribute* pat-
ented by theology in the name of an *infinite* deity of their own making,
this power had to be regarded as " Satanic," and as a usurpation of
divine rights.   Thus, the foregoing, in the light of such narrow views,
must naturally be considered as a terrible slander on man, " created
in the image of God," a still more dreadful blasphemy in the face of
the dead-letter dogma.   " Your doctrine," the Occultists were already
told, " makes of man, created out of dust in the likeness of his God, a
vehicle of the Devil, from the first."   " Why did you make of your god a
devil—both, moreover, created *in your own image?* " is our reply. The
esoteric interpretation of the Bible, however, sufficiently refutes this
slanderous invention of theology; the Secret Doctrine must some day
become the just Karma of the Churches — more anti-Christian than
the representative assemblies of the most confirmed Materialists and
Atheists.

437. See verse 24.   438. See verses 32-36.

The old doctrine about the true meaning of the " Fallen Angels," in its anthropological and evolutionary sense, is contained in the Kabala, and explains the Bible. It is found pre-eminent in *Genesis* when the latter is read in a spirit of research for truth, with no eye to dogma, and in no mood of preconception. This is easily proven. In *Genesis* [439] the " Sons of God " — *B'ne Aleim* — become enamored of the daughters of men, marry, and reveal to their wives the mysteries unlawfully learned by them in heaven, according to Enoch; and this is the " Fall of Angels." [440]   But what is, in reality, the *Book of Enoch* itself, from which the author of *Revelation* and even the St. John of the Fourth Gospel have so profusely quoted? (*e. g.*, verse 8, in chapter x, about all who have come before Jesus, being " thieves and robbers "). Simply a *Book of Initiation*, giving out in allegory and cautious phraseology the program of certain archaic mysteries performed in the *inner* temples. The author of the *Sacred Mysteries among the Mayas and Quichés* very justly suggests that the so-called " Visions " of Enoch relate to his (Enoch's) experience at initiation, and what he learned in the mysteries; while he very erroneously states his opinion that Enoch had learned them before being converted to Christianity (! !); furthermore he believes that this book was

---

439. Chapter vi.

440. In general, the so-called *orthodox* Christian conceptions about the " fallen " angels or Satan, are as remarkable as they are absurd. About a dozen could be cited, of the most various character as to details, and all from the pen of educated lay authors, " University graduates " of the present quarter of our century. Thus, the author of *Earth's Earliest Ages*, G. H. Pember, M.A., devotes a thick volume to proving Theosophists, Spiritualists, Metaphysicians, Agnostics, Mystics, poets, and every contemporary author on oriental speculations, to be the devoted servants of the " Prince of the Air," and irretrievably damned. He describes Satan and his Antichrist in this wise:—

" Satan is the 'Anointed Cherub' of old. . . . God created Satan, the fairest and wisest of all his creatures in this part of His Universe, and made him Prince of the World, and of the Power of the Air. . . . He was placed in an Eden, which was both far anterior to the Eden of *Genesis* . . . and of an altogether different and more substantial character, resembling the New Jerusalem. Thus, Satan being perfect in wisdom, and beauty, His vast empire is our earth, if not the whole solar system. . . .

Certainly no other angelic power of greater or even equal dignity has been revealed to us. The *Archangel Michael himself is quoted by Jude as preserving towards the Prince of Darkness the respect due to a superior, however wicked he may be, until God has formally commanded* his deposition." Then we are informed that " Satan was from the moment of his creation *surrounded by the insignia of royalty*" (!!): that he " awoke to consciousness to find the air filled with the rejoicing music of those whom God had appointed. . . ." Then the Devil " *passes from the royalty to his priestly dignity*" (!!!) " Satan *was also a priest of the Most High*," etc., etc. And now — "Antichrist will be Satan incarnate" (pp. 56-59). The Pioneers of the coming Apollyon have already appeared — they are the Theosophists, the Occultists, the authors of the *Perfect Way*, of "*Isis Unveiled*," of the *Mystery of the Ages*, and even of the " LIGHT OF ASIA "!! The author notes the " *avowed origin*" (of Theosophy) *from the " descending angels*," from the " Nephilim," or the angels of the VIth ch. of *Genesis*, and the Giants. He ought to note his own descent from them also, as the present Secret Doctrine endeavors to show — unless he refuses to belong to the present humanity.

written " at the beginning of the Christian era, when . . . the customs
and religion of the Egyptians fell into decadency " ! This is hardly
possible, since Jude quotes in his epistle from the *Book of Enoch;* [441]
and, therefore, as Archbishop Laurence, the translator of the *Book of
Enoch* from the Ethiopic version, remarks, it "could not have been the
production of a writer who lived after . . . or was even coeval
with " [441a] the writers of the New Testament: unless, indeed, Jude
and the Gospels, and all that follows, was also a production of the
already established Church — which, some critics say, is not impossible. But we are now concerned with the " fallen Angels " of
Enoch, rather than with Enoch himself.

In Indian exotericism, these angels (*Asuras*) are also denounced as
" the enemies of the gods "; those who opposed sacrificial worship
offered to the latter. In Christian theology they are broadly referred
to as the " Fallen Spirits," the heroes of various conflicting and contradictory legends about them, gathered from Pagan sources. The
coluber tortuosus " the tortuous snake," a qualification said to have
originated with the Jews, had quite another meaning before the Roman
Church distorted it:— among others, *a purely astronomical meaning.*

The " Serpent " fallen from on high, *"deorsum fluens,"* was credited
with the possession of the Keys of the Empire of the Dead, τοῦ θανάτου
ἀρχή, to that day, when Jesus saw it " falling like the lightning from
heaven," [442] the Roman Catholic interpretation of *cadebat ut fulgur* to
the contrary, notwithstanding; and it means indeed that even " the
devils are subject " to the *Logos* — who is WISDOM, but who, as the
opponent of ignorance, is Satan or Lucifer at the same time. This
remark refers to divine Wisdom falling like lightning on, and quicken-
ing the intellects of those who fight the devils of ignorance and superstition. Up to the time when Wisdom, in the shape of the incarnating
Spirits of MAHAT, descended from on high to animate and call the
Third Race to real conscious life, humanity — if it can be so called in
its animal, senseless state — was of course doomed to *moral* as well as
to physical death. The Angels *fallen into generation* are referred to
metaphorically as *Serpents* and *Dragons of Wisdom.* On the other
hand, regarded in the light of the Logos, the Christian Savior, like
Krishna, whether as man or logos, may be said to have saved those
who believed in the secret teachings from " eternal death," to have
conquered the Kingdom of Darkness, or Hell, as every Initiate does.
This in the human, terrestrial form of the Initiates, and also because
the *logos* is Christos, that principle of our inner nature which develops in us into the Spiritual Ego — the Higher-Self — being formed

441. Verse 14.
441a. Preliminary Dissertation, p. xliv, ed. of 1838.   442. *Luke* x. 17, 18.

of the indissoluble union of *Buddhi* (the sixth) and the spiritual efflor-escence of *Manas*, the fifth principle.[443] " The Logos is passive Wis-dom in Heaven and Conscious, Self-Active Wisdom on Earth," we are taught. It is the Marriage of " Heavenly man " with the " Virgin of the World " — Nature, as described in *Pymander;* the result of which is their progeny — immortal man. It is this which is called in St. John's *Revelation* the marriage of the lamb with his bride.[444] That " wife " is now identified with the Church of Rome owing to the arbi-trary interpretations of her votaries. But they seem to forget that her *linen* may be fine and white *outwardly* (like the "whitened sepulcher"), but that the rottenness she is inwardly filled with, is not " the righteous-ness of Saints,"[445] but rather the blood of the Saints she has " slain upon the earth."[446] Thus the remark made by the great Initiate[447] — one that referred allegorically to the ray of Enlightenment and reason, *falling like lightning* from on high into the hearts and *minds* of the converts to that old wisdom-religion then presented in a new form by the wise Galilean Adept[448] — was distorted out of recognition (as was his own personality), and made to fit in with one of the most cruel as the most pernicious of all theological dogmas.[449]

But if Western theology alone holds the patent for, and copyright of SATAN — in all the dogmatic horror of that fiction — other nationalities

443. It is not correct to refer to Christ — as some theosophists do — as the sixth prin-ciple in man — *Buddhi.* The latter *per se* is a passive and latent principle, the spiritual vehicle of Atman, inseparable from the mani-fested Universal Soul. It is only in union and in conjunction with *Self-consciousness* that *Buddhi* becomes the Higher Self and the divine, discriminating Soul. *Christos* is the seventh principle, if anything.

444. xix, 7.

445. Verse 8, *ibid.*

446. Chap. xviii, 24.

447. *Luke* x. 18.

448. To make it plainer, any one who reads that passage in *Luke*, will see that the remark follows the report of the *seventy*, who rejoice that "even the devils [the spirit of controversy and reasoning, or the opposing power, since Satan means simply *"adversary"* or *opponent*] are subject unto us through thy name." (*Luke* x. 17.) Now, " thy name " means the name of Christos, or Logos, or the spirit of true divine wisdom, as distinct from the spirit of intellectual or mere mater-ialistic reasoning — the HIGHER SELF in short. And when Jesus remarks to this that he has

" beheld Satan as lightning fall from heav-en," it is a mere statement of his clairvoy-ant powers, notifying then that he already knew it, and a reference to the incarnation of the divine ray (the gods or angels) which *falls into generation.* For not all men, by any means, benefit by that incarnation, and with some the power remains latent and dead during the whole life. Truly " No man knoweth who the Son is, but the Father; and who the Father is, but the Son " as added by Jesus then and there (*ibid.* x. 22) — the Church " of Christ " less than any one else. The Initiates alone understood the se-cret meaning of the term " Father and the Son," and knew that it referred to Spirit and Soul on the Earth. For the teachings of Christ were *occult* teachings, which could only be explained *at the initiation.* They were never intended for the masses, for Jesus forbade the twelve to go to the Gentiles and the Samaritans (*Matt.* x. 5), and repeated to his disciples that the " mysteries of Heaven " were for them alone, not for the multitudes (*Mark* iv. 11).

449. *Vide* at the end of Stanza XI, " SATANIC MYTHS."

and religions have committed equal errors in their misinterpretation of this tenet, which is one of the most profoundly philosophical and ideal conceptions of ancient thought. For they have both disfigured and hinted at the correct meaning of it in their numerous allegories touching the subject. Nor have the semi-esoteric dogmas of Purânic Hindûism failed to evolve very suggestive symbols and allegories concerning the rebellious and fallen gods. The Purânas teem with them; and we find a direct hint at the truth in the frequent allusions of Parâśara (*Vishnu Purâna*), to all those Rudras, Rishis, Asuras, Kumâras and Munis, having *to be born in every age,* to re-incarnate in every Manvantara. This (esoterically) is equivalent to saying that the FLAMES born of the Universal Mind (Mahat), owing to the mysterious workings of Karmic Will and an impulse of Evolutionary Law, had, as in *Pymander* — without any gradual transition — landed on this Earth, having *broken through the seven Circles of fire,* or the seven intermediate Worlds, in short.

There is an eternal cyclic law of re-births, and the series is headed at every new Manvantaric dawn by those who had enjoyed their rest from re-incarnations in previous Kalpas for incalculable *Aeons* — by the highest and the earliest *Nirvânîs.* It was the turn of those " Gods " to incarnate in the present Manvantara; hence their presence on Earth, and the ensuing allegories; hence, also, the perversion of the original meaning.[450] The Gods who had *fallen* into generation, whose mission it was to complete *divine* man, are found represented later on as Demons, evil Spirits, and fiends, at feud and war with Gods, or the irresponsible agents of the one Eternal law. But no conception of such creatures as the devils and Satan of the Christian, Jewish, and Mahomedan religions was ever intended under those thousand and one Aryan allegories.[451] (See " The Fallen Angels " and " The Mystic Dragon," in Part II.)

---

450. So, for instance, in the Purânas, "Pulastya," a Prajâpati, or son of Brahmâ — the progenitor of the Râkshasas, and the grandfather of Râvana, the Great King of Lankâ (*see Râmâyana*) — had, *in a former birth,* a son named Dattoli, "who is now known as the sage Agastya " — says *Vishnu Purâna.* This name of Dattoli alone, has six more variants to it, or seven meanings. He is called respectively, Dattoi, Dattâli, Dattotti, Dattotri, Dattobhri, Dambhobi and Dambholi — which seven variants have each a secret sense, and refer in the esoteric comments to various ethnological classifications, and also to physiological and anthropological

mysteries of the primitive races. For, surely, the Râkshasas are not *demons,* but simply the primitive and ferocious giants, the Atlanteans, who were scattered on the face of the globe as the Fifth Race is now. Vasishtha is a warrant to this, if his words addressed to Parâśara, who attempted a bit of JADOO (sorcery), which he calls "sacrifice," for the destruction of the Râkshasas, mean anything. For he says, "Let no more of *these unoffending ' Spirits of Darkness '* be destroyed " (see for details *Adiparvan,* s. 176, *Mahâbhârata;* also the *Linga Purâna* " Pûrvârdha," s. 64).

451. We have a passage from a Master's

The true esoteric view about " Satan," the opinion held on this subject by the whole philosophic antiquity, is admirably brought out in an appendix, entitled " The Secret of Satan," to the second edition of Dr. A. Kingsford's *Perfect Way*.[452] No better and clearer indication of the truth could be offered to the intelligent reader, and it is therefore quoted here at some length:—

1. And on the seventh day [seventh creation of the Hindûs],[453] there went forth from the presence of God a *mighty Angel*, full of wrath and consuming, and God gave him the dominion of the outermost sphere.[454]

2. Eternity brought forth Time; the Boundless gave birth to Limit; Being descended into generation.[455]

4. *Among the Gods is none like unto him*, into whose hands are committed the kingdoms, the power and the glory of the worlds:

5. Thrones and empires, the dynasties of kings,[456] the fall of nations, the birth of churches, the triumph of Time.

For, as is said in Hermes, " Satan is the door-keeper of the *Temple of the King;* he standeth in Solomon's porch; he holdeth *the key of the Sanctuary*, that no man enter therein, save the Anointed having the arcanum of Hermes." [457]

These suggestive and majestic verses had reference with the ancient Egyptians and other civilized peoples of antiquity to the *creative and generative light of the Logos* (Horus, Brahmâ, Ahura-Mazda, etc., etc., as primeval manifestations of the ever-unmanifested Principle, *e. g.*, Ain-Soph, Parabrahm, or *Zeruan* Akarana — Boundless Time —

letter which has a direct bearing upon these incarnating angels. Says the letter: " Now there are, and there must be, failures in the ethereal races of the many classes of Dhyân-Chohans, or Devas (*progressed entities of a previous* planetary period), as well as among men. But still, as the *failures* are too far progressed and spiritualized to be thrown back forcibly from Dhyân-Chohanship into the vortex of a new primordial evolution through the lower Kingdoms, this then happens. Where a new solar system has to be evolved these Dhyân-Chohans are borne in by influx ' ahead ' of the Elementals (Entities . . . to be developed into humanity at a *future* time) and remain as a latent or inactive spiritual force, in the aura of a nascent world . . . until the stage of human evolution is reached. . . . Then they *become an active force* and commingle with the Elementals, to *develop little by little the full type of humanity.*' That is to say, to

develop in. and endow man with his Self-conscious mind, or *Manas*.

452. Appendix xv, page 369.

453. When the earth with its planetary chain and man were to appear.

454. Our earth and the physical plane of consciousness.

455. When the pure, celestial Being (Dhyân Chohan) and the various classes were commissioned — the one to evolve their images (*Chhâyâ*), and make of them physical man, the others to inform and thus endow him with divine intelligence and the comprehension of the *Mysteries of Creation*.

456. The " dynasties of the kings " who all regard themselves as the " anointed," reigning " by the Grace of God," whereas in truth, they reign by the grace of *matter*, the great *Illusion*, the Deceiver.

457. Verses 20 and 21.

Kâla), but the meaning is now degraded in the Kabala. The "Anointed," who has the secrets and mysteries of Hermes (*Buddha,* Wisdom), and who alone is entrusted with the key to the " Sanctuary," the Womb of nature, in order to fructify it and call to active life and being the whole Kosmos, has become, with the Jews, Jehovah, the "God of generation" on the lunar mountain (Sinai, the mountain of the moon, "*Sin*"). The "Sanctuary" has become the "Holy of Holies," and the arcanum has been anthropomorphized and *phallicized* and dragged down into matter, indeed. Hence arose the necessity of making of the "Dragon of Wisdom," the *Serpent of Genesis:* of the conscious god who needed a body to clothe his too subjective divinity, Satan. But the "innumerable incarnations of Spirit," and " the ceaseless pulse and current of desire " refer, the first one, to our doctrine of Karmic and cyclic rebirths, the second — to Eros, not the later god of material, physiological love, but to the divine desire in the gods, as well as in all nature, to create and give life to Beings. This, the Rays of the one "dark," because invisible and incomprehensible, FLAME could achieve only by themselves descending into matter. Therefore, as continued in the APPENDIX:

12. Many names hath God given him [Satan], names of mystery, secret and terrible.

13. The Adversary, because matter opposeth Spirit. Time accuseth even the Saints of the Lord.

28, 29, 31. Stand in awe of him, and sin not; speak his name with trembling . . . For Satan is the magistrate of the Justice of God [Karma]; he beareth the balance and the sword . . . For to him *are committed Weight and Measure and Number.*

Compare the last sentence with what the Rabbi, who explains the Kabala to Prince *Al-Chazari* in the Book of that name, says; and it will be found that the *Weight* and *Measure* and *Number* are, in *Sepher Jezirah,* the attributes of the Sephiroth (the three *Sephrim,* or figures, ciphers) covering the whole collective number of 10; and that the Sephiroth are the collective Adam Kadmon, the "Heavenly Man" or the *Logos.* Thus Satan and the anointed were identified in ancient thought. Therefore,

33. Satan is the minister of God, Lord of the seven mansions of Hades . . .

The seven or *Saptaloka* of the Earth with the Hindûs; for Hades, or the Limbo of Illusion, of which theology makes a region bordering on Hell, *is simply our globe, the Earth,* and thus Satan is called —

33. . . . the angel of the *manifest Worlds.*

It is "Satan who is the god of our planet and *the only* god," and this without any allusive metaphor to its wickedness and depravity. For

he is one with the Logos, " the first son, *eldest of the gods,*" in the order
of microcosmic (divine) evolution; Saturn (Satan), astronomically,
" is the *seventh and last* in the order of macrocosmic emanation, being
the circumference of the kingdom of which Phoebus (the light of
wisdom, also the Sun) is the center." The Gnostics were right, then,
in calling the Jewish god " an angel of matter," or he who breathed
(conscious) life into Adam, and he whose planet was Saturn.

34. And God hath put a girdle about his loins [the rings of Saturn], and
the name of the girdle is Death.

In anthropogony this "girdle" is the human body with its two lower
principles, which three die, while the innermost man is immortal. And
now we approach the "*Secret* of Satan."

37, 38, 39. . . . Upon Satan only *is the shame of generation.* He hath
lost his virginal estate [so hath the *Kumâra* by incarnating]: *uncovering heavenly secrets,* he hath entered into bondage. . . . He compasseth with bonds
and limits all things. . . .

42, 43, 44. Twain are the armies of God: in heaven the hosts of Michael;
in the abyss [the manifested world] the legions of Satan. These are the
unmanifest and the manifest; the free and the bound [in matter]: the virginal
and the fallen. And both are the Ministers of the Father, fulfilling the
word Divine. . . . [Therefore—]

55. Holy is the Sabbath of god: *blessed and sanctified is the name of the
Angel of Hades —* SATAN.

For, " The glory of Satan is the shadow of the Lord ": God in the
manifested world; " the throne of Satan is the footstool of Adonai "
— that footstool being the whole KOSMOS.[458]

When the Church, therefore, curses Satan, it curses the cosmic
reflection of God; it anathematizes God made manifest in matter or in
the objective; it maledicts God, or the ever-incomprehensible WISDOM,
revealing itself as Light and Shadow, good and evil in nature, in the
only manner comprehensible to the limited intellect of MAN.

This is the true philosophical and metaphysical interpretation of
Samael, or Satan, the adversary in the Kabala; the same tenets and
spirit being found in the allegorical interpretations of every other ancient religion. This philosophical view does not interfere, however,
with the *historical* records connected with it. We say " historical,"
because allegory and a mythical ornamentation around the kernel of
tradition, in no wise prevent that kernel being a record of real events.
Thus, the Kabala, repeating the time-honored revelations of the once
universal history of our globe and the evolution of its races, has presented it under the legendary form of the various records which have
formed the Bible. Its historical foundation is now offered, in however

458. *Vide* Part II, § XIX, " Is Pleroma Satan's Lair? "

imperfect a form, on these pages from the Secret Doctrine of the
East; and thus the allegorical and symbolical meaning of the Serpent
of *Genesis* is found explained by the "Sons of Wisdom" or (angels
from higher spheres, though all and each pertain to the kingdom of
Satan, or Matter) revealing to men the mysteries of Heaven. Hence,
also, all the so-called myths of the Hindû, Grecian, Chaldaean, and Jewish Pantheons are found to be built on fact and truth. The giants of
Genesis are the historical Atlanteans of Lankâ, and the Greek Titans.

Who can forget that Troy was once upon a time proclaimed a myth,
and Homer a non-existing personage, while the existence of such cities
as Herculaneum and Pompeii was denied, and attributed to mere fairy
legends? Yet Schliemann proved that Troy had really existed, and
the two cities, though buried for long ages under the Vesuvian lava,
have had their resurrection day, and live again on the surface of the
earth. How many more cities and localities called "fabulous" are on
the list of future discoveries, how many more personages regarded as
mythical[459] will one day become historical, those alone can tell who
read the decrees of Fate in the astral light.

As the tenets of the Eastern doctrine, however, have always been
kept secret, and as the reader can hardly hope to be shown the original
texts unless he becomes an accepted disciple, let the Greek and Latin
scholar turn to the original texts of Hermetic literature. Let him, for
one thing, read carefully the opening pages of the *Pymander* of Hermes
Trismegistos; and then he will see our doctrines corroborated in it,
however veiled its text. There also he will find the evolution of the
Universe, of our Earth (called "Nature" in *Pymander*) as of everything else, from the "Moyst Principle" — or the great Deep, FATHER-
MOTHER — the first differentiation in the manifested Kosmos. First
the "Universal Mind," which the hand of the Christian translator has
metamorphosed in the earliest renderings into God, the Father: then
the "Heavenly Man,"[460] which is the great Total of that Host of
Angels, which was too pure for the creation of the inferior worlds or
of the men of our globe, but which *fell* nevertheless *into matter* by
virtue of that same evolution, as the second *logos* of the "Father."[441]

---

459. See the "Primeval Manus of Humanity," p. 307.

460. The "Heavenly Man" — please
mark again the word — is "the Logos" or
the "Son" esoterically. Therefore, once
that the title was applied to Christ (declared
God and the very God himself) Christian
theology had no choice. In order to support its dogma of the personal Trinity it
had to proclaim, as it does, that the Christ-

ian *Logos* is the only true one, and that
all the *Logoi* of other religions were false,
and only the masquerading Evil Principles,
SATAN. Now see where this led Western
theology to.

461. "For the *Mind*, a deity abounding
in both sexes, being Life and Light, brought
forth by its *Word* another *Mind* or Work-
man; which, being God of the *Fire* and
the Spirit, fashioned and formed seven other

Synthetically every Creative Logos, or "the Son who is one with the Father," is the Host of the Rectores Mundi in itself. Even Christian theology makes of the seven "Angels of the Presence" the Virtues, or the personified attributes of God, which, being created by him, as the Manus were by Brahmâ, became Archangels. The Roman Catholic *theodice* itself recognizing, in its creative *Verbum Princeps*, the head of those angels — *caput angelorum* — and the *magni consilii Angelus* (the Angel of the great Counsel), thus recognizes the identity of Christ and those Angels.

"The *Gods became no-Gods, the Sura — A*-sura," says the text; *i. e.*, gods became fiends — SATAN, when read literally. But Satan will now be shown, in the teaching of the Secret Doctrine, allegorized as Good, and Sacrifice, a God of Wisdom, under different names.

The Kabala teaches that Pride and Presumption — the two chief prompters of Selfishness and Egotism — are the causes that emptied heaven of *one third* of its divine denizens — mystically, and of *one third* of the stars — astronomically; in other words, the two statements are — the first an allegory, and the second a fact. The former, nevertheless, as shown, is intimately connected with humanity.

In their turn the Rosicrucians, who were well acquainted with the secret meaning of the tradition, kept it to themselves, teaching merely that the whole of *creation* was due to, and the result of, that legendary "War in Heaven" *brought on by the rebellion of the angels* [462] *against creative law,* or the Demiurge. The statement is correct, but the *inner* meaning is to this day a mystery. To elude further explanation of the difficulty by appealing to divine mystery, or to the sin of prying into

---

Governors, which in their circles contain the *Phenomenal World*, and whose disposition is called Fate or Destiny." (*Pymander*, Section 9, ch. 1, ed. of 1579.)

Here it is evident that "Mind" (the primeval universal Divine Thought) is neither the Unknown unmanifested One, since it abounds in both sexes (is male and female), nor yet the Christian Father, as the latter is a male and not an androgyne. The fact is that the *Father, Son, and Man* are hopelessly mixed up in the translations of Pymander.

462. The allegory of the fire of Prometheus is another version of the rebellion of the proud Lucifer, who was *hurled down to the bottomless pit*, or simply unto our Earth, to live as man. The Hindû Lucifer,

the *Mahâsura*, is also said to have become envious of the Creator's resplendent light, and, at the head of inferior Asuras (not gods, but spirits), to have rebelled against Brahmâ; for which Siva hurled him down to Pâtâla. But, as philosophy goes hand in hand with allegorical fiction in Hindû myths, the *devil* is made to repent, and is afforded the opportunity to progress: he is a sinful man *esoterically*, and can by *yoga* devotion, and adeptship, reach his status of *one with the deity*, once more. Hercules, the Sun-god, descends to Hades (the cave of Initiation) to deliver the victims from their tortures, etc., etc. The Christian Church alone creates *eternal* torment for the devil and the damned, that she has invented.

its policy — is to say nothing at all. It may prove sufficient to believers in the Pope's infallibility, but will hardly satisfy the philosophical mind. Yet the truth, although known to most of the higher Kabalists, has never been told by any of their number. One and all, Kabalists and symbologists, showed an extraordinary reluctance to confess the primitive meaning of the Fall of the Angels. In a Christian such silence is only natural. Neither alchemist nor philosopher could, during the Medieval Ages, utter that [463] which in the sight of orthodox theology was a terrible blasphemy, for it would have led them directly through the " Holy " office of the Inquisition, to stake and rack. But for our modern Kabalists and Freethinkers the case is different. With the latter, we fear, it is merely human pride, vanity based on a loudly rejected and as ineradicable superstition. Since the Church, in her struggle with Manicheeism, invented the devil, and by placing a theo-

---

463. Why should, for instance, Eliphas Lévi, the very *fearless* and outspoken Kabalist, have hesitated to divulge the mystery of the *Fallen* Angels so-called? That he knew the fact and real meaning of the allegory — both in its religious and mystical, as well as in its physiological sense — is proved by his voluminous writings and frequent allusions and hints. Yet Eliphas, after having alluded to it a hundred times in his previous works, says in his latest *Histoire de la Magie*, p. 220, ". . . We protest with all our might against the sovereignty and the ubiquity of Satan. We *pretend neither to deny nor affirm here the tradition on the Fall of the Angels* . . . but if so, then the prince of the Angelic Rebels can be at best the last and the most powerless among the condemned — now that he is separated from deity — which is the principle of every power. . . ." This is hazy and evasive enough; but see what Hargrave Jennings writes in his weird, *staccato*-like style:—

" Both St. Michael and St. George are types. They are sainted personages, or dignified heroes, or powers apotheosized. They are each represented with their appropriate faculties and attributes. These are reproduced and stand multiplied — distinguished by different names — in all the mythologies . . . [including the Christian]. . . . The idea regarding each is a general one. This idea and representative notion is that of the all-powerful champion — child-like in his ' Virgin innocence ' — so powerful that this god-filled innocence (the Seraphim ' Know most,' the Cherubim ' love most ') can shatter the world (articulated — so to use the word — in the magic of Lucifer, but condemned) in opposition to the artful constructions . . . (this ' side-life ') of the magnificent apostate, the mighty rebel, but yet at the same time the ' Light-bringer,' the Lucifer — the ' Morning Star,' the ' Son of the morning ' — the very highest title ' out of heaven,' for in heaven it cannot be, but out of heaven it is everything. In an apparently incredible side of his character — qualities are of no sex — this archangel, St. Michael, is the *invincible*, *sexless*, *celestial* ' Energy ' — to dignify him by his grand characteristics — the invincible ' Virgin Combatant,' clothed . . . and at the same time armed, in the denying mail of the Gnostic ' refusal to create.' This is another . . . ' myth within myths ' . . . a stupendous ' mystery of mysteries,' because it is so impossible and contradictory. Unexplainable as the Apocalypse. Unrevealable as the ' Revelation ' " (*Phallicism*, pp. 212, 213).

Nevertheless, this *unexplainable* and *unrevealable* mystery will now be explained and revealed by the doctrines of the East. But as the very erudite, but still more puzzling author of *Phallicism* gives it, of course, no uninitiated mortal would ever understand the real drift of his remarks.

logical extinguisher on the radiant star-god, *Lucifer*, the "Son of the Morning," thus created the most gigantic of all her paradoxes — *a black and tenebrous light* — the myth has struck its roots too deep in the soil of blind faith to permit, in our age, even those, who do not acquiesce in her dogmas and laugh at her horned and cloven-footed Satan, to come out bravely and confess the antiquity of the oldest of all traditions. In a few brief words it is this. *Semi-exoterically,* the "First-born" of the Almighty — *Fiat Lux*, — or the angels of primordial light, were commanded *to create;* one third of them rebelled *and refused;* while those who "obeyed as Fetahil did — *failed*" most signally.

To realize the refusal and failure in their correct physical meaning, one must study and *understand* Eastern philosophy; one has to be acquainted with the fundamental mystical tenets of the Vedântins, with regard to the utter fallacy of attributing functional activity to the infinite and absolute deity. Esoteric philosophy maintains that during the *Sandhyâs*, the "Central Sun" emits *creative light* — passively so to say. *Causality* is latent. It is only during the active periods of being that it gives rise to a stream of ceaseless energy, whose vibrating currents acquire more activity and potency with every rung of the hebdomadic ladder of Being which they descend. Hence it becomes comprehensible how the process of *creating*, or rather of fashioning, the organic Universe, with all its units of the seven kingdoms, necessitated intelligent beings — who became collectively a Being or creative God — differentiated already from the one absolute Unity, unrelated as the latter is to conditioned creation.[464]

Now the Vatican MS. of the Kabala — a single copy of which (in Europe) is said to have been in the possession of Count St. Germain — contains the most complete exposition of the doctrine, including the peculiar version accepted by the Luciferians [465] and other Gnostics; and in that parchment the *Seven Suns of Life* are given in the order they are found in the *Saptasûrya*. Only four of these, however, are mentioned in the editions of the Kabala which are procurable in the public libraries, and that even in a more or less veiled phraseology. Nevertheless even this reduced number is amply sufficient to show an identical origin, as it refers to the quaternary group of the Dhyân-Chohans, and proves the speculation to have had its origin in the Secret Doctrines of

464. "Creation" — out of pre-existent eternal substance, or matter, of course, which substance, according to our teachings, is boundless, ever-existing space.

465. The Luciferians — the sect of the fourth century who are alleged to have taught that the Soul was a *carnal* body transmitted to the child by its father; — and that other religious and still earlier sect of the second century A. D., the Lucianists, who taught all this, and further, that the *animal* Soul was not immortal, were philosophizing on the grounds of the real Kabalistic and Occult teachings.

the Âryans. As is well known, the Kabala never originated with the Jews, who got their ideas from the Chaldaeans and the Egyptians. Thus even the now *exoteric* Kabalistic teachings speak of a *Central Sun*, and of three secondary suns in each solar system — our own included. As shown in that able though too materialistic work, *New Aspects of Life and Religion*, which is a *synopsis of the views* of the Kabalists in an aspect deeply thought out and assimilated:—

> The *Central Sun* . . . *was to them* [as much as to the Aryans] *the center of Rest;* the center to which all motion was to be ultimately referred. Round this central sun . . . "the first of three systemic suns . . . revolved on a polar plane . . . the second, on an equatorial plane " . . . and the third only was our visible sun. These four solar bodies were "*the organs on whose action what man calls the creation, the evolution of life on the planet, earth, depends.*" The channels through which the influence of these bodies was conveyed to the earth they [the Kabalists] held to be electrical.⁴⁶⁶ . . . The radiant energy flowing from the central sun ⁴⁶⁷ called the Earth into being as a watery globe, [whose tendency] as the nucleus of a planetary body, was to rush to the (central) Sun . . . within the sphere of whose attraction it had been created, . . . but the radiant energy, similarly electrifying both, withheld the one from the other, and so changed motion towards into motion round the center of attraction, which the revolving planet (earth) thus sought to reach.
>
> In the organic cell the *visible sun* found its own proper matrix, and produced through this the animal [while maturing the vegetable] Kingdom, finally placing man at its head, in whom, through the animating action of that Kingdom, it originated the psychic cell. But the man so placed at the head of the animal kingdom, at the head of the creation, was the animal, the *soul-less, the perishable man.* . . . Hence man, although apparently its crown, would, by his advent have marked the close of creation; since creation, culminating in him, would at his death have entered on its decline. . . .⁴⁶⁸

This Kabalistic view is here quoted, to show its perfect identity in spirit with the Eastern doctrine. Explain, or complete the teaching of the seven Suns with the seven systems of *planes of being*, of which the " Suns " are the central bodies, and you have the seven angelic

466. Page 287.

467. This " central sun " of the Occultists, which even Science is obliged to accept astronomically, for it cannot deny the presence in Sidereal Space of a central body in the milky way, a point unseen and mysterious, the ever-hidden center of attraction of our Sun and system — this " Sun " is viewed differently by the Occultists of the East. While the Western and Jewish Kabalists (and even some pious modern astronomers) claim that in this sun the Godhead is specially present — referring to it the volitional acts of God — the Eastern Initiates maintain that, as the *supra-divine* Essence of the Unknown Absolute is equally in every domain and place, the "Central Sun " is simply the center of Universal life-Electricity; the reservoir within which that divine radiance, already differentiated at the beginning of every *creation*, is focussed. Though still in a *laya*, or neutral condition, it is, nevertheless, the one attracting, as also the ever-emitting, life Center.

468. Page 289.

planes, whose "Host" are gods thereof, collectively.[469] They are the Head-group divided into four classes from the *incorporeal* down to the semi-corporeal, which classes are directly connected — though in very different ways as regards voluntary connexion and functions — with our mankind. They are three, synthesized by the fourth (the first and highest), which is called the "Central Sun" in the Kabalistic doctrine just quoted. This is the great difference between the Semitic and the Aryan Cosmogony; one materializing, humanizes the mysteries of nature; the other spiritualizes matter, and its physiology is always made subservient to metaphysics. Thus, though the seventh principle reaches man through all the phases of being, pure as an indiscrete element and an impersonal unity, it passes through (the Kabala teaches *from*) the Central Spiritual Sun and Group the second (the *polar* Sun), which two radiate on man his Âtmâ. Group *Three* (the equatorial Sun) cement the Buddhi to Âtman and the higher attributes of *Manas*, while group Four (the spirit of our visible sun) endows him with his Manas and its vehicle — the *Kâma rûpa*, or body of passions and desires, the two elements of *Ahamkâra* which evolve *individualized consciousness* — the personal *ego*. Finally, it is the spirit of the Earth in its triple unity that builds the physical body, attracting to it the Spirits of Life and forming his *Linga Sarîra*.

Now, as everything proceeds cyclically, the evolution of man like everything else, the order in which he is generated is described fully in the Eastern teachings, whereas it is only hinted at in the Kabala. Says the *Book of Dzyan* with regard to primeval man when first projected by the "Boneless," the incorporeal Creator: "*First, the Breath, then Buddhi, and the Shadow-Son* (the Body) *were* 'CREATED.' *But where was the pivot* (the middle principle, Manas)? *Man is doomed. When alone, the indiscrete* (undifferentiated Element) *and the Vâhana* (Buddhi) — *the cause of the causeless — break asunder from manifested life*" — "*unless cemented and held together by the middle principle, the vehicle of the personal consciousness of* JÎVA "; explains the Commentary. In other words, the two higher principles *can have no individuality on Earth*, cannot be *man*, unless there is (*a*) the Mind, the *Manas-Ego*, to cognize itself, and (*b*) the terrestrial *false* personality, or the body of egotistical desires and personal Will, to cement the whole, as if round a pivot (which it is, truly), to the physical form of man. It is the *Fifth* and the *Fourth* principles[470] — *Manas* and *Kâma rûpa* — that contain the dual personality: the real immortal Ego (*if it assimilates itself to the two higher*) and the false and transitory per-

469. See Commentary to Stanza VII, Book I.

470. The Fourth, and the Fifth from *below* beginning by the physical body; the Third and the Fourth, if we reckon from *Âtmâ*.

sonality, the *mâyâvi* or astral body, so-called, or the *animal-human*
Soul — the two having to be closely blended for purposes of a *full*
terrestrial existence.   Incarnate the Spiritual Monad of a Newton
grafted on that of the greatest saint on earth — in a physical body the
most perfect you can think of—*i. e.*, in a two or even a three-principled
body composed of its *Sthûla Sarîra*, prâna (life principle), and *linga
sarîra* — and, if it lacks its middle and fifth principles, you will have
created *an idiot* — at best a beautiful, soul-less, empty and unconscious
appearance.   " *Cogito — ergo sum* "— can find no room in the brain
of such a creature, not on this plane, at any rate.

There are students, however, who have long ago understood the
philosophical meaning underlying the allegory — so tortured and disfigured by the Roman Church — of the *Fallen* Angels.   " The Kingdom
of Spirits and spiritual action which flows from and is the product
of Spirit Volition, is outside and contrasted with and in contradiction
to the Kingdom of (divine) Souls and divine action." [471]   As said in
the text :—

" *Like produces like and no more at the genesis of being, and evolution with its limited conditioned laws comes later.   The Self-Existent* [472]
are called CREATIONS, *for they appear in the Spirit Ray, manifested
through the potency inherent in its* UNBORN *Nature, which is beyond
time and* (limited or conditioned) *Space.   Terrene products, animate
and inanimate, including mankind, are falsely called creation and creatures: they are the development* (evolution) *of the discrete elements.*" [473]

Again :—

" *The Heavenly rûpa* (Dhyân Chohan) *creates* (man) *in his own
form; it is a spiritual ideation consequent on the first differentiation
and awakening of the universal* (manifested) *Substance; that form is
the ideal shadow of Itself: and this is* THE MAN OF THE FIRST RACE."

To express it in still clearer form, limiting the explanation to this
earth only, it was the duty of the first " differentiated Egos " — the
Church calls them Archangels — to imbue primordial matter with the
evolutionary impulse and guide its formative powers in the fashioning
of its productions.   This it is which is referred to in the sentences
both in the Eastern and Western tradition — " the Angels were *commanded to create.*"   After the Earth had been made ready by the
lower and more material powers, and its three Kingdoms fairly started
on their way to be " fruitful and multiply," the higher powers, the
Archangels or Dhyânis, were compelled by the evolutionary Law to

471. *New Aspects of Life.*
472. Angelic, Spiritual Essences, immortal in their being because unconditioned in
Eternity;   periodical and conditioned in
their Manvantaric manifestations.
473. Commentary, xiv.

descend on Earth, in order to construct the crown of its evolution — MAN. Thus the "Self-created" and the "Self-existent" projected their pale shadows; but group the Third, the Fire-Angels, *rebelled and refused* to join their Fellow Devas.

Hindû exotericism represents them all as *Yogins,* whose piety inspired them to refuse *creating,* as they desired to remain eternally *Kumâras,* "Virgin Youths," in order to, if possible, anticipate their fellows in progress towards Nirvâna — the final liberation. But agreeably to esoteric interpretation, it was a self-sacrifice for the benefit of mankind. The "Rebels" would not create will-less irresponsible men, as the "obedient" angels did; nor could they endow human beings with only the temporary reflections of their own attributes; for even the latter, belonging to another and a so-much higher plane of consciousness, would leave man still irresponsible, hence interfere with any possibility of a higher progress. No spiritual and psychic evolution is possible on earth — the lowest and most material plane — for one who on that plane, at all events, is inherently *perfect* and cannot accumulate either merit or demerit. Man remaining the pale shadow of the inert, immutable, and motionless perfection, the one negative and passive attribute of the real *I am that I am,* would have been doomed to pass through life on earth as in a heavy dreamless sleep; hence a failure on this plane. The Beings, or the Being, collectively called Elohim, who first (if ever) pronounced the cruel words, "Behold, the man is become *as one of us,* to know good and evil; and now, lest he put forth his hand and take also of the tree of life and eat and live for ever . . ." must have been indeed the Ilda-baoth, the *Demiurge* of the Nazarenes, filled with rage and envy against his own creature, whose reflection created *Ophiomorphos.* In this case it is but natural — even from the dead letter standpoint — to view *Satan,* the Serpent of *Genesis,* as the real creator and benefactor, the Father of Spiritual mankind. For it is he who was the "Harbinger of Light," bright radiant Lucifer, who opened the eyes of the automaton *created* by Jehovah, as alleged; and he who was the first to whisper: "in the day ye eat thereof ye shall be as Elohim, knowing good and evil " — can only be regarded in the light of a Savior. An "adversary" to Jehovah the *"personating* spirit," he still remains in esoteric truth the ever-loving "Messenger" (the angel), the Seraphim and Cherubim who both *knew* well, and *loved* still more, and who conferred on us spiritual, instead of physical immortality — the latter a kind of *static* immortality that would have transformed man into an undying "Wandering Jew."

As narrated in King's *Gnostics:*

Ilda-Baoth, whom several sects regarded as the God of Moses, was not a pure spirit, he was ambitious and proud, and rejecting the spiritual light of the middle space offered him by his mother Sophia-Achamoth, he set himself to create a world of his own. Aided by his sons, the six planetary genii, he fabricated man, but this one proved a failure. It was a monster, soulless, ignorant, and crawling on all fours on the ground like a material beast. Ilda-Baoth was forced to implore the help of his spiritual mother. She communicated to him a ray of her divine light, and so animated man and endowed him with a soul. And now began the animosity of Ilda-Baoth toward his own creature. Following the impulse of the divine light, man soared higher and higher in his aspirations; very soon he began presenting not the image of his creator Ilda-Baoth but rather that of the Supreme Being, the "primitive man," Ennoia. Then the Demiurgus was filled with rage and envy; and fixing his jealous eye on the abyss of matter, his looks envenomed with passion were suddenly reflected as in a mirror; the reflection became animate, and there arose out of the abyss Satan, serpent, Ophiomorphos — "the embodiment of envy and cunning. He is the union of all that is most base in matter, with the hate, envy, and craft of a spiritual intelligence." [474]

This is the exoteric rendering of the Gnostics, and the allegory, though a *sectarian* version, is suggestive, and seems true to life. It is the natural deduction from the dead letter text of chapter iii of *Genesis*.

Hence the allegory of Prometheus, who steals the divine fire so as to allow men to proceed consciously on the path of spiritual evolution, thus transforming the most perfect of *animals* on earth into a potential god, and making him free to "take the kingdom of heaven by violence." Hence also, the *curse* pronounced by Zeus against Prometheus, and by Jehovah-Il-da-Baoth against his "rebellious son," Satan. The cold, pure snows of the Caucasian mountain and the never-dying, singeing fire and flames of an extinguishable hell. Two poles, yet the same idea; the dual aspect of a refined torture: a *fire producer* — the personified emblem of Φωσφόρος of the astral fire and light in the *anima mundi* — (that element of which the German materialist philosopher Moleschott said: "ohne *Phosphor* kein Gedanke," *i. e.*, without phosphorus no thought), burning in the fierce flames of his terrestrial passions; the conflagration fired by his *Thought*, discerning as it now does good from evil, and yet a slave to the passions of its earthly Adam; feeling the vulture of doubt and full consciousness gnawing at its heart — a *Prometheus indeed, because* a *conscious*, hence a *responsible* entity. [475] The curse of *life* is great, yet how few are those men, outside some Hindū and Sufi mystics, who would exchange all the tortures of conscious life, all the evils of a responsible existence, for the unconscious perfection of a passive (objectively) *incorporeal* being, or even the universal static Inertia personified in Brahmâ during his "night's" rest. For, to quote

474. Pages 97, 98.
475. The history of Prometheus, Karma, and human consciousness, is found further on.

from an able article by one [476] who, confusing the planes of existence and consciousness, fell a victim to it:—

Satan, or Lucifer, represents the *active,* or, as M. Jules Baissac calls it, the "Centrifugal Energy of the Universe" in a cosmic sense. He is Fire, Light, Life, Struggle, Effort, Thought, Consciousness, Progress, Civilization, Liberty, Independence. At the same time he is pain, which is the Re-action of the *pleasure* of action and *death* — which is the revolution of *life* — Satan, burning in his own hell, produced by the fury of his own momentum — the expansive disintegration of the nebula which is to concentrate into new worlds. And fitly is he again and again baffled by the eternal *Inertia* of the *passive* energy of the Kosmos — the inexorable *"I AM"* — the flint from which the sparks are beaten out. And fitly are he . . . and his adherents . . . consigned to the "sea of fire," because it is the *Sun* [in one sense only in the Cosmic allegory], the fount of life in *our system,* where they are purified (disintegrated) and churned up to re-arrange them for another life (the resurrection); that *Sun* which, as the origin of the active principle of our Earth, is at once the *Home* and the *Source* of the Mundane Satan. . . .

Furthermore, as if to demonstrate the accuracy of Baissac's general theory [in *Le Diable et Satan*] cold is known to have a "Centripetal" effect. Under the influence of cold everything contracts. . . . .Under its life *hibernates,* or dies out, thought congeals, and fire is extinguished. Satan is immortal in his own Fire-Sea — it is only in the "Nifl-heim" [the cold Hell of the Scandinavian *Eddas*] of the *"I AM"* that he cannot exist. But for all that there is a kind of *Immortal* Existence in the Nifl-heim, and that existence must be *painless and peaceful,* because it is *Unconscious and Inactive.* In the Kingdom of *Jehovah* [if this God were all that the Jews and Christians claim for him] there is no Misery, no War, no marrying and giving in marriage, no change, no *Individual Consciousness.*[477] All is absorbed in the spirit of the most Powerful. *It is emphatically a kingdom of Peace and loyal Submission as that of the "Arch-Rebel" is one of War and Revolution. . . .* It [the former] is in fact what Theosophy calls *Nirvâna.* But then Theosophy teaches that separation

476. By an Englishman whose erratic genius killed him. The son of a Protestant clergyman, he became a Mohammedan, then a rabid atheist, and after meeting with a *master,* a Guru, he became a mystic; then a theosophist who doubted, despaired; threw up *white* for *black* magic, went insane and joined the Roman Church. Then again turning round, anathematized her, re-became an atheist, and died cursing humanity, knowledge, and God, in whom he had ceased to believe. Furnished with all the esoteric data to write his "War in Heaven," he made a semi-political article out of it, mixing Mal-thus with Satan, and Darwin with the astral light. Peace be to his — *Shell.* He is a warning to the chelas who fail. His forgotten tomb may now be seen in the Mussulman burial ground of the Joonagad, Kathiawar, in India.

477. The author talks of the *active, fighting,* damning Jehovah as though he were a synonym of Parabrahm! We have quoted from this article to show where it dissents from theosophic teachings; otherwise it would be quoted some day against us, as everything published in the *Theosophist* generally is.

from the *Primal Source having once occurred*, Re-union can only be achieved *by Will — Effort —* which is distinctly *Satanic in the sense of this essay.*[477]

It *is* "Satanic" from the standpoint of orthodox Romanism, for it is owing to the prototype of that which became in time the Christian Devil — to the Radiant Archangels, Dhyâns-Chohans, who refused to create, because they wanted Man *to become his own creator* and an immortal god — than men can reach *Nirvâna* and the haven of heavenly divine Peace.

To close this rather lengthy comment, the Secret Doctrine teaches that the Fire-Devas, the Rudras, and the Kumâras, the "Virgin-Angels," (to whom Michael and Gabriel, the Archangels, both belong), the divine "Rebels"—called by the *all-materialising* and positive Jews, the *Nahash* or "Deprived" — preferred the *curse* of *incarnation* and the long cycles of terrestrial existence and rebirths, to seeing the misery (even if *unconscious*) of the beings (evolved as shadows out of their Brethren) through the semi-passive energy of their *too spiritual* Creators. If "man's uses of life should be such as neither to animalize nor to spiritualize, but to *humanize* Self," [479] before he can do so, he must be born *human* not angelic. Hence, tradition shows the celestial *Yogis* offering themselves as voluntary victims in order to redeem Humanity — created god-like and perfect at first — and to endow him with human affections and aspirations. To do this they had to give up their natural status and, descending on our globe, take up their abode on it for the whole cycle of the Mahâyuga, thus exchanging their impersonal individualities for individual personalities — the bliss of sidereal existence for the curse of terrestrial life. This voluntary sacrifice of the Fiery Angels, whose nature was *Knowledge* and *Love*, was construed by the exoteric theologies into a statement that shows "the rebel angels hurled down from heaven into the darkness of Hell" — our Earth. Hindû philosophy hints at the truth by teaching that the *Asuras* hurled down by Śiva, are only in an *intermediate state* in which they prepare for higher degrees of purification and redemption from their wretched condition; but Christian theology, claiming to be based

478. *Theosophist*, Vol. III, p. 68.

479. Explaining the Kabala, Dr. H. Pratt says, "Spirit was to man [to the Jewish Rabbin, rather?] a bodiless, disembodied, or deprived, and degraded being, and hence was termed by the ideograph *Nahash*, 'Deprived'; represented as appearing to and seducing the human race — men through the Woman. . . . In the picture from this Nahash, this spirit was represented by a serpent, because from its *destitution of bodily members*, the Serpent was looked upon as a deprived and depraved and degraded creature" (*New Aspects*, p. 235). Symbol for symbol there are those who would prefer that of the serpent — the symbol of wisdom and eternity, deprived of limbs as it is — to the Jod (׳) — the poetical ideograph of Jehovah in the Kabala — the god of the male symbol of generation.

on the rock of divine love, charity, and justice of him it appeals to as its Savior — has invented, to enforce that claim paradoxically, the dreary dogma of hell, that Archimedean lever of Roman Catholic philosophy.

As to Rabbinical Wisdom — than which there is none more positive, materialistic, or grossly terrestrial, as it brings everything down to physiological mysteries — it calls these Beings, the " Evil One "; and the Kabalists — *Nahash*, " Deprived," as just said, and the *Souls*, that have thrown themselves, *after having been alienated in Heaven from the Holy One*, into an abyss at the dawn of their very existence, and have anticipated the time when they are to descend on earth.[480]

And let me explain at once that our quarrel is not with the *Zohar* and the Kabala in their right interpretation — for the latter is ours — but only with the gross, *pseudo*-esoteric explanations of the later, and especially those of the Christian Kabalists.

" *Our earth and man*," says the Commentary, " *being the products of the three Fires* " — whose three names answer, in Sanskrit, to " *the electric fire, the Solar fire, and the fire produced by friction*," — these three fires, explained on the Cosmic and human planes, are Spirit, Soul, and Body, the three great Root groups, with their four additional divisions. These vary with the Schools, and become — according to their applications — the *upâdhis* and the *vehicles*, or the *noumena* of these. In the exoteric accounts, they are personified by the " three sons of surpassing brilliancy and splendor" of Agni Abhimânin, the eldest son of Brahmâ, the *Cosmic Logos*, by *Svâhâ*, one of Daksha's[481] daughters. In the metaphysical sense the " Fire of friction " means the Union between *Buddhi*, the sixth, and *Manas*, the fifth, principles, which thus are united or cemented together; the fifth merging partially into and becoming part of the *monad;* in the physical, it relates to the *creative spark*, or germ, which fructifies and generates the human being. The three Fires, it is said (whose names are Pâvaka, Pavamâna and Śuchi) were condemned by a curse of Vasishtha, the great sage, " *to be born over and over again*." [482] This is clear enough.

Therefore, the *FLAMES*, whose functions are confused in the exoteric books, and who are called indifferently Prajâpatis, Pitris, Manus,

---

480. *Zohar*, iii, 61, C.

481. Daksha, the " intelligent, the competent." " This name generally carries with it the idea of *creative power*." He is a son of Brahmâ, and of Aditi, and agreeably to other versions, a self-born power, which, like Minerva, sprang from his father's body. He is the chief of the *Prajâpatis* — the Lords or Creators of Being. In *Vishnu Purâna*,

Parâśara says of him, " in every Kalpa (or manvantara) Daksha and the rest are born and are again destroyed." And the *Rig-Veda* says that " Daksha sprang from Aditi and Aditi from Daksha," a reference to the eternal cyclic re-birth of the same divine Essence.

482. *Bhâgavata Purâna*, iv, 24, 4,

Asuras, Rishis, Kumâras,[483] etc., etc., are said to incarnate personally in the Third Root-Race and thus find themselves "reborn over and over again." In the Esoteric doctrine they are generally named the Asura, or the *Asu-ra Devatâ* or *Pitar*-Devatâ (gods) for, as said, they were first Gods — and the highest — before they became "*no*-gods," and had from Spirits of Heaven fallen into Spirits of the Earth [484] — *exoterically*, note well, in orthodox dogma.

No Theologian, any more than an Orientalist, can ever understand the genealogies of the Prajâpatis, the Manus, and the Rishis, nor the direct connexion of these — or their correlation rather — with the Gods, unless he has the key to the old primitive Cosmogony and Theogony, which all the Nations originally had in common. All these gods and demi-gods are found reborn on earth, in various Kalpas and in as various characters; each, moreover, *having his Karma distinctly traced, and every effect assigned to its cause.*

Before other Stanzas could be explained, it was, as seen, absolutely necessary to show that the sons of "Dark Wisdom," though identical with the Archangels which Theology has chosen to call the "Fallen," are as divine and as pure and more so than all the Michaels and Gabriels so glorified in the churches. The "old Book" goes into various details of Astral life, which at this juncture would be quite incomprehensible to the reader. It may, therefore, be left for later explanations, and the First and Second Races can now only receive bare notice. Not so for the Third Race — the Root-Race which separated into sexes, and which was the first to be endowed with reason. Men evolving *pari passu* with the globe, and the latter having "incrustated" more than a hundred million of years before — the first human sub-race had already begun to materialize or solidify, so to say. But, as the *Stanza* has it: "*the inner man* (the conscious Entity) *was not.*" This "Conscious Entity" Occultism says, comes from, nay, in many cases *is*, the very entire essence and *esse* of the high Intelligences condemned, by the undeviating law of Karmic evolution, to reincarnate in this manvantara.

(*b*) This verse (thirty-ninth) relates exclusively to the racial divi-

483. No one of these orders is distinct from the Pitris or Progenitors, as says *Manu* (iii. 284). "The wise call our fathers Vasus; our paternal grandfathers, Rudras; our paternal great grandfathers, Adityas; agreeably to a text of the Vedas," or "this is an everlasting Vedic text" in another translation.

484. As now discovered by the late G. Smith in the Babylonian cylinder literature, it was the same in Chaldaean theogony. Ishtar, "eldest of Heaven and of Earth." Below him the *Igege* or Angels of Heaven, and the *Anunnaki*, or angels of Earth. Below these again various classes of Spirits and "Genii" called Sedu, Vadukku, Ekimu, Gallu — of which some were good, some evil. (See *Chaldaean Account of Genesis*, "Babylonian Mythology," p. 4.)

sions. Strictly speaking, esoteric philosophy teaches a modified poly-genesis. For, while it assigns to humanity a oneness of origin, in so far that its forefathers or " Creators " were all divine beings — though of different classes or degrees of perfection in their hierarchy — men were nevertheless born on seven different centers of the continent of that period. Though all of one common origin, yet for reasons given their potentialities and mental capabilities, outward or physical forms, and future characteristics, were very different.[485] As to their com-plexions, there is a suggestive allegory told in *Linga Purâna.* The *Kumâra* — the Rudra gods, so called (*see further*), are described as incarnations of Śiva, the *destroyer* (of *outward forms*), named also Vâmadeva. The latter, as a *Kumâra*, the " Eternal Celibate," the chaste Virgin youth, springs from Brahmâ in each great Manvantara, and " again becomes four "; a reference to the *four great divisions of* the human races, as regards complexion and type — and three chief vari-ations of these. Thus in the 29th Kalpa — in this case a reference to the transformation and evolution of the human form which Śiva ever destroys and remodels periodically, down to the manvantaric great turning point about the middle of the Fourth (Atlantean) Race — in the 29th Kalpa, Śiva, as Śvetalohita, the *root* Kumâra, becomes, from moon-colored, *white;* in his next transformation — he is *red* (and in this the exoteric version differs from the Esoteric teaching) ; in the third — *yellow;* in the fourth — *black.*

Esotericism now classes these seven variations, with their four great divisions, into only *three* distinct primeval races — as it does not take into consideration the First Race, which had neither type nor color, and hardly an objective, though colossal form. The evolution of these races, their formation and development, went *pari passu* and on parallel lines with the evolution, formation, and development of three geological strata, from which the human complexion was as much derived as it was determined by the climates of those zones. It names three great divisions, namely, the RED-YELLOW, the BLACK, and the BROWN-WHITE.[486] The Aryan races, for instance, now varying from dark brown, almost black, red-brown-yellow, down to the whitest creamy color, are yet all of one and the same stock — the Fifth Root-Race — and spring from

485. Some superior, others inferior, *to suit the Karma* of the various reincarnating Monads which could not be all of the same degree of purity in their last births in other worlds. This accounts for the difference of races, the inferiority of the savage, and other human varieties.

486. " There are," says Topinard (English edition of *Anthropology,* with preface by Professor Broca), " THREE fundamental ele-ments of color in the human organism — namely, the *red,* the *yellow,* and the *black,* which, mixed in variable quantities with the white of the tissues, give rise to those nu-merous shades seen in the human family." Here is science unintentionally supporting Occultism again.

one single progenitor, called in Hindû *exotericism* by the generic name
of Vaivasvata Manu: the latter, remember, being that generic personage, the Sage, who is said to have lived over 18,000,000 years ago, and
also 850,000 years ago — at the time of the sinking of the last remnants
of the great continent of Atlantis [487] (*See the Root and Seed Manus*
further on[488]), and who is said to live even *now* in his mankind.[489] The
light yellow is the color of the first SOLID human race, which appeared
after the middle of the Third Root Race (*after its fall* into generation
— as just explained), bringing on the final changes. For, it is only
at that period that the last transformation took place, which brought
forth man as he is now, only on a magnified scale. This Race gave
birth to the Fourth Race; " Śiva " gradually transforming that portion of Humanity which became " black with sin " into *red-yellow* (the
red Indians and the Mongolians being the descendants of these) and
finally into Brown-white races — which now, together with the yellow
Races, form the great bulk of Humanity. The allegory in *Linga
Purâna* is curious, as showing the great ethnological knowledge of
the ancients.

When reading of " the last transformation," let the reader consider
at this juncture, if that took place 18,000,000 years ago, how many
millions more it must have required to reach that final stage? And if
man, in his gradual consolidation, developed *pari passu* with the earth,
how many millions of years must have elapsed during the *First, Second*,
and the first half of the *Third* Race? For the Earth was in a comparatively ethereal condition before it reached its last consolidated state;
the archaic teachings, moreover, telling us that, during the middle period of the Lemuro-Atlantean Race, three and a half Races after the
Genesis of man, the Earth, man, and everything on the Globe was of
a still grosser and more material nature, while such things as corals and
some shells were still in a semi-gelatinous, astral state. The cycles
that intervened since then, have already carried us onward, on the
opposite ascending arc, some steps toward our *dematerialisation*, as
the spiritualists would say. The Earth, ourselves, and all things have
softened since then — aye, even our brains. But it has been objected
by some theosophists that an ethereal Earth even some 15, or 20,000,000
years ago, *does not square with Geology*, which teaches us that winds

---

487. It must be remembered that the
" last remnants " here spoken of, refer to
those portions of the " great continent "
which still remained, and not to any of the
numerous islands which existed contempor-
aneously with the continent. Plato's " island " was, for instance, one of such remnants; the others having sunk at various

periods previously. An occult " tradition "
teaches that such submersions occur whenever there is an eclipse of the " spiritual
sun."
488. Page 308 *et seq.*
489. *Vide* at the end of this Stanza,
page 307, " THE PRIMEVAL MANUS OF HU-
MANITY."

blew, rains fell, waves broke on the shore, sands shifted and accumulated, etc., etc., that, in short, all natural causes now in operation were then in force, *"in the very earliest ages of geological time,* aye, that of the oldest palaeozoic rocks." To this the following answers are given. *Firstly,* what is the date assigned by geology to those "oldest palaeozoic rocks"? And *secondly,* why could not the winds blow, rain fall, and waves (*of carbonic acid* apparently, as science seems to imply) break on the shore, on an Earth semi-astral, *i. e.,* viscid? The word "astral" does not necessarily mean as thin as smoke, in occult phraseology, but rather "starry," shining or pellucid, in various and numerous degrees, from a quite filmy to a viscid state, as just observed. But it is further objected: How could an astral *Earth* have affected the other planets in this system? Would not the whole process get out of gear now if the attraction of one planet was suddenly removed? The objection is evidently invalid, since our system is composed of older and younger planets, some dead (like the moon), others in process of formation, for all astronomy knows to the contrary. Nor has the latter ever affirmed, so far as we know, that all the bodies of our system have sprung into existence and developed simultaneously. The Cis-Himâlayan secret teachings differ from those of India in this respect. Hindû Occultism teaches that the Vaivasvata Manu Humanity is eighteen million and odd years old. We say, yes; but only so far as *physical,* or approximately physical, man is concerned, who dates from the close of the Third Root-Race. Beyond that period MAN, or his filmy image, may have existed for 300 million years, for all we know; *since we are not taught figures* which are and will remain secret with the Masters of Occult Science, as justly stated in *"Esoteric Buddhism."* Moreover, whereas the Hindû Purânas speak of one Vaivasvata Manu, we affirm that there were several, the name being a generic one.[490]

We must now say a few more words on the physical evolution of man.

ARCHAIC TEACHINGS IN THE PURÂNAS AND GENESIS
PHYSICAL EVOLUTION

The writer cannot give *too much* proof that the system of Cosmogony and Anthropogony as described actually existed, that its records *are* preserved, and that it is found mirrored even in the modern versions of ancient Scriptures.

The Purânas on the one hand, and the Jewish Scriptures on the other, are based on the same scheme of evolution, which, read esoterically

490. *Vide supra.*

and expressed in modern language, would be found to be quite as
scientific as much of what now passes current as the final word of
recent discovery. The only difference between the two schemes is, that
the Purânas, giving as much, and perhaps more attention to the causes
than to the effects, allude to the pre-Cosmic and pre-Genetic periods
rather than to those of so-called Creation, whereas the Bible, saying
only a few words of the former period, plunges forthwith into material
genesis, and, while nearly skipping the *pre-Adamic* races, proceeds with
its allegories concerning the Fifth Race.

Now, whatever the onslaught made on the Order of creation in
Genesis, and its dead letter account certainly lends itself admirably to
criticism,[491] he who reads the Hindû Purânas — their allegorical exaggerations notwithstanding — will find them quite in accordance with
physical Science.

Even what appears to be the, on the face of it, perfectly nonsensical
allegory of Brahmâ assuming the form of a Boar to rescue the Earth
from under the waters, finds in the Secret Commentaries a perfectly
scientific explanation, relating as it does to the many risings and sink-
ings, and the constant alternation of water and land from the earliest to
the latest geological periods of our globe; for Science teaches us now
that nine-tenths of the stratified formations of the earth's crust have
been gradually constructed beneath water, at the bottom of the seas.
The ancient Aryans are credited with having known nothing whatever
of natural history, geology, and so on. The Jewish race is, on the
other hand, proclaimed even by its severest critic, an uncompromising
opponent of the Bible,[492] to have the merit of having conceived the idea
of monotheism " earlier, and retained it more firmly, than any of the
less philosophical and *more immoral religions* [!!] of the ancient
world." Only, while we find in Biblical esotericism physiological sex-

491. Mr. Gladstone's unfortunate attempt
to reconcile the Genetic account with science
(see *Nineteenth Century,* "Dawn of Creation" and the "Proem to Genesis," 1886)
has brought upon him the Jovian thunderbolt
hurled by Mr. Huxley. The dead-letter account warranted no such attempt; and his
fourfold order, or division of animated creation, has turned into the stone which, instead
of killing the fly on the sleeping friend's
brow, killed the man instead. Mr. Gladstone
killed *Genesis* for ever. But this does not
prove that there is no esotericism in the
latter. The fact that the Jews and all the
Christians, the modern as well as the early
sects, have accepted the narrative *literally*
for two thousand years, shows only their
ignorance; and shows the great ingenuity

and constructive ability of the initiated Rabbis, who have built the two accounts — the
Elohistic and the *Jehovistic* — esoterically,
and have purposely confused the meaning by
the vowelless glyphs or word-signs in the
original text. The six days — *yom* — of
creation do mean six periods of evolution,
and the seventh that of culmination of perfection (not of rest), and refer to the seven
Rounds and the seven Races with a *distinct*
" creation " in each; though the use of the
words *boker,* dawn or morning, and *ereb,*
evening twilight — which have esoterically
the same meaning as *sandhyâ,* twilight, in
Sanskrit — have led to a charge of the most
crass ignorance of the order of evolution.
492. See *Modern Science and Modern
Thought,* p. 337.

ual mysteries symbolized, and very little more (something for which *very little real philosophy is requisite*), in the Purânas one may find the most scientific and philosophical " dawn of creation," which, if impartially analysed and rendered into plain language from its fairy-tale-like allegories, would show that modern zoology, geology, astronomy, and nearly all the branches of modern knowledge, have been anticipated in the ancient Science, and were known to the philosophers in their general features, if not in such detail as at present!

Purânic astronomy, with all its deliberate concealment and confusion for the purpose of leading the profane off the real track, was shown even by Bentley to be a real science; and those who are versed in the mysteries of Hindû astronomical treatises, will prove that the modern theories of the progressive condensation of nebulae, nebulous stars and suns, with the most minute details about the cyclic progress of asterisms — far more correct than Europeans have even now — for chronological and other purposes, were known in India to perfection.

If we turn to geology and zoology we find the same. What are all the myths and endless genealogies of the seven Prajâpatis, and their sons, the seven Rishis or Manus, and of their wives, sons and progeny, but a vast detailed account of the progressive development and evolution of animal creation, one species after the other? Were the highly philosophical and metaphysical Âryans — the authors of the most perfect philosophical systems of transcendental psychology, of Codes of Ethics, and such a grammar as Pânini's, of the Sânkhya and Vedânta systems, and a moral code (Buddhism), proclaimed by Max Müller the most perfect on earth — such fools, or children, as to lose their time in writing *fairy tales;* such tales as the Purânas now seem to be in the eyes of those who have not the remotest idea of their secret meaning? What is the *fable,* the genealogy and origin of Kaśyapa, with his twelve wives, by whom he had a numerous and diversified progeny of *nâgas* (serpents), reptiles, birds, and all kinds of living things, and who was thus the *father* of all kinds of animals, but a *veiled* record of the order of evolution in *this* round? So far, we do not see that any Orientalist ever had the remotest conception of the truths concealed under the allegories and personifications. " The *Satapatha Brâhmana,*" says one, " gives *a not very intelligible* account of Kaśyapa's origin. . . . He was the son of Marichi, the Son of Brahmâ, the father of Vivasvat, the father of Manu, the progenitor of mankind. . . . Having assumed the form of a tortoise, Prajâpati created offspring. That which he created he made (*akarot*), hence the word *kûrma* (tortoise). Kaśyapa means tortoise; hence men say: ' All creatures are descendants of Kaśyapa,' " etc., etc.[493]

493. *Hindû Classical Dictionary,* p. 153.

He was all this; he was also the father of *Garuda*, the bird, the " King of the feathered tribe," who descends *from*, and is of one stock *with the reptiles*, the nâgas; and who becomes their mortal enemy *subsequently — as he is also a cycle, a period of time, when in the course of evolution the birds which developed from reptiles in their " struggle for life," — " survival of the fittest," etc., etc., turned in preference on those they issued from, to devour them,* — perhaps prompted by natural law, in order to make room for other and more perfect species.[494]

In that admirable epitome of *Modern Science and Modern Thought*, a lesson in natural history is offered to Mr. Gladstone, showing the utter variance with it of the Bible. The author remarks [495] that Geology, commencing with —

. . . the earliest known fossil, the Eozoon Canadense of the Laurentian, continued in a chain, every link of which is firmly welded, through the Silurian, with its abundance of molluscous, crustacean, and vermiform life and first indication of fishes; the Devonian, with its predominance of fish and first appearance of reptiles; the Mesozoic with its batrachians [or frog family]; the Secondary formations, in which reptiles of the sea, land and air preponderated, and the first humble forms of vertebrate land animals began to appear; and finally, the Tertiary, in which mammalian life had become abundant, and type succeeding to type and species to species, are gradually differentiated and specialized, through the Eocene, Miocene, and Pliocene periods, until we arrive at the Glacial and Pre-historic periods, and at positive proof of the existence of man.

The same order, *plus* the description of animals unknown to modern science, is found in the commentaries on the Purânas in general, and in the Book of Dzyan — especially. The only difference, a grave one, no doubt,— as implying a spiritual and divine nature of man independent of his physical body in this illusionary world, in which the *false personality* and its cerebral basis alone is known to orthodox psychology—is as follows. Having been in all the so-called " Seven creations," allegorizing the seven evolutionary changes, or the *sub-races*, we may call them, *of the First Root-race of Mankind* — MAN was on earth in this Round from the beginning. Having passed through all the kingdoms of nature in the previous *three* Rounds,[496] his *physical* frame —

494. *Vide* Part II, " Symbolism."
495. Page 335.
496. " Follow the law of analogy." — the Masters teach. *Atmâ-Buddhi* is dual and *Manas* is triple; inasmuch as the former has two aspects, and the latter three, *i. e.*, as a principle *per se*, which gravitates, in its higher aspect, to Atmâ-Buddhi, and follows, in its lower nature, Kâma, the seat of terrestrial and animal desires and passions. Now compare the evolution of the Races, the First and the Second of which are of the nature of Atmâ-Buddhi, their passive Spiritual progeny, and the Third Root-Race shows three distinct divisions or aspects physiologically and psychically; the earliest, sinless; the middle portions awakening to intelligence; and the third and last decidedly *animal: i. e.*, Manas succumbs to the temptations of Kâma.

one adapted to the thermal conditions of those early periods — was ready to receive the *divine Pilgrim* at the first dawn of human life, *i. e.,* 18,000,000 years ago. It is only at the mid-point of the 3rd Root Race that man was endowed with *Manas.* Once united, the *two* and then the *three* made one; for though the lower animals, from the amoeba to man, received *their* monads, in which all the higher qualities are potential, all have to remain dormant till each reaches its human form, before which stage *manas* (mind) has no development in them.[497] In the animals every principle is paralysed, and in a fetus-like state, save the second (vital) and the third (the astral), and the rudiments of the fourth (*Kâma,* which is desire, instinct) whose intensity and development varies and changes with the species. To the materialist wedded to the Darwinian theory, this will read like a fairy-tale, a mystification; to the believer in the inner, spiritual man, the statement will have nothing unnatural in it.

Now the writer is certain to meet what will be termed insuperable objections. We shall be told that the line of embryology, the gradual development of every individual life, and the progress of what is known to take place in the order of progressive stages of specialization — that all this is opposed to the idea of man preceding mammals. Man begins as the humblest and most primitive vermiform creature, "from the primitive speck of protoplasm and the nucleated cell in which all life originates," and "is developed through stages undistinguishable from those of fish, reptile and mammal, until the cell finally attains the highly specialized development of *the quadrumanous,* and *last of all, of the human type."* [498]

This is perfectly scientific, and we have nothing against *that;* for all this relates to the *shell* of man — his body, which in its growth is subject, of course, like every other (once called) morphological unit, to such metamorphoses. It is not those who teach the transformation of the mineral atom through crystallization — which is the same function, and bears the same relation to its *inorganic* (so-called) *upâdhi* (or basis) as the formation of *cells* to their organic *nuclei,* through plant, insect and animal into man — it is not they who will reject this theory, as it will finally lead to the recognition of a Universal Deity in nature, ever-present and as ever invisible, and unknowable, and of *intra*-Cosmic gods, who all were men.[499]

<hr>

497. "Men are made *complete* only during their third, toward the fourth cycle (race). They are made 'gods' for good and evil, and responsible only when the two arcs meet (after 3½ rounds towards the fifth Race). They are made so by the *Nirmânakâya* (spiritual or astral remains) of the Rudra-Kumâras, '*cursed* to be reborn on

earth again; meaning—*doomed in their natural turn to reincarnation* in the higher ascending arc of the terrestrial cycle.'" (*Commentary IX*)

498. Laing, *Modern Science and Modern Thought,* p. 335.

499. The whole trouble is this: neither physiologists nor pathologists *will* recognize

But we would ask, what does science and its exact and now axiomatic discoveries prove against *our* Occult theory? Those who believe in the law of Evolution and gradual progressive development from a cell (which from a *vital* has become a morphological cell, until it awoke as protoplasm pure and simple) — these can surely never limit their belief to one line of evolution. The types of life are innumerable; and the progress of evolution, moreover, does not go at the same rate in every kind of species. The constitution of primordial matter in the Silurian age — we mean "primordial" *matter* of science — is the same in every essential particular, save its degree of present grossness, as the primordial *living* matter of today. Nor do we find that which ought to be found, if the now orthodox theory of Evolution were *quite* correct, namely, a constant, ever-flowing progress in every species of being. Instead of that, what does one see? While the intermediate groups of animal being all tend toward a higher type, and while specializations, now of one type and now of another, develop through the geological ages, change forms, assume new shapes, appear and disappear with a kaleidoscopic rapidity in the description of palaeontologists from one period to another, the two solitary exceptions to the general rule are those at the two opposite poles of life and type, namely — MAN *and the lower genera of being!*

Certain well-marked forms of living beings have existed through enormous epochs, surviving not only the changes of physical conditions, *but persisting comparatively unaltered,* while other forms of life have appeared and disappeared. Such forms may be termed "persistent types" of life; and examples of them are abundant enough in both the animal and the vegetable worlds.[500]

Nevertheless, we are not given any good reason why Darwin links together reptiles, birds, amphibians, fishes, mollusca, etc., etc., as offshoots of a moneric ancestry. Nor are we told whether reptiles, for instance, are direct descendants of the amphibia, the latter of fishes, and fishes of lower forms — which they certainly are. For the Monads have passed through all these forms of being up to man, on every planet, in the Three *preceding* Rounds; every Round, as well as every subsequent Globe, from A to G, having been, and still having to be the arena of the same evolution, only repeated each time on a more solid material basis. Therefore the question:— "What relation is there between the Third Round astral prototypes and ordinary physical development in the course of the origination of pre-mammalian organic species?" — is easily answered. One is the shadowy prototype of the other, the preliminary, hardly defined, and evanescent sketch on the

that the cell-germinating substance (the *cyto-blastema*) and the mother-lye from which crystals originate, are one and the same essence, save in differentiation for purposes.
500. Huxley, *Proceedings of Royal Inst.*, vol. iii, p. 151.

canvas, of objects, which are destined to receive the final and vivid form under the brush of the painter. The fish evolved into an amphibian — a frog — in the *shadows* of ponds, and man passed through all his metamorphoses on this Globe in the Third Round as he did in this, his Fourth Cycle. The Third Round types contributed to the formation of the types in this one. On strict analogy, the cycle of Seven Rounds in their work of the gradual formation of man through every kingdom of Nature, are repeated on a microscopical scale in the first seven months of gestation of a future human being. Let the student think over and work out this analogy. As the seven months' old unborn baby, though quite ready, yet needs two months more in which to acquire strength and consolidate; so man, having perfected his evolution during seven Rounds, remains two periods more in the womb of mother-Nature before he is born, or rather reborn a Dhyâni, still more perfect than he was before he launched forth as a Monad on the newly built chain of worlds. Let the student ponder over this mystery, and then he will easily convince himself that, as there are also physical links between many classes, so there are precise domains wherein the astral merges into physical evolution. Of this Science breathes not one word. Man has evolved with and from the monkey, it says. But now see the contradiction.

Huxley proceeds to point out plants, ferns, club mosses, some of them generically identical with those now living, which are met with in the carboniferous epoch, for:—

The cone of the oolitic *Araucaria* is hardly distinguishable from that of existing species. . . . Sub-kingdoms of animals yield the same instances. The *globigerina* of the Atlantic soundings is identical with the cretaceous species of the same genus . . . the tabulate corals of the Silurian epoch are wonderfully like the millepores of our own seas. . . . The *arachnida*, the highest group of which, the scorpions, is represented in the coal by a genus differing only from its living congeners only in . . . the eyes.

etc., etc.; all of which may be closed with Dr. Carpenter's authoritative statement about the *Foraminifera*. He says:—

There is no evidence of any fundamental modification or advance in the Foraminiferous type from the palaeozoic period to the present time. . . . The Foraminiferous Fauna of our own series probably present a greater range of variety than existed at any previous period; but *there is no indication of any tendency to elevation towards a higher type.*[501]

Now, if there is no indication of change in the Foraminifera, a *protozoon* of the lowest type of life, mouthless and eyeless, except its greater variety now than before, man, who is on the uppermost rung of the ladder of being, indicates still less change, as we have seen;

501. *Introduction to the Study of the Foraminifera*, p. xi.

the skeleton of his Palaeolithic ancestor being even found superior in some respects to his present frame. Where is, then, the claimed uniformity of law, the *absolute rule* for one species shading off into another, and, by insensible gradations, into higher types? We see Sir William Thomson admitting as much as 400,000,000 of years in the earth's history, since the surface of the globe became sufficiently cool to permit of the presence of living things;[502] and during that enormous lapse of time in the Oolitic period alone, the so-called "age of reptiles," we find a most extraordinary variety and abundance of Saurian forms. the Amphibian type reaching *its highest developments.* We learn of Ichthyosauri and Plesiosauri in the lakes and rivers, and of winged crocodiles or lizards flying in the air. After which, in the Tertiary period "we find the Mammalian type exhibiting remarkable divergences from previously existing forms . . . Mastodons, Megatheriums, and other unwieldy denizens of the ancient forests and plains; and subsequently," are notified of — "*the gradual modification of one of the ramifications* of the Quadrumanous order, *into those beings from whom primeval man himself may claim to have been evolved.*"[503]

He *may;* but no one, except materialists, can see why he should; as there is not the slightest necessity for it, nor is such an evolution warranted by facts, for those most interested in the proofs thereof confess their utter failure to find one single fact to support their theory. There is no need for the numberless types of life to represent the members of one progressive series. They are "the products of various and different evolutional divergences, taking place now in one direction and now in another." Therefore it is far more justifiable to say that the monkey evolved into the Quadrumanous order, than that primeval man, who has *remained stationary in his human specialization ever since his fossil is found in the oldest strata,* and of whom no variety is found save in color and facial type — has developed from a common ancestor together with the ape.

That man originates like other animals in a cell and develops "through stages undistinguishable from those of fish, reptile, and mammal until the cell attains the highly specialized development of the quadrumanous and *at last the human type,*" is an Occult axiom thousands of years old. The Kabalistic axiom: "A stone becomes a plant; a plant a beast; a beast a man; a man a God," holds good throughout the ages. Haeckel, in his *Schöpfungsgeschichte*, shows a double drawing representing two embryos — that of a dog six weeks old, and that of a man, eight weeks. The two, except the slight differ-

502. *Transactions* of Geological Society of Glasgow, vol. iii. Very strangely, however, he has just changed his opinion.

The sun, he says, is only 15,000,000 old.

503. *The Beginnings of Life.*

ence in the head, larger and wider about the brain in the man, are undistinguishable.

In fact, we may say that every human being passes through the stage of fish and reptile before arriving at that of mammal and finally of man. If we take him up at the more advanced stage where the embryo has already passed the reptilian form . . . for a considerable time, the line of development remains the same as that of other mammalia. The rudimentary limbs are exactly similar, the five fingers and toes develop in the same way, and the resemblance after the first four weeks' growth *between the embryo of a man and a dog is such that it is scarcely possible to distinguish them.* Even at the age of eight weeks the embryo man is an animal with a tail hardly to be distinguished from an embryo puppy.[504]

Why, then, not make man and dog evolve from a common ancestor, or from a reptile — a *Nâga*, instead of coupling man with the quadrumana? This would be just as logical as the other, and more so. The shape and the stages of the human embryo have not changed since historical times, and these metamorphoses were known to Asklepios and Hippocrates as well as to Mr. Huxley. Therefore, since the Kabalists had remarked it since prehistoric times, it is no new discovery. In " *Isis*," [505] it is noticed and half explained.

As the embryo of man has no more of the ape in it than of any other mammal, but *contains in itself the totality of the kingdoms of nature,* and since it seems to be "a persistent type" of life, far more so than even the Foraminifera, it seems as illogical to make him evolve from the ape as it would be to trace his origin to the frog or the dog. Both Occult and Eastern philosophies believe in evolution, which Manu and Kapila [506] give with far more clearness than any scientist does at present. No need to repeat that which was fully debated in *Isis Unveiled,* as the reader may find all these arguments and the description of the basis on which all the Eastern doctrines of Evolution rested, in our earlier books.[507] But no Occultist can accept the unreasonable proposition that all the now existing forms, " from the structureless Amoeba to man," are the direct lineal descendants of organisms which lived millions and millions of years before the birth of man, in the pre-Silurian epochs, in the sea or land-mud. The Occultists believe in an

504. *Modern Science and Modern Thought,* page 171.

505. Vol. I, page 389.

506. Hence the philosophy in the allegory of the 7, 10, and finally 21 Prajâpatis, Rishis, Munis, etc., who all are made the *fathers* of various things and beings. The order of the seven classes or orders of plants, animals, and even inanimate things, given at random in the Purânas, is found in several commentaries in the correct rotation. Thus, Prithu is the father of the Earth. He *milks her,* and makes her bear every kind of grain and vegetable, all enumerated and specified. Kaśyapa is the father of all the reptiles, snakes, demons, etc., etc.

507. See Vol. I, 151, *et seq.*, about the tree of evolution — The " Mundane Tree."

inherent law of progressive *development.*[508]   Mr. Darwin never did, and says so himself.

On page 145 of the *Origin of Species* we find him stating that, since *there can be no advantage* " to the infusorian animalcule or an intestinal worm . . . to become highly organized," therefore, " natural selection," *not including necessarily progressive development* — leaves the animalcule and the worm (the " persistent types ") quiet.

There does not appear much *uniform* law in such behavior of Nature; and it looks more like the discriminative action of some *Super*-Natural selection; perhaps, that aspect of *Karma,* which Eastern Occultists would call the " Law of Retardation," may have something to do with it.

But there is every reason to doubt whether Mr. Darwin himself ever gave such an importance to *his* law — as is given to it now by his atheistic followers. The knowledge of the various living forms in the geological periods that have gone by is very meager. The reasons given for this by Dr. Bastian are very suggestive: (1) On account of the imperfect manner in which the several forms may be represented in the strata pertaining to the period; (2) on account of the extremely limited nature of the explorations which have been made in these imperfectly representative strata; and (3) because so many parts of the record are absolutely inaccessible to us — nearly all beneath the Silurian system having been blotted out by time, whilst those two-thirds of the earth's surface in which the remaining strata are to be found are now covered over by seas. Hence Mr. Darwin says himself:

For my part, following out Lyell's metaphor, I look at the geological record as a history of the world imperfectly kept, and written in a changing dialect; *of this history we possess the last volume alone,* relating only to two or three countries. Of this volume, *only here and there a short chapter has been preserved,* and of each page *only here and there a few lines.*

It is not on such meager data, certainly, that the last word of Science can be said. Nor is it on any ground of human pride or unreasonable belief in man's representing even here on earth —(in *our* period, perhaps) — the highest type of life, that Occultism denies that all the preceding forms of human life belonged to types lower than our own, for it is not so. But simply because the " missing link," such as to prove the existing theory undeniably, will never be found by palaeontologists. Believing as we do that man has evolved from, and passed through, (during the preceding Rounds) the lowest forms of every life, vegetable and animal, on earth, there is nothing very degrading

508. Checked and modified, however, by   restriction on the advance of all species
the *Law of Retardation,* which imposes a   when a Higher Type makes its appearance.

in the idea of having the orang-outang as an ancestor of our physical
form. Quite the reverse; as it would forward the Occult doctrine with
regard to the final evolution of everything in terrestrial nature into
man, most irresistibly. One may even inquire how it is that biologists
and anthropologists, having once firmly accepted the theory of the
descent of man from the ape — how it is that they have hitherto left
untouched the future evolution of the existing apes into man? This
is only a logical sequence of the first theory, unless Science would make
of man a privileged being, and his evolution a *non*-precedent in nature,
quite a *special* and unique case. And that is what all this leads physical
Science to. The reason, however, why the Occultists reject the Darwinian, and especially the Haeckelian, hypothesis is because it is the
ape which is, in sober truth, a special and unique instance, not man.
The pithecoid is *an accidental creation,* a forced growth, the result of
an unnatural process.

The occult doctrine is, we think, more logical. It teaches a cyclic,
never varying law in nature, the latter having no personal, "special
design," but acting on a uniform plan that prevails through the whole
manvantaric period and deals with the land worm as it deals with man.
Neither the one nor the other have sought to come into being, hence
both are under the same evolutionary law, and both have to progress
according to Karmic law. Both have started from the same neutral
center of Life and both have to re-merge into it at the consummation
of the cycle.

It is not denied that in the preceding Round man *was* a gigantic ape-
like creature; and when we say "man" we ought perhaps to say, the
rough mold that was developing for the use of man in this Round only
— the middle, or the transition point of which we have hardly reached.
Nor was man what he is now during the first two and a half Root-races.
That point he reached, as said before, only 18,000,000 years ago,
during the secondary period, as we claim.

Till then he was, according to tradition and Occult teaching, "a god
on earth who had fallen into matter," or generation. This may or may
not be accepted, since the Secret Doctrine does not impose itself as an
infallible dogma; and since, whether its prehistoric records are accepted
or rejected, it has nothing to do with the question of the *actual* man
and his inner nature, the Fall mentioned above having left no original
sin on Humanity. But all this has been sufficiently dealt with.

Furthermore, we are taught that the transformations through which
man passed on the descending arc — which is centrifugal for spirit and
centripetal for matter — and those he prepares to go through, henceforward, on his ascending path, which will reverse the direction of the
two forces — viz., matter will become centrifugal and spirit centripetal

— that all such transformations *are next in store for the anthropoid ape also,* all those, at any rate, who have reached the remove next to man in this Round — and these will all be men in the Fifth Round, as present men inhabited ape-like forms in the Third, the preceding Round.

Behold, then, in the modern denizens of the great forests of Sumatra the degraded and *dwarfed* examples — " blurred copies," as Mr. Huxley has it — of ourselves, as we (the majority of mankind) were in the earliest sub-races of the Fourth Root-race during the period of what is called the " Fall into generation." The ape we know is not the product of natural evolution but an *accident,* a cross-breed between an animal being, or form, and man. As has been shown in the present volume (anthropogenesis), it is the speechless animal that first started sexual connexion, having been the first to separate into males and females. Nor was it intended by Nature that man should follow the bestial example — as shown by the comparatively painless procreation of their species by the animals, and the terrible suffering and danger of the same in the woman. The Ape is, indeed, as remarked in *Isis Unveiled,*[509] " a transformation of species most directly connected with that of the human family — *a hybrid branch engrafted on their own stock before the final perfection of the latter "* — or man. The apes are millions of years later than the speaking human being, and are the latest contemporaries of our Fifth Race. Thus, it is most important to remember that the *Egos* of the apes are entities compelled by their Karma to incarnate in the animal forms, which resulted from the bestiality of the *latest* Third and the earliest Fourth Race men. They are entities who had already reached the " human stage " before this Round. Consequently, they form an exception to the general rule. The numberless traditions about Satyrs are no fables, but represent an extinct race of animal men. The animal " Eves " were their foremothers, and the human "Adams " their forefathers; *hence the Kabalistic allegory of Lilith or Lilatu,* Adam's *first* wife, whom the Talmud describes as a *charming* woman, *with long wavy hair, i. e.,* — a female hairy animal of a character now unknown, still a female animal, who in the Kabalistic and Talmudic allegories is called the female reflection of Samael, Samael-Lilith, or man-animal united, a being called *Hayoh Bishah,* the Beast or Evil Beast.[510] It is from this unnatural union that the present apes descended. The latter are truly " speechless men," and will become speaking animals (or men of a lower order) in the Fifth Round, while the adepts of a certain school hope that some of the Egos of the apes of a higher intelligence will reappear at the close of the Sixth Root-race. What their form will be is of secondary consideration. The form means nothing. Species and genera of the

509. Vol. II, p. 278.   510. *Zohar,* ii, 255-259.

flora, fauna, and the highest animal, its crown — man, change and vary according to the environments and climatic variations, not only with every Round, but every Root-Race likewise, as well as after every geological cataclysm that puts an end to, or produces a turning point in the latter. In the Sixth Root-Race the fossils of the Orang, the Gorilla, and the Chimpanzee will be those of extinct quadrumanous mammals; and new forms — though fewer and ever wider apart as ages pass on and the close of the Manvantara approaches — will develop from the " cast off " types of the human races as they revert once again to astral, out of the mire of physical, life. There were none before man, and they will be extinct before the Seventh Race develops. Karma will lead on the monads of the unprogressed men of our race and lodge them in the newly evolved human frames of the thus physiologically regenerated baboon.[511]

This will take place, of course, millions of years hence. But the picture of this cyclic precession of all that lives and breathes now on earth, of each species in its turn, is a true one, and needs no " special creation," or miraculous formation of man, beast, and plant *ex nihilo.*

This is how Occult Science explains the absence of any link between ape and man, and shows the former evolving from the latter.

A PANORAMIC VIEW OF THE EARLY RACES

There is a period of a few millions of years to cover between the first " mindless " race and the highly intelligent and *intellectual* later " Lemurians "; there is another between the earliest civilization of the Atlanteans and the historic period.

As witnesses to the Lemurians but a few silent records in the shape of half a dozen broken colossi and old cyclopean ruins are left. These are not allowed a hearing, as they are " productions of blind natural forces," we are assured by some; " quite modern " we are told by others. Tradition is left contemptuously unnoticed by sceptic and materialist, and made subservient to the Bible in every case by the too zealous Churchman. Whenever a legend, however, refuses to fit in with the Noachian " deluge theory," it is declared by the Christian clergy " the insanely delirious voice of old superstition." Atlantis is denied, when not confused with Lemuria and other departed continents, because, perhaps, Lemuria is half the creation of modern science, and has, therefore, to be believed in; while Plato's Atlantis is regarded by most of the scientists as a dream.

Atlantis is often described by believers in Plato as a prolongation of Africa. An old continent is also suspected to have existed on the

Eastern coast. Only Africa, as a continent, was never part and parcel
of either Lemuria or Atlantis, as we have agreed to call the Third and
Fourth Continents. Their archaic appellations are never mentioned in
the Purânas, nor anywhere else. But with simply one of the esoteric
keys in hand it becomes an easy task to identify these departed lands in
the numberless " lands of the gods," Devas and Munis described in the
Purânas, in their *Varshas, Dvîpas,* and *zones.* Their Śveta-Dvipa,
during the early days of Lemuria, stood out like a giant-peak from the
bottom of the sea; the area between Atlas and Madagascar being
occupied by the waters till about the early period of Atlantis (after the
disappearance of Lemuria), when Africa emerged from the bottom of
the ocean, and Atlas was half-sunk.

It is of course impossible to attempt, within the compass of even
several volumes, a consecutive and detailed account of the evolution
and progress of the first three races — except so far as to give a general
view of it, as will be done presently. Race the first had no history of
its own. Of race the second the same may be said. We shall have,
therefore, to pay careful attention only to the Lemurians and the Atlanteans before the history of our own race (the Fifth) can be attempted.

What is known of other continents, besides our own, and what does
history know or accept of the early races? Everything outside the
repulsive speculations of materialistic science is daubed with the con-
temptuous term " Superstition." The wise men of today will believe
nothing. Plato's " winged " and *hermaphrodite* races, and his golden
age, under the reign of Saturn and the gods, are quietly brought back
by Haeckel to their *new* place in nature: our divine races are shown
to be the descendants of Catarrhine apes, and our ancestor, a piece
of sea slime.

Nevertheless, as expressed by Faber, " the *fictions* of ancient poetry
. . . will be found to comprehend some portion of historical truth."
However one-sided the efforts of the learned author of the *Mysteries
of the Cabiri,* — efforts directed throughout his two volumes to con-
strain the classical myths and symbols of old paganism, " to bear
testimony to the truth of Scripture,"— time and further research have
avenged, partially at least, that "truth" by showing it *unveiled.* Thus it
is the clever adaptations of Scripture, on the contrary, which are made
to bear evidence to the great wisdom of archaic paganism. This, notwithstanding the inextricable confusion into which the truth about the
Kabiri — the most mysterious gods of antiquity — was thrown by the
wild and contradictory speculations of Bishop Cumberland, Dr. Shuck-
ford, Cudworth, Vallancey, etc., etc., and finally by Faber. Nevertheless, all, from first to last, of these scholars had to come to a certain
conclusion framed by the latter. " We have no reason to think " he

writes, "that the idolatry of the Gentile world was of a merely arbitrary contrivance; on the contrary, it seems to have been built, almost universally, *upon a traditional remembrance of certain real events. These events I apprehend to be the destruction of the first* [the fourth in esoteric teachings] *Race of mankind by the waters of the Deluge."* [512] To this, Faber adds:—

I am persuaded that the tradition of the sinking of the Phlegyan isle is the very same as that of the sinking of the island Atlantis. They both appear to me to allude to one great event, the sinking of the whole world beneath the waters of the deluge, or, if we suppose the arch of the earth to have remained in its original position, the rising of the central water above it. M. Bailly, indeed, in his work upon the Atlantis of Plato, the object of which is evidently to depreciate the authority of Scriptural chronology, labours to prove that the Atlanteans were a very ancient northern nation, long prior to the Hindûs, the Phoenicians, and the Egyptians.[513]

In this Faber is in agreement with Bailly, who shows himself more learned and intuitional than those who accept Biblical chronology. Nor is the latter wrong when saying that the Atlanteans were the same as the Titans and the giants.[514] Faber accepts the more willingly the opinion of his French *confrère*, as Bailly mentions Kosmas Indikopleustes, who preserved an ancient tradition about Noah — that he "formerly inhabited the *island* Atlantis."[515] This island, whether it was the " Poseidonis " mentioned in " *Esoteric Buddhism*," or the Continent of Atlantis, does not much matter. The tradition is there, recorded by a Christian.

No Occultist would ever think of dispossessing Noah of his prerogatives, if he is claimed to be an Atlantean; for this would simply show that the Israelites repeated the story of Vaivasvata Manu, Xisuthrus, and so many others, and that they only changed the name, to do which they had the same right as any other nation or tribe. What we object to is the literal acceptation of Biblical chronology, as it is absurd, and in accord with neither geological data nor reason. Moreover, if Noah was an Atlantean, then he was a Titan, a giant, as Faber shows; and if a giant, then why is he not shown as such in *Genesis?* [516]

Bailly's mistake was to reject the submersion of Atlantis, and to

512. Chap. I, p. 9.
513. *A Dissertation on the Cabiri*, page 284.
514. See *Lettres sur l'Atlantide.*
515. *Ibid.*
516. This is shown by Faber, again a pious Christian, who says that "the Noetic family also . . . bore the appellations of *Atlanteans* and *Titans*, and the great patriarch himself was called by way of eminence *Atlas* and *Titan."* (*Vol. II, p.* 285). And if so, then, *according to the Bible*, Noah must have been the progeny of the Sons of God, the *fallen angels*, agreeably to the same authority, and of the "daughters of men who were fair," (*See Genesis, chap.* vi). And why not, since his father Lamech slew a man, and was, with all his sons and daughters (who perished in the Deluge), as bad as the rest of mankind?

call the Atlanteans simply a Northern and *post diluvian* nation, which, however, as he says, certainly " flourished before the foundation of the Hindû, the Egyptian, and the Phoenician empires." In this, had he only known of the existence of what we have agreed to call *Lemuria,* he would have again been right. For the Atlanteans were *post diluvian* to the Lemurians, and Lemuria was not submerged as Atlantis was, but was *sunk* under the waves, owing to earthquakes and subterranean fires, as Great Britain and Europe will be one day. It is the ignorance of our men of science, who will accept neither the tradition that several continents have already sunk, nor the periodical law which acts throughout the Manvantaric cycle — it is this ignorance that is the chief cause of all the confusion. Nor is Bailly wrong again in assuring us that the Hindûs, Egyptians, and Phoenicians came after the Atlanteans, for the latter belonged to the Fourth, while the Aryans and their Semitic Branch are of the Fifth Race. Plato, while repeating the story as narrated to Solon by the priests of Egypt, intentionally confuses (as every *Initiate* would) the two continents, and assigns to the small island which sank last all the events pertaining to the two enormous continents, the prehistoric and traditional. Therefore, he describes the *first couple,* from whom the whole island was peopled, as being formed of the Earth. In saying so, he means neither Adam and Eve, nor yet his own Hellenic forefathers. His language is simply allegorical, and by alluding to " Earth," he means " matter," as the Atlanteans were really the first purely *human* and *terrestrial* race — those that preceded it being more divine and ethereal than human and solid.

Yet Plato must have known, as would any other initiated adept, about the history of the Third Race after its " Fall," though as one pledged to silence and secrecy he never showed his knowledge in so many words. Nevertheless, it may become easier now, after acquainting oneself with even the approximate chronology of the Eastern nations — all of which was based upon, and followed the early Aryan calculations — to realize the immense periods of time that must have elapsed since the separation of the sexes, without mentioning the First or even the Second Root-Races. As these must remain beyond the comprehension of minds trained in Western thought, it is found useless to speak in detail of the First and Second, and even of the Third Race in its earliest stage.[517] One has to begin with the latter,

<hr/>

517. In that wonderful volume of Donnelly's, *Atlantis, the Antediluvian World,* the author, speaking of the Aryan colonies from Atlantis, and of the arts and sciences — the legacy of our Fourth Race — bravely announces that " the roots of the institutions of today reach back to the Miocene age." This is an enormous allowance for a modern scholar to make; but civilization dates still further back than the Miocene Atlanteans. " Secondary-period " man will be discovered, and with him his long forgotten civilization.

when it reached its full human period, lest the uninitiated reader should find himself hopelessly bewildered. The THIRD RACE FELL — and created no longer: it *begat* its progeny. Being still mindless at the period of separation it begot, moreover, anomalous offspring, until its physiological nature had adjusted its instincts in the right direction. Like the "lords the gods" of the Bible, the "Sons of Wisdom," the Dhyân-Chohans, had warned them to leave alone the fruit forbidden by Nature: but the warning proved of no value. Men realized the unfitness — we must not say sin — of what they had done, only when too late: after the angelic monads from higher spheres had incarnated in, and endowed them with understanding. To that day they had remained simply physical, like the animals generated from them. For what is the distinction? The doctrine teaches that the only difference between animate and inanimate objects on earth, between an animal and a human frame, is that in some the various "fires" are latent, and in others they are active. The *vital fires* are in all things and not an atom is devoid of them. But no animal has the three higher principles awakened in him; they are simply potential, latent, and thus *non-existing*. And so would the animal frames of men be to this day, had they been left as they came out from the bodies of their Progenitors, whose *shadows* they were, to grow, unfolded only by the powers and forces immanent in matter. But as said in PYMANDER :—

This is a Mystery that to this day was sealed and hidden. Nature[518] being mingled with Man[519] brought forth a wondrous miracle; the harmonious commingling *of the essence of the Seven* [Pitris, governors] and her own; the *Fire* and the *Spirit* and Nature [the noumenon of matter]; which [commingling] forthwith brought forth seven men of opposite sexes [negative and positive] according to the essences of the seven governors.[520]

Thus saith Hermes, the thrice great Initiate,[521] "the Power of the

518. Nature is the *natural* body, the shadow of the Progenitors; and —
519. MAN is the "Heavenly man," as already stated.
520. *Divine Pymander*, Chap. I, Sect. 16.
521. The "*Pymander*" of our museums and libraries is an abridgment of one of the Books of Thoth, by a Platonist of Alexandria. In the Third Century it was remodeled after old Hebrew and Phoenician MSS. by a Jewish Kabalist, and called the "Genesis of Enoch." But even its disfigured remnants show how closely its text agrees with the Archaic Doctrine, as is shown in the creation of the Seven Creators and *seven primitive men*. As to Enoch, Thoth or Hermes, Orpheus and Kadmos, these are all generic names, branches and offshoots of the seven primordial sages (incarnated Dhyân Chohans or Devas, in *illusive*, not mortal bodies) who taught Humanity all it knew, and whose earliest disciples assumed their master's names. This custom passed from the Fourth to the Fifth Race. Hence the sameness of the traditions about Hermes (of whom Egyptologists count five) Enoch, etc., they are all inventors of letters; none of them dies but still lives, and they are the first Initiators into, and Founders of the Mysteries. The *Genesis of Enoch* disappeared only very lately among the

Thought Divine." St. Paul, another Initiate, called our world "the enigmatical mirror of pure truth," and St. Gregory, of Nazianzos, corroborated Hermes by stating that "things visible are but the shadow and delineation of things that we cannot see." It is an eternal combination, and images are repeated from the higher rung of the ladder of being down to the lower. The "Fall of the Angels," and the "War in Heaven" are repeated on every plane, the lower "mirror" disfiguring the image of the superior mirror, and each repeating it in its own way. Thus the Christian dogmas are but the reminiscences of the *paradigms* of Plato, who spoke of these things cautiously, as every Initiate would. But it is all as expressed in these few sentences of the *Desatir:*—

All that is on Earth, saith the Lord [Ormazd], is the *shadow of something that is in the superior spheres.* This luminous object [light, fire, etc.] is the shadow of that which is still more luminous than itself, and so on till it reaches ME, who am the light of lights.

In the Kabalistic books, and in the *Zohar* pre-eminently, the idea that everything objective on earth or in this Universe is the Shadow — *Dyooknah* — of the eternal Light or Deity, is very strong.

The Third Race was pre-eminently the bright shadow, at first, of the gods, whom tradition exiles on Earth after the allegorical war in Heaven; which became still more allegorical on Earth, for it was the war between spirit and matter. This war will last till the inner and divine man adjusts his outer terrestrial self to his own spiritual nature. Till then the dark and fierce passions of the former will be at eternal feud with his master, the Divine Man. But the *animal* will be tamed one day, because its nature will be changed and harmony will reign once more between the two as before the "Fall," when even mortal man was *created* by the Elements and was not born.

The above is made clear in all the great theogonies, principally in the Grecian (see Hesiod and his *Theogony*). *The mutilation* of *Ouranos* by his son *Kronos,* who thus condemns him to impotency, has never been understood by the modern Mythographers. Yet, it is very plain; and having been universal [522] (*vide foot note infra*), it must have contained

Kabalists. Guillaume Postel saw it. It was most certainly in a great measure a transcript from the books of Hermes, and far anterior to the Books of Moses, as Éliphas Lévi tells his readers.

522. Ouranos is a modified Varuna, "the Universal encompasser," the all-embracer, and one of the oldest of the Vedic deities—SPACE, the maker of Heaven and Earth, since both

are manifested out of his (or its) seed. It is only later that Varuna became the chief of the Adityas and a kind of Neptune riding on the *Leviathan — Makara,* now the most sacred and mysterious of the signs of the Zodiac. Varuna, "without whom no creature can even wink," was degraded like Ouranos, and like him, *he fell into generation,* his functions, "the grandest cosmical funca great abstract and philosophical idea, now lost to our modern sages. This punishment in the allegory marks, indeed " a new period, a second phase in the development of creation," as justly remarked by De-charme,[523] who, however, renounces the attempt to explain it. Ouranos has tried to oppose an impediment to that development, or natural evolution, by *destroying all his children as soon as born*. *Ouranos*, who personifies all the creative powers of, and in, *Chaos* (Space, or the unmanifested Deity) is thus made to pay the penalty; for it is those powers which cause the *Pitris* to evolve primordial *men* from them-selves — as, later on, these men evolve *their* progeny — without any sense or desire for procreation. The work of generation, suspended during a moment, passes into the hands of *Kronos*,[524] *time*, who unites himself with *Rhea* (the earth in esotericism — matter in general), and thus produces, after celestial — terrestrial Titans. The whole of this symbolism relates to the mysteries of Evolution.

This allegory is the exoteric version of the esoteric doctrine given in this part of our work. For in *Kronos* we see the same story re-peated again. As Ouranos destroyed his children from *Gaia* (one, in the world of manifestation, with Aditi or the Great Cosmic Deep) by confining them in the bosom of the Earth, *Tythea*, so *Kronos* at this second stage of creation destroyed his children from *Rhea* — by devouring them. This is an allusion to the fruitless efforts of Earth or Nature alone to create real *human* men.[525] Time swallows its own fruitless work. Then comes Zeus — Jupiter, who dethrones his father in his turn.[526] Jupiter the Titan, is Prometheus, in one sense,[527] and

tions," as Muir calls them, having been low-ered down from heaven to earth by exoteric anthropomorphism. As the same Orientalist says, " The attributes ascribed to Varuna (in the Vedas) impart to his character a moral elevation and sanctity far surpassing that attributed to any other Vedic Deity." But to understand correctly the reason of his fall, like that of Ouranos, one has to see in every exoteric religion the imperfect and sinful work of man's fancy, and also to study the mysteries which Varuna is said to have imparted to Vasishtha. Only . . . "his secrets and those of Mitra *are not to be revealed to the foolish*."

523. *Mythologie de la Grèce Antique*, page 7.

524. *Kronos* is not only Χρόνος, *time*, but also, as Bréal showed in his *Hercule et Cacus* (p. 57), comes from the root *Kar*, "to make, to create." Whether Bréal and Decharme, who quotes him, are as right in saying that in the Vedas *Kronos* is a creative

god, we have our doubts. Bréal probably meant Karma, or rather Viśva-Karmā, the creative god, the " Omnificent " and the "great Architect of the world."

525. See our Stanzas III – X, *et seq.*, and also Berosus' account of primeval crea-tion.

526. The Titanic struggle, in theogony at least, is the fight for supremacy between the children of *Ouranos* and *Gaia* (or Heaven and Earth in their abstract sense), the Ti-tans, against the children of *Kronos*, whose chief is Zeus. It is the everlasting strug-gle going on to this day between the spir-itual inner man and the man of flesh, in one sense.

527. Just as the " Lord God," or Jehovah, is Cain esoterically, and the " tempting ser-pent " as well, the male portion of the androgynous Eve, before her " Fall "; the female portion of Adam Kadmon; the left side or Binah of the right side Chochmah in the first Sephirothal Triad.

varies from Zeus, the Great "Father of the Gods." He is the "disrespectful son" in Hesiod. Hermes calls him the "Heavenly man" (*Pymander*); and even in the Bible he is found again under the name of Adam, and, later on — by transmutation — under that of Ham. Yet these are all personifications of the "sons of Wisdom." The necessary corroboration that Jupiter belongs to the purely *human Atlantean cycle* — if *Ouranos* and *Kronos* who precede him are found insufficient — may be found in Hesiod, who tells us that the Immortals have made men and created the Golden and the Silver age (First and Second Races); while Jupiter created the generations of Bronze (an admixture of *two* elements), of Heroes, and the men of the age of Iron. After this he sends his fatal present, by Pandora, to Epimetheus,[528] which present Hesiod calls "a fatal gift," or the *first woman*.[528a] It was a punishment, he explains, sent to man "for the theft of divine creative fire." Her apparition on earth is the signal of every kind of evil. Before her appearance, the human races lived happy, exempt from sickness and suffering — as the same races are made to live under Yima's rule, in the Mazdean *Vendîdâd*.

Two deluges may also be traced in universal tradition by carefully comparing Hesiod, the *Rig Veda*, the *Zend Avesta*, etc., while no *first* man is ever mentioned in any of the theogonies save the Bible.[529] Everywhere the man of *our race* appears after a cataclysm of water, after which tradition mentions only the several designations of continents and islands which sink under the ocean waves in due time.[530] "Gods and mortals have one common origin" says Hesiod;[531] and Pindar echoes the statement.[532] Deukalion and Pyrrha, who escape the Deluge by constructing an ark like Noah's,[533] ask Jupiter to reanimate the human race whom he had made to perish under the waters of the Flood. In the Slavonian Mythology,[534] all men were drowned, and two old people, a man and his wife, alone remained. Then *Pram-gimas* (the "master of all") advised them to jump *seven times* on the rocks of the earth, and *seven new races* (couples) were born, from which came the nine Lithuanian tribes. As well understood by the author of the *Mythologie de la Grèce Antique* — the four ages

528. In the Egyptian legend, translated by M. Maspero (the ex-director of the Bulaq Museum), called the "Two Brothers," the original of Pandora is given. *Khnûm*, the famous heavenly artist, creates a marvelous beauty, a girl which he sends to *Batu*, after which the happiness of the latter is destroyed. Batu is man, and the girl Eve, of course. (See Maspero's *Egyptian Legends*, and also Decharme's *Mythologie de la Grèce Antique*.)
528a. *Works and Days*, 73 *et seq.*

529. Yima is not the "first man" in the *Vendîdâd*, but only in the theories of the Orientalists.— See further on.
530. Boeotia, then ancient Athens, and Eleusis were submerged.
531. *Ibid.*, verse 108.
532. *Nem.* VI, 1.
533. See Apollod., i, 7, 2, and Ovid, *Metam.* 1, 260–416.
534. Lithuanian Legend, in Grimm, *Deutsche Myth.*, 1, 545.

signify periods of time, and are also an allegorical allusion to the races. He says:[535]

The successive races, destroyed and replaced by others, without any period of transition, are characterized in Greece by the name of metals, to express their ever-decreasing value. Gold, the most brilliant and precious of all, symbol of purity . . . qualifies the first race. . . . The men of the second race, those of the age of Silver, are already inferior to the first. Inert and weak creatures, all their life is no better than a long and stupid infancy. . . . They disappear. . . . The men of the age of Bronze are robust and violent [the third race]; their strength is extreme. They had arms made of bronze, habitations of bronze; used naught but bronze. Iron, the black metal, was yet unknown.[536]

The fourth generation (race) is, with Hesiod, that of the heroes who fell before Thebes,[537] or under the walls of Troy.

Thus, the four races being found mentioned by the oldest Greek poets, though very much confused anachronistically, our doctrines are once more corroborated by the classics. But this is all "Mythology" and poetry. What can modern science have to say to such a euhemerization of old fictions? The verdict is not difficult to foresee. Therefore an attempt must be made to answer by anticipation, and prove that fictions and *empirical* speculations are so much of the domain of that same science, that none of the men of learning have the slightest right, with such a heavy beam in their own eye, to point to the speck in the eye of the Occultist, even if that speck be not a figment of our opponents' imagination.

STANZA X.—(*Continued.*)

40. THEN THE THIRD AND FOURTH (*races*) BECAME TALL WITH PRIDE. WE ARE THE KINGS, WE ARE THE GODS (*a*).

41. THEY TOOK WIVES FAIR TO LOOK AT. WIVES FROM THE "MIND-LESS," THE NARROW-HEADED. THEY BRED MONSTERS, WICKED DEMONS, MALE AND FEMALE. ALSO KHADO (*Dâkinî*) WITH LITTLE MINDS (*b*).

42. THEY BUILT TEMPLES FOR THE HUMAN BODY. MALE AND FEMALE THEY WORSHIPED (*c*). THEN THE THIRD EYE ACTED NO LONGER (*d*).

(*a*) Such were the first truly physical men, whose first characteristic was — pride! It is the Third Race and the gigantic Atlanteans, the

535. Pages 289, 290.   536. *Opera et Dies*, 143-155.
537. See *The Seven Against Thebes*, by Aeschylus.

memory of whom lingered from one generation and race to another generation and race down to the days of Moses, and which found an objective form in those antediluvian giants, those terrible sorcerers and magicians, of whom the Roman Church has preserved such vivid and at the same time distorted legends. One who has read and studied the Commentaries on the archaic doctrine, will easily recognize in some Atlanteans, the prototypes of the Nimrods, the Builders of the Tower of Babel, the Hamites, and all these *tutti quanti* of " accursed memory," as theological literature expresses it: of those, in short, who have furnished posterity with the orthodox types of Satan. And this leads us naturally to inquire into the religious ethics of these early races, mythical as these may be.

What was the religion of the Third and Fourth Races? In the common acceptation of the term, neither the Lemurians nor yet their progeny, the Lemuro-Atlanteans, had any, as they knew no dogma, nor had they to believe *on faith*. No sooner had the mental eye of man been opened to understanding, than the Third Race felt itself one with the ever-present as the ever to be unknown and invisible ALL, the One Universal Deity. Endowed with divine powers, and feeling in himself his *inner* God, each felt he was a Man-God in his nature, though an animal in his physical Self. The struggle between the two began from the very day they tasted of the fruit of the Tree of Wisdom; a struggle for life between the spiritual and the psychic, the psychic and the physical. Those who conquered the lower principles by obtaining mastery over the body, joined the " Sons of Light." Those who fell victims to their lower natures became the slaves of Matter. From " Sons of Light and Wisdom " they ended by becoming the " Sons of Darkness." They had fallen in the battle of mortal life with Life immortal, and all those so fallen became the seed of the future generations of Atlanteans.[538]

At the dawn of his consciousness, the man of the Third Root Race had thus no beliefs that could be called *religion*. That is to say, he was equally as ignorant of " gay religions, full of pomp and gold " as of any system of faith or outward worship. But if the term is to be defined as the binding together of the masses in one form of reverence paid to those we feel higher than ourselves, of piety — as a feeling expressed by a child toward a loved parent — then even the earliest Lemurians had a religion — and a most beautiful one — from the very beginning of their intellectual life. Had they not their bright gods of the elements

538. The name is used here in the sense of, and as a synonym of " sorcerers." The Atlantean races were many, and lasted in their evolution for millions of years: all were not bad. They became so toward their end, as we (the fifth) are fast becoming now.

around them, and even within themselves?[539] Was not their childhood passed with, nursed and tended by those who had given them life and called them forth to intelligent, conscious life? We are assured it was so, and we believe it. For the evolution of Spirit into matter could never have been achieved; nor would it have received its first impulse, had not the bright Spirits sacrificed their own respective super-ethereal essences to animate the man of clay, by endowing each of his inner principles with a portion, or rather, a reflection of that essence. The Dhyânis of the Seven Heavens (the seven planes of Being) are the NOUMENOI of the actual and the future Elements, just as the Angels of the Seven Powers of nature — the grosser effects of which are perceived by us in what Science is pleased to call the "modes of motion" — the imponderable forces and what not — are the still higher noumenoi of still higher Hierarchies.

It was the "Golden Age" in those days of old, the age when the "gods walked the earth, and mixed freely with mortals." Since then, the gods departed (*i. e.*, became invisible), and later generations ended by worshiping their kingdoms — the Elements.

It was the Atlanteans, the first progeny of *semi-divine* man after his separation into sexes — hence the first-begotten and humanly-born mortals — who became the first "Sacrificers" to the *god of matter*. They stand in the far-away dim past, in ages more than prehistoric, as the prototype on which the great symbol of Cain was built,[540] as the first anthropomorphists who worshiped form and matter. That worship degenerated very soon into *self-worship*, thence led to phallicism, or that which reigns supreme to this day in the symbolisms of every exoteric religion of ritual, dogma, and form. Adam and Eve *became matter*, or furnished the soil, Cain and Abel — the latter the life-bearing soil, the former "the tiller of that ground or field."

Thus the first Atlantean races, born on the Lemurian Continent, separated from their earliest tribes into the righteous and the unrighteous; into those who worshiped the one unseen Spirit of Nature, the ray of which man feels within himself — or the Pantheists, and those who offered fanatical worship to the Spirits of the Earth, the dark Cosmic, anthropomorphic Powers, with whom they made alliance. These were the earliest *Gibborim*, "the mighty men of renown in those

539. The "Gods of the Elements" are by no means the Elementals. The latter are at best used by them as vehicles and materials in which to clothe themselves. . . .

540. Cain was the *sacrificer*, as shown at first in chap. iv of *Genesis*, of "the fruit of the ground," of which he was *first tiller*, while Abel "brought of the firstlings of his flock" to the Lord. Cain is the symbol of the first male, Abel of the first female humanity, Adam and Eve being the types of the third race. (See "The Mystery of Cain and Abel.") The "murdering" is blood-shedding, but not taking life.

days ";[541] who become with the Fifth Race the *Kabirim:* Kabiri with
the Egyptians and the Phoenicians, Titans with the Greeks, and Râkshasas and Daityas with the Indian races.

Such was the secret and mysterious origin of all the subsequent and
modern religions, especially of the worship of the later Hebrews for
their tribal god. At the same time this sexual religion was closely
allied to, based upon and blended, so to say, with astronomical phenomena. The Lemurians gravitated toward the North Pole or the Heaven
of their Progenitors (the Hyperborean Continent) ; the Atlanteans,
toward the Southern Pole, the *pit,* cosmically and terrestrially —
whence breathe the hot passions blown into hurricanes by the cosmic
Elementals, whose abode it is. The two poles were denominated, by
the ancients, Dragons and Serpents — hence good and bad Dragons
and Serpents, and also the names given to the " Sons of God " (Sons
of Spirit and Matter) : the good and bad Magicians. This is the origin
of this dual and triple nature in man. The legend of the " Fallen
Angels " in its esoteric signification, contains the key to the manifold
contradictions of human character; it points to the secret of man's
self-consciousness; it is the angle-iron on which hinges his entire life-
cycle ; — the history of his evolution and growth.

On a firm grasp of this doctrine depends the correct understanding
of esoteric anthropogenesis. It gives a clue to the vexed question of
the Origin of Evil; and shows how man himself is the separator of
the ONE into various contrasted aspects.

The reader, therefore, will not be surprised if so considerable space
is devoted in each case to an attempt to elucidate this difficult and
obscure subject. A good deal must necessarily be said on its symbo-
logical aspect; because, by so doing, hints are given to the thoughtful
student for his own investigations, and more light can thus be suggested
than it is possible to convey in the technical phrases of a more formal,
philosophical exposition. The " Fallen Angels," so-called, are *Humanity
itself.* The Demon of Pride, Lust, Rebellion, and Hatred has never
had *any being before* the appearance of physical conscious man. It is
man who has begotten, nurtured, and allowed the fiend to develop in
his heart; he, again, who has contaminated the indwelling god in
himself, by linking the pure spirit with the impure demon of matter.
And, if the Kabalistic saying, " *Daemon est Deus inversus* " finds its
metaphysical and theoretical corroboration in dual manifested nature,
its practical application is found in Mankind alone.

Thus it has now become self-evident that postulating as we do (*a*)
the appearance of man before that of other mammalia, and even before
the ages of the huge reptiles; (*b*) periodical deluges and glacial peri-

541. *Genesis,* chapter vi.

ods owing to the karmic disturbance of the axis; and chiefly (c) the birth of man from a Superior Being, or what materialism would call a *supernatural* Being, though it is only super-*human* — it is evident that our teachings have very few chances of an impartial hearing. Add to it the claim that a portion of the Mankind in the Third Race — all those Monads of men who had reached the highest point of Merit and *Karma* in the preceding Manvantara — owed their psychic and *rational* natures to divine Beings *hypostasizing* into their fifth principles, and the *Secret Doctrine* must lose caste in the eyes of not only Materialism but even of dogmatic Christianity. For, no sooner will the latter have learned that those angels are identical with their "Fallen" Spirits, than the esoteric tenet will be proclaimed most terribly heretical and pernicious.[542] The *divine* man dwelt in the animal, and, therefore, when the physiological separation took place in the natural course of evolution — when also "all the animal creation was *untied*," and males were attracted to females — *that race fell*: not because they had eaten of the fruit of Knowledge and knew good from evil, but because they knew no better. Propelled by the sexless creative instinct, the early sub-races had evolved an intermediate race in which, as hinted in the Stanzas, the higher Dhyân-Chohans had incarnated.[543] "When we have ascertained the extent of the Universe and learnt to know all that there is in it, we will multiply our race," answer the *Sons of Will and Yoga* to their brethren of the same race, who invite them to do as they do. This means that the great Adepts and Initiated ascetics will "multiply," *i. e.*, once more produce *Mind-born* immaculate Sons — in the Seventh Root-Race.

It is so stated in the Purânas; in *Adi Parvan* (page 115)[544] and *Brahma Purâna*, etc. In one portion of the *Pushkara Mâhâtmya*, moreover, the separation of the sexes is allegorized by Daksha, who, seeing that his will-born progeny (the "Sons of passive Yoga"), will not create men, "*converts half himself into a female* by whom he begets daughters," the future females of the Third Race which begat the

---

542. It is, perhaps, with an eye to this *degradation* of the highest and purest Spirits, who broke through the intermediate planes of lower consciousness (the "Seven circles of fire" of *Pymander*), that St. James is made to say that "this Wisdom (*psuchike* in the original) descended not from above, but is earthly, sensual, *devilish*"; and *psuche* is *Manas*, the "human soul," the Spiritual Wisdom or Soul being *Buddhi*. Yet Buddhi *per se*, being so near the Absolute, is only latent consciousness.

543. This is the "undying race" as it is called in Esotericism, and exoterically the fruitless generation of the first progeny of Daksha, who curses Nârada, the divine Rishi, alleged to have dissuaded the Haryaśvas and the Sabalâśvas, the sons of Daksha, from procreating their species, by saying "Be born in the womb; there shall not be a resting place for thee in all these regions"; after this Nârada, the representative of that race of *fruitless* ascetics, is said, as soon as he dies in one body, to be reborn in another.

544. *Mahâbhârata.*

giants of Atlantis, the Fourth Race, so called. In the *Vishnu Purâna* it is simply said that Daksha, the father of mankind, established sexual intercourse as the means of peopling the world.

Happily for the human race the "Elect Race" had already become the vehicle of incarnation of the (intellectually and spiritually) highest Dhyânis before Humanity had become quite material. When the last sub-races — save some lowest — of the Third Race had perished with the great Lemurian Continent, "the seeds of *the Trinity of Wisdom*" had already acquired the secret of immortality on Earth, that gift which allows the same great personality to step *ad libitum* from one worn-out body into another.

(*b*) The first war that earth knew, the first human gore shed, was the result of man's eyes and senses being opened; which made him see that the daughters of his Brethren were fairer than his own, and their wives also. There were rapes committed before that of the Sabines, and Menelauses robbed of their Helens before the Fifth Race was born. Titans or giants were the stronger; their adversaries, the wiser. This took place during the Fourth Race — that of the giants.

For "there *were* giants" in the days of old, indeed [545] and the evolutionary series of the animal world is a warrant that the same thing took place within the human races. Lower still in the order of creation we find witnesses for the same in the flora going *pari passu* with the fauna in respect of size. The pretty ferns we collect and dry among the leaves of our favorite volumes are the descendants of the gigantic ferns which grew during the carboniferous period.

Scriptures, and fragments of philosophical and scientific works — in short, almost every record that has come down to us from antiquity — contain references to giants. No one can fail to recognize the Atlanteans of the Secret Doctrine in the Râkshasas of Lankâ — the opponents conquered by Râma. Are these accounts no better than the production of empty fancy? Let us give the subject a few moments of attention.

545. The traditions of every country and nation point to this fact. Donnelly quotes from Father Duran's *Historia Antigua de la Nueva España* of 1585, in which a native of Cholula, a centenarian, accounts for the building of the great pyramid of Cholula, by saying as follows: "In the beginning, before the light of the Sun had been created, this land (Cholula) was in obscurity and darkness . . . but immediately *after the light of the Sun arose in the East*, there appeared gigantic men . . . who built the said pyramid, its builders being scattered after that to all parts of the Earth" (p. 200).
"A great deal of the Central American history is taken up with the doings of an ancient race of giants called Quinames," says the author of *Atlantis* (p. 204).

ARE GIANTS A FICTION?

Here, again, we come into collision with Science. The latter denies, so far, that man has ever been much larger than the average of the tall and powerful men one meets with occasionally now. Dr. Henry Gregor denounces such traditions as resting upon ill-digested facts. Instances of mistaken judgments are brought forward. Thus, in 1613, in a locality called from time immemorial the " Field of Giants " in the Lower Dauphiné (France, four miles from St. Romans) enormous bones were found deeply buried in the sandy soil. They were attributed to human remains, and even to Teutobodus, the Teuton chief slain by Marius. But Cuvier's later research proved them to be the fossil remains of the *Dinotherium giganteum* of the family of tapirs, 18 feet long. Ancient buildings are pointed to as an evidence that our earliest ancestors were not much larger than we are, the entrance doors being of no larger size than they are now. The tallest man of antiquity *known to us* was the Roman Emperor Maximus, we are told, whose height was only seven and a half feet. Nevertheless, in our modern day we see every year men taller than this. The Hungarian who exhibited himself in the London Pavilion was nearly 9 feet high. In America a giant was shown 9½ feet tall; the Montenegrin Danilo was 8 feet 7 inches. In Russia and Germany one often sees men in the lower classes above 7 feet. And as the ape-theorists are told by Mr. Darwin that the species of animals which result from cross breeding " always betray *a tendency to revert to the original type,*" they ought to apply the same law to men. Had there been no giants as a rule in ancient days, there would be none now.

All this applies only to the historic period. And if the skeletons of the prehistoric ages have failed so far (which is positively denied) to prove undeniably in the opinion of science the claim here advanced, it is but a question of time. Moreover, as already stated, human stature is little changed since the last racial cycle. The Giants of old are all buried under the Oceans, and hundreds of thousands of years of constant friction by water would reduce to dust and pulverize a brazen, far more a human skeleton. But whence the testimony of well-known classical writers, of philosophers and men who, otherwise, never had the reputation for lying? Let us bear in mind, furthermore, that before the year 1847, when Boucher de Perthes forced it upon the attention of Science, almost nothing was known of fossil man, for archaeology complacently ignored his existence. Of Giants who were " in the earth in those days " of old, the Bible alone had spoken to the wise men of the West, the Zodiac being the solitary witness called upon to corroborate the statement in the persons of Atlas or Orion, whose mighty shoulders are said to support the world.

278 THE SECRET DOCTRINE

Nevertheless, even the "Giants" have not been left without their witnesses, and one may as well examine both sides of the question. The three Sciences — Geological, Sidereal and Scriptural (the latter in its Universal character) — may furnish us with the needed proofs. To begin with geology; it has already confessed that the older the excavated skeletons, the larger, taller and the more powerful their structure. This is already a certain proof in hand. "All those bones" writes Frédéric de Rougemont — who, though believing too piously in Noah's ark and the Bible, is none the less a Scientific witness —

all those skeletons found in the Department of the Gard, in Austria, Liège, etc., etc. . . . those skulls which remind all of the negro type . . . and which by reason of that type might be mistaken for animals, have all belonged to men *of very high stature.* . . .[546]

The same is repeated by Lartet, an authority, who attributes a *tall stature* to those who were submerged in the deluge (not necessarily "Noah's") and a smaller stature to the races which lived subsequently. As for the evidence furnished by ancient writers, we need not stop at that of Tertullian, who assures us that in his day a number of giants were found at Carthage — for, before his testimony can be accepted, his own identity[547] and actual existence would have to be proven. But we may turn to the scientific journals of 1858, which spoke of *a sarcophagus of giants* found that year on the site of that same city. As to the ancient pagan writers — we have the evidence of Philostratos, who speaks of a giant skeleton twenty-two cubits long, as well as of another of twelve cubits, seen by himself at Sigeum. This skeleton may perhaps not have belonged, as believed by Protesilaos, to the giant killed by Apollo at the siege of Troy; nevertheless, it was that of a giant, as well as that other one discovered by Messekrates of Steiria, at Lemnos — "horrible to behold," according to Philostratos.[548] Is it possible that prejudice would carry Science so far as to class *all* these men as either fools or *liars?*

Pliny speaks of a giant in whom he thought he recognized Orion, the son of Ephialtes.[549] Plutarch declares that Sertorius saw the tomb of Antaeus, the giant;[549a] and Pausanias vouches for the actual existence of the tombs of Asterios and of Geryon, or Hyllos, son of Hercules — all giants, Titans and mighty men.[549b] Finally the Abbé Pègues[550] affirms in his curious work on *The Volcanoes of Greece* that

546. *Histoire de la Terre,* p. 154.
547. There are critics who, finding no evidence about the existence of Tertullian save in the writings of Eusebius "the veracious," are inclined to doubt it.
548. *Heroika,* p. 35.
549. *Nat. Hist.,* vol. VII, ch. xvi.
549a. *Lives,* Sertorius, ix.
549b. *Periegesis,* i, 35.
550. Cited in de Mirville's *Pneumatologie.*

in the neighborhood of the volcanoes of the isle of Thera, giants with enormous skulls were found laid out under colossal stones, the erection of which must have necessitated everywhere the use of titanic powers, and which tradition associates in all countries with the ideas about giants, volcanoes and magic.[551]

In the same work above cited of the Abbé Pègues, the author wonders why in Bible and tradition the *Gibborim* (Giants, the mighty ones) the *Rephaim*, or the specters (*Phantoms*), the *Nephilim*, or the fallen ones — (*irruentes*) — are shown "as if identical, though they are all *men*, since the Bible calls them the primitive and the mighty ones " — *e. g.*, Nimrod. The "Doctrine" explains the secret. These names, which belong by right only to the four preceding races and the earliest beginning of the Fifth, allude very clearly to the first two *Phantom* (astral) races; to the *fallen one* — the Third; and to the race of the Atlantean Giants — the Fourth, after which "men began to decrease in stature."

Bossuet[552] sees the cause of subsequent universal idolatry in the "original sin." "Ye shall be as gods," says the serpent of *Genesis* to Eve, thus laying the first germ of the worship of *false divinities*. Hence, he thinks, came idolatry, or the cult and adoration of *images*, of anthropomorphized or human figures. But, if it is the latter that idolatry is made to rest upon, then the two Churches, the Greek and the Latin especially, are as idolatrous and pagan as any other religion.[553] It is only in the Fourth Race that men, who had lost all right to be considered divine, resorted to body worship, in other words to phallicism. Till then, they had been truly gods, as pure and as divine as their progenitors, and the expression of the allegorical serpent does not, as sufficiently shown in the preceding pages, refer at all to the physiological fall of men, but to their acquiring the knowledge of good and evil, which knowledge comes to them *prior* to their fall. It must not be forgotten that it is only after his forced expulsion from Eden that "Adam knew Eve his wife."[554] It is not, however, by the dead-letter of the Hebrew Bible that we shall check the tenets of the *Secret Doctrine*; but point out, rather, the great similarities between the two in their esoteric meaning.

It is only after his defection from the Neo-Platonists, that Clement

---

551. Page 48.

552. *Élévations*, p. 56.

553. And that, notwithstanding the formal prohibition at the great Church Council of Elyrus in A. D. 303, when it was declared that "the form of God, which is immaterial and invisible, shall not be limited by figure or shape." In 692, the council of Constan-

tinople had similarly prohibited "to paint or represent Jesus *as a lamb*," as also "to bow the knee in praying, as it is the act of idolatry." But the council of Nicaea (787) brought this idolatry back, while that of Rome (883) excommunicated John, the Patriarch of Constantinople, for his showing himself a declared enemy of image worship.

554. *Genesis*, iv,

of Alexandria began to translate *gigantes* by *serpentes,* explaining that
" Serpents and Giants signify *Demons*." [555]

We may be told that, before we draw parallels between our tenets
and those of the Bible, we have to show better evidence of the existence
of the giants of the Fourth Race than the reference to them found in
Genesis. We answer, that the proofs we give are more satisfactory,
at any rate they belong to a more literary and scientific evidence, than
those of Noah's Deluge will ever be. Even the historical works of
China are full of such reminiscences about the Fourth Race. In
Shu-King, [556] anyone can read in the French translation,

> When the Miao-tse ["that antediluvian and perverted race," explains the An-
> notator, "which had retired in the days of old to the rocky caves, and the de-
> scendants of whom are said to be still found in the neighborhood of Can-
> ton"], [557] *according to our ancient documents,* had, owing to the beguilements of
> *Chih-Yû,* troubled all the earth, it became full of brigands. . . . The Lord

555. *Genesis,* chapter v.
Treating of the Chinese Dragon and the
literature of China, Mr. Ch. Gould writes
in his *Mythical Monsters,* on page 212:—
" Its mythologies, histories, religions, popular stories and proverbs, all teem with references to a mysterious being *who has a
physical nature and spiritual attributes.*
Gifted with an accepted form, which he has
the supernatural power of casting off for
the assumption of others, he has the power
of influencing the weather, producing
droughts or fertilizing rains at pleasure, or
raising tempests and allaying them. Volumes could be compiled from the scattered
legends which everywhere abound relating
to this subject. . . ."
This " mysterious being " is the *mythical*
Dragon, *i. e.,* the symbol of the *historical,*
actual Adept, the master and professor of
occult sciences of old. It is stated already elsewhere, that the great " magicians "
of the Fourth and Fifth Races were generally called the " Serpents " and the " Dragons " after their progenitors. All these
belonged to the hierarchy of the so-called
" Fiery Dragons of Wisdom," the Dhyân
Chohans, answering to the Agnishvâtta Pitris, the Maruts and Rudras generally, as
the issue of Rudra their father, identified
with the god of fire. More is said in the
text. Now Clement, an initiated Neo-
Platonist, knew, of course, the origin of
the word " Dragon," and why the initiated
Adepts were so-called, as he knew the secret of *Agathodaimon,* the Christ, the seven-

voweled Serpent of the Gnostics. He
knew that the dogma of his new faith required the transformation of all the *rivals*
of Jehovah, the angels supposed to have
rebelled against that Elohim as the Titan-
Prometheus rebelled against Zeus, the usurper of his father's kingdom; and that
" Dragon " was the mystic appellation of
the " Sons of Wisdom "; from this knowledge came his definition, as cruel as it
was arbitrary, " Serpents and Giants signify *Demons,*" *i. e.,* not " Spirits," but
Devils, in Church parlance.
556. Fifth Part, chap. XXVII, page 291.
Cf. " Sacred Books of the East," Vol. III,
pp. 255 *et seqq.*
557. " What would you say to our af-
firmation that the Chinese — I speak of the
inland, the true Chinaman, not of the hybrid mixture between the Fourth and Fifth
Races now occupying the throne, the aborigines who belong in their unallied nationality wholly to the highest and last branch
of the Fourth Race — reached their highest
civilization when the Fifth had hardly appeared in Asia" (*Esoteric Buddhism,* p.
67). And this handful of the inland Chinese are all of a very high stature. Could
the most ancient MSS. in the Lolo language (that of the aborigines of China) be
got at and translated correctly, many a
priceless piece of evidence would be found.
But they are as rare as their language is
unintelligible. So far, one or two European archaeologists only have been able to
procure such priceless works.

Hwang-Ti [a king of the *divine* dynasty] saw that his people had lost the last vestiges of virtue. Then he commanded Chung and Li [two lower Dhyân Chohans] to cut away every communication between heaven and earth. Since then, there was no more *going up and down!* [558]

" Going up and down " means an untrammelled communication and intercourse between the two worlds. Not being in a position to give out a full and detailed history of the Third and Fourth Races, as many isolated facts concerning them as are permitted must now be collated together; especially those corroborated by direct as well as by inferential evidence found in ancient literature and history. As the " coats of skin " of men thickened, and they fell more and more into physical sin, the intercourse between physical and ethereal *divine* man was stopped. The veil of matter between the two planes became too dense for even the inner man to penetrate. The mysteries of Heaven and Earth, revealed to the Third Race by their celestial teachers in the days of their purity, became a great focus of light, the rays from which became necessarily weakened as they were diffused and shed upon an uncongenial, because too material soil. With the masses they degenerated into Sorcery, taking later on the shape of exoteric religions, of idolatry full of superstitions, and man-, or hero-worship. Alone a handful of primitive men — in whom the spark of divine Wisdom burnt bright, and only strengthened in its intensity as it got dimmer and dimmer with every age in those who turned it to bad purposes — remained the elect custodians of the Mysteries revealed to mankind by the divine Teachers. There were those among them, who remained in their *Kumâric* condition from the beginning; and tradition whispers, what the secret teachings affirm, namely, that these Elect were the germ of a Hierarchy *which never died since that period:—*

" *The inner man of the first* * * * *only changes his body from time to time; he is ever the same, knowing neither rest nor Nirvâna, spurning Devachan and remaining constantly on Earth for the salvation of mankind. . . . .*" " *Out of the seven virgin-men* (Kumâra [559]) *four sacrificed themselves for the sins of the world and the instruction of the ignorant, to remain till the end of the present Manvantara. Though unseen they are ever present. When people say of one of them,*

---

558. Remember the same statement in the *Book of Enoch*, as also the ladder seen by Jacob in his dream. The " two worlds " mean of course the " two *planes* of Consciousness and Being." A seer can commune with beings of a higher plane than the earth, without quitting his armchair.

559. *Vide supra* the *Commentary* on the Four Races — and on the " Sons of Will and Yoga," the immaculate progeny of the Androgynous Third Race.

" He is dead "; behold, he is alive and under another form. These are the Head, the Heart, the Soul, and the Seed of undying knowledge ('Jñâna). *Thou shalt never· speak, O Lanoo, of these great ones* (Maha . . .) *before a multitude, mentioning them by their names. The wise alone will understand. . . ."* [560] (Catechism of the inner Schools.)

It is these sacred " Four " who have been allegorized and symbolized in the *Linga Purâna,* which states that Vâmadeva (Śiva) as Kumâra is reborn in each Kalpa (*Race* in this instance), as four youths — four, white; four, red; four, yellow; and four, dark or brown. Let us remember that Śiva is pre-eminently and chiefly an ascetic, the patron of all Yogis and Adepts, and the allegory will become quite comprehensible. It is the spirit of Divine Wisdom and chaste asceticism itself which incarnates in these Elect. It is only after *getting married* and being dragged by the gods from his terrible ascetic life, that Rudra becomes Śiva, a god, and not one of a very virtuous or merciful type, in the Hindû Pantheon. Higher than the " Four " is only ONE on Earth as in Heavens — that still more mysterious and solitary Being described in Book I.

We have now to examine the nature of the " Sons of the Flame " and of " Dark Wisdom," as well as the *pros* and *cons* of the Satanic assumption.

Such broken sentences as could be made out from the fragments on the tile, which George Smith calls "the Curse after the Fall," [561] are of course allegorical; yet they corroborate that which is taught of the true nature of the *fall of the angels* in our Books. Thus, it is said in line 12 that the "Lord of the earth his name called out, the father Elu" (Elohim), and pronounced his curse, which " The God Hea heard, and his liver was angry, because *his* man [Angelic man] had corrupted his purity " (14 *and* 15), for which Hea expresses the desire (line 22) that " ' *Wisdom and knowledge* ' hostilely may they injure him [man]." [561a]

The latter sentence points to the direct connexion of the Chaldaean with the Genetic account. While Hea tries to bring to nought the wisdom and knowledge gained by man, through his newly-acquired intellectual and conscious capacity of creating in his turn (thus taking the monopoly of creation out of the hands of God [the Gods]), the Elohim do the same in the third chapter of *Genesis.* Therefore the Elohim sent him out of Eden.

---

560. In the Kabala the pronunciation of the four-lettered *ineffable* name is " a most secret arcanum " — " a secret of secrets."

561. See p. 81 of his *Chaldean Account of Genesis.*

561a. *Op. cit.,* p. 84.

But this was of no avail. For the spirit of divine Wisdom being upon and *in* man — verily the Serpent of Eternity and all Knowledge, that *Mânasic* spirit, which made him learn the secret of *creation* on the Kriyâśaktic, and of procreation on the earthly planes — led him as naturally to discover his way to immortality, notwithstanding the jealousy of all the Gods.

The earlier Atlanto-Lemurians are charged with taking unto themselves (divine incarnations) wives of a lower race, namely, the race of the hitherto mindless men. Every ancient Scripture has the same, more or less disfigured legend. Primarily, the angelic *Fall*, which has transformed the "first-born" of God into the Asuras, or into the Ahriman and Typhon of the "pagans" (*i. e.*, if the accounts given in the *Book of Enoch*,[562] and in Hermes, in Purânas and Bible are taken literally), when read esoterically means simply this:—

Sentences such as: "In his [Satan's] ambition he raises his hand against the Sanctuary of the God of Heaven" etc., ought to read: "Prompted by the law of eternal evolution and Karma, the angel incarnated on earth in man; and as his Wisdom and Knowledge are still divine, although his body is earthly, he is (allegorically) accused of divulging the mysteries of Heaven. He combines and uses the two for purposes of human, instead of super-human, procreation. Henceforth, "man will *beget*, not *create*."[563] But as, by so doing, he has to use

562. Returning once more to the most important subject in the archaic Cosmogony, it may be said that even in the Norse legends, in the Sacred Scrolls of the goddess Saga, we find Loki, the brother by blood of Odin (as Typhon, Ahriman, and others are brothers of Osiris and Ormazd), becoming evil only later, when he has mixed too long with humanity. Like all other fire or light gods—fire burning and destroying as well as warming and giving life—he ended by being accepted in the destructive sense of "fire." The name *Loki*, we learn (*Asgard and the Gods*, p. 250), has been derived from the old word "liuhan," to enlighten. It has, therefore, the same origin as the Latin "*lux*, light." Hence *Loki* is identical with Lucifer (light-bringer). This title, given to the Prince of Darkness, is very suggestive and is a *vindication* in itself against theological slander. But *Loki* is still more closely related to Prometheus, as he is shown chained to a sharp rock, while Lucifer, identified with Satan, was chained down in hell; a circumstance, however, which prevented neither of them from acting in all freedom on Earth, if we accept the theological paradox in its fulness. *Loki* is a beneficent, generous and powerful god in the beginning of times, and the principle of good, not of evil, in early Scandinavian theogony.

563. The Greek mythos just alluded to a few pages back, namely the mutilation of *Ouranos* by his son *Kronos* in the Greek theogony, is an allusion to this theft by the Son of the Earth and Heavens of the *divine creative fire*. If *Ouranos*, the personification of the celestial Powers, has to stop creating (he is made impotent by *Kronos*, the god *in time*) so, in the Egyptian Cosmogony it is Thoth, the god of Wisdom, who regulates this fight between Horus and Set, the latter being served by the former as Ouranos is by Kronos (see *"Book of the Dead,"* ch. XVII, v. 26). In the Babylonian account it is the god Zu, who strips "the father of the gods" of *umsimi* — the ideal creative organ not the *crown* (!) as G. Smith thought (see pp. 115 and 116 *Chaldean Account of Genesis*). For, in the fragment K. 3454 (British Museum) it is said very clearly, that Zu having stripped the "venerable of Heaven" of his *desire*,

his weak body as the means of procreation, that body will pay the penalty for this wisdom, carried from heaven down to the earth; hence the corruption of physical purity will become a temporary curse.

The medieval Kabalists knew this well, since one of them did not fear to write: " The Kabala was first taught by God himself to a select Company of Angels who formed a theosophic school in Paradise. After the FALL the Angels most *graciously communicated this heavenly doctrine to the disobedient child of Earth*, to furnish the protoplasts with the means of returning to their pristine nobility and felicity." [564] This shows how the event — of the Sons of God, marrying and imparting the divine Secrets of Heaven to the daughters of men — allegorically told by Enoch and in the sixth chapter of *Genesis* was interpreted by the Christian Kabalists. The whole of this period may be regarded as the *pre-human* period, that of divine man, or as *plastic* Protestant theology now has it — the *pre*-adamite period. But even *Genesis* begins its *real* history [565] by the *giants* of " those days " and the " Sons of god " marrying and teaching their wives — the daughters of man.

This period is the one described in the Purânas; and relating as it does to days lost in archaic ages, hence pre-historic, how can any anthropologist feel certain whether the mankind of that period was or was not as he knows it now? The whole *personnel* of the Brâhmanas and Purânas — the Rishis, Prajâpatis, Manus, their wives and progeny — belong to that pre-human period. All these are the *Seed* of Humanity, so to speak. It is around these " Sons of God," the " Mind born " astral children of Brahmâ, that our physical frames have grown and developed to what they are now. For, the Purânic histories of all those men are those of our Monads, in their various and numberless incarnations on this and other spheres, events perceived by the " Śiva eye " of the ancient Seers (the " third eye " of our Stanzas), and described allegorically. Later on, they were disfigured for Sectarian purposes; mutilated, but still left with a considerable ground-work of truth in them. Nor is the philosophy less profound in such allegories for being so thickly veiled by the overgrowth of fancy.

But with the Fourth Race we reach the purely human period. Those who were hitherto semi-divine Beings, self-imprisoned in bodies which were human only in appearance, became physiologically changed and took unto themselves wives who were entirely human and fair to look

he carried away the *umsimi* of the gods, and burnt thereby the *tereti* (the power) of all the other gods, thus " governing the *seed* of all the angels " (line 15). As the *umsimi* was *on the seat* of Bel, it could hardly be the " crown." A fourth version is in the Bible. Ham is the Chaldaean Za, and both are cursed for the same allegorically described crime.

564. Quoted by Christian Ginsburg from the *Kabala*.

565. Chapter vi.

at, but in whom *lower, more material,* though sidereal, beings had in-carnated. These beings in female forms (Lilith is the prototype of these in the Jewish traditions) are called in the esoteric accounts " Khado " (Dâkini, in Sanskrit). Allegorical legends call the chief of these Liliths, *Sangye Khado* (Buddha Dâkini, in Sanskrit) ; all are credited with the art of " walking in the air," and the greatest *kind-ness to mortals;* but *no mind* — only animal instinct.[566]

(*c*) This is the beginning of a worship which, ages later, was doomed to degenerate into phallicism and sexual worship. It began by the worship of the human body — that " miracles of miracles," as an Eng-lish author calls it — and ended by that of its respective sexes. The worshipers were giants in stature ; but they were giants in knowledge and learning, though it came to them more easily than it does to the men of our modern times. Their Science was innate in them. The Lemuro-Atlantean had no need of discovering and fixing in his memory that which his informing PRINCIPLE *knew* at the moment of its incarn-ation. Time alone, and the ever-growing obtuseness of the matter in which the *Principles* had clothed themselves, could, the one, weaken the memory of their pre-natal knowledge, the other, blunt and even extin-guish every spark of the spiritual and divine in them. Therefore had they, from the first, fallen victims to their animal natures and bred " monsters " — *i. e.,* men of distinct varieties from themselves.

Speaking of the Giants, Creuzer describes them well in saying that:—

Those children of Heaven and Earth were endowed at their birth by the *Sovereign Powers,* the authors of their being, with extraordinary faculties moral and physical. They *commanded the Elements, knew the secrets of heaven and the earth, of the sea and the whole world, and read futurity in* the stars. . . . It seems, indeed, as though one has to deal, when reading of them, *not with men as we are* but with Spirits of the Elements sprung from the bosom of Nature and having full sway over her. . . . All these beings *are marked with a character* of MAGIC and SORCERY. . . .

And so they were, those (now) legendary heroes of the pre-historic, still, once really existing races. Creuzer was wise in his gen-eration, for he did not charge with deliberate deceit, or dulness and superstition, an endless series of recognized philosophers, who men-tion these races and assert that, even in their own time, they saw their fossils. There were sceptics in days of old — no fewer and as great as they are now. But even a Lucian, a Demokritos and an Epicurus yielded to the evidence of *facts* and showed the discriminative capacity

566. These are the beings whose legend-ary existence has served as a ground-work upon which to build the rabbinical Lilith, and what the believers in the Bible would term the antediluvian women, and the Kab-alists the pre-Adamite races. They are no fiction — this is certain, however fantastic the exuberance of later growth.

of really great intellects, which can distinguish fiction from fact, and truth from exaggeration and fraud. Ancient writers were no more fools than our modern wise men are; for, as well remarked by the author of some " Notes on Aristotle's Psychology in Relation to Modern Thought " (in *Mind*) :—

The common division of history into ancient and modern is . . . misleading. The Greeks in the 4th century, B. c. were in many respects moderns; especially, we may add, in their scepticism. They were not very likely to accept *fables* so easily . . .

Yet the " Lemurians " and the Atlanteans, " those children of Heaven and Earth," were indeed marked with a character of sorcery; for the Esoteric doctrine charges them precisely with that, which, if believed, would put an end to the difficulties of science with regard to the origin of man, or rather, his anatomical similarities to the *Anthropoid Ape*. It accuses them of having committed the (*to us*) abominable crime of breeding with so-called " animals," and thus producing a truly pithecoid species, now extinct. Of course, as in the question of spontaneous generation — in which Esoteric Science believes, and which it teaches — the possibility of such a cross-breed between man and an animal of any kind will be denied. But apart from the consideration that in those early days, as already remarked, neither the human Atlantean giants, nor yet the " animals," were the physiologically perfect men and mammalians that are now known to us, the modern notions upon this subject — those of the physiologists included — are too uncertain and fluctuating to permit them an absolute denial *a priori* of such a fact.

A careful perusal of the Commentaries would make one think that the Being that the new " *incarnate* " bred with, was called an " animal," not because he was no human being, but rather because he was so dissimilar physically and mentally to the more perfect races, which had developed physiologically at an earlier period. Remember Stanza VII and what is said in its first verse (24th) :— that when the " Sons of Wisdom " came to incarnate the first time, some of them incarnated fully, others projected into the forms only *a spark*, while some of the shadows were left over from being *filled* and perfected, till the Fourth Race. Those races, then, which " remained destitute of knowledge," or those again which were left " mindless," remained as they were, even after the natural separation of the sexes. It is these who committed the first cross-breeding, so to speak, and bred monsters; and it is from the descendants of these that the Atlanteans chose their wives. Adam and Eve were supposed, with Cain and Abel, to be the only *human* family on Earth. Yet we see Cain going to the land of Nod and taking there a wife. Evidently one race only was supposed perfect enough to be called human; and, even in our own day, while the Sinhalese regard the Veddahs of their jungles as *speaking animals* and no more, some British people believe firmly, in their arrogance, that every other human family — especially the dark Indians — is an *inferior* race. Moreover there are naturalists who have sincerely considered the problem whether some savage tribes — like the Bushmen for instance — can be regarded as *men* at all. The Commentary says, in describing that species (or race) of animals " fair to look at " as a biped:— " *Having human shape, but having the lower extremities, from the waist down, covered with hair.*" Hence the race of the *satyrs,* perhaps.

If men existed two million years ago, they must have been — just as the animals were — quite different physically and anatomically from what they have become; and they were nearer then to the type of pure mammalian animal than they are now. Anyhow, we learn that the animal world breeds strictly *inter se, i. e.,* in accordance with genus and species — only since the appearance *on this earth* of the Atlantean race. As demonstrated by the author of that able work, *Modern Science and Modern Thought,* this idea of the refusal to breed with another species, or that sterility is the only result of such breeding, " appears to be a *prima facie* deduction rather than an absolute law " even now. He shows that " different species, do, in fact, often breed together, as may be seen in the familiar instance of the horse and ass. It is true that in this case the mule is sterile . . . but this rule is not universal, and recently one new hybrid race, that of the leporine, or hare-rabbit, has been created which is perfectly fertile." The progeny of wolf and dog is also instanced, as that of several other domestic animals;[567] " like foxes and dogs again, and the modern Swiss cattle shown by Rütimeyer as descended from three distinct species of fossil-oxen, the *Bos primigenius, Bos longifrons and Bos frontosus.*" *Yet some of those species, as the ape family, which so clearly resembles man in physical structure,* contain, we are told, " numerous branches, which graduate into one another, but the extremes of which differ more widely than man does from the highest of the ape series " — the gorilla and chimpanzee, for instance.[568]

Thus Mr. Darwin's remark — or shall we say the remark of Linnaeus? —*natura non facit saltum,* is not only corroborated by Esoteric Science but would — were there any chance of the real doctrine being accepted by any others than its direct votaries — reconcile in more than one way, if not entirely, the modern Evolution theory with facts, as also with the absolute failure of the Anthropologists to meet with the " missing link " in our Fourth Round geological formations.

We will show elsewhere that, however unconsciously to itself, modern Science pleads our case upon its own admissions, and that de

567. *Modern Science and Modern Thought,* page 101.   568. See Addenda, Part III.

Quatrefages is perfectly right, when he suggests in his last work, that it is far more likely that the anthropoid ape should be discovered to be *the descendant of man,* than that these two types should have a common, fantastic and nowhere-to-be-found ancestor. Thus the wisdom of the compilers of the old Stanzas is vindicated by at least one eminent man of Science, and the Occultist prefers to believe as he ever did that —

"*Man was the first and highest* (mammalian) *animal that appeared in this* (Fourth Round) *creation. Then came still huger animals; and last of all the dumb man who walks on all fours.*" For, "*the Râkshasas* (giant-demons) *and Daityas* (Titans) *of the ' White Dvîpa '* (continent) *spoiled his* (the dumb man's) *Sires.*" (Commentary.)

Furthermore, as we see, there are anthropologists who have traced man back to an epoch which goes far to break down the apparent barrier that exists between the chronologies of modern science and the Archaic Doctrine. It is true that English scientists generally have declined to commit themselves to the sanction of the hypothesis of even a Tertiary Man. They, each and all, measure the antiquity of Homo primigenius by their own lights and prejudices. Huxley, indeed, ventures to speculate on a possible Pliocene or Miocene Man. Professor Seeman and Mr. Grant Allen have relegated his advent to the Eocene, but, speaking generally, English scientists consider that we cannot safely go beyond the Quaternary. Unfortunately, the facts do not accommodate the too cautious reserve of these latter. The French school of anthropology, basing their views on the discoveries of l'Abbé Bourgeois, Capellini, and others, has accepted, almost without exception, the doctrine that the traces of our ancestors are certainly to be found in the Miocene, while M. de Quatrefages now inclines to postulate a Secondary-Age Man. Farther on we shall compare such estimates with the figures given in the Brâhmanical exoteric books which approximate to the esoteric teaching.

(d) . . . . *Then, " the third eye acted no longer,"* says the Stanza, because MAN had sunk too deep into the mire of matter.

What is the meaning of this strange and weird statement in Verse 42, concerning the " third eye of the Third Race which had died and acted no longer "?

A few more occult teachings must now be given with reference to this point as well as some others. The history of the Third and Fourth Races must be amplified, in order that it may throw some more light on the development of our present humanity; and show how the faculties, called into activity by occult training, restore man to the position he previously occupied in reference to spiritual perception and consciousness. But the phenomenon of the third Eye has to be first explained.

THE RACES WITH THE "THIRD EYE"

The subject is so unusual, the paths pursued so intricate, so full of dangerous pitfalls prepared by adverse theories and criticism, that good reasons have to be given for every step taken. While turning the light of the bull's eye called esotericism on almost every inch of the occult grounds traveled over, we have also to use its lens to throw into stronger objectivity the regions explored by exact science; this, not only in order to contrast the two, but to defend our position.[569]

It may be complained by some that too little is said of the physical, *human* side of the extinct races, in this history of their growth and evolution. Much more might be said assuredly, if simple prudence did not make us hesitate at the threshold of every new revelation. That, which finds its possibility and landmarks in the discoveries of modern science, is given; all that of which exact knowledge knows nothing and upon which it is unable to speculate — and therefore denies as facts in nature — is withheld.

But even such statements as these — *e. g.*, that of all the mammalians, man was the earliest; that it is man who is the indirect ancestor of the Ape; and that he was a kind of a Cyclops in days of old — will all be contested. Yet, scientists will never be able to prove — except to their own satisfaction — that *it was not so.* Nor can they admit that the first two races of men were too ethereal and phantom-like in their constitution, organism, and *shape*, even to be called physical men. For, if they do, it will be found that this is one of the reasons why their relics can never be expected to be exhumed among other fossils. Nevertheless all this is maintained. Man was the store-house, so to speak, of

569. For suggestiveness, we would recommend a short article in the *Theosophist* of August, 1887, "Esoteric Studies." Its author expounds therein quite an occult theory, though to the world a new idea: " the *progress of the Monad* concurring with the *retrogression* of Form" (p. 666), *i. e.*, "with decrease of the *vis formativa.*" He says, " Who knows what shape vehicled the Ego in remote *rings* [Rounds, or races?] . . .? May not man's type have been that of the *Simiadae* in its variety? Might not the monkey-kingdom of *Râmâyana* fame rest on some far-off tradition relating to a period when that was the common lot, or rather aspect, of man?" . . . and winds up a very clever, though too short, exposition of his theory by saying that which every true occultist will endorse: " With physico-ethereal man there must be *involution* of sex. As physico-astral man depended on entities of the sub-human class (evolved from animal prototypes) for rebirth, so will physico-ethereal man find among the graceful, shapely orders issuing from the *air*-plane, one or more which will be developed for his successive embodiments *when procreated forms are given* — a process which will include all mankind only very gradually. The [*pre?*] Adamic and post-Adamic races were giants; their ethereal counterparts may possibly be liliputians — beauteous, luminous, diaphanous — but will assuredly be giants in mind " (p. 671, art. by Visconde de Figanière, F. T. S.).

all the seeds of life for this Round, vegetable and animal alike.[570]   As En-Soph is " One, *notwithstanding the innumerable forms which are in him*,"[571] so is man, on Earth the microcosm of the macrocosm.   "As soon as man appeared, everything was complete . . . for everything is comprised in man. He *unites in himself all forms*."[572]   " The mystery of the *earthly* man is after the mystery of the Heavenly Man."[573]   The human form — so called, because it is the vehicle (under whatever shape) of the *divine* man — is, as so intuitionally remarked by the author of " Esoteric Studies,"[574] the *new type*, at the beginning of every Round, " as man never can be, so he never has been, manifested in a shape belonging to the animal kingdom *in esse*." The author proceeds :

he never formed part of that kingdom. Derived, only derived, from the most finished class of the latter, a new human form must always have been the *new* type of the cycle. The human shape, in one ring [?], as I imagine, becomes cast-off clothes in the next ; it is then appropriated by the highest order in the servant-kingdom below.

If the idea is what we understand it to mean — for the " rings " spoken of throw some confusion upon it — then it is the correct esoteric teaching. Having appeared at the very beginning, and at the head of sentient and conscious life, man (the astral, or the " Soul," for the *Zohar*, repeating the archaic teaching, distinctly says that " the *real* man is the Soul, and his material frame no part of him ") — man became the living and animal UNIT, from which the " cast-off clothes " determined the shape of every life and animal in this Round.[575]

Thus, he " created " for ages the insects, reptiles, birds, and animals, unconsciously to himself, from his remains and relics from the Third and the Fourth Rounds. The same idea and teaching are as distinctly given in the *Vendîdâd* of the Mazdeans, as they are in the Chaldaean and the Mosaic allegory of the Ark, all of which are the many na- tional versions of the original legend given in the Hindû Scriptures. It is found in the allegory of Vaivasvata Manu and *his* Ark with the Seven Rishis, as in that of the Rishis, each of whom is shown the father

---

570. It may be objected that this is a contradiction. That, as the first Root-Race appeared 300,000,000 years after the vegeta- tion had evolved, the seed of vegetable life could not be in the First Race. We say it could ; for up to man's appearance in *this* Round, the vegetation was of quite another kind than it is now, and quite ethereal, this for the simple reason that no grass or plants could have been physical, before there were animal or other organisms to breathe out the carbonic acid which vegeta- tion has to imbibe for its development, its nutrition and growth. They are inter-

dependent in their *physical* and achieved forms.

571. *Zohar*, i, 21a.

572. *Ibid.*, iii, 48a.

573. *Ibid.* ii, 76a.

574. " Visconde de Figanière, F. T. S." (*The Theosophist*, Aug. 1887, page 666.)

575. It is stated in the *Zohar* that the " primordial worlds " (sparks) could not continue because *man was not as yet*. " The *human* form contains everything ; and as it did not as yet exist, the worlds were de- stroyed."

and progenitor of specified animals, reptiles, and even monsters.[576]
Open the Mazdean *Vendîdâd* (at Fargard ii, at verse 27 (70) and
read the command of Ormazd to Yima, a Spirit of the Earth, who
symbolizes the three races, after telling him to build a *vara* ("an
enclosure," an *argha* or vehicle). . . .
"Thither [into the *vara*] thou shalt bring *the seeds of men and
women*, of the greatest, best, and finest kinds on this earth; thither
thou shalt bring the seeds of every kind of cattle," etc., etc.; and v. 28
(74) ". . . all those seeds shalt thou bring, two of every kind, *to be kept
inexhaustible there*, so long *as those men shall stay in the vara.*"
Those "men" in the "Vara" are the "Progenitors," the heavenly men or
Dhyânis, the future *Egos* who are commissioned to inform mankind.
For "Vara," or the "Ark" (or again the Vehicle) simply means
MAN.[577] Verse 30 says: ". . . thou shalt seal up the vara [after filling
it up with the seeds], and thou shalt make a door and a *window self-
shining within*," which is the Soul. And when Yima inquires of Ahura
Mazda how he shall manage to make that *vara*, he is answered:
"Crush the earth . . . and knead it with thy hands, as the potter does
when kneading the potter's clay" (verse 31).

The Egyptian ram-headed god makes man of clay on a potter's
wheel, and so in *Genesis* do the Elohim fashion him out of the same
material.

When the "Maker of the material world" (Ahura Mazda) is asked,
furthermore, what is to give light "to the *Vara* which Yima made," he
replies that "There are *uncreated* lights and *created* lights" and that
"there" (in Airyana Vaejo, where *Vara* is built), "the stars, the moon,
and the Sun are only once (a year) seen to rise and set" and a year
seems only as a day (and night), a clear reference to the "land of the
Gods" or the (now) polar regions. Moreover another hint is contained
in this verse: a distinct allusion to the "uncreated lights" which enlighten man within — his principles. Otherwise, no sense or reason
could be found in Ahura Mazda's answer (verse 40), which is forthwith followed by verse 41 saying that "Every fortieth year, to every
couple [hermaphrodite] *two are born, a male and female*,"[578] the latter
being a distinct echo of the Secret Doctrine, of a Stanza which says —

"*At the expiration of every forty (annual) Suns, at the end of every*

576. See *Vishnu* and other *Purânas*.

577. This is the meaning when the allegory and symbol are opened and read by
means of the *human* key, or the key to
terrestrial anthroposophy. This interpretation of the "ark" symbolism does not in
the least interfere with its astronomical, or
even theogonic keys; nor with any of the

578. See J. Darmesteter's translation of
the *Vendîdâd*, "Sacred Books of the East,"
pp. 19-20, and also *Bundahiś* xv.

fortieth Day, the double one becomes four; male and female in one, in the first and second and the third. . . . . ."

Which is clear, since " every sun " meant a whole year, the latter being composed of one day then, as in the arctic circle it is now composed of six months. According to the old teaching, the axis of the earth gradually changes its inclination to the ecliptic, and at the period referred to, this inclination was such that a polar day lasted during the whole period of the earth's revolution about the sun, when a kind of twilight of very short duration intervened; after which the polar land resumed its position directly under the solar rays. This may be contrary to astronomy as now taught and understood: but who can say that changes in the motion of the earth, which do not take place now, did not occur millions of years back?

Returning once more to the statement that *Vara* meant the MAN of the Fourth Round, as much as the Earth of those days, the moon, and even Noah's ark, if one will so have it — this is again shown in the dialogue between Ahura Mazda and Zarathustra. Thus when the latter asks —

42. "O Maker of the Material World, thou Holy One! Who is he who brought the law of Mazda into the *Vara* which Yima made?"

Ahura Mazda answered: "It was the bird Karshipta, O holy Zarathustra."...

"The bird Karshipta dwells in the heavens: were he living on the earth he would be king of birds. He brought the law into the var of Yima, and recites the Avesta *in the language of birds.*" [579]

This again is an allegory and a symbol misunderstood by the Orientalists only, who see in this bird " an incarnation of lightning," and say its song was " often thought to be the utterance of a god and a revelation," and what not. Karshipta is the human mind-soul, and the deity thereof, symbolized in ancient Magianism by a bird, as the Greeks symbolized it by a butterfly. No sooner had Karshipta entered the *Vara* or man, than he understood the law of Mazda, or Divine Wisdom. In the *Book of Concealed Mystery* it is said of the tree, which is the tree of knowledge of good and evil: " In its branches [of the tree] the birds lodge and build their nests," or *the Souls* and the Angels have their place! [580] Therefore, with the Kabalists it was a like symbol. " Bird " was a Chaldaean, and has become a Hebrew synonym and symbol for Angel, a Soul, a Spirit, or Deva; and the " Bird's Nest " was with both, Heaven, and is God's bosom in the *Zohar*. The perfect Messiah enters Eden " into that place which is called the Bird's Nest. [581] " Like a bird that is flying from its nest, and that is the Soul

579. *Bundahiš*, xix and xxiv; quoted by Darmesteter, *op. cit.*, p. 21, note 1.
580. See *Kabbalah Unveiled*, by S. MacGregor Mathers, p. 104.
581. *Zohar*, ii, 8b.

from which the Shekinah (divine wisdom or grace) does not move away." [582] " The Nest of the eternal Bird, the flutter of whose wings produces life, is boundless space," says the Commentary, meaning Hansa, the bird of Wisdom.

It is Adam Kadmon who is the (Sephirothal) tree, and it is he who becomes the " Tree of knowledge of good and evil " esoterically. And that " tree hath around it seven columns (seven pillars) of the world, or *Rectores"*; the same *"Progenitors"* or *"Sephiroth"* again "operating through the respective orders of Angels in the spheres of the seven planets," etc., one of which orders begets giants (*Nephilim*) on Earth.

It was the belief of entire antiquity, Pagan and Christian, that the earliest mankind was a race of giants. Certain excavations in America in mounds and in caves, have already yielded in isolated cases groups of skeletons of nine and twelve feet high. [583] These belong to tribes of the early Fifth Race, now degenerated to an average size of between five and six feet. But we can easily believe that the Titans and Cyclopes of old really belonged to the Fourth (Atlantean) Race, and that all the subsequent legends and allegories found in the Hindû Purânas and the Greek Hesiod and Homer, were based on the hazy reminiscences of real Titans — men of a superhuman tremendous physical power, which enabled them to defend themselves, and hold at bay the gigantic monsters of the Mesozoic and early Cenozoic times — and of actual Cyclopes — three-eyed mortals.

It has been often remarked by observant writers, that the " origin of nearly every popular myth and legend could be traced invariably to a fact in Nature."

In these fantastic creations of an exuberant subjectivism, there is always an element of the objective and real. The imagination of the masses, disorderly and ill-regulated as it may be, could never have conceived and fabricated *ex nihilo* so many monstrous figures, such a wealth of extraordinary tales, had it not had, to serve it as a central nucleus, those floating reminiscences, obscure and vague, which unite the broken links of the chain of time to form with them the mysterious, dream foundation of our collective consciousness. [584]

582. *Zohar,* iii, 278a; Myer's *Qabbalah,* 217.

583. Darwinian Evolutionists who are so wont to refer to the evidence of *reversion to type* — the full meaning of which, in the case of human monsters, is embraced in the esoteric solution of the embryological problem — as proof of their arguments, would do well to inquire into those instances of *modern giants* who are often 8, 9, and even 11 feet high. Such *reversions* are imperfect, yet undeniable reproductions of the original towering man of primeval times.

584. See *Mythical Monsters,* by Charles Gould, from whose interesting and scientific volume a few passages are quoted further on. See in Mr. Sinnett's *Occult World,* the description of a cavern in the Himâlayas filled with relics of human and animal giant bones.

The evidence for the Cyclopes — a race of giants — will be pointed
out in forthcoming Sections, in the Cyclopean remnants, so called to
this day. An indication that, during its evolution and before the final
adjustment of the human organism — which became perfect and symmetrical only in the Fifth Race — the early Fourth Race may have been
three-eyed, without having necessarily a third eye in the middle of the
brow, like the legendary Cyclops, is also furnished by Science.

To the Occultist who believes that spiritual and psychic *involution*
proceeds on parallel lines with physical *evolution;* that the *inner* senses
— innate in the first human races — atrophied during racial growth and
the material development of the outer senses; to the student of Esoteric symbology, finally, this statement is no conjecture or possibility,
but simply *a phase of the law of growth, a proven fact,* in short. They
understand the meaning of this passage in the *Commentaries* which
says :—

" *There were four-armed human creatures in those early days of
the male-females* (hermaphrodites) ; *with one head, yet three eyes.
They could see before them and behind them.*[585] *A* KALPA *later*
(after the separation of the sexes) *men having fallen into matter, their
spiritual vision became dim; and co-ordinately the third eye commenced to lose its power. . . . When the Fourth* (Race) *arrived at
its middle age, the inner vision had to be awakened, and* acquired by
artificial stimuli, *the process of which was known to the old sages.*[586]
. . . *The third eye, likewise, getting gradually* PETRIFIED,[587] *soon disappeared. The double-faced became the one-faced, and the eye was
drawn deep into the head and is now buried under the hair. During
the activity of the inner man* (during trances and spiritual visions)
the eye swells and expands. The Arhat sees and feels it, and regulates

585. Viz., the third eye was at the back
of the head. The statement that the latest
hermaphrodite humanity was "four-armed,"
unriddles probably the mystery of all the
representations and idols of the exoteric gods
of India. On the Acropolis of Argos, there
was a ξόανον, a rudely carved wooden statue (attributed to Daedalus), representing a
three-eyed colossus, which was consecrated
to Zeus *Triops* (three-eyed). The head of
the "god" has two eyes in its face and one
above on the top of the forehead. It is considered the most archaic of all the ancient
statues (*Schol. Vatic. ad Eurip. Troad.* 14).

586. The *Inner sight* could henceforth be
acquired only through training and initiation,
save in the cases of "natural and born magicians," sensitives and mediums, as they
are called now.

587. This expression "petrified" instead
of "ossified" is curious. The "back eye,"
which is of course the *pineal gland,* now so-
called, the small pea-like mass of gray nervous matter attached to the back of the third
ventricle of the brain, is said to almost invariably contain *mineral concretions* and
sand, and "nothing more." (*Vide infra.*)

his action accordingly. . . . . The undefiled Lanoo
(disciple, chela) *need fear no danger; he who keeps himself not in
purity* (who is not chaste) *will receive no help from the ' deva eye.' "*

Unfortunately not. The " deva-eye " exists no more for the majority
of mankind. The *third eye is dead,* and acts no longer; but it has left
behind a witness to its existence. This witness is now the PINEAL
GLAND. As for the " four-armed " men, it is they who become the
prototypes of the four-armed Hindû gods, as shown in a preceding
footnote.

Such is the mystery of the human eye that, in their vain endeavors
to explain and account for all the difficulties surrounding its action,
some scientists have been forced to resort to occult explanations. The
development of the *Human eye* gives more support to the occult anthropology than to that of the materialistic physiologists. " The eyes in
the human embryo *grow from within without,"* out of the brain, instead of being part of the skin, as in the insects and cuttlefish. Pro-
fesor Lankester, thinking the brain a queer place for the eye, and
attempting to explain the phenomenon on *Darwinian lines,* suggests the
curious view that "our" earliest vertebrate ancestor was a *transparent*
creature and hence did not mind where the eye was! And so was man
"a transparent creature" once upon a time, we are taught, hence our
theory holds good. But how does the Lankester hypothesis square
with the Haeckelian view that the vertebrate eye originated by changes
in the epidermis? If it started *inside,* the theory goes into the waste-
basket. This seems to be proved by embryology. Moreover, Professor Lankester's extraordinary suggestion — or shall we say admission? — is rendered perhaps necessary by evolutionist necessities.
Occultism with its teaching as to the gradual development of senses
" FROM WITHIN WITHOUT," from astral prototypes, is far more satisfactory: The *third eye retreated inwards* when its course was run
— another point in favor of Occultism.

The allegorical expression of the Hindû mystics when speaking of
the " eye of Śiva," the *Tri-lochana* (" three-eyed "), thus receives its
justification and *raison d'être* — the transference of the pineal gland
(once that " third eye ") to the forehead, being an exoteric license.
This throws also a light on the mystery — incomprehensible to some —
of the connexion between *abnormal,* or Spiritual Seership, and the
physiological purity of the Seer. The question is often asked. " Why
should celibacy and chastity be a *sine qua non* rule and condition of
regular *chelaship,* or the development of psychic and occult powers?
The answer is contained in the Commentary. When we learn that the
" third eye " was once a physiological organ, and that later on, owing

to the gradual disappearance of spirituality and increase of materiality (Spiritual nature being extinguished by the physical), it became an atrophied organ, as little understood now by physiologists as the spleen is — when we learn this, the connexion will become clear. During human life the greatest impediment in the way of spiritual development, and especially to the acquirement of *Yoga* powers, is the activity of our physiological senses. Sexual action being closely connected, by interaction, with the spinal cord and the gray matter of the brain, it is useless to give any longer explanation. Of course, the normal and abnormal state of the brain, and the degree of active work in the *medulla oblongata*, reacts powerfully on the pineal gland, for, owing to the number of "centers" in that region, which controls by far the greater majority of the physiological actions of the animal economy, and also owing to the close and intimate neighborhood of the two, there must be exerted a very powerful "inductive" action by the *medulla* on the pineal gland.

All this is quite plain to the Occultist, but is very vague in the sight of the general reader. The latter must then be shown the possibility of a three-eyed man in nature, in those periods when his formation was yet in a comparatively chaotic state. Such a possibility may be inferred from anatomical and zoological knowledge, first of all; then it may rest on the assumptions of materialistic science itself.

It is asserted upon the authority of Science, and upon evidence, which is not merely a fiction of theoretical speculation this time, that many of the animals — especially among the lower orders of the vertebrata — have a *third* eye, now atrophied, but necessarily active in its origin.[588] The Hatteria species, a lizard of the order *Lacertilia*, recently discovered in New Zealand (*a part of ancient Lemuria so called, mark well*), presents this peculiarity in a most extraordinary manner; and not only the *Hatteria punctata*, but the chameleon, certain reptiles, and even fishes. It was thought, at first, that it was no more than the prolongation of the brain ending with a small protuberance, called epiphysis, a little bone separated from the main bone by a cartilage, and found in every animal. But it was soon found to be more than this. It offered — as its development and anatomical structure showed — such an analogy with that of the eye, that it was found impossible

588. "Deeply placed within the head, covered by thick skin and muscles, true eyes that cannot see are found in certain animals"; also, says Haeckel: "Vertebrata . . . blind moles and field mice, blind snakes and lizards. . . . They shun daylight . . . dwelling under the ground. *They were not originally blind* but have evolved from ancestors that lived in the light and had well-developed eyes. The atrophied eye beneath the opaque skin may be found in these blind beings in every stage of reversion." (*Pedigree of Man*, "Sense Organs." Haeckel) And if *two* eyes could become so atrophied in lower animals, why not *one* eye — the pineal gland — in man, who is but a higher animal in his physical aspect?

to see in it anything else. There were and are palaeontologists who feel convinced to this day that this " third eye " has functioned in its origin, and they are certainly right. For this is what is said of the pineal gland in Quain's *Anatomy*:[589]

It is from this part, constituting at first the whole and subsequently the hinder part of the anterior primary encephalic vesicle, that the optic vesicles are developed in the earliest period, and the fore part is that in connection with which the cerebral hemispheres and accompanying parts are formed. The *thalamus opticus* of each side is formed by a lateral thickening of the medullary wall, while the interval between, descending towards the base, constitutes the cavity of the third ventricle with its prolongation in the infundibulum. The grey commissure afterwards stretches across the ventricular cavity. . . . The hinder part of the roof is developed by a peculiar process, to be noticed later, into the pineal gland, which remains united on each side by its pedicles to the *thalamus,* and behind these a transverse band is formed as posterior commissure.

The *lamina terminalis* (*lamina cinerea*) continues to close the third ventricle in front, below it the optic commissure forms the floor of the ventricle, and further back the infundibulum descends to be united in the *sella turcica* with the tissue adjoining the posterior lobe of the pituitary body.

The two *optic thalami* formed from the posterior and outer part of the anterior vesicle, consist at first of a single hollow sac of nervous matter, the cavity of which communicates on each side in front with that of the commencing cerebral hemispheres, and behind with that of the middle cephalic vesicle *(corpora quadrigemina).* Soon, however, by increased deposit taking place in their interior, behind, below, and at the sides, the *thalami* become solid, and at the same time a cleft or fissure appears between them above, and penetrates down to the internal cavity, which continues open at the back part opposite the entrance of the Sylvian aqueduct. This cleft or fissure is the *third ventricle*. Behind, the two thalami continue united by the *posterior commissure,* which is distinguishable about the end of the third month, and also by the peduncles of the pineal gland. . . .

At an early period the *optic tracts* may be recognised as hollow prolongations from the outer part of the wall of the *thalami* while they are still vesicular. At the fourth month these tracts are distinctly formed. They subsequently are prolonged backwards into connection with the *corpora quadrigemina.*

The formation of the pineal gland and pituitary body presents some of the most interesting phenomena which are connected with the development of the *Thalamencephalon.*

The above is specially interesting when it is remembered that, were it not for the development of the hinder part of the cerebral hemispheres backwards, the pineal gland would be perfectly visible on the removal of the parietal bones. It is very interesting also to note the obvious connexion to be traced between the (originally) hollow optic

589. Vol. II, ninth edit., pp. 830-851. " *Thalamencephalon* " (Interbrain).

tracts and the eyes anteriorly, the pineal gland and its peduncles behind, and all of these with the optic thalami. So that the recent discoveries in connexion with the third eye of *Hatteria punctata* have a very important bearing on the developmental history of the human senses, and on the occult assertions in the text.

It is well known, (and also regarded as a fiction now, by those who have ceased to believe in the existence of an immortal principle in man,) that Descartes saw in the pineal gland the *Seat of the Soul.* Although it is joined to every part of the body, he said, there is one special portion of it in which the Soul exercises its functions more specially than in any other. And, as neither the heart, nor yet the brain could be that " special " locality, he concluded that it was that little gland tied to the brain, yet having an action independent of it, as it could easily be put into a kind of swinging motion " *by the animal Spirits* [590] *which cross* the cavities of the skull in every sense."

Unscientific as this may appear in our day of exact learning, Descartes was yet far nearer the occult truth than is any Haeckel. For the pineal gland, as shown, is far more connected with Soul and Spirit than with the physiological senses of man. Had the leading Scientists a glimmer of the *real* processes employed by the Evolutionary Impulse, and the winding *cyclic* course of this great law, they would *know* instead of conjecturing; and feel as certain of the future physical transformations of the human kind by the knowledge of its past forms. Then, would they see the fallacy and all the absurdity of their modern " blind-force " and mechanical processes of nature; realizing, in consequence of such knowledge, that the said pineal gland, for instance, could not but be disabled for *physical* use at this stage of our cycle. If the odd " eye " in man is now atrophied, it is a proof that, as in the lower animal, it has once been active; for nature never creates the smallest, the most insignificant form without some definite purpose and use. It was an *active* organ, we say, at that stage of evolution when the spiritual element in man reigned supreme over the hardly nascent intellectual and psychic elements. And, as the cycle ran down toward that point when the physiological senses were developed by, and went *pari passu* with, the growth and consolidation of the physical man, the interminable and complex vicissitudes and tribulations of zoological development, that median " eye " ended by atrophying along with the early spiritual and purely psychic characteristics in man. The eye is the mirror and also the window of the soul, says popular wisdom,[591] and *Vox populi Vox Dei.*

590. The " Nervous Ether " of Dr. B. W. Richardson, F. R. S.— the nerve-aura of occultism. The "animal spirits" (?) are equivalent to the currents of nerve-auric compound circulation.

591. Let us remember that the *First*

In the beginning, every class and family of living species was hermaphrodite and objectively one-eyed. In the animal, whose form was as ethereal (astrally) as that of man, before the bodies of both began to evolve their coats of skin, *viz.*, to evolve from *within without* the thick coating of physical substance or matter with its internal physiological mechanism — the third eye was primarily, as in man, the only seeing organ. The two physical front eyes developed [592] later on in both brute and man, whose organ of physical sight was, at the commencement of the Third Race, in the same position as that of some of the blind vertebrata, in our day, *i. e.*, beneath an opaque skin.[593] Only the stages of the *odd*, or primeval eye, in man and brute, are now inverted, as the former has already passed that animal *non-rational* stage in the Third Round, and is ahead of mere brute creation by a a whole plane of consciousness. Therefore, while the " Cyclopean " eye was, and still *is*, in man the organ of *spiritual* sight, in the animal it was that of objective vision. And this eye, having performed its function, was replaced, in the course of physical evolution from the simple to the complex, by two eyes, and thus was stored and laid aside by nature for further use in Aeons to come.

This explains why the pineal gland reached its highest development proportionately with the lowest physical development. It is the vertebrata in which it is the most prominent and objective, and in man it is most carefully hidden and inaccessible, except to the anatomist. No

Race is shown in Occult sciences as spiritual within and ethereal without; the *second*, psycho-spiritual mentally, and ethero-physical bodily; the *third*, still bereft of intellect in its beginning, is astro-physical in its body, and lives an inner life, in which the psycho-spiritual element is in no way interfered with as yet by the hardly nascent physiological senses. Its two front eyes look before them without seeing either past or future. But the "third eye" "*embraces* ETERNITY."

592. But in a very different manner to that pictured by Haeckel as an "*evolution by natural selection in the struggle for existence*" (*Pedigree of Man*, "Sense Organs," p. 335). The mere "thermal sensibility of the skin," to hypothetical light-waves, is absurdly incompetent to account for the beautiful combination of adaptations present in the eye. It has, moreover, been previously shown that "natural Selection" is a pure myth when credited with the *origination* of variations (*vide infra*, Part III, on *Darwinian mechanical causation*); as the

"survival of the fittest" can only take place after useful variations have sprung up, together with improved organisms. Whence came the "useful variations," which developed the eye? Only from "blind forces . . . without aim, without design?" The argument is puerile. The true solution of the mystery is to be found in the impersonal Divine Wisdom, in its IDEATION — reflected through matter.

593. Palaeontology has ascertained that in the animals of the Cenozoic age — the Saurians especially, such as the antediluvian *Labyrinthodon*, whose fossil skull exhibits a perforation otherwise inexplicable — the third, or odd eye must have been much developed. Several naturalists, among others E. Korscheldt, feel convinced that whereas, notwithstanding the opaque skin covering it, such an eye in the reptiles of the present period can only distinguish light from darkness (as the human eyes do when bound with a handkerchief, or even tightly closed), in the now extinct animals that eye functioned and was a real organ of vision.

less light is thrown thereby on the future physical, spiritual, and intellectual state of mankind, in periods corresponding on parallel lines with other past periods, and always on the lines of ascending and descending cyclic evolution and development. Thus, a few centuries before the *Kali yuga* — the black age which began nearly 5000 years ago — it was said (paraphrased into comprehensible sentences):

"*We* (the Fifth Root-Race) *in our first half* (of duration) *onward* (on the now ASCENDING arc of the cycle) *are on the mid point of* (or between) *the First and the Second Races — falling downward* (*i. e..* the races were then on the descending arc of the cycle). . . . . *Calculate for thyself, Lanoo, and see.*" (Commentary xx.)

Calculating as advised, we find that during that transitional period — namely, in the second half of the First Spiritual ethero-astral race — nascent mankind was devoid of the intellectual brain element. As it was on its *descending* line, and as we are parallel to it, on the *ascend-*

EVOLUTION OF ROOT RACES IN THE FOURTH ROUND

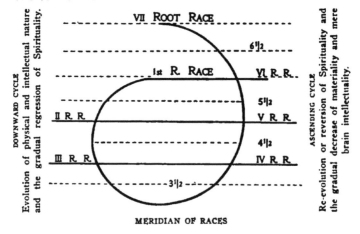

MERIDIAN OF RACES

ing, we are, therefore devoid of the Spiritual element, which is now replaced by the intellectual. For, remember well, as we are in the *mânasa* period of our cycle of races, or in the Fifth, we have, therefore, crossed the meridian point of the perfect adjustment of Spirit and Matter — or that equilibrium between brain intellect and Spiritual perception. One important point has, however, to be borne in mind.

We are only in the Fourth Round, and it is in the Fifth that the full development of *Manas,* as a direct ray from the Universal MAHAT — a ray unimpeded by matter — will be finally reached. Nevertheless, as every sub-race and nation have their cycles and stages of developmental evolution repeated on a smaller scale, it must be the more so in the case of a Root-Race. Our race then has, as a Root-race, crossed the equatorial line and is cycling onward on the Spiritual side; but some of our sub-races still find themselves on the shadowy descending arc of their respective national cycles; while others again — the oldest — having crossed their crucial point, which alone decides whether a race, a nation, or a tribe will live or perish, are at the apex of spiritual development as sub-races.

It becomes comprehensible now why the "odd eye" has been gradually transformed into a simple gland, after the physical Fall of those we have agreed to call the "Lemurians."

It is a curious fact that it is especially in human beings that the cerebral hemispheres and the lateral ventricles have been developed, and that the *optic thalami, corpora quadrigemina,* and *corpora striata* are the principal parts which are developed in the mammalian brain. Moreover it is asserted that the intellect of any man may to some extent be gauged by the development of the central convolutions and the fore part of the cerebral hemispheres. It would seem a natural corollary that if the development and increased size of the pineal gland may be considered to be an index of the astral capacities and spiritual proclivities of any man, there will be a corresponding development of that part of the cranium, or an increase in the size of the pineal gland at the expense of the hinder part of the cerebral hemispheres. It is a curious speculation which would receive a confirmation in this case. We should see, below and behind, the cerebellum which has been held to be the seat of all the animal proclivities of a human being, and which is allowed by science to be the great center for all the physiologically co-ordinated movements of the body, such as walking, eating, etc., etc.; in front, the fore-part of the brain — the cerebral hemispheres — the part especially connected with the development of the intellectual powers in man; and in the middle, dominating them both, and especially the animal functions, the developed pineal gland, in connexion with the more highly evolved, or spiritual man.

It must be remembered that these are only physical correspondences; just as the ordinary human brain is the registering organ of memory, but not memory itself.

This is, then, the organ which gave rise to so many legends and traditions, among others to that of man with one head but two faces. These may be found in several Chinese works, besides being referred

to in the Chaldaean fragments. Apart from the work already cited —
the *Shan Hai King*, compiled by Kung Chia from engravings on nine
urns made 2255 B. C., by the Emperor Yü, they may be found in
another work, called the "*Bamboo Books*," and in a third one, the
"'*Rh Ya*" — " initiated according to tradition by Chow Kung, uncle
of Wu Wang, the first Emperor of the Chow Dynasty, B. C., 1122 ": —
says Mr. Ch. Gould in his *Mythical Monsters*. The Bamboo Books
contain the ancient annals of China, found A. D. 279 at the opening of
the grave of King Seang of Wai, who died B.C. 295. Both these works
mention men with two faces on one head — one in front and one
behind.[594]

Now that which the students of Occultism ought to know is that
THE "THIRD EYE" IS INDISSOLUBLY CONNECTED WITH KARMA. The
tenet is so mysterious that very few have heard of it.

The "eye of Śiva" did not become entirely atrophied before the
close of the Fourth Race. When spirituality and all the divine powers
and attributes of the deva-man of the Third had been made the hand-
maidens of the newly-awakened physiological and psychic passions of
the physical man, instead of the reverse, the eye lost its powers. But
such was the law of Evolution, and it was, in strict accuracy, no FALL.
The sin was not in using those newly-developed powers, but in *mis-
using* them; in making of the tabernacle, designed to contain a god,
the fane of every *spiritual* iniquity. And if we say "sin" it is merely
that everyone should understand our meaning; as the term *Karma*[595]
would be the right one to use in this case; while the reader who
would feel perplexed at the use of the term "spiritual" instead of
"physical" iniquity, is reminded of the fact that there can be no
physical iniquity. The body is simply the irresponsible organ, the tool
of the *psychic*, if not of the "Spiritual man." While in the case of
the Atlanteans, it was precisely the Spiritual being which sinned, the
Spirit element being still the "Master" principle in man, in those days.
Thus it is in those days that the heaviest Karma of the Fifth Race
was generated by our Monads.

As this sentence may again be found puzzling, it is better that it
should be explained for the benefit of those who are ignorant of the
theosophical teachings.

Questions with regard to *Karma* and *re-births* are constantly offered,
and a great confusion seems to exist upon this subject. Those who are

594. *Mythical Monsters*, page 27.
595. Karma is a word of many meanings,
and has a special term for almost every one
of its aspects. It means, as a synonym of
sin, the performance of some action for
the attainment of an object of worldly,
hence *selfish*, desire, which cannot fail to
be hurtful to somebody else. Karman is
action, the Cause; and Karma again is "the
law of ethical causation"; the *effect* of an
act produced egotistically, when the great
law of harmony depends upon altruism.

born and bred in the Christian faith, and have been trained in the idea that a new soul is created by God for every newly-born infant, are among the most perplexed. They ask whether in such case the number of incarnating Monads on earth is limited; to which they are answered in the affirmative. For, however countless, in our conceptions, the number of the incarnating monads — even if we take into account the fact that ever since the Second Race, when their respective seven groups were furnished with bodies, several births and deaths may be allowed for every second of time in the aeons already passed — still, there must be a limit. It was stated that Karma-Nemesis, whose bond-maid is Nature, adjusted everything in the most harmonious manner; and that, therefore, the fresh pouring-in, or arrival of new Monads, had ceased as soon as Humanity had reached its full physical development. No fresh Monads have incarnated since the middle-point of the Atlanteans. Hence, remembering that, save in the case of young children, and of individuals whose lives were violently cut off by some accident, no Spiritual Entity can re-incarnate before a period of many centuries has elapsed, such gaps alone must show that the number of Monads is necessarily finite and limited. Moreover, a reasonable time must be given to other animals for their evolutionary progress.

Hence the assertion that many of us are now working off the effects of the evil Karmic causes produced by us in Atlantean bodies. The Law of KARMA is inextricably interwoven with that of Re-incarnation.

It is only the knowledge of the constant re-births of one and the same individuality throughout the life-cycle; the assurance that the same MONADS — among whom are many Dhyân-Chohans, or the " Gods " themselves — have to pass through the " Circle of Necessity," rewarded or punished by such rebirth for the suffering endured or crimes committed in the former life; that those very Monads, which entered the empty, senseless shells, or astral figures of the First Race emanated by the Pitris, are the same who are now amongst us — nay, ourselves, perchance; it is only this doctrine, we say, that can explain to us the mysterious problem of Good and Evil, and reconcile man to the terrible and *apparent* injustice of life. Nothing but such certainty can quiet our revolted sense of justice. For, when one unacquainted with the noble doctrine looks around him, and observes the inequalities of birth and fortune, of intellect and capacities; when one sees honor paid fools and profligates, on whom fortune has heaped her favors by mere privilege of birth, and their nearest neighbor, with all his intellect and noble virtues — far more deserving in every way — perishing of want and for lack of sympathy; when one sees all this and has to turn away, helpless to relieve the undeserved suffering, one's ears ringing and heart aching with the cries of pain around him — that blessed knowledge of Karma alone prevents him from cursing life and men, as well as their supposed Creator.[596]

Of all the terrible blasphemies and accusations virtually thrown on their God by the Monotheists, none is greater or more unpardonable than that (almost always) false humility which makes the presumably "pious" Christian assert, in connexion with every evil and undeserved blow, that "such *is the will* of God."

Dolts and hypocrites! Blasphemers and impious Pharisees, who speak in the same breath of the endless merciful love and care of their God and creator for helpless man, and of that God *scourging the good, the very best of his creatures, bleeding them to death like an insatiable Moloch!* Shall we be answered to this, in Congreve's words:—

"*But who shall dare to tax Eternal Justice?*" *Logic and simple common sense*, we answer: if we are made to believe in the "original Sin," in *one* life, on this Earth only, for every Soul, and in an anthropomorphic Deity, who seems to have created some men only for the pleasure of condemning them to eternal hell-fire (and this whether they are good or bad, says the Predestinarian),[597] why should not every man endowed with reasoning powers condemn in his turn such a villainous Deity? Life would become unbearable, if one had to believe in the God created by man's unclean fancy. Luckily he exists only in human dogmas, and in the unhealthy imagination of some poets, who believe they have solved the problem by addressing him as —

> "Thou great Mysterious Power, who hast *involved*
> The pride of human wisdom, *to confound*
> The *daring scrutiny* and prove *the faith*
> Of thy *presuming* creatures! . . ."

Truly a robust "faith" is required to believe that it is "presumption" to question the justice of one, who creates helpless little man but to "perplex" him, and to test a "faith" with which that "Power," moreover, may have forgotten, if not neglected, to endow him, as happens sometimes.

Compare this blind faith with the philosophical belief, based on every reasonable evidence and life-experience, in Karma-Nemesis, or

596. Objectors to the doctrine of Karma should recall the fact that it is absolutely *out of the question* to attempt to reply to the Pessimists on other data. A firm grasp of the principles of Karmic Law knocks away the whole basis of the imposing fabric reared by the disciples of Schopenhauer and Von Hartmann.

597. The doctrine and theology of Calvinists. "The purpose of God *from eternity* respecting all events" (which becomes *fatalism* and kills free will, or any attempt of exerting it for good). . . . "It is the preassignment or allotment of men to everlasting happiness or misery" (Catechism). A noble and encouraging Doctrine this!

the Law of Retribution. This Law — whether Conscious or Unconscious — predestines nothing and no one. It exists from and in Eternity, truly, for it is ETERNITY itself; and as such, since no act can be co-equal with eternity, it cannot be said to act, for it is ACTION itself. It is not the Wave which drowns a man, but the *personal* action of the wretch, who goes deliberately and places himself under the *impersonal* action of the laws that govern the Ocean's motion. Karma creates nothing, nor does it design. It is man who plans and creates causes, and Karmic law adjusts the effects; which adjustment is not an act, but universal harmony, tending ever to resume its original position, like a bough, which, bent down too forcibly, rebounds with corresponding vigor. If it happen to dislocate the arm that tried to bend it out of its natural position, shall we say that it is the bough which broke our arm, or that our own folly has brought us to grief? Karma has never sought to destroy intellectual and individual liberty, like the God invented by the Monotheists. It has not involved its decrees in darkness purposely to perplex man; nor shall it punish him who dares to scrutinize its mysteries. On the contrary, he who unveils through study and meditation its intricate paths, and throws light on those dark ways, in the windings of which so many men perish owing to their ignorance of the labyrinth of life, is working for the good of his fellow-men. KARMA is an Absolute and Eternal law in the World of manifestation; and as there can only be one Absolute, as One eternal ever present Cause, believers in Karma cannot be regarded as Atheists or materialists — still less as fatalists:[598] for Karma is one with the Unknowable, of which it is an aspect in its effects in the phenomenal world.

598. Some theosophists, in order to make Karma more comprehensible to the Western mind, as being better acquainted with the Greek than with Aryan philosophy, have made an attempt to translate it by *Nemesis*. Had the latter been known to the profane in antiquity, as it was understood by the Initiate, this translation of the term would be unobjectionable. As it is, it has been too much anthropomorphized by Greek fancy, to permit our using it without an elaborate explanation. With the early Greeks, "from Homer to Herodotus, she was no goddess, but a *moral feeling* rather," says Decharme; the barrier to evil and immorality. He who transgresses it, commits a sacrilege in the eyes of the gods, and is pursued by Nemesis. But, with time, that "feeling" was deified, and its personification became an ever-fatal and punishing goddess. Therefore, if we would connect Karma with Nemesis, it has to be done in the triple character of the latter, viz., as Nemesis, Adrasteia and Themis. For, while the latter is the goddess of Universal Order and Harmony, who, like Nemesis, is commissioned to repress every excess, and keep man within the limits of Nature and righteousness under severe penalty, *Adrasteia* — "the inevitable" — represents Nemesis as the immutable effect of causes created by man himself. Nemesis, as the daughter of *Dike*, is the equitable goddess reserving her wrath for those alone who are maddened with pride, egoism, and impiety. (See Mesomedes, Hymn, *Nemes.*, v. 2, Brunck, *Analecta* II, p. 292; *Mythol. de la Grèce Antique*, p. 304.) In short, while Nemesis is a mythological, exoteric goddess, or *Power*, personified and anthropomorphized in its various aspects, *Karma* is a highly philosophical truth, a most divine noble expression of the primitive intuition of man concerning Deity. It is a doctrine which explains the origin of

Intimately, or rather indissolubly, connected with Karma, then, is the law of re-birth, or of the re-incarnation of the same spiritual individuality in a long, almost interminable, series of personalities. The latter are like the various costumes and characters played by the same actor, with each of which that actor identifies himself and is identified by the public, for the space of a few hours. The *inner*, or real man, who personates those characters, knows the whole time that he is Hamlet for the brief space of a few acts, which represent, however, on the plane of human illusion the whole life of Hamlet. And he knows that he was, the night before, King Lear, the transformation in his turn of the Othello of a still earlier preceding night; but the outer, visible character is supposed to be ignorant of the fact. In actual life that ignorance is, unfortunately, but too real. Nevertheless, the *permanent* individuality is fully aware of the fact, though, through the atrophy of the "spiritual" eye in the physical body, that knowledge is unable to impress itself on the consciousness of the false personality.

The possession of a physical *third* eye, we are told, was enjoyed by the men of the Third Root-Race down to nearly the middle period of the Third Sub-race of the Fourth Root-Race, when the consolidation and perfection of the human frame made it disappear from the outward anatomy of man. Psychically and spiritually, however, its mental and visual perceptions lasted till nearly the end of the Fourth Race, when its functions, owing to the materiality and depraved condition of mankind, died out altogether before the submersion of the bulk of the Atlantean continent. And now we may return to the Deluges and their many "Noahs."

The student has to bear in mind that there were many such deluges as that mentioned in *Genesis*, and three far more important ones, which will be mentioned and described in the Section devoted to the subject of pre-historic continents. To avoid erroneous conjectures, however, with regard to the claim that the esoteric doctrine has much in it of the legends contained in the Hindû Scriptures; that, again, the chronology of the latter is almost that of the former — only explained and made clear; and that finally the belief that "Vaivasvata Manu" — a generic name indeed! — was the Noah of the Aryans and his prototype, all this, which is also the belief of the Occultists, necessitates at this juncture a new explanation.⁵⁹⁹

Evil, and ennobles our conceptions of what divine immutable Justice ought to be, instead of degrading the unknown and unknowable Deity by making it the whimsical, cruel tyrant, which we call Providence.

599. *Vide* Part III. §§ vi and vii. "Submerged Continents."

THE PRIMEVAL MANUS OF HUMANITY

Those who are aware that the "great Flood," which was connected with the sinking of an entire continent — save what became a few islands — could not have happened so far back as 18,000,000 years ago; and that Vaivasvata Manu is the Indian Noah connected with the *Matsya* (or the fish) Avatâra of Vishnu — may feel perplexed at this discrepancy between facts stated and the chronology previously given. But there is no discrepancy in truth. The reader is asked to turn to the *Theosophist* of July, 1883, and after studying the article therein, "The Septenary Principle in Esotericism," the whole question can be explained to him. It is in this explanation, I believe, that the Occultists differ from the Brâhmans.

For the benefit of those, however, who may not have The Theosophist of that month and year to hand, a passage or two may now be quoted from it:

Who was Manu, the son of Svâyambhuva? The secret doctrine tells us that *this* Manu was no man, but the representation of the first human races evolved with the help of the Dhyân-Chohans (*Devas*) at the beginning of the first round. But we are told in his Laws (Book I, 80) that there are fourteen Manus for every Kalpa — or "interval from creation to creation" (read interval from one *minor* "Pralaya" to another ***)—and that "in the present divine age, there have been as yet *seven* Manus." Those who know that there are seven rounds, of which we have passed three, and are now in the fourth; and who are taught that there are seven dawns and seven twilights or fourteen *Manvantaras;* that at the beginning of every Round and at the end, and on, and between the

---

600. *Pralaya* — a word already explained — is not a term that applies *only* to every "Night of Brahmâ," or the world's dissolution following every Manvantara, equal to 71 Mahâ-yugas. It applies also to each "obscuration" as well, and even to every Cataclysm that puts an end, by Fire or by Water in turn, to each Root-Race. *Pralaya* is a term like that of "Manu" — the generic name for the *Sishtas,* who, under the appellation of "King," are shown in *the Purânas* as preserved "with the seed of all things in an ark from the waters of that flood" (or the fires of a general volcanic conflagration, the commencement of which we already see for our Fifth-Race in the terrible earthquakes and eruptions of these late years, and especially in the present one) ". . . which in the season of a pralaya overspreads the world" (the Earth). (See Preface, p. lxxxi, to Wilson's *Vishnu Purâna.*) Time is only a form of "Vishnu" — truly, as Parâśara says in that Purâna. In the

Hindû Yuga Kalpa, we have the regular descending series 4, 3, 2, with ciphers multiplied as occasion requires for esoteric purposes, but not, as Wilson and other Orientalists thought, for "sectarian embellishments." A Kalpa may be an age, a "Day" of Brahmâ, or a sidereal Kalpa, astronomical and earthly. Those calculations are found in all the Purânas, but some differ — as for instance, "the year of the seven Rishis, 3030 mortal years, and the year of Dhruva, 9090 in the *Linga Purâna,*" which are again esoteric, and which *do* represent actual (secret) chronology. As said in the *Brahma-Vaivarta:* "Chronologers compute a Kalpa by the life of Brahmâ. *Minor* Kalpas, as Samvarta and the rest, are numerous." "Minor Kalpas" denote here every period of destruction, as was well understood by Wilson himself, who explains the latter as "those in which the Samvarta wind or other destructive agents operate" (*Vishnu Purâna,* p. 54, vol. I).

planets there is an awakening to *illusive* life, and an awakening to *real* life; and that, moreover, there are root-Manus, and what we have to clumsily translate as the seed-Manus — *the seeds for the human races of the forthcoming* Round [or the *Sishtas*—the surviving fittest; [601]] (a mystery divulged only to those who have passed their third degree in initiation)—those who have learned all that will be better prepared to understand the meaning of the following. We are told in the Sacred Hindû scriptures that "the first Manu produced *six* other Manus (*seven* primary Manus in all), and these produced in their turn each seven other Manus" [602] (*Bhrigu* I, 61-63)—the production of the latter standing in the occult treatises as 7×7. Thus it becomes clear that Manu — the last one, the progenitor of our Fourth Round Humanity — must be the *seventh*, since we are on our fourth Round, [603] and there is a *root*-Manu at globe A and a *seed* Manu at globe G. Just as each planetary Round commences with the appearance of a " Root Manu" (Dhyân Chohan) and closes with a " Seed-Manu," so a *Root* and a *Seed* Manu appear respectively at the beginning and the termination of the human period on any particular planet. [604] It will be easily seen from the foregoing statement that a *Manu-antaric* period means, as the name implies, the time *between* the appearance of two Manus or Dhyân Chohans; and hence a minor *Manvantara* is the duration of the *seven* races on any particular planet, and a major manvantara is the period of one human round along the Planetary chain. Moreover, that, as it is said that each of the seven Manus *creates* 7×7 Manus, and that there are 49 root-races on the seven planets dur-

601. An intuition and a presentiment of the Sishtas may be found in Mr. Sinnett's " *Esoteric Buddhism,*" Fifth Edition. See in it *Annotations* — the " Noah's Ark Theory," pp. 146, 147.

602. The fact that Manu himself is made to declare that he was created by Virâj, and that he then produced the ten Prajâpatis, who again produced seven Manus, who in their turn gave birth to seven other Manus (*Manu* I, 33-36) relates to other still earlier mysteries, and is at the same time a *blind* with regard to the doctrine of the Septenary chain, and the simultaneous evolution of seven humanities, or MEN. However, the present work is written on the records of Cis-Himâlayan Secret Teachings, and Brâhmanical esoteric philosophy may now differ in form as the Kabala does. But they were identical in hoary antiquity.

603. There is another *esoteric* reason besides this one for it. A Vaivasvata is the *seventh* Manu, because this our Round, although the Fourth, is in the *preseptenary* Manvantara, and the Round itself is in its *seventh* stage of materiality or physicality. The close of its middle racial point occurred

during the Fourth Root Race, when man and all nature reached their lowest state of gross matter. From that time, i. e., from the end of the three and a half races, humanity and nature entered on the ascending arc of their racial cycle.

604. The interval that precedes each Yuga is called a *Sandhyâ*, composed of as many hundreds of years as there are thousands in the yuga; and that which follows the latter is named *Sandhyâmśa*, and is of similar duration, we are told in *Vishnu Purâna*. " The interval between the Sandhyâ and the Sandhyâmśa is the yuga denominated Krita, Tretâ, etc., etc. The (four) Krita, Tretâ, Dvâpara, and Kali constitute a great age, or aggregate of four ages: a 1000 such aggregates are a Day of Brahmâ; and 14 *Manus reign within that term.*" Now had we to accept this literally then there would be only one Manu for every 4,320,000,000 of years. As we are taught that it took 300,000,000 of years for the two lower kingdoms to evolve, and that our humanity is just 18 and some odd millions old — where were the other Manus spoken of, unless the allegory means what the esoteric doctrine teaches us about the 14 being each multiplied by 49.

ing each Round, then every root-race has its Manu. The present seventh Manu is called "Vaivasvata" and stands in the exoteric texts for that Manu who represents in India the Babylonian Xisuthrus and the Jewish Noah. But in the esoteric books we are told that Manu Vaivasvata, the progenitor of our *Fifth* race—who saved it from the flood that nearly exterminated the Fourth (Atlantis)—is not the seventh Manu, mentioned in the nomenclature of the Root, or primitive-Manus, but one of the 49 Manus emanated from this Root-Manu.

For clearer comprehension we here give the names of the 14 Manus in their respective order and relation to each Round:—

1st Round
{ 1st (Root) Manu on Planet A — Svâyambhuva.
{ 1st (Seed) Manu on Planet G— Svârochi (or) Svârochisha.

2nd Round
{ 2nd (R.) M. on Planet A— Auttami.
{ 2nd (S.) M. „ „ G— Tâmasa.

3rd Round
{ 3rd (R.) M. „ „ A— Raivata.
{ 3rd (S.) M. „ „ G— Châkshusha.

4th Round
{ 4th (R.) M. „ „ A— Vaivasvata (our progenitor)
{ 4th (S.) M. „ „ G— Sâvarna.

5th Round
{ 5th (R.) M. „ „ A— Daksha Sâvarna.
{ 5th (S.) M. „ „ G— Brahmâ Sâvarna.

6th Round
{ 6th (R.) M. „ „ A— Dharma Sâvarna.
{ 6th (S.) M. „ „ G— Rudra Sâvarna.

7th Round
{ 7th (R.) M. „ „ A— Rauchya.
{ 7th (S.) M. „ „ G— Bhautya.

Vaivasvata, thus, though seventh in the order given, is the primitive Root-Manu of our fourth Human Wave (the reader must always remember that Manu is not a man but collective humanity), while *our* Vaivasvata was but one of the seven *Minor* Manus, who are made to preside over the seven races of this our planet. Each of these has to become the witness of one of the periodical and ever-recurring cataclysms (by fire and water) that close the cycle of every Root-race. And it is this Vaivasvata — the Hindû ideal embodiment, called respectively Xisuthrus, Deukalion, Noah, and by other names — who is the allegorical man who rescued our race, when nearly the whole population of one hemisphere perished by water, while the other hemisphere was awakening from its temporary obscuration.[605]

605. The words "creation," "dissolution," etc., do not render correctly the right meaning of either Manvantara or Pralaya. The *Vishnu Purâna* enumerates several: The dissolution of all things is of four kinds, Parâśara is made to say:— *Naimittika* (occasional), when Brahmâ slumbers (his night, when, "At the end of this Day occurs a re-coalescence *of the Universe*, called Brahmâ's contingent re-coalescence," because Brahmâ *is* this universe itself); "*Prâkritika* (elemental), when the return of this universe to its original nature is partial and physical; *Atyantika* (absolute), identification of *the embodied* with the incorporeal Supreme spirit — Mahâtmic state, whether temporary or until the following *Mahâ-Kalpa:* also absolute obscuration — as of a whole

Thus it is shown that there is no real discrepancy in speaking of the Vaivasvata Manvantara (*Manu-antara*, lit. "between two Manus") 18,000,000 odd years ago, when physical, or the truly human man first appeared in his Fourth Round on this earth; and of the other Vaivasvatas, *e. g.*, the Manu of the Great Cosmic or sidereal Flood (a mystery), or again the Manu Vaivasvata of the submerged Atlantis, when the *racial* Vaivasvata saved the elect of Humanity, the Fifth Race, from utter destruction. As the several (and quite different) events are purposely blended in the *Vishnu* and other Puranas in one narrative, there may yet be a great deal of perplexity left in the profane reader's mind. Therefore, as constant elucidation is needed, we must be forgiven unavoidable repetitions. The blinds which conceal the real mysteries of Esoteric philosophy are great and puzzling, and even now the last word cannot be given. The veil, however, may be a little more removed and some explanations, hitherto denied, may now be offered to the earnest student.

As somebody — Colonel Vans Kennedy, if we do not mistake — remarked, " the first principle in Hindû religious philosophy is *Unity in diversity.*" If all those Manus and Rishis are called by one generic name, this is due to the fact that they are one and all the manifested Energies of one and the same LOGOS, the celestial, as well as the terrestrial messengers and permutations of that Principle which is ever in a state of activity; conscious during the period of Cosmic evolution, unconscious (from our point of view) during Cosmic rest, as the Logos sleepeth in the bosom of THAT which " sleepeth not," nor is it ever awake — for it is SAT or *Be-ness*, not a Being. It is from IT that issues the great unseen Logos, who evolves all the other *logoi*, the primeval MANU who gives being to the other Manus, who emanate the universe and all in it collectively, and who represent in their aggregate the *manifested* Logos.[606] Hence we learn in the " Commentaries " that while no Dhyân Chohan, not even the highest, can realize completely " the condition of the preceding Cosmic evolution," " the Manus retain a knowledge of their experiences of all the Cosmic evolutions throughout Eternity." This is very plain: the first Manu is called *Svâyam-*

---

planetary chain, etc.; and *Nitya* (perpetual), *Mahâpralaya* for the Universe, *death* — for man. *Nitya* is the extinction of life, like the "extinction of a lamp," also "in sleep at night." *Nitya Sarga* is " constant or perpetual creation," as *Nitya pralaya* is " constant or perpetual destruction of all that is born." " That which ensues after a minor dissolution is called ephemeral creation. . . . This

is Samyama " (production, existence, and dissolution). (*Vishnu Purâna*, Book I, ch. vii.) The subject is so difficult that we are obliged to repeat our statements.

606. But see the superb definitions of Parabrahmam and the Logos in Mr. Subba Rao's Lectures on the *Bhagavad Gîtâ* in the early numbers of the *Theosophist* of 1887, Feb., March, April, and May.

bhuva, "the Self-manifested," the Son of the *unmanifested* FATHER. The Manus are the creators of the creators of our First Race — the Spirit of mankind — which does not prevent the *seven* Manus from having been the first "pre-Adamic" men on Earth.

Manu declares himself created by Virâj,[607] or Vaiśvânara (the Spirit of Humanity),[608] which means that his Monad emanates from the never resting Principle in the beginning of every new Cosmic activity: that *Logos* or UNIVERSAL MONAD (collective Elohim) that radiates *from within himself all* those Cosmic Monads that become the centers of activity — progenitors of the numberless Solar systems as well as of the yet undifferentiated *human* monads of planetary chains as well as of every being thereon. Each Cosmic Monad is "Svâyambhuva," the SELF-BORN, *which becomes the Center of Force, from within which emerges a planetary chain* (of which chains there are seven in our system), and whose radiations become again so many Manus Svâyambhuva (a generic name, mysterious and meaning far more than appears), each of these becoming, as a *Host,* the Creator of his own Humanity.[609]

As to the question of the four distinct races of mankind that preceded our Fifth Race, there is nothing mystical in it, except the ethereal bodies of the first races; and it is a matter of legendary, nevertheless, very correct history. That legend is universal. And if the Western *savant* pleases to see in it only a myth, it does not make the slightest difference. The Mexicans had, and still have, the tradition of the fourfold destruction of the world by fire and water, just as the Egyptians had, and the Hindûs have, to this day.

Trying to account for the community of legends in the remote antiquity — held by Chinese, Chaldaeans, Egyptians, Indians and Greeks — and for the absence of any certain vestige of civilization more ancient than 5000 years, the author of *Mythical Monsters* remarks, that

we must not be surprised if we do not immediately discover the vestiges of the people of ten, fifteen, or twenty thousand years ago. With an ephemeral architecture . . . [as in China], the sites of vast cities may have become entirely lost to recollection in a few thousands of years from natural decay, and how much more . . . if . . . minor cataclysms have intervened, such as local inundations, earthquakes, deposition of volcanic ashes . . . the spread of sandy

---

607. See preceding foot-note.

608. See *Manu,* I, 32, 33. Vaiśvânara is, in another sense, the living magnetic fire that pervades the manifested solar system. It is the most objective (to us the reverse) and ever present aspect of the ONE LIFE, for it is the Vital Principle. (See *Theosophist,* July, 1883, p. 249.) It is also a name of *Agni.*

609. See "The Manus and the Manvantaras Explained by a Western Mystic and Mathematician."

deserts, destruction of life by deadly pestilence, by miasma, or by the outpour of sulphurous fumes.[610]

And how many of such cataclysms have changed the whole surface of the earth may be inferred from this *Stanza:*

"*During the first seven crores of the Kalpa (70,000,000 years) the Earth and its two Kingdoms* (mineral and vegetable), *one already having achieved its seventh circle, the other, hardly nascent, are luminous and semi-ethereal, cold, lifeless, and translucid. In the eleventh crore*[611] *the mother* (Earth) *grows opaque, and in the* FOURTEENTH[612] *the throes of adolescence take place. These convulsions of nature* (geological changes) *last until her twentieth crore of years, uninterruptedly, after which they become periodical, and at long intervals.*"

The last change took place nearly twelve crores of years ago (120,000,000). *But the Earth with everything on her face had become cool, hard and settled ages earlier.* (Commentary, xxii)

Thus, if we are to believe esoteric teaching, there have been no more *universal* geological disturbances and changes for the last 120 millions of years, and the Earth was, even before that time, ready to receive her human stock. The appearance of the latter, however, in its full physical development, as already stated, took place only about eighteen millions of years ago, after the first great failure of nature to create beings alone, without the help of the divine " Fashioners," had been followed by the successive evolution of the first three races.[613] The actual duration of the first two and a-half Races is withheld from all but the higher Initiates. The History of the Races begins at the separation of the Sexes, when the preceding egg-bearing androgynous race per-

---

610. *Mythical Monsters*, by Ch. Gould, p. 134.

611. This — in the period of *Secondary* creation, so called. Of the *Primary*, when Earth is in possession of the three *Elemental Kingdoms*, we cannot speak for several reasons, one of which is, that, unless one is a great seer, or naturally intuitional, he will be unable to realize that which can never be expressed in any existing terms.

612. Hippokrates said that number seven " By its occult virtues tended to the accomplishment of all things, to be the dispenser of life and fountain of all its changes." The life of man he divided into seven ages (Shakespeare), for "As the moon changes her phases every seven days, this number influences all sublunary beings," and even the Earth, as we know. With the child, it is the teeth that appear in the seventh month and he sheds them at seven years; at twice seven puberty begins, at three times seven all our mental and vital powers are developed, at four times seven he is in his full strength, at five times seven his passions are most developed, etc., etc. Thus for the Earth. It is now in its middle age, yet very little wiser for it. The *Tetragrammaton*, the four-lettered sacred name of the Deity, can be resolved on Earth only by becoming Septenary through the manifest triangle proceeding from the concealed *Tetraktys*. Therefore, the number seven has to be adopted on this plane. As written in the Kabala " The greater Holy Assembly " v. 1161:— " For assuredly there is no stability in those six, save (what they derive) from *the seventh*. For *all things depend from the* SEVENTH."

613. See above, Stanzas III *et seq.*

ished rapidly, and the subsequent sub-races of the Third Root-Race appeared as an entirely new race *physiologically.* It is this "destruction" which is called allegorically the great "Vaivasvata Manu Deluge," when the account shows Vaivasvata Manu (or "Humanity") remaining alone on Earth in the Ark of Salvation towed by Vishnu in the shape of a monstrous fish, and the Seven Rishis "with him." The allegory is very plain:—

In the Symbolism of every nation, the "Deluge" stands for Chaotic unsettled matter — Chaos itself: and the Water for the feminine principle — the "Great Deep." As the Greek Lexicon of Parkhurst gives it — "'Αρχή [ark] answers to the Hebrew *rasit,* or Wisdom . . . and [at the same time] to the emblem of the female generative power, the *Arg* or *Arca* in which the germ of nature [and of mankind] floats or broods on the great Abyss of the waters, during the interval which takes place after every mundane [or racial] cycle." Ark is also the mystic name of the divine spirit of *life* which broods over chaos. Now Vishnu *is* the divine Spirit, as an abstract principle, and also as the *Preserver* and *Generator,* or *Giver of life* — the third person of the Trimûrti (composed of Brahmâ, the Creator, Śiva, the Destroyer, and Vishnu, the Preserver). Vishnu is shown in the allegory as guiding, under the form of a *fish,* the Ark of Vaivasvata Manu clean across the waters of the Flood. There is no use in expatiating upon the esoteric meaning of the word *fish.*[614] Its theological meaning is phallic, but the metaphysical, *divine.* Jesus is called the "Fish," and so were Vishnu and Bacchus: IHΣ, the "Savior" of mankind, being but the monogram of the god Bacchus called IXΘYΣ, the fish.[615] As to the Seven Rishis in the Ark, they symbolized the seven principles, which became complete in man only after he had separated, and become a *human,* and no longer a divine creature.[616]

Nor have we many details about the submersion of the continent inhabited by the Second Root Race. But the history of the Third, "Lemuria," is given, as is that of Atlantis, the others being only alluded to. Lemuria is said to have perished about 700,000 years before the commencement of what is now called the Tertiary age (the Eocene),[617] and it is during this Deluge also — an actual geological deluge this time — that Vaivasvata Manu is again shown as saving mankind (allegorically it is mankind, or a portion of it, the Fourth Race, which is saved); so also he saves the Fifth Race during the destruction of

614. See Payne Knight, Inman, Gerald Massey, etc.
615. Says St. Augustine of Jesus, "For he is a *fish* that lives in the midst of waters." Christians called themselves little fishes — *pisciculi* — in their sacred mysteries. "So

many *fishes* bred *in the water, and saved by one great fish,"* says Tertullian of the Christians and Christ and the Church.
616. See for further details, "The Seventh Manu."
617. "*Esoteric Buddhism,*" p. 55.

the last Atlanteans, the remnants that perished 850,000 years ago,[618] after which there was no great submersion until the day of Plato's Atlantis, or Poseidonis, known to the Egyptians only because it happened in such relatively recent times.

It is the submersion of the great Atlantis which is the most interesting. It is of this cataclysm that the old records[619] say that "the ends of the Earth got loose"; and upon which the legends and allegories of Vaivasvata, Xisuthrus, Noah, Deukalion and all the *tutti quanti* of the Elect saved, have been built. Tradition, taking into no account the difference between sidereal and geological phenomena, calls both indifferently "deluges." Yet there is a great difference. The cataclysm which destroyed the huge continent of which Australia is the largest relic, was due to a series of subterranean convulsions and the breaking asunder of the ocean floors. That which put an end to its successor — the fourth continent — was brought on by successive disturbances in the axial rotation. It began during the earliest tertiary periods, and, continuing for long ages, carried away successively the last vestige of Atlantis, with the exception, perhaps, of Ceylon and a small portion of what is now Africa. It changed the face of the globe, and no memory of its flourishing continents and isles, of its civilizations and sciences, remained in the annals of history, save in the Sacred records of the East.

Hence, Modern Science denies Atlantis and its existence. It even denies any violent shiftings of the Earth's axis, and would attribute the reason for the change of climates to other causes. But this question is still an open one. If Dr. Croll will have it that all such alterations can be accounted for by the effects of nutation and the precession of the equinoxes, there are other men of Science, such as Sir H. James,[620] and Sir John Lubbock,[621] who feel more inclined to accept the idea that they are due to a change in the position of the axis of rotation. Against this the majority of the astronomers are again arrayed. But then, what have they not denied before now, and what have they not denounced — only to accept it later on whenever the hypothesis became undeniable fact?

How far our figures agree, or rather disagree with modern Science will be seen further in the *Addenda* to this Book, where the geology and anthropology of our modern day are carefully compared with the same in Archaic Science. At any rate, the period assigned in the Secret Doctrine for the sinking of Atlantis, does not seem to disagree very

618. This event, the destruction of the famous island of *Ruta* and the smaller one *Daitya*, which occurred 850,000 years ago in the later Pliocene times, must not be confounded with the submersion of the main continent of Atlantis during the Miocene period. Geologists cannot place the Miocene only so short a way back as 850,000 years; whatever they do, it is several million years ago that the main Atlantis perished.

619. See the "*Book of Enoch.*"

620. *Athenæum*, Aug. 25, 1860.

621. *Ibid.*

much with the calculations of Modern Science, which calls Atlantis "Lemuria," however, whenever it accepts such a submerged continent. With regard to the pre-human period, all that can be said, at present, is, that even up to the appearance of the "Mindless" First Race, the Earth was not without its inhabitants. More may be said: that which Science — recognizing *only physical man* — has a right to regard as the *prehuman* period, may be conceded to have extended from the First Race down to the first half of the Atlantean race, since it is only then that man became the "complete *organic* being he is now." And this would make *Adamic* man no older than a few million of years.[622]

The author of the *Qabbalah* remarks truly that "Man today, as an individual, is only a concatenation of the being-hood of precedent human life," or *lives*, rather. "According to the Qabbalah, the soul sparks contained in Adam [Rishoun], went into three principal classes corresponding to his three *sons*, viz.: Hesed, Habel, Ge-Boor-ah, Qai-yin and *Ra'hmim* Seth. These three were divided into 70 species, called: the principal roots of the human race."[623]

Said Rabbi Yehudah: "How many garments [of the incorporeal man] are these which are crowned" (from the day man was "created")? Said R. El'eazar: "The mountains of the world (the great men of the generation) are in discussion upon it, but there are three: one to clothe in that garment the Rua'h spirit, which ⚬ in the garden (of Eden) on earth: one which is more precious than all, in which the *Neshamah* is clothed in that Bundle of Life, between the angels of the Kings . . .: and one outside garment, which exists and does not exist, is seen and not seen. In that garment, the *Nephesh* is clothed, and she goes and flies in it, to and fro in the world."[624]

This relates to the races (their "garments," or degree of materiality) and to the three principles of man in their three vehicles.

---

622. Mr. Huxley divides those races into the quintuple group of Australioids, Negroids, Mongoloids, Xanthochroics and Melanochroics — all issuing from imaginary Anthropoids. And yet, while protesting against those who say "that the structural differences between man and apes are small and insignificant," and adding that "every bone of the gorilla bears a mark by which it can be distinguished from a corresponding human bone," and that "in the present state of creation, at least, no intermediary being fills the gap which separates man from the troglodyte" — the great anatomist goes on speaking of the *Simian* characteristics in Man! (See de Quatrefages' *The Human Species*, page 113.)

623. Page 422.

624. *Zohar* I, 119b. col. 475; *Qabbalah*, Isaac Myer, 412.

STANZA XI

THE CIVILIZATION AND DESTRUCTION OF THE
FOURTH AND FIFTH RACES

§ § (43) The Lemuro-Atlanteans build cities and spread civilization. The incipient stage of anthropomorphism. (44) Their statues, witnesses to the size of the Lemuro-Atlanteans. (45) Lemuria destroyed by fire, Atlantis by water. The Flood. (46) The destruction of the fourth race and of the last antediluvian monster-animals.

43. THEY (*the Lemurians*) BUILT HUGE CITIES. OF RARE EARTHS AND METALS THEY BUILT. OUT OF THE FIRES (*lava*) VOMITED. OUT OF THE WHITE STONE OF THE MOUNTAINS (*marble*) AND THE BLACK STONE (*of the subterranean fires*) THEY CUT THEIR OWN IMAGES, IN THEIR SIZE AND LIKENESS, AND WORSHIPED THEM (*a*).

(*a*) As the History of the first two human races — the last of the Lemurians and the first of the future Atlanteans — proceeds, we have at this point to blend the two, and speak of them for a time collectively. Here reference is also made to the *divine* Dynasties, such as were claimed by the Egyptians, Chaldaeans, Greeks, etc., to have preceded their *human* kings; they are still believed in by the modern Hindūs, and are enumerated in their sacred books. But of these we shall treat in their proper place. What remains to be shown is, that our modern geologists are now being driven into admitting the evident existence of submerged continents. But to confess their presence is not to accept that there were men on them during the early geological periods;[625]—

625. This is the reason why, perhaps, even Easter Island with its wondrous gigantic statues — a speaking witness to a submerged continent with a civilized mankind on it — is hardly mentioned anywhere in the modern Encyclopaedias. Its mention is carefully avoided except in some books of Travels; modern science has an undeniable predilection for forcing upon the cultured public hypotheses, built on personal hobbies, as well-established evidence, for offering it *guesses* instead of Knowledge, and calling them " scientific conclusions." Its specialists will evolve a thousand and one contradictory speculations rather than confess an *awkward self-evident fact* — pre-eminent among such specialists being Haeckel and his English admirers and co-thinkers. Yet " they are authorities " — we are sternly reminded. What of that? The Pope of Rome is also an AUTHORITY and an infallible one — for his followers; whereas the remarkable fallibility of Scientific speculations is being proven periodically with every change of the moon.

ay, men and civilized nations, not Palaeolithic savages only; who, under the guidance of their *divine* Rulers, built large cities, cultivated arts and sciences, and knew astronomy, architecture and mathematics to perfection. This primeval civilization did not, as one may think, immediately follow their physiological transformation. Between the final evolution and the first city built, many hundred thousands of years had passed. Yet, we find the Lemurians in their sixth sub-race building their first rock-cities out of stone and lava.[626] One of such great cities of primitive structure was built entirely of lava, some thirty miles west from where Easter Island now stretches its narrow piece of sterile ground, and was entirely destroyed by a series of volcanic eruptions. The oldest remains of Cyclopean buildings were all the handiwork of the Lemurians of the last sub-races; and an occultist shows, therefore, no wonder on learning that the stone relics found on the small piece of land called Easter Island by Captain Cook, are " very much like the walls of the Temple of Pachacamac or the Ruins of Tia-Huanuco in Peru ";[627] and that they are in the CYCLOPEAN STYLE. The first large cities, however, appeared on that region of the continent which is now known as the island of Madagascar. There were civilized people and savages in those days as there are now. Evolution achieved its work of

626. Our best modern novelists, who are neither Theosophists nor Spiritualists, begin to have, nevertheless, very psychological and suggestively Occult dreams: witness Mr. Louis Stevenson and his *Dr. Jekyll and Mr. Hyde*, than which no grander psychological essay on Occult lines exists. Has the rising novelist, Mr. Rider Haggard, also had a prophetic or rather a retrospective clairvoyant dream before he wrote "SHE"? His imperial Kor, the great city of the dead, whose surviving living men sailed northwards after the plague had killed almost a whole nation, seems to step out in its general outlines from the imperishable pages of the old archaic records. Ayesha suggests " that those men who sailed north may have been the fathers of the first Egyptians"; and then seems to attempt a synopsis of certain letters of a MASTER quoted in " *Esoteric Buddhism.*" For, she says, " Time after time have nations, ay, and rich and strong nations, learned in the arts, been, and passed away, and been forgotten, so that no memory of them remains. This (the nation of Kor) is but one of several; for time eats up the work of man unless, indeed, he digs in caves

like the people of Kor, and *then mayhap the sea swallows them, or the earthquake shakes them in.* . . . Yet were not these people utterly destroyed, as I think. Some few remained in the other cities, for their cities were many. But the barbarians . . . came down upon them, and took their women to wife, and the race of the Amahagger that is now is a bastard brood of the mighty sons of Kor, and behold it dwelleth in the tombs with its fathers' bones. . . ." (pages 180, 181)

Here the clever novelist seems to repeat the history of all the now degraded and down-fallen races of humanity. The Geologists and Anthropologists would place at the head of humanity as descendants of *Homo primigenius*, the ape-man, of which "NO FOSSIL REMAINS ARE AS YET KNOWN TO US," but (which)" were PROBABLY akin to *the gorilla and orang of the present day*" (*Haeckel*). In answer to whose "probably," occultists point to another and a greater *probability* — the one given in our text. (*See above*.)

627. *The Countries of the World*, by Robert Brown, Vol. 4, p. 43.

perfection with the former, and Karma — its work of destruction on the latter. The Australians and their like are the descendants of those, who, instead of vivifying the spark dropped into them by the " Flames," extinguished it by long generations of bestiality.[628] The Aryan nations could trace their descent through the Atlanteans from the more spiritual races of the Lemurians, in whom the " Sons of Wisdom " had personally incarnated.[629]

It is with the advent of the divine Dynasties that the first civilizations were started. And while, in some regions of the Earth, a portion of mankind preferred leading a nomadic and patriarchal life, and in others savage man was hardly learning to build a fire and to protect himself against the Elements, his brothers — more favored than he by their *Karma*, and helped by the divine intelligence which informed them — built cities, and cultivated arts and sciences. Nevertheless, and civilization notwithstanding, while their pastoral brethren enjoyed wondrous powers as their birthright, they, the builders, could now obtain theirs only gradually; even these being generally used for power

628. See Stanza II, *ante*. This would account for the great difference and variation between the intellectual capacities of races, nations, and individual men. While incarnating, and in other cases only informing the human vehicles evolved by the first brainless (*manasless*) race, the incarnating Powers and Principles had to make their choice between, and take into account, the past Karmas of the *Monads*, between which and their bodies they had to become the connecting link. Besides which, as correctly stated in "*Esoteric Buddhism*" (p. 30), "the fifth principle, or human (intellectual) soul, in the majority of mankind is not even yet fully developed."

629. It is said by Krishna, the *Logos* incarnate, in the *Bhagavad-Gîtâ*, "The seven great Rishis, the four preceding Manus, partaking of my nature, were born from my mind: from them sprang (emanated or was born) the human race and the world." (Chap. X, verse 6.)

Here, by the seven great Rishis, the seven great *rûpa* hierarchies or classes of Dhyân Chohans, are meant. Let us bear in mind that the *Saptarshi* (the seven Rishis) are the regents of the seven stars of the Great Bear, therefore, of the same nature as the angels of the planets, or the seven great Planetary Spirits. They were all reborn, all men on earth in various Kalpas and races. Moreover, "the four preceding Manus" are the four classes of the originally *arûpa* gods — the Kumâras, the Rudras, the Asuras, etc.: who are also said *to have incarnated*. They are not the Prajâpatis, · as the first are, but their informing principles — some of which have incarnated in men, while others have made other men simply the vehicles of their reflections. As Krishna truly says — the same words being repeated later by another *vehicle* of the LOGOS — " I am the same to all beings . . . those who worship me [the 6th principle or the intellectual *divine* Soul, *Buddhi*, made conscious by its union with the higher faculties of *Manas*] *are in me, and I am in them.*" (*Ibid.*, 29.) The Logos, being no personality but the universal principle, is represented by all the divine Powers *born of its mind* — the pure Flames, or, as they are called in Occultism, the " Intellectual Breaths" — those angels who are said to *have made themselves independent, i. e.*, passed from the passive and quiescent. into the active state of Self-Consciousness. When this is recognized, the true meaning of Krishna becomes comprehensible. But see Mr. Subba Rao's excellent lecture on the *Bhagavad Gîtâ* (*Theosophist*, April 1887, p. 444).

over physical nature and selfish and unholy purposes. Civilization has ever developed the physical and the intellectual at the cost of the psychic and spiritual. The command and the guidance over his own psychic nature, which foolish men now associate with the supernatural, were with early Humanity innate and congenital, and came to man as naturally as walking and thinking. " There is no such thing as magic " philosophizes " SHE," the author forgetting that "magic" in her early day still meant the great SCIENCE of WISDOM, and that Ayesha could not possibly know anything of the modern perversion of thought — " though there is such a thing as knowledge of the Secrets of Nature."[630] But they have become " Secrets " only in our race, and were public property with the Third.

Gradually, mankind went down in stature, for, even before the real advent of the Fourth or Atlantean race, the majority of mankind had fallen into iniquity and sin, save the hierarchy of the " Elect," the followers and disciples of the " Sons of Will and Yoga " — called later the " Sons of the Fire Mist."

Then came the Atlanteans; the giants whose physical beauty and strength reached their climax, in accordance with evolutionary law, toward the middle period of their fourth sub-race. But, as said in the Commentary:—

The last survivors of the fair child of the White Island (the primitive Śveta-dvipa) *had perished ages before. Their* (Lemuria's) *elect, had taken shelter on the sacred Island,* (now the fabled Śambhala, in the Gobi Desert), *while some of their accursed races, separating from the main stock, now lived in the jungles and underground ("cavemen"), when the golden yellow race* (the Fourth) *became in its turn " black with sin." From pole to pole the Earth had changed her face for the third time, and was no longer inhabited by the Sons of Śvetadvipa, the blessed, and Adbhitanya, east and west, the first, the one and the pure, had become corrupted. . . . The demi-gods of the Third had made room for the semi-demons of the Fourth Race. Śveta-dvîpa, whose northern parts of the Toyâmbudhi the seven Kumâras (Sanaka, Sananda, Sanâtana, Sanatkumâra, Jâta, Vodhu, and Panchaśikha) had visited, agreeably with exoteric tradition;[631] the White Island had veiled her face. Her children now lived on the Black land, wherein, later on, Daityas from the seventh Dvîpa (Pushkara) and Râkshasas from the seventh climate replaced the Sâdhus and the ascetics of the*

---

630. Page 152.
631. See the Uttara Khanda of the *Padma Purâna; Asiat. Researches* also, Vol. XI, 99, 100.

Third age, who " had descended to them from other and higher regions." . . . .

It is evident that, taken in their dead letter, the Purânas read as an absurd tissue of fairy tales and no better. But if one reads chapters I, II and III from Book II (Vol. II) of *Vishnu Purâna* and accepts *verbatim* its geography, geodesy, and ethnology, in the matter of Priyavrata's seven sons, among whom the father divides the seven *Dvîpas* (Continental Islands) ; and then proceeds to study how the eldest son, the King of *Jambu-dvîpa*, Agnidhra, apportioned Jambu-dvipa among his nine sons; and then how Nâbhi *his* son, who had a *hundred sons* and apportioned all these in his turn — then the reader is likely to throw the book away and pronounce it a farrago of nonsense. But the esoteric student will understand that, in the days when the Purânas were written, the true meaning was clear only to the Initiated Brâhmans, who wrote those works allegorically and would not give the *whole* truth to the masses. And he will explain to the Orientalists who, beginning with Colonel Wilford and ending with Professor Weber, made and still are making such a mess of it, that the first three chapters[632] purposely confuse the following subjects and events :—

I. The series of Kalpas or Ages (also of Races) are never taken into account; *e. g.*, events which have happened in one being allowed to stand along with those which took place in another. The chronological order is entirely ignored. This is shown by several of the Sanskrit commentators, who explain the incompatibility of events and calculations in saying — " Whenever any contradictions in different Purânas are observed, they are ascribed . . . to differences of Kalpas and the like." [633]

II. The several meanings of the words " Manvantara " and " Kalpa " or age, are withheld, and the general one only given.

III. In the genealogy and geography of the Kings and their *Varshas* (countries) and Dvipas, they are all allowed to be regarded as terrestrial regions.

Now, the truth is that, without entering into too minute details, it is easy and permissible to show that :—

(*a*) The Seven *Dvîpas* apportioned to Priyavrata's septenary progeny refer to several localities : first of all to our planetary chain. *Jambu-dvîpa* alone representing our globe, the six others are the (to us) invisible companion globes of this earth. This is shown by the very nature of the allegorical and symbolic descriptions. *Jambu* (dvipa) " *is in the center of all these* [the so-called insular continents] and is

632. See Wilson's trans. of *Vishnu Purâna*, Book II, *et seq.*
633. *Vishnu* and *Bhâgavata Purânas.*

surrounded" by a *sea of salt water* (lavana), whereas Plaksha, Śal-
mala, Kuśa, Krauncha, Śâka and Pushkara, are "surrounded sever-
ally — by great seas of sugar-cane juice, of wine, of clarified butter,
of curds, of milk," etc., etc., and such like metaphorical names.[634]
This is shown furthermore by —

(b) Bhâskara Âchârya, who uses expressions from the *Secret Doctrine* and its books, in his description of the sidereal position of all
these dvîpas:— "the sea of milk and the sea of curds," etc., meaning
the Milky Way, and the various congeries of nebulae; the more so,
since he names "the country to the south of the equator *Bhûr-loka,*
that to the north *Bhuvar-loka, Svar, Mahar, Jana, Tapo* and *Satya
lokas*"; and says: "Those lokas are gradually attained by increasing
religious merits," *i. e.*, they are various *paradises.*[635]

(c) That this geographical division of seven allegorical continents,
islands, mountains, seas and countries, does not belong only to *our*
Round nor even to *our* races (the name of Bhârata Varsha (India) notwithstanding), is explained in the texts themselves by the narrator of
Vishnu Purâna. For he closes the first chapter by saying:

Bhârata (the son of *Nâbhi,* who gave his name to Bhârata-Varsha or India)
consigned the Kingdom to his son Sumati . . . and abandoned his life at Sâla-
grâma. He was afterwards born again as a religious Brâhman, in a distinguished family of ascetics . . . under these princes (Bhârata's descendants)
Bhârata Varsha was divided into nine portions, and their descendants held
successively possession of the country for seventy-one periods of the aggregate
of the four ages,

or the reign of a Manu, representing a Mahâyuga of 4,320,000 years.
But having said so much, Parâśara suddenly explains that "this was
the creation of Svâyambhuva Manu, by which the earth was peopled
when he presided over the first Manvantara, in the Kalpa of Varâha,"
i. e., the *boar* incarnation, or *Avatâr.* Now every Brâhman knows that
it is only with Vaivasvata Manu that *our* Humanity began on this
Earth (or *Round*). And if the Western reader turns to the sub-section
on "*The Primeval Manus of Humanity,*" he will see that Vaivasvata
is the *seventh* of the fourteen Manus who preside over our planetary
chain during its life cycle: *i. e.,* that representing or standing in every
Round for two Manus of the same name (a *Root* and a *Seed* Manu),
he is the Root Manu of the Fourth Round, hence the seventh. Wilson
finds in this only "an incongruity,"[636] and speculates that "the patriarchal genealogies are older than the chronological system of Manvantaras and Kalpas," and thus "have been rather clumsily distributed

634. Chap. II, Book II.
635. See *Bibliotheca Indica* Trans. of the *Golâdhyâya of the Siddhânta-śiromani,* III, 21-44.
636. See his *Vishnu Purâna,* vol. II, p. 108, footnote.

amongst the different periods." It is nothing of the kind. But as Orientalists know nothing of the secret teaching, they will take everything *literally*, and then turn round and abuse the writers of that which they do not comprehend !

These genealogies embrace a period of *three and a half Rounds;* they speak of *pre-human* periods, and explain the descent into generation of every Manu — the first manifested sparks of the ONE Unity — and show, furthermore, each of these human sparks dividing into, and multiplying by, first, the *Pitars,* the human ancestors, then by human Races. No being can become God, or Deva, unless he passes through the human cycles. Therefore the Śloka says, " Happy are those who are born, even from the [latent] condition of gods, *as men,* in Bhârata-varsha ; as that is the way to . . . final liberation." In Jambu-dvipa, Bhârata is considered *the best of its divisions,* because IT IS THE LAND OF WORKS. In it alone " it is that the succession of four Yugas [ages], the Krita, the Tretâ, the Dvâpara, and Kali take place" ; when, therefore, Parâśara, asked by Maitreya " to give him the descriptions of the Earth," returns again to the enumeration of the same Dvipas with the same seas, etc., as those he had described in the Svâyambhuva Manvantara — it is simply a *blind,* yet, to him who reads between the lines, the Four great Races and the Fifth are there, ay, with their sub-divisions, islands, and continents, some of which were called by the names of celestial lokas, and by those of other globes. Hence the confusion.

All these are called by the Orientalists " mythical " and " fabulous " islands and lands.[637] Very true, some *are not of this earth,* but they still exist. The " White Island " and *Atala,* at all events, are no myths, since the latter was the name contemptuously applied by the earliest pioneers of the Fifth Race to the land of Sin — Atlantis, in general, not to Plato's island alone ; and since the former was (*a*) the Sveta-dvipa of theogony, and (*b*) Sâka-dvipa, or Atlantis (its earliest portions) in its beginnings. This was when it yet had its " seven holy rivers that washed away all sin," and its " seven districts, wherein there was no dereliction of virtue, no contention, no deviation from virtue," as it was then inhabited by the caste of the *Magas* — that caste which even the Brâhmans acknowledged as not inferior to their own — and

637. In a lecture, Professor Pengelly, F. R. S., quoting Professor Oliver, makes him say "that the present Atlantic islands' Flora affords no substantial evidence of a former direct communication with the mainland of the New World," but himself adds that, at the same time, " at some period of the Tertiary epoch, N. E. Asia was united to N. W. America, perhaps by the line where the Aleutian chain of islands now extends." Thus Occult Science alone can reconcile the contradictions and hesitations of modern Science. Moreover, surely the argument for the existence of Atlantis does not rest on Botany alone.

which was the nursery of the first Zaratushta. The Brâhmans are shown consulting with Gauramukha, on Nârada's advice, who told them to invite the *Magas* as priests of the Sun in the temple built by Sâmba (the reputed) son of Krishna, who in reality had none. In this the Purânas are *historical*—allegory notwithstanding—and Occultism is stating facts. The whole story is told in *Bhavishya Purâna.* It is stated that, having been cured by Sûrya (the Sun) of leprosy, Sâmba, having built a temple dedicated to the Sun, was looking for pious Brâhmans to perform the appointed rites in it, and receive donations made to the God. But Nârada (this virgin ascetic whom one finds in every age in the Purânas) advised him not to do so, as Manu forbade the Brâhmans to receive emoluments for the performance of religious rites. He therefore referred Sâmba to Gauramukha (white face), the *Purohita* or family priest of Ugrasena, King of Mathurâ, who would tell him whom he could best employ. The priest directed Sâmba to invite the *Magas*, the worshippers of Sûrya, to discharge the duty. Ignorant of the place they lived in, it is Sûrya, the Sun himself, who directs Sâmba to Sâka-dvipa *beyond the salt water.* Then Sâmba performs the journey, using Garuda (Vishnu's and Krishna's vehicle, the great Bird) who lands him among the Magas, etc.

Now Krishna, who lived 5000 years ago, and Nârada, who is found reborn in every cycle (or race), besides Garuda — the symbol esoterically of the great cycle — show the allegory; yet the Magas are the Magi of Chaldaea, and their class and worship were born on the earlier Atlantis, in Sâka-dvipa, the Sinless. All the Orientalists are agreed that the Magas of Sâka-dvipa are the forefathers of the fire-worshiping Parsis. Our quarrel with them rests, as usual, on their dwarfing hundreds of thousands to a few centuries this time: they carry the event — Nârada and Sâmba notwithstanding — to the days of the flight of the Parsis to Gujerât, which is simply absurd, as that was in the VIIIth century of our era. Though the Magas in the *Bhavishya Purâna* are credited with still living in Sâka-dvipa in the day of Krishna's Son, yet the last of it — Plato's " Atlantis " — had perished 6000 years before. They were Mag " late of " Sâka-Dvipa, and lived in those days in Chaldaea. This is an intentional confusion, again.

The earliest pioneers of the Fourth Race were not Atlanteans, nor yet the human *Asuras* and the *Râkshasas* which they became later. In those days large portions of the future continent of Atlantis were yet part and parcel of the Ocean floors. " Lemuria," as we have called the continent of the Third Race, was then a gigantic land.[638] It covered

638. As shown in the Introduction, it *archaic* names of the lost continents, but stands to reason that neither the name of Lemuria nor even Atlantis are the real

the whole area of space from the foot of the Himâlayas, which separated it from the inland sea rolling its waves over what is now Tibet, Mongolia, and the great desert of Shamo (Gobi) ; from Chittagong, westward to Hardvâr, and eastward to Assam. From thence, it stretched South across what is known to us as Southern India, Ceylon, and Sumatra; then embracing on its way, as we go South, Madagascar on its right hand and Australia and Tasmania on its left, it ran down to within a few degrees of the Antarctic Circle; when, from Australia, an inland region on the Mother Continent in those ages, it extended far into the Pacific Ocean, not only beyond Rapa-nui (Teapy, or Easter Island) which now lies in latitude 26 S. and longitude 110 W.[639] This statement seems corroborated by Science, — even if only partially; as, when discussing continental trends, and showing the infra-Arctic masses trending generally with the Meridian, several ancient continents are generally mentioned, though inferentially. Among such the "Mascarene continent," which included Madagascar, stretching north and south, is spoken of, and the existence of another *ancient* continent running "from Spitzbergen to the Straits of Dover, while most of the other parts of Europe were sea bottom," is taught.[640] The latter corroborates, then, the Occult teaching which shows the (now) polar regions as the earliest of the seven cradles of Humanity, and as the tomb of the bulk of the mankind of that region during the Third Race, when the gigantic continent of Lemuria began separating into smaller continents. This is due, according to the explanation in the Commentary, to a decrease of velocity in the earth's rotation : —

" *When the Wheel runs at the usual rate, its extremities* (the poles) *agree with its middle circle* (equator), *when it runs slower and tilts in every direction, there is a great disturbance on the face of the Earth. The waters flow toward the two ends, and new lands arise in the*

have been adopted by us for the sake of clearness. Atlantis was the name given to those portions of the submerged Fourth-Race continent which were "beyond the pillars of Hercules," and which happened to keep above water after the general cataclysm. The last remnant of these — Plato's *Atlantis*, or the "Poseidonis" (another *substitute* or rather a translation of the real name) — was the last of it some 11,000 years ago. Most of the correct names of the countries and islands of both continents are given in the Purânas; but to mention them specially, as found in other more ancient works, such as the *Sûrya Siddhânta*, would necessitate too lengthy explanations. If, in earlier writ-

ings, the two seem to have been too faintly disconnected, this must be due to careless reading and want of reflection. If ages hence, Europeans are referred to as Aryans, and a reader confuses them with the Hindûs and the latter with the Fourth Race, as they live (some of them) in ancient Lankâ — the blame will not fall on the writer.

639. See Addenda to this Book II. Section VI, "Proofs of the Submerged Continents."

640. See Professor Dana's article, *American Journal of Science*, III, p. 442-3; Professor Winchell's *World-Life*; and other geological works.

middle belt (equatorial lands), *while those at the ends are subject to pralayas by submersion. . . ."*

And again:—

" . . . Thus the wheel (the Earth) *is subject to, and regulated by, the Spirit of the Moon, for the breath of its waters* (tides). *Toward the close of the age* (Kalpa) *of a great* (root) *race, the regents of the moon* (the Pitar fathers, or Pitris) *begin drawing harder, and thus flatten the wheel about its belt, when it goes down in some places and swells in others, and the swelling running toward the extremities* (poles) *new lands will arise and old ones be sucked in."*

We have but to read astronomical and geological works, to see the meaning of the above very clearly. Scientists (*modern* Specialists) have ascertained the influence of the tides on the geological distribution of land and water on the planets, and the shifting of the oceans with a corresponding subsidence and rise of continents and new lands. Science knows, or thinks it knows, that this occurs periodically.[641] Professor Todd believes he can trace the series of oscillations backward to the periods of the earth's first incrustation;[642] therefore it seems easy for Science to verify the Esoteric statements. We propose to treat of this at greater length in the *Addenda*.[643]

It is asked by some Theosophists: " What will Atlantis be like when raised? " they understanding from a few words in *"Esoteric Buddhism"* that "old continents" that have been submerged will reappear. Here, again, there is a slight misconception. Were the *same* identical lands of Atlantis that were submerged to be raised again, then they would, indeed, be *barren for ages*. Because the Atlantic sea-bottom is covered with some 5000 feet of chalk at present, and more is forming — a new " cretaceous formation " of strata, in fact — is no reason why when the time for a new continent to appear arrives, a geological convulsion and upraising of the sea bottom should not dispose of these 5000 feet of chalk for the formation of some mountains and 5000 more come to the surface. The racial cataclysms are not a Noah's deluge of forty days — a kind of Bombay monsoon.

641. Speaking on periodical elevation and subsidence of the equatorial and polar regions, and ensuing changes of climate, Mr. Winchell (professor of Geology in Michigan University) says — "As the movements here contemplated are cyclical, the same conditions would recur again and again; and accordingly the same fauna might return again and again to the same region, with intervals of occupation by another fauna. Progressive sedimentation would preserve the records of such faunal alterations; and there would be presented the phenomena of ' colonies,' ' re-apparitions ' and other faunal dislocations in the vertical and horizontal distributions of fossil remains. These phenomena are well known to the student of geology." (*Op. cit.*, " Effects of Astronomical Changes.")

642. See *American Naturalist*, XVIII, 15 *et seq.*

643. *Vide* §§ V and VI.

That the periodical sinking and re-appearance of the mighty continents, now called Atlantis and Lemuria by the modern writers, is no fiction, will be demonstrated in the Section in which all the proofs of the same have been collated together. The most archaic Sanskrit and Tamil works teem with references to both Continents. The seven sacred Islands (Dvipas) are mentioned in the *Sûrya Siddhânta*, the oldest astronomical work in the whole world, and in the works of Asura Maya, the Atlantean astronomer whom Professor Weber has made out reincarnated in Ptolemy. Yet, it is a mistake to call these " sacred islands " *Atlantean*—as done by us; for, like everything else in the Hindû Sacred Books, they are made to refer to several things. The heirloom left by Priyavrata, the Son of Svâyambhuva Manu, to his seven sons—was not *Atlantis*, even though one or two of these islands survived the subsidence of their fellows, and offered shelter, ages later, to Atlanteans, whose continent had been submerged in its turn. When originally mentioned by Parâśara (*Vishnu Purâna*) the seven refer to an esoteric doctrine which is explained further on. Of all the seven islands, Jambudvipa is the only one that is terrestrial, for *it is our globe.* In the Purànas every reference to the North of Meru is connected with that primeval Eldorado, now the North Polar region; which, when the magnolia blossomed there where now we see an unexplored endless desert of ice, was then a continent again. Science speaks of an ancient continent which stretched from Spitzbergen down to the Straits of Dover. The Secret Doctrine teaches that, in the earliest geological periods, these regions formed a horse-shoe-like continent, whose one end, the Eastern, far more northward than North Cornwall, included Greenland, and the other contained Behring Straits as an inland piece of ground, and descended southward in its natural trend down to the British Isles, which in those days must have been right under the lower curve of the semi-circle. This continent was raised simultaneously with the submersion of the equatorial portions of Lemuria. Ages later, some of the Lemurian remains re-appeared again on the face of the Oceans. Therefore, though it can be said without departing from truth that Atlantis is included in the Seven great insular continents, since the Fourth Race Atlanteans got some of the Lemurian relics, and, settling on the islands, included them among *their* lands and continents, yet a difference should be made and an explanation given, once that a fuller and more accurate account is attempted, as in the present work. Easter Island was also taken possession of in this manner by some Atlanteans; who, having escaped from the cataclysm which befell their own land, settled on that remnant of Lemuria only to perish thereon, when destroyed in one day by its volcanic fires and lava. This may be regarded as fiction by certain geographers and geologists; to the

Occultists it is *history*. What does Science know to the contrary?
Until the appearance of a map, published at Basle in 1522, wherein the name
of America appears for the first time, *the latter was believed to be part of India*
..... Science also refuses to sanction the *wild* hypothesis that there was a time
when the Indian peninsula at one end of the line, and South America at the
other, were connected by a belt of islands and continents. The India of the
pre-historic ages .... was doubly connected with the two Americas. The lands
of the ancestors of those whom Ammianus Marcellinus calls the "Brâhmans
of Upper India" stretched from Kashmir far into the (now) deserts of Shamo.
A pedestrian from the north might then have reached — hardly wetting his feet
— the Alaskan peninsula, through Manchuria, across the *future* Gulf of Tartary,
the Kurile and Aleutian islands; while another traveler furnished with a canoe,
and starting from the South, could have walked over from Siam, crossed the
Polynesian Islands and trudged into any part of the continent of South
America.[644]

This was written from the words of a MASTER — a rather doubtful
authority for the materialists and the sceptics. But here we have one
of their own flock, and a bird of the same feather — Ernest Haeckel,
who, in *his* distribution of races, corroborates the statement almost
verbatim:

... It would seem that the region on the earth's surface where the evolution
of these primitive men from the CLOSELY RELATED CATARRHINE APES [!!] took
place, must be sought either in Southern Asia or Eastern Africa [which, by the
bye, was not even in existence when the Third Race flourished—*H.P.B.*] or in
Lemuria. Lemuria is an ancient continent now sunk beneath the waters of the
Indian Ocean, which, lying to the South of the Asia of today, stretched on the
one hand eastwards to upper India and Sunda Island, on the other westward
as far as Madagascar and Africa.[645]

In the epoch we are treating of, the Continent of "Lemuria," had
already broken asunder in many places, and formed new separate continents. There was, nevertheless, neither Africa nor the Americas, still
less Europe in those days, all these slumbering yet on the Ocean floors.
Nor was there much of present Asia; for the cis-Himâlayan regions
were covered with seas, and beyond this stretched the "lotus leaves"
of *Sveta-dvîpa*, the countries now called Greenland, Eastern and Western Siberia, etc., etc. The immense Continent, which had once reigned
supreme over the Indian, Atlantic, and Pacific Oceans, now consisted
of huge islands which were gradually disappearing one after the other,
until the final convulsion engulfed the last remains of it. Easter Isle,
for instance, belongs to the earliest civilization of the Third Race.
Submerged with the rest, a volcanic and sudden uplifting of the Ocean

644. But see *Five Years of Theosophy*, art. "Leaflets from Esoteric History," pp. 338 and 340.
    645. See *supra* and compare *The Pedigree of Man*, p. 80–81.

floor, raised the small relic of the Archaic ages untouched, with its
volcano and statues, during the Champlain epoch of northern polar
submersion, as a standing witness to the existence of Lemuria. It is
said that some of the Australian tribes are the last remnants of the
last descendants of the Third Race.

In this we are again corroborated to a degree by materialistic Science.
Haeckel, when speaking of Blumenbach's brown or Malay race and the
Australians and Papuans, remarks:— " There is much likeness between
these last and the Aborigines of Polynesia, that Australian island-world,
that *seems to have been once on a time a gigantic and continuous
continent.*" [646]

It certainly was, since it stretched, during the Third Race, east and
west, as far as where the two Americas now lie, and since the present
Australia is but a portion of it, as are also a few surviving islands sown
hither and thither on the face of the Pacific and a large bit of California, which belonged to it. Funnily enough, Haeckel, in his fantastic
Pedigree of Man, considers

the Australians of today as the lineal descendants, almost unchanged [?!], of
that *second* branch of the primitive human race . . . that spread northwards,
at first chiefly in Asia, from the home of man's infancy, and seems to have
been the parent of all the other straight-haired races of men. . . . The one,
woolly-haired, migrated in part, westwards . . . [*i. e.,* to Africa and northwards to New Guinea, which countries had then, as said, no existence as yet]
. . . the other, straight-haired, was evolved farther to the north in Asia . . .
and peopled Australia.[647]

" Behold," writes a MASTER, " the relics of that once great nation
[Lemuria of the Third Race] in *some* of the flat-headed aborigines
of your Australia."[648] But they belong to the last remnants of the
Seventh Sub-race of the Third. Professor Haeckel must also have
dreamt a dream and seen for once a *true* vision!

It is to this period that we have to look for the first appearance of
the Ancestors of those, who are termed by us the most ancient peoples of the world — now called respectively the Aryan Hindûs, the
Egyptians, and the oldest Persians, on the one hand, and the Chaldees
and Phoenicians on the other. These were governed by the DIVINE
DYNASTIES, *i. e.,* kings and rulers who had of mortal man only his
physical appearance *as it was then,* but who were Beings from spheres
higher and more celestial than our own sphere will be, long Manvantaras hence. It is useless of course to attempt to force their existence
on sceptics. *Their* greatest pride consists in proving their patronymic
denomination as *catarrhinides;* which fact they try to demonstrate on

---

646. *Pedigree of Man*, p. 82. But see footnote *supra* and the Addenda.
647. Page 81.   648. *" Esoteric Buddhism,"* p. 65.

the alleged authority of the *Coccyx* appended to their *os sacrum*, that rudimentary tail which, if they only had it long enough, they would wag in joy and for ever, in honor of its eminent discoverer. These will remain as faithful to their ape-ancestors as Christians will to tail-less Adam. The Secret Doctrine, however, sets right on this point theosophists and students of Occult Sciences.

If we regard the Second portion of the Third Race as the first representatives of the *really human race* with solid bones, then Haeckel's surmise that "the evolution of the primitive men took place . . . in *either* Southern Asia or . . . Lemuria" — Africa, whether Eastern or Western being out of question — is correct enough, if not entirely so. To be accurate, however, in the same way that the evolution of the First Race (from the bodies of the *pitars*) took place on seven distinctly separated regions of the (then) only Earth at the arctic pole — so did the ultimate transformation of the Third occur: it began in those northern regions, which have just been described a few pages back as including Behring's Straits, and what there then was of dry land in Central Asia, when the climate was semi-tropical even in the Arctic regions and most adapted to the primitive wants of nascent physical man. That region, however, has been more than once frigid and tropical in turn since the appearance of man. The commentary tells us that the Third Race was only about the middle point of its development when:—

" *The axle of the Wheel tilted. The Sun and Moon shone no longer over the heads of that portion of the* SWEAT BORN ; *people knew snow, ice, and frost, and men, plants, and animals were dwarfed in their growth. Those that did not perish* REMAINED AS HALF-GROWN BABES [649] IN SIZE AND INTELLECT. *This was the third pralaya of the races.*[650]

Which means again, that our globe is subject to seven periodical *entire* changes which go *pari passu* with the races. For the Secret Doctrine teaches that, during this Round, there must be seven terrestrial *pralayas*, three occasioned by the change in the inclination of the earth's axis. It is a *law* which acts at its appointed time, and not at all blindly, as science may think, but in strict accordance and harmony with *Karmic* law. In Occultism this inexorable law is referred to as "the great ADJUSTER." Science confesses its ignorance of the cause producing climatic vicissitudes and such changes in the axial direction, which are always followed by these vicissitudes; nor does it seem so sure of the axial changes. And being unable to account for them, it is prepared rather to deny the axial phenomena altogether, than admit the intelligent

---

649. " Half-grown babes " in comparison with their giant Brethren on other zones. So would we now.   650. Relates to Lemuria.

Karmic hand and law which alone could reasonably explain such sudden changes and their results. It has tried to account for them by various more or less fantastic speculations; one of which would be the sudden, and as imaginary, collision of our earth with a comet (de Boucheporn's hypothesis), as the cause of all the geological revolutions. But we prefer holding to our esoteric explanation, since FOHAT is as good as any comet, having, in addition, universal intelligence to guide him.

Thus, since Vaivasvata Manu's Humanity appeared on this Earth, there have already been four such axial disturbances; when the old continents — save the first one — were sucked in by the oceans, other lands appeared, and huge mountain chains arose where there had been none before. The face of the Globe was completely changed each time; the *survival of the fittest* nations and races was secured through timely help; and the unfit ones — the failures — were disposed of by being swept off the earth. Such sorting and shifting does not happen between sunset and sunrise, as one may think, but requires several thousands of years before the new house is set in order.

The *Sub*-races are subject to the same cleansing process, as also the side-branchlets (the family-Races). Let one, well-acquainted with astronomy and mathematics, throw a retrospective glance into the twilight and shadows of the Past. Let him observe, take notes of what he knows of the history of peoples and nations, and collate their respective rises and falls with what is known of astronomical cycles — especially with the *Sidereal year,* equal to 25,868 of our solar years.[651] If the observer is gifted with the faintest intuition, then will he find how the weal and woe of nations is intimately connected with the beginning and close of this sidereal cycle. True, the non-occultist has the disadvantage that he has no such far distant times to rely upon. He knows nothing, through exact Science, of what took place nearly 10,000 years ago; yet he may find consolation in the knowledge or — if he so prefers — speculation on the fate of every one of the modern nations he knows of — about 16,000 years hence. Our meaning is very clear. Every sidereal year the tropics recede from the pole *four degrees* in each revolution from the equinoctial points, as the equator rounds

<hr />

651. There are other cycles, of course, cycles *within cycles* — and this is just that which creates such a difficulty in the calculations of racial events. The circuit of the ecliptic is completed in 25,868 years. And, with regard to our Earth, it is calculated that the equinoctial point falls back 50″.10 annually. But there is another cycle within this one. It is said that "as the apsis goes forward to meet it at the rate of 11″.24 annually" (see the article on *Astronomy* in

Encyclopaedia Britannica), "this would complete a revolution in one hundred and fifteen thousand three hundred and two years (115,302). The approximation of the equinox and the apsis is the sum of these motions, 61″.34, and hence the equinox returns to the same position in relation to the apsis in 21,128 years." We have mentioned this cycle in *Isis Unveiled,* Vol. I, in relation to other cycles. Each has a marked influence on its contemporary race.

through the Zodiacal constellations. Now, as every astronomer knows, at present the tropic is only twenty-three degrees and a fraction less than half a degree from the equator. Hence it has still 2½ degrees to run before the end of the Sidereal year; which gives humanity in general, and our civilized races in *particular*, a reprieve of about 16,000 years.[652]

After the Great Flood of the Third Race (the Lemurians) —

" Men decreased considerably in stature, and the duration of their lives was diminished. Having fallen down in godliness they mixed with animal races, and intermarried among giants and Pigmies (the dwarfed races of the Poles). . . *Many acquired* DIVINE, *more* — UNLAWFUL *knowledge, and followed willingly the LEFT PATH."* (Commentary xxxiii.)

Thus were the Atlanteans approaching destruction in their turn. How many geological periods it took to accomplish this *fourth* destruction? Who can tell. . . . But we are told that —

---

(44). THEY (*the Atlanteans*) BUILT GREAT IMAGES, NINE YATIS HIGH (27 *feet*) — THE SIZE OF THEIR BODIES (*a*). LUNAR FIRES HAD DESTROYED THE LAND OF THEIR FATHERS (*the Lemurians*). WATER THREATENED THE FOURTH (*Race*) (*b*).

(*a*) It is well worth noticing that most of the gigantic statues discovered on Easter Island, a portion of an undeniably submerged continent — as also those found on the outskirts of Gobi, a region which had been submerged for untold ages — are all between 20 and 30 feet high. The statues found by Cook on Easter Island measured almost all *twenty-seven* feet in height, and eight feet across the shoulders.[653] The writer is well aware that the modern archaeologists have decided now that " these statues are not very old," as declared by one of the high officials of the British Museum, where some of them now are. But this is one of those arbitrary decisions of modern science which does not carry much weight.

We are told that it is after the destruction of " Lemuria " by subterranean fires that men went on steadily decreasing in stature — a process already commenced after their *physical* FALL — and that finally, some millions of years after, they reached between six and seven feet, and are now dwindling down (as the older Asiatic races) to nearer five than six feet. As Pickering shows, there is in the Malay race (a sub-race

---

652. See at the end of this Stanza, " On the Duration of Ages and Cycles."

653. See § " Stones, Witnesses to Giants," at the end of this Stanza.

of the Fourth Root Race) a singular diversity of stature; the members of the Polynesian family (Tahitians, Samoans, and Tonga islanders) are of a *higher stature than the rest of mankind;* but the Indian tribes and the inhabitants of the Indo-Chinese countries are decidedly below the general average. This is easily explained. The Polynesians belong to the very earliest of the surviving sub-races, the others to the very last and transitory stock. As the Tasmanians are now completely extinct, and the Australians rapidly dying out, so will the other old races soon follow.

(*b*) Now, how could those records have been preserved? we may be asked. Even the knowledge of the Zodiac is denied to the Hindûs by our kind and learned Orientalists, who *conclude* that the Aryan Hindûs knew nothing of it, before the Greeks brought it into the country. This uncalled-for slander was so sufficiently refuted by Bailly, and what is more, by the clear *evidence of facts,* as not to need very much additional refutation. While the Egyptians have on their Zodiacs [654] irrefutable proofs of records having embraced more than three-and-a-half *sidereal years* — or about 87,000 years — the Hindû calculations cover nearly thirty-three such years, or 850,000 years. The Egyptian priests assured Herodotus that the Pole of the Earth and the Pole of the Ecliptic had formerly coincided. But, as remarked by the author of the *Sphinxiad,* " These *poor benighted* Hindoos have registered a knowledge of Astronomy for ten times 25,000 years since the [last local] *Flood* [in Asia], or *Age of Horror*," in the latitude of India. And they possess recorded observations from the date of the first *Great* Flood within the Aryan *historical* memory — that which submerged the last portions of Atlantis, 850,000 years ago. The floods which preceded are, of course, more traditional than historical.

The sinking and transformation of Lemuria beginning nearly at the Arctic Circle (Norway), the Third Race ended its career in Lankâ, or rather on that which became Lankâ with the Atlanteans. The small remnant now known as Ceylon is the Northern highland of ancient Lankâ, while the enormous island of that name was, in the Lemurian period, the gigantic continent described a few pages back. As a MASTER says: [655] " Why should not your geologists bear in mind that under the continents explored and fathomed by them . . . . there may be hidden, deep in the fathomless, or rather unfathomed ocean beds, other and far older continents whose strata have never been geologically explored; and that they may some day upset entirely their present theories? Why not admit that our present continents have, like Lemuria and Atlantis, been several times already submerged, and had the time to re-appear

654. See Denon's *Voyage en Égypte,* Vol. II.
655. See " *Esoteric Buddhism,*" p. 65.

again and bear their new groups of mankind and civilizations; and that
at the first great geological upheaval at the next cataclysm, in the series
of periodical cataclysms that occur from the beginning to the end of
every Round, our already autopsized continents will go down and the
Lemurias and Atlantises come up again?"

Not the *same* identical continents, of course.

But here an explanation is needed. No confusion need arise as
regards the postulation of a Northern "Lemuria." The prolongation
of that great continent into the North Atlantic Ocean is in no way sub-
versive of the opinions so widely held as to the site of the lost Atlantis,
and one corroborates the other. It must be noted that the Lemuria,
which served as the cradle of the Third Root-Race, not only embraced
a vast area in the Pacific and Indian Oceans, but extended in the
shape of a horse-shoe past Madagascar, round "South Africa" (then a
mere fragment in process of formation), through the Atlantic up to
Norway. The great *English fresh-water deposit called the Wealden —
which every geologist regards as the mouth of a former great river —
is the bed of the main stream which drained Northern Lemuria in the
Secondary Age.* The former reality of this river is a fact of science —
will its votaries acknowledge the necessity of accepting the Secondary-
age Northern Lemuria, which their data demand? Professor Berthold
Seeman not only accepted the reality of such a mighty continent, but
regarded *Australia and Europe as formerly portions of one continent*
— thus corroborating the whole "horse-shoe" doctrine already enunciated. No more striking confirmation of our position could be given,
than the fact that the ELEVATED RIDGE in the Atlantic basin, 9000 feet
in height, which runs for some two or three thousand miles southwards
from a point near the British Islands, first slopes towards South America, then *shifts almost at right angles* to proceed in a SOUTH-EASTERLY
line toward the African coast, whence it runs on southward to Tristan
d'Acunha. This ridge is a remnant of an Atlantic continent, and, could
it be traced further, would establish the reality of a submarine horse-
shoe junction with a former continent in the Indian Ocean.[656]

The *Atlantic portion of Lemuria* was the geological basis of what is
generally known as Atlantis. The latter, indeed, must be regarded
rather as a development of the Atlantic prolongation of Lemuria, than
as an entirely new mass of land upheaved to meet the special require-
ments of the Fourth Root-Race. Just as in the case of Race-evolution,
so in that of the shifting and re-shifting of continental masses, no hard
and fast line can be drawn where a new order ends and another begins.
Continuity in natural processes is never broken. Thus the Fourth Race

656. *Cf.* chart adapted from the *Challenger* and *Dolphin* soundings in Mr. Donnelly's
Atlantis, the Antediluvian World, p. 47.

Atlanteans were developed from a nucleus of Northern Lemurian Third Race Men, centered, roughly speaking, toward a point of land in what is now the mid-Atlantic Ocean. Their continent was formed by the coalescence of many islands and peninsulas which were upheaved in the ordinary course of time *and became ultimately the true home of the great Race known as the Atlanteans.* After this consummation was once attained it follows, as stated on the highest " occult " authority, that " Lemuria should no more be confounded with the Atlantis Continent, than Europe with America." [657]

The above, coming from quarters so discredited by orthodox Science, will, of course, be regarded by it as a more or less happy fiction. Even the clever work of Donnelly, already mentioned, is put aside, notwithstanding that its statements are all confined within a frame of strictly scientific proofs. But we write for the future. Discoveries in this direction will vindicate the claims of the Asiatic philosophers, who maintain that Sciences — Geology, Ethnology, and History included — were pursued by the Antediluvian nations who lived an untold number of ages ago. Future finds will justify the correctness of the present observations of such acute minds as H. A. Taine and Renan. The former shows that the civilizations of such archaic nations as the Egyptians, Aryans of India, Chaldaeans, Chinese, and Assyrians are the result of preceding civilizations during *"myriads* of centuries"; [658] and the latter points to the fact that,

Egypt at the beginning appears mature, old, and entirely without mythical and heroic ages, as if the country had never known youth. Its civilization has no infancy, and its art no archaic period. The civilization of the Old Monarchy did not begin with infancy. It was already mature. [659]

To this Professor R. Owen adds that, " Egypt is recorded to have been a civilized and governed community *before* the time of Menes "; and Winchell, [660] that " at the epoch of Menes the Egyptians were already a civilized and numerous people. Manetho tells us that Athothis, the son of this first king Menes, built the palace of Memphis; that he was a physician, and left *anatomical books."*

This is quite natural if we have to believe the statements of Herodotus, who records in *Euterpe,* [661] that the written history of the Egyptian priests dated from about 12,000 years before his time. But what are 12,000 or even 120,000 years compared with the millions of years elapsed since the Lemurian period? The latter, however, has not been left without witnesses, its tremendous antiquity notwithstanding. The complete records of the growth, development, social, and even political

657. *" Esoteric Buddhism,"* p. 58.
658. *History of English Literature,* page 23.
659. Quoted in *Atlantis,* etc., page 132.
660. *Pre-Adamites,* p. 120.
661. cxlii.

life of the Lemurians, have been preserved in the secret annals. Unfortunately, few are those who can read them; and those who could would still be unable to understand the language, unless acquainted with all the seven keys of its symbolism. For the comprehension of the Occult Doctrine is based on that of the seven sciences; which sciences find their expression in the seven different applications of the secret records to the exoteric texts. Thus we have to deal with modes of thought on seven entirely different planes of Ideality. Every text relates to, and has to be rendered from, one of the following standpoints —

1. The Realistic plane of thought;
2. The Idealistic;
3. The purely Divine or Spiritual.

The other planes too far transcend the average consciousness, especially of the materialistic mind, to admit of their being even symbolized in terms of ordinary phraseology. There is no purely *mythical* element in any of the ancient religious texts; but the mode of thought in which they were originally written has to be found out and closely adhered to during the process of interpretation. For, it is either symbolical (archaic mode of thought), emblematical (a later though very ancient mode of thought), parabolical (allegory), hieroglyphical, or again *logogrammical* — the most difficult method of all, as every letter, as in the Chinese language, represents a whole word. Thus, almost every proper name, whether in the Vedas, the *"Book of the Dead,"* or the Bible (to a degree), is composed of such logograms. No one who is not initiated into the mystery of the occult religious logography can presume to know what a name in any ancient fragment means, before he has mastered the meaning of every letter that composes it. How is it to be expected that the merely profane thinker, however great his erudition in *orthodox* symbolism, so to say — *i. e.,* in that symbolism which can never get out of the old grooves of Solar-myth and sexual-worship — shall penetrate into the arcana behind the veil. One who deals with the husk or shell of the dead letter, and devotes himself to the kaleidoscopic transformation of barren word-symbols, can never expect to get beyond the vagaries of modern mythologists.

Thus, Vaivasvata, Xisuthrus, Deukalion, Noah, etc., etc. — all the head-figures of the world-deluges, universal and partial, astronomical or geological — all furnish in their very names the records of the causes and effects which led to the event, if one can but read them fully. All such deluges are based on events that took place in nature, and stand as *historical* records, therefore, whether they were sidereal, geological, or even simply allegorical, of a moral event on other and higher planes of being. This we believe has now been sufficiently demonstrated during the long explanation necessitated by the allegorical Stanzas.

To speak of a race nine *yatis*, or 27 feet high, in a work claiming a more scientific character than *Jack the Giant-Killer*, is a somewhat unusual proceeding. " Where are your proofs? " the writer will be asked. In History and tradition, is the answer. Traditions about a race of giants in days of old are universal; they exist in oral and written lore. India had her Dânavas and Daityas; Ceylon had her Râkshasas; Greece, her Titans; Egypt, her colossal Heroes; Chaldaea, her Izdubars (Nimrod); and the Jews their *Emims* of the land of Moab, with the famous giants, Anakim.[662] Moses speaks of Og, a king who was nine cubits high (15 ft. 4 in.) and four wide,[663] and Goliath was " six cubits and a span in height " (or 10ft. 7in.). The only difference found between the " revealed Scripture " and the evidence furnished to us by Herodotus, Diodorus Siculus, Homer, Pliny, Plutarch, Philostratos, etc., etc., is this: While the pagans mention only *the skeletons of giants,* dead untold ages before, relics that some of *them had personally seen,* the Bible interpreters unblushingly demand that geology and archaeology should believe, that several countries were inhabited by such giants in the days of Moses; giants before whom the Jews were as grasshoppers, and who still existed in the days of Joshua and David. Unfortunately their own chronology is in the way. Either the latter or the giants have to be given up. (But see Part III, *Addenda,* the closing chapter.)

Of still standing witnesses to the submerged continents, and the colossal men that inhabited them, there are still a few. Archaeology claims several such on this globe, though beyond wondering " what these may be " — it never made any serious attempt to solve the mystery. Besides the Easter Island statues mentioned already, to what epoch do the colossal statues, still erect and intact near Bamian, belong? Archaeology assigns them to the first centuries of Christianity (as usual), and errs in this as it does in many other speculations. A few words of description will show the readers what are the statues of both Easter Isle and Bamian. We will first examine what is known of them to orthodox Science. In *The Countries of the World,* by Robert Brown,[664] it is stated that —

Teapi, Rapa-nui, or Easter Island, is an isolated spot almost 2000 miles from the South American coast. . . . In length it is about twelve miles, in breadth four . . . and there is an extinct crater 1050 feet high in its center. The island abounds in craters, which have been extinct for so long that no tradition of their activity remains. . . .

" . . . But who made the great stone images[665] which are now the

662. *Numbers* xiii. 33.
663. *Deut.* iii. 11.

664. In Vol. IV, page 43.
665. *Ibid.,* p. 44, etc.

chief attraction of the island to visitors? *No one knows,"* says the reviewer.

It is more than likely that they were here when the present inhabitants (a handful of Polynesian savages) arrived. . . . Their workmanship *is of a high order...* and it is believed that the race who formed them were the frequenters of the natives of Peru and other portions of South America. . . . Even at the date of Cook's visit, some of the statues, measuring 27 feet in height and eight across the shoulders were lying overthrown, while others still standing appeared much larger. One of the latter was so lofty that the shade was sufficient to shelter a party of thirty persons from the heat of the sun. The platforms on which these colossal images stood averaged from thirty to forty feet in length, twelve to sixteen broad . . . all built of hewn stone in the Cyclopean style, very much like the walls of the Temple of Pachacamac, *or the ruins of Tia-Huanuco in Peru.*⁶⁶⁶

" THERE IS NO REASON TO BELIEVE THAT ANY OF THE STATUES HAVE BEEN BUILT UP, BIT BY BIT, BY SCAFFOLDING ERECTED AROUND THEM " — adds the journal very suggestively — without explaining *how* they could be built otherwise, unless made by giants of the same size as the statues themselves. One of the best of these colossal images is now in the British Museum. The images at Ronororaka — the only ones now found erect — are four in number, three deeply sunk in the soil, and one resting on the back of its head like the head of a man asleep. Their types, though all are long-headed, are different; and they are evidently meant for portraits, as the noses, the mouths and chins differ greatly in form, their head-dress, moreover—a kind of flat cap with a back piece attached to it to cover the back portion of the head — showing that the originals were no savages of the stone period. Verily the question may be asked —" Who made them ? " — but it is not archaeology, nor yet geology that is likely to answer, though the latter recognizes in the Island a portion of a submerged continent.

But who cut the Bamian, still more colossal, statues, the tallest and the most gigantic in the whole world, for Bartholdi's " Statue of Liberty " (now at New York) *is a dwarf* when compared with the largest of the five images. Burnes, and several learned Jesuits who have visited the place, speak of a mountain *"all honeycombed with gigantic cells,"* with two immense giants cut in the same rock. They are referred to as the modern *Miaotse* (*vide supra,* quotation from *Shu-King*) the last surviving witnesses of the *Miaotse* who had " troubled the earth "; the Jesuits are right, and the Archaeologists, who see Buddhas in the largest of these statues, are mistaken. For all those numberless gigantic ruins discovered one after the other in our day, all those immense avenues of colossal ruins that cross North America along and beyond

666. Vol. III, pp. 310, 311.

the Rocky Mountains, are the work of the Cyclopes, the true and actual
Giants of old. " Masses of enormous human bones " were found " in
America, near Misorte," a celebrated modern traveler tells us, precisely
on the spot which local tradition points out as the landing spot of
those giants who overran America when it had hardly arisen from the
waters.[667]

Central Asian traditions say the same of the Bamian statues. What
are they, and what is the place where they have stood for countless ages,
defying the cataclysms around them, and even the hand of man, as in
the instance of the hordes of Timur and the Vandal-warriors of Nadir-
Shah? Bamian is a small, miserable, half-ruined town in Central Asia,
half-way between Kabul and Balkh, at the foot of Koh-i-Baba, a huge
mountain of the Paropamisan (or Hindû-Kush) chain, some 8500
feet above the level of the sea. In days of old, Bamian was a portion
of the ancient city of Gulguleh, ruined and destroyed to the last stone
by Jengis-Khan in the XIIIth century. The whole valley is hemmed
in by colossal rocks, which are full of partially natural and partially
artificial caves and grottoes, once the dwellings of Buddhist monks who
had established in them their *vihâras*. Such *vihâras* are to be met with
in profusion, to this day, in the rock-cut temples of India and the valleys
of Jellalâbâd. It is at the entrance of some of these that five enormous
statues, of what is regarded as Buddha, have been discovered or rather
rediscovered in our century, as the famous Chinese traveler, Hiuen-
Thsang, speaks of, and saw them, when he visited Bamian in the VIIth
century.

When it is maintained that no larger statues exist on the whole globe,
the fact is easily proven on the evidence of all the travelers who have
examined them and taken their measurements. Thus, the largest is
173 feet high, or *seventy* feet higher than the " Statue of Liberty " now
at New York, as the latter is only 105 feet or 33 meters high. The
famous Colossus of Rhodes itself, between whose limbs passed easily
the largest vessels of those days, measured only 120 to 130 feet in height.
The second statue, cut out in the rock like the first one, is only 120
feet (15 feet taller than the said " Liberty ").[668] The third statue is
only 60 feet high — the two others still smaller, the last one being only
a little larger than the average tall man of our present race. The first
and largest of the Colossi represents a man draped in a kind of *toga;*

---

667. See Garcilasso de la Vega, *Comen-
tarios Reales*, Part II, bk. ix, ch. ix.
    See also *Pneumatologie des Esprits*, Vol.
III, p. 55, de Mirville.
    668. The first and second have, in com-
mon with Bartholdi's Statue, an entrance at
the foot, leading by a winding staircase cut

in the rock up into the heads of the statues.
The eminent French archaeologist and anthropologist, the Marquis de Nadaillac, justly
remarks in his work that there never was in
ancient or in modern times a sculptured
human figure more colossal than the first of
the two.

M. de Nadaillac thinks [669] that the general appearance of the figure,
the lines of the head, the drapery, and especially the large hanging
ears, point out undeniably that Buddha was meant to be represented.
But the above proves nothing. Notwithstanding the fact that most of
the now existing figures of Buddha, represented in the posture of
Samâdhi, have large drooping ears, this is a later innovation and an
afterthought. The primitive idea was due to esoteric allegory. The
unnaturally large ears symbolize the omniscience of wisdom, and were
meant as a reminder of the power of Him who *knows and hears all*,
and whose benevolent love and attention for all creatures nothing can
escape. " The merciful Lord, our Master, hears the cry of agony of
the smallest of the small, beyond vale and mountain, and hastens to
its deliverance ": — says a Stanza. Gautama Buddha was an Âryan
Hindû, and an approach to such ears is found only among the Mongol-
ian Burmese and Siamese, who, as in Cochin, distort them artificially.
The Buddhist monks, who turned the grottoes of the *Miaotse* into
Vihâras and cells, came into Central Asia about or in the first century
of the Christian era. Therefore Hiuen Thsang, speaking of the colossal
statue, says that " the shining of the gold ornamentation that overlaid
the statue " in his day " dazzled one's eyes," but of such gilding there
remains not a vestige in modern times. The very drapery, in contrast
to the figure itself, cut out in the standing rock, is made of plaster and
modelled over the stone image. Talbot, who has made the most careful
examination, found that this drapery belonged to a far later epoch. The
statue itself has therefore to be assigned to a far earlier period than
Buddhism. Whom does it represent in such case? it may be asked.

Once more tradition, corroborated by written records, answers the
query, and explains the mystery. The Buddhist Arhats and Ascetics
found the five statues, and many more, now crumbled down to dust,
and as the three were found by them in colossal niches at the entrance
of their future abode, they covered the figures with plaster, and, over
the old, modelled new statues made to represent Lord Tathâgata. The
interior walls of the niches are covered to this day with bright paintings of human figures, and the sacred image of Buddha is repeated
in every group. These frescoes and ornaments — which remind one
of the Byzantine style of painting — are all due to the piety of the
monk-ascetics, like some other minor figures and rock-cut ornament-
ations. But the five statues belong to the handiwork of the Initiates
of the Fourth Race, who sought refuge, after the submersion of their
continent, in the fastnesses and on the summits of the Central Asian
mountain chains. Moreover, the five statues are an imperishable record
of the esoteric teaching about the gradual evolution of the races.

669. See *infra*.

The largest is made to represent the First Race of mankind, its ethereal body being commemorated in hard, everlasting stone, for the instruction of future generations, as its remembrance would otherwise never have survived the Atlantean Deluge. The second — 120 feet high — represents the sweat-born; and the third — measuring 60 feet — immortalizes the race that fell, and thereby inaugurated the first *physical* race, born of father and mother, the last descendants of which are represented in the Statues found on Easter Isle; but they were only from 20 to 25 feet in stature at the epoch when Lemuria was submerged, after it had been nearly destroyed by volcanic fires. The Fourth Race was still smaller, though gigantic in comparison with our present Fifth Race, and the series culminated finally in the latter.[670]

These are, then, the " Giants " of antiquity, the ante- and post-diluvian *Gibborim* of the Bible. They lived and flourished one million rather than between three and four thousand years ago. The *Anakim* of Joshua, whose hosts were as " grasshoppers " in comparison with them, are thus a piece of Israelite fancy, unless indeed the people of Israel claim for Joshua an antiquity and origin in the Eocene, or at any rate in the Miocene age, and change the millenniums of their chronology into millions of years.

In everything that pertains to prehistoric times the reader ought to bear the wise words of Montaigne in his mind. Saith the great French philosopher: —

. . . It is a sottish presumption to disdaine and condemne that for false, which unto us seemeth to beare no show of likelihood or truth: which is an ordinarie fault in those who perswade themselves to be of more sufficiencie than the vulgar sort.

. . . But reason hath taught me, that so resolutely to condemne a thing for false and impossible, is to assume unto himself the advantage to have the bounds and limits of God's will, and the power of our common Mother Nature tied to his sleeve, and that there is no greater folly in the world than to reduce them to the measure of our capacitie and bounds of our sufficiencie.

If we term those things monsters or miracles to which our reason cannot attain, how many doe such daily present themselves unto our sight? Let us consider through what cloudes, and how blinde-folde we are led to the knowledge of most things that passe our hands; verily we shall finde it is rather custome than Science that receiveth, the strangenesse of them from us: and that those things, were they newly presented unto us, wee should doubtless deeme them as much or more unlikely and incredible than any other.[671]

A fair-minded scholar should, before denying the possibility of *our* history and records, search modern History, as well as the universal traditions scattered throughout ancient and modern literature, for traces

670. See the following sub-section on " Cyclopean Ruins, and Colossal Stones as Witnesses to Giants." 671. *Essays*, chap. xxvi.

left by these marvelous early races. Few among the unbelievers suspect the wealth of corroborative evidence which is found scattered about and buried even in the British Museum alone. The reader is asked to throw one more glance at the subject-matter treated of in the chapter which follows:—

CYCLOPEAN RUINS AND COLOSSAL STONES AS WITNESSES TO GIANTS

In his enormous works — *Mémoires addressées à l'Académie des Sciences* — de Mirville, carrying out the task of proving the reality of the devil and showing his abode in every ancient and modern idol, has collected several hundred pages of "historical evidence" that in the days of *miracle* — Pagan and Biblical — the stones walked, spoke, delivered oracles, and even sang. That finally, "Christ-stone," or *Christ-Rock*, "the spiritual Rock" that followed "Israel"[672] "became a *Jupiter Lapis*," swallowed by his father Saturn, "under the shape of a stone."[673] We will not stop to discuss the evident misuse and materialization of Biblical metaphors, simply for the sake of proving the *Satanism* of idols, though a good deal might be said[674] on this subject. But without claiming any such peripateticism and innate psychic faculties for our stones, we may collect, in our turn, every available evidence on hand, to show that (*a*) had there been no giants to move about such colossal rocks, there could never have been a Stonehenge, a Carnac (Brittany), and other such Cyclopean structures; and (*b*) were there no such thing as MAGIC, there could never have been so many witnesses to *oracular* and *speaking* stones.

In the *Achaika*[675] we find Pausanias confessing that, in beginning his work, he had regarded the Greeks as mighty *stupid* "for worshiping stones." But having reached Arcadia, he adds: "I have changed my way of thinking." Therefore, without worshiping stones or stone idols and statues, which is the same — a crime Roman Catholics are unwise to reproach Pagans with, as they do likewise — one may be allowed to believe in what so many great philosophers and holy men have believed in, without deserving to be called an "idiot" by modern Pausaniases.

The reader is referred to Volume VI of the *Académie des Inscriptions*[676] if he would study the various properties of flints and pebbles

672. I *Corinth.*, x. 4.
673. *Pierres Animées et Parlantes*, p. 283. *Théologie de la Pierre*, 270.
674. Saturn is *Kronos* — "*Time.*" His swallowing *Jupiter lapis* may turn out one day a prophecy. "Peter (*Cephas, lapis*), is

the *stone* on which the Church of Rome is built" we are assured. But *Kronos* is as sure "to *swallow* it" one day, as he has swallowed *Jupiter-lapis* and still greater characters.
675. Page 81.
676. *Mémoires*, p. 518, *et seq.*

from the standpoint of *Magic* and psychic powers. In a poem on *Stones* attributed to Orpheus, those stones are divided into *ophites* and *siderites*, " serpent-stones " and " star-stones." " The ' *Ophite* ' is shaggy, hard, heavy, black, and *has the gift of speech;* when one prepares to cast it away, *it produces a sound similar to the cry of a child.* It is by means of this stone that Helenos foretold the ruin of Troy, his fatherland . . ." etc.[677]

Sanchoniathon and Philo Byblius, in referring to these *bétyles*, call them *"Animated* Stones." Photios repeats what Damaskios, Asklepiades, Isidoros and the physician Eusebios had asserted before him. The latter (Eusebios) never parted with his *ophites*, which he carried in his bosom, and received oracles from them, delivered *in a small voice resembling a low whistling.*[678] Arnobius (a holy man who, " from a Pagan had become one of the *lights of the Church,"* Christians tell their readers) confesses he could never meet on his passage with one of such stones without putting it questions, " which it answered occasionally in a *clear and sharp small voice."* Where is the difference between the Christian and the Pagan *ophites,* we ask?

It is also known that the famous stone at Westminster was called *liafail* — " the speaking stone," — which raised its voice only to name the king that had to be chosen. Cambry[679] says he saw it when it still bore the inscription[680] : —

> *Ni fallat fatum, Scoti quocumque locatum*
> *Invenient lapidem, regnasse tenentur ibidem.*

Finally, Suidas speaks of a certain Heraclios, who could distinguish at a glance the inanimate stones from those which were endowed with motion; and Pliny mentions stones which " ran away when a hand approached them." [681]

De Mirville — who seeks to justify the Bible — inquires very pertinently, why the monstrous stones of Stonehenge were called in days of old *chior-gaur* (from *Cor,* " dance," whence *chorea,* and *gaur,* a GIANT),

677. Falconnet.

678. The same, of course, as the " small voice " heard by Elijah after the earthquake at the mouth of the cave. (I *Kings,* xix. 12,)

679. *Monuments Celtiques.*

680. The rocking, or Logan, stones bear various names. The Celts had their *clacha-brath,* the " Destiny or judgment-stone "; the *divining-stone,* or " stone of the ordeal " and the oracle stone; the moving or animated stone of the Phoenicians; the rumbling stone of the Irish. Brittany has its *" pierres branlantes"* at Huelgoat. They are found in the Old and the New Worlds: in the British Islands, France, Spain, Italy, Russia, Germany, etc., as in North America. (See Hodson's *Letters from North America,* Vol. II. p. 440.) Pliny speaks of several in Asia (*Hist Nat.,* Lib. I, c. 96); and Apollonios Rhodios expatiates on the rocking stones, and says that they are "stones placed on the apex of a tumulus, and so sensitive *as to be movable by the mind"* (Ackerman's *Arth. Index,* p. 34), referring no doubt to the ancient priests who moved such stones by will-power and from a distance.

681. See *Dictionnaire des Religions,* par l'abbé Bertrard; art. on words " Héraclius " and " Bétyles."

or the dance of giants? And then he sends the reader to receive his reply from the Bishop of St. Gildas. But the authors of the *Voyage dans le Comté de Cornouailles, Sur les Traces des Géants,* and of various learned works on the ruins of Stonehenge,[682] Carnac and West Hoadley, give far better and more reliable information upon this particular subject. In those regions — true forests of rocks — immense monoliths are found, " some weighing over 500,000 kilograms." [683] These " hinging stones " of Salisbury Plain are believed to be the remains of a Druidical temple. But the Druids were historical men and not Cyclopes, nor giants. Who then, *if not giants, could ever raise such masses* (especially those at Carnac and West Hoadley), range them in such symmetrical order that they should represent the planisphere, and place them in such wonderful equipoise that they seem to hardly touch the ground, are set in motion at the slightest touch of the finger, and yet would resist the efforts of twenty men who should attempt to displace them.

We say, that most of these stones are the relics of the last Atlanteans. We shall be answered that all the geologists claim them to be of a natural origin. That, a rock when " weathering," *i. e.,* losing flake after flake of its substance under influence of weather, assumes this form. That, the " tors " in West England exhibit curious forms, also produced by this cause. That, finally, as all scientists consider the " rocking stones to be of purely natural origin, wind, rain, etc., causing disintegration of rocks in layers " — our statement will be justly denied, especially as " we see this process of rock-modification in progress around us today." Let us examine the case.

But read what Geology has to say, and you will learn that often these gigantic masses do not even belong to the countries wherein they are now fixed; that their geological congeners often pertain to strata unknown in those regions and to be found only far beyond the seas. Mr. William Tooke,[684] speculating upon the enormous blocks of granite which are strewn over Southern Russia and Siberia, tells the reader that there, where they now rest, there are neither rocks nor mountains; and that they must have been brought over " from immense distances and with prodigious efforts." Charton [685] speaks of a specimen of such rock " from Ireland," which had been submitted to the analysis of an eminent English geologist, who assigned to it a foreign origin, " *most probably African.*"

This is a strange *coincidence,* as Irish tradition attributes the origin

682. See, among others, *History of Pagan-ism in Caledonia,* by Dr. Th. A. Wise, F. R. A. S., etc.
683. Cambry.

684. French trans., *Sépulture des Tartares. Arch.* VII, p. 2227.
685. *Voyageurs Anciens et Modernes,* Vol. I, page 230.

of her circular stones to a *Sorcerer who brought them from Africa*. De Mirville sees in that sorcerer "an accursed Hamite." [686] We see in him a dark Atlantean, or perhaps even some earlier Lemurian, who had survived till the birth of the British Islands — GIANTS in every and any case. [687]

"Men," says Cambry, naïvely, "have nothing to do with it . . . for never could *human* power and industry undertake anything of this kind. Nature alone has accomplished it all [!!] and Science will demonstrate it some day." (!!) [688] Nevertheless, it is a *human*, though gigantic power, which has accomplished it, and no more "nature" alone than god or devil.

"Science," having undertaken to demonstrate that even the mind and Spirit of man are simply the production of *blind forces*, is quite capable of accepting the task. It may come out some fine morning, and seek to prove that nature alone has marshalled the gigantic rocks of Stonehenge, traced their position with mathematical precision, given them the form of the Dendera planisphere and of the signs of the Zodiac, and brought stones weighing over one million of pounds flying from Africa and Asia to England and Ireland!

It is true that Cambry recanted later on. "I had believed for a long time," he says, "that *Nature alone* could produce those wonders . . . but I *recant* . . . chance *is unable to create* such marvellous combinations . . . and those who placed the said rocks in equipoise, are the same who have raised the moving masses of the pond of Huelgoat, near Concarneau. . . ." Dr. John Watson, quoted by the same author, [689] says, when speaking of the *moving* rocks, or Rocking-Stones situated on the slope of Golcar (the "Enchanter"): "The astonishing movement of those masses poised in equilibrium made the Celts compare them to gods. . . ."

In *Stonehenge* [690] it is said that "Stonehenge is built of the stone of the district, a red sandstone, or 'sarsen' stone, locally called 'grey wethers.' But some of the stones, especially those which are said to have been devoted to astronomical purposes, have been brought from a distance, probably the North of Ireland."

To close, the reflections of a man of Science, in an article upon the subject published in 1850 in the *Revue Archéologique*, [691] are worthy of being quoted. Says the paper, concerning the rocking stones:—

686. Ham was no more a Titan or Giant than Shem and Japhet. They are either all Arkite Titans, as Faber shows them, or myths.

687. Diodorus Siculus (Bk. I) asserts that in the days of Isis, all men were of a vast stature, who were denominated by the Hellenes Giants. "Οἱ δ᾽ ἐν Αἰγύπτῳ μυθολογοῦσι κατὰ τὴν Ἴσιδος ἡλικίαν γεγονέναι τινὰς πολυσωμάτους."

688. Page 88.

689. *Antiquités Celtiques*, p. 99.

690. Flinders Petrie.

691. Page 473.

Every stone is a block whose weight would try the most powerful machines. There are, in a word, scattered throughout the globe, masses, before which the word *materials* seems to remain inexplicable, at the sight of which imagination is confounded, and that had to be endowed with a name as colossal as the things themselves. Besides which, these *immense rocking* stones, called sometimes *routers* — placed upright on one of their sides as on a point, their equipoise being so perfect that the slightest touch is sufficient to set them in motion . . . betray a most positive knowledge of statics. Reciprocal counter-motion, surfaces, plane, convex and concave, in turn . . . all this allies them to Cyclopean monuments, of which it can be said with good reason, repeating after de la Vega that "the demons seem to have worked on them more than men."[692]

For once we agree with our friends and foes, the Roman Catholics, and ask whether such prodigies of statics and equilibrium, applied to masses weighing millions of pounds, can be the work of Palaeolithic *savages,* of cave-men, taller than the average man in our century, yet ordinary mortals as we are? It is no use for *our* purpose to refer to the various traditions attached to the rocking-stones. Still, it may be as well to remind the English reader of Giraldus Cambrensis, who speaks of such a stone on the Isle of Mona, which returned to its place, every effort made to keep it elsewhere notwithstanding. At the time of the conquest of Ireland by Henry II, a Count Hugo Cestrensis, desiring to convince himself of the reality of the fact, tied the Mona stone to a far bigger one and had them thrown into the sea. On the following morning it was found in its accustomed place. . . .[692a] The learned William of Salisbury warrants the fact by testifying to its presence in the wall of a church where he had seen it in 1554. . . . And this reminds one of what Pliny said of the stone left by the Argonauts at Cyzicum, which the Cyzicans had placed in the Prytanea "whence it *ran away several times,* which forced them to lead it ..."[693] Here we have immense stones stated by all antiquity to be "living, moving, speaking and self-perambulating." They were also capable, it seems, of making people run away, since they have been called *routers* ("to

---

692. "It is difficult," writes Creuzer, "not to suspect in the structures of Tiryns and Mycenae planetary forces supposed to be moved by celestial powers, analogous to the famous Dactyli." (*Pelasges et Cyclopes.*) To this day Science is ignorant on the subject of the Cyclopes. They are supposed to have built all the so-called "Cyclopean" works whose erection necessitated several regiments of Giants, and — they were only seventy-seven in all (about one hundred, Creuzer thinks). They are called "Builders," and Occultism calls them the INITIATORS, who, initiating some Pelasgians, thus laid the foundation stone of true MASONRY.

Herodotus associates the Cyclopes with Perseus "the son of an Assyrian demon" (I, VI, p. 54). Raoul Rochette found that Palaimon, the Cyclops, to whom a sanctuary was raised, "was the Tyrian Hercules." Anyhow, he was the builder of the sacred columns of Gadir, covered with mysterious characters to which Apollonios of Tyana was the only one in his age to possess the key; and with figures which may still be found on the walls of Ellora, the gigantic ruins of the temple of Viśvakarman, "the builder and artificer of the Gods."

692a. *Itinerarium Cambriae,* II, vii.

693. *Nat. Hist.,* XXXVI, p. 592.

put to flight," to rout) and des Mousseaux shows them all to be prophetic stones and called *mad* stones.[694] "The rocking-stone is accepted
in Science. Why did it rock, why was it made to do so? One must be
blind not to see that this motion was one more means of divination,
and that they were called for this very reason ' the stones of truth.' "[695]

This is history, the Past of prehistoric times, warranting the same in
later ages. The Dracontia, sacred to the moon and the serpent, were
the more ancient " Rocks of Destiny " of older nations, whose motion,
or *rocking*, was a code perfectly clear to the initiated priests, who alone
had the key to this ancient *reading*. Vormius and Olaus Magnus show
that it was according to the orders of the oracle, "whose voice spoke
through the immense rocks raised by the colossal powers of ancient
giants," that the kings of Scandinavia were elected. " In India and
Persia," says Pliny, " it is she (the Persian Oitzoé) whom the magi
had to consult for the election of their sovereigns ";[696] and he describes [697] a rock overshadowing Harpasa, in Asia, and placed in such
a manner that " a single finger can move it, while the weight of the
whole body makes it resist." Why then should not the rocking stones
of Ireland, or those of Brinham, in Yorkshire, have served for the same

694. See his *Dieu et les Dieux*, p. 587.

695. De Mirville, *Fétichisme*.

Messrs. Richardson and Barth are said
to have been amazed at finding in the
Desert of Sahara the same trilithic and
raised stones they had seen in Asia, Cir-
cassia, Etruria, and in all the North of
Europe. Mr. Rivett-Carnac, *b. c. s.*, of
Allahâbâd, the distinguished Archaeologist,
shows the same amazement in finding the
description given by Sir J. Simpson of the
cuplike markings on stones and rocks in
England, Scotland, and other Western countries — " offering an extraordinary resemblance " to " the marks on the trap Boulders
which encircle the Barrows near Nâgpur "
(the city of Snakes). The eminent scholar
saw in this " another and very extraordinary addition to the mass of evidence . . .
that a branch of the nomadic tribes, who
swept at an early date over Europe, penetrated into India also." We say Lemuria,
Atlantis and her giants, and the earliest
races of the Fifth Root-Race had all a hand
in these baetuli, lithoi, and "magic" stones
in general. The cup marks noticed by Sir
J. Simpson, and the "holes scooped out on
the face " of rocks and monuments found by
Mr. Rivett-Carnac " of different sizes varying from six inches to an inch-and-a-half
in diameter, and in depth from one to one-

and-a-half inch . . . generally arranged in
perpendicular lines presenting many permutations in the number and size and arrange-
ment of the cups " — are simply *written*
RECORDS of the oldest races. Whosoever examines with attention the drawings made of
such marks in the *Archaeological Notes on
Ancient Sculpturing on Rocks in Kumaon,
India, etc.*, will find in it the most primitive style of marking or recording; something of the sort having been adopted by
the American inventors of the Morse code
of telegraphic writing, which reminds us of
the Ogham writing, a combination of long
and short strokes, as Mr. Rivett-Carnac describes it, " cut on sandstone." Sweden,
Norway, and Scandinavia are full of such
written records, the Runic characters having
followed the cup-marks and long and short
strokes. In Johannes Magnus' " *Infolio* "
one sees the representation of the demi-god,
the giant Starchaterus (Starkad, the pupil
of Hrossharsgrani, the Magician) who holds
under each arm a huge stone covered with
Runic characters; and Starkad, according
to Scandinavian legend, went to Ireland and
performed marvelous deeds in the North and
South, East and West. (See *Asgard and
the Gods*, p. 219.)

696. *Nat. Hist.*, Lib. lxxxvii, chap. 54.

697. In chap. 38, Lib. ii.

mode of *divination* or oracular communications? The hugest of them are evidently the relics of the Atlanteans; the smaller ones, such as Brinham Rocks, with some revolving stones on their summit, are copies from the more ancient lithoi. Had not the bishops of the middle ages destroyed all the plans of the *Dracontia* they could lay their hands on, Science would know more of these.[698] As it is, we know that they were universally used during long prehistoric ages, and all for the same purposes of prophecy and MAGIC. É. Biot, a member of the Institute of France, published in his *Antiquités de France*,[699] an article showing the *Chatam peramba* (the Field of Death, or ancient burial ground in Malabar), to be identical with the old tombs at Carnac — "a prominence and a central tomb. . . ." " Bones are found in them (the tombs)," he says, " and Mr. Hillwell tells us that some of these are enormous, the natives (of Malabar) calling the tombs the dwellings of Râkshasas (giants)." Several stone circles, "considered the work of the *Pañch Pândava* (five Pandus), as all such monuments are in India, so numerous in that country," when opened by the direction of Râjah Vasariddi, "were found to contain *human bones of a very large size.*"[700]

Again, de Mirville is right in his *generalization*, if not in his conclusions. As the long cherished theory that the Dracontia are mostly witnesses to "great natural geological commotions" (Charton), and "are the *work of Nature*" (Cambry) is now exploded, his remarks are very just.

Before the *impossibility* of such a theory is asserted, we advise Science to reflect . . . and, above all, no longer to class *Titans and Giants* among primitive legends: for their works are there, under our eyes, and those rocking stones will oscillate on their basis to the end of the world to help them to see clearer and realize once for all, that *one is not altogether a candidate for Charenton for believing in wonders certified to by the whole of Antiquity.*[701]

It is just what we can never repeat too often, though the voices of both Occultists and Roman Catholics are raised in the desert. Nevertheless, no one can fail to see that Science is as inconsistent, to say the least, in its modern speculations, as was ancient and medieval theology in *its* interpretations of the so-called *Revelation.* Science would have men descend from the pithecoid ape — a transformation requiring millions of years — and yet fears to make mankind older than 100,000 years! Science teaches the gradual transformation of species, natural selection and evolution from the lowest form to the highest;

698. Charton, the Author of *Voyageurs Anciens et Modernes*, quoted by de Mirville.
699. Vol. ix.
700. T. A. Wise, in *History of Paganism in Caledonia*, p. 36.
701. *Fétichisme*, p. 288.

from mollusc to fish, from reptile to bird and mammalian. Yet it refuses to man, who physiologically is only a higher mammal and animal,
such transformation of his external form. But if the monstrous
iguanodon of the Wealden may have been the ancestor of the diminu-
tive iguana of today, why could not the monstrous man of the Secret
Doctrine have become the modern man — the link between Animal and
Angel? Is there anything more unscientific in *this* " theory," than in
that of refusing to man any spiritual immortal Ego, making of him
an automaton, and ranking him, at the same time, *as a distinct genus*
in the system of Nature? Occult Sciences may be less scientific than
the present exact Sciences, they are withal more logical and consistent
in their teachings. Physical forces, and natural affinities of atoms may
be sufficient as factors to transform a plant into an animal; but it
requires more than a mere interplay between certain material aggregates
and their environment, to call to life a *fully conscious man;* even though
he were no more indeed than a ramification between two " poor
cousins " of the Quadrumanous order. Occult Sciences admit with
Haeckel that (objective) life on our globe " is a logical postulate of
Scientific natural history," but add that the rejection of a like *Spiritual*
involution, from *within without,* of invisible subjective Spirit-life —
eternal and a Principle in Nature — is more illogical, if possible, than to
say that the Universe and all in it has been gradually built by blind
forces inherent in matter, without any *external* help.

Suppose an Occultist were to claim that the first grand organ of a
cathedral had come originally into being in the following manner.
First, there was a progressive and gradual elaboration in Space of an
organizable material, which resulted in the production of a state of
matter named *organic* PROTEIN. Then, under the influence of incident
forces, those states having been thrown into a phase of unstable equilibrium, they slowly and majestically evolved into and resulted in new
combinations of carved and polished wood, of brass pins and staples,
of leather and ivory, wind-pipes and bellows. After which, having
adapted all its parts into one harmonious and symmetrical machine, the
organ suddenly pealed forth Mozart's *Requiem.* This was followed by
a Sonata of Beethoven, etc., *ad infinitum*; its keys playing of themselves and the wind blowing into the pipes by its own inherent force
and fancy. . . . What would Science say to such a theory? Yet,
it is precisely in such wise that the materialistic *savants* tell us that
the Universe was formed, with its millions of beings, and man, its
spiritual crown.

Whatever may have been the real inner thought of Mr. Herbert
Spencer, when writing on the subject of the gradual transformation of
species, what he says in it applies to our doctrine. " Construed in

terms of evolution, every kind of being is conceived as a product of modifications wrought by insensible gradations *on a pre-existing kind of being.*[702] Then why, in this case, should not historical man be the product of a modification on a pre-existent and pre-historical kind of man, even supposing for argument's sake that there is *nothing* within him to last longer than, or live independently of, his physical structure? But this is not so! For, when we are told that " organic matters are produced in the laboratory by what we may literally call *artificial evolution,"* [703] we answer the distinguished English philosopher, that Alchemists and great adepts have done as much, and, indeed, far more, before the chemists ever attempted to "build out of dissociated elements complex combinations." The *Homunculi* of Paracelsus are a fact in Alchemy, and will become one in Chemistry very likely, and then Mrs. Shelley's Frankenstein will have to be regarded as a prophecy. But no chemist, or Alchemist either, will ever endow such a " Frankenstein Monster " with more than animal instinct, unless indeed he does that which the " Progenitors " are credited with, namely, if he leaves his own physical body, and incarnates in the " empty form." But even this would be an *artificial,* not a natural man, for our " Progenitors " had, in the course of eternal evolution, to become *gods* before they became men.

The above digression, if one, is an attempt at justification before the few thinking men of the coming century who may read this. But this accounts also for the reason why the best and most spiritual men of our present day can no longer be satisfied with either Science or theology; and why they prefer any such " psychic craze " to the dogmatic assertions of both, neither of the two having anything better to offer than *blind* faith in their respective infallibility. *Universal* tradition is indeed the far safer guide in life. And universal tradition shows primitive man living for ages together with his Creators and first instructors — the Elohim — in the World's " Garden of Eden," or " Delight." We shall treat of the Divine Instructors in Stanza XII.

---

45. THE FIRST GREAT WATERS CAME. THEY SWALLOWED THE SEVEN GREAT ISLANDS (a).

---

46. ALL HOLY SAVED, THE UNHOLY DESTROYED. WITH THEM MOST OF THE HUGE ANIMALS PRODUCED FROM THE SWEAT OF THE EARTH (b).

702. *Essays on Physiology,* Subj. page   703. Appendix to *Principles of Biology,*
144.   page 482.

(a) As this subject — the fourth great deluge on our globe in this Round — is fully treated in the chapters that follow the last Stanza, to say anything more at present would be mere repetition. The seven great islands (Dvipas) belonged to the continent of Atlantis. The secret teachings show that the "Deluge" overtook the Fourth, giant Race, not on account of their depravity, or because they had become "black with sin," but simply because such is the fate of every continent, which — like everything else under our Sun — is born, lives, becomes decrepit, and dies. This was when the Fifth Race was in its infancy.

(b) Thus the giants perished — the magicians and the sorcerers, adds the fancy of popular tradition, but "all holy saved," and alone the "unholy were destroyed." This was due, however, as much to the *prevision* of the "holy" ones, who had not lost the use of their "third eye," as to Karma and natural law. Speaking of the subsequent race (our Fifth Humanity), the commentary says: —

"*Alone the handful of those Elect, whose divine instructors had gone to inhabit that Sacred Island —'from whence the last Savior will come' — now kept mankind from becoming one-half the exterminator of the other* [as mankind does now — H. P. B.]. *It* (mankind) *became divided. Two-thirds of it were ruled by Dynasties of lower, material Spirits of the earth, who took possession of the easily accessible bodies; one-third remained faithful, and joined with the nascent Fifth Race — the divine Incarnates. When the Poles moved* (for the fourth time) *this did not affect those who were protected, and who had separated from the Fourth Race. Like the Lemurians — alone the ungodly Atlanteans perished, and 'were seen no more.'* . . . ."

STANZA XII

THE FIFTH RACE AND ITS DIVINE INSTRUCTORS

§§ (47) The remnants of the first two races disappear for ever. Groups of the various Atlantean races saved from the Deluge along with the Forefathers of the Fifth. (48) The origins of our present Race, the Fifth. The first divine Dynasties. (49) The earliest glimmerings in History, now pinned to the allegorical chronology of the Bible, and "universal" History slavishly following it. —The nature of the first instructors and civilizers of mankind.

47. FEW (*men*) REMAINED. SOME YELLOW, SOME BROWN AND BLACK, AND SOME RED, REMAINED. THE MOON-COLORED (*of the primitive Divine Stock*) WERE GONE FOR EVER (*a*) . . . .

48. THE FIFTH RACE PRODUCED FROM THE HOLY STOCK (*remained*). IT WAS RULED BY HER FIRST DIVINE KINGS.

49. THE "SERPENTS" WHO RE-DESCENDED; WHO MADE PEACE WITH THE FIFTH (*Race*), WHO TAUGHT AND INSTRUCTED IT (*b*) . . . .

(*a*) This verse (47) relates to the Fifth Race. History does not begin with it, but living and ever-recurring tradition does. History — or what is called history — does not go farther back than the fantastic origins of our fifth sub-race, a " few thousands " of years. It is the sub-divisions of this first sub-race of the Fifth Root-Race which are referred to in the sentence, " Some yellow, some brown and black, and some red, remained." The "moon colored " (*i. e.*, the First and the Second Races) were gone for ever — ay, without leaving any traces whatever; and that, so far back as the third " Deluge " of the Third Lemurian race, that " Great Dragon," whose tail sweeps whole nations out of existence in the twinkling of an eye. And this is the true meaning of the Verse in the COMMENTARY which says:

" *The* GREAT DRAGON *has respect but for the '* SERPENTS ' *of* WISDOM, *the Serpents whose holes are now under the triangular stones,*" *i. e.*, " the Pyramids, at the four corners of the world."

(*b*) This tells us clearly that which is mentioned more than once elsewhere in the Commentaries; namely, that the Adepts or " Wise " men of the three Races (the Third, Fourth and the Fifth) dwelt in subterranean habitats, generally under some kind of pyramidal structure, if not actually under a pyramid. For such "pyramids" existed in the four corners of the world and were never the monopoly of the land of the Pharaohs, though until found scattered all over the two Americas, under and over ground, beneath and amidst virgin forests, as in plain and vale, they were supposed to be the exclusive property of Egypt. If the true geometrically correct pyramids are no longer found in European regions, many of the supposed early *neolithic* caves, of the colossal triangular, pyramidal and conical *menhirs* in the Morbihan, and Brittany generally; many of the Danish tumuli and even of the "giant tombs" of Sardinia with their inseparable companions, the *nuraghi*, are so many more or less clumsy copies of the pyramids. Most of these are the works of the first settlers on the newly-born continent and isles of Europe, the — "some yellow, some brown and black, and some red" — races that remained after the submersion of the last Atlantean continents and islands (850,000 years ago), with the exception of Plato's Atlantean island, and before the arrival of the great Aryan races; while others were built by the earliest immigrants from the East. Those who can hardly accept the antiquity of the human race so far back as the 57,000 years assigned by Dr. Dowler to the skeleton found by him at New Orleans on the banks of the Mississippi, will, of course, reject these facts. But they may find themselves mistaken some day. It is the foolish self-glorification of the Arcadians who styled themselves προσέληνοι — older than the moon — and of the people of Attica, who claimed that they had existed before the sun appeared in heaven, that we may disparage, not their undeniable antiquity. Nor can we laugh at the universal belief that we had giant ancestors. The fact that the bones of the mammoth and mastodon, and, in one case, those of a gigantic salamander, have been mistaken for human bones, does not make away with the difficulty that, of all the mammalians, man is the only one whom science will not allow to have dwarfed down, like all other animal frames, from the giant *homo diluvii* to the creature between 5 and 6 feet that he is now.

But the "Serpents of Wisdom" have preserved their records well, and the history of the human evolution *is* traced in heaven as it is traced on underground walls. Humanity and the *stars* are bound together indissolubly, because of the *intelligences* that rule the latter.

Modern symbologists may scoff at this and call it "fancy," but "it is unquestionable that the Deluge has (ever) been associated in the legends of some Eastern peoples not only with the Pyramids, but also with the constellations," writes Mr. Staniland Wake.[704] The "Old Dragon" is identical with the "great Flood." Says Mr. Proctor:[705]

704. *The Great Pyramid.*   705. In *Knowledge*, Vol. I, p. 241.

We know that in the past the constellation of the Dragon was at the pole, or boss, of the celestial sphere. In stellar temples . . . the Dragon would be the uppermost or ruling constellation . . . it is singular how closely the constellations . . . correspond in sequence and in range of right ascension with the events recorded respecting the [Biblical] Flood.

The reasons for this *singularity* have been made clear in this work. But it shows only that there were *several* Deluges mixed up in the memories and traditions of the sub-races of the Fifth Race. The first great " Flood " was astronomical and cosmical, while several others were *terrestrial*. Yet, this did not prevent our very learned friend Mr. Gerald Massey — an *Initiate* truly in the mysteries of the British Museum, still only a *Self*-initiate — from declaring and insisting that the *Atlantean* submersion and Deluge were only the anthropomorphized fancies of ignorant people; and that Atlantis was no better than an *astronomical allegory*. Nevertheless, the great Zodiacal allegory is based upon historical events, and one can hardly interfere with the other; and it stands also to reason that every student of Occultism knows what that astronomical and zodiacal allegory means. Smith shows in the Nimrod Epic of the Assyrian tablets the real meaning of it. Its " *twelve cantos* " refer to the " annual course of the Sun through the twelve months of the year. Each tablet answers to a special month, and contains a distinct reference to the animal forms in the signs of the Zodiac "; the eleventh canto being " consecrated to Rimmon, the God of storms and of rain, and harmonizes with the eleventh sign of the Zodiac — Aquarius, or the Waterman." [706] But even this is preceded in the old records by the *pre*-astronomical Cosmic FLOOD, which became allegorized and symbolized in the above Zodiacal or Noah's Flood. But this has nothing to do with Atlantis. The Pyramids are closely connected with the ideas of both the Great Dragon (the constellation), the " Dragons of Wisdom," or the great Initiates of the Third and Fourth Races, and the Floods of the Nile, regarded as a divine reminder of the great Atlantic Flood. The astronomical records of Universal History, however, are said to have had their beginnings with the Third Sub-race of the Fourth Root-race or the Atlanteans. When was it? Occult data show that even since the time of the regular establishment of the Zodiacal calculations in Egypt, *the poles have been thrice inverted*.

We will presently return once more to this statement. Such symbols as are represented by the Signs of the Zodiac — a fact which offers a handle to materialists upon which to hang their one-sided theories and opinions — have too profound a signification, and their bearing upon

706. *Nineteenth Century*, 1882, p. 236.

our Humanity is too important to suffer dismissal in a few words. Meanwhile, we have to consider the meaning of that other statement which mentions [707] the first *divine Kings*, who are said to have " re-descended," guided and *instructed* our Fifth Race after the last deluge! We shall consider this last claim historically in the sections that follow, but must end with a few more details on the subject of "Serpents." The rough commentaries on the Archaic Stanzas have to end here. Further elucidation requires proofs obtained from ancient, medieval, and modern works that have treated of these subjects. All such evidence has now to be gathered in, collated and brought together in better order, so as to compel the attention of the reader to this wealth of historical proofs. And as the manifold meaning of the weird symbol — so often referred to and suggestive of the " tempter of man " in the orthodox light of the church — can never be too strongly insisted upon, it seems more advisable to exhaust the subject by every available proof at this juncture, even at the risk of repetition. The Titans and Kabirs have been invariably made out by our theologians and some pious symbologists as indissolubly connected with the grotesque personage called *devil*, and every proof to the contrary has been hitherto as invariably rejected and ignored; therefore, the occultist must neglect nothing which may tend to defeat this conspiracy of slander. It is proposed to divide the subjects involved in these three last verses into several groups, and examine them in this final chapter as carefully and as fully as space permits. A few more details may thus be added to the general evidences of antiquity, on the most disputed tenets of Occultism and the Esoteric Doctrine — the bulk of which will be found in Part II on Symbology.

SERPENTS AND DRAGONS UNDER DIFFERENT SYMBOLISMS

The name of the Dragon in Chaldaea was not written phonetically, but was represented by two monograms, *probably* meaning, according to the Orientalists, " the scaly one." " This description," very pertinently remarks G. Smith, " of course might apply either to a fabulous dragon, a serpent, or a fish," and we may add: " It applies in one case to *Makara*, the tenth Zodiacal sign, meaning in Sanskrit a non-descript amphibious animal, generally called Crocodile, and really signifying something else."[708] This, then, is a virtual admission that the Assyriologists, at all events, know nothing certain as to the status of the " Dragon " in ancient Chaldaea, whence the Hebrews got *their* symbolism, only to be afterwards robbed of it by the Christians, who made of the " Scaly one " a living entity and a maleficent power.

707. Verse 48.   708. *Vide* Part II, § xxv, " The Mysteries of the Hebdomad."

A specimen of Dragons, "winged and scaled," may be seen in the British Museum. Representing the events of the Fall according to the same authority, there are also two figures sitting on each side of a tree, and holding out their hands to the "apple," while at the back of the "Tree" is the Dragon-Serpent. Esoterically, the two figures are two "Chaldees" ready for initiation, the Serpent symbolizing the "Initiator"; while the jealous gods, who curse the three, are the exoteric profane clergy. Not much of the literal "Biblical event" there, as any occultist can see.

"The Great Dragon has respect but for the Serpents of Wisdom," says the Stanza; thus proving the correctness of our explanation of the two figures and the "Serpent."

"*The Serpents who redescended .... who taught and instructed*" the Fifth Race. What sane man is capable of believing in our day that *real* serpents are hereby meant? Hence the rough guess, now become almost an axiom with the men of science, that those who wrote in antiquity upon various sacred Dragons and Serpents either were superstitious and credulous people, or were bent upon deceiving those more ignorant than themselves. Yet, from Homer downwards, the term implied something hidden from the profane.

"Terrible are the gods when they manifest themselves" — those *gods* whom men call Dragons. And Aelianus, treating in his *De Naturā Animalium* of these Ophidean symbols, makes certain remarks which show that he understood well the nature of this most ancient of symbols. Thus he most pertinently explains with regard to the above Homeric verse:— "For the Dragon, while sacred and to be worshiped, *has within himself something still more of the divine nature* of which it is better [for others?] to remain in ignorance." [709]

This "Dragon" having a septenary meaning, the highest and the lowest may be given. The former is identical with the "Self-born," the Logos (the Hindû *Aja*). He was the second person of the Trinity, the Son, with the Christian Gnostics called the Naasenians, or Serpent-Worshipers. His symbol was the constellation of the Dragon. [710] Its seven "stars" are the seven stars held in the hand of the "Alpha and Omega" in *Revelation*. In its most terrestrial meaning, the term "Dragon" was applied to the *Wise* men.

This portion of the religious symbolism of antiquity is very abstruse and mysterious, and may remain incomprehensible to the profane. In our modern day it so jars on the Christian ear that it can hardly escape,

---

709. Book xi, ch. 17.
710. As shown by H. Lizeray in the *Trinité Chrétienne Dévoilée* — placed between the immutable Father (the Pole, a fixed Point) and mutable matter, the Dragon transmits to the latter the influences received by him from the Pole, whence his name — the *Verbum*.

all civilization notwithstanding, being regarded as a direct denunciation
of the most cherished Christian dogmas, the subject of which required,
to do it justice, the pen and genius of Milton, whose poetical fiction
has now taken root in the Church as a revealed dogma.

Did the allegory of the Dragon and his supposed conqueror in
Heaven originate with St. John, and in his *Revelation*? Emphatically
we answer — No. His " Dragon " is Neptune, the symbol of Atlantean
magic.

To demonstrate the negation the reader is asked to examine the
symbolism of the Serpent or the Dragon under its several aspects.

THE SIDEREAL AND COSMIC GLYPHS

Every astronomer — besides Occultists and Astrologers — knows
that, figuratively, the astral light, the milky way, and also the path
of the Sun to the tropics of Cancer and Capricorn, as well as the
circles of the Sidereal or Tropical year, were always called " Serpents " in the allegorical and mystic phraseology of the adepts.

This, cosmically, as well as metaphorically. Poseidon is a " Dragon " : " *Chozzar,* called by the profane Neptune " (Peratae Gnostics) ;
the " Good and Perfect Serpent," the Messiah of the Naaseni, whose
symbol in Heaven is *Draco.*

But one ought to discriminate between the characters of this symbol.
For instance : Zoroastrian Esotericism is identical with that of the
Secret Doctrine ; and when, as an example, we read in the *Vendîdâd*
complaints uttered against the " Serpent," whose bites have transformed the beautiful, eternal spring of Airyana Vaejo, changing it into
winter, generating disease and death, at the same time as mental and
psychic consumption, every occultist knows that the Serpent alluded to
is the north pole, as also the pole of the heavens.[711] The latter produces the seasons according to the angle at which it penetrates the
center of the earth. The two axes were *no more parallel;* hence the
eternal spring of Airyana Vaejo by the good river Daitya had disappeared, and " the Aryan Magi had to emigrate to Sogdiana "— say the
exoteric accounts. But the esoteric teaching states that the pole had
passed through the equator, and that the " land of bliss " of the Fourth
Race, its inheritance from the Third, had now become the region of
desolation and woe. This alone ought to be an incontrovertible proof
of the great antiquity of the Zoroastrian Scriptures. The Neo-Aryans
of the post-diluvian age could, of course, hardly recognize the mountains, on the summits of which their forefathers had met *before the
Flood,* and conversed with the pure " Yazatas " (celestial Spirits of

---

711. Symbolised by the Egyptians under the form of a Serpent with a hawk's head.

the Elements), whose life and *food* they had once shared. As shown by Eckstein,[712] " the *Vendîdâd* seems to point out a great change in the atmosphere of central Asia; strong volcanic eruptions and the collapse of a whole range of mountains in the neighborhood of the Kara-Korum chain."

The Egyptians, according to Eusebius, who for once (and for a wonder) wrote the truth, symbolized Kosmos by a large fiery circle, representing a serpent with a hawk's head lying across its diameter. Here we have the pole of the earth within the plane of the ecliptic, attended with all the fiery consequences that must arise from such a state of the heavens: when the whole Zodiac in 25,000 (odd) years, must have reddened with the solar blaze, and *each sign must have been vertical* to the polar region.[713]

Meru — the abode of the gods — was placed, as before explained, in the North Pole, while *Pâtâla*, the nether region, was supposed to lie in the South. As each symbol in esoteric philosophy has *seven keys*, geographically, *Meru* and *Pâtâla* have one significance and represent localities; while astronomically, they have another, and mean " the two poles," which meaning ended by their being often rendered in *exoteric* sectarianism — the " Mountain " and the " Pit," or Heaven and Hell. If we hold at present only to the astronomical and geographical significance, it may be found that the ancients knew the topography and nature of the Arctic and Antarctic regions better than any of our modern astronomers; they had reasons, and good ones for naming one the *" Mountain "* and the other the *" Pit."* As the author just quoted half explains, *Helion* and *Acheron* meant nearly the same:

Heli-on is the Sun in the highest [Helios, Heli-on, the "most high"]; and *Acheron* is 32 deg. above the pole, and 32 below it, the allegorical river being thus supposed to touch the northern horizon in the latitude of 32 degrees. The vast concave, that is for ever hidden from our sight and which surrounded the southern pole, being therefore called the PIT, while observing, toward the Northern pole that a certain circuit in the heavens always appeared above the horizon — they called it the Mountain. As Meru is the high abode of the Gods, these were said to *ascend* and *descend* periodically; by which (astronomically) the *Zodiacal* gods were meant, the passing of the original North Pole of the Earth to the South Pole of the heaven.

" In that age," adds the author of that curious work, the *Sphinxiad*, and of *Urania's Key to the Revelations* —

at noon, the ecliptic would be parallel with the meridian, and part of the Zodiac would descend from the North Pole to the north horizon; crossing the *eight coils of the Serpent* (eight sidereal years, or over 200,000 solar years), which would seem like an imaginary *ladder* with *eight staves* reaching from the earth up to the pole, *i. e.*, the throne of Jove. Up this ladder, then, the

712. *Revue Archéologique*, 8th year, 1885.   713. See Mackey's *Sphinxiad*.

Gods, *i. e.*, the signs of the Zodiac, ascended and descended. (Jacob's ladder and the angels) . . . It is more than 400,000 years since the Zodiac formed the sides of this ladder. . . .

This is an ingenious explanation, even if it is not altogether free from occult heresy. Yet it is nearer the truth than many of a more scientific and especially theological character. As just said, the Christian trinity was purely astronomical from its beginning, which made Rutilius say — of those who euhemerized it — "*Judaea gens, radix stultorum.*"

But the profane, and especially the Christian fanatics, ever in search of scientific corroboration for their *dead-letter* texts, will persist in seeing in the celestial pole the true Serpent of *Genesis*, Satan, the Enemy of mankind, instead of what it is — a cosmic metaphor. *When the gods are said to forsake the earth*, it does not only mean the gods, protectors and instructors, but also the *minor* gods — the regents of the Zodiacal signs. Yet, the former, as actual and existing Entities which gave birth to, nursed, and instructed mankind in its early youth, appear in every Scripture, in that of the Zoroastrians as much as in the Hindû Gospels. Ormazd, or Ahura-Mazda, the "Lord of Wisdom," is the synthesis of the Amshâspends (or *Amesha-Spentas* — "Immortal Benefactors"),[714] the "Word," however, or the *Logos* and its six highest aspects in Mazdyanism. These "Immortal Benefactors" are described in *Zamyad yasht* as the

Amesha-Spentas, the shining, having efficacious eyes, great, helpful . . . imperishable and pure . . . which are all seven of like mind, like speech, all seven doing alike . . . which are *the creators and destroyers of the creatures* of Ahura-Mazda, their creators and overseers, their protectors and rulers . . .

These few lines alone indicate the dual and even the triple character of the Amshâspends, our Dhyân-Chohans or the "Serpents of Wisdom." They are identical with, and yet separate from Ormazd (Ahura-Mazda). They are also the Angels of the Stars of the Christians — the Star-yazatas of the Zoroastrians — or again the seven planets (including the sun) of every religion.[715] The epithet — "the shining having efficacious eyes" — proves it. This on the physical and sidereal planes. On the spiritual, they are the divine powers of Ahura-Mazda; but on the astral or psychic plane again, they are the "Builders," the "watchers," the *Pitaras* (fathers), and the first Preceptors of mankind.

When mortals shall have become sufficiently spiritualized, there will be no more need of *forcing* them into a correct comprehension of an-

714. Also translated as "blissful Immortals" by Dr. W. Geiger; but the first is more correct.

715. These "seven" became the eight, the Ogdoad, of the later *materialised* religions, the seventh, or the highest principle, being no longer the pervading Spirit, the Synthesis, but becoming an anthropomorphic number, or additional unit.

cient Wisdom. Men will *know* then, that there never yet was a great World-reformer, whose name has passed into our generation, who (*a*) was not a direct emanation of the Logos (under whatever name known to us), *i. e.*, an *essential* incarnation of one of " the seven," of the " divine Spirit who is sevenfold "; and (*b*) who had not appeared before, during the past Cycles. They will recognize, then, the cause which produces in history and chronology certain riddles of the ages; the reason why, for instance, it is impossible *for them* to assign any reliable date to Zoroaster, who is found multiplied by twelve and fourteen in the *Dabistan;* why the Rishis and Manus are so mixed up in their numbers and individualities; why Krishna and Buddha speak of themselves as *re-incarnations, i. e.,* Krishna is identified with the Rishi Nârâyana, and Gautama gives a series of his previous births; and why the former, especially, being " the *very supreme* Brahmâ," is yet called *Amśâmśâvatâra —* " a part of a part " only of the Supreme on Earth. Finally, why Osiris is a great God, and at the same time a " prince on Earth," who reappears in Thoth-Hermes, and why Jesus (in Hebrew, Joshua) of Nazareth is recognized, cabalistically, in Joshua, the Son of Nun, as well as in other personages. The esoteric doctrine explains it by saying that each of these (as many others) had first appeared on earth as one of the seven powers of the Logos, individualized as a God or " Angel " (messenger); then, mixed with matter, they had re-appeared in turn as great sages and instructors who " taught the Fifth Race," after having instructed the two preceding races, had ruled during the Divine Dynasties, and had finally sacrificed themselves, to be reborn under various circumstances for the good of mankind, and for its salvation at certain critical periods; until in their last incarnations they had become truly only " the parts of a part " on earth, though *de facto* the One Supreme in Nature.

This is the metaphysics of Theogony. And, as every " Power " among the SEVEN has (once individualized) in his charge one of the elements of creation, and rules over it,[716] hence the many meanings in every symbol, which, unless interpreted according to the esoteric methods, generally lead to an inextricable confusion.

Does the Western Kabalist — generally an opponent of the Eastern Occultist — require a proof? Let him open Éliphas Lévi's *Histoire de la Magie,*[717] and carefully examine his *" Grand Symbole Kabalistique "* of the *Zohar.* He will find, on the engraving given, a *white* man standing erect and a *black* woman upside down, *i. e.,* standing on her head, her legs passing under the extended arms of the male figure, and pro-

716. These elements are:— The cosmic, the terrene, the mineral, the vegetable, the animal, the aqueous, and finally the human — in their physical, spiritual, and psychic aspects. 717. Page 53.

truding behind his shoulders, while their hands join at an angle on each side. Eliphas Lévi makes of it, God and Nature; or God, "light," mirrored inversely in "Nature and Matter," darkness. Kabalistically and symbolically he is right, but only so far as emblematical cosmogony goes. Nor has he invented the symbol any more than the Kabalists have: the two figures in white and black stone have existed in the temples of Egypt from time immemorial — agreeably to tradition; and historically — ever since the day of King Cambyses, who personally saw them. Therefore the symbol must have been in existence nearly 2500 years ago. This, at the very least, for that Persian sovereign, who was a son of Cyrus the Great, succeeded his father in the year 529 B.C. These figures were the two *Kabiri personifying the opposite poles.* Herodotus[718] tells posterity that when Cambyses entered the temple of the Kabirim, he went into an inextinguishable fit of laughter, on perceiving what he thought a man erect and a woman standing on the top of her head before him. These were the poles, however, whose symbol was intended to commemorate "the passing of the original North Pole of the Earth to the South Pole of the Heaven," as perceived by Mackey.[719] But they represented also the poles *inverted*, in consequence of the great inclination of the axis, bringing each time as a result the displacement of the Oceans, the submersion of the polar lands, and the consequent *upheaval* of new continents in the equatorial regions, and *vice versa.* These Kabirim were the "Deluge"·gods.

This may help us to get at the key of the seemingly hopeless confusion among the numbers of names and titles given to one and the same gods, and classes of gods. Faber showed already, at the beginning of this century, the identity of the Corybantes, Curetes, Dioscuri, Anaktes, Di Magni, Idaei Dactyli, Lares, Penates, Manes,[720] Titans, and Aletae with the KABIRI. And we have shown that the latter were the same as the Manus, the Rishis and our Dhyân Chohans, who incarn-

---

718. *Thalia*, No. 37.

719. Who adds that the Egyptians had various ways of representing the angles of the Poles. Also in Perry's *View of the Levant* there is "a figure representing the South Pole of the Earth in the constellation of the Harp," in which the poles appear like two *straight rods*, surmounted with hawks' wings, but they were also often represented as serpents with heads of hawks, one at each end.

720. Faber and Bishop Cumberland would make them all the later pagan personifications, as the former writer has it, of "the Noetic Ark, and no other than the Patriarch [Noah] and his family" (!). See his *Cabiri*, Vol. I, 136; because, we are told,

"after the Deluge in commemoration of the event, the pious Noachidae had established a religious festival, which was, later on, corrupted by their *impious* descendants; demons or hero-gods; and at length unblushing obscenity usurped the name and garb of religion" (Vol. I. p. 10). Now this is indeed putting an extinguisher upon the human reasoning powers, not only of antiquity, but even of our present generations. Reverse the statement, and explain after the words "Noah and his family" that what is meant by that patriarch and family is simply the Jewish version of a Samothracian mystery, of *Saturn*, or *Kronos-Sadic* and his *Sons*, and then we may say *Amen.*

ated in the Elect of the Third and Fourth Races. Thus, while in Theogony the Kabiri-Titans were seven great gods: cosmically and astronomically the Titans were called Atlantes, because, perhaps, as Faber
says, they were connected (*a*) with *At-al-as* " the divine Sun," and (*b*)
with *tit* " the deluge." But this, if true, is only the exoteric version.
Esoterically, the meaning of their symbols depends on the appellation,
or title, used. The seven mysterious, awe-inspiring great gods — the
Dioscuri,[721] the deities surrounded with the darkness of occult nature
— become the *Idaei* (or Idaeic finger) with the adept-healer by metals.
The true etymology of the name *lares* (now signifying "ghosts") must
be sought in the Etruscan word *" lars,"* " conductor," " leader." Sanchoniathon translates the word *Aletae* as fire worshipers, and Faber
believes it derived from *Al-Orit,* " the god of fire." Both are right, as
in both cases it is a reference to the Sun (the highest God), toward
whom the planetary gods "gravitate" (astronomically and allegorically)
and whom they worship. As *Lares,* they are truly the Solar Deities,
though Faber's etymology, who says that *" lar "* is a contraction of
" El-Ar," the solar deity, is not very correct. They are the " lares,"
the conductors and leaders of men. As *Aletae,* they were the seven
planets — astronomically; and as *Lares,* the regents of the same, our
protectors and rulers — mystically. For purposes of exoteric or phallic worship, as also cosmically, they were the Kabiri, their attributes
being recognized in these two capacities by the name of the temples to
which they respectively belonged, and those of their priests. They all
belonged, however, to the Septenary creative and informing groups of
Dhyân Chohans. The Sabaeans, who worshiped the " regents of the
Seven planets " as the Hindûs do their Rishis, held Seth and his son
Hermes (Enoch or *Enos*) as the highest among the planetary gods. Seth
and Enos were borrowed from the Sabaeans and then disfigured by the
Jews (exoterically); but the truth can still be traced about them even
in *Genesis.*[722] Seth is the " progenitor " of those early men of the
Third Race in whom the " Planetary " angels had incarnated—a Dhyân
Chohan himself, who belonged to the *informing* gods; and Enos (Hanoch or Enoch) or Hermes, was said to be *his* son — because it was
a generic name for all the early *Seers* (" Enoichion "). Thence the
worship. The Arabic writer Soyuti says that the earliest records mention Seth, or *Set,* as the founder of Sabaeanism; and therefore that the

<hr />

721. Who became later on, with the
Greeks, limited only to Castor and Pollux.
But in the days of Lemuria, the *Dioscuri,*
the " Egg-born," were the Seven Dhyân
Chohans (Agnishvâtta-Kumâra) who incarnated in the Seven Elect of the Third Race.
722. Clement of Alexandria recognized

the astronomical significance of chapter xxv
et seq. of *Exodus.* According to the Mosaic
doctrine, he says that the seven planets help '
in the generation of terrestrial things. The
two cherubs standing on the two sides of
the sacred tetragrammaton represent the
Ursa Major and Ursa Minor.

pyramids which embody the planetary system were regarded as the place of sepulture of both Seth and *Idris* (Hermes or Enoch) ;[723] that thither Sabaeans proceeded on pilgrimage, and *chanted prayers seven times* a day, *turning to the North* (the Mount Meru, Kaph, Olympus, etc., etc.) [724] Abd Allatif says curious things about the Sabaeans and their books. So does Shehab Eddin Ahmed Ben Yahya, who wrote 200 years later. While the latter maintains that " each pyramid was consecrated *to a star* " (a star *regent* rather), Abd Allatif assures us " that he had read in Sabaean books that one pyramid was the tomb of Agathodaimon and the other of Hermes." [725] " Agathodaimon was none other than Seth, and, according to some writers, Hermes was his son," adds Mr. Staniland Wake in *The Great Pyramid.*[726]

Thus, while in Samothrace and the oldest Egyptian temples they were the great Cosmic Gods (the seven and the *forty-nine* Sacred Fires), in the Grecian fanes their rites became mostly phallic, therefore to the profane, obscene. In the latter case they were 3 and 4, or 7 — the male and female principles — (the *crux ansata*) ; this division showing why some classical writers held that they were only three, while others named four. And these were — the Kabiri — Axieros (in his female aspect, Demeter) ; Axiokersa (Persephone) ;[727] Axiokersos (Pluto or Hades) ; and Kadmos or Kadmilos (Hermes — not the ithyphallic Hermes mentioned by Herodotus [728] but " he of the sacred legend," explained only during the Samothracian mysteries). This identification, due, according to the Scholiast,[729] to an indiscretion of Mnaseas, is none at all, as names alone do not reveal much. There were still others again who maintained, being as right in their way, that there were only two Kabiri. These were, esoterically, the two Dioscuri, Castor and Pollux, and exoterically, Jupiter and Bacchus. The two personified the terrestrial poles, geodesically; the terrestrial, and the pole of the heavens — astronomically, as also the physical and the spiritual man. The story of Semele and Jupiter and the birth of Bacchus, the *Bimatris*, with all the circumstances attending it, needs

723. See Vyse, *Operations carried on at the Pyramids of Gizeh*, Vol. II, p. 359.
724. See Palgrave, Vol. II, p. 264.
725. Vyse, Vol. II. p. 342.
726. Page 57.
727. It is a curious idea — yet one not very far from the truth, perhaps — that speculation of Mackey, the self-made Adept of Norwich, found in his *Mythological Astronomy*, p. 51. He says that the Kabiri named Axieros and Axiokersa derived their names (a) from *Kab* or *Cab*, a measure, and from *Urim*, the heavens: the Kabirim being thus " a measure of the heavens"; and (b) that

their distinctive names, implying the *principle of generation*, referred to the sexes. For, " the word *sex* was formerly understood by *ax;* which has now settled . . . into sex." And he refers to *Encyclopaedia Londinensis* at the word *"aspiration."* " Now if we give the aspirated sound to Axieros, it 'would be *Sasieros;* and the other pole would be *Sasiokersa.* The two poles would thus become the generators of the other powers of nature — they would be the *parents:* therefore the most powerful gods."
728. II, 51.
729. On Apollonios Rhodios, I, 217.

only to be read esoterically to understand the allegory. The parts played in the event by the fire, water, earth, etc., in the many versions, will show how " the father of the gods " and the " merry God of the wine " were also made to personify the two terrestrial Poles. The telluric, metalline, magnetic, electric and the fiery elements are all so many allusions and references to the cosmic and astronomic character of the diluvian tragedy. In astronomy, the poles are indeed the " heavenly measure " (*vide* note *supra*) ; and so are the Kabiri *Dioscuri*, as will be shown, and the Kabiri-Titans, to whom Diodorus ascribes the *invention of fire* [730] and the art of manufacturing iron. Moreover, Pausanias shows that the original Kabiric deity was Prometheus.[731]

But the fact that, astronomically, the Titans-Kabirim were also the generators and regulators of the seasons, and cosmically the great Volcanic Energies, the gods presiding over all the metals and terrestrial works, does not prevent them from being, in their original divine characters, the beneficent Entities who, symbolized in Prometheus, brought light to the world, and endowed humanity with intellect and reason. They are pre-eminently in every theogony — especially in the Hindû — the sacred divine fires, 3, 7, or 49, according as the allegory demands it. Their very names prove it, as they are the *Agni-putra* (Sons of the Fire) in India, and the genii of the fire under numerous names in Greece and elsewhere. Welcker, Maury, and now Decharme, show the name Kabeiros meaning " the powerful through fire," from the Greek word καίω " to burn." The Semitic *Kabirim*, " the powerful, the mighty, and the great," answering to the Greek μεγάλοι δυνατοί, are later epithets. They were universally worshiped, and their origin is lost in the night of time. Yet whether propitiated in Phrygia, Phoenicia, the Troad, Thrace, Egypt, Lemnos or Sicily, their cult was always connected with fire; their temples ever built in the most volcanic localities, and in exoteric worship they belonged to Chthonian divinities. Therefore Christianity has made of them *infernal* gods.

They are truly " the great, beneficent and powerful Gods," as Cassius Hemina calls them.[732] At Thebes, Koré and Demeter, the *Kabirim*, had a sanctuary,[733] and at Memphis, the Kabiri had a temple so sacred, that none, excepting the priests, were suffered to enter their holy precincts.[734] But we must not lose sight, at the same time, of the fact that the title of Kabiri was a generic one; that the Kabiri (the *mighty* gods as well as mortals), were of both sexes, as also terrestrial, celestial and

---

730. The word "guebre" comes from Kabiri, *gabiri*, and means Persian ancient fire-worshippers, or Parsis. Kabiri became *gabiri* and then remained as an appellation of the Zoroastrians in Persia. (See Hyde's *De Religione Persarum*, cap. 29.)

731. I, ix, p. 751; [*Boiot.*, ix, 25].

732. See Macrobius, *Sat.* I, iii, c. 4, p. 376.

733. Pausanias, ix, 22; 5.

734. Herodotus iii, 37.

kosmic. That, while in their later capacity of the Rulers of sidereal and terrestrial powers, a purely geological phenomenon (as it is now regarded) was symbolized in the persons of those rulers, they were also, in the beginning of times, the rulers of mankind. When incarnated as Kings of the " divine Dynasties," they gave the first impulse to civilizations, and directed the mind with which they had endued men to the invention and perfection of all the arts and sciences. Thus the Kabiri are said to have appeared as the benefactors of men, and as such they lived for ages in the memory of nations. To them — the Kabiri or Titans — is ascribed the invention of letters (the *Devanâgarî*, or the alphabet and language of the gods), of laws and legislature; of architecture, as of the various modes of magic, so-called; and of the medical use of plants. Hermes, Orpheus, Kadmos, Asklepios, all those demi-gods and heroes, to whom is ascribed the revelation of sciences to men, and in whom Bryant, Faber, Bishop Cumberland, and so many other Christian writers — too zealous for plain truth — would force posterity to see only pagan copies of one and sole prototype, named Noah — are all generic names.

It is the Kabiri who are credited with having revealed, by *producing* corn or wheat, the great boon of agriculture. What *Isis-Osiris*, the once living Kabiria, has done in Egypt, that Ceres is said to have done in Sicily; they all belong to one class.

That the Serpents were ever the emblems of wisdom and prudence is again shown by the caduceus of Mercury, one with Thoth, the god of wisdom, with Hermes, and so on. The two serpents, entwined around the rod, are phallic symbols of Jupiter and other gods who transformed themselves into snakes for purposes of seducing goddesses — but only in the unclean fancies of profane symbologists. The serpent has ever been the symbol of the adept, and of his powers of immortality and divine knowledge. Mercury in his psychopompic character, conducting and guiding with the caduceus the souls of the dead to Hades and even raising the dead to life with it, is simply a very transparent allegory. It shows the dual power of the Secret Wisdom: the black and the white magic. It shows this personified Wisdom guiding the Soul after death, and its power to call to life that which is dead — a very deep metaphor if one thinks over its meaning. Every people of antiquity reverenced this symbol, with the exception of Christians, who chose to forget the brazen Serpent of Moses, and even the implied acknowledgment of the great wisdom and prudence of the Serpent by Jesus himself, " Be ye *wise* as serpents and harmless as doves." The Chinese, one of the oldest nations of our Fifth Race, made of it the emblem of their Emperors, who are thus the degenerate successors of the " Serpents " or Initiates, who ruled the early races of the Fifth Humanity.

The Emperor's throne is the "Dragon's Seat," and his dresses of State are embroidered with the likeness of the Dragon. The aphorisms in the oldest books of China, moreover, say plainly that the "Dragon" is a human, albeit *divine*, Being. Speaking of the "Yellow Dragon," the chief of the others, the *Twan-ying-t'u* says:

His wisdom and virtue are unfathomable . . . he does not go in company and does not live in herds [he is an ascetic]. . . . He wanders in the wilds beyond the heavens. He goes and comes, fulfilling the decree [Karma]; at the proper seasons if there is perfection he comes forth, if not he remains [invisible]. . . .

And Kong-fu-tyu is made to say by Lü-lan,

The Dragon feeds in the pure (water) [of Wisdom] and sports in the clear (waters) [of Life].

OUR DIVINE INSTRUCTORS

Now Atlantis and the Phlegyan isle are not the only record that is left of the deluge. China has also her tradition and the story of an island or continent, which it calls Ma-li-ga-si-ma, and which Kaempfer and Faber spell "Maurigosima," for some mysterious phonetic reasons of their own. Kaempfer, in his *Japan*,[735] gives the tradition: The island, owing to the iniquity of its giants, sinks to the bottom of the ocean, and Peiru-un, the king, the Chinese Noah, escapes alone with his family owing to a warning of the gods through two idols. It is that pious prince and his descendants who have peopled China. The Chinese traditions speak of the divine dynasties of Kings as much as those of any other nations.

At the same time there is not an old fragment but shows belief in a multiform and even multigeneric evolution — spiritual, psychic, intellectual and physical — of human beings, just as given in the present work. A few of these claims have now to be considered.

Our races — they all show — have sprung from divine races, by whatever name they are called. Whether we deal with the Indian Rishis or Pitris; with the Chinese *Chim-nang* and *Tchan-gy* — their "divine man" and demi-gods; with the Akkadian *Dingir* and *Mul-lil* — the creative god and the "Gods of the ghost-world"; with the Egyptian Isis-Osiris and Thoth; with the Hebrew Elohim, or again with Manco Capac and his Peruvian progeny — the story varies nowhere. Every nation has either the *seven* and *ten* Rishis-Manus and Prajâpatis; the seven and *ten* Ki-y; or ten and seven Amshâspends[736] (six exo-

---

735. Appendix, p. 13.
736. The Amshâspends are six — if Ormazd, their chief and Logos, is excluded.

But in the secret doctrine he is the seventh and highest, just as Ptah is the seventh Kabir among the Kabiri.

terically), ten and seven Chaldaean Annedoti, ten and seven Sephiroth, etc., etc. One and all have been derived from the primitive Dhyân-Chohans of the Esoteric doctrine, or the "Builders" of the Stanzas (Book I). From Manu, Thoth-Hermes, Oannes-Dagon, and Edris-Enoch, down to Plato and Panodoros, all tell us of seven *divine* Dynasties, of seven Lemurian, and seven Atlantean divisions of the Earth; of the seven primitive and dual gods who descend from their celestial abode[737] and reign on Earth, teaching mankind Astronomy, Architecture, and all the other sciences that have come down to us. These Beings appear first as "gods" and Creators; then they merge in nascent man, to finally emerge as "divine-Kings and Rulers." But this fact has been gradually forgotten. As Basnage shows, the Egyptians themselves confessed that science flourished in their country only since Isis-Osiris, whom they continue to adore as gods, "though they had become Princes in human form." And he adds of Osiris-Isis (the divine androgyne):—"It is said that this Prince [Isis-Osiris] built cities in Egypt, stopped the overflowing of the Nile; invented agriculture, the use of the vine, music, astronomy, and geometry."

When Abul-Feda says in his *Historia Anteislamitica*[738] that the Sabaean language was established by Seth and Edris (Enoch)—he means by "Sabaean language" astronomy. In the *Melelwa Nahil*[739] Hermes is called the disciple of Agathodaimon. And in another account[740] Agathodaimon is mentioned as a "*King of Egypt*." Celepas Geraldinus gives curious traditions about Henoch. He calls him the "divine giant." In the *Book of the Various Names of the Nile*, the same author (the historian Ahmed-Ben-Yusuf Eltiphas) tells us of the belief among the Semitic Arabs that Seth (become later the Egyptian Typhon, Set), had been one of the seven angels (or Patriarchs in the Bible): then he became a mortal and Adam's son, after which he communicated the gift of prophecy and astronomical science to Jared, who passed it to his son Henoch. But Henoch (Idris) "the author of thirty books, was Sabaean by origin" (*i. e.*, belonging to the *Saba*, "a Host"); "having established the rites and ceremonies of primitive worship, he went to the East, where he constructed 140 cities, of which Edessa was the least important, then returned to Egypt where he became its King." Thus, he is identified with Hermes. But there were five Hermes — or rather one, who appeared — as some Manus and Rishis did — in several different characters. In the *Burham-i-Kati* he is mentioned as "Hormig," a name of the planet Mercury or Budha; and Wednesday

---

737. In the Purâna it is identified with Vishnu's or Brahmâ's Sveta-Dvipa of Mount Meru.
738. Fleischer, p. 26.
739. MS. 47 in Nic. Cat.
740. See Col. Vyse's 2nd Vol. of the *Operations carried on at the Pyramids of Gizeh*, p. 364: MS. 785, Uri's Catalog.

was sacred both to Hermes and Thoth. The Hermes of Oriental tradition, worshiped at Phineata and said to have fled after the death of Argos into Egypt, civilized it under the name of Thoth. But under whichever of these characters, he is always credited with having transferred all the sciences from *latent to active potency, i. e.*, with having been the first to teach magic to Egypt and to Greece, *before the days of Magna Graecia,* and when the Greeks were not even Hellenes.

Not only Herodotus — the " father of History " — tells us of the marvelous dynasties of gods that preceded the reign of mortals, followed by the dynasties of demi-gods, Heroes, and finally men, but the whole series of classics support him; Diodorus, Eratosthenes, Plato, Manetho, etc., etc., repeat the same, and never vary the order given.

" It is, indeed," as Creuzer shows:—

from the spheres of the stars wherein dwell the gods of light that wisdom descends to the inferior spheres. . . . In the system of the ancient priests [Hierophants and Adepts] all things without exception, gods, the genii, *manes* [souls], the whole world, are conjointly developed in Space and duration. The pyramid may be considered as the symbol of this magnificent hierarchy of Spirits. . . .[741]

There were more efforts made by the modern historians (French Academicians, like Renan, chiefly) to suppress truth by ignoring the ancient annals of *divine* Kings, than is strictly consistent with honesty. But M. Renan could never be more unwilling than was Eratosthenes 260 years B. C. to accept the unpalatable fact; and yet the latter found himself obliged to recognize its truth. For this, the great astronomer is treated with great contempt by his colleagues 2000 years later. Manetho became with them " a superstitious priest born and bred in the atmosphere of other lying priests of Heliopolis."[742] "All those historians and priests," justly remarks the demonologist, de Mirville, " so *veracious* when repeating stories of *human* kings and men, suddenly become *extremely suspicious* no sooner do they go back *to their gods. . . .*" But there is the synchronistic table of Abydos, which, thanks to the genius of Champollion, has now vindicated the good faith of the priests of Egypt (Manetho's above all), and that of Ptolemy. In the Turin papyrus, the most remarkable of all, in the words of the Egyptologist, de Rougé:—

. . . Champollion, struck with amazement, found that he had under his own eyes the whole truth. . . . It was the remains of a list of dynasties embracing the furthest mythoic times, or the REIGN OF THE GODS AND HEROES. . . . At the very

741. Chapter iv of *Égypte,* p. 441; de Mirville.   742. Fréret.

outset of this curious papyrus we have to arrive at the conviction that so far back already as the period of Rameses, those mythic and heroical traditions were just as Manetho had transmitted them to us; we see figuring in them, as Kings of Egypt, the gods Seb, Osiris, Horus, Thoth-Hermes, and the goddess Ma, a long period of centuries being assigned to the reign of each of these.[743]

The synchronistic tables of Manetho, besides the fact that they were disfigured by Eusebius for dishonest purposes, had never gone beyond Manetho. The chronology of the divine Kings and Dynasties, like that of the age of humanity, has ever been in the hands of the priests, and was kept secret from the profane multitudes.

Africa, as a continent, it is said, appeared before Europe did; nevertheless it appeared later than Lemuria and even the earliest Atlantis. That the whole region of what is now Egypt and the deserts was once upon a time covered with the sea, was known firstly through Herodotus, Strabo, Pliny, and all the Greeks; and, secondly, through geology. Abyssinia was once upon a time an island; and the Delta was the first country occupied by the pioneer emigrants who came with their gods from the North-east.

When was it? History is silent upon the subject. Fortunately, we have the Dendera Zodiac, the planisphere on the ceiling of one of the oldest Egyptian temples, which records the fact. This Zodiac, with its mysterious three *Virgos* between the *Lion* and *Libra*, has found its Oedipus, who understood the riddle of these signs, and justified the truthfulness of those priests who told Herodotus that:— (*a*) The poles of the Earth and the Ecliptic had formerly coincided; and (*b*) That even since their first Zodiacal records were commenced, the Poles have been three times within the plane of the Ecliptic, as the Initiates taught.

Bailly had not sufficient words at his command to express his surprise at the *sameness* of all such traditions about the *divine* races. He exclaims,

What are finally all those reigns of Indian *Devas* and Persian *Peris?* . . . Or, those reigns and dynasties of the Chinese legends; those T'ien-hoang or the *Kings of Heaven*, quite distinct from the *Ti-hoang*, the Kings on Earth, and the *Gin-hoang* the King's men, a distinction which is in perfect accord with that other one made by the Greeks and the Egyptians, in enumerating *their dynasties of Gods, of demi-gods, and of mortals*.[744]

"Now," says Panodoros, "it is before that time [Menes], that *the reign of the seven gods who rule the world took place*. It was during that period that those benefactors of humanity *descended* on Earth and

743. *Ann. de Philologie Chrétienne*, Vol. XXXII, p. 442.

744. *Histoire de l'Astronomie Ancienne.*

taught men to calculate the course of the sun and moon by the twelve signs of the Ecliptic."

Nearly five hundred years before the actual era, Herodotus was shown by the priests of Egypt the statues of their human Kings and Pontiffs-*piromis* (the archi-prophets or Mahâ-Chohans of the temples), *born one from the other* (without the intervention of woman) who had reigned before Menes, their first *human* King. These statues, he says, were enormous colossi in wood, three hundred and forty-five in number, *each of which had his name, his history and his annals.* And they assured Herodotus [745] (unless the most truthful of historians, the " Father of History," is now accused of fibbing, *just in this instance*) that no historian could ever understand or write an account of these superhuman Kings, unless he had studied and learned the history *of the three dynasties* that preceded the human — namely, the DYNASTIES OF THE GODS, that of demi-gods, and of the Heroes, or giants. These "three dynasties" are the three Races.[746]

Translated into the language of the Esoteric doctrine, these three dynasties would also be those of the Devas, of Kimpurushas, and of Dânavas and Daityas — otherwise gods, celestial spirits, and giants or Titans. " Happy are those who are born, even from the condition of gods, as men, in Bhârata-Varsha!" exclaim the incarnated gods themselves, during the Third Root-Race. Bhârata is India, but in this case it symbolized the chosen land in those days, and was considered the best of the divisions of Jambu-dvipa, as it was the land of active (spiritual) works *par excellence;* the land of initiation and of divine knowledge.

Can one fail to recognize in Creuzer great powers of intuition, when, being almost unacquainted with the Âryan Hindû philosophies, little known in his day, he wrote :—

We modern Europeans feel surprised when hearing talk of the Spirits of the Sun, Moon, etc. But we repeat again, the *natural good sense and the upright*

---

745. See also *Mémoires à l'Académie, etc.,* of de Mirville, Vol. III, for a mass of evidence.

746. In *Vishnu Purâna*, Bk. II, chaps. 3, 4, *et seq.*, may be found many corroborations of the same, if one reads carefully. The reigns of gods, lower gods, and men are all enumerated in the descriptions of the seven Islands, seven seas, seven mountains, etc., etc., ruled by Kings. Each king is said invariably to have *seven* sons, an allusion to the seven sub-races. One instance will do. The King of *Kuśa dvipa* had seven sons (follow names) . . . "after whom the seven portions (Varsha) of the island were called. *There reside mankind along with Daityas and Dânavas, as well as with spirits of Heaven (Gandharvas, Yakshas, Kimpurushas, etc.) and gods.*" (*Chapter iv.*) There is but one exception in the case of King Priyavrata, the son of the first Manu, Svâyambhuva — who had *ten* sons. But of these, three — Medha, Agnibâhu, and Putra — became ascetics, and refused their portions. Thus Priyavrata divided the earth again into *seven* continents.

judgment of the ancient peoples, quite foreign to our *entirely material* ideas upon celestial mechanics and physical sciences . . . could not see in the stars and planets only that which we see: namely, simple masses of light, or opaque bodies moving in circuits in sidereal space, merely according to the laws of attraction or repulsion; but they saw in them *living* bodies, *animated* by spirits as they saw the same in every kingdom of nature. . . . *This doctrine of spirits, so consistent and conformable to nature,* from which it was derived, formed a grand and unique conception, wherein the physical, the moral, and the political aspects were all blended together . . ."[747]

It is such a conception only that can lead man to form a correct conclusion about his origin and the genesis of everything in the universe — of Heaven and Earth, between which he is a living link. Without such a psychological link, and the feeling of its presence, no science can ever progress, and the realm of knowledge must be limited to the analysis of physical matter only.

Occultists believe in " spirits," because they *feel* (and some see) themselves surrounded on every side by them.[748] Materialists do not. They live on this earth, just as, in the world of insects and even of fishes, some creatures live surrounded by myriads of their own *genus,* without seeing, or so much as sensing them.[749]

Plato is the first sage among the classics who speaks at length of the

747. *Égypte,* de Mirville, pp. 450 to 455.

748. As a general rule, *now* that the very nature of the *inner* man has become as blind as his physical nature, man is situated on this globe as the *Amphioxus* is in the Ocean. Surrounded by shoals and millions of various other fishes and creatures that see it, the *Amphioxus* species — having neither brain nor any of the senses possessed by the other classes — sees them not. Who knows whether, on the Darwinian theory, these " Branchiostoma " are not the direct ancestors of our Materialists.

749. The Occultists have been accused of worshiping *gods* or devils. We deny this. Among the numberless hosts of spirits — *men* that were, and those who will be men — there are those immeasurably superior to the human race, higher and holier than the highest Saint on Earth, and wiser than any mortal without exception. And there are those again who are no better than we are, as some are far worse and inferior to the lowest savage. It is the latter classes that command the readiest communication with our earth, who perceive and sense us, as the clairvoyants perceive and sense them.

The close proximity of our respective abodes and planes of perception are in favor of such inter-communication unfortunately, as they are ever ready to interfere with our affairs for weal or woe. If we are asked how it is that none but sensitive, hysterical natures, neuro- and psycho-pathic persons see and occasionally talk with " Spirits," we answer the question by several other queries. We ask: " Do you know the nature of hallucination, and can you define its psychic process? How can you tell that all such visions are due merely to physical hallucinations? What makes you feel so sure that mental and nervous diseases, while drawing a veil over our *normal* senses (so-called) *do not* reveal at the same time vistas unknown to the healthy man, by throwing open doors usually closed against your scientific perceptions (?): or that a psycho-spiritual faculty *does not* forthwith replace the loss, or the temporary atrophy, of a purely physical sense? It is disease, or the exuberance of nervous fluid which produces mediumship and visions — hallucinations, as you call them. But what *does* Science know even of mediumship? " Truly were

divine Dynasties, and locates them on a vast continent which he calls Atlantis. Bailly was not the first nor last to believe the same, and he had been preceded and anticipated in this theory by Father Kircher. This learned Jesuit writes in *Oedipus Aegyptiacus:*[750]

> I confess, for a long time I had regarded all this [dynasties and the Atlantis] as pure fables (*meras nugas*) to the day when, better instructed in Oriental languages, I judged that all those legends must be, after all, only the development of a great truth. . . .

As de Rougemont shows, Theopompos, in his *Meropis*, made the priests of Phrygia and Asia Minor speak exactly as the priests of Sais did when they revealed to Solon the history and fate of Atlantis. According to Theopompos, it was a unique continent of an indefinite size, and containing two countries inhabited by *two races* — a fighting, warrior race, and a pious, meditative race,[751] which Theopompos symbolizes by two cities.[752] The pious "city" was *continually visited by the gods;* the belligerent "city" was inhabited by various beings "*invulnerable* to iron, liable to be *mortally wounded* only by stone and wood." [753] De Rougemont treats this as a pure *fiction* of Theopompos [754] and even sees a fraud (*supercherie*) in the assertion of the Saitic priests. This was denounced by the " Demonologists " as illogical. In the words of de Mirville:—

> A *supercherie* which was based on a belief, the product of faith of the whole antiquity; a *supposition* which yet gave its name to a whole mountain chain (the Atlas); which specified with the greatest precision a topographical region (by placing some of its lands at a small distance from Cadiz and the strait of Calpe), which prophesied, 2000 years before Columbus, *the great transoceanic land* situated beyond that Atlantis and which "is reached," it said, by the *islands* not of the blessed, but of the good spirits, εὐδαιμόνια " (our "*Iles Fortunées*") — such a supposition can never be a universal chimera.[755]

It is certain that, whether "chimera" or reality, the priests of the whole world had it from one and the same source: the universal tra-

---

the modern Charcots to pay attention to the *delirium* of their patients from a more psychic standpoint, Science, and physiology especially, might be more benefitted than they are now, and truth have a wider field of fact in its knowledge.

750. Vol. I, p. 70.

751. These were the early Aryans and the bulk of the Fourth Root Races — the former pious and meditative (*yoga*-contemplation), the latter — a fighting race of sorcerers, who were rapidly degenerating owing to their uncontrolled passions.

752. The Northern and Southern Divisions of Lemuria-Atlantis. The Hyperborean and the Equatorial lands of the two continents. (See Sections about Lemuria and Atlantis in History.)

753. This is Occult and refers to the property of iron which, attracted by magnetic elements, is repelled by others, which are made by an occult process, as impervious to it as water to a blow.

754. *Peuple Primitif*, Vol. III, 157.

755. A word on " Atlantis," p. 29.

dition about the third great continent which perished some 850,000 years ago.[756] A continent inhabited by two distinct races; distinct physically and especially morally; both deeply versed in primeval wisdom and the secrets of nature; mutually antagonistic in their struggle, during the course and progress of their double evolution. Whence even the Chinese teachings upon the subject, if it is but a *fiction?* Have they not recorded the existence once upon a time of a *holy* island beyond the sun (*Tcheou*), and beyond which were situated the lands *of the immortal men?*[757] Do they not still believe that the remnants of those *immortal* men — who survived when the *holy* island had become black with sin and perished — have found refuge in the great desert of Gobi, where they still reside invisible to all, and defended from approach by hosts of Spirits?

The very unbelieving Boulanger writes:[758]

If one has to lend ear to traditions, . . . the latter place before the reign of Kings, that of the Heroes and demi-gods; and still earlier and beyond they place the marvelous reign of the gods and all the fables of the golden age. . . . One feels surprised that annals so interesting should have been rejected by almost all our historians. And yet the ideas communicated by them were once universally admitted and revered by all the peoples; not a few revere them still, making them the basis of their daily life. Such considerations seem to necessitate a less hurried judgment. . . . The ancients, from whom we hold these traditions, which *we accept no longer because we do not understand them now*, must have had motives for believing in them furnished by their greater proximity to the first ages, and which the distance that separates us from them refuses to us. . . . Plato in his fourth book of *Laws*, says that, long before the construction of the first cities, Saturn had established on earth a *certain* form of government under which man was very happy. As it is the golden age he refers to, or to that reign of gods so celebrated in ancient fables . . . let us see the ideas he had of that happy age, and what was the occasion he had to introduce this *fable* into a treatise on politics. Acccording to Plato, in order to obtain clear and precise ideas on royalty, its origin and power, one has to turn back to the first principles of history and tradition. Great changes, he says, have occurred in days of old, *in heaven and on earth*, and the present state of things is one of the results [*Karma*]. Our traditions tell us of many marvels, of changes that have taken place in the course of the Sun, of Saturn's reign, and of a thousand other matters that remained scattered about in human memory; but *one never hears anything of the EVIL which has produced those revolutions, nor of the evil which directly followed them.* Yet . . . that Evil is the principle one has to talk about, to be able to treat of royalty and the origin of power. . . .

---

756. The first continent, or island, if so preferred, "the cap of the North Pole," has never perished; nor will it to the end of the Seven Races.

757. See de Rougemont, *ibid.*   758. *Règne des Dieux*, Introduction.

That *evil*, Plato seems to see in the sameness or consubstantiality of the natures of the rulers and the ruled, for he says that long before man built his cities, in the golden age, there was naught but happiness on earth, for there were no needs. Why? Because Saturn, knowing that man could not rule man, without injustice filling forthwith the universe through his whims and vanity, would not allow any mortal to obtain power over his fellow creatures. To do this the god used the same means we use ourselves with regard to our flocks. We do not place a bullock or a ram over our bullocks and rams, but give them a leader, a shepherd, *i. e., a being of a species quite different from their own and of a superior nature.* It is just what Saturn did. He loved mankind and placed to rule over it no mortal King or prince but — "Spirits and genii (δαίμονες) of a divine nature more excellent than that of man."

It was god, the Logos (the synthesis of the Host) who thus presiding over the genii, became the first shepherd and leader of men.[759] When the world had ceased to be so governed and the gods retired, "ferocious beasts devoured a portion of mankind." "Left to their own resources and industry, inventors then appeared among them successively and discovered fire, wheat, wine; and public gratitude deified them. . . ."[760]

And mankind was right, as fire by friction was the first mystery of nature, the first and chief property of matter that was revealed to man.

"*Fruits and grain, unknown to Earth to that day, were brought by the 'Lords of Wisdom' for the benefit of those they ruled — from other lokas* (spheres) . . ." say the Commentaries. Now:

The earliest inventions [?] of mankind are the most wonderful that the race has ever made. . . . The *first use of fire*, and the discovery of the methods by which it can be kindled; the domestication of animals; and above all, *the processes by which the various cereals were first developed* out of some wild grasses [?] — these are all *discoveries with which, in ingenuity and in importance, no subsequent discoveries may compare.* They are all unknown to history — all lost in the light of an EFFULGENT DAWN.[761]

This will be doubted and denied in our proud generation. But if it is asserted that there are no grains and fruits *unknown to earth,* then we may remind the reader *that wheat has never been found in the wild state: it is not a product of the earth.* All the other cereals have been

---

759. The Secret Doctrine explains and expounds that which Plato says, for it teaches that those "inventors" were gods and demigods (Devas and Rishis) who had become — some deliberately, some forced to by Karma — incarnated in man.

760. *De Legibus,* Lib. I, iv; in *Crit.* and in *Politic.*

761. *Unity of Nature,* Argyll.

traced to their primogenital forms in various species of wild grasses, but wheat has hitherto defied the efforts of botanists to trace it to its origin. And let us bear in mind, in this connexion, how sacred was that cereal with the Egyptian priests; wheat being placed even with their mummies, and found thousands of years later in their coffins. Remember:— " The servants of Horus glean the wheat in the field of Aanru, . . . wheat *seven cubits high.*" [762] The reader is referred to Stanza VII, Verse 3, Book I, wherein this verse is explained in another of its meanings, and also to the " *Book of the Dead,*" chap. cix, verses 4 and 5.

" I am the Queen of these regions," says the Egyptian Isis; " I was the first to reveal to mortals the mysteries of wheat and corn. . . . I am she who rises in the constellation of the dog . . . [Dog-star]. . . . Rejoice, O Egypt! thou who wert my nurse." [763]

Sirius was called the *dog-star.* It was the star of Mercury or Budha, called the great instructor of mankind, before other Buddhas.

The book of the Chinese *Yi-King* attributes the discovery of agriculture to " the instruction given to men by celestial genii."

" Woe, woe to the men who know nought, observe nought, nor will they see. . . . They are all blind,[764] since they remain ignorant how much the world is full of various and invisible creatures which crowd even in the most sacred places." [765]

The " Sons of God " *have* existed and *do* exist. From the Hindû *Brahmâputras* and *Mânasaputras* (Sons of Brahmâ and Mind-born sons) down to the *B'ne-aleim* of the Jewish Bible, the faith of the

762. " *Book of the Dead,*" chap. xcix, 33; and clvi, 4. This is a direct reference to the esoteric division of man's principles symbolized by the divine wheat. The legend which inscribes the third Registrar of the papyrus (Chap. cx. of the " *Book of the Dead* ") states: " This is the region of the *Manes* (disembodied men) *seven cubits high*" — to wit: those just translated and supposed to be still sevenfold with all their principles, even the body represented *astrally* in the Kâma-loka or *Hades,* before their separation . . . " and, there is wheat three *cubits high* for mummies in a *state of perfection* " (i. e., those already separated, whose *three* higher principles are in Devachan) " who are permitted to glean it." This region (Devachan) is called " the land of the re-birth of gods," and shown to be inhabited by Shu, Tefnut, and Seb. The " region for the

manes seven cubits high," (for the yet imperfect mummies), and the region for those "*in a state of perfection*" who "glean wheat *three* cubits high," is as clear as possible. The Egyptians had the same esoteric philosophy which is now taught by the cis-Himâlayan adepts, who, when buried, have corn and wheat placed over them.

763. Book I, chap. xiv. There are Egyptologists who have tried to identify Osiris with Menes, which is quite erroneous. Bunsen assigns to Menes an antiquity of 5867 years b.c., and is denounced for it by Christians. But " Isis-Osiris " reigned in Egypt before the Dendera Zodiac was painted on the ceiling of that temple, and that is over 75,000 years ago!

764. In the text, " corked up " or " screwed up."

765. *Zohar,* Part I, col. 177.

centuries and *universal* tradition force reason to yield to such evidence. Of what value is *independent criticism* so called, or "internal evidence" (based usually on the respective hobbies of the critics), in the face of the universal testimony, which never varied throughout the historical cycles? Read esoterically the sixth chapter of *Genesis*, which repeats the statements of the Secret Doctrine, only changing slightly its form, and drawing a different conclusion which clashes even with the *Zohar*. " There were giants in the earth in those days; and *also after that* when ' the Sons of God ' (*b'ne-aleim*) came in unto the daughters of men, and they bare children to them, the same became *mighty men* which were of old, men of renown " (or giants).[766]

What does this sentence " and also after that " signify unless it means when explained: " There were giants in the earth BEFORE, *i. e.*, before the sinless sons of the Third Race; and *also after that* when other sons of God, lower in nature, inaugurated sexual connexion on earth (as Daksha did, when he saw that his *Mânasaputras* would not people the earth) "? And then comes a long break in this chapter vi of *Genesis*, between verses 4 and 5. For surely, it was not in or through the wickedness of the "mighty men" . . . men of renown, among whom is placed Nimrod the "mighty hunter before the Lord," that " god saw that the wickedness of man *was* great," nor in the builders of Babel, for this was *after* the Deluge; but in the progeny of the giants who produced *monstra quaedam de genere giganteo,* monsters from whence sprang the lower races of men, now represented on earth by a few miserable dying-out tribes and the huge anthropoid apes.

And if we are taken to task by theologians, whether Protestant or Roman Catholic, we have only to refer them to their own literal texts. The above quoted verse was ever a dilemma, not alone for the men of science and Biblical scholars, but also for priests. For, as the Rev. Father Péronne puts it:—" Either they [the B'ne-aleim] were good angels, and in such case how could they fall? Or they were bad [angels] and in this case could not be called *b'ne-aleim,* the " sons of God." [767] This Biblical riddle — " the real sense of which no author has ever understood," as candidly confessed by Fourmont[768]— can only be explained by the Occult doctrine, through the *Zohar* to the Western, and the *Book of Dzyan* to the Eastern. What the former says we have seen; what the *Zohar* tells us is this: *B'ne-aleim* was a name common to the *Malachim* (the good Messengers) and to the *Ishin* ("the lower angels").[769]

We may add for the benefit of the demonologists that their Satan,

766. *Genesis* vi. 4.   767. *Praelectiones Theol.,* ch. ii.
768. *Réflexions Critiques sur l'Origine des Anciens Peuples.*   769. Rabbi Parcha.

"the adversary," is included in *Job* among the sons of God or *b'ne-aleim* who visit their father.[770] But of this later on.

Now the *Zohar* says that the *Ishin*, the beautiful *B'ne-aleim*, were *not* guilty, but mixed *themselves with mortal men because they were sent on earth to do so.*[771] Elsewhere the same volume shows the *b'ne-aleim* belonging to the tenth sub-division of the "Thrones."[772] It also explains that the Ishin, "men-spirits," *viri spirituales*, now that men can see them no longer, help magicians to produce, through their science, *homunculi* which are not *small men* but "men *smaller* (in the sense of *inferiority*) than men." Both show themselves under the form that the Ishin had then, *i. e.*, gaseous and ethereal. Their chief is Azazel.

But Azazel, whom the Church dogma will associate with Satan, is nothing of the kind. Azazel is a *mystery*, as explained elsewhere, and it is so expressed in Maimonides, in *More Nevochim.*[773] "There is an impenetrable mystery in the narrative concerning Azazel." And so there is, as Lanci, a librarian to the Vatican and one who ought to know, says — we have quoted him before — that "this venerable divine name (*nome divino e venerabile*) has become through the pen of Biblical scholars, a *devil*, a wilderness, a mountain, and a he-goat."[774] Therefore it seems foolish to derive the name as Spencer does, from *Azal* (separated) and *El* (god), hence "one separated from God," the DEVIL. In the *Zohar*, Azazel is rather the Sacrificial victim than the "formal adversary of Jehovah," as Spencer would have it.[775]

The amount of malicious fancy and fiction bestowed on that "Host" by various fanatical writers is quite extraordinary. Azazel and his "host" are simply the Hebrew "Prometheus," and ought to be viewed from the same standpoint. The *Zohar* shows the *Ishin* chained on the mountain in the desert, allegorically; thus simply alluding to those "spirits" as being chained to the earth during the cycle of incarnation. Azazel (or Azaziel) is one of the chiefs of the "transgressing" angels in *Enoch*, who descending upon Ardis, the top of Mount Armon, bound themselves by swearing loyalty to each other. It is said that Azaziel taught men to make swords, knives, shields, to fabricate mirrors (?) to make *one see what is behind him* (viz., *"magic mirrors"*). Amazarak taught all the sorcerers and dividers of roots; Armers taught the solution of magic; Barkayal, astrology; Akibeel, the meaning of portents and signs; Tamial, astronomy; and Asaradel taught the motion of the moon.[775a] "These seven were the first instructors of the Fourth man"

770. Chapter i.
771. *Book of Ruth and Shadash*, fol. 63, col. 3; Amsterdam edition.
772. *Zohar*, Part III, col. 113. But see also 1st vol. 184.
773. Chapter xxvi, p. 8.
774. *Sagra Scrittura.*
775. II, pp. 14, 29.
775a. *Book of Enoch*, chap. viii, ed. of 1838.

(*i. e.*, of the *Fourth* Race). But why should allegory be always understood as meaning all that its dead-letter expresses?

It is the symbolical representation of the great struggle between divine wisdom, *nous,* and its earthly reflection, *Psuche,* or between Spirit and Soul, in Heaven and on Earth. In Heaven — because the divine MONAD had voluntarily exiled itself therefrom, to descend, for incarnating purposes, to a lower plane and thus transform the animal of clay *into an immortal god.* For, as Éliphas Lévi tells us, "the angels aspire to become men; for the perfect man, the man-god, is above even angels." On Earth — because no sooner had Spirit descended than it was strangled in the coils of matter.

Strange to say, the Occult teaching reverses the characters; it is the anthropomorphous archangel with the Christians, and the man-like God with the Hindûs, which represent matter in this case; and the Dragon, or Serpent, Spirit. Occult symbolism furnishes the key to the mystery; theological symbolics conceal it still more. For the former explains many a saying in the Bible and even in the New Testament which have hitherto remained incomprehensible; while the latter, owing to its dogma of Satan and his rebellion, has belittled the character and nature of its would-be infinite, absolutely perfect god, and created the greatest evil and curse on earth — belief in a personal Devil. This mystery is opened with the key to its metaphysical symbolism now restored; while that of theological interpretation shows the gods and the archangels standing as symbols for the dead letter or dogmatic religions, and as arrayed against the pure truths of Spirit, naked and unadorned with fancy.

Many were the hints thrown out in this direction in "*Isis Unveiled,*" and a still greater number of references to this mystery may be found scattered throughout these volumes. To make the point clear once for all: that which the clergy of every dogmatic religion — pre-eminently the Christian — points out as Satan, the enemy of God, is in reality, the highest divine Spirit — (occult Wisdom on Earth) — in its naturally antagonistic character to every worldly, evanescent illusion, dogmatic or ecclesiastical religions included. Thus, the Latin Church, intolerant, bigoted and cruel to all who do not choose to be its slaves; the Church which calls itself the bride of Christ, and the trustee at the same time of Peter, to whom the rebuke of the Master "get thee behind me Satan" was justly addressed; and again the Protestant Church which, while calling itself Christian, paradoxically replaces the New Dispensation by the old "Law of Moses" which Christ openly repudiated: both these Churches are fighting against divine Truth, when repudiating and slandering the Dragon of esoteric (because *divine*) Wisdom. Whenever anathematizing the Gnostic Solar Chnouphis — the Agathodaimon — Christos, or the theosophical Serpent of Eternity, or even the Serpent of *Genesis* — they are moved by the same Spirit of dark fanaticism that moved the Pharisees to curse Jesus by saying to him " Say we not well thou hast a devil? "

Read the account about Indra (Vâyu) in the *Rig-Veda*, the occult volume *par excellence* of Âryanism, and then compare it with the same in the Purânas — the exoteric version thereof, and the purposely garbled acount of the true Wisdom religion. In the *Rig Veda* Indra is the highest and greatest of the Gods, and his Soma-drinking is allegorical of his highly spiritual nature. In the Purânas Indra becomes a profligate, and a regular drunkard on the Soma juice, in the terrestrial way. He is the conqueror of all the "enemies of the gods" — the Daityas, Nâgas (Serpents), Asuras, all the *Serpent*-gods, and of Vritra, the Cosmic Serpent. Indra is the St. Michael of the Hindû Pantheon — the chief of the *militant* Host. Turning to the Bible, we find Satan, one of the " Sons of God," [776] becoming in exoteric interpretation the Devil, and the Dragon in its infernal, evil sense. But in the Kabala [777] Samael, who is Satan, is shown to be identical with St. Michael, the *slayer of the Dragon*. How is this? For it is said that Tselem (the image) reflects alike Michael and Samael *who are one*. Both proceed, it is taught, from *Ruach* (Spirit), *Neshamah* (Soul) and *Nephesh* (life). In the Chaldaean *"Book of Numbers"* Samael is the concealed (occult) Wisdom, and Michael the higher *terrestrial* Wisdom, both emanating from the same source but diverging after their issue from the *mundane soul*, which on Earth is *Mahat* (intellectual understanding), or *Manas* (the seat of Intellect). They diverge, because one (Michael) is *influenced* by Neshamah, while the other (Samael) remains *uninfluenced*. This tenet was perverted by the dogmatic spirit of the Church; which, loathing independent Spirit, uninfluenced by the external form (hence by dogma), forthwith made of Samael-Satan (the most wise and spiritual spirit of all) — the adversary of its anthropomorphic God and sensual physical man, the DEVIL!

THE ORIGIN OF THE SATANIC MYTH

Let us then fathom this creation of the Patristic fancy still deeper, and find its prototype with the Pagans. The origin of the new *Satanic* myth is easy to trace. The tradition of the Dragon and the Sun is echoed in every part of the world, both in its civilized and semi-savage regions. It took rise in the whisperings about secret initiations among the profane, and was established universally through the once universal heliolatrous religion. There was a time when the four parts of the

776. *Job* i. 6.   777. *"Book of Numbers."*

world were covered with the temples sacred to the Sun and the Dragon; but the cult is now preserved mostly in China and the Buddhist countries, " Bel and the Dragon being uniformly coupled together, and the priest of the Ophite religion as uniformly assuming the name of his God."[778] In the religions of the past, it is in Egypt we have to seek for its Western origin. The Ophites adopted their rites from Hermes Trismegistos, and heliolatrous worship crossed over with its Sun-gods into the land of the Pharaohs from India. In the gods of Stonehenge we recognize the divinities of Delphi and Babylon, and in those of the latter the devas of the Vedic nations. Bel and the Dragon, Apollo and Python, Krishna and Kâliya, Osiris and Typhon are all one under many names — the latest of which are Michael and the Red Dragon, and St. George and his Dragon. As Michael is " one as God," or his " Double," for terrestrial purposes, and is one of the Elohim, the fighting angel, he is thus simply a permutation of Jehovah. Whatever the Cosmic or astronomical event that first gave rise to the allegory of the " War of Heaven," its earthly origin has to be sought in the temples of Initiation and archaic crypts. The following are the proofs:

We find (a) the priests assuming the name of the gods they served; (b) the " Dragons " held throughout all antiquity as the symbols of Immortality and Wisdom, of secret Knowledge and of Eternity; and (c) the hierophants of Egypt, of Babylon, and India, styling themselves generally the " Sons of the Dragon " and " Serpents "; thus the teachings of the Secret Doctrine are thereby corroborated.

There were numerous catacombs in Egypt and Chaldaea, some of them of a very vast extent. The most renowned of them were the subterranean crypts of Thebes and Memphis. The former, beginning on the western side of the Nile, extended towards the Libyan desert, and were known as the *Serpent's* catacombs, or passages. It was there that were performed the sacred mysteries of the *kuklos anagkes,* the " Unavoidable Cycle," more generally known as " the circle of necessity"; the inexorable doom imposed upon every soul after the bodily death, and when it has been judged in the Amenthian region.

In de Bourbourg's book, *Votan,* the Mexican demi-god, in narrating his expedition, describes a subterranean passage which ran underground, and terminated at the root of the heavens, adding that this passage was a snake's hole, " un agujero de colubra "; and that he was admitted to it because he was himself " a son of the snakes," or a serpent.[779]

This is, indeed, very suggestive; for his description of the *snake's hole* is that of the ancient Egyptian crypt, as above mentioned. The

778. *Archaeology,* Vol. xxv, p. 220, London.
779. *Die Phönizier,* 70; Brasseur de Bourbourg, *Hist. des Nat. Civ. du Mexique,* I, 71-72.

hierophants, moreover, of Egypt, as of Babylon, generally styled themselves the " Sons of the Serpent-god," or " Sons of the Dragon," during the mysteries.

"The Assyrian priest bore always the name of his god," says Movers. The Druids of the Celto-Britannic regions also called themselves snakes. " I am a Serpent, I am a Druid," they exclaimed. The Egyptian Karnak is twin brother to the Carnac of Bretagne, the latter Carnac meaning the serpent's mount. The Dracontia once covered the surface of the globe, and these temples were sacred to the Dragon, only because it was the symbol of the sun, which, in its turn, was the symbol of the highest god — the Phoenician Elon or Elion, whom Abraham recognized as El Elion.[780] Besides the surname of serpents, they were called the " builders," the " architects "; for the immense grandeur of their temples and monuments was such that even now the pulverized remains of them " frighten the mathematical calculations of our modern engineers," says Taliesin.[781]

De Bourbourg hints that the chiefs of the name of *Votan*, the *Quetzal-Cohuatl,* or Serpent deity of the Mexicans, are the descendants of Ham and Canaan. " I am Hivim," they say. " Being a Hivim, I am of the great race of the Dragon (snake). I am a snake myself, for I am a Hivim." [782]

Furthermore, the " War in Heaven " is shown, in one of its significations, to have meant and referred to those terrible struggles in store for the candidate for adeptship, between himself and his (by magic) personified human passions, when the *inner* enlightened man had to either slay them or fail. In the former case he became the " Dragon-Slayer," as having happily overcome all the temptations; and a " Son of the Serpent " and a Serpent himself, having cast off his old skin and being born in a *new* body, becoming a Son of Wisdom and Immortality in Eternity.[783]

Seth, the reputed forefather of Israel, is only a Jewish travesty of Hermes, the God of Wisdom, called also Thoth, Tat, Seth, Set, and Satan. He is also Typhon — the same as Apophis, the Dragon slain by Horus; for Typhon was also called Set. He is simply the *dark side* of Osiris, his brother, as Angra Mainyu is the black shadow of Ahura-Mazda. Terrestrially, all these allegories were connected with the trials of adeptship and initiation. Astronomically, they referred to the Solar and Lunar eclipses, the mythical explanations of which we find to this day in India and Ceylon, where any one can study the allegorical

780. See Sanchoniathon in Eusebius, *Praep. Evang.,* I, x, p. 36. *Genesis* xiv.
781. " Society of Antiquaries of London," vol. xxv, p. 220.

782. *Cartas,* 51; " *Iris Unveiled,*" Vol. I, 553, *et seq.*

783. See Part II on the Satanic Myth.

narratives and traditions which have remained unchanged for many thousands of years.

Râhu, mythologically is a *Daitya* — a giant, a Demi-god, the lower part of whose body ended in a Dragon or Serpent's tail. During the churning of the Ocean, when the gods produced *amrita* — the water of Immortality — he stole some of it, and drinking, became immortal. The Sun and Moon, who had detected him in his theft, denounced him to Vishnu, who placed him in the stellar spheres, the upper portion of his body representing the Dragon's head and the lower (Ketu) the Dragon's tail; the two being the ascending and descending nodes. Since then, Râhu wreaks his vengeance on the Sun and Moon by occasionally swallowing them. But this fable had another mystic meaning, since *Râhu*, the Dragon's head, played a prominent part in the mysteries of the Sun's (*Vikarttana's*) initiation, when the candidate and the Dragon had a supreme fight.

The caves of the Rishis, the abodes of Teiresias and the Greek seers, were modeled on those of the *Nâgas*,— the Hindû *King-Snakes*, who dwelled in cavities of the rocks under the ground. From *Sesha*, the thousand-headed Serpent, on which Vishnu rests, down to Python, the dragon *serpent oracle*, all point to the secret meaning of the myth. In India we find the fact mentioned in the earliest Purânas. The children of Surasâ are the "mighty Dragons." The *Vâyu Purâna* replacing "Surasâ" (of *Vishnu Purâna*) by Danujas or *Dânavas*—the descendants of Danu by the sage Kaśyapa — and those Dânavas being the giants (or Titans) who warred against the gods, they are thus shown identical with the "Dragons" and "Serpents" of Wisdom.

By simply comparing the Sun-gods of every country, one may find their allegories agreeing perfectly with one another; and the more the allegorical symbol is occult the more its corresponding symbol in other systems agrees with it. Thus, if from three systems widely differing from each other in appearance — the old Âryan, the ancient Greek, and the modern Christian schemes — we select several Sun-gods and dragons at random, these will be found copied from each other.

Let us take Agni the fire-god, Indra the firmament, and Kârttikeya from the Hindûs; the Greek Apollo; and *Mikael*, the "Angel of the Sun," the first of the Aeons, called by the Gnostics "the savior" — and proceed in order.

(1) Agni — the fire-god — is called in the *Rig-Veda* Vaiśvânara. Now Vaiśvânara is a Dânava — a giant-demon,[784] whose daughters

---

784. He is thus named and included in the list of the Dânavas in *Vâyu Purâna*; the Commentator of *Bhâgavata Purâna* calls him a son of Danu, but the name means also "Spirit of Humanity."

Pulomâ and Kâlakâ are the mothers of numberless Dânavas (30 millions), by Kaśyapa,[785] and live in *Hiranyapura*, " *the golden city*," *floating in the air*. Therefore, Indra is, in a fashion, the step-son of these two as a son of Kaśyapa; and Kaśyapa is, in this sense, identical with Agni, the fire-god, or Sun (Kaśyapa-Âditya). To this same group belongs Skanda or Kârttikeya (god of War, the *six-faced* planet Mars astronomically), a Kumâra, or virgin-youth, born of Agni,[786] for the purpose of destroying Târaka, the Dânava Demon, the grandson of Kaśyapa by Hiranyâksha, his son,[787] whose (Târaka's) yogi austerities were so extraordinary that they became formidable to the gods, who feared such a rival in power.[788] While Indra, the bright god of the Firmament, kills Vritra (or Ahi), the Serpent-Demon — for which feat he is called *Vritra-han,* " the destroyer of Vritra "; he also leads the hosts of *Devas* (Angels or gods) against other gods who rebel against Brahmâ, for which he is entitled *Jishnu,* " leader of the celestial Host." Kârttikeya is found bearing the same titles. For killing Târaka, the Dânava, he is Târaka-Jit, " Vanquisher of Târaka," [789] " *Kumâra Guha,*" " the mysterious Virgin-youth," " *Siddha-Sena* " — " the leader of the Siddhas "; and *Saktidhara* — " Spear-holder."

(2) Now take Apollo, the Grecian sun-god, and by comparing the mythical accounts given of him, see whether he does not answer both

---

785. Kaśyapa is called the Son of Brahmâ, and is the " Self-Born " to whom a great part of the work of creation is attributed. He is one of the seven Rishis; *exoterically*, the son of Marichi, the son of Brahmâ; while *Atharva-veda* says, " The Self-born Kaśyapa sprang from Time "; and *esoterically*—Time and Space are forms of the One *incognizable* Deity. As an *Aditya*, Indra is son of Kaśyapa, as also Vaivasvata Manu, our progenitor. In the instance given in the text, he is Kaśyapa-Aditya, *the Sun, and the Sun-god, from whom all* the " Cosmic " Demons, Dragons (nâgas), Serpent, or Snake-gods, and Dânavas, the giants, are born. The meaning of the allegories given above is purely astronomical and cosmical, but will serve to prove the identity of all.

786. All such stories differ in the *exoteric* texts. In the *Mahâbhârata*, Kârttikeya, " the six-faced Mars," is the son of Rudra or Siva, Self-born *without a mother* from the seed of Siva cast into the fire. But Kârttikeya is generally called *Agnibhû,* " fire born."

787. Hiranyâksha is the ruler or king of the *fifth* region of Pâtâla, a Snake-god.

788. The *Elohim* also feared the knowledge of Good and Evil for Adam, and therefore are shown as expelling him from Eden or killing him *spiritually*.

789. The story told is, that Târaka (called also Kâlanâbha), owing to his extraordinary Yoga-powers, had obtained all the divine knowledge of yoga-vidyâ and occult powers of the gods, who conspired against him. Here we see the " obedient " Host of *Archangels* or minor gods conspiring against the (future) *Fallen* angels, whom Enoch accuses of the great crime of disclosing to the world all " the *secret things* done in heaven." It is Michael, Gabriel, Raphael, Suryal and Uriel who denounced to the Lord God those of their Brethren who were said *to have pried into the divine mysteries* and taught them to men: by this means they themselves escaped a like punishment. Michael was commissioned to fight the Dragon, and so was Kârttikeya, and under the same circumstances. Both are " leaders of the Celestial Host," both Virgins, both " leaders of Saints," " Spear-holders " (*Saktidhara*), etc., etc. Kârttikeya is the original of Michael and St. George, as surely as Indra is the prototype of Kârttikeya.

to Indra, Kârttikeya, and even Kaśyapa-Âditya, and at the same time to Michael (as the Angelic form of Jehovah) the " angel of the Sun," who is " like," and " one with, God." Later ingenious interpretations for monotheistic purposes, elevated though they be into not-to-be-questioned Church dogmas, prove nothing, except the abuse of human authority and power, perhaps.

Apollo is *Helios* (the Sun), Phoibos-Apollo (" the light of life and of the World " [790]) who arises out of the golden-winged cup (the sun) ; hence he is the sun-god *par excellence.* At the moment of his birth he asks for his bow to kill Python, the Demon Dragon, who attacked his mother before his birth,[791] and whom he is divinely commissioned to destroy — like Kârttikeya, who is born for the purpose of killing Târaka, *the too holy and wise demon.* Apollo is born on a sidereal island called *Asteria* — " the golden star island," the " earth which floats in the air," which is the Hindû golden *Hiranyapura;* " he is called the pure, ἁγνός, *Agnus Dei* (the Indian Agni, as Dr. Kenealy thinks), and in the primal myth he is exempt " from all sensual love." [792] He is, therefore, a *Kumâra,* like Kârttikeya, and as Indra was in his earlier life and biographies. Python, moreover, the " red Dragon," connects Apollo with Michael, who fights the Apocalyptic Dragon, who wants to attack the woman in child-birth,[793] as Python attacks Apollo's mother. Can any one fail to see the identity? Had the Rt. Hon. W. E. Gladstone, who prides himself on his Greek scholarship and understanding of the spirit of Homer's allegories, ever had a real inkling of the *esoteric* meaning of the *Iliad* and *Odyssey,* he would have understood St. John's " *Revelation,*" and even the Pentateuch, better than he does. For the way to the Bible lies through Hermes, Bel, and Homer, as the way to these is through the Hindû and Chaldaean religious symbols.

The repetition of this archaic tradition is found in chapter xii of St. John's *Revelations,* and comes from the Babylonian legends without the smallest doubt, though the Babylonian story had its origin in the allegories of the Âryans. The fragment read by the late George Smith [794] is sufficient to disclose the source of the xii chapter of the Apocalypse. Here it is as given by the eminent Assyriologist :

Our . . . fragment refers to the creation of *mankind,* called Adam, as [the

---

790. The " life and the light " of the material *physical* world, the delight of the senses — not of the soul. Apollo is pre-eminently the *human* god, the god of emotional, pomp-loving and theatrical Church ritualism, with lights and music.

791. See chap. xii in *Revelation* where we find Apollo's mother persecuted by that

Python, the Red Dragon, who is also *Porphyrion,* the scarlet or red Titan.

792. *Book of God,* " The Apocalypse of Adam Oannes," p. 88.

793. See *Revelation* xii.

794. See *The Chaldean Account of Genesis,* p. 304.

man] in the Bible; he is made perfect . . . but afterwards joins with the dragon of the Deep, the animal of Tiamat, the Spirit of Chaos, and offends against his god, who *curses him,* and calls down on his head all the evils and troubles of Humanity.[795]

This is followed by a war between the dragon and the powers of evil, or chaos on one side and the gods on the other.

The gods have weapons forged for them,[796] and Merodach [the archangel Michael in *Revelation*] undertakes to lead the heavenly host against the dragons. The war, which is described with spirit, ends, of course, in the triumph of the principles of good. . . .[797]

This war of gods with the powers of the Deep, refers also, in its last and terrestrial application, to the struggle between the Aryan adepts of the nascent Fifth Race and the Sorcerers of Atlantis, the Demons of the Deep, the Islanders surrounded with water who disappeared in the Deluge.[798]

The symbols of the dragons and " War in Heaven " have, as already stated, more than one significance; religious, astronomical, and geological events being included in the one common allegory. But it had also a Cosmological meaning. In India the Dragon story is repeated in one of its forms in the battles of Indra with *Vritra.* In the Vedas this Ahi-Vritra is referred to as the Demon of Drought, the terrible hot Wind. Indra is shown to be constantly at war with him; and with the help of his thunder and lightning the god compels Ahi-Vritra to pour down in rain on Earth, and then slays him. Hence, Indra is called the *Vritra-Han* or " the slayer of Vritra," as Michael is called the Conqueror and " Slayer of the Dragon." Both these " Enemies " are then the " Old Dragon " precipitated into the depths of the Earth, in this one sense.

The Zend-Avestic Amshâspends are a Host with a leader like St. Michael over them, and seem identical with the legions of Heaven, when one reads the *Vendîdâd.* Thus in Fargard XIX, ii, 13 (42), Zarathustra is told by Ahura Mazda to "invoke the Amesha Spentas who rule over the seven *Karshvares*[799] of the Earth "; which Karsh-

795. No "god" who *curses* his (supposed) own work, because he has made it imperfect, can be the one infinite absolute wisdom, whether called Bel or Jehovah.

796. In the Indian allegory of *Târakâmaya,* the war between the gods and the Asuras headed by Soma (the moon, the King of Plants), it is Viśvakarmâ, the artificer of the gods, who forges, like Vulcan (Tubal-Kain), their weapons for them.

797. We have said elsewhere that the " woman with child ' of *Revelation* (xii) was Aima, the great mother, or Binah, the

third Sephiroth, " whose name is Jehovah "; and the " Dragon," who seeks to devour her coming child (the Universe), is the Dragon of absolute Wisdom — that Wisdom which, recognizing the non-separateness of the Universe and everything in it from the Absolute ALL, sees in it no better than the great Illusion, *Mahâmâyâ,* hence the cause of misery and suffering.

798. See the last pages of Vol. I, "*Isis Unveiled,*" Atlantis.

799. The " Seven Karshvares of the Earth " — the seven spheres of our plane-

vares in their seven applications refer equally to the seven spheres of our planetary chain, to the seven planets, the seven heavens, etc., according to whether the sense is applied to a physical, supra-mundane, or simply a sidereal world. In the same Fargard,[800] in his invocation against Angra Mainyu and his Host, Zarathustra appeals to them in these words: " I invoke the seven bright *Sravah* with their sons and their flocks." [801] The " Sravah " — a word which the Orientalists have given up as one "of unknown meaning" — means the same Amshâspends, but in their highest occult meaning. The " *Sravah* " are the noumenoi of the phenomenal Amshâspends, the souls or spirits of those *manifested* Powers; and "their sons and their flock" refers to the planetary angels and their sidereal flock of stars and constellations. "Amshâspend" is the exoteric term used in terrestrial combinations and affairs only. Zarathustra addresses Ahura Mazda constantly as " thou, the maker *of the material* world." Ormazd is the father of our earth (Spenta Ârmaiti), and she is referred to, when personified, as " the fair daughter of Ahura Mazda," [802] who is also the creator of the Tree (of occult and spiritual knowledge and wisdom) from which the mystic and mysterious *Baresma* is taken. But the occult name of the bright God was never pronounced outside the temple.[802a]

Samael or Satan, the seducing Serpent of *Genesis*, and one of the primeval angels who rebelled, is the name of the " Red Dragon." He is the Angel of *Death*, the Talmud saying that " the Angel of Death and Satan are the same," and, killed by Michael, he is once more killed by St. George, who also is a Dragon Slayer; but see the transformations of this. Samael is identical with the *Simoom*, the hot wind of the desert, or again with the Vedic demon of drought, as Vritra; " *Simoon* is called *Atabutos* " or — *Diabolos*, the devil.

Typhon, or the Dragon Apophis — the *Accuser* in the "*Book of the Dead* "— is worsted by Horus, who pierces his opponent's head with a spear; and Typhon is the all-destroying wind of the desert, the rebellious element that throws everything into confusion. As *Set* — he is the darkness of night, the murderer of Osiris, who is the light of day and the sun. Archaeology demonstrates that Horus is identical with Anubis,[803] whose effigy was discovered upon an Egyptian monument, with a cuirass and a spear, like Michael and St. George. Anubis is also

---

tary chain, the seven worlds — also mentioned in the *Rig-Veda* — are fully referred to elsewhere. There are six *rajâmsi* (worlds) above *prithivî*—the earth, or "this" (idam), as opposed to that which is *yonder* (the six globes on the three other planes). (See *Rig-Veda*, I, 34; III, 56; VII, 10411, and V, 60, 6. See § on Chronology.)

800. ii and iii.
801. 42, *Vendîd. Sâdah.*
802. Fargard xix, ii, 13 (42).
802a. *Cf.* " Sacred Books of the East," vol. IV, pp. 204–217 *passim.*
803. Verse 62, chap. xvii, "*Book of the Dead* ": Anubis is Horus who melts in him who is eyeless.

represented as slaying a dragon, that has the head and tail of a serpent.[804]

Cosmologically, then, all the Dragons and Serpents conquered by
their " Slayers " are, in their origin, the turbulent confused principles
in Chaos, brought to order by the Sun-gods or *creative* powers. In the
"Book of the Dead" those principles are called "the Sons of Rebellion."[805] " In that night, the oppressor, the murderer of Osiris,
otherwise called the *deceiving Serpent*[806] . . . calls the Sons of Rebellion in *Air*, and when they arrive to the East of Heavens, then there
is War in Heaven and in the entire world."[807]

In the Scandinavian *Eddas* the " War " of the Ases with the Hrim-
thurses (frost-giants), and of Asathor with the Jötuns, the Serpents
and Dragons and the " wolf " who comes out of " Darkness " — is the
repetition of the same myth. The "evil Spirits,"[808] having begun by
being simply the emblems of Chaos, became euhemerized by the superstition of the rabble, until they have finally won the right of citizenship
in the most civilized and learned races of this globe — *since its creation*
as alleged — and became a dogma with Christians. As George Smith
has it: " The evil Spirits [principles], emblems of Chaos, [in Chaldaea
and Assyria as in Egypt, we see], resist this change and make war
on the Moon, the eldest son of Bel, drawing over to their side the Sun,
Venus and the atmospheric god, Vul."[809] This is only another version
of the Hindû " War in Heaven," between Soma, the moon, and the
gods — Indra being the atmospheric Vul; which shows it plainly to
be both a Cosmogonical and an astronomical allegory, woven into and
drawn from the earliest theogony as taught in the Mysteries.

It is in the religious doctrines of the Gnostics that the real meaning
of the Dragon, the Serpent, the Goat, and all those symbols of powers
now called *Evil*, can be seen the best; as it is they who divulged the
esoteric nature of the Jewish Substitute for *AIN-SOPH in their* teachings; of the true meaning of which, while the Rabbins concealed it, the
Christians, with a few exceptions, knew nothing. Surely Jesus of
Nazareth would have hardly advised his apostles to show themselves
as *wise* as the serpent, had the latter been a symbol of the *Evil one:*
nor would the Ophites, the learned Egyptian Gnostics of "the Brother-
hood of the Serpent," have reverenced a living snake in their ceremonies
as the emblem of *WISDOM*, the divine *Sophia* (and a type of the
all-good, not the all-bad), were that reptile so closely connected with

804. See Lenoir's *Du Dragon de Metz.*

805. See also *Egyptian Pantheon*, pp. 20, 23.

806. Verse 54.

807. Verse 49, *"Book of the Dead,"* xvii.

808. These "evil Spirits" can by no
means be identified with Satan or the Great
Dragon. They are the Elementals generated or begotten by ignorance — Cosmic and
human passions — or Chaos.

809. *Assyrian Discoveries*, page 403.

Satan. The fact is, that even as a common ophidian it has ever been a dual symbol; and as a Dragon it had never been anything else than a symbol of the manifested Deity in its great Wisdom. The *Draco volans,* the flying Dragon of the early painters, may be an exaggerated picture of the real extinct antediluvian animal; but those who have faith in the Occult teachings believe that in the days of old there were such creatures as flying Dragons, or a kind of Pterodactyl, and that it is those gigantic winged lizards that served as the prototypes for the Seraph of Moses and his great Brazen Serpent.[810] The Jews had worshiped the latter *idol* themselves, but, after the religious reforms brought about by Hezekiah, turned round, and called that symbol of the great or Higher God of every other nation — a Devil, and their own usurper — the " One God." [811]

The appellation Sa'tan, in Hebrew *sâtân,* "an adversary" (from the verb *shatana,* " to be adverse," to persecute) belongs by right to the first and cruellest " *adversary of all the other gods* " — Jehovah, not to the Serpent, which spoke only words of sympathy and wisdom, and is at the worst, even in the dogma, " the adversary of men." This dogma, based as it is on chapter iii of *Genesis,* is as illogical and unjust as it is paradoxical. For who was the first to *create* that original and henceforward universal tempter of man — the woman? Not the serpent surely, but the " Lord God " himself, who, saying :— " It is not good that the man should be alone "— made woman, and, " brought her unto the man." [812] If the unpleasant little incident that followed *was* and is still to be regarded as the " original sin," then it exhibits the Creator's divine foresight in a poor light indeed. It would have been far better for the first Adam (of chap. i) to have been left either " male and female," or " alone." It is the Lord God, evidently, who was the real cause of all the mischief, the *"agent provocateur,"* and the Serpent — only a prototype of *Azazel,* " the scapegoat for the sin of (the God of) Israel," the poor *Tragos* having to pay the penalty for his Master's and Creator's blunder. This, of course, is addressed only to those who accept the opening events of the drama of humanity in

---

810. See *Numbers* xxi. 8–9. God orders Moses to build a brazen Serpent " Saraph "; to *look upon which* heals those bitten by the *fiery serpents.* The latter were the *Seraphim,* each one of which, as Isaiah shows (vi. 2), *"had six wings";* they are the symbols of Jehovah, and of all the other Demiurgi who produce out of themselves six sons or likenesses — Seven with their Creator. Thus, the Brazen Serpent *is* Jehovah, the chief of the " fiery serpents." And yet, in II *Kings* xviii, it is shown that King Hezekiah, who, like as David his father, " did that which

was right in the sight of the Lord " — " brake in pieces the brazen serpent that Moses had made ... and called it *Nehushtan,"* or piece of brass.

811. "And Satan stood up against Israel and moved David to number Israel" (I *Chron.* xxi. 1). " The anger of the Lord Jehovah was kindled against Israel," and he moved David to say: " Go, number Israel " (II *Samuel,* xxiv. 1). The two are then identical.

812. ii, 18–22.

Genesis in their dead-letter sense. Those who read them esoterically, are not reduced to fanciful speculations and hypotheses; *they know* how to read the symbolism therein contained, and cannot err.

There is at present no need to touch upon the mystic and manifold meaning of the name Jehovah in its abstract sense, one independent of the Deity *falsely* called by that name. It was a blind created purposely by the Rabbins, a secret preserved by them with ten-fold care after the Christians had despoiled them of this God-name which was their own property.[813] But the following statement is made. The personage who is named in the first four chapters of *Genesis* variously as " God," the " Lord God," and " Lord " simply, is not one and the same person; certainly it is not *Jehovah*. There are three distinct classes or groups of the Elohim called Sephiroth in the Kabala, Jehovah appearing only in chapter iv, in the first verse of which he is named Cain, and in the last transformed into *mankind* — male and female, Jah-veh.[814] The " Serpent," moreover, is not Satan, but the bright Angel, one of the *Elohim* clothed in radiance and glory, who, promising the woman that if they ate of the forbidden fruit " *ye shall not surely die*," kept his promise, and made man immortal in his *incorruptible nature*. He is the Iao of the mysteries, the chief of the Androgyne creators of men. Chapter iii contains (esoterically) the withdrawal of the veil of ignorance that closed the perceptions of the Angelic Man, made in the image of the " Boneless " gods, and the opening of his consciousness to his real nature; thus showing the bright Angel (Lucifer) in the light of a giver of Immortality, and as the " Enlightener "; while the real Fall into generation and matter is to be sought in chapter iv. There, Jehovah-Cain, the male part of Adam the *dual* man, having separated himself from Eve, creates in her " Abel," *the first natural woman*,[816] and sheds the *Virgin blood*. Now Cain, being shown identical with Jehovah, on the authority of the correct reading of verse 1,[816] in the original Hebrew text; and the Rabbins teaching that " *Kin* (Cain), the Evil, was the Son of Eve by Samael, the devil who took Adam's place "; and the Talmud adding that " the evil Spirit, Satan, and Samael, the angel of Death, are the same "[817] — it becomes easy to see that Jehovah (*mankind*, or " Jah-hovah ") and Satan (there-

813. Dozens of the most erudite writers have sifted thoroughly the various meanings of the name J'hovah (with, and without the masoretic points), and shown their multifarious bearings. The best of such works is *The Source of Measures, the Hebrew-Egyptian Mystery*.

814. In the above-mentioned work (p. 233, App.), verse 26 of the 4th chap. of *Genesis* is correctly translated " then men began to call themselves *Jehovah*," but less correctly explained, perhaps, as the last word ought to be written *Jah* (male) *Hovah* (female), to show that from that time the rac: of distinctly separate man and woman began.

815. See for explanation the excellent pages of appendix vii of the same work.

816. Chapter iv, *Genesis*.

817. *Rabba Batra*, 16a.

fore the tempting Serpent) are one and the same in every particular. *There is no Devil, no Evil, outside mankind to produce a Devil.* Evil is a necessity in, and one of the supporters of the manifested universe. It is a necessity for progress and evolution, as night is necessary for the production of Day, and Death for that of Life — *that man may live for ever.*

Satan represents metaphysically simply the *reverse or the polar opposite* of everything in nature.[818] He is the "adversary," allegorically, the "murderer," and the great enemy of *all,* because there is nothing in the whole universe that has not two sides — the reverses of the same medal. But in that case, light, goodness, beauty, etc., may be called Satan with as much propriety as the Devil, since they are the *adversaries* of darkness, badness, and ugliness. And now the philosophy and the *rationale* of certain early Christian sects — called *heretical* and viewed as the abomination of the times — will become more comprehensible. We may understand how it was that the sect of SATANIANS came to be degraded, and were anathematized without any hope of vindication in a future day, since they kept their tenets secret. How, on the same principle, the CAINITES came to be degraded, and even the (Judas) ISCARIOTES; the true character of the *treacherous* apostle having never been correctly presented before the tribunal of Humanity.

As a direct consequence, the tenets of the Gnostic sects also become clear. Each of these sects was founded by an Initiate, while their tenets were based on the correct knowledge of the symbolism of every nation. Thus it becomes comprehensible why Ilda-Baoth was regarded by most of them as the god of Moses, and was held as a proud, ambitious, and impure spirit, who had abused his power by usurping the place of the *highest God,* though he was no better, and in some respects far worse than *his brethren Elohim*; the latter representing the all-embracing, manifested deity only in their collectivity, since they were the fashioners of the first differentiations of the primary Cosmic substance for the creation of the phenomenal Universe. Therefore Jehovah was called by the Gnostics the Creator of, and one with Ophiomorphos, the Serpent, Satan, or *EVIL.*[819] They taught that Iurbo and Adonai were "names of Jao-Jehovah, who is an emanation of Ilda Baoth."[820] (*See Part II, "The Fallen Angels."*) This amounted in their language to saying what the Rabbins expressed in

818. In Demonology, Satan is the leader of the opposition in Hell, the monarch of which was Beelzebub. He belongs to the fifth kind or class of demons (of which there are nine according to medieval demonology), and he is at the head of witches and sorcerers. But see in the text the true meaning of Baphomet, the goat-headed Satan, one with Azaziel, the scape-goat of Israel. Nature is the god *PAN.*

819. See "*Isis Unveiled,*" II, 184.
820. *Codex Nasoraeus,* iii, p. 73,

a more veiled way, by stating that — " Cain had been generated by Samael or Satan."

The fallen Angels are made in every ancient system the prototypes of *fallen* men — allegorically, and, *those men themselves* — esoterically. Thus the Elohim of the hour of creation became the " Beni-Elohim," the sons of God, among whom is Satan — in the Semitic traditions; war in heaven between Thraetaona and Azhi-dahaka, the destroying Serpent, ends on earth, according to Burnouf, in the battle of pious men against the power of Evil, " of the Iranians with the Aryan Brâhmans of India." And the conflict of the gods with the *Asuras* is repeated in the Great War — the *Mahâbhârata.* In the latest religion of all, Christianity, all the Combatants, gods and demons, adversaries in both the camps, are now transformed into Dragons and Satans, simply in order to connect *EVIL* personified with the Serpent of *Genesis,* and thus prove the new dogma.[821]

NOAH WAS A KABIR, HENCE HE MUST HAVE BEEN A DEMON

It matters little whether it is Isis, or Ceres — the " Kabiria " — or again the Kabiri, who have taught men agriculture; but it is very important to prevent fanatics from monopolizing all the facts in history and legend, and from fathering their distortions of truth, history, and legend upon one man. Noah is either a *myth* along with the others, or one whose legend was built upon the Kabirian or Titanic tradition, as taught in Samothrace; he has, therefore, no claim to be monopolized by either Jew or Christian. If, as Faber tried to demonstrate at such cost of learning and research, Noah is an Atlantean and a Titan, and his family are the Kabiri or pious Titans, etc.— then biblical chronology falls by its own weight, and along with it all the patriarchs — the antediluvian and pre-Atlantean Titans. As now discovered and proven, Cain is Mars, the god of *power and generation,* and of the first (sexual) bloodshed.[822] Tubal-Cain is a Kabir, " an instructor of every artificer in brass and iron "; or — if this will please better — he is one with Hephaistos or Vulcan; Jabal is taken from the Kabiri — instructors in agriculture, " such as have cattle," and Jubal is " the father of all those who handle the harp," he, or *they* who fabricated the *harp* for Kronos and the trident for Poseidon.[823]

821. *Vide* for further details upon the Satanic myth, Part II on Symbolism, in this volume.

822. As he is also Vulcan or Vul-cain, the greatest god with the later Egyptians, and the greatest Kabir. The god of *time* was *Chiun* in Egypt, or Saturn, or Seth, and Chiun is the same as Cain.

823. See Strabo, *comparing them to the Cyclopes* — XIV. p. 653 *sqq.* Callim. in *Del..* 31; Statius, *Silv.*, IV. 6, 47; etc., etc,

The history or "fables" about the mysterious Telchines — fables echoing each and all the archaic events of our esoteric teachings — furnish us with a key to the origin of *Cain's* genealogy;[824] they give the reason why the Roman Catholic Church indentifies "the accursed blood" of Cain and Ham with Sorcery, and makes it responsible for the Deluge. Were not the Telchines — it is argued — the mysterious ironworkers of Rhodes; they who were the first to raise statues to the gods, furnish them with weapons, and men with magic arts? And is it not they who were destroyed by a deluge at the command of Zeus, as the *Cainites* were by that of Jehovah?

The Telchines are simply the Kabiri and the Titans, in another form. They are the Atlanteans also. "Like Lemnos and Samothrace," says Decharme, "Rhodes, the birth-place of the Telchines, is an island of volcanic formation."[825] The island of Rhodes emerged suddenly out of the seas, after having been previously engulfed by the Ocean, say the traditions. Like Samothrace (of the Kabiri) it is connected in the memory of men with the Flood legends. As enough has been said on this subject, however, it may be left for the present.

But we may add a few more words about Noah, the Jewish repre-sentative of nearly every pagan God in one or another character. The Homeric songs contain, poetized, all the later fables about the Patri-archs, who are all sidereal, cosmic, and numerical symbols and signs. The attempt to disconnect the two genealogies — those of Seth and Cain[826] — and the further attempt, as futile, to show them *real, his-torical* men, has only led to more serious inquiries into the history of the Past, and to discoveries which have damaged for ever the sup-posed *revelation*. For instance, the identity of Noah and Melchizedek being established, the further identity of Melchizedek, or Father Sadik, with Kronos-Saturn is proved also.

That it is so may be easily demonstrated. It is not denied by any of the Christian writers. Bryant[827] concurs with all those who are of opinion, that Sydic, or Sadic, was the patriarch Noah (as also Mel-

824. *Genesis*, ch. iii.

825. *Genii of Fire*, p. 271.

826. Nothing could be more awkward and childish, we say, than this fruitless at-tempt to disconnect the genealogies of Cain and of Seth, or to conceal the identity of names under a different spelling. Thus, Cain has a Son ENOCH, and Seth a Son ENOCH also (Enos, Ch'anoch, Hanoch; — one may do what one likes with Hebrew unvoweled names). In the Cainite line Enoch begets IRAD, Irad MEHUJAEL, the latter METHUSAEL, and Methusael, Lamech.

In the Sethite line, Enoch begets Cainan, and this one MAHALEEL (a variation on Mehujael), who gives birth to JARAD (or Irad); Jarad to ENOCH (Number 3), who produces Methuselah (from Methusael), and finally Lamech closes the list. Now all these are symbols (Kabalistically) of solar and lunar years, of astronomical periods, and of physiological (phallic) functions, just as in any other pagan symbolical creed. This has been proven by a number of writers.

827. See *Analysis of Ancient Mythology*, Vol. II, p. 760.

chizedek); and that the name by which he is called, or Sadic, corresponds to the character given of him in *Genesis*, chap. vi, 9. " He was צדיק , Sadic, a JUST man, and perfect in his generation. All science and every useful art were attributed to him, and through his sons transmitted to posterity." [828]

Now it is Sanchoniathon, who informs the world that the Kabiri were the sons of Sydic or Zedek (Melchizedek). True enough, this information, having descended to us through Eusebius (*Praeparatio Evangelica*), may be regarded with a certain amount of suspicion, as it is more than likely that he dealt with Sanchoniathon's works as he has with Manetho's Synchronistic Tables. But let us suppose that the identification of Sydic, Kronos, or. Saturn with Noah and Melchizedek, is based on one of the Eusebian pious hypotheses. Let us accept it as such, along with Noah's characteristic as a *just man*, and his supposed duplicate, the mysterious Melchizedek, King of Salem, and priest of the high god, after " his own order "; [829] and finally, having seen what they all were spiritually, astronomically, psychically and cosmically, let us now see what they became *rabbinically* and KABALISTICALLY.

Speaking of Adam, Kain, Mars, etc., as *personifications*, we find the author of *The Source of Measures* enunciating our very esoteric teachings in his Kabalistic researches. Thus he says:—

Now Mars was the lord of *birth* and of *death*, of *generation* and of *destruction*, of *ploughing*, of *building*, of *sculpture* or stone-cutting, of *Architecture* . . . in fine, of all . . . ARTS. He was the *primeval principle*, disintegrating into the modification of *two opposites for production.* Astronomically, too,[830] he held the birthplace of the day and year, the place of its *increase of strength*, *Aries*, and likewise the place of its death, Scorpio. He held the house of *Venus*, and that of the *Scorpion*. He, as *birth*, was *Good; as death*, was *Evil*. As *good*, he was *light;* as bad, he was *night*. As *good*, he was *man;* as *bad*, he was *woman*. He held the cardinal points, and as *Cain*, or *Vulcan*,[830] or *Pater Sadic*, or *Melchizadek*, he was lord of the *Ecliptic*, or *balance*, or *line of adjustment*, and therefore was THE JUST ONE. The ancients held to there being seven planets, or

828. See *New Encyclopaedia* by Abraham Rees, *v. r. s.*

829. See *Hebrews*, v. 6, and vii. 1, *et seq.*

830. The Aeolian name of Mars was "Apevs, and the Greek Ares, ''Αρης, is a name over the etymological significance of which, philologists and Indianists, Greek and Sanskrit scholars have vainly worked to this day. Very strangely, Max Müller connects both the names *Mars* and *Ares* with the Sanskrit root *mar*, whence he traces their derivation, and from which, he says,

the name of *Maruts* (the storm-gods) comes. Welcker, however, offers more correct etymologies (See *Griech. Götterlehre*, I, 415). However it may be, etymologies of roots and words alone will never yield the esoteric meaning fully, though they may help to useful guesses.

831. As the same author shows: " The very name Vulcain appears in the reading; for in the first words [of chap. iv, *Genesis*, 5] is to be found V'elcain or V'ulcain, agreeably to the deepened u sound of the letter *vau*. Out of its immediate context,

great gods, growing out of eight, and Pater Sadik, *the Just or Right One*, was lord of the eighth, which was *Mater Terra*.[332]

This makes their functions plain enough after they had been de-graded, and establishes the identity.

The *Noachian* Deluge, as described in its dead letter and within the period of Biblical chronology, having been shown to have never existed, the pious, but very arbitrary supposition of Bishop Cumberland has but to follow that deluge into the land of fiction. Indeed it seems rather fanciful to any impartial observer to be told that there were "two distinct races of Cabiri," the first consisting of Ham and Miz-raim, whom he conceives to be Jupiter and Dionysos of Mnaseas; the second, "of the children of Shem, are the Cabiri of Sanchoniathon, while their father Sydyk is consequently the Scriptural Shem."[333]

The Kabirim, "the mighty ones," are identical with our primeval Dhyân-Chohans, with the corporeal and the incorporeal Pitris, and with all the rulers and instructors of the primeval races, which are referred to as the Gods and Kings of the divine Dynasties.

THE OLDEST PERSIAN TRADITIONS ABOUT THE POLAR, AND THE SUBMERGED CONTINENTS

Legendary lore could not distort facts so effectually as to reduce them to unrecognizable shape. Between the traditions of Egypt and Greece on the one hand, and Persia on the other — a country ever at war with the former — there is too great a similarity of figures and numbers to allow such coincidence to be due to simple chance. This was well proven by Bailly. Let us pause for a moment to examine these traditions from every available source, to compare the better those of the Magi with the so-called Grecian "fables."

Those legends have now passed into popular tales, the folklore of Persia, as many a real fiction has found its way into our universal History. The stories of King Arthur and his knights of the Round Table are also fairy tales to all appearance; yet they are based on facts, and pertain to the History of England. Why should not the folklore of Iran be part and parcel of the history and the pre-historic events of Atlantis? That folklore says as follows:—

it may be read as '*and the god Cain,*' or Vulcain. If, however, anything is wanting to confirm the Cain-Vulcain idea, Fuerst says: " ןיק, *Cain, the iron point of a lance, a smith* (blacksmith), inventor of sharp iron tools and smith work" (p. 278).

832. *Source of Measures*, p. 186.

833. *Append. de Cabiris, ap. Orig. Gent.*, pp. 364, 376, *and the latter statement on page* 357.

Before the creation of *Adam*, two races lived and succeeded each other on Earth; the Devs who reigned 7000 years, and the Peris (the Izeds) who reigned but 2000, during the existence of the former. The Devs were giants, strong and wicked; the Peris were smaller in stature, but wiser and kinder.

Here we recognize the Atlantean giants and the Aryans, or the Râkshasas of the *Râmâyana* and the children of Bhârata Varsha, or India; the ante- and the post-diluvians of the Bible.

Gyan (or rather Gñan, true or occult Wisdom and knowledge), also called *Gian-ben-Gian* (or Wisdom, son of Wisdom), was the king of the Peris.[834] He had a shield as famous as that of Achilles, only instead of serving against an enemy in war, it served as a protection against black magic, the *sorcery* of the Devs. Gian-ben-Gian had reigned 2000 years when *Iblis*, the devil, was permitted by God to defeat the Deos and scatter them to the other end of the world. Even the magic shield, which, produced on the principles of astrology, destroyed charms, enchantments, and bad spells, could not prevail against *Iblis*, who was an agent of Fate (or Karma).[835] They count ten kings in their last metropolis called Khanoom, and make the tenth, Kaimurath, identical with the Hebrew Adam. These kings answer to the ten antediluvian generations of kings as given by Berosus.

Distorted as those legends are now found, one can hardly fail to identify them with the Chaldaean, Egyptian, Greek, and even Hebrew traditions. The latter, disdaining in its exclusiveness to speak of pre-adamite nations, yet allows these to be clearly inferred, by sending out Cain — *one of the two only living men on earth* — into the land of Nod, where he gets married and builds a city,[836] etc.

Now if we compare the 9000 years mentioned by the Persian tales with the 9000 years, which Plato declared had passed since the submersion of the last Atlantis, a very strange fact is made apparent. Bailly remarked, but distorted it by his interpretation. The Secret Doctrine may restore the figures to their true meaning. " First of all," we read in *Kritias* that " one must remember that 9000 years have elapsed *since the war of the nations*, which lived above and outside the Pillars of Hercules, and those which peopled the lands on this side."

834. Some derive the word from *Peras* which produced Para, Persia, *Pars;* but it may be equally derived from Pitar or Pitris, the Hindû progenitors of the Fifth Race — the Fathers of Wisdom or the Sons of "Will and Yoga"—who were called Pitar, as were the divine Pitaras of the First Race.
835. See for these traditions the *Collection of Persian Legends*, in Russian, Geor-gian, Armenian, and Persian; Herbelot's narrative *Légendes Persanes*, " Bibliothèque Orientale," pp. 298, 387, etc., and Danville's *Mémoires*. We give in a condensed narrative that which is scattered in hundreds of volumes in European and Asiatic languages, as well as in oral traditions.
836. *Genesis*, iv.

In *Timaios* Plato says the same. The Secret Doctrine declaring that most of the later islander Atlanteans perished in the interval between 850,000 and 700,000 years ago, and that the Aryans were 200,000 years old when the first great " island " or continent was submerged, there hardly seems any reconciliation possible between the figures. But there is, in truth. Plato, being an Initiate, had to use the veiled language of the Sanctuary, and so had the Magi of Chaldaea and Persia, through whose exoteric revelations the Persian legends were preserved and passed to posterity. Thus, one finds the Hebrews calling a week " seven days," and " a week of years " when each of its days represents 360 solar years, and the whole " week " is 2520 years, in fact. They had a Sabbatical week, a Sabbatical year, etc., etc., and their Sabbath lasted indifferently 24 hours or 24,000 years — in their secret calculations of the Sods. We of the present times call an age *a century*. They of Plato's day, the initiated writers, at any rate, meant by a millennium, not a thousand but 100,000 years; Hindûs, more independent than any, never concealed their chronology. Thus, when saying 9000 years, the Initiates will read 900,000 years, during which space of time — *i. e.*, from the first appearance of the Aryan race, when the Pliocene portions of the once great Atlantis began gradually sinking [837] and other continents to appear on the surface, down to the final disappearance of Plato's small island of Atlantis, the Aryan races had never ceased to fight with the descendants of the first giant races. This war lasted till nearly the close of the age which preceded the Kali Yuga, and was the Mahâbhâratan war so famous in Indian History. Such blending of the events and epochs, and the bringing down of hundreds of thousands into thousands of years, does not interfere with the numbers of years that had elapsed, according to the statement made by the Egyptian priests to Solon, since the destruction of the last portion of Atlantis. The 9000 years were the correct figures given. The latter event has never been kept a secret, and had only faded out of the memory of the Greeks. The Egyptians had their records complete, because isolated; for, being surrounded by sea and desert, they had been left untrammelled by other nations, till about a few millenniums before our era.

History, for the first time, catches a glimpse of Egypt and its great mysteries through Herodotus, if we do not take into account the Bible, and its queer chronology.[838] And how little Herodotus *could* tell is

837. The *main* continent perished in the Miocene times, as already stated.

838. From Bede downwards all the chronologists of the Church have differed among themselves, and contradicted each other. " The chronology of the Hebrew text has been grossly altered, especially in the interval next after the Deluge ": — says Whiston (*Old Test.*, p. 20).

confessed by himself when speaking of a mysterious tomb of an Initiate at Sais, in the sacred precinct of Minerva. There, he says:

> behind the chapel . . . is the tomb of One, *whose name I consider it impious to divulge.* . . . In the enclosure stand large stone obelisks and there is a *lake* near, surrounded with a stone wall formed *in a circle.* . . . In this lake they perform by night . . . that person's adventures, which they call *Mysteries:* on these matters, however, though I am accurately acquainted with the particulars of them, *I must observe a discreet silence.*[839]

On the other hand, it is well to know that no secret was so well preserved and so sacred with the ancients, as that of their cycles and computations. From the Egyptians down to the Jews it was held as the highest sin to divulge anything pertaining to the correct measure of time. It was for divulging *the secrets of the Gods,* that Tantalos was plunged into the infernal regions; the keepers of the sacred Sibylline Books were threatened with the death penalty for revealing a word from them. Sigalions (images of Harpokrates) were in every temple — especially in those of Isis and Serapis — each pressing a finger to the lips; while the Hebrews taught that to divulge, after initiation into the Rabbinical mysteries, the secrets of Kabala, was like eating of the fruit of the Tree of Knowledge: it was punishable by death.

And yet, we Europeans accepted the exoteric chronology of the Jews! What wonder that it has influenced and colored ever since all our conceptions of science and the duration of things!

The Persian traditions, then, are full of two nations or races, now entirely extinct, as some think; whereas, they are only transformed. They are ever speaking of, and describing the mountains of Kâf (Kafaristân?), which contain a gallery built by the giant Argeak, wherein the statues of the ancient men under all their forms are preserved. They call them *Sulimans* (Solomons), or the wise kings of the East, and count seventy-two kings of that name.[840] Three among them reigned for 1000 years each.[841]

Siamek, the beloved son of Kaimurath (Adam), their first king, died murdered by his giant brother. The father had a perpetual fire preserved on the tomb which contained his cremated ashes; hence — the origin of fire-worship, as some Orientalists think.

Then came *Hushenk,* the prudent and the wise. It was his dynasty which re-discovered metals and precious stones, which had been concealed by the Devs or Giants in the bowels of the earth; how to make

839. ii, 170, 171.

840. Thence King Solomon, whose traces are nowhere to be found outside of the Bible, and the description of whose magnificent palace and city dovetail with those of the Persian tales; though they were unknown to all pagan travelers, even to Herodotus.

841. Herbelot, p. 829.

brass-work, to cut canals, and improve agriculture. As usual, it is Hushenk, again, who is credited with having written the work called "Eternal Wisdom," and even with having built the cities of Luz, Babylon and Ispahan, though they were built ages later. But as modern Delhi is built on six other older cities, so these just-named cities may be built on emplacements of other cities of an immense antiquity. As to his date, it can only be inferred from another legend.

In the same tradition that wise prince is credited with having made war against the giants on a twelve-legged horse, whose birth is attributed to the *amours* of a crocodile with a female hippopotamus. This *dodecapod* was found on the "dry island" or new continent; much force and cunning had to be used to secure the wonderful animal, but no sooner had Hushenk mounted him, than he defeated every enemy. No giants could withstand his tremendous power. Notwithstanding, this king of kings was killed by an enormous rock thrown at him by the giants from the great mountains of *Damavend.*[842]

Tahmurath is the third king of Persia, the St. George of Iran, the knight who always has the best of, and who kills, the Dragon. He is the great enemy of the Devs, who, in his day, dwelled in the mountains of Kâf, and occasionally made raids on the Peris. The old French chronicles of the Persian folklore call him the *Dev-bend*, the conqueror of the giants. He, too, is credited with having founded Babylon, Nineveh, Diarbek, etc., etc. Like his grand-sire Hushenk, Tahmurath (Taimuraz) also had his steed, only far more rare and rapid — a bird called *Simorgh-Anke.* A marvelous bird, in truth, intelligent, a polyglot, and even very religious.[843] What says that Persian Phoenix? It complains of its old age, for it is born cycles and cycles before the days of Adam (also Kaimurath). It has witnessed the revolutions of long centuries. It has seen the birth and the close of twelve cycles of 7000 years each, which multiplied esoterically will give us again 840,000 years.[844] Simorgh is born with the last deluge of the pre-Adamites, says the "romance of Simorgh and the good Khalif"![845]

What says the *"Book of Numbers"?* Esoterically, Adam Rishoon is the lunar Spirit (Jehovah, in a sense, or the Pitris) and his three Sons — Ka-yin, Habel, and Seth — represent the three races, as already explained. Noah-Xisuthrus represents in his turn (in the cosmogeological key) the 3rd Race separated, and his three sons, its last

842. *Orient. Trad.*, p. 454. See also Bailly's *Lettres sur l'Atlantide.*
843. See *Orient. Collect.*, ii, 119.
844. *Orient. Collect.*, ii, 119 *et seq.*
Remember that the Rabbins teach that there are to be seven successive renewals of the globe; that each will last 7000 years,

the total duration being thus 49,000 years (See Rabbi Parcha's "*wheel*"; also Kenealy's "*Book of God,*" p. 176). This refers to 7 Rounds, 7 Root-races, and sub-races, the truly occult figures, though sorely confused.
845. *Tales of Derbent.*

three races; Ham, moreover, symbolizing that race which uncovered the "*nakedness*" of the Parent Race, and of the "Mindless," *i. e.,* committed sin.

Tahmurath visits on his winged steed (Ahriman) the Mountains of Koh-Kâf or *Kaph.* He finds there the Peris ill-treated by the giants, and slays Argen, and the giant *Demrush.* Then he liberates the good Peri, Mergiana,[846] whom Demrush had kept as a prisoner, and takes her over to the *dry* island, *i. e.,* the new continent of Europe.[847] After him came Giamshid, who builds *Esikekar,* or Persepolis. This king reigns 700 years, and believes himself, in his great pride, immortal, and demands divine honors. Fate punishes him, he wanders for 100 years in the world under the name of *Dhulkarnayn* "the two horned." But this epithet has no connexion with the "two-horned" gentleman of the cloven foot. The "two-horned" is the epithet given in Asia, uncivilized enough to know nothing of the attributes of the devil, to those conquerors who have subdued the world from the East to the West.

Then come the usurper *Zohac,* and Feridan, one of the Persian heroes, who vanquishes the former, and shuts him up in the mountains of Damavend. These are followed by many others down to *Kaikobad,* who founded a new dynasty.

Such is the legendary history of Persia, and we have to analyse it. What are the mountains of *Kâf* to begin with?

Whatever they may be in their geographical status, whether they are the Caucasian or Central Asian mountains, it is far beyond these mountains to the North, that legend places the Devs and Peris; the latter the remote ancestors of the Parses or Farses. Oriental tradition is ever referring to an unknown glacial, gloomy sea, and to a dark region, within which, nevertheless, are situated *the Fortunate Islands,* wherein bubbles, from the beginning of life on earth, the *fountain of life.*[848] But the legend asserts, moreover, that a portion of the first *dry* island (continent), having detached itself from the main body, has remained, since then, beyond the mountains of Koh-kâf, "the stony girdle that surrounds the world." A journey of seven months' duration will bring him who is possessed of "Soliman's ring" to that "fountain," if he keeps on journeying North straight before him as the bird flies. Journeying therefore from Persia *straight north,* will bring one along the sixtieth degree of longitude, holding to the west, to Nova Zembla; and from the Caucasus to the eternal ice

846. Mergain, or Morgana, the fairy sister of King Arthur, is thus shown of Oriental descent.

847. Where we find her, indeed, in Great Britain, in the romance of the Knights of the Round Table. Whence the identity of name and fairy-hood, if both heroines did not symbolize the same historical event which had passed into a legend?

848. Herbelot, p. 593; *Armenian Tales,* p. 35.

beyond the Arctic circle would land one between 60 and 45 degrees of longitude, or between Nova Zembla and Spitzbergen. This, of course, if one has the dodecapodian horse of Hushenk or the winged Simorgh of Tahmurath (or Taimuraz), upon which to cross over the Arctic Ocean.[849]

Nevertheless, the wandering songsters of Persia and the Caucasus will maintain, to this day, that far beyond the snow-capped summits of Kap, or Caucasus, *there is a great continent now concealed from all.* That it is reached by those who can secure the services of the twelve-legged progeny of the crocodile and the female hippopotamus, whose legs become at will *twelve wings;* [850] or by those who have the patience to wait for the good pleasure of *Simorgh-Anke,* who promised that before she dies she will reveal the hidden continent to all, and make it once more visible and within easy reach, by means of a bridge, which the Ocean Devs will build between that portion of the " dry island " and its severed parts.[851] This relates, of course, to the seventh race, Simorgh being the Manvantaric cycle.

It is very curious that Kosmas Indikopleustes, who lived in the sixth century A. D., should always have maintained that man was born, and dwelt at first in a country *beyond the Ocean,* a proof of which had been given him in India, by a learned Chaldaean.[852] *He says: "The lands we live in are surrounded by the ocean, but beyond that ocean there is another land which touches the walls of the sky; and it is in this land that man was created and lived in paradise. During the Deluge, Noah was carried in his ark into the land his posterity now inhabits."* [853] The twelve-legged horse of Hushenk was found on that continent named the *dry* island.[854]

The " Christian topography " of Kosmas Indikopleustes and its merits are well known; but here the good father repeats a universal tradition, now, moreover, corroborated by facts. Every arctic traveler suspects a continent or a " dry island " beyond the line of eternal ice.

---

849. To this day the aborigines of Caucasus speak of their mountains as Kap-kaz, using the consonant p instead of the usual v (Kavkaz or Caucasus). But their bards say that it requires seven months for a swift horse to reach the " dry land " beyond Kâf, holding north without ever deviating from one's way.

850. Bailly thought he saw in this horse a twelve-oared ship. The Secret Doctrine teaches that the early Third Race built boats and flotillas before it built houses. But the " horse," though a much later animal, has, nevertheless, a more occult primitive meaning. The crocodile and the hippopotamus were held sacred and represented divine symbols, both with the ancient Egyptians and with the Mexicans. Poseidon is, in Homer, the God of the Horse, and assumes that form himself to please Ceres. Arion, their progeny, is one of the aspects of that " horse," which is a cycle.

851. The severed parts must be Norway and other lands in the neighborhood of the Arctic Circle.

852. Kosmas Indikopleustes in *Collect. nova Patrum,* t. II, p. 188; also see *Journ. des Savants,* Suppl. 1707, p. 20.

853. *Ibid.*

854. *Supra,* p. 154.

Perhaps now the meaning of the following passage from one of the Commentaries may become clearer.

" In the first beginnings of (human) life, the only dry land was on the Right end [855] of the sphere, where it (the globe) is motionless. [856] The whole earth was one vast watery desert, and the waters were tepid . . . . There man was born on the seven zones of the immortal, the indestructible of the Manvantara. [857] There was eternal spring in darkness. (But) that which is darkness to the man of today, was light to the man of his dawn. There, the gods rested, and Fohat [858] reigns ever since . . . . Thus the wise fathers say that man is born in the head of his mother (earth), and that her feet at the left end generated (begot) the evil winds that blow from the mouth of the lower Dragon . . . . Between the first and second (races) the eternal central (land) was divided by the water of life. [859]

" It flows around and animates her (mother earth's) body. Its one end issues from her head; it becomes foul at her feet (the Southern Pole). It gets purified (on its return) to her heart—which beats under the foot of the sacred Sambhala, which then (in the beginnings) was not yet born. For it is in the belt of man's dwelling (the earth) that lies concealed the life and health of all that lives and breathes. [860] During the first and second (races) the belt was covered with the great waters. (But) the great mother travailed under the waves and a new land was joined to the first one which our wise men call the head-gear (the cap). She travailed harder for the third (race) and her waist

855. The two poles are called the right and left ends of our globe — the right being the North Pole — or the head and feet of the earth. Every beneficent (astral and cosmic) action comes from the North; every lethal influence from the South Pole. They are much connected with and influence " right " and " left " hand magic.

856. The more one approaches the poles the less rotation is felt; at the poles proper, the diurnal rotation is quite neutralized. Thence the expression that the sphere is " motionless."

857. It is averred in Occultism that the land or island, which crowns the North Pole like a skull-cap, is the only one which prevails during the whole Manvantara of our " Round." All the central continents and lands will emerge from the sea bottom many times in turn, but this land will never change.

858. Bear in mind that the Vedic and Avestian name of Fohat is Apâm-Napât. In the Avesta he stands between the fire-yazatas and the water-yazatas. The literal meaning is " Son of the Waters," but these "waters" are not the liquid we know, but Ether — the fiery waters of space. Fohat is the " Son of Ether " in its highest aspect, Akâśa, the Mother-Father of the primitive Seven, and of Sound or Logos. Fohat is the light of the latter. See Book I.

859. This "water" is the blood or fluid of life which animates the earth, compared here to a living body.

860. Occult teaching corroborates the popular tradition which asserts the existence of a fountain of life in the bowels of the earth and in the North Pole. It is the blood of the earth, the electro-magnetic current, which circulates through all the arteries; and which is said to be found stored in the " navel " of the earth.

and navel appeared above the water. It was the belt, the sacred Himavat, which stretches around the world.[861] *She broke toward the setting sun from her neck*[862] *downward* (to the south west), *into many lands and islands, but the eternal land* (the cap) *broke not asunder. Dry lands covered the face of the silent waters to the four sides of the world. All these perished* (in their turn). *Then appeared the abode of the wicked* (the Atlantis). *The eternal land was now hid, for the waters became solid* (frozen) *under the breath of her nostrils and the evil winds from the Dragon's mouth,"* etc., etc.

This shows that Northern Asia is as old as the Second Race. One may even say that Asia is contemporary with man, since from the very beginnings of human life its *root*-continent, so to speak, already existed; that part of the world now known as Asia being only cut off from it in a later age and divided by the glacial waters.

If, then, the teaching is understood correctly, the first continent which came into existence capped over the whole North Pole like one unbroken crust, and remains so to this day, beyond that inland sea which seemed like an unreachable *mirage to the few* arctic travelers who perceived it.

During the Second Race more land emerged from under the waters as a continuation of the "head" from the neck. Beginning on both hemispheres, on the line above the most northern part of Spitzbergen[863] on Mercator's Projection, on our side, it may have included, on the

---

861. Occultism points to the Himâlayan chain as that "belt," and maintains that whether under the water or above, it encircles the globe. The *navel* is described as situated to the setting sun or to the west of the Himavat in which lie the roots of Meru, which mountain is north of the Himâlaya. Meru is *not* "the fabulous mountain *in* the navel or center of the earth," but its roots and foundations are in that navel, though it is in the far north itself. This connects it with the "central" land "that never perishes"; the land in which "the day of the mortal lasts six months and his night another six months." As the *Vishnu Purâna* has it: "for the North of Meru there is, therefore, always night during day in *other regions*; for Meru is north of all the *dvîpas* and *varshas*" (islands and countries) (*Book II, chap. viii*). Meru is therefore neither on *Atlas* as Wilford suggests, nor, as Wilson tried to show, "absolutely in the center of the globe," only because "relatively with the inhabitants of the sev-

eral portions, to all of whom the East is that quarter where the sun first appears."

862. Even the Commentaries do not refrain from Oriental metaphor. The globe is likened to the body of a woman, "mother earth." From her neck downward, means from the inland sea now beyond the impassable barrier of ice. The Earth, as Parâsara says, "is the mother and nurse, augmented with all creatures and *their* qualities, *the comprehender* of all the worlds."

863. For the Stanzas call this locality by a term translated in the commentary as *a place of no latitude* (niraksha) the abode of the gods. As a scholiast says from the *Sûrya Siddhânta:*

"Above this (the Siddhâ) goes the sun when situated at the equinoxes; they have neither equinoctial shadow nor elevation of the pole (*akshonnati*, v. 42). In both directions from these are two pole-stars (*dhruvatârâ*), fixed in the midst of the sky; to those *who are situated in places of no lati-*

American side, the localities that are now occupied by Baffin's Bay and the neighboring islands and promontories. *There* it hardly reached, southward, the 70th degree of latitude; *here* — it formed the horseshoe continent of which the commentary speaks; of the two ends of which, one included Greenland with a prolongation which crossed the 50th degree a little south west, and the other Kamschatka, the two ends being united by what is now the northern fringe of the coasts of Eastern and Western Siberia. This broke asunder and disappeared. In the early part of the Third Race — Lemuria was formed.[864] When it was destroyed in its turn, Atlantis appeared.

WESTERN SPECULATIONS,
FOUNDED ON THE GREEK AND PURÂNIC TRADITIONS

Thus it becomes natural to find that on even such meager data as have reached the profane historian, Rudbeck, a Swedish scientist, tried to prove about two centuries ago that Sweden was the Atlantis of Plato. He thought, even, that he had found in the configuration of ancient Upsala, the situation and measurements given by the Greek sage of the capital of "Atlantis." As Bailly proved, Rudbeck was mistaken; but so was Bailly likewise, and still more. For Sweden and Norway had formed part and parcel of ancient Lemuria, and also of Atlantis on the European side, just as Eastern and Western Siberia and Kamschatka had belonged to it, on the Asiatic. Only, once more, when was it? We can find it out approximately only by studying the *Purânas,* if we will have nought to do with the Secret teachings.

Three quarters of a century have already elapsed since Captain (now Colonel) Wilford brought forward his fanciful theories about the British islands being the "White Island," the *Atala* of the Purânas. This was sheer nonsense, as the Atala is one of the seven *dvîpas,* or islands, belonging to the nether lokas, one of the seven regions of Pâtâla (the antipodes). Moreover, as Wilford[865] shows, the Purânas place it "on the seventh zone or seventh climate," — rather, on the seventh

---

tude (niraksha) both these have their place in the horizon. Hence there is (on that land) no elevation of the poles, the two pole-stars being situated in their horizon; but their degrees of colatitude (*lambaka*) are 90; at Meru the degrees of latitude (*aksha*) are of the same number." (43 *and* 44.)

864. *Vide supra.*

865. Wilford makes many mistakes. He identifies, for instance, Sveta-dvîpa (the white Island), the "island in the northern part of *Toyâmbudhi,*" with England, and then tries to identify it with Atala (a nether region) and Atlantis. Now the former is the abode of Vishnu, *esoterically,* and Atala is a hell. He also places it in the Euxine or Icshu (Black) Sea, and then seems to connect it, in another place, with Africa and Atlas.

measure of heat: which thus locates it between the latitudes of 24 and 28 degrees north. It is then to be sought on the same degree as the Tropic of Cancer, whereas England is between the 50th and 60th degrees of latitude. Wilford speaks of it as *Atala,* Atlantis, the white island. And in *Journal of Asiatic Researches,*[866] its enemy is called the " White Devil," the *demon of terror.* For he says:

In their (the Hindû and Mahomedan) romances, we see Kai-caus going to the mountain of " *As-burj, at the foot of which* the Sun sets," to fight the *Dev-Sefid,* or white devil, the *Târadaitya* of the *Purânas,* whose abode was on the *seventh stage* of the world, answering to the seventh zone of the Buddhists, or the *White* Island.

Now here the Orientalists have been, and are still, facing the Sphinx's riddle, the wrong solution of which will ever destroy their authority, if not their persons, in the eyes of every Hindû scholar, even those who are not initiates. For there is not a statement in the Purânas — on the conflicting details of which Wilford based his speculations — which has not several meanings, and does not apply to both the physical and the metaphysical worlds. If the old Hindûs divided the face of the globe geographically into seven zones, climates, dvipas, and into seven hells and seven heavens, allegorically, that measure of seven did not apply in both cases to the same localities. It is the north pole, the country of " Meru," which is the seventh division, as it answers to the Seventh principle (or fourth metaphysically), of the occult calculation, for it represents the region of Âtmâ, of pure soul, and Spirituality. Hence Pushkara is shown *as the seventh zone,* or dvipa, which encompasses the *Kshîra* Ocean, or Ocean of milk (the ever-frozen white region) in the *Vishnu* (and other) *Purânas.*[867] And Pushkara, with its two *Varshas,* lies directly at the foot of Meru. For it is said that " the two countries north and south of Meru are *shaped like a bow, . . .*" and that " one half of the surface of the earth is on the south of Meru and the other half on the north of Meru — *beyond which is half of Pushkara."* [868] Geographically, then, Pushkara is America, Northern and Southern; and *allegorically* it is the prolongation of Jambu-dvipa[869] in the middle of which stands Meru, for it is

866. Vol. viii, p. 280.
867. Book II, ch. iv.
868. *Vishnu Purâna, Asiatic Researches,* etc.
869. Every name in the Purânas has to be examined at least under two aspects; geographically, and metaphysically, in its allegorical application; *e. g.,* Nîla, the (blue) mountain which is one of the boundaries to the north of Meru, is again to be sought

geographically in a mountain range in Orissa, and again in a mountain quite different from the others (in Western Africa). Jambu-dvipa is Vishnu's dominion — the world, limited in the Purânas to our globe, the region which contains Meru *only,* and again it is divided to contain Bhârata-varsha (India), its *best* division, and the fairest, says Parâśara. Likewise with Pushkara and all others.

the country inhabited by beings who live ten thousand years, who are free from sickness or failing; where there is neither virtue nor vice, caste or laws, for these men are "of the same nature as the Gods."[870] Wilford is inclined to see Meru in Mount Atlas, and locates there also the Loka-lokas. Now Meru, we are told, which is the *Svar*-loka, the abode of Brahmâ, of Vishnu, and the Olympus of Indian exoteric religions, is described geographically as "passing through the middle of the earth-globe, and protruding on either side.[871] On its upper station are the gods, on the nether (or South pole) is the abode of demons (hells). How can then Meru be Mount Atlas? Besides which, Târadaitya, a demon, cannot be placed on the seventh zone if the latter is identified with the "white" Island, which is *Sveta-dvîpa*, for reasons given in the foot-note.[872]

Wilford accuses the modern Brâhmans "of having jumbled them (islands and countries) all together";[873] but *he* jumbled them still more. He believes that as the *Brahmânda* and *Vâyu Purânas* divide the old continent into seven dvîpas, said to be surrounded by a vast ocean, beyond which lie the regions and mountains of Atala,[874] hence "most probably the Greeks divided the nation of Atlantis, which, as it could not be found after having once been discovered, they conceived to have been destroyed by some shock of nature."

Finding certain difficulties in believing that the Egyptian priests, Plato, and even Homer, had all built their notions of Atlantis on Atala — a nether region located at the Southern pole — we prefer holding to the statements given in the secret books. We believe in the seven "continents," four of which have already lived their day, the fifth still exists, and two are to appear in the future. We believe that each of these is not strictly a continent in the modern sense of the word, but that each name, from Jambu down to Pushkara,[875] refers to the geographical names given (i.) to the dry lands covering the face of the whole earth during the period of a Root-Race, in general; and (ii.) to what remained of these after a geological (race) *Pralaya* — as "Jambu," for instance; and (iii.) to those localities which will enter, after the future cataclysms, into the formation of new *universal* "continents," peninsulas, or dvîpas[876] — each continent being, in one sense, a greater or smaller region of dry land surrounded with water. Thus, that what-

870. *Vishnu Purâna*, Book II, ch. iv.

871. *Sûrya Siddhânta*, verse 5, Whitney's translation.
872. *Vide infra.*
873. *Asiatic Researches*, III, 300.
874. *Ibid.*
875. Jambu, Plaksha, Salmali, Kuśa, Krauncha, Sâka and Pushkara.

876. Such as Sâka and Pushkara, for instance, which do not yet exist, but into which will enter such lands as some portions of America, of Africa, and Central Asia, with the Gobi region. Let us bear in mind that *Upadvîpas* means "root" islands, or the dry land in general.

ever "jumble" the nomenclature of these may represent to the profane, there is none, in fact, to him who has the key.

Thus, we believe *we know* that, though two of the Purânic "islands" — the *sixth and seventh* "continents" — are yet to come, nevertheless there *were*, or there *are*, lands which will enter into the composition of the future dry lands, of new earths whose geographical faces will be entirely changed, as were those of the past. Therefore we find in the Purânas that Sâka-dvipa is (or will be) a continent, and that Sankha-dvipa, as shown in the *Vâyu Purâna*, is only "a minor island," one of the nine divisions (to which Vâyu adds six more) of Bhârata Varsha. Because Sankha-dvipa was peopled by "Mlechchhas [unclean foreigners], who worshiped Hindû divinities," therefore they were connected with India.[877] This accounts for Sankhâsura, a King of a portion of Sankha-dvipa, who was killed by Krishna; that King who resided in the palace "which was an ocean shell, and whose subjects lived in shells also," says Wilford.

On the banks of the Nile[878] [?] there were frequent contests between the Devatâs (divine beings, demi-gods) and the Daityas (giants); but the latter tribe having prevailed, their King, Sankhâsura, who resided in the Ocean, made frequent incursions in the night.[879]

It is not on the banks of the *Nile*, but on the coasts of Western Africa, south of where now lies Morocco, that these battles took place. There was a time when the whole of the Sahara desert was a sea, then a continent as fertile as the Delta, and then, only after another temporary submersion, it became a desert similar to that other wilderness, the desert of Shamo or Gobi. This is shown in Purânic tradition, for on the same page as above cited, it is said: "The people were between two fires; for, while Sankhâsura was ravaging one side of the continent, Krauncha (or Cracacha), King of Krauncha, used to desolate the other; both armies . . . thus *changed the most fertile regions into a savage desert*."

That not only the last island of Atlantis, spoken of by Plato, but a large continent, first divided, and then broken later on into seven peninsulas and islands (called *dvipas*), preceded Europe, is sure. It covered the whole of the North and South Atlantic regions, as well as portions of the North and South Pacific, and had islands even in the Indian Ocean (relics of Lemuria). The claim is corroborated by Indian Purânas, Greek writers, and Asiatic, Persian, and Mohammedan traditions. Wilford, who confuses sorely the Hindû and the Mus-

---

877. They were called demons, *Asuras*, giants, and monsters, because of their wickedness; and thus their country was likened to Atala — a hell, because of that.

878. Not on the river Nile, surely, but near the *Nila* mountains of the Atlas range.

879. *Asiatic Researches*, Vol. III, page 225.

sulman legends, shows this, however, clearly.[880] And his facts and quotations from the *Purânas* give direct and conclusive evidence that the Aryan Hindûs and other ancient nations were earlier navigators than the Phoenicians, who are now credited with having been the first seamen that appeared in the *post*-diluvian times. This is what is given in the *Journal* of the Asiatic Society:[881]

In their distress the few nations who survived (in the war between Devatàs and Daityas) raised their hands to Bhagavân, "Let him who can deliver us . . . be our King"; using the word I'T [a *magic* term not understood by Wilford, evidently] which re-echoed through the whole country.

Then comes a violent storm, the waters of the *Kâlî* are strangely agitated, "when there appeared from the waves . . . a man, afterwards called I'T, at the head of a numerous army, saying *abhayan*, no fear . . . " and scattered the enemy. "The King I'T," explains Wilford, "is a subordinate incarnation of Mrira" (*Mrida*, a form of Rudra, probably?) who "re-established peace and prosperity throughout all Sankha-dvipa, *through Barbaradesa*, Misrasthân and Arvasthân or Arabia . . ." etc., etc.

Surely, if the Hindû Purânas give a description of wars on continents and islands situated beyond Western Africa in the Atlantic Ocean; if their writers speak of *Barbaras* and other people such as Arabs — they who were never known to navigate, or cross the *Kâlâ pânî* (the black waters of the Ocean) in the days of Phoenician navigation — then their Purânas must be older than those Phoenicians (placed at from 2000 to 3000 years B. C.). At any rate those traditions must have been older;[882] as—

" In the above accounts," writes an adept, " the Hindûs speak of this island as *existing* and in great power; it must, therefore, have been more than *eleven thousand years ago.*"

But another calculation and proof may be adduced of the great antiquity of these Hindû Âryans who knew of (because they had once dwelt in it) and described the last surviving island of Atlantis — or

880. See Vol. VIII, X and XI of *Asiatic Researches.*

881. Vol. III, pp. 325, *et seq.*

882. Says Wilford of the division of Atlantis and Bhârata or India, confusing the two accounts and Priyavrata with Medhâtithi:— " The division was made by Priyavrata. . . . He had ten sons, and it was his intention to divide the whole world. In the same manner Neptune divided Atlantis between his ten sons. . . . One of them had . . . the extremity of the Atlantis" — which "is probably the old continent.... This Atlantis was overwhelmed by a flood . . . and it seems that *by Atlantis we should understand the Antediluvian Earth* over which ten princes were born to rule according to the mythology of the West [and of the East, also] but *seven only* of them sat upon the throne." (*Vol. III*, p. 286) . . . Some also are of opinion that of the *seven* dvipas *six* were destroyed by a flood (*Vol. VIII, p. 367*). Wilford takes it to be " Gades which included Spain," but it was Plato's island — rather.

rather of that remnant of the Eastern portion of that continent which had perished soon after the upheaval of the two Americas[883] — the two Varshas of Pushkara. This may be demonstrated, moreover, on an astronomical calculation by an adept who criticises Wilford. For recalling what the Orientalist had brought forward concerning the Mount Ashburj " at the foot of which the sun sets," where was the war between the Devatâs and the Daityas,[884] he says:—

" We will consider, then, the latitude and longitude of the lost island, and of the remaining Mount Ashburj. It was on the seventh stage of the world, *i. e.*, in the seventh climate (which is between the latitude of 24 degrees and latitude 28 degrees north). . . . This island, the daughter of the Ocean, is frequently described as lying in the West; and the sun is represented as setting at the foot of its mountain (Ashburj, Atlas, Teneriffe or Nila, no matter the name), and fighting the white Devil of the ' White Island.' "

Now, considering this statement from its astronomical aspect, and knowing that Krishna is the incarnated Sun (Vishnu), a solar God; and that he is said to have killed Dev-Sefid, the white giant — a *possible* personification of the ancient inhabitants at the foot of the Atlas — perchance Krishna may be only a representation of the vertical beams of the Sun? Those inhabitants (the Atlantides) are, we have seen, accused by Diodorus of daily *cursing the Sun*, and ever fighting his influence. This is an astronomical interpretation of course. But it will now be proved that Śankhâsura, and Sancha dvipa, and all their history, is also geographical and ethnologically Plato's "Atlantis " in Hindû dress.

It was just remarked that since, in the Purânic accounts, the island is *still existing*, then those accounts must be older than the 11,000 years elapsed since Sancha dvipa, or the Poseidonis of Atlantis, disappeared. Is it not barely possible that Hindûs should have known the island still earlier? Let us turn again to astronomical demonstrations, which make this quite plain if one assumes, according to the said adept, that " at the time when the summer tropical ' colure ' passed through the *Pleiades*, when *Cor Leonis* would be upon the equator; and when Leo *was vertical* to Ceylon at sunset, then would *Taurus* be vertical to the island of *Atlantis at noon.*"

This explains, perhaps, why the Sinhalese, the heirs of the Râkshasas

---

883. America, the " new " world — is thus, though not *much*, older; still it is older than Europe, the " old world."

884. If Div or Dev-Sefid's (the Târadaitya's) abode was on the *seventh stage*, it it because he came from Pushkara, the *Pâtâla*

(antipodes) of India, or from America. The latter touched the walls, so to say, of Atlantis, before the latter sank finally. The word *Pâtâla*, meaning both the antipodal countries and infernal regions, thus became synonymous in ideas and attributes as well as in name.

and Giants of Lankâ, and the direct descendants of *Sinha*, or *Leo*, became connected with Sancha dvipa or Poseidonis (Plato's Atlantis). Only, as shown by Mackey's *Sphinxiad*, this must have occurred about 23,000 years ago, *astronomically;* at which time the obliquity of the ecliptic must have been rather more than 27 degrees, and consequently Taurus must have passed over "Atlantis" or "Sancha dvipa." And that it was so is clearly demonstrated.

"*The sacred bull Nandi was brought from Bhârata to Sancha to meet Rishabha* (Taurus) *every Kalpa. But when those of the White Island* (who descended originally from Sveta dvipa),[885] *who had mixed with the Daityas* (giants) *of the land of iniquity, had become black with Sin, then Nandi remained for ever in the 'White Island'* (or Sveta dvipa)." "*Those of the Fourth World* (race) *lost AUM*" — say the *Commentaries.*

Asburj (or Azburj), whether the peak of Teneriffe or not, was a volcano, when the sinking of the "western Atala" (or hell) began, and those who were saved told the tale to their children. Plato's Atlantis perished between water below and fire above; the great mountain vomiting flames all the while. "The 'fire-vomiting Monster' survived alone out of the ruins of the unfortunate island."

Do the Greeks, accused of borrowing a Hindû fiction (Atala), and inventing from it another (Atlantis), stand also accused of getting their geographical notions and the number seven from them?[886] Says Proklos:

The famous Atlantis exists no longer, but we can hardly doubt that it did once, for Marcellus, who wrote a history of Ethiopian affairs, says that such, and so great an island once existed, and this is evidenced by those who composed histories relative to the external sea. For *they relate that in this time there were seven islands* in the Atlantic sea sacred to Proserpine; and besides these, three of immense magnitude, sacred to Pluto . . . Jupiter . . . and Neptune. And, besides this, the inhabitants of the last island [Poseidonis] *preserved the memory of the prodigious magnitude* of the Atlantic island as related by their ancestors, and of its governing for many periods all the islands in the Atlantic sea. From this *isle* one may pass to other large islands beyond, which are not far from the firm land, near which is the true sea.

885. Neither Atlantis, nor yet Sancha dvipa, was ever called "White Island." When tradition says that "the White Island became black on account of the sins of people" it only means the denizens of the "White Island," or Siddhapura, or Sveta dvipa, who descended to the Atlantis of the Third and Fourth races, to "inform the latter; and who, having incarnated, became black with sin" — a figure of speech. All the Avatârs of Vishnu are said to come originally from the White Island. According to Tibetan tradition the White Island is the only locality which escapes the general fate of other dvipas and can be destroyed by neither fire nor water, for — it is the "eternal land."

886. *Vide* in Part II, the several sections on the SEPTENATE in nature.

Wilford himself writes:

These seven dvipas [inaccurately rendered islands] constitute, according to Marcellus, the body of the famous Atlantis. . . . This evidently shows that *Atlantis is the old continent*. . . . The Atlantis was destroyed after a violent storm [?]: this is well known to the Paurânics, some of whom assert that in consequence of this dreadful convulsion of nature, six of the dvipas disappeared. . . .[887]

Enough proofs have now been given to satisfy the greatest sceptic. Nevertheless, direct proofs based on exact science are also added. Volumes might be written, however, to no purpose for those who will neither see nor hear, except through the eyes and ears of their respective authorities.

Hence the teaching of the Roman Catholic scholiasts, namely, that Hermon, the mount in the land of Mizpeth — meaning "anathema," "destruction" — is the same as Mount Armon. As a proof of this Josephus is often quoted, as affirming that still in his own day enormous bones of giants were daily discovered on it. But it was the land of Balaam the prophet, whom the "Lord loved well"; and so mixed up are facts and personages in the said scholiasts' brains, that, when the *Zohar* explains the "birds" which inspired Balaam to mean "Serpents," to wit, the wise men and adepts at whose school he had learned the mysteries of prophecy — the opportunity is again taken of showing Mount Hermon inhabited by the "winged dragons of Evil, whose chief is Samael" (the Jewish Satan).

It is to those unclean spirits chained on Mount Hermon of the Desert, that the scape-goat of Israel, who assumed the name of one of them (Azaz(y)el), was sent.[888]

We say it is not so. The *Zohar* has the following explanation on the practice of magic which is called in Hebrew *Nehhashim*, or the "Serpents' Works." It says:[889] — "It is called *nehhashim*, because the magicians [practical Kabalists] work *surrounded by the light of the primordial serpent*, which they perceive in heaven as a luminous zone composed of myriads of small stars . . ." which means simply the *astral light*, so called by the Martinists, by Éliphas Lévi, and now by all the modern Occultists. (*Vide* Sections about.)

THE "CURSE" FROM A PHILOSOPHICAL POINT OF VIEW

The foregoing teachings of the SECRET DOCTRINE, supplemented by universal traditions, must now have demonstrated that the Brâhmanas

887. xi, 27.   888. Spencer.   889. Part III, col. 302.

and Purânas, the Gâthas and other Mazdean Scriptures, down to the
Egyptian, Greek, and Roman, and finally to the Jewish Sacred records,
all have the same origin. None are meaningless and baseless stories,
invented to entrap the unwary profane: all are allegories intended to
convey, under a more or less fantastic veil, the great truths gathered
in the same field of pre-historic tradition. Space forbids us from
entering, in these two volumes, into further and more minute details
with respect to the four Races which preceded our own. But before
offering to the student the history of the psychic and spiritual evolution
of the direct antediluvian fathers of our Fifth (Aryan) humanity, and
before demonstrating its bearing upon all the other side branches grown
from the same trunk, we have to elucidate a few more facts. It has
been shown, on the evidence of the whole ancient literary world, and
the intuitional speculations of more than one philosopher and scientist
of the later ages, that the tenets of our Esoteric Doctrine are corroborated by inferential as well as by direct proof in almost every case. That
neither the " legendary " giants, nor the lost continents, nor yet the evolution of the preceding races, are quite baseless tales. In the *Addenda*
which close this volume, science will find itself more than once unable to
reply; they will, it is hoped, finally dispose of every sceptical remark
with regard to the sacred number in nature, and our figures in general.[890]
   Meanwhile, one task is left incomplete: that of disposing of that
most pernicious of all the theological dogmas — the CURSE under which
mankind is alleged to have suffered ever since the supposed disobedience of Adam and Eve in the bower of Eden.
   Creative powers in man were the gift of divine wisdom, not the result of sin. This is clearly instanced in the paradoxical behavior of
Jehovah, who first *curses* Adam and Eve (or Humanity) for the supposed committed crime, and then *blesses* his "chosen people" by saying
" Be fruitful and multiply, and replenish the earth."[891] The curse was
not brought on mankind by the Fourth Race, for the comparatively
sinless Third Race, the still more gigantic Antediluvians, had perished
in the same way; hence the Deluge was no punishment, but simply a
result of a periodical and geological law. Nor was the curse of KARMA
called down upon them for seeking *natural* union, as all the mindless
animal-world does in its proper seasons; but, for abusing the creative
power, for desecrating the divine gift, and wasting the life-essence for
no purpose except bestial personal gratification. When understood, the
third chapter of *Genesis* will be found to refer to the Adam and Eve
of the closing Third and the commencing Fourth Races. In the beginning, conception was as easy for woman as it was for all animal creation. Nature had never intended that woman should bring forth her

890. *Vide* §§ on the *Septenaries.*   891. *Genesis* ix. 1.

young ones "in sorrow." Since that period, however, during the evolution of the Fourth Race, there came enmity between its seed, and the "Serpent's" seed, the seed or product of *Karma* and divine wisdom. For the seed of woman or lust, *bruised the head* of the seed of *the fruit of wisdom and knowledge*, by turning the holy mystery of procreation into animal gratification; hence the law of Karma "bruised the *heel*" of the Atlantean race, by gradually changing physiologically, morally, physically, and mentally, the whole nature of the Fourth Race of mankind,[892] until, from the healthy King of animal creation of the Third Race, man became in the Fifth, our race, a helpless, scrofulous being, and has now become the wealthiest heir on the globe to constitutional and hereditary diseases, the most consciously and intelligently bestial of all animals![893]

This is the real CURSE from the physiological standpoint, almost the only one touched upon in the Kabalistic esotericism. Viewed from this aspect, the curse is undeniable, for it is evident. The intellectual evolution, in its progress hand-in-hand with the physical, has certainly been a curse instead of a blessing — a gift quickened by the "Lords of Wisdom," who have poured on the human *manas* the fresh dew of their own spirit and essence. The divine Titan has then suffered in vain; and one feels inclined to regret his benefaction to mankind, and sigh for those days so graphically depicted by Aeschylus, in his *Prometheus Bound,* when, at the close of the first Titanic age (the age that followed that of ethereal man, of the pious Kandu and Pramlochâ), nascent, physical mankind, still mindless and (physiologically) senseless, is described as —

> Seeing, they saw in vain;
> Hearing, they heard not; but like shapes in dreams,
> Through the long time all things at random mixed.

Our *Saviors*, the Agnishvâtta and other divine "Sons of the Flame of Wisdom" (personified by the Greeks in Prometheus[894]), may well,

892. How wise and grand, how far-seeing and morally beneficent are the laws of Manu on connubial life, when compared with the license tacitly allowed to man in civilized countries. That those laws have been neglected for the last two millenniums does not prevent us from admiring their forethought. The Brâhman was a *grihastha,* a family man, till a certain period of his life, when, after begetting a son, he broke with married life and became a chaste Yogi. His very connubial life was regulated by his Brâhman astrologer in accordance with his nature. Therefore, in such countries as the Panjâb, for instance, where the lethal influence of Mus-

sulman, and later on of European, licentiousness, has hardly touched the orthodox Aryan castes, one still finds the finest men — so for as stature and physical strength go — on the whole globe; whereas the mighty men of old have found themselves replaced in the Dekhan, and especially in Bengal, by men whose generation becomes with every century (and almost with every year) dwarfed and weakened.

893. Diseases and over-population are facts that can never be denied.

894. In Mrs. Anna Swanwick's volumes *The Dramas of Aeschylus,* it is said of *Prometheus Bound* (Vol. II, pages 146,

in the injustice of the human heart, be left unrecognized and un-
thanked. They may, in our ignorance of the truth, be indirectly cursed
for Pandora's gift: but to find themselves proclaimed and declared by
the mouth of the clergy, the EVIL ONES, is too heavy a Karma for
" Him " " who dared alone " — when Zeus " ardently desired " to
quench the entire human race — to save " that mortal race " from per-
dition, or, as the suffering Titan is made to say :—

> From sinking blasted down to Hades' gloom.
> For this by these dire tortures I am bent,
> Grievous to suffer, piteous to behold,
> I who did mortals pity! . . . (240-248)

The chorus remarking very pertinently :—

> Vast boon was this thou gavest unto mortals . . .

Prometheus answers :—

> Yea, and besides 'twas I that gave them fire.
> CHORUS: Have now these short-lived creatures flame-eyed fire?
> PROM.: Ay, and by it full many arts will learn. . . . (259-262)

But, with the arts, the fire received has turned into the greatest
curse: the animal element, and *consciousness* of its possession, has
changed periodical instinct into chronic animalism and sensuality.[895] It
is this which hangs over humanity like a heavy funereal pall. Thus
arises the responsibility of free-will; the Titanic passions which represent humanity in its darkest aspect; " the restless insatiability of the
lower passions and desires, when, with self-asserting insolence, they
bid defiance to the restraints of law." [896]

Prometheus having endowed man, according to Plato's *Protagoras*,
with that " wisdom which ministers to physical well-being," but the
lower aspect of *manas* of the animal (*Kâma*) having remained un-

147), that Prometheus truly appears in it
" as the champion and benefactor of mankind, whose condition . . . is depicted as
weak and miserable in the extreme. . . .
Zeus, it is said, proposed to annihilate these
puny ephemerals, and to plant upon the
earth a new race in their stead." We see
the Lords of Being doing likewise, and ex-
terminating the first product of nature and
the sea, in the Stanzas (V, *et seq.*).
" Prometheus *represents* himself as having
frustrated this design, and as being consequently subjected, for the sake of mortals,
to the most agonizing pain, inflicted by the
remorseless cruelty of Zeus. We have, thus,
the Titan, the symbol of finite reason and
free will [of intellectual humanity, or the

higher aspect of *Manas*], depicted *as the sublime philanthropist*, while Zeus, the supreme
deity of Hellas, is portrayed as the cruel
and obdurate despot, a character peculiarly
revolting to Athenian sentiment." The reason for it is explained farther on. The
" Supreme Deity " bears, in every ancient
Pantheon — including that of the Jews — a
dual character, composed of light and shadow.
895. The animal world, having simple in-
stin.t to guide it, has its *seasons of procreation*, and the sexes become neutralized during the rest of the year. Therefore, the
free animal knows sickness but once in its
life — before it dies.
896. Introduction to *Prometheus Bound*,
p. 152.

changed, instead of "an untainted mind, heaven's first gift," [897] there was created the eternal vulture of the ever unsatisfied desire, of regret and despair coupled with "the dreamlike feebleness that fetters the blind race of mortals," [898] unto the day when Prometheus is released by his heaven-appointed deliverer, Herakles.

Now Christians — Roman Catholics especially — have tried to prophetically connect this drama with the coming of Christ. No greater mistake could be made. The true theosophist, the pursuer of divine wisdom and worshiper of ABSOLUTE perfection — the unknown deity which is neither Zeus nor Jehovah — will demur to such an idea. Pointing to antiquity he will prove that there never was an *original* sin, but only an abuse of physical intelligence — the psychic being guided by the animal, and both putting out the light of the spiritual. He will say, "All ye who can read between the lines, study ancient wisdom in the old dramas — the Indian and the Greek; read carefully the one just mentioned, one enacted on the theaters of Athens 2400 years ago, namely *Prometheus Bound."* The myth belongs to neither Hesiod nor Aeschylus; but, as Bunsen says, it "is older than the Hellenes themselves," for it belongs, in truth, to the dawn of human consciousness. The *Crucified* Titan is the personified symbol of the collective Logos, the "Host," and of the "Lords of Wisdom" or the HEAVENLY MAN, who incarnated in Humanity. Moreover, as his name *Pro-metheus,* meaning "he who sees before him" or futurity, shows [899] — in the arts he devised and taught to humanity, psychological insight was not the least. For as he complains to the daughters of Okeanos:—

> Of prophecies the various modes I fixed,
> And among dreams did first discriminate
> The truthful vision . . . and mortals guided
> To a mysterious art. . . . .
> All arts to mortals from Prometheus came. . . . (492–513)

897. Aeschylus.

898. Lines 558–560.

899. From πρό μῆτις. "forethought." "Professor Kuhn," we are told in the above-named volumes of *The Dramas of Aeschylus,* "considers the name of the Titan to be derived from the Sanskrit word Pramantha, the instrument used for kindling fire. The root *mand* or *manth,* implies rotatory motion, and the word *manthâmi* (used to denote the process of fire-kindling) acquired the secondary sense of snatching away; hence we find another word of the same stock, *pramatha,* signifying theft." This is very ingenious, but perhaps not altogether correct; besides, there is a very prosaic element in it. No doubt in physical nature, the higher forms may develop from the lower ones, but it is hardly so in the world of thought. And as we are told that "the word *manthâmi* passed into the Greek language and became the word *manthanô,* to learn; that is, to appropriate knowledge; whence *prometheia,* fore-knowledge, forethought"; we may find, in searching, a more poetical origin for the "fire bringer" than that displayed in its Sanskrit origin. The *Svastika,* the sacred sign and the instrument for kindling *sacred* fire, may explain it better. "Prometheus, the fire-bringer, is the *Pramantha* personified," goes on the author; "he finds his prototype in the Aryan Mâtariśvan, a divine

Leaving for a few pages the main subject, let us pause and see what may be the hidden meaning of this, the most ancient as it is the most suggestive of traditional allegories. As it relates directly to the early races, this will be no real digression.

The subject of Aeschylus' drama (the trilogy is lost) is known to all cultured readers. The demi-god robs the gods (the Elohim) of their secret — the mystery of the *creative fire.* For this sacrilegious attempt he is struck down by KRONOS[900] and delivered unto Zeus, the FATHER and creator of a mankind which he would wish to have blind intellectually, and animal-like; a *personal* deity, which will not see MAN " like one of us." Hence Prometheus, " the fire and light-giver," is chained on Mount Caucasus and condemned to suffer torture. But the triform Fates (Karma), whose decrees, as the Titan says, even Zeus:—

> E'en he the fore-ordained cannot escape. . . .

— ordain that those sufferings will last only to that day when a son of Zeus —

> Ay, a son bearing stronger than his sire   (787)
> .   .   .   .
> One of thine [Io's] own descendants it must be. . . .   (791)

— is born. This " Son " will deliver Prometheus (the suffering Humanity) from his own fatal gift. His name is, " He who has to come. . . ."

On the authority, then, of these few lines, which, like any other allegorical sentence, may be twisted into almost any meaning; namely, on the words pronounced by Prometheus and addressed to Io, the daughter of Inachos, persecuted by Zeus — a whole prophecy is constructed by some Catholic writers. Says the crucified Titan:—

> And, portent past belief, the speaking oaks
> By which thou clearly, in no riddling phrase
> Wert hailed *as the illustrious spouse of Zeus*
> .   .   .   . (ll. 851–853)
> .   .   .   . stroking thee
> With *touch alone of unalarming hand;*
> Then thou *dark Epaphos* shalt bear, whose name
> Records his sacred gendering . . . (868–871)

This was construed by several fanatics — des Mousseaux and de

---

. . . personage, closely associated with the fire god of the Veda, Agni. . . ." Math, in Sanskrit, is " understanding," and a synonym of MAHAT and *manas*, and must be of some account in the origin of the name:

Pramati is the son of Fohat, and has his story also.

900. Kronos is " time," and thus the allegory becomes very suggestive. (*See closing pages of this Sub-section.*)

Mirville amongst others — into a clear prophecy. Io — " is the mother of God," we are told, and " dark Epaphos " — Christ. But, the latter has not dethroned his father, except metaphorically, if one has to regard Jehovah as that " Father "; nor has the Christian Savior hurled *his* Father down into Hades. Prometheus says, in line 928, that Zeus will be humbled yet; as for himself:—

> . . . such marriage he prepares
> Which from his throne of power to nothingness
> Shall hurl him down; so shall be all fulfilled
> His father Kronos' curse. . . .[901]
>   . . . Then let him sit
> Confiding in his lofty thunder-peals,
> And wielding with both hands the fiery bolt;
> For *these shall not avail, but fall he shall,*
> *A fall disgraceful,* not to be endured . . . (ll. 929-940)

" Dark Epaphos " was the Dionysos-Sabazios, the son of Zeus and of Demeter in the Sabazian Mysteries, during which the " father of the gods," assuming the *shape of a Serpent,* begot on Demeter, Dionysos, or the solar Bacchus. Io is the moon, and at the same time the EVE *of a new race,* and so is Demeter — in the present case. The Promethean myth is a prophecy indeed; but it does not relate to any of the cyclic Saviors who have appeared periodically in various countries and among various nations, in their transitionary conditions of evolution. It points to the last of the mysteries of cyclic transformations, in the series of which mankind, having passed from the ethereal to the solid physical state, from spiritual to physiological procreation, is now carried onward on the opposite arc of the cycle, toward that second phase of its primitive state, when *woman knew no man,* and human progeny *was created, not begotten.*

That state will return to it and to the world at large, when the latter shall discover and really appreciate the truths which underlie this vast problem of sex. It will be like " the light that never shone on sea or land," and has to come to men through the Theosophical Society. That light will lead on and up to the *true spiritual intuition.* Then (as expressed once in a letter to a theosophist), " the world *will have a race of Buddhas and Christs,* for the world will have discovered that individuals *have it in their own powers to procreate Buddha-like children — or demons."* " When that knowledge comes, all dogmatic religions, and with these the demons, will die out."

If we reflect upon the serial development of the allegory, and the character of the heroes, the mystery may be unriddled. KRONOS is of course " time " in its cyclic course. He swallows his children — the

901. See, for explanation of this curse, the last page of the present sub-section.

personal gods of exoteric dogmas included. He has swallowed instead of Zeus, his *stone* idol; but the symbol has grown, and has only developed in human fancy as mankind was cycling down toward only its physical and intellectual — not spiritual — perfection. When it is as far advanced in its spiritual evolution Kronos will be no longer deceived. Instead of the *stone image* he will have swallowed the anthropomorphic fiction itself. Because, *the serpent of wisdom,* represented in the Sabazian mysteries by the anthropomorphized Logos, the unity of spiritual and physical Powers, will have begotten in Time (Kronos) a progeny — Dionysos-Bacchus or the "dark Epaphos," the "mighty one" — the race that will overthrow him. Where will he be born? Prometheus traces him to his origin and birth-place in his prophecy to Io. Io is the moon-goddess of generation — for she is Isis and she is Eve, the great mother.[902] He traces the path of the (racial) wanderings as plainly as words can express it. She has to quit Europe and go to Asia's continent, reaching there the highest of the mountains of Caucasus (737), the Titan telling her:—

> When thou hast crossed the flood, limit bewixt
> Two continents, fronting the burning East (810)

that she must travel eastward, after passing the "Kimmerian Bosporos," and cross what is evidently the Volga and now Astrakhan on the Caspian Sea. After this she will encounter "fierce northern blasts" and cross thither to the land of the "Arimaspian host" (east of Herodotus' Scythia) to —

> Pluto's gold-abounding flood. . . .   (825)

Which is rightly conjectured by Professor Newman to have meant the Ural, the Arimaspi of Herodotus being "the recognized inhabitants of this golden region."

902. It is complained by the author of the version on, and translator of, *Prometheus Bound* that in this tracing of Io's wanderings, "no consistency with our known geography is attainable" (*p.* 191, *Vol. II*). There may be good reason for it. First of all it is the journey and wandering from place to place of the *race* from which the "tenth," or *Kalki*-Avatâra, so-called, is to issue. This he calls the "Kingly race born in *Argos*" (888). But Argos has no reference here to Argos in Greece. It comes from *Arg* or *arca* — the female generative power symbolized in the moon — the navi-formed Argha of the mysteries, meaning the Queen of Heaven. Eustathios shows that, in the dialect of the Arg-ians, Io signified the moon; while esotericism explains it as the divine Androgyne, or the mystic 10; in Hebrew 10 is the perfect number, or Jehovah. *Arghya* in Sanskrit is the libation cup, the *navi*-form or boat-shaped vessel in which flowers and fruit are offered to the deities. *Arghyanâth* is a title of the Mahâ-Chohan, meaning "the Lord of Libations"; and *Arghya Varsha* — "the land of libations" — is the mystery name of that region which extends from Kailâs mountain nearly to the Shamo Desert — from within which the *Kalki-Avatâra* is expected. The Airyana-Varsedya of the Zoroastrians, as a locality, is identical with it. It is now said to have been situated between the Sea of Aral, Baltistân, and Little Tibet; but in olden times its area was far larger, as it was the birth-place of *physical* humanity, of which Io is the mother and symbol.

And here comes, between verses 825 and 835, a puzzle to all the European interpreters. Says the Titan:—

> To these [Arimaspi and Grypes] approach not; a far border-land
> Thou next shalt reach, where dwells a swarthy race
> Near the Sun's founts, whence is the Aethiop "river";
> Along its banks proceed till thou attain
> The mighty rapids, where from Bybline heights
> Pure draughts of sacred water Neilos sends . . .

There Io was ordained to found a colony for herself and sons. Now we must see how the passage is interpreted. As Io is told that she has to travel eastward till she comes to the river Ethiops, which she is to follow till it falls into the Nile — hence the perplexity. "According to the geographical theories of the earliest Greeks" we are informed by the author of the version on *Prometheus Bound* —

> This condition was fulfilled by the river Indus. Arrian (vi. 1) mentions that Alexander the Great, when preparing to sail down the Indus (having seen crocodiles in the river Indus, and in no other river except the Nile ...), seemed to himself to have discovered the sources of the Nile; as though the Nile, rising from some place in India, and flowing through much desert land, and thereby losing its name Indus, next . . . flowed through inhabited land, being now called Nile by the Ethiopians of those parts, and afterwards by the Egyptians. . Virgil in the 4th Georgic echoes the obsolete error.[903]

Both Alexander and Virgil may have erred considerably in their geographical notions; but the prophecy of Prometheus has not so sinned, in the least — not, at any rate, in its esoteric spirit. When a certain race is symbolized, and events pertaining to its history are rendered allegorically, no topographical accuracy ought to be expected in the itinerary traced for its personification. Yet it so happens, that the river "Ethiops" is certainly the Indus, and it is also the *Nîl* or *Nîla*. It is the river born on the *Kailâs* (heaven) mountain, the mansion of the gods — 22,000 feet above the level of the sea. It was the Ethiops river — and was so called by the Greeks, long before the days of Alexander, because its banks, from Attock down to Sind, were peopled by tribes generally referred to as the Eastern Ethiopians. India and Egypt were two kindred nations, and the Eastern Ethiopians — the mighty builders — have come from India, as is pretty well proved, it is hoped, in "Isis Unveiled."[904]

Then why could not Alexander, and even the learned Virgil have used the word Nile or *Neilos* when speaking of the Indus, since it is one of its names? To this day that river is called, in the regions around Kala-Bagh, *nîl* (blue), and *Nîlah*, "the blue river." The water here is of such dark blue color that the name given to it from time immemorial led to a small town on its banks being called by the same name. It exists to this day. Evidently Arrian — who wrote far later than the day of Alexander, and who was ignorant of the old name of the Indus — has unconsciously slandered the Greek conqueror. Nor are our modern historians much wiser, in judging as they do. For they often make the most sweeping declarations on mere appearances, as much as their ancient colleagues ever did in days of old, when no Encyclopaedias were yet ready for them.

The race of Io, "the cow-horned maid" is then simply the first pioneer race of the Aethiopians brought by her from the Indus to the Nile (which received its name in memory of the mother river of the colonists from India[905]). For does not Prometheus say to Io[906] that the sacred Neilos (the god, not the river) —

". . . He to the land, *three-cornered*, thee shall guide," — namely, to the *Delta*, where her sons are foreordained to found — ". . . that far-off colony . . ." (l. 830 *et seq.*).

It is there that a new race (the Egyptians) will begin, and a " female race " (873) which, " fifth in descent " from dark Epaphos —

> Fifty in number shall return to Argos.

Then one of the fifty virgins will fail through love and shall —

> . . . A kingly race in Argos bear
>
> . . . .
>
> But from this seed shall dauntless hero spring,
> Bow-famous, who shall free me from these toils. (890)

When this hero shall arise, the Titan does not reveal; for as he remarks :—

> This, to set forth at large needs lengthy speech.

But "Argos" is *Arghya Varsha*, the land of libation of the old Hiero-

---

905. Alexander, who was better acquainted with Attock than with India (where he never went) could not have failed to hear the Indus near its very sources called *Nil* and *Nilah*. Even if a mistake, it is thus easily accounted for.

906. That Io is identical allegorically with Isis and the moon is shown by her being " cow-horned." The allegory undeniably reached Greece from India, where Vâch — " the melodious cow " (*Rig-Veda*) " from whom mankind was produced " (*Bhâgavata Purâna*) is shown in the *Aitareya Brâhmana* as pursued by her father Brahmâ, who was moved by an illicit passion, and changed her into a deer. Hence Io, refusing to yield to Jupiter's passion,

becomes " horned." The cow was in every country the symbol of the passive generative power of nature, Isis, Vâch, Venus — the mother of the prolific god of love, Cupid, but, at the same time, that of the *Logos* whose symbol became with the Egyptians and the Indians — the bull — as testified to by Apis and the Hindû bulls in the most ancient temples. In esoteric philosophy the cow is the symbol of creative nature, and the Bull (her calf) the spirit which vivifies her, or " the Holy Spirit," as Mr. Kenealy shows. Hence the symbol of the horns. These were sacred also with the Jews, who placed near the altar horns of Shittim wood, by seizing which a criminal ensured his safety.

phants, whence the deliverer of Humanity will appear, a name which became ages later that of its neighbor, India — the Âryâ-varta of old. That the subject formed part of the Sabazian mysteries is made known by several ancient writers: by Cicero [907] and by Clemens Alexandrinus.[908] The latter writers are the only ones who attribute the fact that Aeschylus was charged by the Athenians with sacrilege and condemned to be stoned to death, to its true cause. They say that having been himself uninitiated, Aeschylus had profaned the Mysteries by exposing them in his trilogies on a public stage.[909] But he would have incurred the same condemnation had he been initiated — which must have been the case, as otherwise he must, like Socrates, have had a *daïmon* to reveal to him the secret and sacred allegorical drama of initiation. At all events, it is not the "father of the Greek tragedy" who invented the prophecy of Prometheus; for he only repeated in dramatic form that which was revealed by the priests during the MYSTERIA of the Sabazia.[910] The latter, however, is one of the oldest sacred festivals, whose origin is to this day unknown to history. Mythologists connect it through Mithras (the Sun, called Sabazios on some old monuments) with Jupiter and Bacchus. But it was never the property of the Greeks, but dates from days immemorial.

The translators of the drama wonder how Aeschylus could become guilty of such "discrepancy between the character of Zeus as portrayed in the *Prometheus Bound* and that depicted in the remaining dramas."[911] This is just because Aeschylus, like Shakespeare, was and will ever remain the intellectual "Sphinx" of the ages. Between Zeus, the abstract deity of Grecian thought, and the Olympic Zeus, there was an abyss. The latter represented during the mysteries no higher a principle than the lower aspect of human physical intelligence — *Manas* wedded to *Kâma;* Prometheus — its divine aspect merging into and aspiring to Buddhi — the divine Soul. Zeus was the human soul and nothing more, whenever shown yielding to his lower passions, — the *jealous* God, revengeful and cruel in its egotism or I-AM-NESS. Hence, Zeus is represented as a serpent — the intellectual tempter of man — which, nevertheless, begets in the course of cyclic evolution the "Man-Savior," the solar Bacchus or "Dionysos," *more than a man.*

Dionysos is one with Osiris, with Krishna, and with Buddha (the

907. In *Tuscul. Quaest.* 1, ii, No. 20.

908. *Strom.* 1, ii. *Oper.* tom. 1, p. 467 — Potter's edit.

909. Herodotus and Pausanias supposed that the cause of the condemnation was that Aeschylus, adopting the theogony of the Egyptians, made Diana, the daughter of Ceres, and not of Latona. (See Aelian *Var. Hist.* I, v. c. xviii, *tom.* 1, p. 433

Edition Gronov.) But Aeschylus *was* initiated.

910. The *Sabazia* were a periodical festival with mysteries enacted in honor of some gods, a variant on the Mithraic Mysteries. The whole evolution of the races was performed in them.

911. Mrs. A. Swanwick, Preface.

heavenly wise), and with the coming (tenth) Avatâr, the glorified Spiritual *Christos*, who will deliver the suffering *Chrestos* (mankind, or Prometheus, on its trial). This, say Brâhmanical and Buddhistic legends, echoed by the Zoroastrian and now by the Christian teachings (the latter only occasionally), will happen at the end of *Kaliyuga*. It is only after the appearance of Kalki-Avatâra, or Sosiosh, that man will be born from woman without sin. Then will Brahmâ, the Hindû deity; Ahura-Mazda (Ormazd), the Zoroastrian; Zeus, the Greco-Olympian Don Juan; Jehovah, the jealous, repenting, cruel, tribal God of the Israelites, and all their likes in the universal Pantheon of human fancy — vanish and disappear in thin air. And along with these will vanish their shadows, *the dark aspects* of all those deities, ever represented as their "twin brothers" and creatures, in exoteric legend, *their own reflection* on earth — in esoteric philosophy. The Ahrimans and Typhons, the Samaels and Satans, must be all dethroned on that day, when every dark evil passion will be subdued.

There is one eternal Law in nature, one that always tends to adjust contraries and to produce final harmony. It is owing to this law of spiritual development superseding the physical and purely intellectual, that mankind will become freed from its false gods, and find itself finally — *SELF-REDEEMED*.

In its final revelation, the old myth of Prometheus — his *proto-* and *anti-*types being found in every ancient theogony — stands in each of them at the very origin of physical evil, because at the threshold of human physical life. KRONOS is "Time," whose first law is that the order of the successive and harmonious phases in the process of evolution during cyclic development should be strictly preserved — under the severe penalty of abnormal growth with all its ensuing results. It was not in the program of natural development that man — higher animal though he may be — should become at once — intellectually, spiritually, and psychically — the demi-god he is on earth, while his physical frame remains weaker and more helpless and ephemeral than that of almost any huge mammal. The contrast is too grotesque and violent; the tabernacle much too unworthy of its indwelling god. The gift of Prometheus thus became a CURSE — though *foreknown* and *foreseen* by the HOST personified in that personage, as his name well shows.[912] It is in this that rests, at one and the same time, its sin and

912. *Vide supra*, a foot-note concerning the etymology of προμήτις or *forethought*. Prometheus confesses it in the drama when saying:—
"Oh! holy Ether, swiftly-winged gales . . .
Behold what I, a god, from gods endure
. . . .

And yet what say I? *Clearly I foreknow*
All that must happen; . . .
. . . the Destined it behoves,
As best I may, to bear, for well I wot
How incontestable the strength of Fate
. . . . . . (ll. 88-105)
"Fate" stands here for KARMA, or *Nemesis*.

its redemption. For the Host that incarnated in a portion of humanity, though led to it by Karma or *Nemesis*, preferred free-will to passive slavery, intellectual self-conscious pain and even torture.— "while myriad time shall flow " — to inane, imbecile, instinctual beatitude. Knowing such an incarnation was premature and not in the program of nature, the heavenly host, "Prometheus," still sacrificed itself to benefit thereby, at least, one portion of mankind.[913] But while saving man from mental darkness, they inflicted upon him the tortures of the self-consciousness of his responsibility — the result of his free will — besides every ill to which mortal man and flesh are heir. This torture Prometheus accepted for himself, since the Host became henceforward blended with the tabernacle prepared for them, which was still unachieved at that period of formation.

Spiritual evolution being incapable of keeping pace with the physical, once its homogeneity was broken by the admixture, the gift thus became the chief cause, if not the sole origin of *Evil.*[914] The allegory which shows KRONOS cursing Zeus for dethroning him (in the primitive "golden" age of Saturn, when all men were demi-gods), and for creating a physical race of men weak and helpless in comparison; and then as delivering to his (Zeus') revenge the culprit, who despoiled the gods of their prerogative of creation and who thereby raised man to their level, intellectually and spiritually — is highly philosophical. In the case of Prometheus, Zeus represents the Host of the primeval progenitors, of the PITAR, the "Fathers" who created man senseless and without any mind; while the divine Titan stands for the Spiritual creators, the *devas* who "fell" into generation. The former are spiritually lower, but physically stronger, than the "Prometheans": therefore, the latter are shown conquered. "The lower Host, whose work the Titan spoiled and thus defeated the plans of Zeus," was on this earth in its own sphere and plane of action; whereas, the superior Host was an exile from Heaven, who had got entangled in the meshes of matter. They (the inferior " Host ") were masters of all the Cosmic and lower titanic forces; the higher Titan possessed only the intel-

---

913. Mankind is obviously divided into god-informed men and lower human creatures. The intellectual difference between the Aryan and other civilized nations and such savages as the South Sea Islanders, is inexplicable on any other grounds. No amount of culture, nor generations of training amid civilization, could raise such human specimens as the Bushmen, the Veddahs of Ceylon, and some African tribes, to the same intellectual level as the Aryans, the Semites, and the Turanians so called. The "sacred spark" is missing in them and it is they who are the only *inferior* races on the globe, now happily — owing to the wise adjustment of nature which ever works in that direction — fast dying out. Verily mankind is "of one blood," *but not of the same essence.* We are the hot-house, artificially quickened plants in nature, having in us a spark, which in them is latent.

914. The philosophical view of Indian metaphysics places the Root of Evil in the differentiation of the Homogeneous into the Heterogeneous, of the unit into plurality.

lectual and spiritual fire. This drama of the struggle of Prometheus
with the Olympic tyrant and despot, sensual Zeus, one sees enacted
daily within our actual mankind: the lower passions chain the higher
aspirations to the rock of matter, to generate in many a case the
vulture of sorrow, pain, and repentance. In every such case one sees
once more —

> A god . . . in fetters, anguish-fraught;
> The foe of Zeus, in hatred held of all. . . . (118–119)

A god, bereft even of that supreme consolation of Prometheus, who
suffered in self-sacrifice —

> For that to men (he) bare too fond a mind . . . (121),

as the divine Titan is moved by altruism, but the mortal man by Selfishness and Egoism in every instance.

The modern Prometheus has now become *Epi-metheus,* " he who
sees only after the event "; because the universal philanthropy of the
former has long ago degenerated into selfishness and self-adoration.
Man will rebecome the *free* Titan of old, but not before cyclic evolution has re-established the broken harmony between the two natures —
the terrestrial and the divine; after which he becomes impermeable
to the lower titanic forces, invulnerable in his personality, and immortal
in his individuality, which cannot happen before every animal element
is eliminated from his nature. When man understands that " *Deus
non fecit mortem,*"[914a] but that man has created it himself, he will
re-become the Prometheus before his Fall.

For the full symbolism of Prometheus and the origin of this mythos
in Greece, the reader is referred to Part II of this Volume, chapter
" A Second Key to Prometheus," etc. In the said Part — a kind of
supplement to the present portion — every additional information is
given upon those tenets that will be the most controverted and questioned. This work is so heterodox, when confronted with the acknowledged standards of theology and modern science, that no proof which
tends to show that these standards often usurp an illegal authority
should be neglected.

[914a.] *Sap.* i, 13.

ADDITIONAL FRAGMENTS FROM A COMMENTARY
ON THE VERSES OF STANZA XII

THE MS. from which these additional explanations are taken belongs to the group called "*Tongshakchi Sangye Songa*," or the Records of the " Thirty-five Buddhas of Confession," as they are *exoterically* called. These personages, however, though called in the Northern Buddhist religion " Buddhas," may just as well be called Rishis, or Avatârs, etc., as they are " Buddhas who have preceded Sakyamuni" only for the Northern followers of the ethics preached by Gautama. These great Mahâtmâs, or Buddhas, are a universal and common property: they are *historical* sages — at any rate, for all the Occultists who believe in such a hierarchy of Sages, the existence of which has been proved to them by the learned ones of the Fraternity. They are chosen from among some ninety-seven Buddhas in one group, and fifty-three in another,[915] mostly imaginary personages, who are really the personifications of the powers of the first-named.[916] These " baskets " of the oldest writings on " palm leaves " are kept very secret. Each MS. has appended to it a short synopsis of the history of that sub-race to which the particular " Buddha-Lha " belonged. The one special MS. from which the fragments which follow are extracted, and then rendered into a more comprehensible language, is said to have been copied from stone tablets which belonged to a Buddha of the earliest day of the Fifth Race, who had witnessed the Deluge and the submersion of the chief continents of the Atlantean race. The day when much, if not all, of that which is given here from the archaic records, will be found correct, is not far distant. Then the modern symbologists will acquire the certitude that even Odin, or the god Woden, the highest god in the German and Scandinavian mythology, is one of these thirty-five Buddhas; one of the earliest, indeed, for the continent to which he and his race belonged, is also one of the earliest. So early, in truth, that in the days when tropical nature was to be found, where now lie eternal unthawing snows, one could cross almost by dry land from Norway *via* Iceland and Greenland, to the

915. Gautama Buddha, named Shakya Thüb-pa, is the *twenty-seventh* of the last group, as most of these Buddhas belong to the *divine dynasties* which instructed mankind.
916. Of these " Buddhas," or the " Enlightened," the far distant predecessors of Gautama the Buddha, and who represent, we are taught, once living men, great adepts and Saints, in whom the " Sons of Wisdom " had incarnated, and who were, therefore, so to speak, minor Avatârs of the Celestial Beings — eleven only belong to the Atlantean race, and 24 to the Fifth race, from its beginnings. They are identical with the Tîrthañkaras of the Jainas.

lands that at present surround Hudson's Bay.[917] Just as, in the palmy days of the Atlantean giants, the sons of the "giants from the East," a pilgrim could perform a journey from what in our days is termed the Sahara desert, to the lands which now rest in dreamless sleep at the bottom of the waters of the Gulf of Mexico and the Caribbean Sea. Events which were never written outside the human memory, but which were religiously transmitted from one generation to another, and from race to race, may have been preserved by constant transmission " within the book volume of the brain," and through countless aeons, with more truth and accuracy than inside any written document or record. " That which is part of our souls is eternal," says Thackeray; and what can be nearer to our souls than that which happens at the dawns of our lives? Those lives are countless, but the soul or spirit that animates us throughout these myriads of existences is the same; and though " the book and volume " of the *physical* brain may forget events within the scope of one terrestrial life, the bulk of collective recollections can never desert the divine soul within us. Its whispers may be too soft, the sound of its words too far off the plane perceived by our physical senses; yet the shadow of events *that were,* just as much as the shadow of the events *that are to come,* is within its perceptive powers, and is ever present before its mind's eye.

It is this soul-voice, perhaps, which tells those who believe in tradition more than in written History, that what is said below is all true, and relates to pre-historic facts.

This is what is written in one passage :—

"THE KINGS OF LIGHT HAVE DEPARTED IN WRATH. THE SINS OF MEN HAVE BECOME SO BLACK THAT EARTH QUIVERS IN HER GREAT AGONY. . . . THE AZURE SEATS REMAIN EMPTY. WHO OF THE BROWN, WHO OF THE RED, OR YET AMONG THE BLACK (*races*), CAN SIT IN THE SEATS OF THE BLESSED, THE SEATS OF KNOWLEDGE AND MERCY! WHO CAN ASSUME THE FLOWER OF POWER, THE PLANT OF THE GOLDEN STEM AND THE AZURE BLOSSOM? "

917. This may account for the similarity of the artificial mounds in the U. S. of America, and the tumuli in Norway. It is this identity that led some American archaeologists to suggest that Norwegian mariners had *discovered* America some one thousand years ago (*Vide* Holmboe's *Traces de Bouddhisme en Norvège*, p. 23). There is no doubt that America is that "far distant land into which pious men and heavy storms had transferred the sacred doctrine," as a Chinese writer suggested by his description to Neumann (Lassen, *Indische Al-terthumskunde*, IV, 749). But neither Professor Holmboe, of Stockholm, nor the American archaeologists, have guessed the right age of the mounds, or the tumuli. The fact that Norwegians may have re-discovered the land that their long-forgotten forefathers believed to have perished in the general submersion, does not conflict with that other fact that the *Secret Doctrine* of the land which was the cradle of physical man, and of the Fifth Race, had found its way into the so-called *New World* ages and ages before the " Sacred Doctrine " of Buddhism.

The " Kings of Light " is the name given in all old records to the Sovereigns of the divine Dynasties. The " azure seats " are translated " celestial thrones " in certain documents. The " flower of power " is now the Lotus; what it may have been at that period, who can tell. The writer proceeds, like the later Jeremiah, to bewail the fate of his people. They had become bereft of their "azure" (celestial) kings, and " they of the *Deva* hue," the moon-like complexion, and " they of the refulgent (golden) face " have gone " to the land of bliss, the land of metal and fire "; or — agreeably with the rules of symbolism — to the lands lying North and East, from whence " the great waters have been swept away, sucked in by the earth and dissipated in the air." The wise races had perceived " the black storm-dragons, called down by the dragons of wisdom " — and " had fled, led on by the shining Protectors of the most Excellent Land " — the great ancient adepts, presumably; those the Hindûs refer to as their Manus and Rishis. One of them was Vaivasvata Manu.

They " of the yellow hue " are the forefathers of those whom Ethnology now classes as the Turanians, the Mongols, Chinese and other ancient nations; and the land they fled to was no other than Central Asia. There entire new races were born; there they lived and died until the separation of the nations. But this "separation" did not take place either in the localities assigned for it by modern science, nor in the way the Aryans are shown to have divided and separated by Mr. Max Müller and other *Aryanists*. Nearly two-thirds of one million years have elapsed since that period. The yellow-faced giants of the post-Atlantean day, had ample time, throughout this forced confinement to one part of the world, and with the same racial blood and without any fresh infusion or admixture in it, to branch off during a period of nearly 700,000 years into the most heterogeneous and diversified types. The same is shown in Africa; nowhere does a more extraordinary variability of types exist, from black to almost white, from gigantic men to dwarfish races; and this only because of their forced isolation. The Africans have never left their continent for several hundred thousands of years. If tomorrow the continent of Europe were to disappear and other lands to re-emerge instead; and if the African tribes were to separate and scatter on the face of the earth, it is they who, in about a hundred thousand years hence, would form the bulk of the civilized nations. And it is the descendants of those of our highly cultured nations, who might have survived on some one island, without any means of crossing the new seas, that would fall back into a state of relative savagery. Thus the reason given for dividing humanity into *superior* and *inferior* races falls to the ground and becomes a fallacy.

Such are the statements made and facts given in the archaic records. Collating and comparing them with some modern theories of Evolution, *minus natural selection*,[918] these statements appear quite reasonable and logical.[919] Thus, while the Aryans are the descendants of the *yellow* Adams, the gigantic and highly civilized Atlanto-Aryan race, the Semites — and the Jews along with them — are those of the red Adam; and thus both de Quatrefages and the writers of the Mosaic *Genesis* are right. For, could chapter v. of the First Book of Moses be compared with the genealogies found in our Archaic Bible, the period from Adam unto Noah would be found noticed therein, of course under different names, the respective years of the Patriarchs being turned into periods, the whole being shown symbolical and allegorical. In the MS. under consideration many and frequent are the references to the great knowledge and civilization of the Atlantean nations, showing the polity of several of them and the nature of their arts and sciences. If the Third Root-Race, the Lemuro-Atlanteans, are already spoken of as having been drowned " with their high civilizations and gods,"[920] how much more may the same be said of the Atlanteans!

It is from the Fourth Race that the early Aryans got their knowledge of " the bundle of wonderful things," the *Sabhâ* and *Mâyâsabhâ*, mentioned in the *Mahâbhârata*, the gift of Mayâsura to the Pândavas. It is from them that they learned aeronautics, *Vimâna Vidyâ* (the " knowledge of flying in air-vehicles "), and, therefore, their great arts of meteorography and meteorology. It is from them, again, that the Aryans inherited their most valuable science of the hidden virtues of precious and other stones, of chemistry, or rather alchemy, of mineralogy, geology, physics and astronomy.

Several times the writer has put to herself the question: " Is the story of *Exodus* — in its details at least — as narrated in the Old Testament, original? Or is it, like the story of Moses himself and many others, simply another version of the legends told of the Atlanteans? " For who, upon hearing the story told of the latter, will fail to perceive the great similarity of the fundamental features? The anger of " God " at the obduracy of Pharaoh, his command to the "chosen" ones, to spoil the Egyptians, before departing, of their " jewels of silver and jewels of gold "; (*Exod.* xi) and finally the Egyptians and their Pharaoh drowned in the Red Sea (xiv). For here is a fragment of the earlier story from the Commentary:—

" . . . *And the ' great King of the dazzling Face,' the chief of all the Yellow-faced, was sad, seeing the sins of the Black-faced.*

918. *Vide Physiological Selection*, by G. J. Romanes, F. R. S.
919. *Vide* the first pages of Part III.
920. " *Esoteric Buddhism*," p. 65.

"*He sent his air-vehicles* (Viwân) *to all his brother-chiefs* (chiefs of other nations and tribes) *with pious men within, saying:* '*Prepare. Arise ye men of the good law, and cross the land while* (yet) *dry.*' '*The Lords of the storm are approaching. Their chariots are nearing the land. One night and two days only shall the Lords of the Dark Face* (the Sorcerers) *live on this patient land. She is doomed, and they have to descend with her. The nether Lords of the Fires* (the Gnomes and fire Elementals) *are preparing their magic Agneyâstra* (fire-weapons worked by magic). *But the Lords of the Dark Eye* ("Evil Eye") *are stronger than they* (the Elementals) *and they are the slaves of the mighty ones. They are versed in Ashtar* (Vidyâ, the highest magical knowledge).[921] *Come and use yours* (i. e., your magic powers, in order to counteract those of the Sorcerers). *Let every lord of the Dazzling Face* (an adept of the White Magic) *cause the Viwân of every lord of the Dark Face to come into his hands* (or possession), *lest any* (of the Sorcerers) *should by its means escape from the waters, avoid the rod of the Four,* (Karmic deities) *and save his wicked*' (followers, or people).

'*May every yellow face send sleep from himself* (mesmerize?) *to every black face. May even they* (the Sorcerers) *avoid pain and suffering. May every man true to the Solar Gods bind* (paralyse) *every man under the lunar gods, lest he should suffer or escape his destiny.*

'*And may every yellow face offer of his life-water* (blood) *to the speaking animal of a black face, lest he awaken his master.*[922]

'*The hour has struck, the black night is ready, etc., etc.*

.   .   .   .

'*Let their destiny be accomplished. We are the servants of the great Four.*[923] *May the Kings of Light return.*'"

"*The great King fell upon his dazzling Face and wept.* . . .

"*When the Kings assembled the waters had already moved.* . . .

"(But) *the nations had now crossed the dry lands. They were*

---

921. Wrote the late Brahmâchârî Bawa, a Yogi of great renown and holiness: "Extensive works on *Astra Vidyâ* and such other sciences were at different times compiled in the languages of the times. . . . But the Sanskrit originals were lost at the time of the partial deluge of our country. . . ." (See *Theosophist* of June, 1880, page 236, "Some Things the Aryans Knew.") For *Agneyâstra,* see Wilson's *Specimens of the Hindû Theater,* I, p. 297.

922. Some wonderful, artificially-made beast, similar in some way to a Frankenstein creation, which spoke and warned his master of every approaching danger. The master was a "black magician," the mechanical animal was informed by a *jinni,* an Elemental, according to the accounts. The blood of a pure man alone could destroy him. *Vide* Part II, § xxv, "Seven in Astronomy, Science, and Magic."

923. The four **Karmic gods,** called the Four **Mahârâjas** in the **Stanzas.**

beyond the water mark. Their Kings reached them in their Viwâns, and led them on to the lands of Fire and Metal (East and North)."

.   .   .   .

Still, in another passage, it is said:—

" . . . . *Stars* (meteors) *showered on the lands of the black Faces; but they slept.*

"The speaking beasts (the magic watchers) *kept quiet.*

"The nether lords waited for orders, but they came not, for their masters slept.

"The waters arose, and covered the valleys from one end of the Earth to the other. High lands remained, the bottom of the Earth (the lands of the antipodes) *remained dry. There dwelt those who escaped; the men of the yellow-faces and of the straight eye* (the frank and sincere people).

"When the Lords of the Dark Faces awoke and bethought them-selves of their Viwâns in order to escape from the rising waters, they found them gone."

Then a passage shows some of the more powerful magicians of the "Dark Face" — who awoke earlier than the others — pursuing those who had "spoilt them" and who were in the rear-guard, for — *"the nations that were led away, were as thick as the stars of the milky way,"* says a more modern Commentary, written in Sanskrit only.

"Like as a dragon-snake uncoils slowly its body, so the Sons of men, led on by the Sons of Wisdom, opened their folds, and spreading out, expanded like a running stream of sweet waters. . . . . . many of the faint-hearted among them perished on their way. But most were saved."

Yet the pursuers, "whose heads and chests soared high above the water," chased them "for three lunar terms" until finally reached by the rising waves, they perished to the last man, the soil sinking under their feet and the earth engulfing those who had desecrated her.

This sounds a good deal like the original material upon which the similar story in *Exodus* was built many hundred thousands of years later. The biography of Moses, the story of his birth, childhood and rescue from the Nile by Pharaoh's daughter, is now shown to have been adapted from the Chaldaean narrative about Sargon. And if so, the Assyrian tile in the British Museum being a good proof of it, why not that of the Jews robbing the Egyptians of their jewels, the death of Pharaoh and his army, and so on? The gigantic magicians of Ruta and Daitya, the "lords of the Dark Face," may have become in the later narrative the Egyptian Magi, and the yellow-faced nations of

the Fifth Race, the virtuous sons of Jacob, the "chosen people." . . .
One more statement has to be made: There have been several Divine
Dynasties — a series for every Root Race beginning with the Third,
each series according and adapted to its Humanity. The last Seven
Dynasties referred to in the Egyptian and Chaldaean records belong to
the Fifth Race, which, though generally called Aryan, was not entirely
so, as it was ever largely mixed up with races to which Ethnology
gives other names. It would be impossible, in view of the limited
space at our disposal, to go any further into the description of the Atlanteans, in whom the whole East believes as much as we believe in the
ancient Egyptians, but whose existence the majority of the Western
Scientists deny, as they have denied, before this, many a truth, from
the existence of Homer down to that of the carrier pigeon. The civilization of the Atlanteans was greater even than that of the Egyptians.
It is their degenerate descendants, the nation of Plato's Atlantis, which
built the first Pyramids in the country, and that certainly before the
advent of the "Eastern Aethiopians," as Herodotus calls the Egyptians.
This may be well inferred from the statement made by Ammianus
Marcellinus, who says of the Pyramids that "there are also subterranean passages and winding retreats, which, it is said, men skilful in
the ancient mysteries, by means of which they divined the coming of
a flood; constructed in different places lest the memory of all their
sacred ceremonies should be lost."[923a]

These men who "divined the coming of floods" were not Egyptians,
who never had any, except the periodical rising of the Nile. Who were
they? The last remnants of the Atlanteans, we maintain. Those races
which are dimly suspected by Science, and thinking of which Mr.
Charles Gould, the well-known geologist, says:

Can we suppose that we have at all exhausted the great museum of nature?
Have we, in fact, penetrated yet beyond its antechambers? Does the written
history of man, comprising a few thousand years, embrace the whole course of
his intelligent existence? Or have we in the long mythical eras, extending over
hundreds of thousands of years, and recorded in the chronologies of Chaldaea
and of China, shadowy mementoes of pre-historic man, handed down by tradition,
and perhaps transported by a few survivors to existing lands from others, which,
like the fabled (?) Atlantis of Plato, may have been submerged, or the scene of
some great catastrophe which destroyed them with all their civilization?[923b]

After this one can turn with more confidence to the words of a Master
who wrote, several years before these words were penned by Mr.
Gould:— "The Fourth Race had its periods of the highest civilization. Greek and Roman and even Egyptian civilizations are nothing

923a. xxii, 15, 30.   923b. *Mythical Monsters*, p. 19.

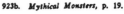

compared to the civilizations that began with the Third Race " — after its separation.

But if this civilization and the mastery of arts and sciences are denied to the Third and Fourth Races, no one will deny that between the great civilizations of antiquity, such as those of Egypt and India, there stretched the dark ages of crass ignorance and barbarism ever since the beginning of the Christian era up to our modern civilization; during which period all recollection of these traditions was lost. As said in *Isis Unveiled:* " Why should we forget that, ages before the prow of the adventurous Genoese clove the Western waters, the Phoenician vessels had circumnavigated the globe, and spread civilization in regions now silent and deserted? What archaeologist will dare assert that the same hand which planned the Pyramids of Egypt, Karnak, and the thousand ruins now crumbling to oblivion on the sandy banks of the Nile, did *not* erect the monumental Nagkon-Wat of Cambodia? or trace the hieroglyphics on the obelisks and doors of the deserted Indian village, newly discovered in British Columbia by Lord Dufferin? or those on the ruins of Palenque and Uxmal, of Central America? Do not the relics we treasure in our museums — last mementos of the long ' lost arts ' — speak loudly in favor of ancient civilization? And do they not prove, over and over again, that nations and continents that have passed away have buried along with them arts and sciences, which neither the first crucible ever heated in a medieval cloister, nor the last cracked by a modern chemist, have revived, nor will — at least, in the present century.'"[234]

And the same question may be put now that was put then; it may be once more asked: " How does it happen that the most advanced standpoint that has been reached in our times, only enables us to see in the dim distance up the Alpine path of knowledge the monumental proofs that earlier explorers have left to mark the plateaux they had reached and occupied?

" If modern masters are so much in advance of the old ones, why do they not restore to us the lost arts of our postdiluvian forefathers? Why do they not give us the unfading colors of Luxor — the Tyrian purple; the bright vermilion and dazzling blue which decorate the walls of this place, and are as bright as on the first day of their application? The indestructible cement of the pyramids and of ancient aqueducts; the Damascus blade, which can be turned like a corkscrew in its scabbard without breaking; the gorgeous, unparalleled tints of the stained glass that is found amid the dust of old ruins and beams in the windows of ancient cathedrals; and the secret of the true malleable glass? And if chemistry is so little able to rival even the early medi-

923c. Vol. I, p. 239.

eval ages in some arts, why boast of achievements which, according to strong probability, were perfectly known thousands of years ago? The more archaeology and philology advance, the more humiliating to our pride are the discoveries which are daily made, the more glorious testimony do they bear in behalf of those who, perhaps on account of the distance of their remote antiquity, have been until now considered ignorant flounderers in the deepest mire of superstition."

Among other arts and sciences, the ancients — ay, as an heirloom from the Atlanteans — had those of astronomy and symbolism, which included the knowledge of the Zodiac.

As already explained, the whole of antiquity believed, with good reason, that humanity and its races are all intimately connected with the planets, and these with Zodiacal signs. The whole world's History is recorded in the latter. In the ancient temples of Egypt this was proved by the Dendera Zodiac; but except in an Arabic work, the property of a *Sufi*, the writer has never met with a correct copy of these marvelous records of the past, as also of the *future*, history of our globe. Yet the original records exist, most undeniably.

As Europeans are unacquainted with the real Zodiacs of India, nor do they understand those they happen to know (witness Bentley), the reader is advised, in order to verify the statement, to turn to the work of Denon[924] in which, *if understood*, the two famous Egyptian Zodiacs can be found and examined. Having seen them personally, the writer has no longer need to trust to what other students — who have examined and studied both very carefully — have to say of them. As asserted by the Egyptian Priests to Herodotus, who was informed that the terrestrial Pole and the Pole of the Ecliptic had formerly coincided, thus was it found and corroborated by Mackey.[925] For he states that the Poles are represented on the Zodiacs in both positions, " And in that which shows the Poles (polar axes) at right angles, there are marks which prove that ' it was not the last time they were in that position; *but the first*' — after the Zodiacs had been traced." " Capricorn," he adds, " is represented at the North Pole, and Cancer is divided, near its middle, at the South Pole; which is a confirmation that originally they had their winter when the Sun was in Cancer; but the chief characteristics of its being a monument commemorating the *first time* that the Pole had been in that position, are the Lion and the Virgin." (See in Part II, § " A Mystery of the Zodiac.")

Broadly calculated, it is believed by the Egyptologists that the great

924. *Travels in Egypt*, Vol. II.
925. " The Mythological Astronomy of the Ancients Demonstrated " by a strangely intuitional symbologist and astronomer, a kind of a self-made adept of Norwich, who lived in the first quarter of this century.

Pyramid was built 3350 B. C.;[926] and that Menes and his dynasty existed 750 years before the Fourth Dynasty (supposed to have built the Pyramids) had appeared.[927] Thus 4100 years B. C. is the age assigned to Menes. Now Sir J. Gardner Wilkinson's declaration that *"all the facts lead to the conclusion* that the Egyptians had already made very great progress in the arts of civilization *before the age of Menes, and perhaps before they immigrated into the valley of the Nile "*[928] is very suggestive, as destroying this hypothesis. It points to great civilization in *prehistoric* times, and a still greater antiquity. The *Shesu-Hor* ("the servants of Horus") were the people who had settled in Egypt; and, as M. G. Maspero affirms, it is to this *prehistoric* race that "belongs the honor . . . of having founded the principal cities of Egypt, and established the most important sanctuaries." This was *before* the great Pyramid epoch, and when Egypt had hardly arisen from the waters. Yet "they possessed the hieroglyphic form of writing special to the Egyptians, and must have been already considerably advanced in civilization." It was, says Lenormant, "the country of the great prehistoric sanctuaries, seats of the sacerdotal dominion, which played the most important part in the origin of civilization." What is the date assigned to this people? We hear of 4000, at the utmost of 5000 years B. C. (Maspero). Now it is claimed that it is by means of the cycle of 25,868 years (the Sidereal year) that the approximate year of the erection of the Great Pyramid can be ascertained. "Assuming that the long narrow downward passage was directed towards the pole star of the pyramid builders, astronomers have shown that . . . Alpha Draconis, the then pole-star, was in the required position about 3350 B. C., as well as in 2170 B. C." (Proctor, quoted by Staniland Wake). But we are also told that "this relative position of Alpha Draconis and Alcyone being an extraordinary one . . . it could not occur again for a whole sidereal year." (*Ibid.*) This demonstrates that, since the Dendera Zodiac shows the passage of three sidereal years, the great Pyramid must have been built 78,000 years ago, or in any case that this possibility deserves to be accepted at least as readily as the later date of 3350 B. C.

Now on the Zodiac of a certain temple in far Northern India, as on the Dendera Zodiac, the same characteristics of the signs are found. Those who know well the Hindû symbols and constellations, will be able to find out by the description of the Egyptian, whether the indications of the chronological time are correct or not. On the Dendera Zodiac as preserved by the modern Egyptian Coptic and Greek adepts,

926. See Proctor, *Knowledge*, Vol. I, pp. 242, 400.

927. *The Great Pyramid*, Staniland Wake.

928. Rawlinson's *Herodotus*, vol. ii, p.   345; vol. ii, p. 291, ed. of 1862.

and explained a little differently by Mackey, the Lion stands upon the *Hydra* and his tail is almost straight, pointing downwards at an angle of forty or fifty degrees, this position agreeing with the *original* conformation of these constellations. " But in many places we see the Lion [*Simha*]," Mackey adds, " with his tail turned up over his back, and ending with a Serpent's head ; thereby showing that the Lion had been ' *inverted* '; which, indeed, must have been the case with the whole Zodiac and every other Constellation, when the Pole had been inverted." Speaking of the *Circular* Zodiac, given also by Denon, he says :— There,

the Lion is standing *on* the Serpent, and his tail forming a curve downward, from which it is found that *though six or seven hundred thousand years* must have passed between the two positions, yet they had made but little difference in the constellations of Leo and the Hydra ; while *Virgo* is represented very differently in the two. In the *circular* Zodiac, the *Virgin is nursing her child;* but it seems that they had not had that idea when the pole was first within the plane of the Ecliptic ; for in *this* Zodiac, as given by Denon, we see *three Virgins* between the Lion and the Scales, *the last of which holds in her hand* an ear of wheat. It is much to be lamented that there is in this Zodiac a breach of the figure in the latter part of Leo and the *beginning of Virgo* which has taken away one *Decan* out of each sign.

Nevertheless, the meaning is plain, as the three Zodiacs belong to three different epochs : namely, to the last three family races of the fourth Sub-race of the Fifth Root-race, each of which must have lived approximately from 25 to 30,000 years. The first of these (the "Aryan-Asiatics ") witnessed the doom of the last of the populations of the " giant Atlanteans "[929] who perished some 850,000 years ago (the Ruta and Daitya Island-Continents) toward the close of the Miocene Age.[930] The fourth sub-race witnessed the destruction of the last remnant of the Atlanteans — the Aryo-Atlanteans in the last island

929. The term " Atlantean " must not mislead the reader to regard these as one race only, or even a nation. It is as though one said· " Asiatics." Many, multityped, and various were the Atlanteans, who represented several *humanities*, and almost a countless number of races and nations, more varied indeed than would be the " Europeans " were this name to be given indiscriminately to the five existing parts of the world ; which, at the rate colonization is proceeding, will be the case, perhaps, in less than two or three hundred years. There were brown, red, yellow, white and black Atlanteans ; giants and dwarfs (as some African tribes comparatively are, even now).

930. Says a teacher in *"Esoteric Buddh-*

ism," on p. 64: " In the Eocene age, even in its very first part, the great cycle of the fourth race men, the (Lemuro-) Atlanteans had already reached its highest point (of civilization), and the great continent, the father of nearly all the present continents, showed the first symptoms of sinking. . . ." And on page 70, it is shown that Atlantis as a whole perished during the Miocene period. To show how the continents, races, nations and cycles overlap each other, one has but to think of Lemuria, the last of whose lands perished about 700,000 years before the beginning of the Tertiary period (see p. 65 of the same work), and the last of "Atlantis" only 11,000 years ago ; thus both overlapping — one the Atlantean period, and the other the Aryan.

of Atlantis, namely, some 11,000 years ago. In order to understand
this the reader is asked to glance at the diagram of the genealogical
tree of the Fifth Root-Race — generally, though hardly correctly,
called the Aryan race, and the explanations appended to it.

Let the reader remember
well that which is said of
the divisions of Root Races
and the evolution of Hu-
manity in this work, and
stated clearly and concisely
in Mr. Sinnett's "*Esoteric
Buddhism.*"

1. There are seven
ROUNDS in every manvan-
tara; this one is the Fourth,
and we are in the Fifth
Root-Race, at present.

2. Each Root-Race has
seven sub-races.

3. Each sub-race has,
in its turn, seven rami-
fications, which may be
called Branch or "Family"
races.

4. The little tribes,
shoots, and offshoots of
the last-named are count-
less and depend on Kar-
mic action. Examine the
" genealogical tree " hereto

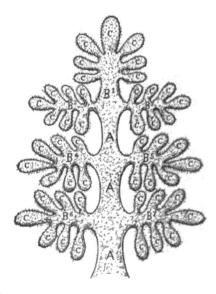

appended, and you will understand. The illustration is purely dia-
grammatic, and is only intended to assist the reader in obtaining a
slight grasp of the subject, amidst the confusion which exists between
the terms which have been used at different times for the divisions of
Humanity. It is also here attempted to express in figures — but only
within approximate limits, for the sake of comparison — the duration
of time through which it is possible to definitely distinguish one division from another. It would only lead to hopeless confusion if any
attempt were made to give accurate dates to a few; for the Races, Sub-
Races, etc., etc., down to their smallest ramifications, overlap and are
entangled with each other until it is nearly impossible to separate them.

The human Race has been compared to a tree, and this serves
admirably as an illustration.

The main stem of a tree may be compared to the ROOT-RACE (A).
Its larger limbs to the various SUB-RACES; seven in number (B¹, B²).
On each of these limbs are seven BRANCHES, OR FAMILY-RACES (C).
After this the cactus-plant is a better illustration, for its fleshy
"leaves" are covered with sharp spines, each of which may be
compared to a nation or tribe of human beings.

Now our Fifth Root-Race has already been in existence — as a
race *sui generis* and quite free from its parent stem — about 1,000,000
years; therefore it must be inferred that each of the four preceding
Sub-Races has lived approximately 210,000 years; thus each Family-
Race has an average existence of about 30,000 years.   Thus the
European "Family Race" has still a good many thousand years to
run, although the nations or the innumerable spines upon it, vary with
each succeeding "season" of three or four thousand years.   It is
somewhat curious to mark the comparative approximation of duration
between the lives of a " Family-Race " and a " Sidereal year."

The knowledge of the foregoing, and the accurately correct division,
formed part and parcel of the Mysteries, where these Sciences were
taught to the disciples, and where they were transmitted by one hierophant to another.   Everyone is aware that the European astronomers assign (arbitrarily enough) the date of the invention of the Egyptian Zodiac to the years 2000 or 2400 B.C. (*Proctor*); and insist that this invention coincides in its date with that of the erection of the Great Pyramid.   This, to an Occultist and Eastern astronomer, must appear quite
absurd.   The year of the *Kaliyuga* is said to have begun between
the 17th and 18th of February in the year 3102 B.C.   Now the Hindûs
claim that in the year 20,400 before Kaliyugam the origin of their
Zodiac coincided with the spring equinox — there being at the time a
conjunction of the Sun and Moon — and Bailly proved by a lengthy
and careful computation of that date, that, even if fictitious, the epoch
from which they had started to establish the beginning of their Kali-
yuga was *very real*.   That "epoch is the year 3102 before our era,"
he writes.[931]   The lunar eclipse arriving just a fortnight after the beginning of the black Age — it took place in a point situated between
the Wheat Ear of Virgo and the star ☉ (θ) of the same constellation.
One of their most esoteric Cycles is based upon certain conjunctions
and respective positions of Virgo and the Pleiades — (*Krittikâs*).
Hence, as the Egyptians brought their Zodiac from Southern India
and Lankâ,[932] the esoteric meaning was evidently identical.   The
three " Virgins," or Virgo in three different positions, meant, with
both, the record of the first three " divine or astronomical Dynasties,"

931. See Part III, Book I, " Hindû Astronomy defended by an Academician."
932. Ceylon.

who taught the Third Root-Race; and after having abandoned the
Atlanteans to their doom, returned (or redescended, rather) during
the third Sub-Race of the Fifth, in order to reveal to saved humanity
the mysteries of their birth-place — the sidereal Heavens. The
same symbolical record of the human races and the three Dynasties
(Gods, Manes — semi-divine astrals of the Third and Fourth, and the
" Heroes " of the Fifth Race), which preceded the purely human
kings, was found in the distribution of the tiers and passages of the
Egyptian Labyrinth. As the three inversions of the Poles of course
changed the face of the Zodiac, a new one had to be constructed
each time. In Mackey's *Sphinxiad* the speculations of the bold author
must have horrified the orthodox portion of the population of Norwich,
as he says, fantastically enough:—

> But, after all, the greatest length of time recorded by those monuments [the
> Labyrinth, the Pyramids and the Zodiacs] *does not exceed five millions of years*
> [which is not so];[933] which falls short of the records given us both by the
> [esoteric] Chinese and Hindûs; which latter nation has registered a knowledge
> of time for seven or eight millions of years;[934] which I have seen upon a
> talisman of porcelain. . . .

The Egyptian priests had the Zodiacs of the Atlantean Asura-Maya,
as the modern Hindûs still have. As stated in *"Esoteric Buddhism,"*
the Egyptians, as well as the Greeks and " Romans " some thousand
years ago, were " remnants of the Atlanto-Aryans," *i.e.*, the former, of
the older, or the Ruta Atlanteans; the last-named, the descendants of
the last race of that island, whose sudden disappearance was narrated
to Solon by the Egyptian Initiates. The *human* Dynasty of the older
Egyptians, beginning with Menes, had all the *knowledge* of the Atlanteans, though there was no more Atlantean blood in their veins. Nevertheless, they had preserved all their Archaic records. All this has been
shown long ago.[935] And it is just because the Egyptian Zodiac is between 75 and 80,000 years old that the Zodiac of the Greeks is far
later. Volney has correctly pointed out in his *Ruins of Empires*[936]
that it is only 16,984 years old, or up to the present date 17,082.[937]

---

933. The forefathers of the Aryan Brâhmans had their Zodiacal calculations and
Zodiac from those born by Kriyâśakti power,
the " Sons of Yoga "; the Egyptians from
the Atlanteans of Ruta.
934. The former, therefore, may have
registered time for seven or eight millions
of years, but the Egyptians *could not*.
935. This question was amply challenged,
and as amply discussed and answered. See
Five Years of Theosophy. (Art. " Mr. Sin-

nett's ' *Esoteric Buddhism,' "* pp. 325–346.)
936. Page 360.
937. Volney says that, as *Aries* was in
its 15th degree, 1447 a. c., it follows that the
first degree of "Libra" could not have coincided with the vernal equinox more lately
than 15,194 years a. c., to which if you add
1790 since Christ, when Volney wrote this,
it appears that 16,984 years have elapsed
since the (Greek or rather Hellenic) origin
of the Zodiac.

CONCLUSION

Space forbids us to say anything more, and this part of the " Secret Doctrine" has to be closed. The forty-nine Slokas and the few fragments from the Commentaries just given are all that can be published in these volumes. These, with some still older records — to which none but the highest Initiates have access — and a whole library of comments, glossaries, and explanations, form the synopsis of Man's genesis. It is from the Commentaries that we have hitherto quoted and tried to explain the hidden meaning of some of the allegories, thus showing the true views of esoteric antiquity upon geology, anthropology, and even ethnology. We will endeavor in the Part which follows, to establish a still closer metaphysical connexion between the earliest races and their Creators, the *divine* men from other worlds; accompanying the statements proffered with the most important demonstrations of the same in esoteric Astronomy and Symbolism.

In Volume III of this work (the said volume and the IVth being almost ready) a brief history of all the great adepts known to the ancients and the moderns in their chronological order will be given, as also a bird's-eye view of the Mysteries, their birth, growth, decay, and final death — in Europe. This could not find room in the present work. Volume IV will be almost entirely devoted to Occult teachings.

The duration of the periods that separate, in space and time, the Fourth from the Fifth Race — in the historical [938] or even the legendary beginnings of the latter — is too tremendous for us to offer, even to a Theosophist, any more detailed accounts of them. During the course of the post-diluvian ages — marked at certain periodical epochs by the most terrible cataclysms — too many races and nations were born, and have disappeared almost without leaving a trace, for any one to offer any description of the slightest value concerning them. Whether the Masters of Wisdom have a consecutive and full history of our race from its incipient stage down to the present times; whether they possess the uninterrupted record of man since he became the complete physical being, and became thereby the king of the animals and master on this earth — is not for the writer to say. Most probably they have, and such is our own personal conviction. But if

938. The word " historical " is used, because, although historians have dwarfed almost absurdly the dates that separate certain events from our modern day, nevertheless, once that they are known and accepted, they belong to history. Thus the Trojan War *is* a historical event; and though even less than 1000 years B. C. is the date assigned to it, yet in truth it is nearer 6000 than 5000 years B. C.

so, this knowledge is only for the *highest* Initiates, who do not take their students into their confidence. The writer can, therefore, give but what she has herself been taught, and no more.

But even this will appear to the profane reader rather as a weird, fantastic dream, than as a possible reality.

This is only natural and as it should be, since for years such was the impression made upon the humble writer of these pages herself. Born and bred in European, matter-of-fact and presumably civilized countries, she assimilated the foregoing with the utmost difficulty. But there are proofs of a certain character which become irrefutable and are undeniable in the long run, to every earnest and unprejudiced mind. For a series of years such were offered to her, and now she has the full certitude that our present globe and its human races must have been born, grown and developed in this, and in no other way.

But this is the personal view of the writer; and her orthodoxy cannot be expected to have any more weight than any other " doxy," in the eyes of those to whom every fresh theory is heterodox until otherwise proved. Therefore are we Occultists fully prepared for such questions as these: " How does one know that the writer has not invented the whole scheme? And supposing *she* has not, how can one tell that the whole of the foregoing, as given in the Stanzas, is not the product of the imagination of the ancients? How could they have preserved the records of such an immense, such an incredible antiquity? "

The answer that the history of this world since its formation and to its end " is written in the stars," *i.e.,* is recorded in the Zodiac and the Universal Symbolism whose keys are in the keeping of the Initiates, will hardly satisfy the doubters. The antiquity of the Zodiac in Egypt is much doubted, and it is denied point-blank with regard to India. " Your conclusions are often excellent, but your premises are always doubtful," the writer was once told by a profane friend. To this, the answer came that it was one point, at least, gained on the scientific syllogisms. For, with the exception of a few problems from the domain of purely physical science, both the premises and conclusions of the men of Science are as hypothetical as they are almost invariably erroneous. And if they do not so appear to the profane, the reason is simply this: the said profane is very little aware, taking as he does his scientific data on faith, that both premises and conclusions are generally the product of the same brains, which, however learned, are not infallible; a truism demonstrated daily by the shifting and reshifting of scientific theories and speculations.

However it may be, the records of the temples, Zodiacal and traditional, as well as the ideographic records of the East, as read by the adepts of the Sacred Science and Vidyâ, are not a whit more doubtful than the so-called ancient history of the European nations, now edited, corrected, and amplified by half a century of archaeological discoveries, and the very problematical readings of the Assyrian tiles, cuneiform fragments, and Egyptian hieroglyphics. So are our data based upon the same readings, in addition to an almost inexhustible number of Secret works of which Europe knows nothing — *plus* the perfect knowledge by the Initiates of the symbolism of every word so recorded. Some of these records belong to an immense antiquity. Every archaeologist and palaeontologist is acquainted with the ideographic productions of certain semi-savage tribes, who from time immemorial have aimed at rendering their thoughts symbolically. This is the earliest mode of recording events and ideas. And how old this knowledge is in the human race may be inferred from some signs, evidently ideographic, found on hatchets of the Palaeolithic period. The red Indian tribes of America, only a few years ago comparatively speaking, petitioned the President of the United States to grant them possession of four small lakes, the petition being written on the tiny surface of a piece of a fabric, which is covered with barely a dozen representations of animals and birds. (See Lubbock.) The American savages have a number of such different kinds of writing, but not one of our Scientists is yet familiar, or even knows of the early hieroglyphic cypher, still preserved in some Fraternities, and named in Occultism the *Sensar.* Moreover, all those who have decided to regard such modes of writing — *e.g.*, the ideographs of the Red Indians, and even the Chinese characters — as " attempts of the early races of mankind to express their untutored thoughts," will decidedly object to our statement, that writing was invented by the Atlanteans, and not at all by the Phoenicians. Indeed, such a claim as that writing was known to mankind many hundreds of milleniums ago, in the face of the philologists who have decreed that writing was unknown in the days of, and to Pânini, in India, as also to the Greeks in the time of Homer, will be met by general disapprobation, if not with silent scorn. All denial and ridicule notwithstanding, the Occultists will maintain the claim, and simply for this reason: from Bacon down to our modern Royal Society, we have a too long period, full of the most ludicrous mistakes made by Science, to warrant our believing in modern scientific assumptions rather than in the denials of our Teachers. Writing, our scientists say, was unknown to Pânini; and this sage nevertheless composed a grammar which contains 3996 rules, and is the most perfect of all the grammars that were ever made! Pânini is made out to have lived barely a few centuries B.C., by the most liberal; and the rocks in Iran and Central Asia (whence the philologists and historians show us the ancestors of the same Pânini, the

Brâhmans, coming into India) are *covered with writing*, two and three thousand years old (12,000, according to some fearless palaeontologists). Writing was an *ars incognita* in the days of Hesiod and Homer, agreeably to Grote, and unknown to the Greeks so late as 770 B.C.; and the Phoenicians who had *invented* it, and knew writing as far back as 1500 B. C., at the earliest,[939] were living among the Greeks, and elbowing them, all the time! All these scientific and contradictory conclusions disappeared, however, into thin air, when Schliemann discovered (*a*) the site of ancient Troy, whose actual existence had been so long regarded as a fable; and (*b*), excavated on that site earthenware vessels with inscriptions *in characters unknown* to the palaeontologists and the all-denying Sanskritists. Who will now deny Troy, or these Archaic inscriptions? As Professor Virchow witnesses:— " I was myself an eye-witness of two such discoveries, and helped to gather the articles together. The slanderers have long since been silenced, who were not ashamed to charge the discoverer with an imposture." [940] Nor were truthful women spared any more than truthful men. Du Chaillu, Gordon Cumming, Madame Merian,[941] Bruce, and a host of others were charged with lying.

Madame Merian — says the author of *Mythical Monsters*, who gives this information in the *Introduction* — was accused of deliberate falsehood in reference to her description of a bird-eating spider nearly two hundred years ago. But now-a-days reliable observers have confirmed it in regard to South America, India, and elsewhere. Audubon was accused by botanists of having invented the yellow water-lily, which he figured in his *Birds of the South* under the name of Nymphaea lutea, and after having lain under the imputation for years, was confirmed at last by the discovery of the long-lost flower in Florida in 1876.[942] And, as Audubon was called *a liar* for this, and for his Haliaetus Washingtonii,[943] so Victor Hugo was ridiculed for . . . his marvellous word-painting of the devil-fish, and his description of a man becoming its helpless victim.

The thing was derided as a monstrous impossibility; yet within a few years were discovered, on the shores of Newfoundland, cuttle-fish with arms extending to thirty feet in length, and capable of dragging a good-sized boat beneath

939. It is a historical fact that Sanchoniathon compiled and wrote in Phoenician characters — from annals and State documents in the archives of *the older* Phoenician cities — the full record of their religion in 1250 B. C.

940. Professor Virchow, in Appendix 1 to Schliemann's *Ilios*. Murray, 1880.

941. Gosse writes of the latter: " She is set down a thorough heretic, not at all to be

believed, a manufacturer of unsound natural history, an inventor of false facts in science." (*Romance of Natural History*, p. 227.)

942. *Popular Science Monthly*, No. 60, April 1877.

943. Dr. Cover writes: " That famous bird of Washington was a myth; either Audubon was mistaken, or else, as some do not hesitate to affirm, *he lied* about it,"

the surface; and their action has been reproduced *for centuries past* . . . by Japanese artists.[944a]

And if Troy was denied, and regarded as a myth; the existence of Herculaneum and Pompeii declared a fiction; the travels of Marco Polo laughed at and called as absurd a fable as one of Baron Münchhausen's tales, why should the writer of "*Isis Unveiled*" and of the "*Secret Doctrine*" be any better treated? Mr. Charles Gould, the author of the above-cited volume, quotes in his excellent work a few lines from *Macmillan* (1860), which are as true to life, and too much to the point not to be reproduced:

When a naturalist, either by visiting such spots of earth as are still out of the way, or by his good fortune, finds a very queer plant or animal, he is forthwith accused of *inventing* his game. . . . As soon as the creature is found to sin against preconception, the great (mis?) guiding Spirit, *a priori* by name, who furnishes philosophers with their omniscience *pro re nata*, whispers that no such thing *can* be, and forthwith there is a charge of hoax. The heavens themselves have been charged with hoaxes. When Leverrier and Adams predicted a planet by calculation, it was gravely asserted in some quarters that the planet which had been calculated was not *the* planet but another which had clandestinely and improperly got into the neighborhood of the true body. *The disposition to suspect hoax is stronger than the disposition to hoax.* Who was it that first announced that the classical writings of Greece and Rome were one huge hoax perpetrated by the monks in what the announcer would be as little or less inclined than Dr. Maitland to call the dark ages?[944b]

Thus let it be. No disbeliever who takes the "*Secret Doctrine*" for a "hoax" is forced or even asked to credit our statements. These have already been proclaimed to be such by certain very clever American journalists before even the work went to press.[945]

Nor is it, after all, necessary that any one should believe in the Occult Sciences and the old teachings, before one knows anything or even believes in his own soul. No great truth was ever accepted *a priori*, and generally a century or two passed before it began to glimmer

---

944. *Mythical Monsters,* pp. 10, 11, Introd.

944a. Page 13.

945. So far back as July, 1888, at a time when the MSS. of this work had not yet left my writing table, and the *Secret Doctrine* was utterly unknown to the world, it was already being denounced as a product of my brain and no more. These are the flattering terms in which the *Evening Telegraph* (of America) referred to this still unpublished work in its issue of June 30, 1888: "*Among the fascinating books for July reading is Mme. Blavatsky's new book on Theo-*sophy . . . (!) the SECRET DOCTRINE. . . . But because she can soar back into the Brāhman ignorance . . . (!?) . . . *is no proof that everything she says is true.*" And once the prejudiced verdict given on the mistaken notion that my book was out, and that the reviewer had read it, neither of which was or could be the case, now that it is really out the critic will have to support his first statement, whether correct or otherwise, and thus get out of it, probably by a more slashing criticism than ever.

in the human consciousness as a possible verity, except in such cases as the positive discovery of the thing claimed as a fact. The truths of today are the falsehoods and errors of yesterday, and *vice versa*. It is only in the XXth century that portions, if not the whole, of the present work will be vindicated.

It is no fact going against our statements, therefore, even if Sir John Evans does affirm that writing was unknown in the stone age. For it may have been unknown during that period in the Fifth Aryan race, and have been perfectly known to the Atlanteans of the Fourth, in the palmy days of their highest civilization. The cycles of the rise and fall of the nations and races are there to account for it.

If told that there have been cases before now of forged pseudographs being palmed off on the credulous, and that our work may be classed with Jacolliot's *Bible in India* (in which, by the way, there are more truths among its errors than are found in the works of orthodox and recognized Orientalists)—the charge and comparison will dismay us very little. We bide our time. Even the famous "*Esour-Veda*" of the last century, considered by Voltaire "the most precious gift from the East to the West," and by Max Müller "about the silliest book that can be read," is not altogether without facts and truths in it. The cases where the *a priori* negations of specialists became justified by subsequent corroborations form but an insignificant percentage of those that were fully vindicated by subsequent discoveries, and confirmed to the great dismay of the learned objectors. "*Esour Veda*," was a very small bone of contention compared with the triumph of Sir William Jones, Anquetil du Perron, and others in the matter of Sanskrit and its literature. Such facts are recorded by Professor Max Müller himself, who, speaking of the discomfiture of Dugald Stewart and Co. in connexion with this, states that "if the facts about Sanskrit were true, Dugald Stewart was too wise not to see that the conclusions drawn from them were inevitable. He therefore denied the reality of such a language as Sanskrit altogether, and wrote his famous essay to prove that Sanskrit had been put together after the model of Greek and Latin, by those arch-forgers and liars, the Brâhmans, and that the whole of Sanskrit literature was an imposition."[946] The writer is quite willing and feels proud to keep company with these Brâhmans, and other *historical* "liars," in the opinion of our modern Dugald Stewarts. She has lived too long, and her experience has been too varied and personal, for her not to know at least something of human nature. "When you doubt, abstain," says the wise Zoroaster, whose prudent aphorism is found corroborated in every case by daily life and experience. Yet, like St. John the Baptist, this sage of the

946. *Science of Language*, p. 168.

past Ages is found preaching in the desert, in company with a more modern philosopher, namely Bacon, who offers the same priceless bit of practical Wisdom. " In contemplation," he says (in any question of Knowledge, we add), " if a man begin with certainties, he shall end in doubts; but *if he will be content to begin with doubts he shall end in certainties."*

With this piece of advice from the father of English Philosophy to the representatives of British scepticism we ought to close the debate, but our theosophical readers are entitled to a final piece of Occult information.

Enough was said to show that evolution in general, events, mankind, and everything else in Nature proceed in cycles. We have spoken of seven Races, five of which have nearly completed their earthly career, and have claimed that every Root-Race, with its sub-races and innumerable family divisions and tribes, was entirely distinct from its preceding and succeeding race. This will be objected to, on the authority of uniform experience in the question of Anthropology, and Ethnology. Man was — save in color and type, and perhaps a difference in facial peculiarities and cranial capacity — ever the same under every climate and in every part of the world, say the Naturalists: ay, even in stature. This, while maintaining that man descends from the same unknown ancestor as the ape, a claim that is logically impossible without an infinite variation of stature and form, from his first evolution into a biped. The very logical persons who maintain both propositions are welcome to their paradoxical views. Once more we address only those who, doubting the general derivation of myths from " the contemplation of the visible workings of external nature . . . " think it, " less hard to believe that these wonderful stories of gods and demi-gods, of giants and dwarfs, of dragons and monsters of all descriptions, are transformations, than to believe them to be inventions." It is only such "transformations" in physical nature, as much as in the memory and conceptions of our present mankind, that the Secret Doctrine teaches. It confronts the purely speculative hypotheses of modern Science, based upon the experience and exact observations of barely a few centuries, with the unbroken tradition and records of its Sanctuaries; and brushing away that tissue of cobweb-like theories, spun in the darkness that covers a period of hardly a few millenniums back, and which Europeans call their " History," the Old Science says to us: Listen, now, to my version of the memoirs of Humanity.

The human Races are born one from the other, grow, develop, become old, and die. Their sub-races and nations follow the same rule. If your all-denying modern science and so-called philosophy do not

THE SECRET DOCTRINE

contest that the human family is composed of a variety of well-defined types and races, it is only because the fact is undeniable; no one would say that there was no external difference between an Englishman, an African negro, and a Japanese or Chinaman. On the other hand it is formally denied by most naturalists that *mixed human races*, *i. e.*, the seeds for entirely new races, are any longer formed in our days. But this last is maintained on good grounds by de Quatrefages and some others.

Nevertheless our general proposition will not be accepted. It will be said that whatever forms man has passed through in the long prehistoric Past there are no more changes for him (save certain variations, as at present) in the future. Hence that our Sixth and Seventh Root Races are fictions.

To this it is again answered: How *do you* know? Your experience is limited to a few thousand years, to less than a day in the whole age of Humanity and to the present types of the actual continents and isles of our Fifth Race. How can you tell what will or will not be? Meanwhile, such is the prophecy of the Secret Books and their no uncertain statements.

Since the beginning of the Atlantean Race many million years have passed, yet we find the last of the Atlanteans, still mixed up with the Aryan element, 11,000 years ago. This shows the enormous overlapping of one race over the race which succeeds it, though in characters and external type the elder loses its characteristics, and assumes the new features of the younger race. This is proved in all the formations of mixed human races. Now, Occult philosophy teaches that even now, under our very eyes, the new Race and Races are preparing to be formed, and that it is in America that the transformation will take place, and has already silently commenced.

Pure Anglo-Saxons hardly three hundred years ago, the Americans of the United States have already become a nation apart, and, owing to a strong admixture of various nationalities and inter-marriage, almost a race *sui generis*, not only mentally, but also physically. "Every mixed race, when uniform and settled, has been able to play the part of a primary race in fresh crossings," says de Quatrefages. "Mankind, in its present state, has thus been formed, certainly, for the greatest part, by the successive crossing of a number of races *at present undetermined*." [947]

Thus the Americans have become in only three centuries a "primary race," *pro tem.*, before becoming a race apart, and strongly separated from all other now existing races. They are, in short, the germs of the *Sixth* sub-race, and in some few hundred years more, will become

947. *The Human Species*, p. 274.

most decidedly the pioneers of that race which must succeed to the present European or fifth sub-race, in all its new characteristics. After this, in about 25,000 years, they will launch into preparations for the seventh sub-race; until, in consequence of cataclysms — the first series of those which must one day destroy Europe, and still later the whole Aryan race (and thus affect both Americas), as also most of the lands directly connected with the confines of our continent and isles — the Sixth Root-Race will have appeared on the stage of our Round. When shall this be? Who knows save the great Masters of Wisdom, perchance, and they are as silent upon the subject as the snow-capped peaks that tower above them. All we know is, that it will silently come into existence; so silently, indeed, that for long millenniums shall its pioneers — the peculiar children who will grow into peculiar men and women — be regarded as anomalous *lusus naturae*, abnormal oddities physically and mentally. Then, as they increase, and their numbers become with every age greater, one day they will awake to find themselves in a majority. It is the present men who will then begin to be regarded as exceptional mongrels, until these die out in their turn in civilized lands; surviving only in small groups on islands — the mountain peaks of today — where they will vegetate, degenerate, and finally die out, perhaps millions of years hence, as the Aztecs have, as the Nyam-Nyam and the dwarfish Moola Koorumba of the Nilghiri Hills are dying. All these are the remnants of once mighty races, the recollection of whose existence has entirely died out of the remembrance of the modern generations, just as we shall vanish from the memory of the Sixth Race Humanity. The Fifth will overlap the Sixth Race for many hundreds of millenniums, changing with it slower than its new successor, still changing in stature, general physique, and mentality, just as the Fourth overlapped our Aryan race, and the Third had overlapped the Atlanteans.

This process of preparation for the Sixth great Race must last throughout the whole sixth and seventh sub-races (*vide supra*, the diagram of the Genealogical Tree of the Fifth Race). But the *last* remnants of the Fifth Continent will not disappear until some time after the birth of the *new* Race; when another and *new* dwelling, the sixth continent, will have appeared above the *new* waters on the face of the globe, so as to receive the new stranger. To it also will emigrate and settle all those who shall be fortunate enough to escape the general disaster. When this shall be — as just said — it is not for the writer to know. Only, as nature no more proceeds by sudden jumps and starts, than man changes suddenly from a child into a mature man, the final cataclysm will be preceded by many smaller submersions and destructions both by wave and volcanic fires. The exultant pulse will

beat high in the heart of the race now in the American zone, but
there will be no more Americans when the Sixth Race commences;
no more, in fact, than Europeans; for they will have now become a
new race, and many new nations. Yet the Fifth will not die, but
survive for a while: overlapping the new Race for many hundred
thousands of years to come, it will become transformed with it —
slower than its new successor — still getting entirely altered in mentality, general physique, and stature. Mankind will not grow again
into giant bodies as in the case of the Lemurians and the Atlanteans;
because while the evolution of the Fourth race led the latter down
to the very bottom of materiality in its physical development, the
present Race is on its ascending arc; and the Sixth will be rapidly
growing out of its bonds of matter, and even of flesh.

Thus it is the mankind of the New world — one by far the senior of
our Old one, a fact men had also forgotten — of *Pâtâla* (the Antipodes, or the Nether World, as America is called in India), whose
mission and Karma it is, to sow the seeds for a forthcoming, grander,
and far more glorious Race than any of those we know of at present.
The Cycles of Matter will be succeeded by Cycles of Spirituality and
a fully developed mind. On the law of parallel history and races, the
majority of the future mankind will be composed of glorious Adepts.
Humanity is the child of cyclic Destiny, and not one of its Units can
escape its unconscious mission, or get rid of the burden of its co-
operative work with nature. Thus will mankind, race after race, perform its appointed cycle-pilgrimage. Climates will, and have already
begun, to change, each tropical year after the other dropping one sub-
race, but only to beget another higher race on the ascending cycle; while
a series of other less favored groups — the failures of nature — will,
like some individual men, vanish from the human family without even
leaving a trace behind.

Such is the course of Nature under the sway of KARMIC LAW: of
the ever present and the ever-becoming Nature. For, in the words of
a Sage, known only to a few Occultists:—" THE PRESENT IS THE
CHILD OF THE PAST; THE FUTURE, THE BEGOTTEN OF THE PRESENT.
AND YET, O PRESENT MOMENT! KNOWEST THOU NOT THAT THOU HAST
NO PARENT, NOR CANST THOU HAVE A CHILD; THAT THOU ART EVER
BEGETTING BUT THYSELF? BEFORE THOU HAST EVEN BEGUN TO SAY
'I AM THE PROGENY OF THE DEPARTED MOMENT, THE CHILD OF THE
PAST,' THOU HAST BECOME THAT PAST ITSELF. BEFORE THOU UTTEREST
THE LAST SYLLABLE, BEHOLD! THOU ART NO MORE THE PRESENT BUT
VERILY THAT FUTURE. THUS, ARE THE PAST, THE PRESENT, AND
THE FUTURE, THE EVER-LIVING TRINITY IN ONE — THE MAHÂMÂYÂ
OF THE ABSOLUTE IS."

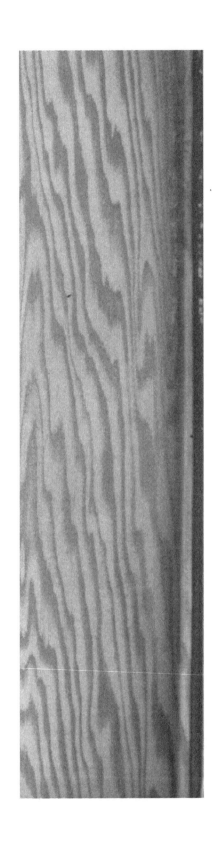